HANDBOOK OF ECONOMIC PSYCHOLOGY

Handbook of Economic Psychology

edited by

W. Fred van Raaij

Erasmus University Rotterdam

Gery M. van Veldhoven

Tilburg University Tilburg

Karl-Erik Wärneryd

Stockholm School of Economics Stockholm

Kluwer Academic Publishers
Dordrecht / Boston / London

Library of Congress Cataloging in Publication Data

Handbook of economic psychology.

Includes indexes.
1. Economics--Psychological aspects. 2. Consumers.
I. Raaij, W. Fred van. II. Veldhoven, Gery M. van.
III. Wärneryd, Karl Erik, 1927- .
HB74.P8H37 1988 330'.01'9 88-12699
ISBN 90-247-3720-6

Published by Kluwer Academic Publishers,
P.O. Box 17, 3300 AA Dordrecht, The Netherlands.

Kluwer Academic Publishers incorporates
the publishing programmes of
D. Reidel, Martinus Nijhoff, Dr W. Junk and MTP Press.

Sold and distributed in the U.S.A. and Canada
by Kluwer Academic Publishers,
101 Philip Drive, Norwell, MA 02061, U.S.A.

In all other countries, sold and distributed
by Kluwer Academic Publishers Group,
P.O. Box 322, 3300 AH Dordrecht, The Netherlands.

Printed in The Netherlands

Table of contents

PART IV. THE SOCIETAL PERSPECTIVE

Preface

The idea to publish a Handbook of Economic Psychology came up as a natural consequence of a discussion concerning appropriate reading material for courses in economic psychology. The discussion took place a few years ago in the Department of Economic Psychology at Tilburg University, The Netherlands. It was noted that there was a surprising lack of collections of pertinent readings, to say nothing about the lack of textbooks in the English language. So the present editors, who had been involved in the discussion, decided to start working on a Handbook. The situation has changed quite a lot since then. There are now a number of books, internationally available in the English language, in economic psychology or behavioral economics. The interest in this field of study is expanding quite impressively. The Journal of Economic Psychology is now (1988) in its ninth volume and many other journals are publishing articles in the field.

The application of psychological theories and methods to economic problems or the study of economic experiences and behavior is variously referred to as *economic psychology* or *behavioral economics*. While in principle we do not want to overdo the differences between the two, we have a feeling that economic psychology has a slightly stronger flavor of psychology than behavioral economics which in its turn seems to be closer to economics. Psychologists tend to feel more at home in economic psychology, while economists seem to favor behavioral economics. Another difference that is sometimes pointed out relates to the fact that economic psychology has its roots and is more widely spread in Europe, whereas the concept of behavioral economics has its strongest support in the U.S. Be these differences as they may, the present volume reflects more of the psychologists' way of thinking about problems than of the economists' way of dealing with economic problems.

The aim of this book is to give an overview of psychology as applied in the study of economic problems, notably economic behavior. The Handbook offers reviews of important areas of psychology and social psychology such as cognition, attitudes, motivation, and social influence with special consideration of and examples from the applications to economic behavior. It also reviews the most current research in a number of

Van Raaij, W.F., van Veldhoven, G.M. and Wärneryd, K.E. (eds) Handbook of Economic Psychology. ISBN 90-247-3720-6.

problem areas for example related to use of leisure, household decision making, fiscal problems, income and wealth and so on.

The Handbook is in the first place aimed at two types of audiences: psychology students and students of marketing. We think that there is a need for more psychology students to devote their attention to problems of economic behavior and become acquainted with what psychologists can contribute in this area of endeavor. Economic behavior is after all a very important part of human behavior. It has certain characteristics which distinguish it from many other areas of behavior, involving the use of money, and which makes it fascinating to study as part of social reality. Students of psychology will discover that the introductory chapters which cover the main fields in psychology are not a mere repetition of their earlier readings, but rather mean up-to-date reviews of the fields with special attention given to economic applications.

Students of marketing often get a good background in the behavioral sciences and are mostly subjected to a fairly intensive study of consumer behavior or buyer behavior. Through the ordinary textbooks they get a rather narrow perspective of consumer behavior and of the behavior of industrial buyers. There is a tendency to focus primarily and sometimes exclusively on such aspects that are assumed to have managerial interest. A myopic focus on brand choice and factors affecting brand choice leads to omission of other important aspects of economic behavior which at least in the long run are highly significant for marketing at the strategic level. We think that this Handbook can be an excellent complement or even alternative to such textbooks since it gives a broadened, more basic perspective on essential sides of economic behavior. The students may fail to get some detailed managerial thinking about brand choices, but will, on the other hand, find richer knowledge about economic-psychological problems that concern all of us and that will also affect marketing, such as environmental problems and unemployment.

Economists who are engaged in advancing their science by means of data about economic behavior will here have a chance to find out about the state of the art, as seen by psychologists who are active in the field since the contributors with only a few exceptions have psychology as their main orientation.

The volume covers many topics. Still some potentially interesting topics are missing. The Handbook can be seen as an attempt to claim certain scientific ground or problem areas as constitutive of economic psychology. There are some areas that we definitely think belong to economic psychology, but which it has not been possible to accommodate, mainly for lack of authors with the necessary time for writing available. We have had to omit such "classical" areas in economic psychology as saving behavior and the psychology of inflation. There is interesting research to report in these areas. We would also have liked to have a chapter on business leadership from the perspective of society, not as an organizational issue, but dealing with the economic and social implications of different types of leadership. There are other chapters that should have been written, but so far there is too little research going on in the areas. We have a feeling that research combining psychological approaches and economic thinking has only just begun and that the near future will see many more joint undertakings in economic psychology.

ACKNOWLEDGEMENTS

As editors of the Handbook we want to thank the authors of the chapters for their contributions. We tested their cooperativeness by suggesting changes in their work, and agree after all that they did not accommodate to all of our proposals. We thank the secretaries of the economic psychology group at Erasmus University, Gemma Schmitz, Joke van Oost and Sylvia Ouwerkerk, for retyping a number of chapters on the word processor. One of the research assistants at Erasmus University, Marietta Haffner, spent several months, as a technical editor, to check the spelling, the layout and the references of the chapters. She prepared the chapter indexes and the subject index as well. Without their enthusiastic contributions and without the support of the publisher this Handbook would never have been finished.

Table of Contents

1. Economic Psychology as a Field of Study

KARL-ERIK WÄRNERYD
Stockholm School of Economics, Stockholm, Sweden

1. ECONOMIC PSYCHOLOGY

1.1. *Introduction*

Judging from mass media treatment of economic affairs – be it in a recession, in a more serious depression or in an upswing period – there should be ample room for psychology when economic issues are dealt with. Economists who appear in the public eye as authors of articles or as interviewees often stress the importance of psychological factors. References to psychological factors are primarily made when the factors studied by economists do not suffice to explain certain economic developments. In such contexts, it is characteristic that no reference is made to the existence of scientific psychology and that comments are based on common-sense notions about man. There seems to be little awareness and recognition of the fact that concepts such as expectations, attitudes, preferences, and motivation are actually studied in psychology and that they are considered to be amenable to measurement. Psychology is used by economists to designate factors that create individual variations in economic behavior and that consequently are responsible for making economic behavior hard to predict (cf. Maital, 1982).

Psychologists are rarely sought by the mass media for the purpose of explaining economic phenomena or even for commenting on them. If a family is hit by economic disaster, a clinical psychologist may be asked for a comment, but events at the macro level, i.e., concerning the whole economy of a nation, are seen as being beyond the scope of the psychologist. In the frame of reference of the mass media, psychologists are visualized as persons who are associated with diagnoses of personal problems and of intellectual capacity or, for those who know a little more, as occupied with laboratory studies of students and sometimes rats. The truth is that most psychologists also see little connection between what they do and economic problems (except maybe their own private economic troubles).

It is likely that economists, like most people, base their views of psycho-

Van Raaij, W.F., van Veldhoven, G.M. and Wärneryd, K.E. (eds) Handbook of Economic Psychology. ISBN 90-247-3720-6.

logists and psychological research mainly on what the mass media communicate about psychology. It is similarly conceivable that psychologists get their impressions of economists and economic research from the mass media where economists are more visible than psychologists. The psychologist's image of an economist can then easily become that of an expert who makes strong statements about how human beings act and how that affects the economic conditions in the country. From there to a criticism of economists for their highly simplified assumptions about human beings is a short step. To psychologists who know a little about economic theory the concept of the economic man often raises an insurmountable wall between economics and psychology; the psychologist tends to think that a science based on such simplified notions about humans must necessarily be wrong.

Despite this rather gloomy picture of relations between economists and psychologists, there is reason for hope for a better understanding on both sides. Some economists have found considerable utility in adopting and using methods and ideas from psychological research and some psychologists have also found that there is a common ground of interest for economists and psychologists (cf. Wärneryd, 1986). This common ground will here be referred to as *economic psychology* and it will be more fully defined and explained in the rest of this chapter.

It is the aim of this Handbook to give reviews of on-going research in different areas of economic psychology and to some extent to suggest new areas for exploration. A fundamental assumption is that many psychologists, if they get better acquainted with the field, will find that economic behavior, which is the main preoccupation of economic psychology, can offer interesting problems for psychological research and that they can learn something from the way economic researchers have grappled with the same problems. It is also assumed that an increasing number of economists will discover new possibilities for bringing economic research problems to better solutions through the use of psychological methods and theories.

There are quite a few examples of attempts to combine knowledge from the two disciplines of economics and psychology, most of them made by economists (see, e.g., Weisskopf, 1955; Shackle, 1955; Scitovsky, 1976; Maital, 1982; Alhadeff, 1982). Usually these attempts have not been well received by other economists. A few psychologists, in the first place George Katona (1975), have successfully worked with economic problems as their main research interest. Katona and his associates have contributed, if not exactly to economic theory, at least to the wealth of empirical data on which economic models can be tested. In some areas of economic interest there has even been a predominance of researchers with some background and sometimes advanced degrees in psychology. A notable example is the study of consumer behavior, which is usually associated with the area of marketing where the use of psychology or more generally expressed the behavioral sciences has been pervasive and sometimes even referred to by consumerists in the mass media as abusive. Consumer behavior study is undoubtedly important to marketing, but as will be seen in this Handbook, there are also other important uses of consumer behavior study in the field of economic psychology.

1.2 *A Brief History of Economic Psychology*

According to the French social psychologist Gabriel Tarde, the concept of economic psychology dates back to 1881. He notes in his two-volume work *La Psychologie Economique* which was published in 1902 that in an article published in 1881, he first used this concept. He claims that he introduced the concept before the economists belonging to the Austrian school, sometimes called the psychological school, used it. Reynaud (1964) comments that there were attempts to combine economics and psychology long before Tarde.

In Tarde's view it was regrettable that Adam Smith who had proved his skill as a psychologist in his *Theory of Moral Sentiments* (1759) did not utilize this knowledge in his economics work *An Inquiry into the Wealth of Nations* (1776). Tarde who directed severe critique against Adam Smith and other economists, based his criticism on the notion that man was a social being and that interaction among people, "l'interpsychologie," should be the appropriate basis for a theory of economic behavior. Economic psychology was to Tarde not a special field of knowledge, since it concerned the fundamental psychological assumptions of economic theory. Tarde who is best known for his work *The Laws of Imitation* (1903) which is still often cited in sociological literature, had formed his views on the proper foundations of economic theory from his own observations and interpretations of social phenomena.

Tarde's voluminous work on economic psychology does not seem to have had much influence on thinking in economics. Reynaud (1964) remarks that economists typically responded that they were interested in acts, not in the states of the soul. The work is mentioned in a footnote in Veblen's book *The Theory of Business Enterprise* (1904), but without a comment. Tarde's work was rediscovered by an American sociologist, who in 1961 published an article where he pointed out how surprisingly modern Tarde's ideas were and commented that there was now even empirical support for some of Tarde's ideas (Hughes, 1961). He especially stressed that Tarde had viewed leisure and the arts of consumption as at least as important as work.

Adam Smith was followed by many other economists who in their development of theory did not pay attention to what there was of psychological knowledge. Maybe the reason was that psychology was not considered to be a well-developed science. Kant had declared that psychology could never become a science because it could not be dealt with in mathematical terms or become experimental (Boring, 1950). Later developments in the nineteenth century proved Kant to be wrong. According to many influential views, psychology started its real progress towards becoming a science when Wundt founded his psychological laboratory in Leipzig in 1879. Wundt's initiative led to the establishing of at least some quantitative relations in psychology, involving a new interpretation of the mind-body problem in the guise of psychophysics.

The members of the Austrian school – also called the psychological or the marginalist school – did not rely on the growing science of psychology for the psychological assumptions of their theoretical work although they began their study at about the same time as Wundt opened his laboratory. Carl Menger published his seminal work *Grundsätze der Volkswirtschaftslehre* in 1871. His idea and that of his associates and followers was that economists could improve economic theory through using common-sense observations and interpretations in judicious combination with some loans from philosophy, such as the notion of hedonism and the calculus of utility.

The Austrian school introduced fundamental economic concepts such as marginal utility and opportunity cost. The former refers to the subjective value contributed by the last added, "marginal" unit of consumption. Opportunity cost is defined as what you have to forego in terms of non-selected alternatives when you make a choice. Menger's discussion of the hierarchy of human needs is still worth reading. It resembles Maslow's (1954) much more recent need hierarchy. Independently of Menger, Jevons (1871) – who did not read German – developed a mathematical utility theory. He apologized as a matter of fact for using mathematics! He saw economics as a "Calculus of Pleasure and Pain." He had taken some advice from Bain who has been called the first British psychologist (see Boring, 1950).

Another example of the Austrian school's use of psychology can be taken from Böhm-Bawerk's well-known, but also heavily criticized (by Schumpeter, 1933, among others) theory of interest on capital. Böhm-Bawerk (1891) stated that the interest rate was a function of technical factors, deriving from conditions of production, and psychological factors. The latter had to do with the uncertainty about the future and the little forethought that most people were willing to devote to the fulfillment of future needs. An interpretation of this is that the acceptable interest rates may vary not only among capital owners and borrowers, but also differ for differently long time periods since they can be characterized by different degrees of subjective uncertainty.

In the early forties, economic psychology was introduced into the U.S.

by the psychologist George Katona who started using psychological theories and methods in research on economic problems in collaboration with a team of economists and sociologists. Among those who know anything about economic psychology, the name of George Katona is the first and often the only association when economic psychology is mentioned. Katona formulated one basic idea for economic psychology: "Buying depends both on ability to purchase and willingness to purchase." Both concepts can be measured according to Katona. This means that psychological factors which here are called willingness to purchase are no longer seen as disturbances making consumer behavior if not unpredictable at least hard to predict.

Katona's contributions to economic psychology were firmly based on empirical data, primarily originating from consumer surveys conducted with regular intervals, usually on a quarterly basis. Katona showed that consumer reactions to economic stimuli could be explained and predicted on the basis of psychological measurements, in time series analysis often combined with macroeconomic statistical data. George Katona was a protagonist in the area of economic psychology for almost forty years (see Wärneryd (1982) for a biography and complete bibliography).

Katona's view of economic psychology is succinctly expressed in the following quotation: "... the basic need for psychology in economic research consists in the need to discover and analyze the forces behind economic processes, the forces responsible for economic actions, decisions and choices...." "Economics without psychology has not succeeded in explaining important economic processes and "psychology without economics"has no chance of explaining some of the most common aspects of human behavior" (Katona, 1951: pp. 9-10).

In his contribution to the Katona Festschrift, the economist Tobin (1972: p. 55) says: "That is why we need George Katona. The wealth model offers him plenty of latitude. He is right that once consumption is not liquidity-constrained it is a highly psychological variable. Wealth itself is highly psychological." He adds, however, a few sentences later:

> But in the long run attitudes and valuations are strongly governed by objective realities, and the purposes for which wealth is desired determine how much is accumulated. That is why the consumption-income relation is stable in trend while volatile quarter-to-quarter and year-to-year. That is why studies of consumer attitudes and behavior need to be embedded in a theoretical framework of rational accumulation.

It should be mentioned that Katona first vacillated between the concepts of economic psychology and psychological economics. He tended to use them interchangeably, but the latter served as title to his most comprehensive book *Psychological Economics* which was published in 1975 after his retirement as professor (although not as researcher). In an even later book, he adopted "behavioral economics" as the most appropriate heading for the field of study.

Since Tarde there is a French tradition in economic psychology with Pierre-Louis Reynaud and Paul Albou as the best-known representatives in modern times. Their conception of the field of study is much broader than what Katona meant by economic psychology. The French approaches are more characterized by a quest for a theoretical framework and development of comprehensive theory than by reliance on empirical data from individuals. Reynaud (1964) who, already in the 1940's, as a young economist became interested in learning and using psychology, preferred to speak of economic psychology rather than of psychological economics which he said was associated with the Austrian school in economics. He devoted much of his attention to the study of the dynamism of economic growth. He adopted concepts relating to "mental energy" from the work of a leading French psychologist and used them as explanatory factors in the study of economic growth. His fundamental assumption derived from the fact that when attempts were made to explain economic growth using labor and capital as explanatory factors, there was still more variance left unexplained than explained and an important part of the unexplained variation was ascribed to the influence of the human factor. Reynaud thus tried to find measures of motivational factors at a level between macro and micro (the meso level) and developed indicators of such factors (Reynaud, 1974, 1981).

Like Reynaud, Paul Albou (1984) includes organizational and industrial psychology in the field of economic psychology. He sees economic behavior as comprising both work and consumption. In Albou's view, it is essential for economic psychology to develop a comprehensive theory in economic psychology that can serve as a basis for more specific models ("modélisation") and that can make the study of reality meaningful. Albou and his associates have carried out empirical studies using survey techniques, e.g., relating to health economics. He has been especially interested in developing the concept of "need" (Albou, 1976).

Research pertaining to economic psychology is now pursued in many university departments and research institutes representing economics, marketing, psychology, and social psychology. There are professorial chairs in economic psychology and research groups connected with those. To some extent the research activities at each place bear the imprint of the environment where the research is conducted. At the Stockholm School of Economics (Sweden), the Aarhus and Helsinki Schools of Economics and Business Administration (in Denmark and Finland, respectively) and at Erasmus University, Rotterdam (The Netherlands), economic psychology is allied with economic and management sciences. At Tilburg University

(The Netherlands) economic psychology is a unit in the department of psychology. Some differences in research orientations can be noticed as a consequence of the different affiliations of the chairs, but their size should not be exaggerated. In many universities in Europe and the U.S., economic psychological research is found in contexts relating to professional training for business. A large part of what is here claimed to be economic psychological research is actually pursued in departments of marketing where consumer behavior is the main focus of study.

2. DELINEATION OF THE FIELD

2.1. *A General Definition*

According to Tarde (1902) economic psychology deals with the psychological foundations of economics, or somewhat differently expressed, the psychological assumptions on which economic theory is based. He did not give any explicit definition of the field (cf. Albou, 1984). There are now several definitions of economic psychology, but all can be subsumed under the label of the study of economic behavior. I shall define economic psychology in three ways:

1. through a general definition,
2. through a model which generates a taxonomy of research areas, and
3. through a brief overview of problem areas which are objects of study.

The first part of economic psychology "economic" has to do with the handling of scarce resources and expresses activities and outcomes of activities in monetary terms. The second part "psychology" indicates that economic psychology is concerned with human experience and behavior. Combining the two components gives the result that economic psychology encompasses the study of human behavior and experience in connection with how scarce resources in terms of money, time and effort are handled so as to satisfy needs.

> Economic psychology as a discipline thus studies the psychological mechanisms and processes that underlie consumption and other economic behavior. It deals with preferences, choices, decisions and factors influencing these, as well as the consequences of decisions and choices with respect to the satisfaction of needs. Furthermore, it deals with the impact of external economic phenomena upon human behavior and well-being. These studies may relate to different levels of aggregation: From the household and individual consumer to the macro level of whole nations.

This definition was agreed upon at the founding of the International Association for Research in Economic Psychology.

Economic psychology is closely related both to psychology and to economics. These two sciences represent highly different approaches to the study of economic problems and human behavior. Economic theory is to a large extent deductive, depending on mathematical reasoning in its development of models. It relies mostly on empirical evidence that is aggregated and highly abstracted. The basic tenets of the theory are generally accepted among economists. Since the basic theory is at a high level of abstraction, the applications of the theory in the study of reality presupposes interpretation through more specific models which contain simplifying assumptions so as to make measurements feasible.

Psychology cannot boast of any generally accepted theory. Theory construction in psychology is characterized by close adherence to the data. Except in the rather exclusive branch of mathematical psychology, mathematics is primarily used for elaboration of data and not for deducing consequences from a few basic postulates. Speculative theories are not encouraged in psychology; demands for more speculation on the basis of research findings have been expounded, e.g., as a quest for more generative theory (see Gergen, 1982). At the low level of abstraction, i.e., close to the empirical data, where psychological research usually operates, there is much room for finding and stressing differences among people, situations, and variables. This may be an explanation of the fact that there is not one, unified psychological theory, but rather a number of theories covering different aspects of behavior. In addition, there are also differences in approaches and methods used, often referred to as differences in schools.

Economic psychology has so far resembled psychology more than economics. It has had an orientation toward empirical observation and data analysis and the theory making attempts have been quite close to the observational level. I shall have more to say about this when later in this chapter, I shall attempt to establish a common frame of reference for the treatment of economic-psychological problems.

2.2. *A Conceptual Scheme Generating a Taxonomy of Problems for Research*

Van Raaij (1981) has proposed a general model for economic psychology which serves the purpose of indicating problem areas for research. The components of the model can be seen in Figure 1.

Van Raaij describes a number of research designs generated by the model in the following way:

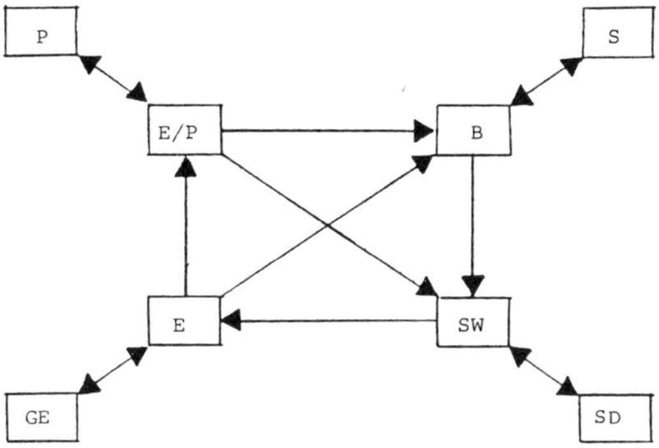

Fig. 1. Van Raaij's conceptual scheme of economic psychology.

GE = general economic conditions
E = economic environment
P = personal factors
E/P = perception of economic conditions
B = behavior
S = situation (events in the environment)
SW = subjective well-being
SD = societal (system) discontent

1. The relationship E → E/P pertains to how people perceive economic realities; mass communication and agenda-setting studies; the money illusion.
2. The relationship E/P → B gives the perceptions, preferences, attitudes, as related to behavior; hierarchy of effect studies.
3. The relationship B → SW pertains to studies on consumer satisfaction and complaints, well-being and welfare.
4. The relationship B → E is the economic research on demand and supply of goods and services.
5. The relationship SW → E relates to studies on the design and development of products, services, and programs based on consumer/participant's satisfactions and experiences; program evaluation studies.
6. The relationship SW → E/P pertains to how confirmed and disconfirmed expectations change consumer perceptions of the market and products.
7. The relationship GE → E are economic studies of the correspondence of general economic conditions and personal finances and opportunities of the household.
8. The relationship P → E/P is related to the effects of personality, cognitive style, and life style on the perception and categorization of economic reality.

9. The relationship $S \rightarrow B$ are the situational influences on economic behavior.
10. The relationship $SD \rightarrow SW$ relates to studies on the correspondence of consumption, economic satisfaction with life, work, and marriage satisfaction.

This model demonstrates in a lucid way that consumer/citizen well-being occupies an important position in economic psychology. The ideas of the model emanate from some of Strümpel's (1974) work and have been elaborated by Van Raaij. Subjective well-being may be seen as corresponding to welfare as this concept is used in economic welfare theory. It stresses, however, the subjective aspects which may deviate from objectively defined welfare, but which do not necessarily do so.

2.3. *A Brief Description of Research Areas in Economic Psychology*

Studies in economic psychology have usually taken their problems from different arenas (where actors meet) in economic reality rather than from theory (see Van Veldhoven (1981) for a discussion of research in economic-psychological problem areas). Economic psychology as a field of study is thus problem-oriented. The problems studied derive from three types of economic reality or arenas:

1. the consumer marketplace where consumer and household behavior is in the center of attention,
2. the business arena where entrepreneurship and business behavior are the focal points, and
3. the citizen/society arena where economic relations such as social benefits/taxes and reactions to economic policy measures are problem areas of special concern.

I do not know exactly when the first empirical studies in economic psychology were made. It seems likely that Katona was the first researcher to start research on a large scale. His first study was *Price Control and Business* which was published in 1945 and which reported on a carefully executed interview survey with business executives. The book contains an interesting discussion of "Interviewing as a Tool of Economic Research" which greatly stimulated economists in the use of interviews for systematic economic research. A few years later Katona presented his first consumer surveys which comprised structured interviews with open-ended follow-up questions posed to consumers in representative samples.

Before Katona there had been little systematic research on consumers except for marketing research and a few laboratory experiments such as Thurstone's (1931) study of one subject's indifference curves for hats and ties. Occasionally, psychologists had ventured to use economic variables in their regular experimentation, not for the sake of contributing to economic knowledge, but for an interest in developing psychological theory. Before Katona there had also been studies of advertising in the laboratory as well as in the field.

Katona was the first psychologist to focus on problems at the macro-economic level: explanations and predictions of expenditures and savings, of reactions to economic stimuli like inflation and to income changes such as introduction of pension plans and tax cuts. The research is characterized by its successful mixing of psychological and economic concepts and measurements. This type of research is still a major area within economic psychology and surveys of consumers and business decision makers in the Katona tradition are now made in many countries. Consumer and business expectations (by Katona and his associates called "sentiment") with respect to future financial conditions for the nation and for the individual household or business firm are the main preoccupation of these surveys.

The psychological variables are viewed as intervening between economic stimuli, on one hand, and consumer reactions, on the other. According to this way of thinking, the effects of economic events cannot be predicted on the sole basis of earlier conjunctions of stimuli and reactions because the effects depend on the states of the changeful intervening variables. Katona used the general label of "attitudes" or "expectations" for these variables. Thus, he maintained that consumer reactions, for example to inflation, could not be predicted in the rather simple way, based on past experiences, that most economic models used. It was, according to Katona, necessary to assess expectations about future developments at the individual level before an accurate prediction at the macro level could be made.

More intensive and more detailed consumer behavior studies, based on much more elaborated models than that of Katona, have proved their value in connection with public consumer policy and marketing. The study of consumer behavior has emerged as the dominant study area in economic psychology. There is a long tradition of employing psychology to market goods and especially to utilize methods and findings from psychology in advertising. Some of the best known experimental psychologists of the first decades of this century were as a matter of fact engaged in advertising as consultants on effect measurements, textbook contributors or – as J.B. Watson, the founder of behaviorism, in his later years – as full-time employee in an advertising agency.

Many aspects of consumer behavior are studied. In marketing-related research beside advertising research, the main interest is placed on factors that can explain and predict product and brand selection. In this context, consumer information processing has recently drawn the attention of many researchers and there have been considerable efforts devoted to developing theory in this area (see, e.g., Bettman, 1979). Research pertinent to public policy has comprised studies of consumer information needs and complaint behavior. The measurement of consumer satisfaction and dissatisfaction remains an important issue to the solution of which economic psychological research can make important contributions.

In the business arena there is as yet comparatively little research. There are behavioral studies of pricing behavior which have indicated that in practice pricing deviates considerably from what economic theory would lead one to expect. This does not by necessity mean that economic theory which is focused on long-run outcomes at the aggregate level, is wrong. Business decision making in marketing and investment activities has been studied quite extensively since it gives valuable background knowledge for the marketing of industrial goods to industrial purchasers. Tracking decision making in business firms as well as in other organizations has since long been a research theme within organizational psychology. Of more recent origin is an interest in studying factors influencing entrepreneurship and innovation.

The Consumer and Business Sentiment studies which were started by George Katona soon spread to other countries all over the world. Since the early seventies such survey data are collected in every country belonging to the European Community. They have proved their value for making short-run forecasts of consumer behavior and business behavior.

The long lasting economic setbacks of recent years in many Western countries have given impetus to a variety of studies which are aimed at elucidating the citizens' problems when they are faced with high taxes and at the same time reductions of benefits. Fiscal psychology has developed into an important subfield of economic psychology (see Lewis, 1982). Schmölders (1959) and Strümpel (1969) were forerunners in the field. They used survey research to find out about attitudes and behavior in fiscal matters. There is now a considerable literature covering tax evasion and tax attitudes (see special issue of the *Journal of Economic Psychology* (1982) and single articles in recent issues).

Special issues of the Journal of Economic Psychology illustrate other areas that have come into focus in recent years. The psychology of unemployment is an example. Unemployment is a growing concern in many countries and economic-psychological research is essential. Another example is the psychology of inflation. Katona (1975) was something of a trailblazer in this field and there is among some economists at least a notable interest in attempts to measure individual expectations using psychological theories and methods. Growing concerns about shrinking natural resources and the pollution of the environment have led to massive research on energy conservation. In this research ideas and methods deriving from economic psychology have played a role. Two special issues of the *Journal of Economic Psychology* (1983) were devoted to the problem area of energy conservation.

Economic psychology does not deal exclusively with problems relating to affluence or minor reductions in affluence within the welfare states. In the less developed countries there is as Reynaud (1974, 1981) emphasized plenty of room for economic-psychological research and application of ideas. There are some studies that can be subsumed under the rubric of economic psychology such as studies of entrepreneurial behavior (e.g., McClelland and Winter, 1969), modernization and economic development (e.g., Rogers, 1969). In the welfare states, especially in the U.S., there is research on poverty. It has become obvious that even in welfare states poverty can arise and that certain population groups easily remain out of reach of government relief actions and can be severely hit by poverty.

The common element in the research which has been briefly surveyed here is the focus on the human aspects. Economic psychology deals with the economic behavior of individuals and attaches great importance to how human actors perceive stimuli, how they handle information, how they make and implement decisions and how motivational forces initiate and sustain behavior. Towards the end of the chapter more will be said about these characteristics of economic psychology.

3. RELATIONS OF ECONOMIC PSYCHOLOGY TO OTHER FIELDS

3.1. *Introduction*

Economic psychology is not and should not be a very strictly defined area or field of study. It is of course desirable and necessary to delineate it and trace its boundaries the way I have done above, but a rigidly defined new field of study may not allow enough room for development. It is essential for the future of the field that there is an openness with respect to what specific contents to give to economic psychology and what specific methods to employ in it within the boundaries of the general definition. A new field of study like economic psychology is naturally conceived as being interdisciplinary which means that its further development rests on the exchange of ideas with the basic disciplines of economics and psychology. I shall now deal with the relations of economic psychology to these two disciplines which are next of kin. With respect to practical applications, the applied discipline of marketing displays important relations with economic psychology. Finally, sociology, in particular the sociological branch of social psychology, overlaps considerably with economic psychology.

3.2. *Psychology and Social Psychology*

The science of psychology encompasses the study of behavior in general and thus in principle also the study of economic behavior. Psychology has with few exceptions been taught as an experimental laboratory science in the universities ever since Wundt founded his experimental laboratory in 1879. Clinical psychologists have also got a dose of training in experimental methods. Although interviewing skills have been taught in psychology, this has typically been done for clinical purposes. The survey methods which are now used in psychology have been adopted from sociology and come in via social psychology.

Little experimental interest has been bestowed on the study of economic behavior despite the fact that it offers good and meaningful ways of measuring the dependent behavioral variables in terms of money. It may be that economic behavior has been assumed to be in no way different from other behavior and that behavioral findings could without change be generalized also to economic behavior. A more plausible reason for the lack of interest in studying economic behavior may be that economic behavior is assumed to have such peculiarities that the study in the laboratory would contribute little to general psychological theory. A notable exception to the common lack of interest in economic behavior is *decision theory* where psychologists have picked up experimental hypotheses and methods from economists representing the theory of games.

The earliest applications of psychological research to economic problems were in the area of consumer behavior. Apart from the fact that psychologists were recruited as market researchers to do research on consumers, there was an early interest in consumer behavior as a testing ground for hypotheses and methods developed in the psychological laboratories. This seems to have been a reason for the interest in advertising shown by some early experimental psychologists. The external validity of experimental results could be tested outside the laboratory and the usefulness of methods and techniques could be demonstrated. Psychological research had an impact on advertising and marketing practice, and it received in return mainly some proof of the validity of its methods. A well-known example from more recent times is the employment of Stephenson's Q-technique for the study of washing powder brand names before the technique was actually ready for scientific presentation (Stephenson, 1953).

Experimental psychology has since roughly fifteen years witnessed a strongly increased interest in cognitive research. This has no doubt facilitated the exchange of ideas between psychology and economics. It has been pointed out that microeconomic theory is cognitive in its general approach (Fels, 1963). The economic man – a postulate heavily criticized by most psychologists – is a calculating, well-informed consumer who is not completely remote from the empirically construed information-processing consumer in experimental consumer research. The major difference is maybe that the economists are first and foremost concerned with the outcomes of the economic man's activities, aggregated over a large population, whereas the cognitive psychologists want to concentrate on a true description of the details of the processes preceding the acts. The purpose of the psychological research when it overlaps with economic research related to cognitions is not in the first place to contribute to economic theory or models, but to develop psychological theory further.

The concept of uncertainty and attempts to measure the effects of uncertainty appear to have brought (some) psychologists and (some) economists closer together (Maital, 1982). In the early sixties psychological researchers became more and more interested in how man interacts with an environment in which relations are not deterministic, but probabilistic. This can be exemplified with the research that the so-called lens model which originated from Egon Brunswick's work and was further developed by Hammond and his associates (1975), inspired. The lens model has been applied in accounting research (Libby, 1981). Game theory inspired economists to start experimenting on uncertainty, employing lottery techniques. Decision making theory has developed into an area of common research interest for psychologists and economists although the objectives for the research may vary.

Social psychology is preoccupied with the effects of social stimuli and social interaction on human behavior. Social interaction involves among other things influences from membership and reference groups, social comparisons, and socialization. The field of study is related both to psychology and to sociology and the subject-matter varies somewhat depending on whether sociology or psychology is seen as next of kin. At an early stage, social psychology contributed to the study of consumer behavior its instinct theories which as could be expected appealed to creators of advertising. McDougall's (1908) instinct theory remained popular in the advertising world from the twenties and on until the fifties. Now it is replaced by more modern motivation theories like that of Maslow (1954) and other dynamic theories (see Chapter 2 of this Handbook). Attitude theory and attitude measurement which is an area of high interest in social psychology have been recurrent issues in the literature and research on consumer behavior since the sixties. More recent loans of concepts and accompanying methods of study can be exemplified by attribution theory which treats how human beings attribute causes to phenomena in order to explain events to themselves. An adoption from social psychology with a sociological bent is the two-step flow of communication hypothesis and the theory of opinion leadership, which play an important role in marketing (see Chapter 5 of this Handbook).

Viewed in the brief historical perspective used above, psychology and social psychology give an impression of having served as a kind of cafetaria of ideas – models, hypotheses, and techniques – for gaining insights into problems of economic behavior in the marketplace. This holds true mainly for the study of consumer behavior related to marketing. Marketing researchers have found a number of tools for potential use and psychologists have found a testing ground. Consumer behavior study has directly contributed rather little to the development of psychological theories or methods. Attitude theory and measurement seem to have got some stimulation from consumer behavior studies and from the debate that has raged in the concerned marketing-oriented journals. Information processing theory has received some, quite important contributions from the study of consumer behavior (see e.g., Van Raaij, 1976; Svenson, 1979; Bettman, 1979). As a matter of fact, consumer behavior appears to offer an ideal area for studying how humans receive and handle information that is meaningful, from the outside world and combine it with memory in decision processes. Except for these two areas economic psychology as hitherto explored offers potentiality rather than boasts of achievement.

Organizational psychology has some important overlap with economic psychology. It has its focus on the individual as a member of an organization with a defined goal and investigates what factors affect the individual's behavior in relation to this goal. Typically the research interest is concerned with factors relating to the productivity of the individual member and of groups in the organization: payment, working conditions, organizational structure, work climate, etc. If industrial psychology and work psychology are seen as part of organizational psychology, problems referring to personnel selection and placement, training and so on are added to the list.

From the preoccupation with one main type of dependent variable, namely productivity or efficiency, there has been a development towards the inclusion of another dependent variable, job satisfaction or in a broader sense quality-of-working-life. Assumptions about the relations between the two types of dependent variables have varied over time and they still vary. For example, less attention is paid to job satisfaction in times of economic recession and unemployment. There is still a clear trend towards increasing efforts being directed to problems of job satisfaction even though job satisfaction may not contribute to productivity. Job satisfaction is a goal in itself and this has affected research in the field of organizational psychology. The area has become concerned with the quality-of-life of workers and the researchers assume some responsibility for advancing it. To some extent the situation could be analogous for economic psychologists with respect to consumers, whose well-being could be a concern.

Economic psychology tends to view the productivity problem from the vantage point of an outside observer. It is treated as a macro problem, not as a problem for the individual organization. Job satisfaction is of course closely related to subjective well-being which is a major dependent variable in the thinking of many economic psychologists. The job is a major determinant of well-being both on account of earnings and on account of other satisfactions and dissatisfactions deriving from it.

Psychology is a descriptive-explanatory science which means that normative propositions involving recommendations for actions are not regarded as part of the scientist's realm. Psychologists who have been steeped in the thinking of scientific psychology, are not inclined to give recommendations for actions based on their research. The same restrictiveness is characteristic of many applications of psychology to problem areas. In clinical psychology there is usually more emphasis on diagnosis than on therapy or therapy recommendations. Economists, on the other hand, distinguish between positive economics which is descriptive-explanatory, and normative economics which is prescriptive (see next section). It is an interesting question whether economic psychology should not only be descriptive-explanatory, but also normative and on the basis of research findings give advice for policy actions to reach defined goals. Being normative in this sense would mean that economic psychology like organizational psychology breaks with what is tradition in psychological research.

3.3. *Macro- and Microeconomics*

After Lionel Robbins (1935; reprinted 1979) economics is often defined as the handling of scarce resources to achieve a given end. This definition would seem to leave some room for psychology in economics. Robbins, however, expresses his aversion toward psychology in a way that is still representative of what many economists think about scientific psychology:

> It is sometimes thought, even at the present day, that this notion of relative valuation depends upon the validity of particular psychological doctrines. The borderlands of Economics are the happy hunting-ground of minds averse to the effort of exact thought, and in these ambiguous regions, in recent years, endless time has been devoted to attacks on the alleged psychological assumptions of Economic Science. Psychology, it is said, advances very rapidly. If, therefore, Economics rests upon particular psychological doctrines, there is no task more ready to hand than every five years or so to write sharp polemics showing that, since psychology has changed its fashion, Economics needs "rewriting from the foundations upwards." Professional economists, absorbed in the exciting task of discovering new truth, have usually disdained to reply; and the

lay public, ever anxious to escape the necessity of recognizing the implications of choice in a world of scarcity, has allowed itself to be bamboozled into believing that matters, which are in fact as little dependent on the truth of fashionable psychology as the multiplication table, are still open questions on which the enlightened man, who, of course, is nothing if not a psychologist, must be willing to suspend judgment (Robbins, 1979: p. 40).

In a similar vein, Gary Becker (1976) has said about economics that what most distinguishes economics as a science from other social sciences, is not its subject matter, but its approach. He says: "The combined assumptions of maximizing behavior, market equilibrium, and stable preferences, used relentlessly and unflinchingly, form the heart of the economic approach as I see it." Furthermore, the economic approach can be successfully applied to all kinds of human behavior, not only economic behavior. "... I contend that the economic approach is uniquely powerful because it can integrate a wide range of human behavior." Becker and his associates and followers have accordingly applied the economic approach to such diverse areas as crime, altruism, marriage, and having children. The theory of public choice applies the economic approach to politicians who are then treated as maximizers of votes (see Buchanan and Tullock, 1962).

Economic theory is said to have two functions: a normative, "prescriptive" function and a positive, "descriptive" function. The normative function is served through the formulation of rules for action in relation to defined goals. There are certain rules to follow if consumers want to maximize their utility, there are rules to follow for entrepreneurs if they want to maximize their profits. Since the assumption is that the consumer and the entrepreneur actually – at least in the long run and on average in large enough groups – behave in accordance with the rules, the theory also serves to explain and predict economic behavior at some level of aggregation. If people behave rationally in the stipulated sense, behavior becomes predictable. Rationality means that given the characteristics of the situation including preferences for alternative actions, any decision maker would make the same, perfectly predictable choice. The assumptions mentioned constitute the much criticized concept of the economic man. It has already been pointed out that psychologists are prone to find the assumptions totally unrealistic at the individual level.

The assumptions about economic man serve as a basis for deriving a number of conclusions about demand and supply curves for commodities and labor and the price mechanisms yielding market prices. They also give a basis for reasoning and conclusions regarding income, saving, and consumption at the aggregate level. The assumptions which point out the consumer and the entrepreneur as maximizers are part of microeconomic theory. The main interest in microeconomics is focussed on how price mechanisms operate (price theory) and relative prices of commodities are determined, how interest rates and wage rates are determined. Macroeconomics involves the study of aggregates in the national economy, i.e., economics in terms of whole systems. It studies key economic quantities, such as national income, savings, investments and balance of payments, and the factors determining them and their interrelationships.

It may look obvious to many psychologists that economic psychology should be busy with the elaboration of the psychological assumptions behind economic theory. It is not likely that this will be a very fruitful allocation of research resources, at any rate in the short run. Psychology is a highly empirical science with few attempts at abstract theorizing of the type that economic theory displays. An important assumption in economic studies is that deviations from rationality, that is from maximizing behavior, have a tendency to balance out over time and in large populations. Becker states simply that rationality at the market level does not presuppose rationality at the household level. An important reason for this is what he calls the existence of opportunity sets which limit the amount of irrationality possible. The psychologist's contention that subjective rationality may be different from objectively defined rationality and that the subjective rationality is decisive for individual behavior is thus to some extent taken care of. Katona (1975) maintained on the basis of his empirical studies that sometimes deviations from rational behavior did not offset one another even in a large population since a majority of decision makers had received and acted on the same information. The economist may grant that the psychologist can give different and more realistic descriptions of individual economic behavior and then ask in Milton Friedman's spirit whether the new assumptions give better predictions than the old ones (see Friedman, 1953). The psychologist may find it difficult to give an affirmative answer to this question.

Economic research typically starts with deductive reasoning and a mathematical model is developed which makes it possible to derive specific consequences. Simplifying assumptions make empirical testing of the consequences feasible. A simplified example can perhaps clarify some of the economist's way of operation. The example is taken from the area of forecasting consumption. Microeconomic theory explains individual consumption of a commodity group as a function of:

1. preferences,
2. relative prices of commodities, and
3. household incomes.

Rationality or maximizing behavior is assumed and is taken to mean that consumers know and follow their preference scales when choosing commodities and that they heed their budget limits, i.e., what they can afford. One simplifying assumption involves that preferences are revealed through behavior in the marketplace and that they are stable over the period considered. Consequently, the market share for a commodity group gives an indication of the group's position on the preference scales of the households. The prices connected with the commodity group are assumed to remain stable in relation to the general price level. On the basis of time series data for a period of, say, ten years, the market share of the commodity group is related to household income and expressed in terms of income elasticities indicating the commodity group's sensitivity to changes in household income. An assumption must be made about the change in total household income during the period to be forecasted and the future consumption of the commodity group can then be calculated.

If the forecast turns out to be far off the actual consumption of the commodity group, which can be checked when the forecast period is over, the search for explanations follows a logical sequence. The first question is whether the assumption about income changes corresponded to the actual development. If not, the model should be tested with the correct level of income change and again checked for accuracy. If the results still do not agree with actual development for the commodity group, the second step is to look at the development of the prices of the commodity group in relation to the prices of other commodities. They may have changed differently from other prices. Thirdly, the assumption of stable preferences may be risky, if the commodity group is too narrowly defined. It may for example be fairly safe to assume that preferences for the whole area of recreation expressed in terms of market share remain stable for a period of many years while there may be many changes in preferences within this group.

Becker (1979) says about the assumed stability of preferences: "The preferences that are assumed to be stable do not refer to market goods and services... These underlying preferences are defined over fundamental aspects of life – such as health, prestige, sensual pleasure, benevolence, or envy – that do not always bear a stable relation to market goods and services." Regrouping goods and services may then be a way of improving consumption forecasts.

This example, in which some omissions and simplifications have been made, serves to illustrate the point that basic microeconomic theory is on the whole left unaffected by possible failures of models derived from it. This means a significant difference in comparison to the common theories in psychological research. The latter are typically at a rather low level of abstraction, the empirical tests relate more directly to the underlying theory, and can be crucial for the theory's survival. The obverse of this is that economists produce more information in terms of conclusions from their use of empirical data than psychologists do. Economic analysis of data yields more implications thanks to the more abstract level of the theory and can perhaps be said to be more parsimonious in its handling of data. Psychological research on economic problems has a tendency to focus on possible interactions between variables and to lead to discussions of under what conditions a relation may hold rather than to generally valid, simple laws. This is another way of saying that psychologists do not believe that individual deviations from rational behavior necessarily cancel out in a population as assumed by economists.

Economics operates with what Maital (1982) calls a two-valued logic or two-question technique:

1. What do I get out of it? (utility)
2. How much do I have to sacrifice? (cost)

Psychologists are often accused by economists of trying to explain and predict behavior on the basis of attractiveness ratings of objects and forgetting about the sacrifice aspects (see, e.g., Meyer, 1982). It is said to be no wonder that attitudes do not predict behavior when costs are not considered. Such critique is pronounced also by psychologists and is to some extent answered by pointing to developments in attitude research concerning the relation between attitudes and behavior. Verhallen and Pieters (1984) review the problems and present a model for handling them. Among other things they extend the sacrifice or cost concept to include behavioral costs, defined as time, physical and mental effort in addition to monetary costs.

In psychology, there are some early attempts to incorporate a two-valued logic in the area of conflict studies. Lewin (1951) dealt with positive and negative valences in his theory of conflict. Positive valence is similar to utility and negative valence is the same as cost in a broad sense. The theory has been applied to situations in which consumers make difficult choices with both advantages and disadvantages (Bilkey, 1951; Kassarjian, 1973). One of the competing conflict theories, proposed by Neal Miller, has been shown to have similarities with microeconomic theory (Holzman, 1958). Miller's approach-avoidance conflict type reflects the idea that an object can have both utility which stimulates to approach and cost aspects leading to avoidance tendencies. Another of Miller's conflict types is called approach-approach and involves a choice between two attractive alternatives. An economist would point out that this type of conflict concerns opportunity cost, i.e., the cost of not being able to select the other alternatives when a choice has been made. Although psychologists may speak of after choice dissonance in such cases, they show little inclination to take into account that expectations of such opportunity costs can be a possible determinant of the choice. Thaler (1980) presents some interesting ideas about opportunity costs derived from the psychological theory called "prospect theory" (Kahneman and Tversky, 1979). Experimental studies cast some doubts on the assumption that businessmen actually consider opportunity costs in their decision making. They seem inclined to exaggerate the value of actual outlays in relation to opportunity costs (Beeker et al., 1974; Neumann and Friedman, 1979; Hoskin, 1983) which is what prospect theory would predict.

Expectation has long been a concept used both by economists and psychologists although their paths of thinking in this area seldom seem to have crossed. Keynes noted in his *General Theory* (1936) that the entrepreneur had to make decisions about production before he could expect any return on his investments. His decisions had to be based on his expectations. The Stockholm School (Myrdal, Ohlin, and Lindahl) even expanded that, in their discussion of business cycles, into "expectations ex ante" and "expectations ex post" (see Hanson, 1982). This meant that there was assumed to be a learning process.

In economics, it has been commonly assumed and to some extent is still assumed that expectations are formed on the basis of past experience and that there are no differences in individual interpretations of past experience. An objective study of price level development over a period of time then gives reliable information about expectations of future price developments. Economic studies have, however, shown that actions based on price level expectations have deviated considerably from what past experience would have suggested. Attempts have been made to improve the theory by weighing in different ways the time series data which serve as proxies for past experience, for example giving extra weight to more recent developments (theories of adaptive expectations). A crucial question in this context is how new information that indicates departures from earlier trends is received and processed. In Katona's (1975) view past experiences give poor predictions when consumers face situations which they think require problem solving rather than routine or habitual behavior.

The theory of rational expectations represents a radically new way of treating expectations. It has caused an intense debate in economics and inspired a large number of theoretical and empirical studies (for summaries, see Sheffrin, 1983; Carter and Maddock, 1984). The theory states that decision makers, whether businessmen or consumers, are so well informed that they can make estimates (educated guesses) of what will happen in the future. They are assumed to utilize information and form their expectations as though they were highly qualified economists and could calculate the future with the help of a set of economic equations. This assumption may simply be replaced by the assumption that the decision makers on the average find the best available forecast and adopt it as their own expectation. A consequence is that people acting on the basis of such expectations tend to make the expected development, for example, level of inflation, come true.

At first view, the theory of rational expectations appears to open up possibilities for interesting psychological research since it is based on the assumption that information is received and acted upon. It is true that some experiments have been carried out to elucidate some assumptions, but on the whole the proponents of the theory are not inclined to presume that measurement attempts at the level of the individual can give any relevant information. Katona (1980) who finds such measurements necessary views the theory of rational expectations as another attempt from inveterate economists to avoid the study of individual behavior. The area of expectations and how expectations are formed on the basis of past experience and information seems to be a potentially interesting one for psychological research. The theory of rational expectations has drawn economists' attention to the influence of information and has led to the introduction into economic literature of such concepts as the credibility of certain sources of information (see, e.g., Backus and Driffill, 1985).

Experimental economics is a relatively new branch of economics. It began in West Germany around thirty years ago and has since then gained some standing which is illustrated by the fact that articles written by experimental economists appear regularly in the most respected economic journals. The approaches used are very similar to those used in experimental psychology. Laboratory experiments are run on problems related to bargaining, coalition formation, competition, pricing, tax evasion etc. (see, e.g., Plott, 1982; Smith, 1982). A growing number of economists have found that controlled experiments offer chances of studying theoretical relationships and of testing hypotheses under conditions that give less bias than introspection, mental experiments, and casual observation of phenomena.

In the periphery of economics, there are other developments that indicate an increased interest in psychological methods and theories. Several books in which the authors have criticized economic theory and suggested more use of psychological research have come out in recent years (Scitovsky, 1976; Maital, 1982; Maital and Maital, 1984; Alhadeff, 1982; Gilad and Kaish, 1986). Economists have for example found common ground with psychologists who work in the tradition of Skinner. Alhadeff (1982) has even formulated a whole new microeconomic theory on the basis of operant conditioning theory. Lea (1978) who is a psychologist, has pointed out that operant conditioning studies of how behavioral acts followed by reinforcements are learned under varying schedules of reinforcements produce something very similar to economic demand curves. He notes some similarities and differences between such psychological demand curves and economic demand curves. It is for the psychologists who study operant conditioning not only a matter of teaching economists some psychology, but also a taking over of concepts and problems from economics (see, e.g., Hursh, 1985)

3.4. *Marketing*

Kotler, one of the leaders in the academic field of marketing, defines marketing as the science of exchange. "Marketing is human activity directed at satisfying needs and wants through exchange processes" (Kotler, 1980: p. 19). Division of labor presupposes exchange to compensate the specialized individual for the shortages that specialization leaves in the non-specialized areas. Specialization and division of labor are a necessary, but not sufficient requisite for mass production. The latter requires a large enough market with a demand for the mass produced goods. Mass production adds special features to exchange relations, involving for example physical distribution of goods and establishing contacts between parties. The concept of marketing brings those to mind. It is often associated with activities directed by a seller toward a large group of potential buyers. Marketing can also be used to designate exchange which is not based on mass production, but where a seller has some kind of initiative. A characteristic feature of marketing is the use of persuasive communication which may be a sign of the fact that one party, namely the seller, who has already invested money in the venture, has a greater interest in the exchange than the other party, the potential buyer or consumer. The idea behind an exchange is otherwise that the potential buyer has a need for something and that this need can be fulfilled through something that the seller is willing to part with.

As Keynes (1936) noted, the manufacturers and sellers of products have to make investments on the basis of their expectations of being able to sell later and get their money back. They need information about what the potential buyers want, preferably before they have incurred too much cost. It is the function of market research to furnish such information. Market research reduces the uncertainty about the consumers' future reactions to the product that is being developed. When the product is launched on the market, the potential buyers must get some knowledge about it before they are able and willing to buy. Since the sellers have incurred costs, they want to influence the purchasing decision in their favor, and they give the information in the shape of more or less persuasive communication. The product is made available through retail outlets, mail ordering, door-to-door selling, or other forms of distribution.

The study of consumer behavior has become one of the cornerstones of marketing which is understandable against the background outlined above.

Consumer behavior research provides ideas for market segmentation and for marketing activities, in particular for advertising, pricing, and product development. It gives ideas about how marketing strategy should be formulated and implemented. Consumer behavior theory has in the first place been developed in connection with marketing management problems. The close connection between consumer behavior study and marketing management is evidenced by the subtitles of some recent textbooks on consumer behavior indicating that managerial implications are given or that the perspective is managerial. This in its turn mirrors the most recent developments in marketing thought where there is a pronounced emphasis on management and strategic decision making (Kotler, 1980). This involves that profitability (return on investment) is stressed and that every activity in the firm is scrutinized from the angle of what it may add to improved decision making and strategy formulation.

Granting that consumer behavior is an important area in marketing does not imply that marketing completely overlaps with economic psychology with respect to consumer behavior study. It is true that economic psychology has a fundamental interest in the study of consumer behavior, but this interest is not exclusively tied to marketing interests. There is also the point of view of public policy makers, who work with problems of consumer information and consumer protection. As a matter of fact most academic consumer behavior researchers make a special point of interpreting their findings both in terms of marketing implications and public policy implications (for an example, see Bettman, 1979). When consumer behavior is discussed, it should also be remembered that there is a demand from government bodies as well as from business firms for data on consumer expenditures and saving behavior, analyzed by consumer researchers.

It is essential for economic psychology that work is done to develop consumer behavior theory in such a way that the theory is independent of immediate interests of application. It should be possible to evolve a theory which can serve as a source of models for such different fields of application as marketing and public policy. A close association with a field of application may be detrimental to the development of the theory that is fundamentally necessary for good applications. Consumer behavior theory which now almost exclusively rests on contributions from marketing contexts has been accused of being narrow in scope, of studying trivial problems like brand selection from among homogeneous goods, and of being tied to rigid ways of thinking which leave little room for development (cf. Arndt, 1981).

Marketing can be seen as a branch of business administration. In passing it should be mentioned that economic psychology has an overlap of interest also with other areas in business administration. An example is so-called behavioral accounting. Accounting deals with figures and report systems which are used to provide information about a firm's economic status and about economic activities pursued. They can be subjected to experimental research modeled after research in cognitive psychology. A rather complete review of the use of laboratory experiments in accounting research is given by Swieringa and Weick (1982). A typical question raised by behavioral accounting researchers is how the receivers of a financial report react to it, to what extent they use the information in it, and how they use it. This also encompasses that reports like annual statements of business firms are planned with a view to secure the attention and comprehension of the target audience (see, e.g., Wright, 1977a, 1977b). A study in which a content analysis, applying psychological attribution theory, was performed on annual statements of a number of big U.S. companies, shows that attributions of success and failure tend to be predictable using hypotheses from attribution theory (Bettman and Weitz, 1983). Even in annual statements which can be expected to be perused by many stakeholders, there is a tendency to explain failures by means of external factors whereas successes are explained with reference to internal factors in the business firms.

3.5. *Sociology*

While psychology is said to focus on the individual, sociology is said to focus on groups and social systems. In the study of consumer behavior there has often been a need to improve explanations through including sociological variables. The effects of belonging to a certain culture or to certain types of social networks turn out to be very important in explaining both individual and market behavior (cf. Van Veldhoven, 1981). Studies of the diffusion and adoption of innovations originated in sociology, but have become a necessary ingredient in theory development relating to consumer behavior.

Within the boundaries of social psychology there is naturally considerable overlap between sociology and psychology in the type of research problems tackled. Sociological variables derived from social class theories, from culture and subculture theories, and from different group theories are juxtaposed with socio-psychological variables like values and attitudes. These variables are also used in sociological theory making. The concept of life style which is commonly used in consumer research, particularly in marketing research, embodies ideas both from sociology and from psychology. Van Raaij (1981) notes in his introductory article in the first issue of the *Journal of Economic Psychology* that there are few contributions of sociology to the study of consumer behavior, but that the use of sociological variables is pervasive. He suggests that there should be no strict boundaries between economic sociology and economic psychology. After some decades with rather low interest paid to economic sociology, it now seems to be coming back into focus as a consequence of widening interests in sociological research. Well-known economists like Joseph Schumpeter and Gunnar Myrdal have done considerable work in sociology. Some of Schumpeter's work has actually been described as being primarily sociological in slant and referred to as economic sociology. His theory of the role of the entrepreneur for economic development is an example.

4. A PERSPECTIVE FOR THE STUDY OF ECONOMIC PSYCHOLOGY

4.1. *Introduction*

In the final section of the chapter, I shall take up two major themes. The first concerns the fundamental character of economic psychology. As I see it, it is a problem-oriented science in which theory development is highly important for its progress and acceptance as a new branch of science. The relation between problem orientation and theory construction in economic psychology is thus discussed. Secondly, the question of relevance or the external validity of the research in the field is brought up. The discussion concerns the three major arenas in economic psychology and in addition also includes some points on the normative vs. the descriptive use of science.

4.2. *Problem Orientation and Theory Construction*

Economic psychology has derived its problems primarily from economic reality. The starting point of research has not been economic theory or psychological theory, but usually the fact that the researcher has become involved in or intrigued by some kind of economic problems and started delving in order to gain a better understanding of the underlying phenomena. Katona's research career is a good illustration. Faced with the enormous inflation in Germany immediately after World War I, he tried to find psychological explanations for the economic situation so as to increase the understanding of the causes.

In economic psychology, the problems are studied with the aid of what there is of potentially applicable theory. This means that available theories are employed in new, perhaps generative ways and makes theory development a necessity. Theory is generally developed in close contact with empirical data, so-called lowlevel theory, which, it is hoped, will in the long run be replaced by theory at a more abstract, comprehensive level.

As mentioned earlier Becker (1976) suggests that a scientific discipline should be defined through its approach to the study of problems and he provides a succinct statement of what constitutes the economic approach, applicable in his view not only to economic behavior, but to human behavior in general. Judging from some of Katona's writings, I think that he would have thought himself able to make an almost equally succinct statement about the economic psychological approach, maybe something like this: "Economic behavior, involving consumption and saving, is in the economic-psychological approach assumed to depend on ability to consume and willingness to consume. Both sets of factors can be measured." For a comparatively young and undeveloped discipline like economic psychology, such a statement of the economic-psychological approach is probably too terse and I shall spell it out further, while conceding that it contains the main ideas of the economic-psychological approach.

The main focus in economic psychology lies on the role of the human agent in economic behavior. It means a concentration of research interest on individual behavior in such terms that aggregation over individuals is made possible. The purpose is to describe and explain behavior at a level of aggregation which can be defined as a market. Descriptions and explanations of individual behavior serve this purpose rather than the purpose of making individual predictions. Economic psychology may still be useful, for instance to budget advisers who work with the economic problems of families.

The fundamental assumptions are that behavioral acts and behavioral patterns are affected by:

1. motivation factors involving discrepancies between actual and desired states which give force and general direction to behavior;
2. value structures that have both stable and volatile components;
3. processing of information from the external and the internal environment, combining new information with information from memory;
4. social comparison processes and social influence;
5. rules for weighing benefits and sacrifices against each other (choice heuristics);
6. attributions of success and failure to causes: learning.

These six characteristics appear in most theories of human behavior although under somewhat differing labels and with varying degrees of empirical referents. The economic-psychological approach implies, as I see it, that the concepts used have a good empirical anchoring.

The predominance of cognitive theories in today's psychological research fits in well with what seems most promising in economic psychology. Bettman's (1986) review of consumer behavior studies gives an impression of a total dominance for cognitive approaches in this research. Influences from external and internal stimuli flow through human perception and affect behavior after information processing of longer or shorter duration. Hilgard (1980) remarks that consciousness is back in psychology after many years of absence and under new labels. Although welcome, this return may have led to an overemphasis of conscious information processing in consumer behavior study, making the consumer look more active and rational with respect to information use than what actually corresponds to reality. Routine, sometimes almost automatic processes must be given due research attention. There must, furthermore, be some room left for testing also more dynamic approaches to the study of economic behavior. Van Raaij (1984), following Zajonc (1980) has drawn attention to the potential effects of emotional reactions that precede cognitive responses.

Becker's observation that there is usually a limit to the amount of irrationality that can be displayed by a household in a market, should serve as a caution for economic psychology. Opportunity sets establish boundaries which restrict the freedom of behavior not only at the market level, but also at the individual level. The impact of the environment is a fundamental tenet in Marxist economics. Psychological research on poverty has to some extent failed because opportunity sets in the environment of the poor or rather the lack of opportunities have been left out of consideration (Strümpel, 1974; Gurin and Gurin, 1970). In many other areas of economic behavior a disregard of restricting or constraining factors in the environment may make the value of a psychological analysis doubtful. Economic psychology must operate with both individual and system variables.

In principle, psychological research aims at finding general relationships between phenomena. These are sometimes referred to as behavioral laws, and they aim at having such scope that individual differences can be neglected. In practice, however, psychological research often faces the responsibility of pointing out the importance of individual differences and, moreover, to divide up the individual differences further by introducing interactions and dependencies between variables. In a somewhat jocular vein, it can be said that the psychologist's typical answer to a question about the relationship between two phenomena is: "It all depends." Then the psychologist tries to find all of the factors, the conditions and the "covariates," that can influence the relationship. This way of thinking is foreign to practitioners who tend to prefer simple cause-and-effect relations, and psychologists working for managerial purposes have often been forced to relinquish it. It is not highly regarded by economists either since they tend to start their work on models of economic behavior with a few simple assumptions about human characteristics. Actually, a fundamental epistemological question is involved here, namely what interactions and dependencies among variables can be safely neglected.

In an examination of Friedman's (1953) assertions about positive economics, the philosopher Musgrave (1981) distinguishes between three types of assumptions in theory development:

1. negligibility assumptions,
2. domain (applicability) assumptions,
3. heuristic assumptions.

The first type of assumption means that some factors are consciously left out of consideration either because their effects can be presumed to be insignificant or because there is simply no way to assess the size of the effects. Psychological factors are for example often assumed to be negligible in macroeconomic analyses and in sociological analyses because they are assumed to cancel out in a population.

The second type of assumption involves that the negligibility assumption may have turned out to be wrong. Then the question is whether the negligibility assumption may still be valid for a specific domain of applicability. Adoption of the domain assumption can be a way out from entangled nets of interactions which cannot be studied effectively. It means that a certain relationship is assumed to be valid only within specified limits.

The heuristic assumption is the provisional use of an hypothesis such as an hypothesis of negligibility. For lack of better knowledge or methods to use, a negligibility assumption can be made at first to make research at all possible. Later this assumption may be replaced by domain assumptions.

It has often happened in psychological research that a relationship between two variables has been found in some research and it has been interpreted as a kind of law with general applicability. Later research has then discovered that the linear relationship holds only under certain conditions. An example is the finding that increasing the fear-arousing contents of a communication decreased its influence on behavior and on attitudes. Later research has demonstrated that there are a number of conditions and interactions that affect this relationship. Strong fear-arousing stimuli can be effective under certain circumstances. Medium scare content is sometimes more effective than low scare content. It is important to find out which these circumstances are. Research has indicated something about what the important conditions are and some domain assumptions can be made. Fear arousing stimuli up to a certain level of scaring content may for example constitute a domain in which a linear relationship holds (see Kroeber-Riel (1984: pp. 71-77) for a similar discussion).

With economics as a springboard economic psychology has the task of challenging some negligibility assumptions, made in economic theory. Katona's introduction of some intervening variables is an example of this kind. Psychological research can provide more of descriptive richness to economics. This richness must not become too cumbersome and overwhelming. The question is where one can stop looking at factors that might possibly exert an influence. With psychology as a starting point, economic psychology faces the necessity of making new negligibility assumptions, since psychology is intent on finding distinguishing details about men. Thereby economic psychology of course risks accusations of superficiality from psychologists, while still being too detailed for the economist's taste.

The experimental approach means that certain types of negligibility assumptions are controlled for in the experimental setting. This is accomplished through the use of one or more control groups. The latter are assigned the role of making sure that the effect of the experimental treatments can be assessed. Other influences than the experimental treatments are assumed to be the same in both experimental and control groups. Negligibility in the laboratory or in other settings where experiments are performed is not equal to negligibility in real-life situations. The external validity of the laboratory experiment is by critics said to be low (see, e.g., the discussion in the *Journal of Consumer Research*, 1982-1983; Lynch, 1982). Experimental psychologists maintain that the external validity is not always of great import since the role of the laboratory experiment is to test theory and establish possibilities of relationships rather than to provide estimates of the external probabilities of relationships (see, e.g., Petrinovitch, 1979; Swieringa and Weick, 1982; Mook, 1983).

If economic psychology, as proposed earlier, aims at describing and predicting economic behavior at the market level (here used to designate aggregation over a large group of people – a mass market), the question arises whether the data at the individual level and at the aggregate level have to give corresponding results. Economists tend to assume that for example (some) irrational behavior at the individual level may appear as rational at the aggregate level. Can psychological relations found at the aggregate level be expected to be valid also at the individual level and vice versa? This question emerged in economic psychology, when Adams (1965) formulated his time-series vs. cross-section paradox. Time series analysis of attitudinal data reflecting optimism-pessimism about future economic conditions showed that these data had considerable predictive power at the aggregate level. In cross-section analysis, the data, which were in fact collected from individuals, turned out to have poor predictive power. Buying intentions or plans, on the other hand, were good predictors of individual household behavior, but contributed little to explaining the variance in time series analyses of aggregate data. Later research by Bouwen (1977) has contributed to making this apparent paradox somewhat clearer.

The economist Kenneth Boulding (1972) said about Katona's Index of Consumer Sentiment (the optimism-pessimism index referred to above):

> Even if we cannot get very reliable measures for the individual, by the famous principle which I have sometimes called "Katona's Law," that

> the summation of ignorance produces knowledge, we may find an operation or instrument with self-cancelling random factors, which will give us a much better measure for a hundred or a thousand individuals than we can get for one (p. 466).

Without claiming that he had found or created his own law, Katona (1979) in an article discussed these problems and pointed out that the law of large numbers operates and that thus a gain can be made through an analysis at the aggregate level. Relations can be discovered that do not appear at the individual level. The problem is now often dealt with in terms of ecological inference (see, e.g., Langbein and Lichtman, 1978). Studies of ecological inference usually grapple with the problem of "aggregation bias" which applies when there are aggregate data and individual level inference is desired. What Katona refers to in his article is called "aggregation gain." He calls it "macropsychology" and pleads for more interest devoted to macrophenomena among psychological researchers.

Other psychological researchers have been worried about the difficulties in psychology to explain any great amounts of behavioral variation. Epstein (1980) has, agreeing with Katona, recommended averaging over large numbers of people as one way of reaching more stable relationships and better explanatory results in psychological research. He also advocates more use of time series data and shows by examples the increases in reliability that are obtainable through such procedures. Gregson (1983) has even devoted a whole book to the use of time series analysis in psychology and is a strong advocate for it.

In conclusion, it should be stressed again that economic psychology embodies the idea that human actors have to be studied for understanding and predicting economic behavior. Understanding is a prerequisite for predicting behavior in situations, where new combinations of factors occur, where it is necessary to try to foresee the effects of specified external stimuli, and where human perception, information processing, emotions, and decisions make straightforward predictions on the sole basis of economic variables inadequate.

4.3. *Problem Orientation and the Question of Relevance*

In the social and behavioral sciences, despite many differences of opinion with respect to the appropriate procedure for theory development, there are certain criteria that are applied to a piece of research to determine, whether it is acceptable or not. These criteria encompass such things as a scrutiny of the procedure used, from correspondence rules between conceptual level and observational level, i.e., the internal validity, to the adequacy of the statistical analysis. Replicability of results and long-term contribution to theory are further major criteria. The last decade or so has seen additional criteria become pervasive as a consequence of a quest for relevance. Scientific research should according to this view not be a search without definite goals and with a long-term expectation that something useful will always come out, but it should be related to some specific, worthy issue, the progress of which could be furthered by the research.

Three main arenas in economic psychology were identified above. One arena relates to the consumer role and has consumer behavior as its focus, another has the business role and business behavior as center of attention, and the third arena focusses on the economic, resource-handling citizens and their relations to society. In the last section, I shall sketch some interpretations of what the quest for relevance may mean to these three arenas. Perhaps I should point out that by relevance I do not mean immediate practical application of the research, but rather the promise of being useful in relation to some purpose.

4.3.1. *The Focus on the Consumer Role*

The quest for research to be relevant to some acceptable use may seem to be in conflict with the earlier expounded demand for consumer behavior theory to become more detached from specific practical uses. Actually the quest for relevance should here be interpreted as applicability to more than one area of use. Marketing management interest has influenced the selection of problems for study and has in return provided empirical data that have been used for theory development. Much of the research and consequently of the existing theories concern the selection of product brands and the factors affecting such choices. This area has for the researcher the tempting advantage of being comparatively simple to investigate and the choice behavior bears much resemblance to what has been studied in psychological learning theories, both in simple mechanistic and more complex cognitive learning theory. Representatives of consumer associations and public policy making in the consumer area tend to find existing theory too limited when it comes to providing a basis for helping consumers make better decisions. It is a problem in itself to clarify, what better decision making means and a better consumer behavior theory may contribute to solving this problem. It is embedded in the bigger problem of what constitutes well-being and the latter is a major concern of economic psychology as it is usually defined.

Both public policy making and marketing can and do contribute to consumer well-being. Some marketing activities (malpractices in some interpretations, intrinsic characteristics of marketing according to others) have been accused of not serving the consumer interest. There is also some debate over public policy making in the consumer area, for example, concerning increased consumer costs as a consequence of some consumer policies, but the questions raised are much less aggravating than with respect to marketing. It is not an easy task to define consumer well-being or the consumer interest in such terms that they will be generally accepted. Research can all the same shed light on the problems and suggest some solutions.

Economic psychology is not in the first place normative with respect to consumer behavior. It contributes knowledge which can be used in the interplay between consumers, marketers, and public policy makers in such a way that consumer well-being is furthered. It is then up to the individual researchers to decide, whether they want to commit themselves further and actively promote the inclusion of well-being considerations into the policy making of government bodies, consumer associations, and marketing firms.

4.3.2. *The Focus on the Business Role*

The treatment of business behavior hints that economic-psychological research is carried out from so-to-speak an outsider's stance. The purpose of the research is not primarily to serve individual business firms with research results relating to business behavior and providing suggestions for changes or actions. The research is rather aimed at developing theories of business behavior that can lend themselves to describing and explaining business behavior in a societal or macroeconomic framework. The relevance of a particular instance of research is determined by such a framework.

Areas of special interest are business decision making in finance, production, and marketing, factors influencing the emergence of innovations and entrepreneurship. Many of the problems towards which research attention is directed originate in a macroeconomic frame of reference, e.g., how do business decision makers react to a certain policy measure before, during and after the measure has been put into effect? What factors influence the appearance and exploitation of inventions in an economy?

The focus of interest is naturally on what the human actors perceive, expect and value. Such subjective phenomena can be studied through inferences from environmental changes – which means using objective data as proxies for subjective phenomena – or through questioning or observing the actors concerned. The latter approach means that economic psychology takes issue with economists like Becker (1979) who says: "Moreover the economic approach does not assume that decision units are necessarily conscious of their efforts to maximize or can verbalize or otherwise describe in an informative way reasons for the systematic patterns in their behavior." It should be noted that in cognitive research there is a more or less continuous discussion of the possibilities of gaining access to cognitive processes. Both inferences about cognitive processes, based on objective indicators, and direct questioning methods are employed and validated in psychological research. More acceptance among psychologists of the fact that good predictions of outcomes can sometimes be more desirable than good descriptions and explanations of processes would facilitate collaboration with economists. Economists should of course also accept to learn a few things about psychological processes.

4.3.3. *The Societal Perspective*

Many of the problems under this heading are usually referred to as macroeconomic. Some of the problem areas are not found in the common macroeconomic texts, since they rather belong to public finance or environmental economics or relate to some other economic aspect that is of concern at the level of government or to some national or international organization. The societal perspective can be said to pervade economic psychology, as should be obvious from the discussions of the consumer and the entrepreneurial roles. This does not preclude that economic psychology can be of use also at less aggregated levels.

Economic-psychological research can serve three major functions at the societal level:

1. Reporting on "the psychological state" of the economy at regular intervals. The studies of optimism-pessimism among consumers and business decision makers are good examples. More in-depth analyses are desirable and possible;
2. Providing analytic foundations for the planning of policy measures. This involves strategy considerations as well as providing ideas for contents of actions intended to change the course of events in some respect.
3. Encouraging considerations of behavioral aspects in economic decision making; this is not necessarily a normative function, rather dissemination of knowledge.

The functions can be fulfilled through judicious use of theory and careful collection of data through surveys and controlled experiments, also in laboratories. An important part of theory development may have to be done in laboratory research.

How far in the direction of being normative should economic psychology go with respect to this kind of research? Lewis (1982) pleads for normative involvement in the area of fiscal policy. It should be admitted that many of the problem areas have such a structure and are characterized by such selections of problems to be studied that some steps in a normative direction are taken already with the starting of a research project. The implications for actions on the basis of certain research results, say in poverty research, may be obvious. Again it appears most prudent to leave to the individual researcher or research team the decision about how far to go in a normative direction. In my opinion there is room for action and intervention research in economic psychology, but I would rather not think of such research as the most characteristic feature of economic-psychological research.

REFERENCES

Adams, F.G., 1965, Prediction with consumer attitudes: The time-series-cross section paradox, Review of Economics and Statistics, 4, 367-378.

Albou, P., 1962, Initiation à la psychologie économique, Bulletin de Psychologie, 16 Octobre, 1-82.

Albou, P., 1976, Besoins et Motivations Economiques, Paris: Presses Universitaires de France.

Albou, P., 1984, La Psychologie Economique, Paris: Presses Universitaires de France.

Alhadeff, D.A., 1982, Microeconomics and Human Behavior. Toward a New Synthesis of Economics and Psychology, Berkeley, CA: University of California Press.

Arndt, J., 1981, Marketing and the quality of life, Journal of Economic Psychology, 1, 283-301.

Backus, D., and J. Driffill, 1985, Rational expectations and policy credibility following a change in regime, Review of Economic Studies, 52, 211-221.

Becker, G.S., 1976, The Economic Approach to Human Behavior, Chicago, IL: The University of Chicago Press.

Becker, G.S., 1979, "Economic analysis and human behavior," in: L. Lévy-Garboua (ed.), Sociological Economics, London: Sage Publications, pp. 7-24.

Beeker, S., J. Ronen, and G. Sorter, 1974, Opportunity costs. An experimental approach, Journal of Accounting Research, 12, 317-329.

Bettman, J.R., 1979, An Information Processing Theory of Consumer Choice, Reading, MA: Addison-Wesley.

Bettman, J.R., 1986, Consumer psychology, Annual Review of Psychology, 37, 257-289.

Bettman, J.R., and B.A. Weitz, 1983, Attributions in the board room: Causal reasoning in corporate annual reports, Administrative Science Quarterly, 28, 165-183.

Bilkey, W.J., 1951, The vector hypothesis of consumer behavior, Journal of Marketing, 16, 137-151.

Böhm-Bawerk, E., 1891, The Theory of Capital, London: MacMillan.

Boring, E., 1950, A History of Experimental Psychology, Englewood Cliffs, NJ: Prentice-Hall (second edition).

Boulding, K., 1972, "Human betterment and the quality of life," in: B. Strümpel, J.N. Morgan, and E. Zahn (eds.), Human Behavior in Economic Affairs, Amsterdam, Elsevier, pp. 455-470.

Bouwen, R., 1977, Anticipation and realization: Attitudes and buying plans in the future time orientation of consumer behavior, Psychologica Belgica, 17, 113-134.

Buchanan, J., and G. Tullock, 1962, The Calculus of Consent: Logical Foundations of Constitutional Democracy, Ann Arbor, MI: University of Michigan Press.

Carter, M., and R. Maddock, 1984, Rational Expectations. Macroeconomics for the 1980s?, London: Macmillan.

Epstein, S., 1980, The stability of behavior. II. Implications for psychological research, American Psychologist, 35, 790-806.

Fels, E., 1963, Hedonistic calculus as seen from a distance, Weltwirtschaftliches Archiv, 91, Heft 1.

Friedman, M., 1953, Essays in Positive Economics. Chicago IL: University of Chicago Press.
Gergen, K., 1982, Toward Transformation in Social Knowledge, New York: Springer Verlag.
Gilad, B., and S. Kaish (eds.), 1986, Handbook of Behavioral Economics. Behavioral Microeconomics, Vol. A, Greenwich, CT: JAI Press.
Gregson, R.A.M., 1983, Time Series in Psychology, Hillstate, NJ: Lawrence Erlbaum.
Gurin, G., and P. Gurin, 1978, Expectancy theory in the study of poverty, Journal of Social Issues, 26, 83-104.
Hammond, K.R., T.R. Stewart, B. Brehmer, and D.O. Steinman, 1975, "Social-judgment theory," in: M.F. Kaplan and S. Schwartz (eds.), Human Judgment and Decision Processes, New York: Academic Press, pp. 271-312.
Hanson, B.A., 1982, The Stockholm School and the Development of Dynamic Method, London: Croom Helm.
Hilgard, E.R., 1980, Consciousness in contemporary psychology, Annual Review of Psychology, 31, 1-26.
Holzman, M., 1958, Theories of choice and conflict in psychology and economics, Journal of Conflict Resolution, 2, 310-320.
Hoskin, R.E., 1983, Opportunity cost and behavior, Journal of Accounting Research, 21, 78-95.
Hughes, E.C., 1961, Tarde's Psychologie Economique. An unknown classic by a forgotten sociologist, American Journal of Sociology, 66, 553-559.
Hursh, S.R., 1985, "Demand analysis: A quantitative model of motivation," in: H. Brandstätter and E. Kirchler (eds.), Economic Psychology, Proceedings of the 10th IAREP Annual Colloquium, Linz, Austria: Rudolf Trauner Verlag, pp. 117-125.
Jevons, W.S., 1871, The Theory of Political Economy (reprint: 1911, London: Macmillan, fourth edition).
Kahneman, D., and A. Tversky, 1979, Prospect theory: An analysis of decision under risk, Econometrica, 47, 263-291.
Kassarjian, H.H., 1973, "Field theory in consumer behavior," in: S. Ward and T.S. Robertson (eds.), Consumer Behavior: Theoretical Sources, Englewood Cliffs, NJ: Prentice-Hall, pp. 118-140.
Katona, G., 1945, Price Control and Business; Field Studies Among Producers and Distributors of Consumer Goods, Bloomington, IN: Cowles Commission and Principia Press.
Katona, G., 1951, Psychological Analysis of Economic Behavior, New York: McGraw-Hill.
Katona, G., 1975, Psychological Economics, New York: Elsevier.
Katona, G., 1979, Toward a macropsychology, American Psychologist, 34, 118-126.
Katona, G., 1980, Essays on Behavioral Economics, Ann Arbor, MI: University of Michigan, Institute for Social Research.
Keynes, J.M., 1936, The General Theory of Employment, Interest and Money, London: Macmillan.
Kotler, P., 1980, Marketing Management, Englewood Cliffs, NJ: Prentice-Hall (fourth edition).
Kroeber-Riel, W., 1984, Konsumentenverhalten, München, FRG: Verlag Franz Vahlen (third edition).
Langbein, L.I., and A.J. Lichtman, 1978, Ecological Inference, Sage University Paper Series on Quantitative Applications in the Social Sciences, 07-010, Beverly Hills, CAA: Sage Publications.
Lea, S.E.G., 1978, The psychology and economics of demand, Psychological Bulletin, 85, 441-466.
Lewin, K., 1951, Field Theory in Social Science. Selected Theoretical Papers, New York: Harper and Row.
Lewis, A., 1982, The Psychology of Taxation, Oxford, UK: Martin Robertson.

Libby, R., 1981, Accounting and Human Information Processing: Theory and Applications, Englewood Cliffs, NJ: Prentice-Hall.
Lynch, J.G., Jr., 1982, On the external validity of experiments in consumer research, Journal of Consumer Research, 9, 225-239.
Maital, S., 1982, Minds, Markets, and Money. Psychological Foundations of Economic Behavior, New York: Basic Books.
Maital, S., and S. Maital, 1984, Economic Games People Play, New York: Basic Books.
Maslow, A.H., 1954, Motivation and Personality, New York: Harper and Row.
McClelland, D.C., and D.G. Winter, 1969, Motivating Economic Achievement, New York: The Free Press.
McDougall, W., 1908, An Introduction to Social Psychology (reprint: 1950, London: Methuen).
Menger, C., 1871, Grundsätze der Volkswirtschaftslehre (reprint: 1923, Vienna: Hölder-Pichler-Tempsky Y.).
Meyer, W., 1982, The research programme of economics and the relevance of psychology, British Journal of Social Psychology, 21, 81-91.
Mook, D.G., 1983, In defense of external invalidity, American Psychologist, 38, 379-387.
Musgrave, A., 1981, Unreal assumptions in economic theory: The F-twist untwisted, Kyklos, 34, 377-387.
Neumann, B.R., and L.A. Friedman, 1978, Opportunity costs: Further evidence through an experimental replication, Journal of Accounting Research, 16, 400-410.
Petrinovich, L., 1979, Probabilistic functionalism: A conception of research method, American Psychologist, 34, 373-390.
Plott, C.R., 1982, Industrial organization theory and experimental economics, Journal of Economic Literature, 20, 1485-1527.
Reynaud, P.L., 1954, Bilans de Psychologie Economique, Paris: Rivière.
Reynaud, P.L., 1964, La Psychologie Economique, "Que-sais-je?," Paris: Presses Universitaires de France.
Reynaud, P.L., 1974, Précis de Psychologie Economique, Paris: Presses Universitaires de France.
Reynaud, P.L., 1981, Economic Psychology, New York: Praeger.
Robbins, L., 1979, "The nature of economic generalizations," in: F. Hahn and M. Hollis (eds.), Philosophy and Economic Theory, Oxford, UK: Oxford University Press, pp. 36-46.
Rogers, E.M., 1969, Modernization Among Peasants: The Impact of Communication, New York: Holt, Rinehart and Winston.
Schmölders, G., 1959, Fiscal psychology: A new branch of public finance, National Tax Journal, 12, 340-345.
Schumpeter, J.A., 1933, The Theory of Economic Development. An Inquiry into Profits, Capital, Credit, Interest, and the Business Cycle, Cambridge, MA: Harvard University Press.
Scitovsky, T., 1976, The Joyless Economy. An Inquiry into Human Satisfaction and Consumer Dissatisfaction, New York: Oxford University Press.
Shackle, G.L., 1955, Uncertainty in Economics, Cambridge, UK: Cambridge University Press.
Sheffrin, S.M., 1983, Rational Expectations, Cambridge, UK: Cambridge University Press.
Smith, A., 1759, The Theory of Moral Sentiments (reprint: 1976, in: D.D. Raphael and A.C. Macfie (eds.), Oxford, UK: Clarendon Press).
Smith, A., 1776, An Inquiry into the Wealth of Nations. Harmondsworth, Middlesex, UK: Penguin Books (reprint: 1982).
Smith, V.L., 1982, Microeconomic systems as an experimental science, American Economic Review, 72, 923-955.

Stephenson, W., 1953, The Study of Behavior, Chicago, IL: University of Chicago Press.
Strümpel, B., 1969, "The contribution of survey research to public finance," in: A.T. Peacock (ed.), Quantitative Analysis in Public Finance, New York: Praeger, pp. 3-22.
Strümpel, B., 1974, "Economic well-being as an object of social measurement," in: B. Strümpel (ed.), Subjective Elements of Well-being, Paris: OECD, pp.
Svenson, O., 1979, Process descriptions of decision making, Organizational Behavior and Human Performance, 23, 86-112.
Swieringa, R.J., and K.E. Weick, 1982, An assessment of laboratory experimentation in accounting, Journal of Accounting Research, 20, 56-101 (supplement).
Tarde, G., 1890, The Laws of Imitation (reprint: 1903, New York: Holt).
Tarde, G., 1902, La Psychologie Economique, Paris: Alcan (2 volumes).
Thaler, R., 1980, Toward a positive theory of consumer choice, Journal of Economic Behavior and Organization, 1, 39-60.
Thurstone, L., 1931, The indifference function, Journal of Social Psychology, 2, 139-167.
Tobin, J., 1972, "Wealth, liquidity, and the propensity to consume," in: B. Strümpel, J.N. Morgan, and E. Zahn (eds.), Human Behavior in Economic Affairs, Amsterdam: Elsevier, pp. 37-56.
Van Raaij, W.F., 1976, Consumer Choice Behavior: An Information-processing Approach, Tilburg, The Netherlands: Tilburg University (doctoral dissertation).
Van Raaij, W.F., 1981, Economic psychology, Journal of Economic Psychology, 1, 1-24.
Van Raaij, W.F., 1984, Affective and Cognitive Reactions to Advertising, 84-111, Cambridge, MA: Marketing Science Institute (working paper).
Van Veldhoven, G.M., 1981, "Economic psychology: A new discipline?," in: W. Molt, H.A. Hartman, and P. Stringer (eds.), Advances in Economic Psychology, Heidelberg, FRG: Edition Meyn, pp. 1-20.
Veblen, T., 1904, The Theory of Business Enterprise, New York: Charles Scribner's Sons (reprint: 1958, as Mentor Book, MD 218).
Verhallen, T.M.M. and R.G.M. Pieters, 1984, Attitude theory and behavioral costs, Journal of Economic Psychology, 5, 223-249.
Wärneryd, K.-E., 1982, The life and work of George Katona, Journal of Economic Psychology, 2, 1-31.
Wärneryd, K.-E., 1986, "Economic and psychological approaches to the study of economic behavior: Similarities and differences," in: B. Brehmer, H. Jungermann, P. Lourens, and G. Sevón (eds.), New Directions in Research on Decision Making, Amsterdam: North-Holland, pp. 29-58.
Weisskopf, W.A., 1955, The Psychology of Economics, Chicago, IL: University of Chicago Press.
Wright, W.F., 1977a, Self-insight into the cognitive processing of financial information, Accounting, Organizations and Society, 2, 323-331.
Wright, W.F., 1977b, Financial information processing models: An empirical study, The Accounting Review, 52, 676-689.
Zajonc, R.B., 1980, Feeling and thinking: Preferences need no inferences, American Psychologist, 35, 151-175.

Part I

Theoretical Background

Introduction to Part I

PSYCHOLOGICAL PROCESSES AND ECONOMIC PHENOMENA: THE INNER SIDE OF ECONOMIC BEHAVIOR

Introduction

In Part I of the Handbook, a number of central psychological concepts will be discussed that are relevant for the explanation of economic behavior. Economic behavior can be studied as part of economic reality: Economic decisions and choices are input variables for the functioning of the economic system. Economic behavior also can be studied as outcome of psychological processes: directed by behavioral mechanisms, such as needs, motives, beliefs, and social references. Psychological variables are thus related to economic phenomena in various ways.

Although psychology and economics as scientific disciplines should be equally involved in the study and analysis of economic phenomena, this is not the starting point for this part of the book. There are several arguments for this. One argument is that there is no simple common classification principle to be applied to economic phenomena and being valid within both disciplines at this moment. Economics and psychology are organized in a totally different way and have developed independently from each other, although both have economic behavior as a central variable. As indicated above, economics deals mainly with the outcomes of economic behavior: aggregated volumes and quantities of economic output-variables and their quantitative relationships. Psychology, on the other hand, deals with the "inner side" of economic behavior: its psychological antecedents and effects. Lacking a common conceptual framework, it is impossible to deal with both disciplines in connection with economic behavior in a balanced and satisfactory way. Both disciplines have their own scientific approach and should thus be treated separately, within the conceptual framework of psychology or within economics.

Van Raaij, W.F., van Veldhoven, G.M. and Wärneryd, K.E. (eds) Handbook of Economic Psychology. ISBN 90-247-3720-6.

The Handbook is aimed at a broad audience. Therefore it is expected that a large part of this audience is probably less familiar with central notions and concepts of psychology. Most of the authors, however, have their scientific background within the behavioral sciences, especially psychology, so it seems to be reasonable to treat the psychological concepts in more detail, as a starting point for the analysis and explanation of economic phenomena. The chapters in this first part will thus be firmly grounded within psychology and its main theoretical orientations.

Discussing the relevance of psychological concepts for economic behavior it may be stated that the psychological explanation of economic behavior can be formulated in two different ways. Either economic behavior is being conceived as the necessary outcome of human nature, where this nature is a composite of assumed psychological laws and characteristics. Or economic behavior is being conceived as the result of a number of psychological processes that occur in connection with economic behavior.

Economic theory has implicitly postulated that general behavioral mechanisms underlie economic behavior. Even before Adam Smith, "human nature" has served to explain central economic phenomena and related processes. Thus, concepts, such as (marginal) utility, elasticity, and scarcity, are basically postulates about behavioral mechanisms and their underlying psychological variables. This approach deviates from the second one, according to which psychological variables should be found and studied in relation to economic behavior in a more descriptive way. This means explaining actual behavior within a given situation, at a given time and with a certain predictability as far as its outcomes may be valid for certain groups of people.

There is a controversy between "human nature" as a normative framework of determinants of economic behavior vs. the inventory of isolated psychological constructs and variables explaining economic behavior in a descriptive way. This is however not an essential but a gradual controversy: "human nature" as a causing system presumes that a certain relation between one or more psychological variables and a specific economic behavioral modality is true, irrespective of individual differences, situational settings or temporal determinants. When an empirically found relationship appears to be valid for more people within more situations and over a longer time period, then it comes close to the concept of "human nature" (or "homo economicus" in the case of economic behavior). At the end however, the difference between both approaches is a matter of more or less specifications that are imposed upon the relationship between psychological variables and economic behavior.

Psychology as a Discipline

Taking psychology as the disciplinary frame of reference for the explanation of economic behavior, the question arises about the characteristics of psychology as a scientific discipline.

Psychology, as a science, is inductive and empirically oriented. Insight in behavioral mechanisms and underlying constructs and variables is gained step by step via hypothesis, experimental testing and validation of the results. Starting point is the reality of behavior in its phenomenal form. This reality can be observed, perceived, known and experienced and exhibits the functional connection of the individual with his environment.

Behavior is being analyzed in an inductive and empirical way: The body of knowledge within psychology is the result of tested findings, hypotheses and theoretical suppositions. Experimental control and manipulation of behavioral aspects play an important role in generating this body of knowledge.

As a result of this inductive and empirical orientation, psychology as a discipline operates on several levels of specification. Sometimes knowledge is gained with respect to isolated variables in experimental conditions, for instance in perception, memory, and information processing. On this level psychology deals with specific variables.

The next level of specification should be indicated as the level of constructs, i.e., abstract explanatory notions consisting and organised as a structure of coherent variables. This level is more general in its explanatory power. Concepts, such as attitudes, motives, personality, and reference group, each explain a number of behavioral phenomena in their interrelationship within one central "idea" or organizing construct.

The third level of specification is reached when theories are being formulated, i.e., explanatory systems, in which a number of theoretical notions and concepts are linked within one overall frame of thinking and interpretation. Substantial parts of behavioral reality are being covered within such theories. There are a large number of theories within psychology. Learning theories, social comparison theory, psychoanalytical theories and other theories are examples of this level. Psychological knowledge thus includes variables, constructs and theories.

Although psychology is characterized by a large number of explanatory factors on various levels of specification, three general aspects are being distinguished within most behavioral processes and phenomena of individuals.

The first dimension refers to the cognitive aspects of human behavior. Cognitive variables have to do with what people know or are aware of about themselves in relation to the world they are living in. Intellectual abilities and rationality, memory, and beliefs are examples of cognitive variables or constructs. Affects have to do with positive and negative evaluations of things: liking, emotions, aggression, anxiousness, love are affective variables based upon evaluation and experiences within the world one is living in. Sometimes they are expressed, sometimes not. Some psychological variables have apparent, dynamic and behavior-steering characteristics: motives, needs, habits and intentions have a drive-impact on behavior.

Cognitions, affects, and dynamic aspects of behavior may be distinguished in an analytical way, but in reality they are integrated within many behavioral forms and processes. Emotions play a role within perception and are "co-organizers" within our learning system; for example, when people tend to see or, in other cases, tend to forget things they fear or are hoping for. Cognitions and beliefs sometimes possess a motivational function, for instance, in that they are self-defensive.

A last remark should be made with respect to the emphasis that can be put upon individual vs. social determinants of economic behavior. Economic behavior can be related to individual psychological factors, such as perception, personality, cognitions and affects. On the other hand, many activities are influenced by the actual or assumed presence of others. Social references are widespread within consumer behavior, serving the social identity of the individual or demonstrating the influence of social categories and group norms on individual behavior. Both aspects do not exclude each other: The same behavioral act may be explained from an individual psychological point of view as well as within a social psychological approach.

Psychology and Economic Behavior

Having discussed some general characteristics of psychology as a scientific discipline, some observations should be made about the particularities of economic behavior as a domain of scientific psychological approach.

The economic world we are living in has marked physical features. This physical reality aspect of economics, dealing with products, properties, money, physical distribution systems and so on, has important bearings upon economic behavior and its psychological explanation.

The first consequence is that within this reality it is necessary to distinguish between psychological processes that precede behavior and psychological processes that result from (changes in) economic circumstances. We are "shaping" economic-micro- reality by our acts and initiatives when saving, buying, borrowing and lending. The economic environment, at the same time, has psychological impact and leads to learning and adaptive behavior, as well as to satisfaction, well-being, feelings of frustration and aggressiveness. Within the domain of economic behavior both types of psychological interaction with the environment could and should be distinguished probably more rigidly than in other behavioral domains.

The next consequence pertains to contingencies within economic behavior. Economic reality may intervene between the intentions, motives and other antecedents of economic behavior, on the one hand, and its actual effects and outcomes on the other hand. This may have large consequences for the attributed or experienced instrumentality of behavior. Bankruptcy is a striking example of discontinuity between saving intentions and saving outcomes, eroding confidence and feelings of security of the savers. Contingency pertains to the link between antecedents and consequences of individual behavior and has important bearings for learning, personality, and the socialization of individuals.

Related to the foregoing is the observation that economic behavior varies largely in its degrees of freedom. Some behavioral acts are more or less free, or discretionary as Katona stated it. Choice behavior, for instance, refers to a free selection and choice among alternatives, based on autonomous preferences and available information. Other behavioral acts are more or less determined by external conditions or are obligatory. Contractual obligations, e.g., in the field of insurance, should be mentioned here, but also changes in external economic conditions, such as income, price level, or taxation rates have a compulsory effect on behavior. In studying economic behavior as the outcome of the interaction between the individual and the environment, the degrees of freedom of this behavior should be kept in mind. It may be quite clear that in the case of compulsory behavior the influence and role of pure psychological explanatory factors will be less than in behavior that has more degrees of freedom.

The last consequence is that it is not easy to classify economic behavioral forms along psychological dimensions or criteria. Many economic behaviors are highly object-specific and are thus not easily reducible to underlying broader psychological categories. This is the reason why in the other chapters of this Handbook more or less specific economic phenomena and issues are being raised instead of using a systematic approach from basic psychological processes into the various categories of economic behavior.

An additional remark should be made with respect to the level of aggregation. Many economic data are aggregates of individual decisions, choices and productive acts. The criterion of aggregation within economics is most of the time the monetary value of the aggregates, be it quantities, volumes, amounts or balances. This however does not necessary correspond with the psychological homogeneity of these aggregates. Economic aggregates are not ipse facto psychologically meaningful. Market segmentation is an example of splitting up economic aggregates ("markets") into psychologically meaningful aggregates ("segments") that correspond with need characteristics, value orientations or other psychological features.

Conclusion

The chapters in Part I of the Handbook offer introductions to various aspects of scientific psychology that are of interest when discussing economic behavior and its psychological basis.

The contribution of Gery van Veldhoven "Dynamic aspects of economic behavior: some determinants" (Chapter 2) might be seen as a condensed summary of behavioral dynamics that originate within the individual. The chapter should be positioned at the theoretical level, thus eliminating discussions about isolated concepts and constructs. The dynamics underlying human behavior are being stressed and a tentative classification of different theoretical approaches is being given.

Chapter 3 of Fred van Raaij has obviously a strong cognitive orientation. Within the paradigm of the "information processing" approach, a number of general functions and restrictions with respect to the role of cognitive factors within consumer decision making are discussed. Indicating the issues and trends within decision making, it is argued that the cognitive aspects are connected with affective and social factors.

Chapter 4 deals with the role of affect within economic behavior. Rik Pieters and Fred van Raaij discuss this interesting and "reanimated" dimension of economic behavior. Due to the impact of the long lasting interest in rational and cognitive aspects of behavior, the role of affects has been badly neglected. Although this chapter starts from the necessity of an integrated treatment of affect with other aspects of behavior, this refers to one of the major drawbacks that should be signaled with respect to this area. Especially the link between cognitive and affective aspects of behavior is still puzzling. The chapter gives a thorough treatment of empirical findings in this field and stresses the central significance of human experience for explaining economic behavior and behavior in general.

Chapter 5 by Rik Pieters is on attitude-behavior relationships. Attitudes refer to one of the central and most studied constructs within social psychology, that has found neither a final definition, nor a univocal status as a construct within various theoretical frameworks. One of the reasons for the continuing discussion about attitudes is that, whatever the theoretical definition and whatever the assessment method, one always seems to be confronted with a number of inconsistencies between attitudes and behavior. There are problems of measurement and there are problems of intervening and moderating variables that should be solved. The attitude-behavior debate is illustrative for the painsteaking efforts that psychology, as an inductive empirical science, has to make in order to gain a better insight and understanding of human behavior.

Karl-Erik Wärneryd in Chapter 6 clearly takes a social-psychological viewpoint on human behavior. Social influences, attribution of social phenomena, and the influence of social systems are being discussed, together with social learning and social transmittance processes. He demonstrates in this general treatment the richness and variety of social factors within human behavior. This area however appears to be rather poor with respect to overall theoretical explanatory systems: the results of empirical research are still somewhat fragmented and lack broad theoretical frameworks.

Gery M. van Veldhoven.

Table of Contents

2. Dynamic Aspects of Economic Behavior: Some Determinants

GERY M. VAN VELDHOVEN
Tilburg University, Tilburg, The Netherlands

1. INTRODUCTION

The ultimate criterion of all economic activities and economic policy is human well-being. In the end, all distribution of scarce means and goods serves the fulfillment of needs and aspirations and the achievement of satisfactions of individuals and groups. Thus, economic reality cannot adequately be understood without the analysis of the subjective and psychological dynamics that underlie and guide economic behavior of both individuals and groups: the motivations, values, and individual drives and states of happiness that are the targets of human activities. Some of these driving factors will be treated under the heading of "behavioral dynamics" in this chapter.

2. DELINEATION OF THE FIELD

Within psychology there is no such area as "behavioral dynamics" which can be treated as an independent field of study and which can be referred to in terms of separate traditions, generalized findings or even theoretical paradigms. "Behavioral dynamics" is a label that is useful for the purpose of this book, to mark the issues to be discussed in this chapter and to keep these issues manageable. "Behavioral dynamics" merges and combines several psychological approaches, such as motivation theory, personality theory, and learning theory, which study the dynamics of human behavior and which have research traditions, generalized findings and theories of their own.

For the purposes of this chapter *behavioral dynamics* deals with human behavior as it is "caused" and governed by processes that originate from motivational states, learning, or personality characteristics. Those aspects

Van Raaij, W.F., van Veldhoven, G.M. and Wärneryd, K.E. (eds) Handbook of Economic Psychology. ISBN 90-247-3720-6.

of human behavior that can be regarded as the reflection and expression of inner states of individuals and their connections with the environment will not be covered.

Rather, this chapter deals with dynamic aspects of behavior, aimed at the achievement of desired states and/or changes in the surroundings of an individual. Furthermore, the object of this chapter is overt behavior based on learning, motivation, and/or personality. Other constructs and variables which precede behavior, such as attitudes, cognitions, preferences and expectations, are left out of the discussion here. See for these concepts Chapters 3, 4, 5, and 13. Although these concepts and constructs are valuable notions in explaining behavior, they will not be treated here, because they are not primarily located within the framework of learning, motivation or personality.

Before proceeding to a more detailed discussion of the concepts of personality, motivation and learning, a definition of these concepts will be presented first. *Personality* refers to the total of an individual's characteristics which are stable over different situations and over time. It can be stated that the *motivation approach* of behavior stresses the direction of behavior towards certain goals or states and the intensity of this behavioral orientation. Finally, *learning* refers to the way in which past experiences are integrated within the behavior of an individual.

An example may clarify the relevance of personality, motivation and learning in explaining and understanding individual behavior. People differ in their saving behavior in many ways: Some people save in a loose, careless way, whereas others save in a rigid way, with severe control and strict and systematic planning. For some people saving is a very complex activity which includes gathering and organizing of (market) information and choosing an acceptable alternative. Although there is not much empirical evidence about the impact of personality factors on saving behavior, one may guess that personality factors may influence saving behavior, as an organizing and "styling" principle.

Saving may reflect different motivational orientations. Saving may be done for the purpose of risk avoidance, wealth accumulation and/or security of one's future or the future of one's children. These saving targets, risk avoidance, wealth accumulation, security, correspond to fundamental motivational processes within the individual.

Saving, to some extent, has to be learned. Sources of information, number and format of available alternatives, market conditions, such as interest rates and other economic indicators, should have their own meaning and weight within optimal saving decisions. Saving thus depends on previous training and experiences and may be viewed as a skill or expertise. Here, learning processes clearly play a role.

Within saving behavior the three components, personality, motivation and learning, interact. Buying shares may reflect a speculative, risk-prone personality, it may serve long-term saving motives, or it may simply be the outcome of learning processes during education and earlier life experiences.

Although more can be said about each of the above mentioned constructs, it can be stated that behavioral dynamics refers to several, more or less independent theoretical approaches to behavior. Each of these approaches is rooted in more or less independent theoretical streams and traditions within psychology and deserves a discussion in somewhat more detail. A short overview may serve this purpose.

2.1. *Personality*

Personality factors as an explanation of human behavior dates back to the ancient Greeks, Plato and Aristoteles, and to later philosophers relating human character to bodily fluids, such as sanguinic, phlegmatic, choleric, and melancholic types of "temperaments" (Galenus). Personality emerged as a legitimate focus of scholarly and scientific inquiry during the thirties. Authors such as Allport (1937), Lewin (1935), Murray (1938) and Murphy (1947), wrote the first comprehensive textbooks on personality and discussed the basic principles and issues that govern modern personality theory. They were preceded, of course, by several historical viewpoints and developments in the fields of psychometrics, medicine and psychiatry, and by general psychological theories, such as the Gestalt-theory and behaviorism. Modern personality theory, however, may be characterized by the interplay of biological, developmental and social forces within the individual's functioning (Jackson and Paunonen, 1980).

Within the concept of personality several issues dominated for some time. Personality assessment by using tests and inventories is an important issue within personality psychology. In various forms of psychometric measurement a number of tests have made several aspects of personality accessible for diagnosis, assessment and scientific research. At the same time, procedures for the evaluation of the validity and reliability of these tests have been developed. Thus, a number of theoretical constructs have emerged that were and still are of substantial interest to personality theorists: Individuals can be characterized by their positions on dimensions such as "need for achievement," "authoritarianism," "extraversion," and "machiavellism." Each of these constructs has been elaborated in psychometric procedures, has been connected with behavioral syndromes and characteristics, has been hypothesized to cause or to correlate with other personality variables and is at the core of research and conceptual efforts and developments. According to this tradition, individual behavior is determined by intrapsychic factors that are personality-bound. Protagonists in this field include Allport (1937) and Cattell (1966).

Situational and contextual variables, on the other hand, also have attracted substantial interest in connection with personality functioning. "Situationism" thereby refers to the predominant role that is attributed to external and circumstantial factors in relation to personality. At the extreme, this viewpoint denies any other behavioral mechanisms than those that originate from a person's environment. According to this point of view personality is exclusively being shaped by the influence of situational processes, and there is no "inner" or psychic reality that corresponds with or interacts with outside events and processes in an autonomous way.

Situationism within personality theory has had a number of advocates, e.g., Skinner (1953) and Bandura (1977), who differ markedly in their position within this issue but who principally agree upon the predominance of situational learning factors.

Although the processes that condition and reinforce behavioral effects from outside have been studied in many laboratory experiments, situational context itself has been investigated only to a minor extent, compared with the so called "trait" adherence within personality theory. For years and years, test and inventory construction have dominated the field. Systematic assessment of situations and their influence on personality, however, is lagging far behind. So this issue has led to the defense and empirical evidence in favor of personalism and trait psychology, rather than to positive and empirically proven evidence in favor of situationalism.

Of course there is a third party in this dispute: interactionism, which takes an intermediate position. Based upon the works of Lewin, Murray and others, modern interactionism stresses that behavior is the result of person-situation interactionism (Endler and Magnussen, 1976; Mischel, 1968). Adaptation to situational influences and integration of these influences with person characteristics play an important role in the individual's functioning. Interactionism, however, is still lacking an empirically based assessment and taxonomy of the situational component.

Another major issue within personality theory is behavioral consistency. Apart from whether individual behavior is determined more by situational factors, by intra-psychic factors or by both, the problem is raised of how far these patterned influences work in a systematic and consistent way so that personality can be seen as an organizing principle that, over time and/or over situations, gives behavior its specificity and recognizable consistency. If there were no behavioral consistency, personality theory would be reduced to the study of principally unpredictable fragmentised behavior in ad hoc situational settings. Consistency probably refers to the most essential postulate within personality theory.

Although consistency, as a postulate, has been widely accepted by personality theorists, a number of problems still have to be solved. Especially within interactionism, consistency is not easy to assess, behavior being connected with clusters of situations as well as with personal factors. Consistency is not an appropriate concept at the level of situation-bound behavior, but is probably valid at a more general level of behavioral and situational settings and may vary over individuals.

Related to this problem is the issue of the predictability of behavior. Consistency and predictability are interdependent. At what level of specificity or generality, however, is individual behavior predictable? Rather than single act prediction, the prediction of clusters or categories of multiple acts should be considered in order to solve the problem of predictability within personality theory (Verhallen and Pieters, 1984).

It may be noted, however, that personalism vs. situationism on the one hand, and behavioral consistency on the other hand, are of central importance to the field of economic behavior. Assuming that economic behavior is organized by the same general behavioral principles that characterize other fields of individual functioning, the controversy between intra-psychic and environmental factors in behavioral determination is probably sharper for economic behavior than for many other behavioral fields, given the real and even materialistic form of many variables that play a role in the economic environment. The same is true for behavioral consistency and prediction.

Assumptions of traditional economic theory are often related to the consistency of human behavior (rationality and utility maximization) and give human behavior a perfect consistency. Psychological research, however, has shown that consistency and predictability depend on a number of restrictive conditions. Personality factors may interact with these conditions.

From the point of view of policy makers, the prediction of economic behavior of different agents – consumers, entrepreneurs, bankers – is of utmost importance. These predictions should finally be based on the consistency of human behavior within changing economic conditions, with regard to economic opportunities and in the development of economic outlook and expectations.

To summarize, personality refers to the integrative organization of person characteristics that gives individual behavior its specificity.

2.2. *Motivation*

Motivational psychology has to do with the causes of intentional action. What are the drives and reasons for individual behavior? Where is the energy coming from and what are the mechanisms and processes that organize the direction and intensity of motivational behavior? On the one hand, the emphasis in answering these questions can be placed on the content of the behavioral mechanisms: the motives themselves, their classification and interdependency. On the other hand, the emphasis can be placed on the processes and mechanisms that moderate and model the satisfaction and actualization of needs and motives.

Adorno et al. (1950), for instance, hypothesized that so-called "authoritarianism" is one of the central motives within human behavior. Others, e.g., Murray (1938) and Maslow (1954), have given complete lists of needs, drives or motives underlying human behavior. These approaches stress the content of motives and are primarily concerned with the classification and taxonomies of motives.

Adams (1963) is one of those who paid attention to the processes that activate and channel motivation, by formulating that social comparison processes are at the basis of many motivational phenomena. Other theoretical orientations such as the arousal/activation theory (Berlyne, 1960) and the attribution theoretical framework (Heider, 1958; Kelley, 1973) can be classified within the same category.

Historically, motivational psychology has developed, like other psychological disciplines, from the biological and physiological roots of psychology. Inspired by authors such as Darwin and later McDougall, Freud and others, early motivation theory was characterized by a strong biological orientation. Human behavior was thought to be reigned by instincts, drives and needs, that all emerged from the biological basis of man, and that derived their function from central functions of the biological organism like preservation of the individual and of the species. Thus, from Darwin's theory, McDougall's (1908) list of instincts developed. Primarily, these instincts serve the purposes of the individual as an organism and only through experience and interaction, they develop into different behavioral patterns and functions.

Likewise Freud's "libido," as a central instinctive force within human behavior, is strongly connected with sexuality as a primarily biological function. These instincts were regarded to be at the basis of the whole plurality of human behavior in its many aspects and varieties.

After this first stage of development, motivational theory also "discovered" social and cultural aspects of psychological motivation, and in fact "soaked" motives off their biological basis. Motivation nowadays is approached from a wide angle of viewpoints that differ markedly in their emphases on biological, social, and cultural aspects of human motives. There are cognitive-oriented theories of motivation, centered around tasks, goals, and, related to them, aspirations and expectations. Psychologists such as Atkinson (1964) and McClelland (1961) should be mentioned here. Another orientation focuses on the organismic arousal-activation paradigm of physiology and places stimulation processes in the center of motivational phenomena (Berlyne, 1960; Helson, 1964). Finally, social motivation theory deals with a number of distinct motives, that have social impact or are elicited by social interaction, such as affiliation, power, aggression, and justice. A number of psychologists should be mentioned here, e.g., Berkowitz and Walster (1976).

The overall trend within motivation psychology is a retreat from need-based theories into more process-oriented approaches. There are several causes for this retreat, partly related to problems of measurement and partly even to the validity of the concept of motives. The classification of motives has never been solved in a satisfactory way and no system has been accepted unanimously, neither on the grounds of content nor on the grounds of assessment. In fact this aspect of motivation theory is being neglected more and more.

From the angle of economic behavior this development is disappointing, for it may be hypothesized that "economic motives" are very relevant and may constitute a category of their own. Motives related to saving and wealth, to competition, selfishness and altruism, to profit making, risk taking and transactions, have a strong economic bearing. They should be helpful in explaining economic behavior as a relatively autonomous but integrated behavioral area.

The processes that activate motivation, however, are also of central importance for economic behavior: Economic incentives elicit many forms of motivated behavior; and intrinsic or added motivational appeals and features explain buying behavior for many products.

2.3. *Learning*

Learning theory deals with dynamics of behavior in a rather formal way. Personality theory and motivation theory both relate dynamic aspects of behavior to "causal factors" within the situation and/or within the individual. Learning theory takes dynamics as the result of previous behavioral processes and analyses structures and patterns of behavior in terms of the constituting elements: stimulus and response, and their several different kinds of connections.

Analogous to other psychological subdisciplines, learning theory emerged from an originally biological approach of behavior. Animal learning is still a powerful source of insight and knowledge. The central hypothesis underlying the biological-physiological learning paradigm is that the stimulus-response sequence is the most fundamental behavioral unit and that, at the end, behavioral complexity can be reduced to these stimulus-response elements. In learning theory, the processes and conditions are studied that guide and determine the building up of behavior out of the original stimulus-response sequences. Several mechanisms, such as generalization and extinction of stimulus-influence, are supposed to condition the building up or destruction of learning effects out of simple stimulus-response sequences. Theorists within this instrumental learning tradition, that originated with the Russian physiologist Pavlov (1906), are Watson (1925) and, later Hull (1943) and Skinner (1953). However there are marked differences between them in the way they deal with the stimulus-response sequences.

Skinner (1953), for instance, deals with this fundamental unit in a purely behavioral way, without any reference to the physiological substratum. In a more revolutionary way, he even reverses the sequence of the fundamental unit stating that sometimes response behavior precedes or elicits stimulus-offering situations in an instrumental way. Within instrumental learning, feedback processes and reinforcing mechanisms (rewarding a response increases the probability of reoccurrence of this response when confronted again with the same stimulus) are of central importance in establishing and maintaining certain learning effects: They direct and correct learning.

Instrumental learning theory developed from hypothesizing a rather simple basic behavioral unit into a more complex theory of behavioral processes and mechanisms. At the same time a more cognitive and social orientation occurred, based upon a less "mechanistic" reduction to behavioral sequences within learning. Bandura's (1977) social learning theory is a good example of this alternative orientation. Although according to this theoretical view, a number of fundamental processes from instrumental learning have a general validity for any form of learning (incentive-working of the stimulus, reinforcement and feedback characteristics), these processes are not mechanically determined, but operate in a more functional and meaningful way. Cognitive factors, such as expectation and self-regulation, accompany and condition learning processes, while within the process itself modelling and imitating play a role in addition to a pure mechanistic stimulus-response effect. The person as a social and cognitive unit is a central factor within social learning theory.

Apart from these forms of instrumental learning, pure cognitive learning processes should be mentioned: the processing and retrieval of information from sensory material. Here also some general hypotheses can be stated about the interaction between presentation and characteristics of stimulus-offerings and cognitive processes that follow this stimulus presentation. Association, repetition, recognition, problem solving and other processes occur in connection with cognitive learning.

Learning theory has several important bearings for economic behavior. Within consumer behavior learning theories especially are of central importance: consumer habits, the learning of prices, advertising and information processing, the stimulus characteristics of products and their impact on learning, and on a more general level market as a system that should be explored and learned before becoming familiar. A thorough overview of learning theories and consumer behavior has been given by Ray (1973).

Also from a marketing-management point of view, learning processes are crucial. The introduction of new products and brands, for instance, can be conceived as an integrated learning-program: names, features and availability of new brands have to be learned. This process of cognitive learning, with phenomena like reinforcement, wear-out, extinction and other learning devices, should result in final trial and acceptance of the product. In an analogous way, brand loyalty and other forms of routinized behavior are the outcomes of learning processes. See also Alhadeff (1982); Lea, Tarpy, and Webley (1987) on learning processes in economic behavior.

Many authors have drawn attention to the cognitive level of learning within consumer buying behavior (Ray, 1973; Robertson, 1976; Engel, Blackwell, and Miniard, 1986; Nord and Peter, 1980). They state that the buying and using of many products may occur under low-involvement circumstances and thus may be learned by simple stimulus-response mechanisms in a rather mechanistic and non-cognitive way. This, of course, means that the analyses of advertising, product promotion and marketing have to start from other behavioral starting points as well than those that dominate the field of behavior regarded as an extended form of cognitive problem solving. Consumer habits and routinized behavior thus may be studied from rather different behavioral learning theories.

3. BEHAVIORAL DYNAMICS: A SIMPLE FRAMEWORK

Given the diversity within personality, motivation, and learning theory and the number of different approaches, theoretical orientations and research traditions within each of these areas, some simplifying device is needed to integrate the fields of behavioral dynamics, in connection with economic behavior. On the other hand, it has to be stated that personality, motivation and learning, although they refer to distinct areas within psychology, do have a clear overlap in issues, approaches and even in content.

Motivation plays a shaping role within personality and influences many learning processes. Learning principles are rooted within personality. In short, personality, motivation and learning do not exclude each other.

Is there any classification principle at hand to structure the field of behavioral dynamics? Although our system also has its shortcomings, and, certainly, will not cover all the relevant theories in detail, we will deal with the problem of behavioral dynamics in connection with economic behavior by following a simple framework. This framework is based upon determinants of human behavior that have already been discussed in the first sections of this chapter. The individual is seen as a "causing" factor of behavioral dynamics, stimulus and stimulus-situation as "eliciting" factors of human behavior, and the interaction between person and environment as a behavioral determinant. As may be clear from the same introduction, another starting-point could have been the level of behavioral processes: the physiological basis, intra-psychic cognitive and social characteristics or the overall cultural embeddedness of behavioral dynamics. In the existing theoretical classifications within personality, motivation and learning theory both principles are explicitly or implicitly being referred to. Other and more complex classification devices also have been used (Hall and Lindzey, 1978). For our framework we will only use the behavioral determinants as a classification principle.

1. Behavioral dynamics, regarded as being determined by the individual, constitute of three sub-classes:
   - Behavioral dynamics as the result of individual, stable properties and characteristics of the person: This will be indicated as "*traits and styles*".
   - Behavioral dynamics directed at the maintenance or (re-) acquisition of internal states of balance of the individual: "*homeostasis*".
   - Behavioral dynamics directed at the fulfillment of desired states for the individual: "*goals and values*".
2. Behavioral dynamics, regarded as being determined by stimulus characteristics, generally falls into one class: "*behavioral activation*".
3. Finally, behavioral dynamics may be the result of the interaction between the individual and his environment in several different ways. This will be indicated by "*interactive dynamics.*"

The framework thus includes five classes that in a certain way exclude each other and that permit a rough overview of the relevant theories. In order to avoid difficulties of space, a detailed discussion of all the relevant theories will not be given here. A short bibliographic summary is given in Table 1. Several general remarks will suffice at this point.

3.1. *Traits and Styles*

Traits and styles have been referred to in connection with motivation and personality. A number of tests and inventories are available to assess behavioral dynamics. Most of the instruments are used for clinical and diagnostic purposes. In connection with perceptual and cognitive processes, however, scales have been developed to assess cognitive styles, i.e. individual characteristics in the processing of sensory input, such as differentiation, discrimination, integration, tolerance for ambiguity, analytic-global functioning, and leveling-sharpening (Pinson, 1978).

Traits refer to the content of behavioral dynamics; styles are connected with cognitive and perceptual processing-characteristics.

Table I. Behavioral dynamics: A bibliographical survey.

Behavioral determinants	General psychology	Macro-economics	Consumer behavior
Traits and styles	*Statistical traits*, Cattell, Eysenck		
	Psycholigical needs/traits, Allport, Murray	Allen	Wells and Beard Cox
	Cognitive style		Pinson
	Attribution theory, Kelley	Elster	Mizerski et al., Settle
Homeostasis	*Cognitive consistency*, Kelley		Venkatesan
	Activation arousal	Scitovsky	Raju
	"Self-concept"		
	Cognitive dissonance	Akerlof and Dickens	
Goals and values	*Social value theory*, Rokeach	Strümpel et al.	Vinson et al., Pitts and Woodside
	Growth theory, Maslow		Hanna
	Achievement theory, McClelland, Atkinson	McClelland	
	Social justice theory, Adams		Walster et al.
Stiumulus-activation	*Behaviorism*, Skinner		Nord and Peter
	Instrumental learning, Hull	Alhadeff	Ray
	Social learning/expectancy theory	Maital, Gurin and Gurin	
Interaction	*Cognitive field theory*, Lewin	Katona	Kassarjian and Sheffet

3.2. *Homeostasis*

Homeostasis is a very broad concept including biological-physiological as well as purely psychic states of balance of the organism or individual. In general, disturbance or threat to a state of balance is followed by counter activity, aimed at the restoration of the original state. Homeostasis has strong motivational aspects. All individuals are supposed to have their own states of balance that serve as anchorage for their motivational (re)actions.

Cognitive theories of balance play a predominant role within recent personality and motivation theory: Individuals are supposed to aspire to a certain level of consistency in their behavior. Sometimes, the "self" of the individual is taken as the cognitive-consistency principle.

3.3. *Goals and Values*

Goals and values within psychology do not belong to any acknowledged major theoretical framework, except behavioral decision making. Most of the time, goals and values are treated in connection with motivation psychology or personality theory with reference to some authors who "stand" for this specific category. Goals and values however are being treated here separately for the following reason: They both are considered of primary importance within many fields of economic behavior. Economic behavior, in many instances, may be characterized as purposeful and goal directed. Economic theory even postulates the individual to maximize his "utility," which cannot be understood without reference to the fulfillment of goals and values. Goals and values have primarily been studied within cognitive-oriented theories of personality and motivation.

3.4. *Behavioral Activation*

Behavioral activation includes a number of rather heterogeneous theories and options. On the one hand within so-called "arousal-activation" theories, behavioral activation has been regarded as a complement to homeostasis: Stimuli elicit behavior as far as they in fact "disturb" existing states of balance and thereby "cause" behavioral responses. The analogy with physiological-based theories is evident. On the other hand, stimulus-response sequences are of central significance within learning theories, without any intervening role for "states of balance": Stimuli are considered to fulfill existing needs and wants in a direct way. As far as economics pertains to the study of choices between alternatives, a stimulus-oriented theoretical framework could be applied. The alternatives may be considered as stimuli. Choice is the response to these stimuli, either in a non-cognitive, habitual and routinized way or as extensive problem solving (information processing and attribute evaluation).

3.5. *Interaction*

Interaction is in many ways the least clearly defined category. Interaction between the individual and the environment is an omnipresent phenomenon and cannot totally be excluded from any of the above mentioned other class. Although this category thus should comprise most references, for reasons of clarity we have made negative choices; only when a theoretical framework is interactive and does not fit into one of the above mentioned classes, it has been positioned within this class. For a more detailed insight the given references should be consulted.

The bibliographic survey is not exhaustive: There is the problem of the autonomy of theories and their ranking within existing hierarchies of theories. There is also the problem of subjectivity in assigning illustrative cases to general categories of theories. Some arbitrariness could not be avoided.

The lack of integration of psychological theories within personality, learning and motivation is quite clear. In addition to the general psychological entries, a column is dedicated to theoretical contributions and reflections on the role of behavioral dynamics with respect to economic behavior. Many of the general theoretical notions from the field of learning, motivation and personality have been used in the fields of economic or consumer behavior. Although the coverage of these "interpretative translations" in some cases is less broad and less fundamental than theories in the first column ask for, they may serve as first references to this interesting intermediate area, where a lot of reflections and analyses still have to be done.

4. ECONOMICS AND BEHAVIORAL DYNAMICS: FIELDS OF APPLICATION

Economic behavior never has been an acknowledged field for theoretical "exercises" of psychologists. There is no systematic entrance leading into the field of economic behavior from theories of learning, motivation or personality. In the past, marketing people, economists in the field of utility, price-mechanisms and supply-demand functions, and behavioral scientists in the field of decision theory and industrial psychology "discovered" some aspects of economic behavior to be accessible from behavior-dynamic points of view. Many "terrae incognitae" are still on the chart of economic behavior, that have not yet been studied in connection with behavioral dynamics. Here no more than a rough and unbalanced indication can be given of the mutual relevance of economic phenomena and issues, on the one hand, and psychological processes of personality, learning and motivation on the other hand.

Following the scope of this book there is a large discrepancy between consumer behavior and other forms of economic behavior. Consumer behavior is relatively well-covered in connection with behavioral constructs, while other forms of economic behavior have only incidently been subject to study within behavioral frameworks. Many phenomena that are manifest within consumer behavior, were approached from a behavioral dynamic point of view. At the same time, it can be stated that many of the theoretical constructs within behavioral dynamics have been used in connection with some form of consumer behavior.

Central areas within consumer behavior are: individual choice and purchase of products, brands and attributes (yielding on an aggregate level "segments" of consumer buying behavior), and information acquisition and communication processes of the consumer.

4.1. *Consumer Buying Behavior*

A rich tradition in the application of personality and motivation theory exists already in the area of purchases, brands and attributes. Personality and motivation theory are applied to the preferences, choices and purchases of almost any kind of product: automobiles, cosmetics, toothpaste, ice cream and other food products, and magazines. All these products have incidental and heavy users who can be characterized by a "profile" in terms of their values, motives and personality traits. For a bibliography see Twedt et al. (1977).

Sometimes assessment occurs with the help of self-designed inventories and so-called "psychographics," which are less abstract, but at the same time less reliable than the standard psychometric instruments. Sometimes more qualitative research into the depths of human needs and motives with regard to the emotional and symbolic meaning of products and brands is used, and sometimes the original clinical-diagnostic tests and inventories were applied.

The purchase of automobiles is a good example of personality and motivation inspired research within consumer behavior. Brands, models and types as well as attributes have been subject to extended forms of research (Evans, 1959).

On the one hand, segments of automobile purchasers have been defined in terms of needs, interests and traits. Personality and motivation dimensions, such as aggressiveness, sportsmanship, comfort, technical interest, and security, have been used to describe these segments and to "predict" aspects of their buying behavior. On the other hand car-buyers have been divided into classes of usership, paid prices, type and model, etc. These classes also have been "profiled" in terms of motivation and personality variables.

In general, the contribution of personality traits to the explanation of buying behavior can only be considered moderate (Jacoby, 1969; Kassarjian and Sheffet, 1981; Van Veldhoven, 1973). This is the result of the use of inappropriate instruments, statistical treatment of data and not least the insufficiency of the "trait-construct" in the field of economic behavior.

In addition to purchase behavior, its antecedents, "brand-loyalty" and "innovativeness," are well-investigated phenomena in terms of traits. Here also in numerous product fields attempts have been made to define the "characteristics" of innovators and brand-loyal people in terms of their underlying personality-structure (Robertson and Myers, 1969; Jacoby and Chestnut, 1978; Carman, 1970).

In connection with innovation, other constructs also have been used. An approach from the cognitive consistency theory and from the arousal-activation theory may be mentioned here (Venkatesan, 1973; Raju, 1981), as well as the application of cognitive style variables such as tolerance for ambiguity (Pinson, 1978; Schaninger and Sciglimpaglia, 1981).

4.2. *Segmentation*

On an aggregate level, psychological constructs have been used in defining segments of consumers. These segments have some homogeneity in buying or other consumption-related characteristics as a result of assumed underlying common psychological mechanisms and variables. Here trait and need inventories can be used as mentioned above.

Besides traits and needs, "values" seem to be a promising explanatory construct, at least at the level of generic product choice behavior (brands and attributes being too specific for the discriminative power of the value-construct).

Systematic patterns in the purchase and usage of products are considered to correspond to underlying value orientations of people. These values can be either general, or more domain-specific (Gutman and Vinson, 1979; Boote, 1981; Pitts and Woodside, 1983).

Finally, segments may be defined in terms of aggregated aspects or elements of buying processes: size of "evoked sets" (range of available alternatives), dissatisfaction and complaining behavior, information-processing characteristics and decision heuristics. Not many systematic approaches have been developed in this area.

4.3. *Consumer Communication*

Another area of application within consumer behavior is that of communicative processes. Here perceptual processes as well as changes of attitudes and beliefs in connection with information-processing characteristics play a central role. Purely cognitive behavioral effects are probably difficult to distinguish from each other, with the result that the behavior-dynamic aspects of advertising and communication have some ambiguities. Nevertheless, it can be stated that attributional processes as well as traits and other personality characteristics play an intervening role.

Attribution is relevant for the credibility of the information and its sources (Settle and Golden, 1974; Van Raaij, 1985). Traits have been used in connection with persuasiveness and other attitude and belief changing processes.

In the processing of sensory information, cognitive style is also a relevant personality variable (Pinson, 1978). Consumer communication processes may be regarded as cognitive learning processes, with intervening influences through factors, such as involvement and risk (Robertson, 1976; Krugman, 1965; Rothschild, 1979).

Finally, advertising has been used widely as a vehicle for symbolic communication and as expression for non-rational need satisfaction in the tradition of (neo-)Freudian psychodynamics (Martineau, 1957). To sum up, it can be stated that the field of advertising and communication because of its multi-facetedness offers a wide variety of applications of behavioral-dynamic theories.

In spite of the omission of several other aspects of consumer behavior, the total impression is one of fragmentation and heterogeneity. Simple, central and appropriate theoretical constructs from personality, learning and motivation are still lacking in the explanation of broad areas of consumer behavior.

4.4. *Some Blind Spots Within Consumer Behavior*

An enumeration of issues within consumer behavior, that have been made accessible to behavioral dynamics, should be followed by the question of still undiscovered areas. To name a few, it might be indicated that phenomena, such as elasticity and substitution, fit perfectly into an approach utilizing the "goals and values" dimensions. These are rather uncovered topics, given the importance they have in real life: Consumers do not always have a free choice, but do experience restrictions in their choice behavior due to availability, time pressure, and other circumstances.

Other interesting areas are the learning of tastes, and preferences, in their physiological as well as in their cultural context. Tastes and preferences are "given" within traditional microeconomic theory. In a consumer's life, however, they have to be learned along the lines of each of the above mentioned learning principles: instrumental, cognitive and social.

Finally, it may be mentioned that an issue like generic product choice (in contrast with brand choice and attribute evaluation) is a relatively undeveloped area for research within one of the behavioral dynamic traditions, particularly within the "traits and styles" and the "goals and values" categories. The effects of promotional activities on the other hand should be investigated more intensively in terms of attributional processes. Of course, this is only a limited summary.

4.5. *Other Areas of Economic Behavior*

Diversity may be the predominant characteristic of consumer behavior as a subject for behavioral dynamics; the other areas of economic behavior are only partially covered. Within household management several budget allocation functions may be distinguished: consumer spending behavior, but also saving, installment debts and credits, insurance, and the managerial dealing with these functions within financial planning. Motives and traits have been used to explain intensity and forms of saving and to characterize different groups of savers.

"Standard" instruments, such as inventories, have rarely been used, and the same is true for theoretical concepts and frameworks from behavioral dynamics.

In contrast with consumer behavior, where a large number of fragmented contributions and transpositions can be found concerning constructs from personality, motivation and learning theories, the opposite can be stated for more general economic issues and problem areas. With respect to problems of economic growth, public transfers and taxation, and the distribution of income and welfare, only a small number of contributions can be mentioned that have their starting point in well-defined areas of behavioral dynamics and that treat a number of issues in a consequent way along the lines of the chosen theoretical construct.

Well-known, for instance, is McClelland's *Achieving Society* (1961), in which economic growth in a broad cultural-historical and psychological context is related to an underlying motivational syndrome or factor, called "need for achievement." The analysis is based upon individual motivation in its processes and characteristics, as it has been studied in laboratory-experiments by early need-achievement psychologists. McClelland (1961) applies this to the field of economic efforts and growth of many countries during a number of periods in history. This is a major contribution, indeed, from psychology to the study of societal problems.

Scitovsky's *Joyless Economy* (1976) is another example of a broad, motivation-based analysis of macroeconomic phenomena. Taking Berlyne's "arousal-activation-theory" as a guiding principle, Scitovsky attacks the rigidity and boring characteristics that man is being doomed to by economic theory: maximizing his utility and minimizing his sorrows; man can only be clean and rational. Observation shows that there is more in life: pleasant risks, irresponsible pleasures, extravagance, variety-for-its-own-merits. This only can be understood in a scenario where some stimuli have charms of their own and where the organism sometimes wants to be stimulated for the sake of stimulation. This, clearly motivational, approach is valid for individuals, but it is also valid for many features within economic life. Scitovsky gives many descriptive examples (1976). His approach may be labeled under the heading of "homeostasis."

In 1982 Maital published his *Minds, Markets and Money.* Maital employs several constructs to explain the many facets of economic life, in particular the "prisoner's dilemma" situation is used as a model to study the problems of pollution, inflation, and waste of energy and natural resources. The main approach, however, falls within the "social learning" theory developed and formulated by Rotter (1966) and Bandura (1977). Behavior in economic situations has to be learned. By imitation, feedback and reinforcement, by modelling and by self-efficacy, behavioral patterns are being transferred during the process of socialization of the individual. According to Maital, social learning occurs in connection with many economic institutions and values: money, justice, competition, and interest. These institutions are discussed with a behavioral perspective based on social learning and socialization (Maital, 1982).

More implicitly, in the work of Katona social learning also plays a central role. Being trained as a Gestalt-psychologist, Katona stresses the general economic outlook of people with regard to inflation, recession, and the business cycle. Many attitudes and subsequent behaviors to these phenomena are learned through the process of social learning. Although he does not belong to a particular tradition within psychology, Katona considered himself to be a Lewinian (Katona, 1975).

These major publications in the field of macroeconomic phenomena can be complemented by a number of contributions toward more specific issues and topics. In the tradition of "equity theory" and social justice some problems of welfare and income distribution have been studied (Von Grumbkow, 1980). Aspects of transfers like taxation, have been studied in connection with personality (Groenland and Van Veldhoven, 1983) and motivation (Von Grumbkov and Wärneryd, 1986).

Although many aspects of economic behavior have been studied in connection with behavioral-dynamic concepts, many areas have still to be covered. Economic phenomena and institutions, such as money, property, distribution of income and wealth, have strong motivational and personality impact, but are still relatively uncovered. Well-being, poverty, social security and other "eco-psychological" states have motivational and personality bearings. Learning behavior applies to many aspects of the economic socialization of the individual.

Economic behavior is at the basis of many aggregated economic phenomena and processes, but at the same time individual behavioral dynamics in the field of personality, motivation and learning are at the basis of many forms of economic behavior!

REFERENCES

Adams, J.S., 1963, Toward an understanding of inequity, Journal of Abnormal and Social Psychology, 67, 422-436.

Adorno, T.W., E.F. Brunswik, D.J. Levinson, and R.N. Sanford, 1950, The Authoritarian Personality, New York: Harper and Row.

Akerlof, G.A., and W.T. Dickens, 1982, The economic consequences of cognitive dissonance, American Economic Review, 72, 307-319.

Alhadeff, D.A., 1982, Microeconomics and Human behavior. Toward a New Synthesis of Economics and Psychology, Berkeley, CA: University of California Press.

Allen, V.L., 1970, "Personality correlates of poverty," in: V.L. Allen (ed.), Psychological Factors in Poverty, Chicago, IL: Markham, pp. 242-265.

Allport, G.W., 1937, Personality, a Psychological Interpretation, New York: Holt, Rinehart and Winston.

Atkinson, J.W., 1964, Introduction to Motivation, Princeton, NJ: Van Nostrand.

Bandura, A., 1977, Social Learning Theory, Englewood Cliffs, NJ: Prentice-Hall.

Berkowitz, L., and E. Walster, 1976, Advances in Experimental Social Psychology, New York: Academic Press.

Berlyne, D.E., 1960, Conflict, Arousal and Curiosity, New York: McGraw-Hill.

Boote, A.S., 1981, Market segmentation by personal values and salient product attributes, Journal of Advertising Research, 21, 29-35.

Carman, J.M., 1970, Correlates of brand loyalty: Some positive results, Journal of Marketing Research, 7, 67-76.

Cattell, R.B., 1966, The Scientific Analysis of Personality, Chicago, IL: Aldine.

Cox, D.F. (ed.), 1967, Risk Taking and Information Handling in Consumer Behavior, Cambridge, MA: Harvard University Press.

Elster, J., 1982, Sour-grapes utilitarianism and the genesis of wants, in: A.K. Sen and B. Williams (eds.), Utilitarianism and Beyond, Cambridge, UK: Cambridge University Press.

Endler, N.S., and D. Magnusson, 1976, Toward an interactional psychology of personality, Psychological Bulletin, 83, 956-974.

Engel, J.F., R.D. Blackwell, and P.W. Miniard, 1986, Consumer Behavior, Chicago, IL: The Dryden Press (fifth edition).

Evans, F.B., 1959, Psychological and objective factors in the prediction of brand choice. Ford versus Chevrolet, Journal of Business, 32, 340-369.

Eysenck, H.J., 1960, The Structure of Human Personality, London: Methuen.

Groenland, E.A.G., and G.M. van Veldhoven, 1983, Tax evasion behavior: A psychological framework, Journal of Economic Psychology, 3, 129-144.

Gurin, G., and P. Gurin, 1970, Expectancy theory in the study of poverty, Journal of Social Issues, 26, 83-104.

Gutman, J., and D.E. Vinson, 1979, Value structures and consumer behavior, Advances in Consumer Research, 6, 335-339.

Hall, C.S., and G. Lindzey, 1978, Theories of Personality, New York: John Wiley (third edition).

Hanna, J.G., 1980, "A typology of consumer needs," in: J.N. Sheth (ed.), Research in Marketing, Vol. 3, Greenwich, CT: JAI Press, pp. 83-104.
Heider, F., 1958, The Psychology of Interpersonal Relations, New York: John Wiley.
Helson, H., 1964, Adaptation Level Theory, New York: Harper and Row.
Hull, C.L., 1943, Principles of Behavior, New York: Appleton-Century-Crofts.
Jackson, D.N., and S.V. Paunonen, 1980, "Personality structure and assessment," in: M.R. Rosenzweig and L.W. Porter (eds.), Annual Review of Psychology, Vol. 31, Palo Alto, CA: Annual Reviews, pp. 503-551.
Jacoby, J., 1969, Personality and consumer behavior: How not to find relationships, Purdue Papers in Consumer Psychology.
Jacoby, J., and R.W. Chestnut, 1978, Brand Loyalty: Measurement and Management, New York: John Wiley.
Kassarjian, H.H., and M.J. Sheffet, 1981, "Personality and consumer behavior: An update," in: H.H. Kassarjian and T.S. Robertson (eds.), Perspectives in Consumer Behavior, Glenview, IL: Scott and Foresman, pp. 160-180.
Katona, G., 1975, Psychological Economics, Amsterdam: Elsevier.
Kelley, H.H., 1973, The process of causal attribution, American Psychologist, 28, 107-128.
Krugman, H.E., 1965, The impact of television advertising: Learning without involvement, Public Opinion Quarterly, 29, 349-356.
Lea, S.E.G., R.M. Tarpy, and P. Webley, 1987, The Individual in the Economy. A Survey of Economic Psychology, Cambridge, UK: Cambridge University Press.
Lewin, K., 1935, A Dynamic Theory of Personality, New York: McGraw-Hill.
Maital, S., 1982, Minds, Markets and Money, New York: Basic Books.
Martineau, P., 1957, Motivation in Advertising, New York: McGraw-Hill.
Maslow, A.H., 1954, Motivation and Personality, New York: Harper and Row.
McClelland, D.C., 1961, The Achieving Society, Princeton, NJ: Van Nostrand.
McDougall, W., 1908, An Introduction to Social Psychology, Boston, MA: Luce.
Mischel, W., 1968, Personality and Assessment, New York: John Wiley.
Mizerski, R.W., 1982, An attribution explanation of the disproportionate influence of unfavorable information, Journal of Consumer Research, 9, 301-310.
Mizerski, R.W., L.L. Golden, and J.B. Kernan, 1979, The attribution process in consumer decision making, Journal of Consumer Research, 6, 123-140.
Murphy, G., 1947, Personality: A Biosocial Approach to Origins and Structure, New York: Harper.
Murray, H.A., 1938, Explorations in Personality, New York: Oxford University Press, New York.
Nord, W.R., and J.P. Peter, 1980, A behavior modification perspective on marketing, Journal of Marketing, 44, 36-47.
Pavlov, I.P., 1906, The scientific investigation of the psychical faculties or processes in the higher animals, Science, 24, 613-619.
Pinson, C.R.A., 1978, "Consumer cognitive styles: Review and implications for marketers," in: E. Topritzhofer (ed.), Marketing. Neue Ergebnisse aus Forschung und Praxis, Wiesbaden: FRG, Gabler, pp. 163-184.
Pitts, R.E., and A.G. Woodside, 1983, Personal value influences on consumer product class and brand preferences, Journal of Social Psychology, 119, 37-53.
Raju, P.S., 1981, "Theories of exploratory behavior: Review and consumer research implications," in: J.N. Sheth (ed.), Research in Marketing, Vol. 4, Greenwich, CT: JAI Press, pp. 223-249.
Ray, M.L., 1973, "Psychological theories and interpretations of learning," in: S. Ward and T.S. Robertson (eds.), Consumer Behavior: Theoretical Sources, Englewood Cliffs, NJ: Prentice-Hall, pp. 45-117.

Robertson, T.S., 1976, Low-commitment consumer behavior, Journal of Advertising Research, 16, 19-24.

Robertson, T.S., and J.H. Myers, 1969, Personality correlates of opinion leadership and innovative buying behavior, Journal of Marketing Research, 6, 164-168.

Rokeach, M., 1973, The Nature of Human Values, New York: Macmillan.

Rothschild, M.L., 1979, "Advertising strategies for high and low involvement situations," in: J. Maloney and B. Silverman (eds.), Attitude Research Plays for High Stakes, Chicago, IL: American Marketing Association, pp. 74-93.

Rotter, J.B., 1966, Generalized expectancies for internal vs. external control of reinforcement, Psychological Monographs, 80, no. 609.

Schanigner, C.M., and D. Sciglimpaglia, 1981, The influence of cognitive personality traits and demographics on consumer information acquisition, Journal of Consumer Research, 8, 208-216.

Scitovsky, T., 1976, The Joyless Economy, London: Oxford University Press.

Settle, R.B., and L.L. Golden, 1974, Attribution theory and advertiser credibility, Journal of Marketing Research, 11, 181-185.

Skinner, B.F., 1953, Science and Human Behavior, New York: Macmillan.

Strümpel, B., R.T. Curtin, and M.S. Schwartz, 1973, "Economic life styles, values and subjective welfare. An empirical approach," in: E. Sheldon (ed.), A Family Economic Behavior: Problems and Prospects, New York: Lippincott.

Twedt, D.W., L.E. Dawson, H.G. Wales, and G.N. Bruner, 1977, Personality Research in Marketing: A Bibliography, Chicago, IL: American Marketing Association.

Van Raaij, W.F., 1985, Attribution of causality to economic actions and events, Kyklos, 38, 3-19.

Van Veldhoven, G.M., 1973, Personality and individual economic behavior, ESOMAR Seminar, Maidenhead, Berks, UK, pp. 1-17.

Verhallen, T.M.M., and R.G.M. Pieters, 1984, Attitude theory and behavioral costs, Journal of Economic Psychology, 5, 223-249.

Venkatesan, M., 1973, "Cognitive consistency and novelty seeking," in: S. Ward and T.S. Robertson (eds.), Consumer Behavior: Theoretical Sources, Englewood Cliffs, NJ: Prentice-Hall, pp. 354-384.

Vinson, D.E., J.E. Scott, and K.M. Lamont, 1977, The role of personal values in marketing and consumer behavior, Journal of Marketing, 41, 44-50.

Von Grumbkow, J., 1980, Sociale vergelijking van salarissen (Social Comparison of Salaries), Tilburg, The Netherlands: Tilburg University (dissertation).

Von Grumbkov, J., and K.-E. Wärneryd, 1986, Does the tax system ruin the motivation to seek advancement?, Journal of Economic Psychology, 7, 221-243.

Walster, E., G.W. Walster, and E. Berscheid, 1978, Equity: Theory and Research, Boston, MA: Allyn and Bacon.

Watson, J.B., 1925, Behaviorism, New York: Norton.

Wells, W.D., and A.D. Beard, 1973, "Personality and consumer behavior," in: S. Ward and T.S. Robertson (eds.), Consumer Behavior: Theoretical Sources, Englewood Cliffs, NJ: Prentice-Hall, pp. 141-199.

Table of Contents

3. Information Processing and Decision making Cognitive Aspects of Economic Behaviour

W. FRED VAN RAAIJ
Erasmus University, Rotterdam, The Netherlands

1. INTRODUCTION

Decision making is a recurrent behavior of both consumers and business people. The economic behavior of consumers, entrepreneurs, and investors largely consists of comparing alternative options and making a decision about which option(s) to select under several kinds of constraints. It is then expected that a "best" alternative leads to reaching a desired goal or avoiding an undesirable situation.

Motivation is therefore an important part of decision making. Consumers, entrepreneurs, and investors try to accomplish goals and to reach desired situations. Information about the characteristics of the available options is often instrumental in the decision making process.

For some choices, the information stored in memory (internal information and habits) may be sufficient. Choice may then be based on earlier decision-making processes (e.g., brand loyalty) or known characteristics of alternatives. If the stored information is not sufficient, additional information may be actively sought. Especially for choices involving perceived risk of negative consequences and uncertainty about outcomes, information may be functional in reducing the risk and uncertainty.

The first topic to be discussed in this chapter is the function of information in decision making and choice (section 2). Then a model of information processing is described (section 3), followed by a description of levels of processing and internal representation of information (section 4). A behavioral methodology to trace information processing (section 5) is followed by an overview of decision rules (section 6). In section 7 the limitations to information search and processing are described. Section 8 concludes with some issues and trends in decision-making research.

Van Raaij, W.F., van Veldhoven, G.M. and Wärneryd, K.E. (eds) Handbook of Economic Psychology. ISBN 90-247-3720-6.

2. FUNCTIONS OF INFORMATION

2.1. *Introduction*

What is information? Information is often described as relevant data about choice alternatives, e.g., their scores on attributes or characteristics. These data become information, if they are relevant for a better choice among the alternatives. Information may be in a spoken or written verbal or a pictorial format, and may come from personal, commercial, or neutral sources. Information may serve decision makers in several ways:

1. Consumers may expect a better decision outcome after information retrieval, acquisition and processing.
2. Information may reduce the perceived risk of the choice.
3. Consumers may feel more confident after using information, although their decision is not necessarily better.
4. Information is needed to trade-off the present costs and expected future benefits of information processing.
5. Information processing may be useful in finding desirable alternatives or ruling out undesirable ones.
6. Information may be used in an ego-defensive way to justify one's behavior after the decision has been made.

In economic behavior, as in most other behavior, decision making is a process of evaluating alternatives and selecting one or more (or none) "optimal" alternative(s). The decision may be on a generic level ("whether to go on vacation or not"), a modal level ("which type of vacation"), or a specific level ("which destination or travel agency"). While a generic decision is largely based on the time, financial budget and general benefits, modal and specific decisions generally require more specific information on the attributes of the alternatives acquired from external sources.

Internal and external search of information should be distinguished. Internal search of information stored in memory employs information from previous learning and experience that may be suitable for similar decisions. Search of information from external sources employs information obtained from the mass media and conversations with others, and from one's own observations. Apart from active search for internal and external information, people may be confronted with information they did not search for, and learn consciously or unconsciously from it (incidental learning). See Bettman (1979: p. 109) for a framework of consumer information acquisition.

2.2. *Better Decision Outcome*

Consumers may expect to make a better decision after information acquisition and processing, due to a cultural norm that all decisions should be based on reason and documentation. Compliance with this cultural norm will generally be stronger for "important" decisions, involving a major financial outlay or affecting other persons. Impulsive behavior is not appreciated, except for minor choices or "spontaneous" gifts.

Normative approaches to decision making presume that collecting and comparing information and "structuring the problem" will help the decision maker. Decision aiding does not only help in making the decider aware of all aspects of his/her decision, but may also influence the decision making process. Borcherding (1983) distinguishes between a normative and a prescriptive approach. In a normative approach, generally accepted decision goals are defined for an optimal decision. In a prescriptive approach, subjective decision goals are defined in order to reach an optimal decision for the subject.

In this chapter, the emphasis is on the description of consumer decision processes, not on the normative and prescriptive approaches of helping persons to make better decisions. However, descriptive knowledge of how consumers make decisions may be helpful in designing "better ways" of information presentation. In this way we can help de decision-maker, consumers and producers, to make better decisions.

2.3. *Reduction of Perceived Risk*

Economic decision-makers may perceive risk in their decisions. Cox (1967) employs the concept of perceived risk in consumer choice, including uncertainty and importance. Reduction of uncertainty is not the same as reducing risk. Better knowledge of probabilities reduces the "uncertainty intervals" (ambiguity, see below) around risk, although not risk itself. Information may reduce some uncertainty about the alternatives but may also state the risk in a more precise way, e.g., as in the case of knowing the side-effects of a drug.

Within the uncertainty dimension, Einhorn and Hogarth (1985) propose five components:

(1) the expected attribute or product outcome level,
(2) its probability of occurrence,
(3) the certainty/uncertainty with which this probability is held (ambiguity),
(4) unknown attribute or outcome levels not anticipated,
(5) the ambiguity surrounding unanticipated levels.

Cunningham (1967) measured certainty in choice. Hansen (1972) proposed a conflict model, based on Berlyne's (1963) arousal theory. The degree of conflict is related to four factors: the number of competing alternatives, the perceived equality of the alternatives, the importance and the incompatibility of the alternatives. More uncertainty will be experienced, if many alternatives compete, if these alternatives are very similar, and if a large financial outlay is required.

Economic decisions are often characterized by a financial, temporal and/or effort risk. For some decisions, a physical risk becomes relevant, e.g., automobile driving, some sports, food and drugs. Risk reduction methods (Roselius, 1971) include information processing, brand loyalty, store loyalty, relying on recommendations, and money-back guarantees. Most risk-reduction methods pertain to the probability component (brand or store loyalty, recommendation, reputation); the money-back guarantee reduces the negative effects of a risky decision.

2.4. *Confidence*

Many decision makers feel more confident after acquiring information, even if this information is not really processed to reach a decision (Oskamp, 1965). Consumers may feel confident with nutrition information on the packages, although they may not fully understand this information. People may feel confident having access to documentation, but often do not use the information in their choice process.

The function of information in increasing confidence with the outcome may be dysfunctional for a better decision ("illusion of knowledge"). Jacoby and his co-researchers (Jacoby, Speller, and Kohn, 1974a, 1974b) and Van Raaij (1977) find that consumers use only a small part of the available information but are more confident with their decision, if much information is available. The quality of the decision may even decrease under conditions of information overload, due to the fact that irrelevant information obscures the access to relevant information. Due to all the trees one fails to see the forest!

On the one hand, consumers have the "right" to have access to relevant information, although information overload may have its dysfunctional effects. This is due to the human limitations in encoding and storing this information; to the human limitations in information processing; and to the fact that relevant information is often confounded with irrelevant information. From a consumer policy perspective, one should carefully design ways of information presentation for consumers, in such a way that "optimal" decisions are facilitated.

2.5. *Information About Costs/Benefits of Information Processing*

Information acquisition and processing involves behavioral, and sometimes even financial costs. Financial costs include travel and telephone costs; behavioral costs include the time and effort spent to obtain the information. These financial and behavioral costs are traded off against expected gain of information and expected future benefits of a better decision. In shopping behavior, not only the price of a product, but also travel time, costs and effort should be considered in comparing shopping trips.

Economic decision makers often process information on the costs and benefits of information processing. In this "thinking about thinking" decision makers assess, whether it is worthwhile to process information.

The "cost of thinking" (Shugan, 1980) is related to the similarity and complexity of the alternatives. It is relatively "costly" to decide between similar alternatives or between alternatives with many attributes (characteristics). However, it is not always necessary to process all information that is available. "Heuristics" and simple decision rules may facilitate the decision task, although one is not certain to obtain the "optimal" alternative.

In many choice situations it is almost impossible to select the "optimal" alternative. This is the case, if the information comes sequentially, i.e., not all information about the choice alternatives is available simultaneously. Consumer decision processes for sequential information are a neglected area of research. The available studies show that a *satisficing* notion is appropriate. Maximizing utility is almost impossible, because the new information may change the attractiveness of former choice alternatives. The consumer sets a certain level (threshold), above which an alternative is satisficing. This level depends on the person's expectations of what kind of alternatives will occur and on his/ her own needs. The threshold level is adapted based on the apparent alternatives.

Ölander (1975: p. 318) states that it seems altogether possible that choices among alternatives well-known to the decision-maker (already before or as a consequence of search) are based on a multi-valued utility scale and some kind of expected utility calculation at the same time as decisions about whether to search for further behavior alternatives are based on whether the best of the accessible alternatives exceeds a certain level of aspiration or not. In such a situation satisficing behavior is likely to occur. The costs of finding the optimal alternative are sometimes higher than the expected benefits. If product differences are small, the information processing costs of finding the better alternative may be high in comparison with the benefits of selecting a slightly better alternative. Shugan (1980) developed a "confusion index" for the costs of information processing, i.e., a pairwise comparison (tournament) of choice alternatives. In Shugan's (1980) approach, the information is freely available; the costs pertain only to the information processing and not to the acquisition of information. The costs of information processing are traded off against expected decision outcomes.

2.6. *Desirable and Undesirable Alternatives*

Consumers and other economic agents do not necessarily derive utility from products as such, but from product characteristics. Lancaster (1966) postulates that products are bundles of characteristics. Information use is instrumental in making a better "matching" of the product characteristics and one's needs and desires. It is assumed that consumers have more or less detailed specifications of the products and services they want, subject to cost restrictions, and try to match these specifications with actual product characteristics. The product with the optimal matching will then be selected. Product specifications may include price and size intervals, desired product features, acceptable levels of operating costs. The specifications may have minimum and maximum values, or optimum values.

Considering minimum values only, consumers could use a conjunctive decision. This means that all alternatives with attribute values above a minimum cutoff value are acceptable. Assuming only two attributes, a number of possibilities are given in Figure 1. In Figure 1a, an acceptable alternative should have a value on attribute 1 (a_1) with $a_2 > p$, and on attribute 2 with $a_2 > r$.

Considering minimum and maximum values, alternatives are acceptable with attribute values between the minimum and maximum. In Figure 1b, an acceptable alternative should have a value on attribute 1 with $p < a_1 < q$ and on attribute 2 with $r < a_2 < s$.

Considering maximum values only, the conjunctive rule could be used as well. An alternative with attribute values below the maximum, is acceptable. In Figure 1c, an acceptable alternative should have a value on attribute 1 with $a_1 < q$ and on attribute 2 with $a_2 < s$.

Combinations of the above cases are also possible. In Figure 1d, an acceptable alternative should have a value $a_1 < q$ and $a_2 > r$. In Figure 1e, an acceptable alternative should have a value $p < a_1 < q$ and $a_2 < s$.

Applying the conjunctive rule for minima and maxima, provides a region of acceptable alternatives. It does not tell which alternative in the acceptability region will be selected. This may be the first alternative found with acceptable attribute values ("satisficing"), or the consumer may proceed and searches the "best" alternative within the acceptability region. The conjunctive rule is then applied to discriminate between acceptable and unacceptable alternatives. A more complex, e.g., compensatory, rule could then be applied to the acceptable alternatives.

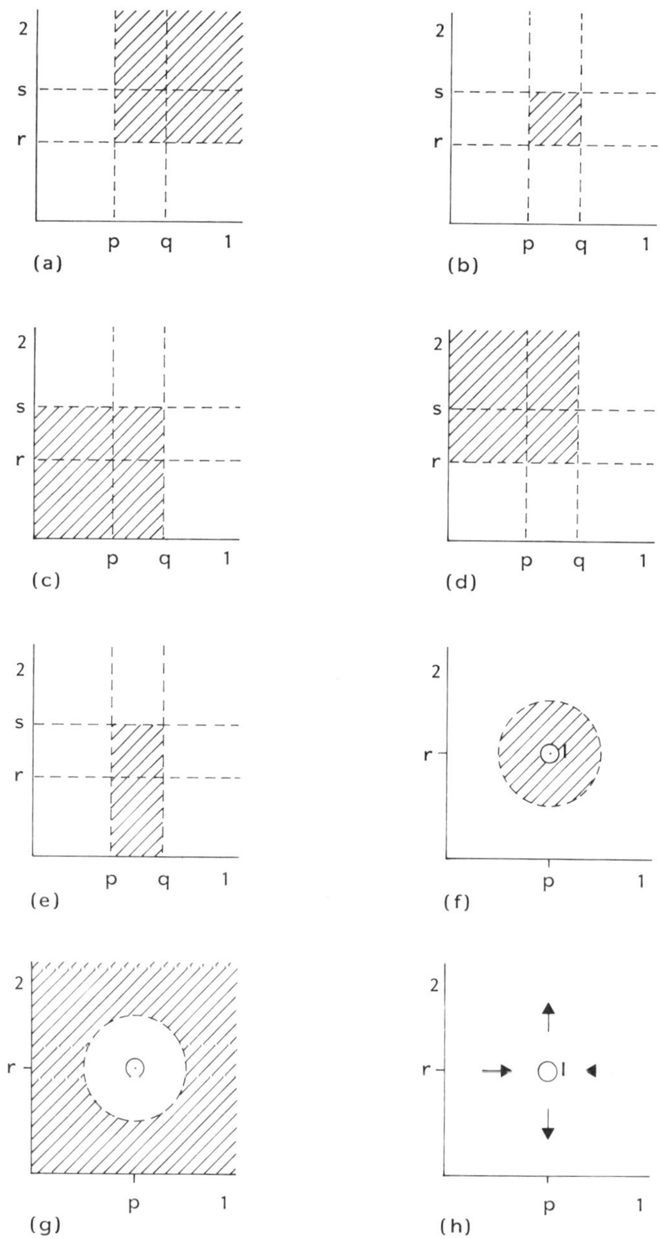

Fig. 1. Examples of acceptable regions.

Another approach starts from ideal values. Let us assume that a consumer has an ideal value on both attributes 1 and 2 (Figure 1f). Alternatives with attribute values within a circle with the ideal point I as a center will be selected. In Figure 1g, a negative ideal point is depicted. Alternatives outside the circle are acceptable, whereas alternatives close to I are unacceptable. In Figure 1h, a combination of a positive-negative ideal point is given. It is a positive ideal point for attribute 1 at value p and a negative ideal point for attribute 2 at value r.

The "ideal point" examples (Figures 1f, 1g) may be interpreted not only as acceptability regions, but as optimal isopreference concentric circles with I as a center. Alternatives on an isopreference (= equal preference) circle close to I will be preferred to alternatives on an isopreference circle further away from I (Figure 1f). Alternatives on an isopreference circle further away from I will be preferred to alternatives on an isopreference circle close to I (Figure 1g). Figure 1h is an example of a "saddle point" with a maximum for attribute 1 and a minimum for attribute 2.

In this approach it is assumed that consumers have correct insights in their needs, desires, and budget constraints. It is further assumed that these needs and desires remain constant over time. Through the interaction with alternatives that are available on the market, consumers may change their needs, desires and acceptability levels. The available alternatives shape or change needs and desires, which should be included in a dynamic model.

2.7. *Justification*

An often neglected function of information is the justification. In many instances, one has to defend after a decision, why one bought the product or service. For this defense, a consumer could effectively use information from advertising or other sources to obtain arguments favoring the decision. On the one hand, it is an ego-defensive mechanism to reduce post-purchase cognitive dissonance; on the other hand, information serves to produce arguments to defend oneself against the possible critical remarks of others. Murray (1979) states that important functions of advertising are not only:

1. to induce trial,
2. to keep the brand in the consumer's evoked set, but also:
3. to reassure and reinforce the decision that has been made.

Information serves thus not only before a decision, but also after a decision to keep or make a person satisfied with the selected product or service. In early consumer research, e.g., Ehrlich et al. (1957), it was found that recent purchasers of an automobile that had long deliberated about which brand to choose, tended to read more advertisements of the selected brand than of not-selected brands.

3. AN INFORMATION PROCESSING MODEL

3.1. *A Model of Information Processing*

In most information-processing models it is assumed that information acquisition, perception and processing ("cognition") precedes the evaluation ("affect") of the available alternatives. The hierarchy is thus: cognition → affect → conation (behavioral intention). This model complies with the model of rational economic man. It does not explain, why consumers attend to some advertisements and not to others; and why we like some people and dislike others at a first impression. Psychological research (Broadbent, 1977) provides evidence that an affective reaction precedes cognition. Van Raaij (1984) states that a *primary affective reaction* is needed, before a consumer pays attention to an advertisement. In information as well, the triggering mechanism may be affective. At an early stage, a consumer develops an affect toward a certain alternative. A certain level of affect and arousal is needed to be motivated to engage in information processing. The primary affect may serve as a selection mechanism to find acceptable and attractive alternatives (cf. conjunctive rule). A third function of the primary affective reaction is to make quick selections from a large number of alternatives based on an affective reaction toward familiar and attractive alternatives ("impulse buying").

The "primary affective reaction" is however not the first reaction. Before this the object or person has to be perceived. This could be called a simple cognitive process. In the cognitivistic approach, cognition precedes affect. (Birnbaum, 1981; Lazarus, 1984).

The information processing model of this chapter is given in Figure 2. There are essentially two ways, by which choice alternatives enter the system.

First, consumers may recognize a consumption problem (defective automobile or a need for a restaurant) and search for alternatives to solve the problem. Alternatives that are found from memory and from external search, are evaluated in general affective terms ("primary affective reaction;" like or dislike). Alternatives are not only obtained by active search (intentional learning), but also by incidental learning, if a consumer is unexpectedly confronted with an alternative. Such an unexpected confrontation might even create problem recognition (food triggering a hunger signal). Or, being aware of a problem, this might increase the number of incidental learning occasions (Hungry persons see more food items).

The primary affective reaction or global evaluation may lead to direct action, as in the case of impulse buying. Especially for products with low levels of risk and involvement, consumers tend to try the products and

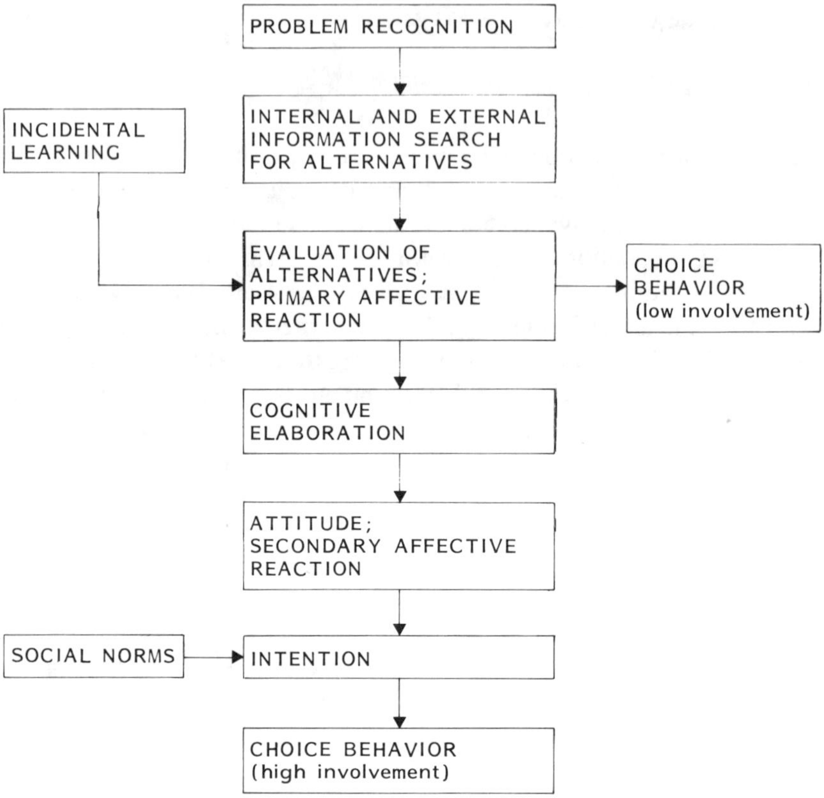

Fig. 2. Model of information processing.

perform some *cognitive elaboration* and evaluation afterwards, in order to make the same or better decision next time (repeat buying).

The primary affective reaction may also lead to process of cognitive elaboration, i.e., the collection and processing of detailed information about the alternatives. After the cognitive elaboration process, a more detailed evaluation (secondary affective reaction or attitude) may be formed or revised.

The *attitude* toward the act, according to Fishbein and Ajzen (1975), consists of beliefs (b_i) about acting toward the alternative (cognitive elements) and evaluations of beliefs (e_i) in terms of favorableness (see also Chapter 5)::

$$A_{act} = \sum_{i=1}^{n} b_i e_i \quad (1)$$

The attitude towards an act (A_{act}) is the summation of the belief * evaluation products. In (1), b_i and e_i are the i-th belief and i-th evaluation of this belief, respectively. n is the number of beliefs (attributes) about the object (alternative).

In expected utility theory the equivalent formula is:

$$U_o = \sum_{i=1}^{n} p_i u_i \tag{2}$$

The utility of an object (U_o) depends on the probability (p_i) that the object has an attribute i and on the utility of attribute i. Instead of the probability, importance weights are sometimes used in the utility models. U_o is the summation of the probability * utility products.

Behavioral intention (BI) is a function of attitude and social norms in the Fishbein & Ajzen-model:

$$B \sim BI = w_1 \underbrace{\sum_{i=1}^{n} b_i e_i}_{\text{attitude}} + w_2 \underbrace{\sum_{i=1}^{n} NB_i MC_i}_{\text{social norms}} \tag{3}$$

NB_i is the i-th normative belief and MC_i is the motivation to comply with the i-th normative belief. This means that not only a personal attitude, but also social norms influence behavioral intention (BI). Behavior (B) is thought to be closely related to BI. A normative belief is a belief that referent persons may favorably or unfavorably evaluate one's behavior. The motivation to comply with these evaluations is the degree to which one conforms to these normative beliefs. The behavioral intention (BI) leads to choice behavior (B), if anticipated or unanticipated constraints do not inhibit the choice behavior (e.g., the product is sold out), and if the budget of the consumer is sufficient.

3.2. *Cognitive Elaboration*

Cognitive elaboration is more detailed information processing about the alternatives obtained from internal and external search (intentional learning) and from incidental learning. Cognitive elaboration can be considered as an argumentation process with the following elements (Wright, 1980; Petty, Brock, and Ostrom, 1981):

A. *Support argumentation*: Information from one source is supported by information from other source(s), e.g., own experience (internal search), advertising, and product tests. In attribution theory terms, it is the consistency criterion, that information elements from different sources support each other.

B. *Counter argumentation*: Information from one source is not supported by information from other sources, e.g., one's own experience. Then, the person tends to refute the information from the external source, especially if this external source is biased or unreliable, e.g. advertising. A moderate form of counter argumentation is curious disbelief; this disbelief is normally changed into a positive interest by procssing the information.

C. *Source derogation* is a means to solve the problem of inconsistency of information sources. It is the derogation of the expertness and/or trustworthiness of the information source, with the consequence not to believe the information. Information sources, such as advertising or salespersons, may be easily derogated, because of their one-sidedness and persuasive intentions.

D. *Thoughts about the medium* and the *form/layout of the message* may inhibit or reinforce the information acquisition and understanding. The way information is presented has a strong effect on the persuasiveness of the message. Media effects may operate as well. Print media (newspaper, magazine) allow the readers to process the information in their own speed, read the texts twice, and skip parts of the message (internal pacing). With audiovisual media (television, radio) the speed of information transmission is controlled by the sender and not by the receiver (external pacing). Externally paced media do not allow for much cognitive elaboration, if the speed of information transmission is high (Van Raaij, 1984).

4. INFORMATION PROCESSING

4.1. *Levels of Information Processing*

The level of information processing is relevant in order to assess the impact that information may have on the formation and change of knowledge about the choice alternatives. Levels of information processing will be approached from two perspectives: central vs. peripheral route, and depth of processing.

Petty and Cacioppo (1986) state that under conditions of high involvement information processing is thought to occur via the central route, i.e. product attributes will be thoroughly scrutinized and information will be processed at a deep level (extensive problem solving; Howard and Sheth, 1969). In contrast, if involvement is low, consumers tend to base their judgment mainly on context and peripheral message cues, such as the style or the credibility of the communicator. Product information is then often ignored or processed at an undeep level. In most information processing research it is assumed that consumers follow the central route and are willing and able to process information on the attribute values of the alternatives.

An *undeep level* of information processing implies that only the surface level of information has been processed. Craik and Tulving (1975) assert that information that is processed at an undeep level, is stored in memory in an isolated and episodic manner. No or limited connections with existing information will be established, if there is little cognitive elaboration. If no time or opportunity is available, information processing will normally be at an undeep (shallow) level, because cognitive elaboration takes time and effort.

A *deep level* of information processing implies that the consumer spends more time and effort on information processing. With some degree of cognitive elaboration, the content and meaning of the information could be understood. Cognitive elaboration consists of support and counter argumentation, and comparison of new information with existing knowledge. Information processed at a deep level is stored in memory in an integrated manner (large width of information storage), imbedded in a meaningful structure of concepts and relations between concepts. A deep level of information processing is a prerequisite to memorize the information, and to understand the meaning. The major differences between undeep and deep levels of information processing are given in Table 1.

Table 1. Undeep and deep levels of information processing

Undeep (shallow) level:	Deep level:
physical, sensory, coding	semantic coding
emphasis on form and layout	emphasis on content and meaning
little or no elaboration	much elaboration
low involvement	high involvement
episodic, isolated storage of information	integrated storage of information
low level of generation of cognitive responses	high level of generation of cognitive responses

An undeep level of information processing is instrumental in memorizing information for a brief period, e.g., a telephone number before dialing. For products that evoke only a low level of involvement (low physical, financial, or social risk), a deep level of information processing is unlikely. For economic agents that are very much involved in a product (e.g., prospective buyers of durables), one could expect a deep level of information processing.

Information that is stored in memory in an integrated manner, has relations with other concepts in the memory. This could be called a cognitive structure or network. Concepts are the nodes (synapses) in this network. Relations between concepts are the connections or links between the nodes (Anderson, 1983). The "memory spread" theory asserts that nodes may be activated through internal or external stimulation. From the activated nodes, neural activity spreads to connecting nodes. In this way connections are reinforced. New nodes and connections could also be formed.

The following levels of information processing may be distinguished:

1. automatic processes of association and discrimination; often a primary affective or cognitive reaction, e.g., habits and routines;
2. structural processing of information, i.e., form, color, design, layout, esthetics;
3. semantic processing of sentences, parts of the message;
4. semantic processing of the total message; and
5. self-reference, i.e., relating the message to oneself.

In general, deep levels of processing ask more time and effort than undeep levels. However, this is not always true. Rogers, Kuiper and Kirker (1977) designed an experiment, in which the subjects had to memorize adjectives. Active recall was measured afterwards. Four conditions were created. In a structural condition, subjects were instructed to pay attention to type/form of printing. In a phonemic condition, they had to pay attention to rhyme. In a semantic condition, subjects focussed on the meaning of the adjectives. In a self-reference condition, subjects checked, whether the adjectives applied to themselves or not. Active recall was highest in the self-reference condition and lowest in the structural and phonemic conditions. The subjects in the four conditions of this experiment obtained equal amounts of time to memorize the adjectives. The obtained results cannot be explained from differences in time allowances. Deep levels of information processing and especially self-reference, results in a better active recall. Self-reference may have affective overtones, reinforcing recall.

4.2. *Internal Representation*

As noted before about the primary affective reaction, impression formation is important for subsequent information processing. People form first impressions of another person based on discrete and often limited amounts of information. Asch (1946) and Kelly (1955) varied the adjectives warm and cold in person descriptions and found large differences in the evaluation of the persons. First impressions and previous information ("primacy effects") tend to change the information processing, in the sense that with a favorable first impression, the cognitive elaboration tends to focus on positive attributes. With an unfavorable first impression, the focus is on negative attributes.

Bruner and Tagiuri (1954) suggested that people have implicit personality theories. This theory involves an understanding of which personality traits are associated with or are implied by other traits. This may even lead to erroneous and stereotypic views of other persons (prejudice and racial discrimination) and halo effects.

Not only with persons, also with objects, attributes are implicitly combined. Price may become an indicator of quality (Gabor and Granger, 1966). The brand name may stand for quality and service. In fact, product attributes may be hierarchically ordered with "chunking" attributes at the top, standing for a number of detailed or unknown attributes. Products may be categorized according to some top attributes (price, brand name). Within a category, minor attributes may play a role in the discrimination between the products.

This has an interesting parallel in Kelly's (1955) psychology of personal constructs. Kelly contends that people differ in the constructs they assign to other people (and to objects). A construct is a set of bipolar traits. In ambiguous situations, and probably based on first impressions, people may use different constructs in the evaluation of persons and objects. This shows that information processing is not a "cool," rational, but a value-laden, often affective, process. Attributes of persons and objects are thus often interdependent.

Impression formation is not only built on a primacy effect. A "recency effect" may be distinguished as well. A favorable score on an important and lasting attribute, already at an early stage, may influence the subsequent information processing. Subsequent information may, however, replace earlier information, if it is more accurate or from a superior information source. In this case a recency effect may apply.

Product attributes may also be inferred from product performance and the information one obtains about product performance and consumer satisfaction. Kelley's (1967) consistency and consensus criteria apply for the attribution of "attribute values" to products. The assignment of attributes to objects and the resultant evaluation of objects is only one part of attaching meaning to the world of objects. Another approach starts from the multitude of objects around us and the ways people classify and categorize these objects. Bruner, Goodnow and Austin (1956) describe the processes of categorizations: perceptual, if the objects are present to immediate perception, and conceptual, on a more abstract level.

Categorization is instrumental for at least five reasons:

1. It reduces the complexity of the environment, from individual objects to classes and categories.

2. It is a way to identify the objects around us (as category members).
3. It reduces the necessity of constant learning (a similarity of objects in a class is assumed).
4. It provides direction for instrumental activity, e.g. product positioning.
5. It permits ordering and relating classes of objects and events, e.g., market segmentation.

Sujan (1985) and Cohen and Basu (1987) review the information processing issues in categorization. The classical view (Bruner et al., 1956) departs from an analytical information processing rule in order to classify objects based on a number of attributes, although a unique set of attributes for assigning an object to a class is often absent. The prototype/probabilistic view starts from a set of common attributes (features); objects that come close to the prototype will be assigned to that class. Finally, the exemplar view starts from the category members that are easily accessible during the categorization process (cf. the availability heuristic).

A brand name may reduce the necessity of constant inquiry about product attributes. The brand name may function as a "chunk, i.e. stand for other attributes. A well-known brand name may be a chunk for a good quality of the product. "Package information ("poisonous," X-rated) is instrumental in avoiding or seeking the use of a product.

Bruner et al. (1956) stress the anticipatory and exploratory aspects of categorizing. We attempt to categorize an animal as dangerous, as early as possible and as sure as possible to maintain control over the situation. We cannot always check the edibility of food by eating it; we must have prior signs ("cues") to categorize the food as edible or inedible. The validation of the categorizing is partly an attribution process, especially Kelley's (1967) consistency and consensus criteria (See Chapter 6). Two other validation criteria have to be mentioned. First, recourse to an ultimate criterion, e.g., eating the mushrooms in order to find out their edibility. Second, a test by affective congruence, i.e., a belief or feeling that objects are related or signs of a supernatural force. God's presence may be inferred from the experience of the beauty of nature. Works of arts may be categorized according to affective criteria, just as food or other products and services.

In consumer research, product categorization is important for advertising and market segmentation. How do consumers perceive the products, and which products are competing or not? Rossiter and Percy (1987, p. 47-50) give an example of different categorizations of yogurt, by flavor or by brand, and deodorants categorized by type of package (spray vs. non-spray) and by applicator (aerosol, pump, roll-on, sticks, and powder). Each of these categorization requires another advertising and competition strategy. Sujan and Dekleva (1987) studied inference making and product categorization with regard to comparative advertising. Comparative advertising generates different inferences than noncomparative advertising, and thus affects product categorization.

5. BEHAVIORAL METHODOLOGY

The process of information search can be simulated with a behavioral methodology. It is a simulation of the amount and order of information acquired to reach a decision. Note that neither internal information search (from memory) nor internal representation are part of this methodology. Only external information search is considered. This means that the behavioral methodology is only suitable for simulation of information search for new alternatives with limited or no information already stored in memory and for simulation with information that is not represented in memory too differently from the presentation.

Van Raaij (1983) describes process tracing research, in which information is presented either in *information display matrices* (IDM) or on product packages. An IDM is a matrix with two or more alternatives (as columns) and two or more attributes (as rows). With eight alternatives (A through H) and seven attributes, 56 items of information are presented (see Figure 3).

Each information item is on a separate card that can be consulted by the decision maker. In a "blind" IDM, each card has to be turned over to read the information. It is studied, how many cards are consulted, before the decision maker selects an alternative. The order of cards is also important, either to find the "important" attributes, of which many cards are selected.

		Alternatives							
		A	B	C	D	E	F	G	H
Attributes	1	A1	B1	C1	D1	E1	F1	G1	H1
	2	A2	B2	C2	D2	E2	F2	G2	H2
	3	A3	B3	C3	D3	E3	F3	G3	H3
	4	A4	B4	C4	D4	E4	F4	G4	H4
	5	A5	B5	C5	D5	E5	F5	G5	H5
	6	A6	B6	C6	D6	E6	F6	G6	H6
	7	A7	B7	C7	D7	E7	F7	G7	H7

Fig. 3. Information Display Matrix (IDM) for 8 alternatives and 7 attributes.

Some attributes, e.g., price, may be important to select a small number of acceptable alternatives from the alternatives presented. Consumers may select more information on the acceptable alternatives in order to select the "best" alternative.

In order to characterize information processing, four transition types are distinguished for a sequence of information items as acquired by the consumer. The (n + 1)th item is either from the same or from a different alternative and either from the same or from a different attribute as the n-th item of information. Table 2 gives the four transition types that can be distinguished.

Table 2. Transition types

Transition type	Alternative	Attribute	Indicates
Type 1	same	same	repetition
Type 2	same	different	processing by alternative
Type 3	different	same	processing by attribute
Type 4	different	different	pattern shift

The transition type analysis has been developed by Jacoby, Chestnut, Weigl, and Fisher (1976) and Payne (1976). Type 2 transitions identify "processing by alternative," i.e., the processing of information of the attributes of one alternative at a time. Type 3 transitions identify "processing by attribute," i.e., comparing many alternatives on one attribute at a time. A type 1 transition is merely a repetition, whereas type 4 transitions point to a pattern shift or a random process: a different alternative and a different attribute. Van Raaij (1977) finds that type 3 transitions often dominate in the first part of the information acquisition, in order to find the acceptable alternatives. Type 2 transitions are dominant in the last part, in order to select the "best alternative" from the set of acceptable alternatives.

Note that the information in an IDM is well-structured, so that the consumer can easily find the desired information. In real life, this is the case with product information tables, provided by consumer organizations and testing bureaus. Often, however, information in real life is not very well structured. In that case, consumers have to search for the information they desire. For instance, on product packages and in advertising, information on one alternative is usually presented. In other cases, information is not simultaneously available, but becomes available after visiting stores or reading advertisements. Non-simultaneous information makes it impossible to find the "optimal" alternative, especially if new alternatives enter the market and old alternatives are "sold out" (Ölander, 1975). In other choice situations, alternatives may be only comparable at an abstract level (Johnson,

1984); then processing by attribute is only possible for abstract attributes.

For information on product packages or in advertising, eye-movement recording techniques may be used (Van Raaij, 1983). The eye-movement recorder records the subject's discrete visual fixation point within the field of view. In this way, the order of fixation points, and thus of the information acquired, can be recorded. It is assumed that subjects "process" the information they fixate, i.e., that an eye fixation corresponds with a mental activity.

One of the weaknesses of the behavioral methodology is the fact that external information search is not connected with existing knowledge and memory of the consumer and internal representation of the information. One way to overcome this, is to use *verbal protocols*, i.e., "thinking aloud" of the decision maker. One could start assessing the existing knowledge of the consumer and then ascertain the degree and content of external information search. The verbal protocols could also provide information, why consumers search for specific information. Verbal protocols provide evaluations and categorizations of the information: "price too high," "A is better than B," etc. Verbal protocols show (Svenson, 1983: p. 131) "that many different decision rules seem to be used when making a choice. These rules are used in sequence in a decision process and different types of rules tend to be applied during different stages of the process."

6. DECISION RULES

6.1. *Taxonomy of Decision Rules*

Consumers are subject to limitations in their ability and willingness to process information. This means that detailed and complex calculations ("mental algebra") or comparisons are the exception rather than the rule. Information processing by attribute or by alternative are examples of decision rules. A *decision rule* specifies the process by which an alternative is evaluated, i.e., assigning a value (evaluation) to an alternative. A decision rule should also specify the choice criterion, i.e., the alternative(s) to be chosen (Wright, 1975). Thirdly, a decision rule should specify the form of processing, such as processing by attribute or by alternative.

Following Bettman (1979), a number of decision rules may be distinguished. In order to reach a decision, i.e., choice among the alternatives, one decision rule or a sequence of decision rules may be employed.

A. *Affect referral* is a simple decision rule. No attributes are examined, a simple affective reaction determines, which alternative is selected: the alternative you like best or the brand you are loyal to. In fact, little or no cognitive elaboration takes place (Wright, 1975). Affect referral will often be used at impulse and repeat buying.

B. *Linear compensatory* decision rules are complex. Alternatives are described as having many attributes. Each attribute is weighed according to its importance or its probability. Utility theory (see formula (2)) provides an example of a linear-compensatory decision rule. The decision rule is linear, because the weighted attributes are added in a linear fashion. It is compensatory, because "poor" attributes may be compensated by "strong" ones. A specific case is the *linear averaging* decision rule, in which the summation of all weights p_i is equal to one. Note that an importance weight p_i is used, rather than a probability p_i.

$$U_o = \sum_{i=1}^{n} p_i u_i \qquad (2)$$

$$\text{with} \quad \sum_{i=1}^{n} p_i = 1 \qquad (4)$$

C. *Nonlinear compensatory* decision rules employ another, nonlinear, function to integrate the information and evaluation for each alternative. A multiplicative or other polynomial function may be used in this case. An empirical example of a multiplicative compensatory rule for automobile choice is given by Lehtinen (1974).

D. *Conjunctive* decision rules were already discussed in section 2.6 (Figure la-1e). Minimum cutoffs are assumed for each attribute. If an attribute does not pass the minimum, it will be rejected. Alternatives are thus categorized as acceptable vs. unacceptable. If two or more alternatives are acceptable, another decision rule, for instance a linear-compensatory one, could be used. Conjunctive decision rules are useful in the first stage of a selection process to eliminate unacceptable alternatives. This is related to Simon's (1976) "satisficing" concept, in the sense that the first satisfactory alternative is selected. The conjunctive choice rule is further developed as a constrained optimization problem by Grether and Wilde (1984).

E. *Disjunctive* decision rules are based on positive or even extremely positive values on one attribute. An alternative is selected based on at least one superior attribute value, disregarding other attributes. Just as the conjunctive decision rule, the disjunctive decision rule is noncompensatory.

F. *Lexicographic* decision rules start from an ordering of the attributes in terms of importance. Alternatives are first compared on the most important attribute. If one alternative is superior to all others (disjunctive decision rule), that alternative is selected. If two or more form a tie, they are compared on a second attribute, and so on. The lexicographic decision rule assumes information processing by attribute and is non-compensatory.

G. *Sequential elimination* is conjunctive in the sense that minimum cutoffs are stated for each attribute. Alternatives are eliminated, considering one attribute at a time. There is no rule for the order of the attributes. Information processing by attribute is assumed. A specific case is Tversky's (1972) *elimination by aspects*. An attribute (aspect) is selected with a probability proportional to its weight. All alternatives with unsatisfactory values are eliminated.

H. The *lexicographic semiorder* decision rule is closely related to the lexicographic decision rule. A second attribute is used to break the tie on a first attribute, not only when the values on the first attribute are equal but also when the difference is small, insignificant or not noticeable.

I. The *additive-difference* decision rule assumes pairwise comparison of alternatives. The differences between both alternatives are added with equal or differential weighing. If u and v are attributes of U and V, U is preferred to V, if:

$$\sum_{i=1}^{n} p_i (u_i - v_i) > 0 \quad (5)$$

With equal weights $p_i = 1$ for all i; otherwise $\sum p_i = 1$.
This binary decision rule yields only relative evaluations of U and V. For a large set of alternatives, the number of pairwise comparisons becomes very large; for ten alternatives, 45 pairwise comparisons should be made. This decision rule assumes information processing by alternative. It may be used in a "tournament" fashion, i.e., comparing pairs of alternatives and retaining the winner each time for use in the next comparison.

Some decision rules mentioned above assume information processing by alternative (linear-compensatory, non-linear-compensatory, conjunctive, disjunctive), whereas other decision rules assume information processing by attribute (lexicographic, sequential elimination, lexicographic semiorder, additive difference). The additive difference decision rule could be called paired comparison of alternatives, a mixture of both processing styles.

As mentioned before, decision rules are often used in sequence (phased strategies). Conjunctive decision rules are used in a first phase to select acceptable alternatives (Pras and Summers, 1975). Information processing by attribute, in a first stage or as the total process, does not necessarily lead to attitude formation or change. Attitude formation is more likely with information processing by alternative. However, alternatives may be accepted or rejected based on a primary affective reaction (affect referral), Wright (1975), Van Raaij (1984)). For the final alternative(s), a secondary, more elaborated, affective reaction (attitude) may be formed, based on information processing by alternative.

The data requirements of the decision rules mentioned above allow for the following classification. The linear and non-linear compensatory decision rules require ratio-scale data, allowing for multiplication. The additive-difference decision rule requires interval data, allowing the computation of differences. The other decision rules have the most relaxed data requirements: ordinal data.

Decision rules may be stored in memory to be used in actual choice situations, or they may be constructed during the decision process. In the latter case, decision rules will be built up rather than recalled as units. The way the information is presented, has a strong effect on the decision rule constructed for the decision process. The use of rules stored in memory can be seen as the result of decision processes in the past. Howard and Sheth (1969) distinguish:

1. routinized response behavior, in which a stored decision rule is used, e.g., affect referral,
2. limited problem solving, in which there is some simple construction or cutoff, e.g., conjuctive rule, and
3. extensive problem solving, in which a decision rule is constructed or used after information search, e.g., compensatory rules (under conditions of high involvement).

6.2. *Contingency of the Use of Decision Rules*

The more time and opportunity for cognitive elaboration and information processing, and the more involved the decision maker, the more complex the decision rules will be. Under constraints of time pressure, distraction, competing activities, social pressure, and risk perception, certain decision rules may be preferred to others. Wright (1974) found that under strainful conditions, elimination of alternatives based on negative evidence may occur, because there is no opportunity for compensatory decision rules. If only small differences are perceived and/or limited risk is involved, a conjunctive decision rule may be used to select the first acceptable alternative ("satisficing").

Dawes (1975) argues that the information processing models are primarily models of the task structure. Understanding the task requirements (contingency) yields an understanding of the subject who performs more or less adequately in the given situation. Instead of considering individual differences, the direction should be to the information structure, format, and the environmental factors determining consumer choice behavior.

7. LIMITATIONS TO INFORMATION SEARCH AND PROCESSING

7.1. *Rationality?*

Humans have limited capacities and are not always motivated to maximize utility. Etzioni (1986) even asserts that "rationality" is the exception, not the rule in human behavior, because "rationality" involves costs of information acquisition, cognitive elaboration, information processing, selection of an alternative, and the implementation of the choice. Habits, such as brand loyalty, involve almost no costs and will thus be preferred, unless the habitual choice is no longer attractive (or available).

The limitation to information search and processing may be classified under the headings: information environment, situational environment, information stored in memory, and individual differences.

7.2. *The Information Environment*

The structure and format of the available information is an important determinant of information search and processing. Information *structure* pertains to structuring of information (Van Raaij, 1977):

1. structuring by alternatives, such as in advertising,
2. structuring by matrix, such as in the IDM, and
3. non-simultaneous structuring.

Structuring by alternatives facilitates processing by alternatives; structuring by matrix facilitates processing by attributes, although processing by alternatives is still feasible; non-simultaneous structuring facilitates "satisficing" and the use of conjunctive decision rules.

The *format* of the information pertains to the type and unit of information. Examples of formats are: ratio-scale numbers, such as weight and price; in ordinal numbers, such as hotel classifications; in binary form, such as hotel classifications; in binary form, such as the presence or absence of an attribute; and pictorial format, such as pictures or video. Information may be given quantitatively (as "facts") or qualitatively (as 'evaluations'), e.g., a price in dollars and the evaluation 'low price,' respectively. A quantitative item will not necessarily be processed as such via the central route, but is often transformed into a qualitative evaluation and processed via the peripheral route (Petty and Cacioppo, 1986; Yalch and Elmore-Yalch,

1984). This will happen if the consumer is unwilling or unable to process the quantitative information.

Edell and Staelin (1983) studied the information processing of pictures in print advertising. They conclude that information processing depends on the "framing" of the pictures, i.e. an unframed picture does not refer to the accompanying text and distracts the attention away from the text, while a framed picture supports the information processing of the text. See Rossiter and Percy (1983) for more details on the processing of visual information.

The way information is presented influences information processing in other ways as well. This is also called "framing". Kahneman and Tversky (1979) found that the framing of the information is important, in this case, stressing positive or negative consequences. This affects the preference for and choice of alternatives. According to Kahneman and Tversky (1979, 1984) people reformulate ("edit" or "frame") risky decisions into "prospects", and then select the prospect with the highest gain or the lowest loss. In the domain of gains people are risk-averse and prefer a sure gain over a chance to gain. In the domain of losses people are risk-seeking and prefer a chance not to lose over a sure loss. Puto (1987) found that people use reference points for comparing choice alternatives. A choice alternative with a value below the reference value is perceived ("framed") as a loss, whereas a choice alternative with a value above the reference value is perceived as a gain.

Some other heuristics, e.g., representativeness and availability, also depend on the way in which the information is presented to the decision-maker (Tversky and Kahneman, 1974). These heuristics are briefly described in Chapter 11 of this Handbook.

The *amount* of information available may constitute a situation of information overload. Overload means that (too) many alternatives with (too) many attributes compete for attention; cf. the advertising environment in media and in stores. Although a certain amount of information is needed to make a good decision, too much information may lower the quality of the decision. This may be due to irrelevant information obscuring relevant facts, or due to human capacity constraints to process that much information. Another explanation is that with ample information a consumer feels overconfident and takes a worse decision than with less information (Oskamp, 1965). Additional information may not always increase the quality of the decision. Jacoby, Speller, and Kohn (1974a, 1974b) find that too many alternatives is more detrimental to choice quality than too many attributes. Malhotra (1982) finds that both too many attributes and too many alternatives decrease choice accuracy. Keller and Staelin (1987) conclude that information quantity decreases information effectiveness, while information quality keeping the quantity constantr improves decision effectiveness, although too high levels of quality may be detrimental to the evaluations.

The understandability and usability of information plays an important role. New information should be easily integrated in the existing knowledge in memory. If the new information is hard to categorize in existing categories, e.g., new attributes, it is likely that the information cannot be used in an easy way. The person has to spend time and effort (cognitive work) to obtain the integration of new and existing information in the nodes and links of the brain network.

Consumers may use stores and catalogs as external memories. Instead of searching information from several sources (active search or need formulation), they may be influenced by the products available in the store or in the catalog (passive search or need recognition). Instead of preparing a shopping list, consumers may walk through the supermarket to recognize the products that are needed. In-store information processing (Is the product needed or not?: conjunctive decision rule) replaces out-store information processing. It is likely that a "passive" shopper is more easily persuaded by an attractive product presentation than an "active" shopper. In many cases, shopping behavior is a mixture of active and passive search.

In the case of complete information use of decision rules is facilitated, whereas in the case of incomplete information the problem has to be "framed" and a decision rule often has to be constructed (Bettman and Sujan, 1987). In the case of complete information, attributes that are common to all or most choice alternatives, are used more frequently than attributes that are not common. Common attributes that are necessary for a lexicographic decision rule to compare alternatives. Product differences are more difficult to assess with uncommon or unique attributes. In the case of incomplete information but common attributes, consumers tend to make inferences about the missing attributes. Attribute information about a partly described alternative has greater influence than that of a fully described one. Consumers do not always ignore the attributes for which no information is available. They make inferences about missing information. Johnson and Levin (1985) find that alternatives with much missing information obtain a less favorable evaluation. Consumers complete the information by a same-alternative strategy (Ford and Smith, 1987), i.e. use the available information about a alternative to infer the missing information (halo effect). To a much lesser degree they use information of other alternatives to infer missing information.

7.3. *Situational Environment*

The store environment with the presentation of products is an example of a situational environment with product information. The same is true for the mass media with advertisements and commercials. Information search and processing also takes place in social conversation with friends and relatives.

Wright (1974) examined time pressure and distraction conditions and predicted that under time pressure or distraction consumers will overweight negative evidence in order to eliminate unsatisfactory alternatives (without compensation). Distraction may be created by crowding in a store or by concurrent activities, e.g., watching television while eating and talking. Time pressure did increase the reliance on negative evidence; distraction showed a tendency toward this effect. Wright and Weitz (1977) studied the impact of time horizons on information processing. Negative evidence is more heavily weighted for outcomes that are expected to come sooner. Store atmospherics may change the mood of the shoppers and thus induce them to use other decision rules (see Chapter 4).

7.4. *Information in Memory*

It seems to be reasonable to expect that external information search is complementary to internal information search (Bettman, 1979). Consumers who know less of a product class, should spend more time and effort to compensate for this lack of knowledge. However, one may state the opposite hypothesis. Consumers who know more of a product class, are better equipped to process new information, because they already know the basic categories to judge the alternatives. They are probably also more interested in new information, or they want to check the validity of the information they possess. The latter hypotheses are not in favor of the complementarity hypothesis.

Not only information in memory, but also memory for rules, heuristics, and operations plays an important role in information processing. Knowledge of facts is useful, but knowing how to obtain and how to evaluate information may be just as important.

Information in memory may direct the type of information sought and the interpretation of information. Prior knowledge may led to less information search, due to either the information already stored in memory, or to a more efficient information search (Katona and Mueller, 1955; Moore and Lehman, 1980). On the other hand, prior knowledge may lead to more information search, because information search and interpretation is facilitated by the categories and attributes one already knows (Johnson and Russo, 1984). The manner of coding and storage of product information in memory may also determine the additional information one searches. It may bne concluded that prior knowledge and external search for information have an inverted U-shaped relationship. Consumers with an intermediate level of knowledge search more than consumers with either limited or elaborate knowledge.

Biehal and Chakravarti (1983, 1986) conclude that choice tasks that require both internal and external information simultaneously are more difficult than tasks that require only internal or only external search for information. Differences in the accessibility of prior information in memory affects brand choice outcomes.

Brucks (1985) finds that prior knowledge facilitates the acquisition of new information and increases search efficiency. The categories one employs, may create an open mind for products fitting the categories, and probably a closed mind for products that do not fit the categories. In her study it is assumed that prior knowledge in memory gives direction to the external search. Furse, Punj, and Stewart (1984) distinguish six search patterns for external information among purchasers of a new automobile, including low, moderate, high search, and, interestingly, purchase-pal assisted search (shopping with the assistance of a more experienced person).

7.5. *Individual Differences*

A certain level of arousal is needed for information processing. Individuals differ to the degree of arousal they already have, or the arousal that is activated by advertising or the product presentation. Berlyne (1963) defines the optimal level of arousal potential in the environment. Too low levels of arousal potential stimulate the desire to increase stimulation (and to search for more information). Too high levels of arousal potential lead to avoidance of stimulation (and to stop searching for more information). Individuals with a higher education level and/or living in urban environments have generally a higher optimal level of arousal potential. One may expect that these individuals are able and willing to process more information, experience less information overload, and use more complex decision rules.

Van Raaij (1977) found among housewives more information processing by alternatives as compared with students. In an IDM task design, students process more information by attribute. Processing by alternative is probably stimulated by the experience of information presentation by alternatives in daily life (advertising, packages). The rather abstract IDM task contains a two-dimensional presentation in a table, more easily employed by students.

Individual differences, and more specifically differences between student and housewife samples, limit the generalization of the results of laboratory experiments. Individual differences can affect a number of aspects of the decision process. Bettman (1979: p. 223) mentions

1. the particular decision rules known by the individual,
2. the processing abilities (e.g., cognitive skills, intelligence, or speed of processing),

3. perceptions of the degree of difficulty and the potential for leading to good choices of various decision rules,
4. the amount and organization of product-related information in memory (The elderly have more retrieval problems), and
5. the degree to which various methods are used for implementing choice (e.g., recall vs. recognition, prior vs. in-store information processing, and stored rules vs. construction of rules).

Gensch and Javalgi (1987) distinguish high- and low-involvement segments, and find that high-involvement consumers use (difficult) simultaneous or alternative processing decision rules, e.g., compensatory rules, while low-involvement consumers employ (easy) sequential or attribute decision rules, e.g., lexicographic or sequential elimination rules.

8. ISSUES AND TRENDS IN RESEARCH ON INFORMATION PROCESSING AND DECISION MAKING

The cognitive approach to economic behavior tends to emphasise the rational and reasoned aspects of behavior, assuming that information processing precedes decision making. In many instances, the degree of information processing before a decision is low or even non-existent. In many low-involvement choice situations, habits and brand loyalty influence the decision without much information processing. Ray (1977) even questions, whether consumer information processing research has anything to do with consumer information processing at all. In many experiments artificial conditions have been created that have little to do with actual choice situations. The first issue is clearly the *external validity* of the theory generated by these experiments.

A second issue is the role of *affective factors* in decision making. A primary affective preference for one of the alternatives may influence the information processing in that direction. Information, thus, is not so much an a priori process toward a better choice, but a posteriori justification of the preference. Thus affective factors play not only a role in the (detailed) evaluation of choice alternatives after cognitive elaboration (attitude); also before cognitive elaboration choice alternatives are (globally) evaluated. The emphasis in information processing research is too much on the choice between specific choice alternatives. In a broader context, budget allocation, the generic choice between expenditure categories, store patronage often precede the specific choice (Gredal, 1966; Olshavsky and Granbois, 1979). Especially, for low-income households, the budget allocation decision may take more time and effort than the specific decision between brands.

A fourth issue is the neglected one of *group decision making*. Households, as a small group, take many decisions together. Dominance of one partner, bargaining, coalition formation, and conflict resolution are part of the decision process. Due to a fuzzy attribution of responsibility, households may take a riskier option than any one in the family would have taken individually ("risky shift or polarization"). Resources may be exchanged (concessions vs. love), or a concession of one family member against a concession of the other partner in another choice process. Too little is known of these group processes, especially over time. See Rudd and Kohout (1983) and Chapter 7 of this Handbook.

Finally, cognitive limitations may be remedied by *decision aids*, such as computer simulation or decision charts or trees. Decision aids may be helpful in finding the relevant choice alternatives, their attributes, and the processing of information. Affective factors and aspects that are difficult to quantify, are often not part of the decision aids. Decision aids may increase the "procedural rationality" (Simon, 1976), but cannot replace human information processing and decision making.

REFERENCES

Anderson, J.R., 1983, The Architecture of Cognition, Cambridge, MA: Harvard University Press.

Asch, S.F., 1946, Forming impressions of personality, Journal of Abnormal and Social Psychology, 41, 258-290.

Beatty, S.E., and S.M. Smith, 1987, External search effort: An investigation across several product categories, Journal of Consumer Research, 14, 83-95.

Berlyne, D.E., 1963, "Motivational problems raised by exploratory and epistemic behavior," in: S. Koch (ed.), Psychology: A study of a Science, Vol. 5, New York: McGraw-Hill, pp. 284-364.

Bettman, J.R., 1979, An Information Processing Theory of Consumer Choice, Reading, MA: Addison-Wesley.

Bettman, J.R., and M. Sujan, 1987, Effects of framing on evaluation of comparable and noncomparable alternatives by expert and novice consumers, Journal of Consumer Research, 14, 141-154.

Biehal, G., and D. Chakravarti, 1983, Information accessibility as a moderator of consumer choice, Journal of Consumer Research, 10, 1-14.

Biehal, G., and D. Chakravarti, 1986, Consumers' use of memory and external information in choice: Macro and micro perspectives, Journal of Consumer Research, 12, 382-405.

Birnbaum, M.H., 1981, Thinking and feeling: A skeptical review, American Psychologist, 36, 99-101.

Borcherding, K., 1983, "Entscheidungstheorie und Entscheidungshilfeverfahren für komplexe Entscheidungssituationen," in: M. Irle (ed.), Methoden und Anwendungen in der Marktpsychologie, Göttingen, FRG: Verlag für Psychologie, Dr. C.J. Hogrefe, pp. 64-173.

Broadbent, D.E., 1977, The hidden pre-attentive processes, The American Psychologist, 32, 109-118.

Brucks, M., 1985, The effects of product class knowledge on information search behavior, Journal of Consumer Research, 12, 1-16.

Bruner, J.S., and R. Tagiuri, 1954, "Person perception," in: G. Lindzey (ed.), Handbook of Social Psychology, Vol. 2, Reading, MA: Addison-Wesley, pp. 634-654.
Bruner, J.S., J.J. Goodnow, and G.A. Austin, 1956, A Study of Thinking, New York: John Wiley.
Capon, N., and R. Davis, 1984, Basic cognitive ability measures as predictors of consumer information processing strategies, Journal of Consumer Research, 11, 551-563.
Cohen, J.B., and K. Basu, 1987, Alternative models of categorization: Toward a contingent processing framework, Journal of Consumer Research, 13, 455-472.
Cox, D.F., 1967, Risk Taking and Information Handling in Consumer Behavior, Boston, MA: Harvard Business School.
Craik, F.I.M., and E. Tulving, 1975, Depth of processing and the retention of words in episodic memory, Journal of Experimental Psychology: General, 104, 268-294.
Cunningham, S.M., 1967, "Perceived risk and brand loyalty," in: D.F. Cox (ed.), Risk Taking and Information Handling in Consumer Behavior, Boston, MA: Harvard Business School, pp. 507-523.
Dawes, R.M., 1975, "The mind, the model, and the task," in: H.L. Castellon and F. Restle (eds.), Proceedings of the 7th Annual Indiana Theoretical and Cognitive Psychology Conference, pp. 119-129.
Edell, J.A., and R. Staelin, 1983, The information processing of pictures in print advertisements, Journal of Consumer Research, 10, 45-61.
Ehrlich, D., L. Guttman, P. Schonback, and J. Mills, 1957, Post-decision exposure to relevant information, Journal of Personality and Social Psychology, 54, 98-102.
Einhorn, H.J., and R.M. Hogarth, 1985, Ambiguity and uncertainty in probabilistic inference, Psychological Bulletin, 92, 433-461.
Etzioni, A., 1986, Rationality is anti-entropic, Journal of Economic Psycholoy, 7, 17-36.
Etzioni, A., 1988, Normative-affective factors: Toward a new decision-making model, Journal of Economic Psychology, 9, in press.
Fishbein, M., and I. Ajzen, 1975, Belief, Attitude, Intention, and Behavior, Reading, MA: Addison-Wesley.
Ford, G.T., and R.A. Smith, 1987, Inferential beliefs in consumer evaluations: An assessment of alternative processing strategies, Journal of Consumer Research, 14, 363-371.
Furse, D.H., G.N. Punj, and D.W. Stewart, 1984, A typology of individual search strategies among purchasers of new automobiles, Journal of Consumer Research, 10, 417-431.
Gabor, A., and C.W.J. Granger, 1966, Price as an indicator of quality, Economica, 33, 43-70.
Gensch, D.H., and R.G. Javalgi, 1987, The influence of involvement on disaggregate attribute choice models, Journal of Consumer Research, 14, 71-82.
Gredal, K., 1966, "Purchasing behavior in households," in: M. Kjaer-Hansen (ed.), Readings in Danish Theory of Marketing, Copenhagen: Einar Harcks Forlag, pp. 84-100.
Grether, D., and L. Wilde, 1984, An analysis of conjunctive choice: Theory and experiments, Journal of Consumer Research, 10, 373-385.
Hansen, F., 1972, Consumer Choice Behavior. A Cognitive Theory, New York: The Free Press.
Holbrook, M.B., and E.C. Hirschman, 1982, The experiential aspects of consumption: Consumer fantasies, feelings, and fun, Journal of Consumer Research, 9, 132-140.
Howard, J.A, and J.N. Sheth, 1969, The Theory of Buyer Behavior, New York: John Wiley.
Jacoby, J., D.E. Speller, and C.A. Kohn, 1974a, Brand choice behavior as a function of information load, Journal of Marketing Research, 11, 63-69.
Jacoby, J., D.E. Speller, and C.A. Kohn, 1974b, Brand choice behavior as a function of information load: Replication and extension, Journal of Consumer Research, 1, 33-42.
Jacoby, J., R.W. Chestnut, K.C. Weigl, and W. Fisher, 1976, Prepurchase information acquisition: Description of a process methodology, research paradigm, and pilot investigation, Advances in Consumer Research, 3, 306-314.

Johnson, E., and J.E. Russo, 1984, Product familiarity and learning new information, Journal of Consumer Research, 11, 542-550.

Johnson, R.D., and I.P. Levin, 1985, More than meets the eye: The effect of missing information on purchase evaluations, Journal of Consumer Research, 12, 169-177.

Kahneman, D., and A. Tversky, 1979, Prospect theory; An analysis of decision under risk, Econometrica, 47, 263-291.

Kahneman, D., and A. Tversky, 1984, Choices, values, and frames, American Psychologist, 39, 341-350.

Katona, G., and E. Mueller, 1955, "A study of purchase decisions," in: L.H. Clark (ed.), Consumer Behavior. The Dynamics of Consumer Reaction, New York: New York University Press, pp. 30-87.

Keller, K.L., and R. Staelin, 1987, Effects of quality and quantity of information on decision effectiveness, Journal of Consumer Research, 14, 200-213.

Kelley, H.H., 1967, "Attribution theory in social psychology," in: D. Levine (ed.), Nebraska Symposium on Motivation, Vol. 15, Lincoln, NB: University of Nebraska Press, pp. 192-238.

Kelly, G.A., 1955, The Psychology of Personal Constructs, New York: W.W. Norton.

Klein, N.M., and S.W. Bither, 1987, An investigation of utility-directed cutoff selection, Journal of Consumer Research, 14, 240-256.

Lancaster, K.J., 1966, A new approach to consumer theory, Journal of Political Economy, 74, 132-157.

Lazarus, R.S., 1984, On the primacy of cognition, American Psychologist, 39, 124-129.

Lehtinen, U., 1974, A brand choice model. Theoretical framework and empirical results, European Research, 2, 51-68, 83.

Malhotra, N.K., 1982, Information load and consumer decision making, Journal of Consumer Research, 8, 419-430.

Moore, W.L., and D.R. Lehmann, 1980, Individual differences in search behavior for a nondurable, Journal of Consumer Research.

Murray, H., 1979, So you know how advertising works?, Management Decision, 17, 369-390.

Ölander, F., 1975, "Search behavior in non-simultaneous choice situations: Satisficing or maximizing?" in: D. Wendt and C. Vlek (eds.), Utility, Probability, and Human Decision Making, Dordrecht, The Netherlands: Reidel, pp. 297-320.

Olshavsky, R.W., and D.H. Granbois, 1979, Consumer decision making – fact or fiction?, Journal of Consumer Research, 6, 93 100.

Oskamp, S., 1965, Overconfidence in case-study judgments, Journal of Consulting Psychology, 29, 261-265.

Payne, J.W., 1976, Task complexity and contingent processing in decision making: An information search and protocol analysis, Organizational Behavior and Human Performance, 16, 366-387.

Petty, R.E., and J.T. Cacioppo, 1986, "The elaboration likelihood model of persuasion", in: L. Berkowitz (ed.), Advances in Experimental Social Psychology, Vol. 19, New York: Academic Press, pp. 123-205.

Petty, R.E., T.C. Brock, and T.M. Ostrom (eds.), 1981, Cognitive Responses in Persuasion, Hillsdale, NJ: Lawrence Erlbaum.

Pras, B., and J.O. Summers, 1975, A comparison of linear and nonlinear evaluation process models, Journal of Marketing Research, 12, 276-281.

Puto, C.P., 1987, The framing of buying decisions, Journal of Consumer Research, 14, 301-315.

Ray, M.L., 1977, When does consumer information processing research actually have anything to do with consumer information processing?, Advances in Consumer Research, 4, 372-375.

Roedder John, D., and C.A. Cole, 1986, Age differences in information processing: Understanding deficits in young and elderly consumers, Journal of Consumer Research, 13, 297-315.

Rogers, T.B., N.A. Kuiper, and W.S. Kirker, 1977, Self-reference and the encoding of personal information, Journal of Personality and Social Psychology, 35, 677-688.

Roselius, T., 1971, Consumer rankings of risk reduction methods, Journal of Marketing, 35, 56-61.

Rossiter, J.R., and L. Percy, 1983, "Visual communication in advertising," in: R.J. Harris (ed.), Information Processing Research in Advertising, Hillsdale, NJ: Lawrence Erlbaum, pp. 83-125.

Rossiter, J.R., and L. Percy, 1987, Advertising and Promotion Management, New York: McGraw-Hill.

Rudd, J., and F.J. Kohout, 1983, Individual and group consumer information acquisition in brand choice situations, Journal of Consumer Research, 10, 303-309.

Shugan, S.M., 1980, The cost of thinking, Journal of Consumer Research, 7, 99-111.

Simon, H.A., 1976, "From substantial to procedural rationality," in: S.J. Latsis (ed.), Method and Appraisal in Economics, Cambridge, UK: Cambridge University Press, pp. 129-148.

Sujan, M., 1985, Consumer knowledge: Effects on evaluation strategies mediating consumer judgments, Journal of Consumer Research, 12, 31-46.

Sujan, M., and C. Dekleva, 1987, Product categorization and inference making: Some implications for comparative advertising, Journal of Consumer Research, 14, 372-378.

Svenson, O., 1983, "Decision rules and information processing in decision making," in: L. Sjöberg, T. Tyszka, and J.A. Wise (eds.), Human Decision Making, Bodafors, Sweden: Doxa AB, pp. 131-162.

Tversky, A., 1972, Elimination by aspects: A theory of choice, Psychological Review, 79, 281-299.

Tversky, A., and D. Kahneman, 1974, Judgment under uncertainty: Heuristics and biases, Science, 185, 1124-1131.

Van Raaij, W.F., 1977, Consumer information processing for different information structures and formats, Advances in Consumer Research, 4, 176-184.

Van Raaij, W.F., 1983, "Techniques for process tracing in decision making,"in: L. Sjöberg, T. Tyszka, and J.A. Wise (eds.), Human Decision Making, Bodafors, Sweden: Doxa AB, pp. 179-196.

Van Raaij, W.F., 1984, Affective and Cognitive Reactions to Advertising, 84-111, Cambridge, MA: Marketing Science Institute (working paper).

Wright, P.L., 1974, The harassed decision maker: Time pressures, distractions, and the use of evidence, Journal of Applied Psychology, 59, 555-561.

Wright, P.L., 1975, Consumer choice strategies: Simplifying vs. optimizing, Journal of Marketing Research, 12, 60-67.

Wright, P.L., 1980, Message-evoked thoughts: Persuasion research using thought verbalizations, Journal of Consumer Research, 7, 151-175.

Wright, P.L., and B. Weitz, 1977, Time horizon effects on product evaluation strategies, Journal of Marketing Research, 14, 429-443.

Yalch, R.F., and R. Elmore-Yalch, 1984, The effect of numbers on the route to persuasion, Journal of Consumer Research, 11, 522-527.

Zajonc, R.B., 1984, On the primacy of affect, American Psychologist, 39, 117-123.

alternatives and 7 attributes.

Table of Contents

4. The Role of Affect in Economic Behavior

RIK G.M. PIETERS

and

W. FRED VAN RAAIJ

Erasmus University, Rotterdam, The Netherlands

> *"For many years the writer has been of the opinion that "emotion" as a scientific concept, is worse than useless" (Duffy, 1941 : p. 283).*

> *"And what is the role of emotion in the study of cognition? We leave it to the poet, the playwright, the novelist. As people, we delight in art and in music. We fight, get angered, have joy, grief, happiness. But as students of mental events, we are ignorant of why, how" (Norman, 1985 : p. 326).*

1. INTRODUCTION

Many economic behaviors cannot be explained by the economist's approach that people behave according to reasoning and try to maximize some utility function. Emotions do not seem to serve a role in this approach. Many human emotions seem to be irrational. But are emotions and affect not a integral part of our lives? Which functions do emotions serve? Are emotions counterproductive and disruptive for "normal" rational behavior? Why are consumers emotional about the products and brands they use? Which emotions play a role in investment behavior? Why do people actively seek sensations in sports and in watching movies? In this chapter, we distinguish several functions of affective processes in general and in economic behavior in particular, and withdraw from the notion that emotions are only irrational and dysfunctional.

After a long period that was dominated by cognitive theories of economic behavior (see Chapter 3), we are now witnessing a period in which affect gets a prominent place in our theories. Several questions come to mind, when analyzing the interrelationships between cognition, affect, and behavior. First, in which respects does affect differ from cognition? Isn't it the current fashion that dictates the incorporation of affect in theories of

Van Raaij, W.F., van Veldhoven, G.M. and Wärneryd, K.E. (eds) Handbook of Economic Psychology. ISBN 90-247-3720-6.

economic behavior? Isn't affect another name for long known cognitive concepts and processes? Second, if affect cannot be reduced to some form of cognition, do we really need it to describe, explain, and predict economic behavior? If affect is an entity conceptually independent of cognition, does it have any impact on economic behavior? Third, if affect does have an impact on economic behavior, is this effect large and consistent enough? Is the impact of affect predictable, and how much weight does it carry? In this chapter, we hope to show that affect is something different from cognition, and that its effects on economic behavior are large and consistent enough to justify this chapter.

Our present knowledge about affective processes and their relationships with cognitive processes and behavior is still limited, although, more than a century ago, Darwin (1872) already theorized about the expression of affect in man and animal. Despite the enormous amounts of research on aspects of mood, preferences and emotion, a unified conception of the interface between affect, cognition and behavior does not yet exist. As mentioned by Norman (1985), it should be a conception that integrates research findings and our day-to-day observations and experiences.

Confronted with this state of affairs, theorists seem to be following one of two roads to describe the role of affect in economic behavior: the road to synthesis, and to analysis. The road to synthesis leads, almost necessarily given the state of knowledge, to models, in which all possible components of affect, cognition, and behavior are linked together with bi-directional arrows. In such an approach everything is related to everything all of the time (Candland, 1977; Holbrook, 1986).

On the other road, analysis is the focus of attention. Here, specific functions of affect in cognitive processes and/or behavior, or functions of cognitive processes in the experience and expression of affect are investigated (Ray and Batra, 1983). The disadvantage of such an approach is its incapacity to deal with all the interactions and complexities of the interplay between affect, cognition and behavior. Very few theorists nowadays will still adhere to Duffy's third road, i.e., the conception of affect as only an extreme state of motivation (Duffy, 1941).

In concert, the roads to analysis and to synthesis lead to an enhanced knowledge about the complexities of economic behavior. In this chapter, the analysis approach to the specification of the interplay between affect, cognition and behavior is chosen. A number of functions of affect and of components of affect in economic behavior will be described. Special emphasis will be placed on the impact of affect on economic behavior and on the (active) management and control of one's affect.

2. FORMS OF AFFECT

Affect is a generic term for all kinds of emotions, attitudes, evaluations, preferences and moods. Some affect refers to the evaluation of objects, behaviors, ideas, or persons, such as attraction, liking, and prejudice. This is called: *attitude*, *evaluation*, or *preference*. This kind of affect is related to a specific target, object or behavior. *Mood* is a type of affect with no or a less specific target. Moods are less intense in the subjective experience and more diffuse, and often originate in the glandular system of the person (Nowlis, 1970). *Emotion*, however, is intense, related to a specific target, and often involves a somatic expression (joy and elation vs. distress and despair). All these types of affect are accompanied by *feeling*, i.e., a subjective experience of the state of pleasantness or unpleasantness of the organism.

A broad class of affect consists of object-related affect, such as attitudes, evaluations, and preferences. These kinds of affect are a product of associative and cognitive learning processes, such as belief formation and change. Based on information processing, objects, behaviors, persons, or ideas are categorized on dimensions of favorableness, attractiveness or likability (e.g., Fishbein and Ajzen, 1975). In later stages, after an enduring encounter with the object or person, one may gradually forget the cognitions and associations, but retain the overall attitude, evaluation or preference. In fact, a summary notion (residual) may be kept in memory (Zajonc and Markus, 1982). Chapter 5 treats the object-related types of affect.

Other kinds of affect are to a lesser degree mediated by cognitive processes: emotion and mood. These kinds of affect will be discussed here. First, we will define the terms "emotion" and "mood."

Emotion is a strong affective reaction to a person, an experience, a message, or a situation, for instance, bad or good news about one's health. Emotion, as a strong affect, is usually related to a specific cause, is localized, and has a strong somatic manifestation, such as arousal of the autonomic nervous system (ANS) and motor exprcssion (weeping, crying, laughter, facial and other body changes).

Mood is less intense and more diffuse than emotion (Ewert, 1970; Nowlis, 1970). The determinants of mood are often obscure, remote, and, although sometimes obvious, hard to manipulate. As a consequence, mood is often difficult to verbalize and to attribute to a specific cause. A person might get out of bed on the wrong side without actually realizing it, until others draw his or her attention to it. Although mood is transient, i.e., particularized to specific items (Gardner, 1985), it is a more enduring kind of affect than emotion (Eckenrode, 1984).

More or less invariant feeling states, e.g., optimism or pessimism, come close to an (affective) *personality characteristic* (Gardner, 1985). Personality is partly the "sediment" of socialization processes and experiences from the past, especially during childhood. Emotional experiences may leave traces (traumata) that have a permanent influence on personality. Affect-based personality characteristics include happiness, intra/extraversion and neuroticism (Costa and McCrae, 1980).

In Table 1, emotion, mood, and affect-based personality characteristics are compared on four aspects (antecedents or "causes," intensity, duration, and specificity).

Table 1. Differences between emotion, mood, and affective personality characteristics

Aspect:	Emotion	Mood	Personality
Antecedents:	often known	often unknown	often unknown
Intensity:	high	intermediate	low[1]
Duration:	short/long	intermediate[2]	long
Specificity:	high	intermediate	low

[1] e.g., Kassarjian (1971).
[2] e.g., Stone and Neale (1984).

The antecedents of an emotion are often specific and known, e.g., a person pointing a gun at you in a dark alley. Mood can have multiple antecedents that are often vague or unknown. Mood may be the remainder (residual) of a strong emotion (Stone and Neale, 1984). Mood may also be the result of one or more small pleasant or unpleasant events, i.e., the unexpected finding of a dime in a telephone booth (Isen and Shalker, 1982). It may be the result of thinking about or imagining pleasant or unpleasant events (Srull, 1984), or of glandular changes in the body, e.g., the pre-menstruation period in women (Smith, 1975). If the person is unaware of the real cause of the affect (mood), incidental experiences may be perceived as a cause in a process of rationalization or justification of the affect: "I'm in a good/bad mood, and I'm looking for a plausible cause for my good/bad mood." This is an attribution process of ascribing causes to one's mood (compare Schachter and Singer, 1962).

People may only sometimes have an emotion, but they are always in some kind of mood (Nowlis, 1970).

The antecedents of personality characteristics may be specific and unique, e.g., a traumatic experience that has taken place in the past. Usually, however, the process in which personality characteristics are acquired, is complex and extended over time. Consequently, the exact antecedents of the personality characteristics are often unknown to the person. The real causes may have been forgotten or repressed, but might be made conscious in psychotherapy.

The intensity of an emotion, both in experience and in expres-sion, is stronger than the experience of mood. The intensity of a personality characteristic is normally low, unless in case of mental illness.

The duration of an emotion is often shorter than the duration of a mood, although, as was noted before, an emotion of (un)pleasant character may be transferred to a (un)pleasant mood. Some severe emotions may have a longer duration. Personality characteristics have, by definition, an almost permanent duration.

The specificity of affect may be related to its cause, if the person is aware of the cause. The specificity may also be related to the circumstances, e.g., hormonal changes, of which the person may be unaware. Becoming aware of the cause (attribution processes) may change the direction (content or quality) and intensity of the affect.

In this study, the relationships between the affective and cognitive components of human functioning, especially the functions of affect, are investigated, with special reference to economic behavior. We will say little of the taxonomies of affect; these may be found in a number of other publications, e.g., Izard (1977) and Holbrook (1986). Neither will we elaborate on the measurement and physiology of affect or the components of affect; such technical descriptions may be found in Klebba (1985) and Kroeber-Riel (1979).

3. AFFECTIVE-COGNITIVE INTERFACE

3.1. *Representations*

Fundamental questions arise studying the interactions of cognition and affect. In research on decision processes, affect is often neglected. Research on emotion struggles over the role of cognitive processes in affect. The study of cognition and of affect has been largely done in separate "schools" in psychology, without much interaction and cooperation. Some researchers have even argued that affect and cognition are separate systems that operate independently (Zajonc, 1980). Others assume causal relationships between affect and cognition. Candland (1977) suggests to view the relationship between cognitive appraisal and affective experience as a continuous loop system.

The interface of cognition and affect is often thought to exist in memory, where cognitive and affective structures are associated in memory schemata. Zajonc and Markus (1984) assume the "hard" interface of cognition and affect to exist in somatic expressions. Motor responses could serve representational and mnestic functions as well. The "hard" representation of affect comprises

1. *arousal*, and
2. *motor expression.*

Arousal is the activation of the autonomous nervous system (ANS). Frequently, emotions have a strong arousal component. Motor expression in emotion (and in other types of affect) refers to facial expressions, action tendencies, body postures, and inhibitions. Most of the motor expressions are observable behaviors. The "soft" representation of affect is

3. the *experience* of pleasantness or unpleasantness, i.e., the feelings about the state of one's own organism.

The experience of affect is not homogeneous. At one time we may feel elated; at another time in deep anger, or fear is experienced.

3.2. *Typologies*

Several typologies of the kinds of emotions have been developed. Based on introspection, James (1884) distinguished between grief, fear, hatred, and more subtle emotions such as the pleasure derived from a mathematical demonstration or musical perceptions. There are at least three procedures to arrive at a typology of emotions (Holbrook, 1986): introspection, logical derivation, and statistical data reduction.

By logical derivation we develop a typology by checking all possible emotions from a set of proposed dimensions of emotions. De Rivera (1977) developed a classification of emotions based on a combination of five dimensions, four of which are two-leveled, and one of which has three levels.

Statistical data reduction techniques, such as factor analysis or cluster analysis, can be used to "extract" the basic emotions from the responses to a large set of emotion statements (see Russell, 1980).

All three procedures mentioned (introspection, logical derivation, statistical data reduction) have serious weaknesses. Introspection may easily lead to omissions. Logical derivation may lead to typologies that are more fine-grained than valid. Using a statistical data reduction technique may hide the lack of a good theory.

A fourth procedure is based on the development of a theory, from which hypotheses are derived that are empirically tested. For instance, Plutchik (1980) systematically develops a framework in which eight primary emotions are distinguished. These primary emotions are: acceptance, disgust, fear, anger, joy, sadness, surprise, and expectancy. Research (Plutchik, 1980; Holbrook, 1986) indicates the validity of the classification. Plutchik's classification does not seem the definite answer to the question, which emotions can be distinguished. The emotional experience is a rich one.

Although more and less basic emotions can be distinguished, and Plutchik's classification seems to be a valid starting point for further research, the statement of James (1884) that "... there is no limit to the number of possible different emotions which may exist ..." (pp. 453-454) still has much appeal. Accepting this statement, this leads to questions about the antecedents and consequences of emotions, that is, to the question, how a specific emotion is invoked, and the question, what the effects of emotions are, once they have been invoked.

Mehrabian and Russell (1974) distinguish three basic dimensions in affect: pleasure, arousal, and dominance. In a recent consumer study, in which the Mehrabian-Russell and the Plutchik schemes were compared, it was concluded that "In general, the three dimensions of pleasure, arousal, and dominance captured more information about the emotional character of consumption experiences than did their measurement via the eight basic emotional categories recommended by Plutchik" (Havlena and Holbrook, 1986). However, research on emotional experiences, in which theoretical models are empirically tested, has just begun.

3.3. *Theories of the Cognitive-affective Interface*

Since the early days of psychology, numerous authors have developed theories, frameworks and models of the antecedents and consequences of emotions. Different classes of emotion theories can be distinguished. Strongman (1978) mentions six classes of emotion theories. Recently, Leventhal and Tomarken (1986), discussing the state-of-the-art in research on emotion, distinguish four classes. For the present purpose, a more global distinction may be made.

Based on the focus of attention, either experience or expression, two main classes of theories of affect can be distinguished: cognitive and somatic theories (Zajonc and Markus, 1984). In the *cognitive* theories of affect it is assumed that affect (arousal) needs a cognitive interpretation, based on the present external and internal cues.

3.4. *Cognitive Theories*

Four approaches to the cognitive theory of affect may be distinguished: misattribution of arousal to emotional cues; misattribution of arousal to neutral cues; excitation transfer; and bogus physiological feedback (Leventhal and Tomarken, 1986). Although most of the daily attributions of arousal to external and internal cues are correct, the studies on the cognitive-affective interface mainly employ misattributions.

1. *Misattribution of arousal to emotional cues.*
   Subjects experiencing arousal, without knowing the real cause of their arousal, attribute their arousal to external cues (Schachter, 1964; Schachter and Singer, 1962). It resembles Bem's (1972) self-perception theory in the sense that people perceive a state of their organism and attribute this state to some external cause. E.g., after injection with adrenaline, causing arousal, subjects were, under certain conditions an unaware of the real cause, friendly in a friendly environment and hostile in a hostile environment.
2. *Misattribution of arousal to neutral cues.*
   Nisbett and Schachter (1966) demonstrated that low-fear subjects who expected that a inert placebo would arouse them, subsequently tolerated more intense shocks and rated their shocks as less painful. These subjects attributed their arousal to a neutral cue, the placebo, and were thus able to tolerate more pain, anxiety, stress or other adverse stimulation.
3. *Excitation transfer.*
   Arousal does not terminate abruptly but dissipates slowly. Residual arousal from a prior situation will still be there in a subsequent situation. Subjects tend to attribute the residual arousal to the external cues in the subsequent situation (Zillman, 1971). For example, residual excitation from physical exertion may intensify feelings of anger, enjoyment of music, and aggressive behavior. Just as in the case of misattribution of arousal to emotional cues, economic agents with a high level of arousal may show more extreme reactions than agents with a lower level of arousal. This might explain why gamblers take high-risk bets after loosing or winning a large sum of money. It might also explain vandalism of some supporters after a football match.
4. *Bogus physiological feedback.*
   Actual arousal is not needed to make these attributions. False feedback on the state of arousal may be sufficient to misattribute the perceived arousal to an external cue present. Valins (1966) demonstrated this by giving subjects false heart-rate feedback while presenting pictures; these subjects then gave higher rates of sexual attractiveness to the persons on these pictures.

3.5. *Somatic Theories*

The other class are the *somatic* theories of affect (Izard, 1977). The representation of affect in these theories derives mainly from kinesthetic and proprioceptive feedback that is generated by emotional arousal. Here too, the cognitive system is involved in the representation of affect. The cognitive theories are mainly concerned with the experience of affect, whereas the somatic theories were developed mainly to describe the expression of affect.

4. FUNCTIONS OF AFFECT

4.1. *Introduction*

Recently, the attention for the affective-cognitive interface has increased enormously, both in psychology and in consumer research. Researchers from the cognitive sciences have started to study the effects of affect on decision making and behavior. Much progress in understanding the role of affect in behavior, specifically consumer behavior, has been made. However, the perennial problems in the field of emotion, that Arnold (1970) formulated more than 15 years ago, have not been answered yet. In Arnold's view these questions are:

1. the question of how emotion is related to action,
2. how emotion is aroused,
3. what is the difference between an emotion that accompanies goal-directed striving, and an emotion that interferes with it, and
4. how the physiological changes that go with emotion, are produced.

In this chapter the following four major functions of affect in economic behavior are distinguished.

4.2. *Interpretation and Organization (Function A)*

Interpretation and organization of information about one's own somatic and psychic functioning, and about the physical and social environment. Affect in this function is instrumental in knowing oneself and the environment, apart from or in co-operation with the cognitive system. Pain and fatigue indicate one's somatic constraints. Fear and anxiety indicate, how far one dares to go. Appreciation and disgust indicate, what one likes or dislikes. Boredom and stress tell about the lack or overdosis of stimulation of the environment. Affect in this sense is a direct and quick way of knowing oneself, others and the physical environment.

Affect also provides a simple structure of the world (Katz' (1960) knowledge function) distinguishing and categorizing objects, persons, and ideas on the basis of attractiveness and to give meaning to an otherwise chaotic universe. One may have forgotten the salient beliefs, but retained the overall impression of favorableness. Affect is then a residual of a reasoning process of attitude formation in the past.

A third aspect of function A is the motivation to complete a task. Zeigarnik (1927) postulated that a certain level of arousal exists when one is performing a task. If a task is completed, the arousal decreases. But if a task is interrupted, the arousal remains at a high level, until one completes the task. Affect, and especially the arousal component, is thus instrumental in completing tasks.

Finally, mood, as a form of affect, has an effect on memory. It affects what one remembers, how much and how long one remembers what one has learned. The effects of mood on memory are discussed in a separate paragraph.

4.3. *Mobilization and Allocation (Function B)*

Mobilization and allocation of resources is affected by the affective state of the organism. In strong emotional states of the organism, somatic energy resources are mobilized (peak performance) or inhibited (freezing). A separate paragraph is devoted to the release and inhibition of resources.

Affect is a task interruptor as well. A sudden danger, a loud noise, or a fast moving object creates an emergency reaction with fear and a fight or flight tendency. Resources are then mobilized, adrenaline output is enhanced, and allocated to the more urgent task to cope with the danger.

Affect is aroused, if a long and important relationship is discontinuated by death or separation (Berscheid, 1982). After the discontinuation, one discovers how much affect was invested in the relationship and how much affect comes "free" after the interruption of the relationship. Mourning processes could be understood in this perspective.

"Acting out" frustrations may be a consequence of the blocking of a goal. This could be understood in a similar way, as a discontinuation of the way to a goal. The blocking of a desired goal may create fury and frustration, even aggression (Dollard et al., 1939). It may be therapeutic ("catharsis") to act out one's frustrations in showing affect to others and to oneself.

Finally, affect may be a choice heuristic. It is a simple way of selecting a product to buy (affect referral; Wright, 1975) or an advertisement to attend to (primary affective reaction; Van Raaij, 1984). In this situation, consumers just select the products they like or attend to the advertisements or commercials they like.

4.4. *Sensation Seeking and Avoiding (Function C)*

Sensation seeking and avoiding may occur in order to reach an optimal level of arousal. Berlyne (1963) postulates that people actively seek an optimal level of stimulation. Stimulation levels that are too low, create low levels of arousal (boredom). Stimulation levels that are too high, create high levels of arousal (stress). People try to avoid these extreme levels of arousal by actively seeking or avoiding stimulation (sensation). Separate paragraphs are devoted to sensation seeking and avoidance, and to affect experience management.

4.5. *Communication (Function D)*

"One cannot overemphasize the interpersonal aspect of emotion: emotional behaviors are, above all, a key system for interpersonal communication" (Leventhal and Tomarken, 1986: p. 599).

Affect is communicated with others. Facial expressions, body postures (Morris, 1977), and exclamations all tell others about one's feelings and preferences. Affect is communicated to other people and to oneself, e.g., through the reactions of others. Affect of others is also quickly understood (see function A). Affect is a much quicker communication system than the cognitive system, and this is very useful in dangerous situations. A separate paragraph is devoted to affect expression (communication) management.

4.6. *Summary*

These four major functions of affect will be discussed in this chapter. Note that the functions A and C pertain to the experience of affect, whereas the functions B and D refer to the expression of affect. Note also that the functions A and B may constitute a decision-making process, going from reception and interpretation of information to the mobilization of resources and to choice.

We will discuss the functions of affect under different headings. However, these four basic functions can be distinguished in the discussions below.

5. EFFECTS OF MOOD ON MEMORY (Function A).

Recently, a number of studies have investigated the effects that mood states might have on memory (e.g., Bower, 1981; Bower and Cohen, 1982; Isen, Shalker, Clark, and Karp, 1978; Srull, 1984). Three main topics have been analyzed in depth:

1. the effects of mood on the *encoding* of material in memory,
2. the effects of mood on the *retrieval* of material from memory,
3. the *state-dependency* effects of mood on memory.

Research by Bower and his associates (Bower, 1981; Bower and Cohen, 1982; Bower, Gilligan, and Monteiro, 1981) demonstrated that stimuli that are congruent with the mood state of the subject, are learned better than incongruent stimuli. When being in a sad mood, Bower's subjects encoded material that referred to sadness, better, while when the subjects were in a good mood, happy material was encoded better. This so-called *mood-congruency* effect relates to the content of the material encoded in memory.

A second encoding effect, the *mood–valence* effect is not related to the content of the material, but to the specific memory processes during encoding. Leight and Ellis (1981) report that, experimentally induced, depressed individuals encoded material considerably worse than individuals that were either in a neutral or an elated mood. This effect was explained by the effect of mood on the cognitive effort, or, as others (Duffy, 1941) would call it, motivation, with which the encoding of material in memory takes place.

The congruency effect refers to the content, the information elements, of memory and memory processes in different mood states. The valence effect refers to the form of memory and memory processes in different mood states.

Congruency and valence effects of mood on the retrieval of material from memory have been demonstrated as well. Lawson (1985) asked his subjects to listen to and to read objective reports about six consumer products (children's bookpacks, electric bug killers, electric citrus juicers, interior wall paint, gas barbecue grills, and bathroom scales). Next, using a procedure adapted from Srull (1984), either a happy or a sad mood was induced in the subjects. The results of the analyses showed that sad subjects retrieved more negative than positive material about the products from memory. The happy subjects recalled about the same levels of positive and negative material about the products. Goldberg and Gorn (1987) studied the effects of program content on the reactions to commercials inserted in the program. A happy program induced a happy mood of the viewers, more affectively positive cognitive responses to the commercial, a greater perceived commercial effectiveness, and to some extent a better recall of the commercial. This study supports the mood congruency hypothesis, because the commercials had an upbeat, fun content. Teasdale and Fogarty (1979) report that their depressed subjects took longer to retrieve pleasant material from memory than their happy subjects. However, the opposite did not hold for the retrieval of unpleasant material. There is much anecdotal evidence for such a mood-congruency effect on the retrieval of information memory.

Discussing the results of survey research on consumer spending and saving behavior, Katona (1975) noted that "rarely do many people mention both favorable and unfavorable business news at the same time. According to whether they feel that business conditions are improving or deteriorating, only good news or bad news are salient to them" (p. 200). This may be the consequence of selectivity in perception and/or retrieval, or of a tendency toward cognitive consistency.

Research indicates that the retrieval of material from memory is better, if the moods at the time of encoding and of retrieval match, independent of the specific mood involved. This is referred to as the *state-dependent* effect of mood on memory. Several studies have demonstrated this effect (Bower, Monteiro, and Gilligan, 1978; Leight and Ellis, 1981). State dependence may have both valence and congruency effects (Srull, 1984).

Although some fruitful specific (e.g., Isen, Shalker, Clark, and Karp, 1978) and general (Bower, 1981) explanations for mood effects on memory have been formulated, the exact nature of the process is yet unknown (Simon, 1982; Lawson, 1985). A promising candidate for a general explanation of mood effects on memory is provided by the network theory of memory. In this network theory it is assumed that feelings, thoughts, somatic manifestations and even physiological arousal are linked together in memory in a network of nodes and connections. Activation of one of the nodes of the network spreads to other nodes. Some authors (Zajonc and Markus, 1984; Zajonc, 1986) add that memory is not only a cerebral (brain) process, but that it can be represented in other parts of the body as well.

The effects of mood on memory have important implications for consumer and marketing policy. If consumers are in a good mood ("happy") when they watch or read advertising messages (encoding), we may expect positive effects for advertisements in general (mood-valence effect) and for "happy" advertisements in particular (mood-congruency effect). Advertisers could select situations, where consumers are generally "happy," e.g., amusement parks and shopping malls. Or they could advertise in media that induce a good mood and during periods in which consumers are generally happy, e.g., weekends and vacations.

Consumers in a good mood retrieve more positive elements from a message than consumers in a bad mood (mood-congruency effect). This is especially important in a shopping situation, where the atmosphere of a store (Kotler, 1974) may induce a good mood through friendly personnel, background music, store design, and even through a nice smell. Consumers in a good mood will probably spend more than consumers in a neutral mood. The state-dependency effect may be enhanced by eliciting the "same" mood in the store as in the advertisements. We should however be aware that these mood induction procedures in stores might be misleading for consumers, who are distracted from the intrinsic product qualities, might forget the negative aspects of the products, and might buy products they would not buy in less attractive environments. From a consumer policy viewpoint, however, consumers should be distrustful and critical rather than euphoric during shopping.

6. EFFECTS OF MOOD ON DECISION MAKING (Functions A and B).

6.1. *Introduction*

Especially in the 1960's and in the 1970's, multi-attribute attitude models and subjective expected utility models have become the cornerstone of research on consumer decision making and reasoned action. The basic assumptions of these models are that consumers form expectations about the outcomes of a choice for a certain alternative, and that these expectations are combined with the utilities of the outcomes. After combining the expectation-utility parts, an overall evaluation (attitude) of the alternative results (Schoemaker, 1982; Fishbein and Ajzen, 1975).

Mood may affect decision making in several ways. Mood may affect the content of the expectations people form about certain outcomes. It may affect, directly or indirectly, the utilities or values associated with the specific outcomes, and it may affect the form in which the expectation-utility parts are combined (combination rules).

6.2. *Expectations*

In one study (Bower and Cohen, 1982), subjects were asked to estimate on a 0-to-100 scale the "objective" probability of possible future events. U.S. subjects were asked, for instance, to estimate the probability that within the next three years they would take a vacation in Europe, or, that within the next ten years there would be a major disaster at a nuclear power plant in California. Experimentally, either a happy or a depressed mood had been induced in the subjects. Analyses of the probability estimates showed that happy subjects elevated their probability estimates of positive future events, e.g., the vacation trip to Europe, and reduced their estimates of negative future events, e.g., the nuclear power plant disaster. Exactly the opposite results were obtained for depressed subjects.

Johnson and Tversky (1983) asked two groups of subjects, respectively in a neutral and in a depressed mood to indicate the degree of risk and their own degree of worry about a number of possible causes of death, as well as their likelihood estimate of each type of cause. Depressed mood enhanced the risk and likelihood estimates of causes of death, as compared with the neutral mood.

Since the late 1940's Katona and his collaborators have surveyed consumer spending and saving behavior. The expectations that consumers have about personal and general future economic cir-cumstances are a central component in this research program. In the course of years, Katona (1975) developed a measure of consumer attitudes, including expectations. This Index of Consumer Sentiment (ICS) represents expectations colored by affect. As Wärneryd (1982) notes, the ICS expresses the degree of optimism and pessimism in society, based on five survey questions. These questions cover the expectations about the business cycle, inflation and personal finances.

The ICS can be conceptualized as a measure of specific consequences of the consumers' mood at an aggregate level. The words "mood" and "sentiment" have similar meanings. Research with the ICS indicates that the consumers' mood is relatively stable over time and contributes to the prediction of consumer spending and saving. Katona (1975) states that the relative stability of the consumers' mood is the result of mass media information and interpersonal communication processes. Large groups of consumers receive regular mass media information about the economic situation in general. Interpersonal communication stimulates the dissemination of such information. Together with other factors, e.g., personal experiences, this information influences the consumers' mood in a positive or in a negative direction. Such differences in mood influence the expectations, consumers and investors form about the future economic conditions. These expectations then influence their spending, investment, saving, and borrowing.

Mood is a relevant concept in economic behavior and marketing. Consumers and speculators in a good mood form more positive ex-pectations about a product, a service or a stock. They are willing to take more risk and are thus more easily convinced to buy the particular product, service or stock. Consumers and speculators in a bad mood form more negative expectations; take less risk; and are thus less likely to buy. Katona (1975) found that a positive (optimistic) mood enhances spending, especially on durables, luxury services, and consumer credit, and tends to decrease consumer saving.

6.3. *Mood and Decision Making*

The effect of mass media information on mood and decision making is reported in other contexts as well. Veitch and Griffit (1976) found that the content of a radio broadcast (good news vs. bad news) influenced the opinions people formed about other people on the basis of written descriptions of these other people. If not reinforced, a mood may fade away after a short while. Isen, Clark and Schwartz (1978) report that the effect of a positive mood induction lasted approximately twenty minutes. Stone and Neale (1984) found that serious negative experiences affected mood negatively only during the same day. If, however, a specific mood is reinforced, the mood may remain relatively stable over time.

We are not aware of research on the effects of mood on decision rules, except for Wright's (1975) affect-referral decision rule. But one could expect that consumers in a good mood are more likely to use the disjunctive and elimination rules, rather than conjunctive and linear-compensatory rules. This means that alternatives are not judged on their full profile, but accepted on one or some salient positive attributes or rejected on one or some salient negative attributes only.

7. AFFECT AND TASK INTERRUPTION (Functions A and B)

Norman (1985: p. 310), discussing central issues for cognitive science, remarks that he has become "more and more dissatisfied with the conventional view of information processing." One of the sources of his dissatisfaction is "the lack of consideration (in cognitive science) of the special problems and issues confronting an animate organism that must survive as both an individual and as a species." Dangerous situations require immediate attention and immediate reactions of the organism. The same holds for sudden opportunities to reach important goals. For such events, perception, knowledge and language must be called into play. However, interpretation of the situation and the event must operate with immediacy, interrupting whatever task was going on. The cognitive system does not seem to be equipped to invoke such an interruption alone.

Interruption of a task may originate from different sources. Sensory stimuli, such as a loud noise or the sudden confrontation with a saber-toothed hungry tiger, will attract the attention, and consequently will distract attention from the ongoing task. This task is then interrupted. Stimuli from the autonomic nervous system (ANS), for instance, hunger, and affect-colored experiences from long-term memory, e.g., the recall of the experiences one had when one's house burned down, may equally lead to an interruption of the task (Simon, 1967, 1982).

Affect is present in these sources of task interruption. Pribram (1970) states that the mechanisms of emotion are of two sorts. One tends to open, the other tends to close the organism to further input. In either case, however, the orderly progression of "the growth of the PLAN being executed is brought to a halt." Thus, affect may function as a "gate keeper" of the organism, in particular as a gate-keeper that acts with a high speed.

Affect is not only a source of task interruption (function B); some authors even speak about goal interruption (Simon, 1967). It may also be a consequence of task interruption (function A). Zeigarnik (1927) described the effects of task interruption and postulated that interrupted tasks are remembered better, because people maintain a higher level of arousal with incomplete tasks as compared with completed tasks. People also have the tendency to complete the interrupted task as soon as this is possible. There are individual differences in this tendency, which makes it possible to use it for diagnostic purposes. Entrepreneurs are, for instance, disposed to show a low tolerance for the Zeigarnik effect; they are eager to complete unfinished tasks (Brockhaus, 1980).

Berscheid (1982) analyzed affect in interpersonal relationships. She described the "hot" emotions that arise in the partners of a relationship that is interrupted, i.e., broken up by death or by separation. Such a strong affect may not be visible in the normal day-to-day interactions between the partners. But the potential of emotion exists and it shows up vigorously when the relationship is interrupted. This is function B: the mobilization of affect in order to overcome a severe loss and to reorganize one's world. Or as pop singer Tom Waits formulated: "I never knew I needed you, until I nearly went insane."

The affect in acting out of frustrations should be mentioned as well. This pertains to affect and aggression that shows up after one discovers that a desired goal cannot be attained. This is the frustration-aggression hypothesis of Dollard et al. (1939).

Thus, affect seems to be, under certain conditions, a source of task or goal interruption (function B), in order to replace the present task with a more urgent task, and, under other conditions, a consequence of the interruption (function A), especially of a long-time relationship.

The implications of affect interrupting tasks for consumer and marketing policy are related to stimulus competition and attention, e.g., in advertising. Many advertisements compete for attention. Advertisements with certain characteristics (color, layout, size, picture, or headline) that attracts the attention or elicits affect, have a higher chance to be attended to (Van Raaij, 1984). The advertisement or the commercial has often to interrupt an ongoing activity of the consumer. These attention-getting characteristics are of a cognitive (collative; Berlyne, 1963) or an affective nature.

Affect is also a consequence of task interruption. Consumers often have an "affective investment" in a brand (loyalty). They don't like to discontinue their relationship with the brand. Such a relationship might be even stronger with a shopkeeper, a supplier, a barber, or a physician.

8. RELEASE AND INHIBITION OF HUMAN RESOURCES (Function B)

Almost everybody has at one time in his or her life run one hun-dred yards in less than twenty seconds. Terrified with fear for being bitten by a ferocious dog, one will run faster than one ever expected or imagined to run. Or one is nailed to the floor, unable to move. Many examples from novels and own experiences indicate that humans possess far greater resources than are normally allocated to our daily activities. The cited examples below pertain to extreme cases and strong emotions, however one could find examples in daily experience as well.

Peak performance may be defined as behavior that exceeds the probable or predictable boundaries, and may occur in any facet of human activity, intellectual, physical, and emotional. Peak performance is more efficient, more productive, or in some other way better than modal behavior. Privette and Landsman (1983) conclude that acts of superior performance arouse widespread interest, but have scarcely been investigated. The conditions under which peak performance occurs, are varied, but in many instances strong affect seems to be one of these conditions. One of the respondents in the Privette-Landsman study reported the following:

> The barn caught fire from a brush fire! The children were safe, but animals in an adjacent shed were not. There was a lot of smoke and heat from the raging fire. I had no tools, and the oak boards were thick- nailed with twenty-penny nails! I pulled at a board with my hands, and it came off with ease, as if a wrecking bar was being used. The animals were free. After the fire died away, it took five minutes to straighten the nails and remove them from the oak plank. The pen was singed but not burned. On inspection we verified that the oak board was well attached to the locust posts, and removing it by hand was virtually impossible. But it happened to me.

Duffy (1941) argues that strong affect represents a change in the energy level, or degree of reactivity, of the individual. The excited person, for instance, has an energy level higher than normal. Energy level refers to the degree of resources mobilized.

Clearly, strong affect may release exceptional amounts of human resources. These resources may be allocated efficiently, as in the case of the burning barn. However, they may also be allocated inefficiently. Extreme, undirected or misdirected states of the organism may occur, e.g., in panic reactions. Such reactions are labeled *catastrophe reactions* (Frijda, 1986). Often fugitives from floods or fires try to rescue futile belongings rather than valuables or necessities: They save their tax-free liquor in an airplane crash! In some cases, catastrophe reactions may be effective in reaching a short-term goal, but they are certainly not efficient, contrary to peak performance.

Individual catastrophe reactions that are communicated and transferred to other individuals, may lead to large-scale detrimental effects. If one of the persons in a crowd starts pushing wildly, out of fear of being overrun, others may start pushing too, and more others. In the chain reaction that follows, many people may in fact be overrun. Something that would probably not have happened, if everybody had remained "cool."

Such individual catastrophe reactions, leading to crowd catastrophe reactions, occur in economic situations as well. For instance, when the unjustified fear of scarcity leads to large-scale excessive hoarding, this leads to the scarcity expected, with all consequences of rising prices, long waiting lines, and even fighting that may go with it. Similar self-fullfilling prophecies, driving by strong either positively or negatively toned emotions, may arise on the financial and stock market.

Strong affect does not always lead to increased resource mobilization. In situations of extremely high arousal, this arousal may be internally directed and one may become immobilized, a paralysis of terror (Scitovsky, 1976) or *freezing* ("freezing 1"). This can be observed in terrified animals. The "keeping dead" reflex may be functional for them in diverting the attention of the beast of prey. At the other extreme, in severe depression, an individual may give up, "resign" or fall in a state of "depressive stupor" ("freezing 2"). In the first case of freezing, extreme levels of arousal are internally directed; in the second case there is no resource mobilization at all (Frijda, 1986).

All four types of extreme changes in resource mobilization and allocation, as influenced by strong affect, are given in Table 2.

Table 2. Resource mobilization and allocation in affect-based behaviors

Type of behavior	Mobilization	Resources direction	Allocation
Peak performance	high	external	efficient
Catastrophe reactions	high	external	inefficient
Freezing 1	high	internal	inefficient
Freezing 2	low	irrelevant	irrelevant

Whether peak performance, catastrophe reactions, or freezing will occur, is not dependent on the quality of affect. Both positive and negative affect may have the mentioned reactions as their consequence. In peak performance, the resources are allocated to the dominant goal. The task as defined by the individual becomes prominent, and events seem "like a mission" (Privette and Landsman, 1983). In catastrophe reactions activities are not very well directed and coordinated. In freezing, the focus of attention seems to be the person's self. However, such hypotheses are only general. A number of hypotheses have been advanced to explain the phenomena, e.g., response competition, attentional capacity, and mental disorganization. To date, no empirical results seem to favor one of the hypotheses over the others. Little is known about the exact conditions that invoke these extreme states of resource mobilization and allocation.

9. SENSATION SEEKING AND AVOIDING (Function C)

Our daily observations provide illustrations of consumers deliberately looking for new stores to visit and for variety in the products they buy. If a T-bone steak is served every night, one would soon tire of it and look for another dish. This is an example of variety seeking as a result of boredom with the present situation. This may be instrumental in learning about new alternatives. Variety seeking in consumer behavior is discussed by Faison (1977) and Venkatesan (1973).

Variety seeking is in conflict with instrumental learning (operant conditioning) and with cognitive consistency theories. These theories are based on the notion that persons strive for a low level of conflict and ambiguity, and thus for a low level of stimulation from the environment. According to these theories people strive for a consistent and familiar environment. These theories fail to explain, why people purposefully engage in new activities and learn about new alternatives.

A number of theories have been proposed to explain variety seeking behavior. These theories are based on the concept of an optimal level of stimulation (OLS) as preferred by the individual. The optimal level of stimulation of the environment corresponds with an optimal level of arousal in the individual. Individuals do not prefer a minimal, but an optimal level of arousal. The optimal level varies from individual to individual.

Stimuli possess certain properties which have an "arousal potential," e.g., novelty, incongruity, ambiguity, and uncertainty. These properties are considered to increase the level of arousal of the individual. If the actual level of arousal of the organism deviates from the optimal level, the individual will engage in "exploratory behavior" (Berlyne, 1963) in order to increase or to decrease his/her arousal level. An increase of arousal potential is reached by a further exploration of existing stimuli or by exploring new stimuli (diversive exploratory behavior). A decrease of arousal potential is reached by "solving" the inconsistencies in the present stimulus field or by attending to less stimuli (specific exploratory behavior).

Raju and Venkatesan (1980) discuss four theories to explain sen-sation seeking and avoiding, by Berlyne (1960, 1963), Fiske and Maddi (1961), Hunt (1963), and Driver and Streufert (1965).

Berlyne (1960, 1963) states that persons try to alter their stimulus field so as to attain an optimal level of arousal potential, i.e., the potential to create arousal in the person. If the actual arousal level is below the optimal level, discomfort in the form of boredom results. If the arousal level is above the optimal level, it produces discomfort in the form of stress. Discomfort, either boredom or stress, are negative affective states. In Berlyne's theory, exploratory behavior is evoked under both conditions. If the arousal potential is below optimum, exploratory behavior is directed toward more aspects of the present stimuli or toward stimuli with higher arousal potential (diversive exploration). If the arousal potential is above optimum, specific exploratory behavior is undertaken in order to become more familiar with the stimulus and to "solve" inconsistencies in the stimulus field.

Fiske and Maddi (1961) use a concept called "activation," similar to arousal, and propose that individuals prefer an optimal level of activation. Similar to Berlyne (1960, 1963), they state that individuals seek a stimulation level that is close to their optimum. Stimulation may be reduced by withdrawal from novel or incongruous stimuli. Stimulation may be increased by attending to novel and "interesting" stimuli.

Hunt (1963) postulates an intrinsic motivation "inherent in information processing and action" to explore incongruities in perceptions and expectations. Individuals prefer an optimal level of incongruity. This causes approach behaviors to increase incongruity, if one is below the optimal level, and avoidance behaviors to decrease incongruity, if one is above the optimal level. States of non-optimal incongruity are experienced as unpleasant.

Driver and Streufert (1965) state, as Hunt (1963), that individuals expect a certain level of incongruity in their environment. This expectation is at the optimum and represents the adaptation level (AL) of the organism. More

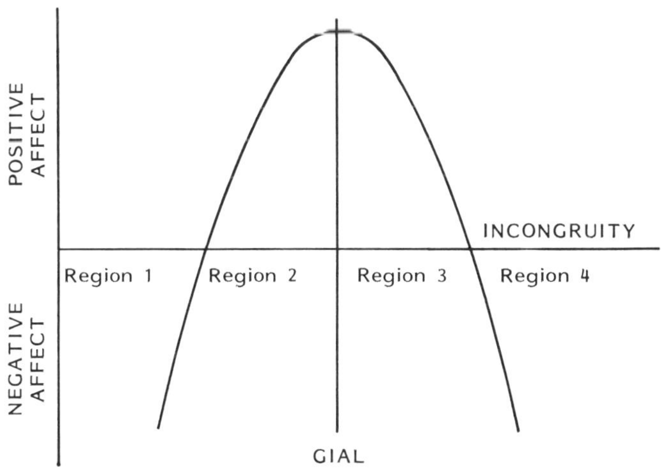

Fig. 1. Relationship between environmental stimulation and affect (according to Driver and Streufert, 1965).

or less incongruity than the expected level is experienced as uncomfortable. The expectation of general incongruity is labeled General Incongruity Adaptation Level (GIAL). Deviations from GIAL motivate actions (exploratory behavior) to get back to GIAL. See Figure 1 from Driver and Streufert (1965).

In Region 1, the stimulation is very low. This creates a negative affect due to boredom. Efforts to find novel aspects are likely to be unsuccessful. Hence, the most likely behavior is an escape from the boring situation to a more stimulating environment.

In Region 2, the stimulation is slightly below optimum, but is associated with a positive affect. The individual will probably look for new aspects of the environment to increase the stimulation (cf. diversive exploration).

In Region 3, the stimulation is somewhat above optimum and the affect is positive. The individual will probably try to reduce the complexity of the environment by familiarizing him/herself more with the present stimuli and reducing their novelty and incongruity (cf. specific exploration).

In Region 4, the stimulation is very high. This creates a negative affect due to overstimulation and stress. Since it is not likely that the stimulation could be brought down, the individual tries to escape from this situation to a less stimulating environment.

Howard and Sheth (1969: pp. 27-28) discuss the "psychology of simplification" and the "psychology of increasing complexity" in a similar way. In Region 3 individuals will try to simplify the situation, moving toward routinization and having a lower tendency for active search behavior. In Region 2 individuals tend to complicate their situation by, for instance, considering new choice alternatives.

It is easy to see that the above effects of stimulation levels have impacts on economic behavior. Product and brand familiarity may lead to brand switching (Region 1) or to distinguishing more aspects in a brand (complication), if these are available (Region 2). Brands might not be selected due to complexity and unfamiliarity (Region 4) or should be simplified and explained as much as possible (Region 3). Similar differences could be expected for the complexity of advertisements and the optimal level of advertising repetition.

Zuckerman (1979) developed a Sensation Seeking Scale (SSS) to measure individual differences in the optimal level of stimulation and arousal. He distinguishes four factors:

1. thrill and adventure seeking, e.g., preference for risk seeking and adventurous activities,
2. experience seeking, i.e., arousal through the mind and senses,
3. disinhibition, i.e., release through drinking, partying, gambling, and sex, and

4. boredom susceptibility, i.e., aversion for repetitive experience, routine work, dull and boring people.

Sensation seeking is rather individualistic, even egocentric. High scores on these factors are related to a high optimal level of stimulation and arousal. Mehrabian and Russell (1974) developed an Arousal Seeking Tendency scale to measure the optimal stimulation level. This scale was used by Raju (1980) in a consumer behavior study.

Active and passive sports, adventure trips, amusement parks, movie theaters offer opportunities for people to find sensations and to escape the (boring) everyday life. In the section on affect experience management, sensation seeking and avoiding is developed further.

10. AFFECT MANAGEMENT (Functions C and D)

10.1. *Impression Management*

In most research on affect, the effects of a certain affective state on decision making and behavior are studied. This emphasis on the effects of affective states, once they have been induced, may lead to the impression that affective states befall individuals, and are more or less involuntary states of the organism. However, often, individuals deliberately attempt to influence their experience of affect (e.g., sensation seeking and watching horror movies). Attempts to influence their expression of affect may be undertaken in order to communicate to others and/or to influence others and/or to influence oneself.

In using the term "affect management" we do not want to imply that such behaviors are completely deliberate or reasoned. Many acts of affect management have been learned in the course of time, or have been transformed from one generation to another, and are thus hardly open to conscious reasoning. We merely want to stress that considering affect as something that unwantedly befalls us, is too narrow a view. People actively strive for affect for many reasons. Some of these affect management strategies will be discussed in this section.

Tedeschi and his colleagues (Tedeschi, 1972; Tedeschi and Norman, 1985; Tedeschi, Bonoma, and Schlenker, 1972) postulated that a basic motive of human social behavior is a desire to maximize one's potential of influencing others. This desire for social power is expressed by self-presentation (Goffman, 1973). Self-presentations are attempts to control the identities attributed to the actor by an audience, i.e., to manage the impressions one makes to an audience.

On the basis of two dimensions, Tedeschi and Norman (1985) have proposed four kinds of impression management. These two dimensions are:

1. *Defensive and assertive* impression management:
   Defensive impression management occurs when a person believes others may attribute some negative or undesirable quality or identity to him or her. Assertive impression management occurs when a person performs certain behaviors to actively establish a certain identity or attribute of him/herself in the mind of the audience.
2. *Tactical and strategic* impression management:
   Tactical impression management has short term goals, whereas strategic impression management has long term goals, i.e., over time and situations. Tetlock and Manstead (1985) have argued that impression management theory does not provide answers to the question, which behavioral tactics individuals employ to achieve the desired impressions in the audience. There are an indeterminate number of tactics, individuals may employ to pursue certain goals. For a number of other reasons as well, Tetlock and Manstead (1985) conclude that impression management theory should be regarded as "... a metatheoretical framework, in which one can formulate and seek answers to questions on the causes and consequences of human social behavior" (p. 62). Research on the ways individuals actively deal with the experience and expression of affect, may develop in the further development of the impression management framework. Aspects of the experience and expression of affect are not only controlled in social situations, to exert influence on others. Individuals may attempt to manage the experience and expression of affect to influence themselves as well. In this respect, impression management theory may be extended to incorporate the self as the audience to influence.

Affect management may occur by attempts to influence directly your own experience of affect, and by attempts to influence directly your own expression of affect.

10.2. *Affect Experience Management* (Function C)

In some occasions individuals attempt to influence the experience of affect. These influence attempts may be performed either directly or indirectly. In both cases, the affective state that one wants to experience, is different from the one one is experiencing. According to Berlyne (1963) people strive for an optimal level of arousal. Under conditions of a suboptimal level of positive affect, people strive for a more intense affect. Under conditions of a supra-optimal level of affect, people strive for a less intense affect.

Three forms of affect experience management are thus:

1. striving for a more intense affect (Region 2),
2. striving for a less intense affect (Region 3), and
3. striving for a different affect than the one experienced (Regions 1 and 4).

The forms 1. and 2. pertain to the intensity of the affect, whereas form 3. refers to the quality and direction of the affect.

On many occasions, people are experiencing an affect, while they actually want to be in an affectively (more) neutral state. When applying for a job, some people may feel insecure, emotionally aroused, and afraid. Most of them, probably all, will consciously try to control their affect, to control themselves, so as not to make mistakes, and in order to give the right answers to the questions asked. Much cognitive, and other activity may be needed to control one's affective state, to experience a neutral affect. Notice how tired people may become after having gone through such an interview.

On other occasions people may also strive for an affect, experiencing no affect at all, or they may strive for a different affect than the one they experience. People may be in a "neutral" mood, not feeling bad and not feeling good, and strive for excitement, thrills, adventure, love or fear. People may try do this directly by recalling certain items from memory, or by recalling or imagining certain situations (self stimulation). People may also try to change this indirectly by performing certain behaviors.

Manucia, Baumann and Cialdini (1984) studied the effect of the quality of mood (either good or bad) and the perceived stability of mood (either stable or unstable) on helping behavior. Half of the subjects in their experiment were brought into a positive mood, and half of the subjects in a bad mood. The results of the experiment showed that subjects in a good mood performed the helping behavior irrespective of the perceived stability of the mood. Of the subjects in a bad mood, only those who perceived that their mood was unstable, performed the helping behavior. Those who perceived the bad mood to be outside the realm of their personal control, did not help. Manucia, Baumann and Cialdini (1984) argue that helping is instrumental in pursuing a good mood for people who are in a bad mood. If the bad mood is perceived to be unstable, people in such a bad mood will help. When being in a good mood, helping may reinforce the good mood, if it is perceived to be under personal control, or it may be a mere side-effect of the good mood, if it is perceived not to be under personal control.

Services, such as the movies, theaters, sports, and amusement parks, are directed toward customer affective experiences. These customers want a reasonable part of sensation, fear and anxiety, and of romance and tenderness. They escape the day-to-day reality in order to experience certain affects. Fantasies, day-dreaming, the reading of novels may serve the same purpose of reaching an optimal level of stimulation.

10.3. *Affect Expression Management* (Function D)

Individuals often attempt to exert influence over the expression of affect. In that case, the expression and experience of affect do not match. Three forms of this affect expression management are:

1. expressing no signs of affect when experiencing affect,
2. expressing signs of an affective state without experiencing it, and
3. expressing signs of a different affect than the one experiencing.

On some occasions people experience a strong affect, but bite their teeth and act "cool." Contrary to inhibition, which is nonvoluntary, this is a form of deception (Buck, 1980). Affect expression management is a central component in human communication and education. Zajonc and Markus (1984) describe, for instance, the education at an English boarding school. The pupils in these schools are taught to repress the expression of many emotions. They learn to keep a stiff upper lip in most situations. In this case, affect expression management is strategic; it is meant to be advantageous in the British culture for the pursuit of long-term goals. In the course of time, such affect expression management may lead to a highly overlearned habit, never to show affect, the original functions of which individuals have long forgotten (Tetlock and Manstead, 1985). Acting "cool" while being in an affective state may have tactical functions, when it only serves short-term goals, confined to a specific situation and to a short-time period.

For most people it is hardly possible to express no signs of affect at all, when experiencing affect. Some experience of affect and the attempts not to show the expression seem to "leak away," e.g., via the hands, the feet, and the face (Darwin, 1872; Buck, 1984). To an observer and to a receiver of the message these leaks are relevant, nonverbal cues in the detection of deception by the sender of the message.

Sometimes, individuals display all external signs of affect without actually experiencing the affect. Notice how realistic some actors know how to express certain emotions on stage or on the screen. Professional mourners may shed real tears. In some occasions, the audience may feel they are witnessing real grief, joy or fear. In this case, affect is expressed to influence others, the audience.

Affect expression management may also indirectly influence the experience of affect. This notion fits well into the network theories of emotion that have been proposed recently (see, e.g., Bower and Cohen, 1982; Leventhal, 1980). According to these theories, affect is a network of feelings, expressive-motor reactions, thoughts and memories, and, as Zajonc and Markus (1984) suggest, the affective arousal, i.e., the physiological correlates of affect. In the emotion network the different components are linked together, so that activation of one component increases the likelihood that other components will be activated as well. Thus, activating the (motor) expression of affect may activate the experience of affect (the James-Lange theory of emotion; see James, 1884). If this view is correct, the experience of affect may be influenced through the expression of affect: We do not tremble because we are afraid, but we are afraid because we tremble.

Research testing the facial feedback hypothesis is particularly relevant for this issue. According to this hypothesis, the experience of emotion is in part controlled by feedback of information about the state of certain facial muscles.

Laird (1974) asked his subjects to relax and contract certain specified facial muscles as they looked at one of two sets of pictures. There were four conditions in his experiment. Subjects either saw a set of pictures displaying members of the Ku Klux Klan or a set of pictures displaying a number of children happily at play. While looking at the pictures, subjects either contracted their face so as to show a smile, or so as to frown. The results of the analyses showed that the subjects' mood ratings were influenced both by the picture type and the facial expression type. Subjects were more elated by the happy pictures, when they had a smile on their face, and more hostile towards the Ku Klux Klan pictures, when they had a frown on their face. In other words, the expression of either positive or negative affect reinforced the compatible affective state evoked by the picture type.

Although the results of studies finding support for the facial feedback hypothesis, have been questioned (Buck, 1980), the literature suggests that, in general, changes in the expression of affect can alter its experience (Leventhal and Tomarken, 1986).

Research of Wells and Petty (1980) points in the same direction. Wells and Petty asked subjects to rate the performance of stereo headphones ("walkmen"). The subjects were asked to move their head in a specified direction, while listening to a taped message through the headphones. The specified head movements mimicked the movements of disagreeing with a certain statement or issue (left-right movement), or mimicked the movements of agreeing with a certain statement or issue (up-down movement). Afterwards, the subjects were asked to rate the performance of the headphone, and to indicate their level of agreement or disagreement with the content of the audio-taped message. The analyses revealed that subjects shaking their head when listening to the message, were less in favor of the issue than subjects moving their head up and down. In this experiment, the attitude towards an issue was, in part, determined by the body movements belonging to a certain attitude. Although the dependent variable in this study was the attitude and not the mood or another affective state, the results of this experiment are in agreement with the present analysis.

People are well aware that they may indirectly influence the experience of affect by influencing the expression of affect. In the fifties, rock singer Johnny Ray expressed this, singing "Smile when your heart is aching, smile when your heart is breaking." The exact process that takes place when expression becomes experience, is not yet exactly known (James, 1884). In many cases, cognitive activity will be involved, for instance, when people interpret their bodily states as expressions of their "true" affect (Schachter and Singer, 1962). However, hardly any cognitive activity may be involved at all (Laird, 1974; Wells and Petty, 1980).

Expression of a desired affect not only becomes experience through an intraindividual process, a social process may be involved as well. Showing a specific emotion in public may lead to congruent reinforcements (feedback) from others, and thus to the experience of the desired affect. An example is the advice to a woman in sex therapy to simulate the desired orgasm (expression of affect). Her partner then will experience this and become more confident of himself. This confidence increases his sexual performance and thus her real orgasm (arousal and experience).

It has been noted that people often show close motor mimicry of the affective state of other persons, such as wincing when someone else is injured, crying at the distress of others, or smiling at another's delight. This phenomenon has traditionally been explained by heightened feeling, i.e., people become so involved in the emotional state of the other that they too experience that emotional state (Darwin, 1872). However, there may be another explanation. Recently, motor mimicry has been explained as an act of communication. Facial and other nonverbal expressions of affect are conspicuously visible to others. Thus, close motor mimicry of affective states may serve functions of affect expression management. In movies and commercials "canned laughter" is used to induce laughing by the audience, and thus to increase appreciation of the movie or the commercial.

Bavelas, Black, Lemery, and Mullett (1986) hypothesized that motor mimicry is communicative. Thus the probability of being observed by a perceiver should affect the sender's display of facial mimicry, and receivers should interpret such displays consistently. If motor mimicry would reflect a private experience that happens to result in overt nonverbal behavior, the presence or absence of observers should have no effect. In an intricate study, Bavelas et al. (1986) found support for their hypotheses that motor mimicry is partly an act of communication. Affect expression management is relevant for consumer services, such as hospitals, funeral services, airlines, and restaurants. The employees in these services should either show the desired affect or not show their real affect, in order to assist their customers. Hochschild (1983) states that the emotional labor of the flight attendants encourages a cheerful and secure flying experience in the face of anxieties that might otherwise escalate into a dread fear of air travel.

11. SUMMARY AND CONCLUSIONS

11.1. *Integration*

Three representations of affect were distinguished: the "hard" representations *arousal* and *expression* and the "soft" representation *experience*. The relationships between these representations are summarized in Figure 2.

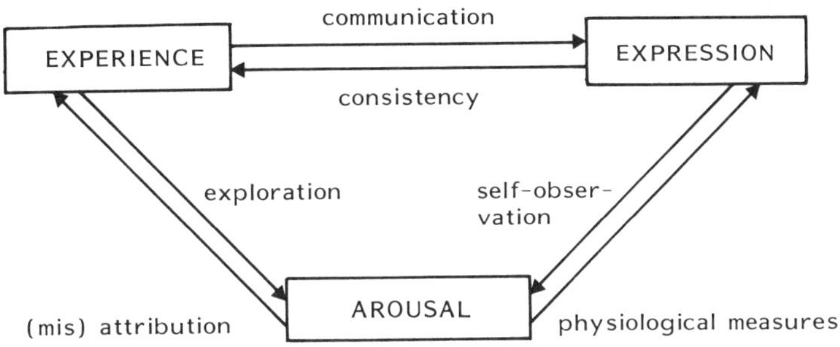

Fig. 2. Relationships between arousal, experience and affect.

The effect of arousal on experience may be described by attribution and misattribution processes (Schachter and Singer, 1962; Zillman, 1971). But on the other hand, experience may increase one's arousal through diversive exploratory behavior or decrease one's arousal through specific exploration (Berlyne, 1963). Fantasies and day-dreaming processes may be part of this exploratory behavior.

Arousal expresses itself in observable body changes and can be measured with physiological measures (Klebba, 1985). Self-observation in a mirror is an example of a direct effect of the expression of affect on arousal. But more often, experience seems to be a necessary mediator of how expression affects arousal.

Experience of affect may lead to the expression (communication) of the affect to oneself and to others. Reversely, affective expression might influence one's experience: If we are induced to laugh we feel happy. This could be explained as a tendency of consistency between expression and experience (Laird, 1974) or self-perception (Bem, 1972).

11.2. *Conclusions*

The "separate systems" view of cognition and affect is an overly simplistic approach to human functioning. Affect and cognition are both thoroughly intertwined, each system partly acting as a control of the other system and an entity to be controlled. Consciously and unconsciously, individuals strive for certain affective states and goals. In such behaviors, cognitive activity may be involved to control, to interpret and to accompany this process.

Cognitive activity is needed to make decisions that lead to these goals. In such behaviors affective states may be involved to control the process, to quickly categorize incoming stimuli, to gate-keep the process, and to interrupt the performance of ongoing tasks.

The more the research on the interplay between affect and cognition will accumulate, the more we may find that the processes we are studying, cannot be completely separated from each other. We should look at the conditions under which the components of the cognitive-affective system function in certain ways. This is not a revolutionary conclusion, nor does it satisfy our desire for a theory, in which clear, independent elements may be distinguished. However, it may prove to be the most realistic conclusion at the moment.

Economic behavior, as economists study it, is modeled with cognitive factors. Psychology could bring in affect to increase the value of models of economic behavior. Affect may contribute to the explanation of "irrational" behaviors. The affective system may help to provide organization and interpretation of the economic environment. Affect may explain, why people may use large resources of energy in certain situations. Lastly, the affective system is a communication system to others and to oneself.

To return to the issues formulated at the onset of this chapter, in our opinion, affect is something different from cognition. The effects of affect on economic behavior are considerable and consistent enough to justify this attention.

REFERENCES

Arnold, M.B., 1970, "Perennial problems in the field of emotion," in: M.B. Arnold (ed.), Feelings and Emotions. The Loyola Symposium, New York: Academic Press, pp. 169-185.

Bavelas, J.B., A. Black, C.R. Lemery, and J. Mullett, 1986, "I show how you feel": Motor mimicry as a communicative act, Journal of Personality and Social Psychology, 50, 322-329.

Bem, D.J., 1972, "Self-perception theory," in: L. Berkowitz (ed.), Advances in Experimental Social Psychology, Vol. 6, New York: Academic Press, pp. 2-62.

Berlyne, D.E., 1960, Conflict, Arousal, and Curiosity, New York: McGraw-Hill.

Berlyne, D.E., 1963, "Motivational problems raised by exploratory and epistemic behavior," in: S. Koch (ed.), Psychology: A study of a Science, Vol. 5, New York: McGraw-Hill, pp. 284-364.

Berscheid, E., 1982, "Attraction and emotion in interpersonal relations," in: M.S. Clark and S.T. Fiske (eds.), Affect and Cognition, Hillsdale, NJ: Lawrence Erlbaum, pp. 37-54.

Bower, G.H., 1981, Mood and memory, American Psychologist, 36, 129-148.

Bower, G.H., and P.R. Cohen, 1982, "Emotional influences in memory and thinking: Data and theory," in: M.S. Clark and S.T. Fiske (eds.), Affect and Cognition, Hillsdale, NJ: Lawrence Erlbaum, pp. 291-331.

Bower, G.H., S.G. Gilligan, and K.P. Monteiro, 1981, Selectivity of learning caused by affective states, Journal of Experimental Psychology: General, 110, 451-473.

Bower, G.H., K.P. Monteiro, and S.G. Gilligan, 1978, Emotional mood as a context for learning and recall, Journal of Verbal Learning and Verbal Behavior, 17, 573-585.

Brockhaus, R.H., Sr., 1980, Risk-taking propensity of entrepreneurs, Academy of Management Journal, 23, 509-520.

Buck, R., 1980, Nonverbal behavior and the theory of emotion: The facial feedback hypothesis, Journal of Personality and Social Psychology, 38, 811-824.

Candland, D.K., 1977, "The persistent problems of emotion," in: D.K. Candland, J.P. Fell, E. Keen, A.I. Leshner, R. Plutchik, and R.M. Tarpy (eds.), Emotion, Monterey, CA: Brooks/Cole, pp. 1-84.

Costa, P.T., and R.R. McCrae, 1980, Influence of extraversion and neuroticism on subjective well-being: Happy and unhappy people, Journal of Personality and Social Psychology, 38, 668-678.

Darwin, C., 1872, The Expression of Emotions in Man and Animals, London: John Murray (reprint: 1965, Chicago, IL: University of Chicago Press).

De Rivera, J., 1977, A Structural Theory of the Emotions, New York: International Universities Press.

Dollard, J., L.W. Doob, N.E. Miller, O.H. Mowrer, and R.R. Sears, 1939, Frustration and Aggression, New Haven, CT: Yale University Press.

Driver, M.J., and S. Streufert, 1965, The "General Incongruity Adaptation Level" (GIAL) Hypothesis: An Analysis and Integration of Cognitive Approaches to Motivation, 114, Lafayette, IN: Purdue University, Krannert Graduate School of Management (working paper).

Duffy, E., 1941, An explanation of "emotional" phenomena without the use of the concept "emotion," Journal of General Psychology, 25, 283-293.

Eckenrode, J., 1984, Impact of chronic and acute stressors on daily reports of mood, Journal of Personality and Social Psychology, 46, 907-918.

Ewert, O., 1970, "The attitudinal character of emotion," in: M.B. Arnold (ed.), Feelings and Emotions. The Loyola Symposium, New York: Academic Press, pp. 233-240.

Faison, E.W.J., 1977, The neglected variety drive: A useful concept for consumer behavior, Journal of Consumer Research, 4, 172-175.

Fishbein, M., and I. Ajzen, 1975, Belief, Attitude, Intention, and Behavior: An Introduction to Theory and Research, Reading, MA: Addison-Wesley.

Fiske, D.W., and S.R. Maddi, 1961, Functions of Varied Experience, Homewood, IL: Dorsey Press.

Frijda, N.H., 1986, The Emotions, New York: Cambridge University Press.

Gardner, M.P., 1985, Mood states and consumer behavior: A critical review, Journal of Consumer Research, 12, 281-300.

Goffman, E., 1973, The Presentation of Self in Everyday Life, Woodstock, NY: The Overlook Press.

Goldberg, M.E., and G.J. Gorn, 1987, Happy and sad TV programs: How they affect reactions to commercials, Journal of Consumer Research, 14, 387-403.

Havlena, W.J., and M.B. Holbrook, 1986, The varieties of consumption experience: Comparing two typologies of emotion in consumer behavior, Journal of Consumer Research, 13, 394-404.

Hochschild, A.R., 1983, The Managed Heart: Commercialization of Human Feeling, Berkeley, CA: University of California Press.

Holbrook, M.B., 1986, "Emotion in the consumption experience: Toward a new model of the human consumer," in: R.A. Peterson, W.D. Hoyer, and W.R. Wilson (eds.), The Role of Affect in Consumer Behavior, Lexington, MA: Heath, pp. 17-52.

Howard, J.A., and J.N. Sheth, 1969, The Theory of Buyer Behavior, New York: John Wiley.

Hunt, J. McV., 1963, "Motivation inherent in information processing and action," in: O.J. Harvey (ed.), Motivation and Social Interaction: Cognitive Determinants, New York: Ronald Press, pp. 35-94.

Isen, A.M., and T.E. Shalker, 1982, The effect of feeling state on evaluation of positive, neutral, and negative stimuli: When you "accentuate the positive," do you "eliminate the negative?," Social Psychology Quarterly, 45, 58-63.

Isen, A.M., M.S. Clark, and M.F. Schwartz, 1978, Duration of the effect of good mood on helping: Footprints on the sands of time, Journal of Personality and Social Psychology, 36, 1-12.

Isen, A.M., T.E. Shalker, M.S. Clark, and L. Karp, 1978, Positive affect, accessibility of material in memory and behavior: A cognitive loop?, Journal of Personality and Social Psychology, 36, 1-12.

Izard, C.E., 1977, Human Emotions, New York: Plenum Press.

James, W., 1884, What is an emotion?, Mind, 19, 188-205.

Johnson, E., and A. Tversky, 1983, Affect, generalization and the perception of risk, Journal of Personality and Social Psychology, 45, 20-31.

Kassarjian, H.H., 1971, Personality and consumer behavior: A review, Journal of Marketing Research, 8, 409-418.

Katona, G., 1975, Psychological Economics, New York: Elsevier.

Katz, D., 1960, The functional approach to the study of attitudes, Public Opinion Quarterly, 24, 163-204.

Klebba, J.M., 1985, Physiological measures of research: A review of brain activity, electrodermal response, pupil dilation, and voice analysis methods and studies, Current Issues & Research in Advertising, 53-76.

Kotler, P., 1974, Atmospherics as a marketing tool, Journal of Retailing, 49, 48-64.

Kroeber-Riel, W., 1979, Activation research: Psychobiological approaches in consumer research, Journal of Consumer Research, 5, 240-250.

Laird, J.D., 1974, Self-attribution of emotion: The effects of expressive behavior on the quality of emotional experience, Journal of Personality and Social Psychology, 29, 475-486.

Lawson, R., 1985, The effects of mood on retrieving consumer product information, Advances in Consumer Research, 12, 399-403.

Leight, K.A., and H.C. Ellis, 1981, Emotional mood states, strategies, and state dependency in memory, Journal of Verbal Learning and Verbal Behavior, 20, 251-266.

Leventhal, H., 1980, "Toward a comprehensive theory of emotion," in: L. Berkowitz (ed.), Advances in Experimental Social Psychology, Vol. 13, New York: Academic Press, pp. 140-207.

Leventhal, H., and A.J. Tomarken, 1986, Emotion: Today's problems, Annual Review of Psychology, 37, 565-610.

Manucia, G.K., D.J. Baumann, and R.B. Cialdini, 1984, Mood influences on helping: Direct effects or side effects, Journal of Personality and Social Psychology, 46, 357-364.

Mehrabian, A., and J.A. Russell, 1974, An Approach to Environmental Psychology, Cambridge, MA: MIT Press.

Morris, D., 1977, Manwatching, London: Book Club Associates.

Nisbett, R.E., and S. Schachter, 1966, Cognitive manipulation of pain, Journal of Experimental Social Psychology, 2, 227-236.

Norman, D.A., 1985, "Twelve issues for cognitive science," in: A.M. Aitkenhead and J.M. Slack (eds.), Issues in Cognitive Modeling, London: Lawrence Erlbaum.

Nowlis, V., 1970, "Mood, behavior and experience," in: M.B. Arnold (ed.), Feelings and Emotions. The Loyola Symposium, New York: Academic Press, pp. 261-278.

Plutchik, R., 1962, The Emotions: Facts, Theories, and a New Model, New York: Random House.

Plutchik, R., 1980, Emotion, A Psychoevolutionary Synthesis, New York: Harper and Row.

Pribram, K.H., 1970, "Feelings as monitors," in: M.B. Arnold (ed.), Feelings and Emotions. The Loyola Symposium, New York: Academic Press, pp. 39-54.

Privette, G., and T. Landsman, 1983, Factor analysis of peak performance: The full use of potential, Journal of Personality and Social Psychology, 44, 195-200.

Raju, P.S., 1980, Optimum stimulation level: Its relationship to personality, demographics, and exploratory behavior, Journal of Consumer Research, 7, 272-282.

Raju, P.S., and M. Venkatesan, 1980, Exploratory behavior in the consumer context: A state of the art review, Advances in Consumer Research, 7, 258-263.

Ray, M.L., and R. Batra, 1983, Emotion and persuasion in advertising: What we know and don't know about affect, Advances in Consumer Research, 10, 543-548.

Russell, J.A., 1980, A circumplex model of affect, Journal of Personality and Social Psychology, 39, 1161-1178.

Schachter, S., 1964, "The interactions of cognitive and physiological determinants of emotional state," in: L. Berkowitz (ed.), Advances in Experimental Social Psychology, Vol. 1, New York: Academic Press, pp. 49-80.

Schachter, S., and J.E. Singer, 1962, Cognitive, social, and physiological determinants of emotional state, Psychological Review, 69, 379-399.

Schoemaker, P.J.H., 1982, The expected utility model: Its variants, purposes, evidence and limitations, Journal of Economic Literature, 20, 529-563.

Scitovsky, T., 1976, The Joyless Economy, New York: Oxford University Press.

Simon, H.A., 1967, Motivational and emotional controls of cognition, Psychological Review, 74, 29-39.

Simon, H.A., 1982, "Comments," in: M.S. Clark and S.T. Fiske (eds.), Affect and Cognition, Hillsdale, NJ: Lawrence Erlbaum, pp. 333-342.

Smith, S.L., 1975, "Mood and the menstrual cycle," in: E.J. Sachar (ed.), Topics in Psychoendocrinology, New York: Grune and Stratton, pp. 19-58.

Srull, T.K., 1984, The effects of subjective affective states on memory and judgment, Advances in Consumer Research, 11, 530-533.

Stone, A.A., and J.M. Neale, 1984, Effects of severe daily events on mood, Journal of Personality and Social Psychology, 46, 137-144.

Strongman, K.T., 1978, The Psychology of Emotion, New York: John Wiley.

Teasdale, J.D., and S.J. Fogarty, 1979, Differential effects of induced mood on retrieval of pleasant and unpleasant events from episodic memory, Journal of Abnormal Psychology, 88, 248-257.

Tedeschi, J.T. (ed.), 1972, The Social Influence Processes, Chicago, IL: Aldine.

Tedeschi, J.T., and N. Norman, 1985, "Social power, self-presentation, and the self," in: B.R. Schlenker (ed.), The Self in Social Life, New York: McGraw-Hill, pp. 293-322.

Tedeschi, J.T., T.V. Bonoma, and B.R. Schlenker, 1972, "Influence, decision, and compliance," in: J.T. Tedeschi (ed.), The Social Influence Processes, Chicago, IL: Aldine, pp. 346-418.

Tetlock, P.E., and A.S.R. Manstead, 1985, Impression management versus intrapsychic explanations in social psychology: A useful dichotomy?, Psychological Review, 92, 59-77.

Valins, S., 1966, Cognitive effects of false heart-rate feedback, Journal of Personality and Social Psychology, 4, 400-408.

Van Raaij, W.F., 1984, Affective and Cognitive Reactions to Advertising, 84-111, Cambridge, MA: Marketing Science Institute (working paper).

Veitch, R., and W. Griffit, 1976, Good news-bad news: Affective and interpersonal effects, Journal of Applied Social Psychology, 6, 69-75.

Venkatesan, M., 1973, "Cognitive consistency and novelty seeking," in: S. Ward and T.S. Robertson (eds.), Consumer Behavior. Theoretical Sources, Englewood Cliffs, NJ: Prentice-Hall, pp. 354-384.

Wärneryd, K.-E., 1982, The life and work of George Katona, Journal of Economic Psychology, 2, 1-31.

Wells, G.L., and R.E. Petty, 1980, The effect of overt head movement on persuasion: Compatibility and incompatibility, Psychology Today, 1, 219-230.

Wright, P.L., 1975, Consumer choice strategies: Simplifying vs. optimizing, Journal of Marketing Research, 7, 60-67.

Zajonc, R.B., 1980, Feeling and thinking: Preferences need no inferences, American Psychologist, 35, 151-175.

Zajonc, R.B., 1986, "Basic mechanisms of preference formation," in: R.A. Peterson, W.D. Hoyer, and W.R. Wilson (eds.), The Role of Affect in Consumer Behavior, Lexington, MA: Heath, pp. 1-16.

Zajonc, R.B., and H. Markus, 1982, Affective and cognitive factors in preferences, Journal of Consumer Research, 9, 123-131.

Zajonc, R.B., and H. Markus, 1984, "Affect and cognition: The hard interface," in: C.C. Izard, J. Kagan, and R.B. Zajonc (eds.), Emotions, Cognition and Behavior, Cambridge, MA: Cambridge University Press, pp. 73-102.

Zeigarnik, B., 1927, Über das Behalten von erledigten und unerledigten Handlungen, Psychologische Forschungen, 9, 1-85.

Zillman, D., 1971, Excitation transfer in communication-mediated aggressive behavior, Journal of Experimental Social Psychology, 7, 419-434.

Zillman, D., 1978, "Attribution and misattribution of excitatory reaction," in: J.H. Harvey, W.J. Ickes, and R.F. Kidd (eds.), New Directions in Attribution Research, Hillsdale, NJ: Lawrence Erlbaum, pp. 335-368.

Zuckerman, M., 1979, Sensation Seeking: Beyond the Optimal Level of Arousal, Hillsdale, NJ: Lawrence Erlbaum.

Table of Contents

5. Attitude-behavior Relationships

RIK G.M. PIETERS
Erasmus University, Rotterdam, The Netherlands

1. INTRODUCTION

It is both artificial and impractical to split behavior into clearly distinct compartments, economic behavior vs. non-economic behavior (MacFadyen and MacFadyen, 1986). Psychology and economics share the common problem of developing and testing models which describe, explain and predict the behavior of individuals alone and in groups. Both disciplines have tackled this problem proficiently, albeit with different emphasis. One of the differences is that psychology has been engaged heavily in explaining behavior, sometimes at the expense of trying to predict behavior – assuming that explanation naturally leads to prediction. Economics, on the other hand, has focussed mainly on the prediction of behavior, sometimes neglecting the explanation of behavior – assuming that explanation lies in the prediction.

In recent years both disciplines have come more closely to each other. Many papers illustrate and several reviews describe this development (see, e.g., Earl, 1983; MacFadyen and MacFadyen, 1986; Furnham and Lewis, 1986). In psychology, more than before, emphasis is placed on the prediction of (economic) behavior, and on the formalization of the relationships between the determinants and the behavior that is to be predicted. In economics, the explanation of behavior has gained more importance.

In this development, attitude theory takes a central position. Attitude is a motivational concept. Attitude theory deals with the motivations underlying behavior, including economic behavior. Attitude theory does not deal with the deep corners of the human mind. Attitudes are at the surface of human functioning, and open to empirical investigation. The prediction of the behavior of individuals from knowledge of their attitudes has been one of the most profoundly studied issues in attitude theory. Attitude surveys are widespread in consumer and market research. Katona was one of the first to infuse attitude theory in economics (for an overview see Katona,

Van Raaij, W.F., van Veldhoven, G.M. and Wärneryd, K.E. (eds) Handbook of Economic Psychology. ISBN 90-247-3720-6.

1975). Using a survey approach, Katona studied the effect of aspirations, expectations, and attitudes on economic behavior. He advocated to develop a "macropsychology" dealing with aggregate measures of attitudes and economic behavior.

In developing a realistic account of economic behavior, a micro-psychology is needed. Without denying the importance of firms and households and other collectivities, Leibenstein (1976) argues that such groups are the molecules of economic organization, and that their behavior can only be understood by understanding the behavior of their atoms. Individuals are the basic units of the economy, only they make decisions. Findings of attitude research can prove their utility in developing a micro-psychology of economic behavior. Evidently, the characteristics of individuals cannot simply be summated to obtain collective characteristics (Van Raaij, 1984). Attitude theory is not all encompassing. However, research on the formation and change of attitudes, and on the relationship between attitudes and behavior can help to provide more sound behavior assumptions of economic theory, one of the three major conditions economic theories should fulfill according to Leibenstein (1976: p. 19). Using the findings of attitude research can lead to developing better models of economic behavior, both in terms of prediction and explanation.

2. ATTITUDE THEORY

Some 50 years ago Allport (1935) wrote that "the concept of attitude is probably the most distinctive and indispensable concept in contemporary American social psychology. No other term appears more frequently in the experimental and theoretical literature" (p. 798). In a recent review of the literature on attitude and attitude change, McGuire (1985) noted that since the 1920's and 1930's the interest in attitudes, although it has waxed and waned, has always been substantial. Few will contradict that attitudes have been a perennial, and sometimes the paramount, topic of social psychological and consumer research (Kassarjian and Kassarjian, 1979; McGuire, 1986).

Attitudes are not studied for the sake of beauty, nor does the attitude area merely form a convenient arena for eager scientists to measure their intellectual strengths. Attitude has gained its status in social psychological research and theorizing for several reasons. First, attitudes are thought to serve certain psychological functions for the person holding the attitudes. Theorists have considered one of the major functions served by attitudes to be that of organizing and structuring a rather chaotic world (Katz, 1960; Smith, Bruner, and White, 1956). Attitudes are thought to provide ready aids in sizing up objects and events in the environment. Other functions that attitudes may serve can be distinguished (see, e.g., Katz, 1960; Lutz, 1981).[1] Second, attitudes are thought to direct and thus to explain and predict behavior (Fishbein and Ajzen, 1975).

At least two research lines can be distinguished in the study of attitudes. First, much attention has been focussed on the question of attitude-behavior consistency. If attitudes do not direct, or at least precede, behavior, one of the elements of the utility of the attitude concept would be absent. Second, behavior change via attitude change has been and is still a prominent research line. Here, the main attention will be devoted to the topic of attitude-behavior relations, particularly to the consistency of attitudes and behavior. The topic of attitude change will be given less attention. This is not to suggest that the latter topic is of less theoretical or practical relevance. Rather, the question whether attitudes relate to and precede behavior, should be answered satisfactorily, before one can turn to the topic, how to change behavior via attitude change.

Research on attitude-behavior consistency has a long tradition in social psychology. LaPiere (1934) investigated whether the behavior of hotel and restaurant owners in the United States was consistent with their self-reported attitudes towards discrimination of ethnic groups. Travelling with a Chinese couple, LaPiere visited over 200 hotels and restaurants. The Chinese couple was refused service at only one establishment. A few months later, all the restaurants that had been visited received a letter asking whether one would give service to Chinese guests. Over 90 percent of the places that responded to the letter said that they would not. Although the study can be criticized on a number of points, it has become one of the classics in the collection of failures to find consistency between attitudes and behavior. The issue of attitude-behavior inconsistency will be returned to in section 8.

The LaPiere study addressed the question of whether attitudes relate to behavior. It is an example of what Zanna and Fazio (1982) call the first generation of research questions on attitude-behavior consistency: the "IS"-questions. The second generation of research questions deals with the conditions upon which attitude-behavior consistency can be observed. Such questions can be called the "WHEN"-questions. Fazio and Zanna (1981) stress the importance of such questions, recommending that "Rather than asking whether attitudes relate to behavior, we have to ask "under what conditions do what kinds of attitudes of what kinds of individuals predict what kinds of behavior?" " (p. 165). The third generation of research questions deals with the processes underlying the mediating effects. These questions can be called the "HOW"-questions.

In recent years, research has shifted from addressing the "IS"-questions to addressing the "WHEN"-questions. Yet, despite the voluminous literature, relatively limited attention has been paid to the processes that give rise to attitude-behavior consistency (Zanna and Fazio, 1982). This situation seems to be changing.

If one is interested in the explanation and prediction of behavior from a broader perspective, the three mentioned questions, the IS, WHEN and HOW questions, of the attitude-behavior relation represent only part of the questions that can be asked. From this perspective the relevant questions are: What determines behavior, and why. Such a perspective calls for taking into account determinants of behavior, apart from attitudes. In this chapter, research with respect to attitude-behavior relationships, and research on other determinants of behavior will be reviewed. Before turning to this topic, some notes on the definition and measurement of attitudes and behavior will be made first.

3. DEFINING ATTITUDES

What exactly is an attitude? Is an opinion about the fuel consumption of your car an attitude? Is a feeling about having a baby an attitude? Is voting for candidate X an attitude? Is a body position, as in ballet, an attitude? Is an attitude a combination of the above mentioned, or is it something completely different?

Theorists have been generous in providing us with definitions and conceptualizations of attitudes. Reviewing the literature on attitudes and opinions, Fishbein and Ajzen (1972) compiled some 500 different operational definitions of what an attitude is. They note that in some studies even several different definitions are used. A closer look indicates that some elements constantly appear.

Many theorists have argued that attitudes are feelings related to some class of stimuli. Such stimuli may include objects, persons, issues and behaviors. Thus, attitudes can be viewed as an object-related type of affect. Petty and Cacioppo (1981) note that "there is widespread agreement among social psychologists that the term *attitude* should be used to refer to a general and enduring positive or negative feeling about some person, object or issue" (p. 7).

Such a conceptualization focusses on the *experience* of attitude, i.e., on the experiential qualities. Some theorists take the point of view that since attitudes are assumed to direct behavior, conceiving attitudes as mere feelings may not be sufficient. Others however stress that the relationship with behavior cannot be part of the definition, as exactly this point is to be proven.

In many definitions and conceptualizations the expressive qualities of attitudes are emphasized, i.e., the *expression* of the feeling. Campbell (1963) suggests that the concept of attitude can be subsumed by the more general term disposition. In this view, attitudes can be defined as dispositions to respond in a consistently positive or negative way to a class of stimuli (Seibold, 1980). Others take a similar position. E.g., Ehrenberg and Goodhardt (1980) argue that a consumer's attitude to a brand may be summarized by his or her expressed intention to buy the brand.

Sometimes, emphasis is placed on the *cognitive antecedents or consequences* of attitudes. The importance of this aspect is frequently not recognized. Attitudes are assumed to be learned, and not innate (Fishbein and Ajzen, 1975). Attitudes are the result, the residual, of past experience (Campbell, 1963). This experience may be direct, i.e., own experience, or indirect, i.e., communicated experience from others. Learning can take place in different forms: from associative (classical and operant conditioning) to cognitive (information processing). If attitudes are the result of cognitive learning, cognitions or beliefs are expected to give rise to the attitude. In the course of time, these cognitions may be forgotten (Zajonc and Markus, 1982). If attitudes are the result of associative learning, cognitions do not have to be involved in attitude formation, although, in the course of time, cognitions may become involved as post hoc explanations or rationalizations of the attitude. Many attitude models deal with the cognitive antecedents or consequences of attitudes.

Few conceptualizations and definitions of attitudes capitalize on (psychophysiological) *concomitants or correlates* of attitudes. Yet, as will be indicated in the next section, attempts to measure the psychophysiological concomitants of attitudes are numerous.

In some conceptualizations, attitudes are considered to consist of several components. In the tripartite attitude model, attitudes are assumed to consist of three parts, a cognitive (knowledge), affective (feeling) and conative (disposition, behavior) part. The tripartite model was popular in the 1950's and 1960's (Breckler, 1984). Despite its popularity in textbooks and reviews of the attitude literature, the bulk of attitude research and theory mainly focussed on the affective component of attitudes (Ostrom, 1969). This has remained until our days. Instead of considering attitude to be composed of three parts, many theorists nowadays investigate the relationships between attitude and the cognitive and conative components of human functioning.

Here, in agreement with most theorists, the term attitude will be used to refer to a positive or negative feeling towards a given class of stimuli. Possible antecedents, consequences and correlates of an attitude are excluded from its definition.

Contrary to the attitude concept, relatively limited attention in social psychology has been devoted to the conceptualization and definition of behavior. What behavior is, is assumed to be self-evident. Often, discussions of attitude-behavior relations include thorough analyses of the attitude concept, but lack any reference to what behavior is (Verhallen and Pieters, 1984), or how it should be measured (Ajzen, 1982).

Usually, the term "behavior" is used to refer to observable acts that are studied in their own right (Fishbein and Ajzen, 1975: p. 13). Questionnaire or verbal responses are instances of overt behavior. Such responses may be used to infer attitudes, cognitions, intentions, or behavior. They may also be studied as instances of the behavior under study, questionnaire behavior. In the latter case questionnaire responses are studied "in their own right."

Fishbein and Ajzen (1975, 1976; Ajzen and Fishbein, 1977, 1980) explain that when studying behavior (and attitudes) four specification elements can be distinguished:

1. the action,
2. the target at which the action is directed,
3. the context in which the action is performed, and
4. the time at which the action is performed.

On the basis of these specification elements, two types of behavior can be recognized: single acts and behavior categories. A single act is a specific behavior that is performed by the observation unit. In a single act all four specification elements are (at least implicitly) defined. A behavior category is a set of single acts that are similar in at least one specification element (Verhallen and Pieters, 1984), usually the action or the target. Buying a solar energy collector (on Monday June the 5th at L-Mart) is a single act. This single act can be an element of the behavior category "energy saving behavior," to which other single acts, such as lowering the thermostat in the winter time with four degrees, belong. In this behavior category, all single acts are aimed at the same target: saving energy. Buying the solar energy collector is also an element of the behavior category "buying at L-Mart." Distinguishing between single acts and behavior categories is important since many behaviors that social scientists are interested in are in fact behavioral categories (see Fishbein, 1980: p. 72).

5. MEASURING ATTITUDES

5.1. *Introduction*

Many techniques to measure attitudes have been developed. These techniques differ in a number of characteristics and assumptions. Although an in-depth analysis of attitude measurement is not provided, some issues concerning the techniques will be introduced. Such an introduction opens the door to discussing the relationships between attitudes and behavior.

Techniques to measure attitudes belong to one of three broad classes. Attitudes can be assessed with verbal self-reports, with observations of non-verbal behavior and with psychophysiological measures. The relevance of such measures for consumer and market research is evident.

5.2. *Self-report Measures*

Self-report measures, in surveys, have been and are being used extensively to assess attitudes. In economics, Katona (1975) was one of the first to use the survey approach to measure attitudes. Attitude self-reports can be obtained either directly or indirectly. The one-item rating scale is a direct measure of attitude. In such a single-response measure an object is usually placed along some affective bipolar dimension, e.g., "I like Marx Brothers movies – I dislike Marx Brothers movies." Most self-reports of attitudes are indirect measures. The attitude, as object-related feeling, is not assessed directly, it is inferred from other verbal responses.[2] The four classic indirect self-report measures of attitudes are the Thurstone, Likert, Guttman, and Semantic Differential scales. A description of these measures is provided by many handbooks, see, e.g., Fishbein and Ajzen (1975).

Often, the ease with which a one item-rating scale can be constructed seems to outweigh its, in comparison to the other scales, relatively low reliability. Petty and Cacioppo (1981: p. 12) note that for many research and survey purposes the one-item rating scale seems to be sufficient.

Several assumptions underlie the mentioned direct and indirect self-report measures of attitudes. It is assumed that:

1. Individuals are motivated to report their "true" attitude.
2. Individuals are able to report their true attitude.
3. The measurement technique doesn't affect the attitude and the behavior.

Campbell and Stanley (1966) indicate that a measure may be considered reactive to the extent that its implementation influences the responses of individuals being observed. Reactivity may threat the validity of the measurement (Cook and Campbell, 1979; Judd and Kenny, 1981). Research has shown that self-reports of attitudes can be troubled by reactivity.

Overt and covert cueing can take place in interview situations. Aspects from the interview situation may inadvertently provide cues as to how the respondent is expected to respond. Also, respondents may react in a manner that the researcher or interviewer is expected to desire, the "good" subject, or in a manner opposite to what the researcher or interviewer is expected to desire, the "bad" subject (see, e.g., Rosenthal and Rosnow (1969) and Barber (1976) on subject roles and evaluation apprehension).

Respondents may try to present themselves in a better light than their actual behavior might reveal. Such *impression management* in surveys can be either offensive, in which case respondents actively present themselves in a better light, or defensive, in which case respondents may give misleading responses to questionnaire items in order to avoid confrontation (see, e.g., Cialdini and Bauman, 1981).

If overt and covert cueing and impression management take place, the assumption that individuals are motivated to report their "true" attitudes and behaviors is not warranted.

There has been some discussion whether individuals are able to report their true attitudes. Nisbett and Wilson (1977) have argued that people sometimes do not know what they are doing and that at times they may be unable to report what has influenced their thoughts and judgments, and how this influence has taken place. In such cases, individuals may rely on their private theories of how judgment and behavior is influenced. If people are motivated but not able to give an account of their internal states and the accompanying processes, interpretations of self-report may be erroneous. This may lower the validity of verbal self-reports. It should be mentioned that most theorists implicitly or explicitly (Wright and Rip, 1980; Rip, 1980) believe that, in general, people do have access to their internal states and to the relationship between these states and behavior.

Finally, self-report measures of attitudes may serve to crystallize or freeze the attitude (Sechrest and Belew, 1983). A request to indicate one's attitudes, may bring attitudes to a higher level of awareness than they were before. Also, the measurement of attitudes may form attitudes that did not exist before. Moreover, several studies have demonstrated that verbal self-reports can change attitudes and behavior (e.g., Schwartz and Orleans, 1967). Sherman (1980) found that asking people to state their intention to perform a certain behavior enhances the likelihood that they will behave in accordance with their intentions.[3] When *attitude crystallization and behavior change* takes place because of self-reports, the assumption that the measurement does not influence the measured phenomenon, is not correct.

The critique on verbal self-reports has stimulated attempts to develop add-on procedures to validly measure attitudes by means of self-reports, and to develop alternative attitude measures.

The bogus pipeline technique (Jones and Sigall, 1971) is an example of such an add-on technique. Individuals are led to believe that their true attitudes can be measured with an intricate technical device. Next, these individuals are asked to predict the attitudes that the device indicates. This procedure aims at motivating individuals to report their true attitudes by minimizing impression management.

The presented measurement techniques are all nondisguised techniques. The respondent is aware that his or her attitude is being assessed. The purpose of the measurement is not deliberately concealed.

Disguised self-report techniques have been developed to minimize overt and covert cueing and impression management by concealing the purpose of the measurement. Here, attitudes are measured indirectly and without the respondent knowing it (For a review of disguised self-reports see, Kidder and Campbell, 1970). Research indicates that disguised techniques should be used with caution (Fishbein and Ajzen, 1975: pp. 89-94; Kidder and Campbell, 1970; Selltiz, Wrightsman, and Cook, 1976). Since, when applying such techniques, attitudes have to be inferred from responses to indirect self-reports, it may be questionable whether such techniques actually measure attitude.

5.3. *Non-verbal Behavior Measures*

Non-verbal behavior measures of attitudes capitalize on the assumption that an attitude predisposes an individual to respond in a consistently favorable or unfavorable manner towards the attitude object. Assuming such response consistency, an attitude toward an object can be assessed by measuring one or more specific single acts with regard to the attitude object, or by measuring the consequences of such acts. Such measures assess attitude indirectly. Non-verbal behavior measures avoid the problems associated with verbal self-reports. The reactivity of the measurement is usually low or absent, leaving little room for impression management. The amount of overt and covert cueing is also minimal or absent.

Sechrest and Belew (1983) provide an overview of non-verbal behavior measures of attitude. One particular ingenious measure is described among many others. A radio reporter, interested in predicting the outcome of an election, had taken a seat on top of a large water tower. He asked his listeners to vote for one of the candidates in the coming election. Listeners could vote for a candidate by flushing the toilet when the name of the candidate they were most positive about would be announced. The measured drop in the water level was used by the reporter as a measure of attitude. Many other non-verbal attitude measures have been developed, including the response to advertisements, the amount of littering of leaflets in favor of a political candidate, the amount and content of bumper stickers, graffiti and published letters to the editor, and the lost letter technique (see, e.g., Milgram, 1969).

Often, non-verbal behavior techniques measure binary events or objects, e.g., flushing or not flushing the toilet. Also, the results can often not be disaggregated, i.e., they cannot be attributed to specific individuals, e.g., graffiti. Consequently, non-verbal measures may at times lack precision. Some of the non-verbal measures do have some reactivity associated with them, e.g., flushing the toilet upon a request to vote. Finally, the assumption of response consistency may sometimes be troublesome. Attitudes are often used to predict behavior. If non-verbal measures of attitude are used to predict behavior, certain specific acts or their consequences, assumed to be indicators of an attitude, are used to predict other acts. Thus, both acts, the one used as predictor and the one used as criterion, are assumed to be under the control of the same hypothetical attitude construct. It is questionable whether littering a leaflet in which candidate X is promoted is always influenced by the same factors as voting for candidate Y. Other issues on the validity of non-verbal behavior measures of attitudes have been raised as well (see, e.g., Forbes and Gromoli (1971) on the lost letter technique). Given the fact that they usually avoid the problem of reactivity, non-verbal behavior measures seem particularly useful when the effect of overt and covert cueing, impression management, and attitude crystallization and behavior change in verbal self-reports is expected to be large. However, given the mentioned issues, great care should be taken when applying such non-verbal behavior measures. General guidelines for their application are not simple. Sechrest and Belew (1983: p. 56) strongly advise those who develop new methods or implement those already used by others to do the groundwork first. That is, compare the results yielded by these measures to results from more established measures. In most instances, non-verbal behavior measures may prove useful as additional attitude measures.

5.4. *Psychophysiological Measures*

Psychophysiological measures of attitude focus on involuntary responses of individuals, thereby avoiding part of the reactivity and ability problems discussed. It is assumed that attitudes have certain psychophysiological concomitants that can be assessed reliably and validly. A number of such indirect attitude measures has been developed, including: measures of pupil dilation, galvanic skin response, body temperature, voice tremor and facial EMG (see, e.g., Cacioppo and Petty, 1983).

Many psychophysiological measures focus on the intensity of arousal associated with attitude (e.g., galvanic skin response). This may decrease their validity as general attitude measures. First, it is not likely that all attitudes are associated with arousal. Also, other factors than attitude may give rise to arousal. Second, the direction of an attitude, positive or negative, cannot be determined when only the intensity of arousal is (can be) measured. Some psychophysiological measures, e.g., facial EMG, can detect gross differences in the direction of one's feelings. However, it is not yet clear whether these measures will also be useful in determining the intensity of feelings (Petty and Cacioppo, 1981: p. 21). This decreases the precision of such measures. Also, many psychophysiological techniques are expensive and time consuming to implement. Some reactivity is undoubtedly inherent in the techniques as well (Sechrest and Belew, 1983).

In a recent review Cacioppo, Losch, Tassinary and Petty (1986: p. 117) conclude that psychophysiological measures of enduring and accessible psychological states have often proved to be expensive, cumbersome, and less sensitive than traditional methods such as verbal self reports or simple variations on these assessments, such as the bogus pipeline technique. Some of the psychophysiological techniques of attitude measurement seem promising, e.g., voice tremor, facial EMG, infra-red photography. But as yet, most of the techniques still remain insufficiently developed and tested to be considered more than a possibility.

5.5. *Summary*

The majority of studies that have measured attitudes rely solely on questionnaire and survey data. Most researchers seem to agree that verbal self-reports, although a number of serious problems can be associated with them, can be valid, reliable and precise techniques to measure attitudes. Many non-verbal behavioral measures of attitudes have been and can be developed. Given the problems associated with non-verbal behavioral measures, care should be taken when applying such measures without any additional, verbal, attitude measures. Most psychophysiological measures of attitude do not seem to have reached a stage of maturity yet. Their further development is awaited.

6. MEASURING BEHAVIOR

6.1. *Introduction*

Although a considerable number of measures of behavior can be distinguished theoretically, most studies in which a measure of behavior is included employ one or more of three general measures. Self-reports, direct observation and artifacts, or resultants of behavior will be briefly introduced.

6.2. *Self-report Measures*

Verbal self-reports of behavior, directly and without disguise, asking whether a person has performed a certain behavior, are very common in social scientific research. Consumers are, e.g., asked to indicate whether they have or have not conserved energy in the previous months, or whether they have or have not bought a particular item. Self-reports of media behavior, often using diaries, are common in marketing research.

Verbal self-reports of behavior are subject to the general reactivity and ability problems of self-reports, which have been discussed in the previous section.

In research on food loss, Adelson et al. (1961, 1963) noted that it was difficult to establish with self-report measures, the amount of once-edible food tossed out by consumers. The amounts that households indicated were unreasonably low in their study. Next to other problems, overt and covert cueing and impression management occurred. Rathje (1984a) notes that reports were biased by the moral implications of admitting to "waste." Also, some of the respondents in the study changed their waste behavior as a consequence of thinking about and reporting it. Verbal self-reports of behavior may be biased if people cannot remember (accurately) what they did in the past (Reilly, 1984; Rathje, 1984b). Reactivity and ability problems of self-reports of behavior may be relatively small if the behavior under study is not socially sensitive and easily retrievable from memory.

Self-report measures of behavior may be biased particularly because of memory errors. It has been observed that when reporting past behavior, individuals often reveal "telescoping" (Sudman, 1983). When telescoping occurs, events are perceived as having occurred more recently than they actually did. When asking a person if s/he read Time magazine at least once last month, the answer may be affirmative, while in fact, the last time the person read it may have been longer ago. Procedures to reduce memory errors such as telescoping have been suggested (Sudman, 1983).

Both if the behavior under study is a single act and if it is a behavior category, measures of behavior can be direct and indirect. In a direct measure of the behavior category dieting behavior, respondents could, e.g., be *asked* to indicate whether they are dieting or not. However, while single acts acts can be *observed*, behavior categories cannot be observed directly. We cannot observe whether an individual is actually performing the behavior category "dieting," or "exercising," or "saving energy." What can be observed are specific single acts that are expected to be valid indicators of such behavior categories.

Ajzen and Fishbein (1977, 1980) have suggested a procedure to measure behavioral categories indirectly. First, a number of judges determine which single acts belong to the behavior category under study. Next, single acts with a sufficient interrater reliability are included in a so called multiple act or behavior category criterion. Subjects are asked to indicate which of the single acts in the criterion they perform. Finally, the total number of single acts that an individual performs is taken as an indicator of behavior in the behavior category.

Some issues have been raised concerning this procedure (Verhallen and Pieters, 1984), e.g., whether it is correct to assign all single acts in the criterion the same weight, which is implicitly done by simply counting the number of acts an individual performs.

Problems may also occur because of *diverging definitions*. In the suggested procedure to measure a behavior category, a *social definition* of a behavior category is employed: Only items with sufficient interrater reliability are chosen. Such a social definition of what comprises a behavior category may diverge from the *individual definition*. An individual may think that "stop eating snacks after 10 pm" belongs to the behavior category "dieting," while such behavior is not included in the behavior category criterion. In such a case the individual's dieting behavior as measured by the behavior category criterion underscores his/her (perceived) dieting behavior. Diverging definitions of what constitutes a behavior category may attenuate the strengths of attitude-behavior (as measured by behavior category criteria) relations.

6.3. *Direct Observation*

Some behaviors can be observed directly. Wells and LoSciuto (1966) provide an early account of the direct observation of purchasing behavior. The main advantage of direct observation is that it avoids the reactivity and ability problems inherent in self-reports. A disadvantage is that it provides information on observable specific acts only, and "behavior cannot always be interpreted easily" (Wells and LoSciuto, 1966: p. 228). This may sometimes lead to experimenter or researcher effects. Silverman (1968) found that some researchers wrongly recorded the responses of their subjects and that these misrecordings were in line with the results that the researchers expected or desired. Others report similar results (e.g., Webb, Campbell, Schwartz, and Sechrest, 1966). Procedures for minimizing such effects have been suggested (see Barber, 1976), one could for instance obtain both direct observations and self-reports.

6.4. *Measures of Artifacts; in Particular Household Waste Analysis*

As Ajzen and Fishbein (1980) stress, resultants of behavior are not always distinguished from actual behavior. Under certain conditions, behavior can be inferred from resultants or artifacts. It is very likely that a person has applied for a certain job, if his/her name appears on a list of job applicants, provided that no one else applied in his/her name.

If specific circumstances independent of, or in interaction with, behavior have certain consequences, these consequences cannot simply be taken as an indicator of behavior. The amount of weight loss can only serve as an indirect indicator of weight-loss behavior, such as dieting, exercise and so on. Other factors outside the personal control of individuals, e.g., physiological, influence the amount of weight loss as well (Cooper and Croyle, 1984). Verhallen and Van Raaij (1981) found that only 26 percent of the variation in the usage of natural gas by households could be attributed to their energy-related behavior. Other factors such as seasonal influence, condition of the building and the heating equipment were also of relevance. The use of natural gas cannot be used as a valid indicator of energy-related behavior of the residents.

If certain consequences are the result of group behavior, these consequences cannot simply be attributed to specific individuals. This is an important issue to social scientific researchers and to criminologists.

In recent years, a methodology to study consumption behavior by measuring artifacts or resultants of behavior has been developed in anthropology and archeology. Since it may be applied to study several aspects of acquiring, using, and disposing of products, it will be briefly introduced.

Household waste analysis can supplement the more traditional techniques to measure consumption behavior, when these fall short, i.e., when problems of reactivity and ability can be expected in self-reports and/or when direct observations are troublesome or for other reasons difficult to perform.

Rathje (1984a) reports an undated study of Rabow and Nueman that illustrates the utility of household waste analysis, sometimes called garbage analysis. Rabow and Nueman investigated the impact of a new liquor outlet on the alcohol consumption in a Los Angeles neighborhood. Both interviews and household waste analyses were conducted. A comparison of the interview data collected before and after the new store opened revealed no change in reported alcohol consumption. However, a comparison of the household waste showed a marked increase in the discard of beer, wine, and hard liquor containers after the new store began selling liquor. The discrepancy between the survey results and the results of the household waste analysis can be attributed, at least in part, to impression management by the respondents in the interviews.

Ability problems that may occur in self-reports of consumption behavior, can also be circumvented by analysing the household waste. Individuals may well be able to report normal or average behaviors, but may have difficulties when reporting infrequent or unusual behaviors, such as how often a half-full container of bleach is discarded (Rathje, 1984a).

Household waste analysis can be performed on several levels of *aggregation*. Some aggregation over time almost always takes place, e.g., when the waste of one person over one day, one week or one year is studied. Aggregation can also take place over individuals, e.g., when the waste of one household, neighborhood, city or country is analyzed. The analysis can be performed on several levels of *specificity*. The total weight of the waste that an observation unit produces in a unit of time can be assessed. On a more specific level, different components in the waste (paper, glass, tins and so on), different products (newspapers or paper wrappers) or brands (New York Times or USA Today) can be distinguished (Hughes, 1984).

The analysis can be performed with or without the prior consent of the unit of observation. Ritenbaugh and Harrison (1984) note that with prior consent, household waste analysis may be subject to reactivity. In their project, one of the households did not discard any whisky bottles during the official ("consented") data collection phase. Yet, it discarded one in each regular waste pick-up both before and after the official data collection phase. Analyzing household waste without prior consent of the households involved may have ethical problems associated with it. Procedures to deal with such problems have been suggested, e.g., safe-guarding anonymity, after-the-fact consent (see, e.g., West and Gunn, 1978).

Household waste analysis can be performed to study many aspects of consumer behavior, such as brand and type switching patterns, market share estimation, lifestyle patterns, ethnic and social differences in consumption, the use of free samples, deal packs, trial sizes and coupons, waste disposition patterns, participating in recycling projects, the effect of unanticipated events on consumption behavior (Reilly, 1984; Cote, 1984; McGuire, 1984).

Measuring artifacts and resultants of behavior has a number of limitations as well (Sechrest and Phillips, 1979). As has been noted before, assumptions about the relationships between the artifacts or resultants, and the behavior of the observation unit have to be made. Artifacts or resultants of behavior may often be aggregate measures of behavior. Apart from that, it is only suitable to study the consumption of daily necessities, not of consumer durables, such as washing machines. Also, something may intervene between behavior and a certain artifact, thus introducing validity problems. Therefore, the assumptions underlying the use of artifacts as measures of behavior may not always be realistic. Also, and more specifically the amount of random error present in unobtrusive measures, such as household waste analysis, is not exactly known (Cote, 1984). Such considerations may preclude household waste analysis and other unobtrusive measures from widespread application. Household waste analysis seems more suited to study disposition and usage behaviors than to study purchasing.

Reviewing the methodology and peculiarities of household waste analysis, Rathje (1984b: p. 76) remarks that it does not represent an unbiased view of reality, but that identifying patterns in the way self-report data and household waste data are interrelated can teach us more about the way each recording method works, and that it can teach us more about reality than each of the methods separately. Such a call for a multi-method approach to measurement can be extended to measures of behavior (and attitude) in general (Campbell and Fiske, 1959).

Several other procedures to obtain data on consumption behavior without the use of self-reports or direct observation have been developed. Computerized scanner data can be used to study purchasing behavior. As with the other procedures, such techniques are subject to certain limitations (see, e.g., Reilly, 1984).

6.5. *Summary*

Several techniques have been used to study behavior. Three broad classes of techniques can be distinguished: self-reports of behavior, direct-observation, artifacts, or resultants of behavior. The techniques in these broad classes all have their limitations, their strengths and weaknesses. Self-reports of behavior may be subject to problems of reactivity and ability. In cases where serious reactivity and/or ability problems are expected, direct-observation, or measures of artifacts or resultants of behavior may supplement or replace self-reports. If direct-observation is laborious, or subject to observation bias, artifacts or resultants of behavior can sometimes be assessed. One specific source of data to study consumption behavior, household waste analysis was introduced. Some of the strengths and weaknesses of this technique were mentioned.

The previous sections have dealt with the definition and measurement of attitudes and behavior. In the next sections, the relationships between attitudes and behavior will be discussed. First, the issue of the explanation of behavior will be introduced. Next, the prediction of behavior through attitudes will be dealt with.

7. EXPECTANCY-VALUE MODELS

7.1. *Introduction*

Uni-dimensional scales to measure attitude directly or indirectly offer a high level of measurement efficiency. The measurement instrument can be short and unstructured, and it provides a summary measure of attitude. Such a uni-dimensional approach does not provide much insight in the determinants of attitudes and behavior. The usefulness of the attitude concept is partly based on its usefulness in explaining behavior. The emergence of expectancy-value models of attitude has stimulated research on the cognitive antecedents of behavior. Such research has led to a better understanding of the reasons for certain behaviors, although not necessarily to better prediction of behaviors.

Expectancy-value models have a number of varied intellectual roots. The basic idea is that expectancies underlie behavior. In this view, behavior is not merely a reflection of reinforcements in the past, as is assumed in traditional learning theory. Instead behavior is perceived to be based on the anticipated future, i.e., on the expected consequences of behavior. Such expected consequences take the form of cognitions. But how can cognitions give rise to behavior? Atkinson (1982) states that an expectation no more implies an action than does the streak of lightning imply the bang of thunder. There is no inherent logic in an observed or presumed correlation. The logical bridge between cognitions, as antecedents, and behavior, as consequent, must be constructed. Theories provide such constructions.

Theories about the relationship between expectations and behavior have been developed in several areas of social scientific enquiry. Both theorists working in the context of animal (Tolman, 1938) and human learning (Lewin, 1938) contributed to this development. In decision theory contributions were made (Von Neuman and Morgenstern, 1944). Also, in research on achievement motivation (McClelland, Atkinson, Clark, and Lowell, 1953) and on social learning (Rotter, 1954) the relationship between expectations and behavior has been a central component.

7.2. *Expectations and Behavior*

Several conceptions of the relationships between expectations and behavior have emerged. Such conceptions sometimes differ considerably, especially in terminology. Many similarities may be recognized as well (Feather, 1982; Van Raaij, 1977). In decision theory the overall approach is known as subjective expected utility. In marketing it is sometimes referred to as multi-attribute attitude models. Here, the general term expectancy-value will be used.

The expectancy-value approach can be used prescriptively or descriptively. Often, the expectancy-value approach has been used prescriptively, normatively. Prescriptively, a decision maker should make some basic steps to reach a decision (Beach and Beach, 1982: p. 366):

1. Identify the available courses of action – the decision alternatives.
2. Identify the possible outcomes (i) of each decision alternative.
3. Assess the utility (U_i) of each outcome.
4. Assess the probability (P_i) of each outcome accruing to the decision maker should that decision alternative be selected.
5. Compute the expectation (usually the Expected Value or SEU) of each decision alternative:

$$SEU = \sum_{i=1}^{n} P_i U_i$$

6. Apply some choice rule, usually maximization, to the expectations in order to select one of the decision alternatives.

Issues pertaining to the validity of the prescriptive uses of expectancy-value and subjective expected utility models are thoroughly discussed by Schoemaker (1982), and by Fischhoff, Goitein and Shapira (1982). Here, the focus is on the descriptive use.

Many expectancy-value models that aim at describing the process by which individuals form attitudes, preferences or make decisions have been developed. Some authors provide lists of such expectancy-value, subjective expected utility or multi-attribute attitude models, e.g., Feather (1982), Mitchell (1974), Van Raaij (1977), Schoemaker (1982), Wilkie and Pessemier (1973). These lists will not be repeated.

Two expectancy-value models have been popular in psychological research. The valence model of Vroom (1964) has been developed in industrial and organizational psychology. It is used to predict and explain occupational choice, effort on the job, and job satisfaction. Until 1974, at least 50 studies applying the model were published (Mitchell, 1974). The number of studies has increased since then (Mitchell, 1982).

The attitude model of Fishbein (1963) has been developed in social psychology. It was originally used to predict and explain attitudes towards objects, but was reformulated to predict and to explain attitudes towards behaviors. Without doubt the Fishbein model and later reformulations of the model by Fishbein and Ajzen (1975) has, almost from its inception, dominated a large part of attitude research in social and consumer psychology. This justifies a somewhat closer look.

Basically the Fishbein attitude model[4] specifies that an attitude towards an act is determined by the added expected salient consequences of performing the act multiplied by their respective evaluation. In formula:

$$A_{act} = \sum_{i=1}^{n} b_i * e_i \qquad (1)$$

In the formula, A_{act} stands for the attitude towards the act; b_i (belief) is expected consequence i; e_i is the evaluation of expected outcome i, and n is the number of outcomes that is salient to an individual.

Several issues with regard to the Fishbein model and related expectancy value models have been raised: issues with regard to theoretical assumptions, issues with regard to the operationalization of concepts, and issues with regard to statistical analysis. Such issues have been treated in several publications (see, e.g., Wilkie and Pessemier, 1973; Ryan and Bonfield, 1975; Mitchell, 1982; Verhallen and Pieters, 1984). Also, the issue of the reliability and validity of the instruments to measure concepts of the Fishbein attitude and related expectancy-value models has been discussed (see Bagozzi, 1981, 1982; Burnkrant and Page, 1982; Bettman, Capon, and Lutz, 1975).

Some authors have questioned whether weighing expected consequences by evaluations, or, as is done in some expectancy-value models, by importance ratings leads to better statistical explanation and prediction of the attitude. This issue may have implications for the utility attributed to expectancy-value models. Although including such weights is theoretically almost self evident, Wilkie and Pessemier (1973) state that "importance weights are not likely to reduce explanatory power… Neither, however, do they add strikingly to prediction" (p. 436). Research indicates that models in which the expected consequences are not weighted by evaluations or importance ratings show an equally strong, or almost as strong, relationship with the attitude as models in which evaluation or importance ratings are included (Bettman, Capon, and Lutz, 1975; Falbo and Becker, 1980; Wahlers, 1982; Midden, 1986). So, although theoretically necessary and intuitively appealing, it may prove empirically less useful to weigh beliefs by evaluations. The *beliefs-only model* can be expressed as:

$$A_{act} = \sum_{i=1}^{n} b_i \qquad (2)$$

To explain such results, some have hypothesized that respondents might implicitly incorporate some evaluation or importance rating into belief-ratings. (Wilkie and Pessemier, 1973). Although theoretically, probabilities (expectations) may be separated from evaluations, individuals may have problems to actually do so (see, e.g., Fischhoff, Goitein, and Shapira, 1982).

The same holds for separating the evaluation from the description of objects or phenomena. It is well established that valuable objects tend to be perceived as larger than they actually are (Furnham, 1983).

Some have argued that researchers inadvertently tend to incorporate some evaluative component in their measures of cognitions, such as expectancies, and conation. McGuire (1986) commenting on the poor results of studies designed to test the tripartite attitude model remarks that the discriminant validity of the affective, cognitive and conative part of the attitude may be poor, because "... investigators typically reduce the information in the cognitive and the conative also to an evaluation score..." (p. 111). Such comments also apply to expectancy-value models. Often belief- or expectancy-statements in questionnaires already contain some evaluative component. A typical belief-statement in a questionnaire on energy saving may, e.g., be worded as: "In order to save energy in my home the next winter, I will have to spend much time. Very likely........ Very unlikely." Spending much time is, in itself, an evaluation of the exact amount of time an individual is expected to spend. When a belief-statement is partly worded as an evaluation, separate evaluation-statements are not likely to contribute much to the explanation of attitudes. In fact, expectancy and value are confounded in such a belief-statement.

Some have argued that importance and evaluation ratings often yield high mean values with little variation available for explanatory value (see Wilkie and Pessemier, 1973). This may be due to the way importance and evaluation-statements are generally worded. Verhallen and Pieters (1984) have discussed this issue more in depth. In general, an evaluation-statement is worded in a nonspecific way, i.e., without reference to a specific behavior. Verhallen and Pieters (1984) note that an expected consequence such as "being tired" is not always evaluated negatively, but that the direction the evaluation will take is dependent on the behavior of which "being tired" is a consequence. As a consequence of "running to catch the train" it will be evaluated differently (negatively) than as a consequence of "doing fitness-training." "Losing weight" is evaluated positively by someone who is on a diet to take off those extra pounds; it is evaluated negatively by someone who wants to gain some weight after a serious illness. Verhallen and Pieters (1984) suggest to make evaluation-statements in questionnaires act- or domain-specific. If such a recommendation should be followed, the expectancy-value approach may lose some of its generality, values are made specific; whether such adaptations improve the contribution of evaluations to explanation of attitudes and behavior remains to be studied.

7.3. *Descriptive Use of Expectancy-value Models*

Theorists seem to agree that expectancy-value models do not always provide a description of the actual decision processes individuals engage in. Two arguments underlie this.

"People do not compute probabilities and values, multiply them together, add the products, and base their choice on these computations. It is far too taxing and complex a process" (Mitchell, 1982: p. 309). Even stronger, combining enormous amounts of information in one's head overwhelms the computational capacity of anyone but an "idiot savant" (Fischhoff, Goitein, and Shapira, 1982). This argument indicates that expectancy-value models may not always or hardly ever provide realistic descriptions of the actual decision making process. Often decision making processes may be simpler (see, e.g., Van Raaij, 1977). The second argument pertains to the robustness of the expectancy-value approach.

The usual decision rule, "heuristic," in expectancy-value models is linear-compensatory: Expectancies are "multiplied" by evaluations, and the expectancy-value combinations are "added" to form an overall index. Research (see, e.g., Anderson and Shanteau, 1977; Dawes and Corrigan, 1974) has shown that such a decision rule may predict actual decisions fairly well, even if the process by which the decision was reached differed completely from the one implied by the linear-compensatory rule. So, expectancy-value models may in some occasions be *paramorphic*, able to replicate the input-output relations of phenomena, instead of *isomorphic*, describing the actual process between input and output. The robustness of the linear-compensatory decision rule may lead to the (implicit) conclusion that the rule describes the way decisions are actually made. This may be a false conclusion.

The expectancy-value approach is popular and is expected to remain alive in the future. Partly, its popularity may derive from "... its being plausible (even banal) and sufficiently quantifiable..." to allow investigation of a number of controversies, such as whether separate expectancy-value scores should be added or averaged (McGuire, 1986: p. 111). Partly, its popularity derives from its providing an elegant framework in which the reasons for (some types of) behavior of (some) individuals can be studied coherently; it points out that behavior-outcome links are important as well as the values that individuals attach to these outcomes (Mitchell, 1982). Identical attitudes and behavior may be the result of different underlying structures of expected outcomes and evaluations. Models that link the perceived consequences of behavior to attitudes and behavior increase understanding and the capacity for favorable action (Wilkie and Pessemier, 1973: p. 439).

In the next sections, attitude-behavior consistency will be shortly introduced. The "is" and "when" questions of attitude-behavior consistency will be dealt with. Some recent research on the "how" question will be touched upon.

8. ATTITUDE-BEHAVIOR CONSISTENCY

The utility of the attitude concept partly derives from its assumed ability to predict behavior. Almost from the beginning of attitude research the consistency between attitudes and behavior has been investigated. The LaPiere (1934) study, described in section 2, provides an early and widely cited example of a failure to find consistency between attitudes and behavior. In 1969, Wicker published a study in which the literature on attitude-behavior consistency was reviewed. Wicker (1969) analyzed some 46 studies that met the following criteria:

1. The unit of observation was the individual rather than the group.
2. At least one attitudinal measure and one overt behavior measure toward the same object were obtained for each subject.
3. The attitude and the behavior were measured on separate occasions.
4. The overt behavior response was not merely the subject's retrospective self-report of his or her behavior.

Three categories of attitude objects were included in his study:

1. jobs,
2. minority group members,
3. miscellaneous objects.

Wicker (1969) concluded:

> taken as a whole, these studies suggest that it is considerably more likely that attitudes will be unrelated to overt behaviors than that attitudes will be closely related to actions. Product-moment correlation coefficients relating the two kinds of responses are rarely above 0.30, and often are near zero. Only rarely can as much as 10% of the variance in overt behavioral measures be accounted for by attitudinal data (p. 65).

As a final remark, he noted that one of the roads future research could follow was "to abandon the attitude concept in favor of directly studying overt behavior" (p. 75).

Wicker was not alone in his conclusions. Deutscher (1966, p. 247) remarked that researchers do not have any reason to expect consistency and every reason to expect inconsistency between attitudes and behavior. Others made similar statements (see, e.g., Ehrlich, 1969; Greenwald, 1965).

McGuire (1986) notes that the failure to find attitude-behavior consistency is one of the scandals of social psychology. Such conclusions and remarks have thrown the gauntlet down to attitude theorists. The conclusions of studies indicating that attitudes do not substantially predict and explain behavior have been reacted upon in one or more of five ways. These five reactions are:

A. The conclusions are (partly) unjustified,

The conclusions are justified, and due to:

B. *incorrect conceptualization* of attitudes,
C. *incorrect measurement methodology*,
D. not taking into account *other determinants* of behavior,
E. not taking into account *conditions* upon which attitude-behavior relationships are *contingent*.

The first reaction will be briefly presented in the remainder of this section. Reactions B to E will be discussed in sections 9 to 12.

Some researchers were not ready to accept completely the conclusions of reviews such as Wicker's study. Seibold (1980: p. 213) notes that when methodological problems, such as measurement unreliability, statistics used, behavior measure distribution, and threshold levels, have been treated in some of the studies showing attitude-behavior inconsistency, the low correlations originally reported are found to be underestimates of the actual consistency. Also, some of the studies reviewed by Wicker were not testing attitude-behavior consistency, but behavior-attitude consistency. In LaPiere's study, for instance, the attitude was assessed after the behavior. The negative results of such studies cannot be taken as proof of attitude-behavior inconsistency. Taking into account these considerations, the conclusion that attitudes do not explain and predict behavior is weakened. However, the conclusion is only weakened. The other reactions carry somewhat more weight.

9. ATTITUDE-BEHAVIOR OR BEHAVIOR-BEHAVIOR CONSISTENCY

In section 3 some aspects of definitions of attitude have been presented. No explicit attention has been given to the conceptualization of attitude.

Two general conceptualizations of attitude can be distinguished:

1. the probability conception, and
2. the latent process conception (Warner and deFleur, 1969).

The way attitude is conceptualized has considerable effects on how failures to find attitude-behavior consistency are dealt with.

In the *probability conception*, it is assumed that an individual's reactions toward an object in a certain situation show organization, structure and predictability. In this view, attitudes are specific probabilities of specific forms of response to specific social objects. Attitude is anchored to observable events, in other words, only an inferred property of the individual's reaction in a specific situation (Foxall, 1983). Thus, the individual's responses to questionnaire items are a specific type of response in a specific situation. From these responses an "attitude" toward an object in the interview situation can be inferred. From the overt responses of the individual also an attitude can be inferred. In the probability conception of attitude, the issue of attitude-behavior consistency is irrelevant. Both "attitude," as measured by verbal self-reports, and overt behavior are classes of behavior, each contingent on different situational conditions. So, the only reason for expecting consistency between two classes of responses,

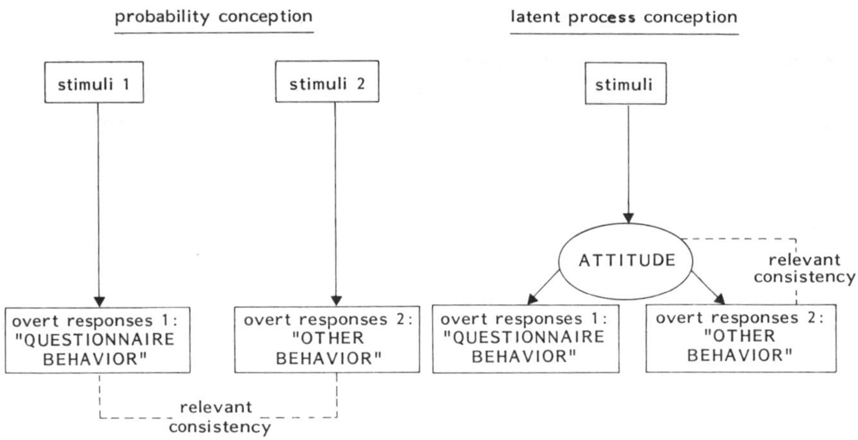

Fig. 1. The probability and latent process conception of attitude.

responses to questionnaire items and overt responses, would be that the situations in which the responses occur have an identical effect on them.

In this conception of attitudes, the issue of attitude-behavior consistency is reformulated to that of attitude-attitude consistency, or, better, to that of behavior-behavior consistency. The probability conception of attitude is depicted in Figure 1.

In the *latent process conception*, attitude is also inferred from the individual's reactions to an object. However, here both verbal behavior reactions (to questionnaire items) and non-verbal behavior reactions are assumed to be determined by a latent construct: attitude. Attitude is assumed to be the factor that directs both classes of behavior reactions. In this conception the issue of attitude-behavior consistency, and that of the direction of causality between attitudes and behaviors take a prominent position. The latent process conception of attitude is depicted in Figure 1.

One solution to the problem that often attitude-inconsistency is found, is to reject the latent process conception of attitude, in favor of the probability conception. Warner and deFleur (1969) do not hide their choice: The question whether the latent process "attitude" determines behavior is analogous to the question, that was asked in the Middle Ages, whether the invisible matter phlogiston caused wood that was heated to burn. Although elegant, the probability conception may leave the organism devoid of reasoning and decision making. Most attitude theorists favor the latent process conception, that is part of the cognitive tradition. The effects of situational influences on (measures of) attitude and behavior have become an important object of research (see section 4, on measurement, and section 11.6).

Most attempts to solve the problem of attitude-behavior inconsistency have followed other roads than accepting the probability conception of attitude.

10. CONSISTENCY AND MEASUREMENT METHODOLOGY

10.1. *Introduction*

In recent years the optimism about establishing attitude-behavior consistency has grown. This spirit is expressed by Ajzen (1982) stating that "... the conclusion that there is no direct relation between attitudes and behavior is, in my opinion, unwarranted" (p. 3). Studies have shown that attitudes can and do predict behavior. The question "when" attitudes predict behavior has been addressed extensively. Here the methodological approach will be presented.

Two conditions concerning the measurement of attitudes and behavior, in particular, have been reported to increase attitude-behavior consistency:

1. correspondence in specification elements, and
2. time interval between attitude and behavior measurement.

10.2. *Correspondence*

In 1977, Ajzen and Fishbein (1977) reviewed 109 studies in which a total of 142 attitude-behavior relations were reported. The four specification elements, action, target, context and time (see also section 3), that attitudes and behavioral entities comprise of were taken as the starting point.

Attitudes and behaviors can be defined on several levels of generality. In the global "attitude towards helping" only the action element is defined. In the specific "attitude towards helping the neighbor to paint the front door on Saturday morning," all four specification elements are defined. Ajzen and Fishbein tested the hypothesis that attitude-behavior consistency can be established when measures of attitude correspond in specification elements with measures of behavior. Thus, a specific attitude was expected to predict a single act, while a global attitude should predict measures of global behavior, a behavior category criterion.

The results confirmed the hypothesis: When attitudes and behavior correspond in specification elements, "significant attitude-behavior relations of considerable magnitude were found." Other research has supported this conclusion (e.g., Ajzen and Fishbein, 1977; Davidson and Jaccard, 1979; Weigel and Newman, 1976).

It should be noted that on some occasions, Ajzen and Fishbein (see, e.g., Ajzen and Fishbein, 1977: p. 912; Fishbein, 1980: p. 87) remark that five, rather than four, specification elements can be distinguished. In studying certain behaviors, a reference to the person, the actor, may be of relevance in measures of attitude. Such a reference to the person in measures of attitude is deemed essential where attitudes towards birth control, smoking and drinking are assessed (Ajzen and Fishbein, 1977: p. 912). Ahtola (1977) suggests that a reference to the person should always be made when studying personal behavior.

10.3. *Time Interval*

If for some reason, the attitude changes between the time that the attitude is measured and the time that the behavior is measured, the original attitude will not predict behavior. Hence, in such cases, the original attitude will be inconsistent with behavior. The longer the time interval between measurement of attitude and measurement of behavior, the larger the probability that the individual may obtain new information or that certain events will occur that change the attitude or the intended behavior (Fishbein and Ajzen, 1975: p. 370). To limit the possibility that attitudes may change before measurement of behavior, some have suggested to measure attitudes in close temporal proximity to the behavior that is to be predicted (Fishbein and Ajzen, 1975: p. 376).

If such a suggestion is followed, the utility of the attitude concept may be limited considerably. What is the value of the attitude concept, if the only attitudes that predict election results are those that are measured five minutes before the election? A considerable amount of research, discussed in section 12, treats the issue of attitude-behavior consistency without recourse to the measurement-proximity condition.

Some other suggestions to increase attitude-behavior consistency have been made from a methodological point of view (see, e.g., Seibold, 1980). The behavior to be predicted should not depend on the behavior of other people or on specific events, and it should not be the end of a sequence of acts all to be performed as a prerequisite to perform the behavior that is to be predicted (Fishbein and Ajzen, 1975: pp. 368-381; Fishbein and Ajzen, 1976; see also Abelson (1973) and Smith (1982) on "enabling conditions").

11. OTHER DETERMINANTS OF BEHAVIOR

11.1. *Introduction*

Failures to find attitude-behavior consistency can be due to the fact that attitude is only one of the variables that influence behavior. Next to this, the effect of attitude on behavior can be mediated by certain variables. In both cases, only measuring attitudes is not sufficient to predict and explain behavior. A large number of possible other determinants of behavior has been suggested. Wicker (1971) provides a list, including: other attitudes held by the individual; the individual's activity level; his or her verbal, intellectual, and social abilities; the presence of other people, social norms; the range of alternative behaviors available; the occurrence of unforeseen events; the expected and/or actual consequences of various actions. The list could easily be extended. Some of the other determinants of behavior received considerable attention, notably social norms, habits and prior behavior, and situational influence. Also, behavioral intention is often included in research models as a mediating variable between attitudes and behavior. In the Reasoned Action (RA) theory, developed by Fishbein and Ajzen (1975), the relationships between attitudes, social norms, intentions and behavior are specified. This theory will be used as a general guideline to discuss the role of other determinants of behavior. The Reasoned Action theory will first be introduced briefly.

11.2. *The Reasoned Action Theory*

Several theorists have argued that social norms influence behavior, independently of attitudes, and that behavioral intentions are the direct antecedents of behavior. Sheth (1974) developed a model of attitude structure and the attitude-behavior relationship in which, next to other factors, behavior is determined by behavioral intentions. A behavioral intention is an individual's subjective probability that s/he will perform a certain behavior.[5] Sheth indicates that behavioral intentions are a function of the expected consequences of behavior, the individual's social environment, and the individual's anticipation of events at the time the behavior is performed. The social environment includes all the social factors that are likely to impinge on and provide a set of normative beliefs to the individual about how s/he should behave toward the object, issue or person at the specified time. Empirical evidence validating Sheth's model is scarce. Also, it has been criticized on the grounds that the variables are weakly specified, theoretically deficient and overlapping measures (Warshaw, 1980: p. 154).

Based on Dulany's (1968) theory of propositional control, Fishbein and Ajzen (1975; Fishbein, 1967; Ajzen and Fishbein, 1980) develop a theory of Reasoned Action (RA). They argue that most behaviors of interest to social scientists are under volitional control and that such behaviors can be predicted from the person's behavioral intentions (Fishbein and Ajzen, 1975: p. 371). In the RA theory, a behavioral intention is a weighted sum of a personal determinant of behavior, the individual's attitude to perform the behavior under study, and a social component, the subjective norm. The central equation of the theory can be presented as follows:

$$B \sim BI = w_1(A_{act}) + w_2(SN) \qquad (3)$$

in which B is the behavior under study, BI represents the behavioral intention, A_{act} is the attitude to perform the behavior, SN is the subjective norm, and w_1 and w_2 are empirically determined weights. The subjective norm is conceived of as the generalized perceived social pressure, i.e., the individual's perception that most people and organizations important to him or her think s/he should or should not perform the behavior.

In the RA theory, the attitude toward the behavior is determined by beliefs, expected consequences of behavior, and the evaluations of these beliefs in an expectancy-value manner (see section 7). Likewise, the subjective norm (SN) is determined by normative beliefs, expectations about what others think one should or should not do, and the motivations to comply with these norms. This can be presented as:

$$SN = \sum_{j=1}^{m} nb_j * mc_j \qquad (4)$$

in which nb_j is the belief concerning the norm of referent j, mc_j is the motivation to comply with referent j, and m is the number of salient referents.

The RA theory has stimulated much research on the determinants of behavior, and on the relationships between these determinants. This warrants a closer look. Here, some aspects of the theory that are relevant for the present discussion of the role of other determinants of behavior, and of the role of behavioral intentions, will be singled out. First, the mediating role of behavioral intentions between attitudes and behavior will be discussed. Second, the conceptualization and measurement of normative influence, and the relationships between normative influence, attitudes, and behavioral intentions. Third the effects of habits and prior behavior, and fourth, the effects of situational influence.

11.3. *Behavioral Intention*

Ajzen and Fishbein (1980) provide considerable support for their two-component model of behavioral intentions, e.g., in the context of dieting and voting. Davidson and Jaccard (1979) found strong relationships between behavioral intentions and family planning practices. Others found similar results, e.g., Cook, Lounsbury and Fontenelle (1980) on alcohol consumption. However, Olshavsky (1981: p. 465) notes that the relationship between behavioral intentions and behavior is not precisely stated in the theory. In his view, behavioral intentions are merely predictions of the individual concerning his or her own future behavior. Consequently, behavior, can under certain conditions, be predicted from behavioral intentions, but it cannot be explained by them. Warshaw (1980) states that the RA theory implies that behavioral intentions "... outperform attitudes, beliefs and other cognitive measures as behavioral correlates" (p. 26). This premise of the RA theory, along with other premises, that will be dealt with in the next sections, has been tested in a number of studies.

Bentler and Speckart (1979), studying tobacco, alcohol and other drug use, found that attitudes determined behavior directly, additionally to their indirect influence via behavioral intentions. In this and a related study (Bentler and Speckart, 1981) self-report measures of behavior were used. Such measures may be inappropriate if accounts of the behavior are difficult to access from memory, or if the behavior is socially sensitive (see section 6). On these and other grounds (see Bagozzi, 1981a, 1981b), the results of Bentler and Speckart's studies have been questioned. Also using self-report measures of behavior, Manstead, Proffitt and Smart (1983) found that, although mother's intentions with respect to infant feeding practices "... accounted for a large and significant proportion of variance in behavior, adding attitudes to the regression equation significantly enhanced the prediction of behavior" (p. 668). Bagozzi (1981a, 1981b, 1982) used nonreactive instead of reactive measures in his research on determinants of blood donation (Red Cross recordings). He found that attitudes influenced behavior only through their impact on behavioral intentions.

Although research is not conclusive on this issue, the results indicate that behavioral intentions, as the Reasoned Action theory specifies, mediate the relationship between attitudes and behavior.

11.4. *Normative Influence*

A social norm can be defined as an expectation shared by group members which specifies behavior that is considered appropriate for a given situation (Midden and Ritsema, 1983). Kelman (1961) suggests that three processes are involved in social influence: compliance, identification, and internalization (see also Chapter 6 of this Handbook). Compliance occurs when an individual accepts influence from a certain norm referent because of a belief that compliance will result in personal benefits or in the avoidance of personal costs. Identification takes place when an individual adopts the role of a norm referent to meet the other's own role expectation. Internalization occurs when an individual accepts normative influence because it is congruent with his/her value system. The three processes are not completely independent but are present in some mix in a given situation. Ryan and Bonfield (1975) argue that internalization of social norms will be manifested in the attitude toward the behavior. Thus, normative influence and attitudes will be closely associated if the degree of internalization of social norms is high (see also Warshaw, 1980).

In recent versions of the Reasoned Action theory, normative influence is only represented by the concept of social norms. In earlier formulations of the Reasoned Action theory, different kinds of norms were distinguished. These different kinds of norms show a considerable similarity with the normative processes distinguished by Kelman. Fishbein (1967) distinguished between personal norms (personal normative beliefs) and social norms. A personal norm is described as "the individual's belief about what he should do" (p. 489). Such personal norms may, in part, be the result of internalization and identification.

Stroebe and Frey (1982), discussing the factors influencing the extent of free-riding in the provision of collective goods, state that individuals often have personal norms, e.g., about fair dealing in business transactions, and that they comply with such norms – even if there is no threat of sanctions when the norms are not adhered to. Situations in which personal norms are salient but not adhered to lead to feelings of guilt. Such feelings, or the expectation that such feelings may arise, can have a considerable impact on behavior.

Margolis (1982) developed a model of social choice in which personal norms are central. In this fair share model, choice is based on both self-interested and group-interested preferences. Group-interested preferences lead to altruistic, socially responsible behavior, such as voting, or genuine concern in political leaders for the public interest. The fair share model is analogous to distinguishing personal norms separately from attitude and social norms as determinants of behavior.

Ajzen and Fishbein note that research led to dropping personal norms from the Reasoned Action theory "... since it seemed to be little more than an alternative way of measuring behavioral intentions" (Ajzen and Fishbein, 1980: p. 247). Some research indicates that this decision may have been premature. Budd and Spencer (1985) analyzed the determinants of intentions to drink beer or spirits in either pubs or university and hall of residence bars. Path analyses revealed that personal norms did not act as an alternative measure of behavioral intentions.

Research has been carried out on the effect of moral obligations on behavioral intentions and behavior. Moral obligations refer to what individuals feel they ought to do. Moral obligations are not personal norms, but they are conceptually closely related to them. Schwartz (1977) developed a theory of altruistic behavior in which feelings of moral obligation and the acceptance of personal responsibility are necessary conditions to arrive at altruistic behavior. Acceptance of responsibility is also a central concept in models of energy saving (Van Raaij and Verhallen, 1983) and ecology-conscious behavior (Kok and Siero, 1985). Schwartz and Tessler (1972) studying organ donation found that moral obligation did significantly contribute to the prediction of behavioral intentions without completely overlapping them. Gorsuch and Ortberg (1983) found that moral obligation significantly (although to a relatively small extent) predicted behavioral intentions in three of the four situations that they studied, after the variance explained by attitude and social norms had been accounted for. Gorsuch and Ortberg (1983: p. 1028) concluded that in situations where moral rules of conduct can be appealed to (in their study: decisions concerning religious behaviors and paying taxes), moral obligation is a necessary component of the Reasoned Action theory.

Other, more technical, issues with respect to the conceptualization of normative influence in the Reasoned Action theory have been raised as well (see Ahtola, 1977; Burnkrant and Page, 1982; Falbo and Becker, 1980; Miniard and Page, 1984; Verhallen and Pieters, 1984; Warshaw, 1980). The available research indicates that personal norms and moral obligations are an important determinant of behavioral intentions, at least in certain situations. This leads to a reformulation of the Reasoned Action theory's central equation as follows:

$$B \sim BI = w_1(A_{act}) + w_2(SN) + w_3(PN) \qquad (5)^6$$

in which PN refers to the personal norms and moral obligations of the individual. However, the exact role that personal norms and moral obligations play in the explanation of behavior is less clear (Budd and Spencer, 1985: p. 309). In view of these results, more research on the effect of personal norms and moral obligations on behavioral intentions and behavior, on the conditions under which significant effects can be observed, and on the processes underlying such effects, is needed.

11.5. *Habit*

A discrepancy between what individuals intend to do and what they actually do may be due to "the force of habit" (Fishbein and Ajzen, 1975: p. 371). Before leaving home one may intend to try a new route to the office, but later one may find oneself driving the same old route again. In fact, it is fortunate that many of our behaviors are governed by habits. It would be too taxing to consciously elaborate every morning on tying one's shoestrings. However, Fishbein and Ajzen (1975: p. 371) argue that most behaviors that social scientists are interested in are under volitional control, and can therefore be predicted from behavioral intentions. Habit or prior behavior is not explicitly modelled in the Reasoned Action theory.

Other theorists have a different view on this issue. Sheth (1974) includes a separate habit-controlled mechanism in his model (partly described in the foregoing). In his view, habit or "conditioning toward object j" influences behavior indirectly, through its impact on attitude. In the subjective culture model specified by Triandis (1977) the probability that a certain act is performed is a weighted function of habits and behavioral intentions, multiplied by facilitating conditions. Here, habit is assumed to influence behavior directly. Habit is defined as "the frequency of the act in the behavioral history of the organism" (Landis, Triandis, and Adamopoulos, 1978: p. 228). In the subjective culture model, it is assumed that behavior that the individual has never performed before, is under the control of behavioral intentions. As a particular behavior repeatedly occurs, the importance of the habit component increases, while that of the behavioral intention component decreases.

Research supports the notions of the subjective culture model. Landis, Triandis and Adamopoulos (1978) investigated the link between teacher habits, intentions and behavior in classrooms. Their results showed that the impact of intentions on classroom behavior was moderate, but that habits had a strong impact. Landis et al (1978: p. 234) concluded that when behavioral intentions and habits are consistent, and an "old" behavior is involved, the weight of the habit component is likely to be large, while that of the behavioral intention component is likely to be small. After finding that habit was an important factor in explaining seat belt usage, Wittenbraker, Gibbs and Kahle (1983) conclude that "although the theory of reasoned action attempts to account for the most variance with the fewest variables, the addition of the habit variable constitutes a useful amendment to the theory in this context" (p. 418). Bentler and Speckart (1979, 1981) found that in the context of alcohol, tobacco and other drug use, past behavior strongly contributed to the occurrence of behavior without the regulation of behavioral intentions. Bagozzi's studies (1981a, 1981b, 1982) on blood donation revealed that the extent of past behavior tended to reduce the impact of behavioral intentions on behavior, as proposed by Triandis (1977).

Such findings lead to the conclusion that habit or past behavior can directly influence many behaviors that are of interest to social scientists. Accordingly, the relevant equation of the Reasoned Action theory could be changed into:

$$B \sim w_1(BI) + w_2(H) \tag{6}$$

in which H refers to past behavior and habit.

This conclusion refers to the direct effect of past behavior or habit on behavior. The effect that past behavior might have on the prediction and explanation of behavior from attitudes will be returned to in the next section.

11.6. *Situational Influence*

An individual may have a very positive attitude towards watching a certain television show at home, but if the television set breaks down, a "context of opportunity" (Sarver, 1983) is absent, and the attitude is not likely to be expressed in overt behavior. Van Raaij (1981: p. 11) notes that behavioral intentions lead to behavior if no anticipated or unanticipated situations arise that prevent the realization of the intentions. One way of minimizing the impact of situational influences on attitude-behavior consistency was described in the previous section: minimizing the time interval between measurement of attitude and measurement of behavior. Such a suggestion indeed makes theories of attitude-behavior relationships parsimonious. However, it does not make them very socially relevant. In many instances, prediction and explanation of behavior is needed well in advance of the behavior (see also section 12).

In Sheth's model (1974) unexpected events are included as determinants of behavior. Foxall (1983) deals extensively with situational influences on consumer choice. Belk (1974) defines a situation as something outside the basic tendencies of the individual (such as traits and response dispositions), but beyond the characteristics of the stimulus object to be acted upon (e.g., product attributes). Belk (1975) describes the situations that consumers are confronted with in terms of five sets of features:

1. physical surroundings, e.g., the lighting and temperature, the weather, the shop's decor, shelf heights,
2. social surroundings, e.g., the presence of other people,
3. temporal perspective, e.g., the time of day and time constraints,
4. task definition, e.g., the role of the buyer, and
5. antecedent states, e.g., acute temporary moods, availability of the proper resources, such as income, and capacity.

Other theorists have described different features of situations, or have provided a different conceptualization of what comprises a situation (Lutz and Kakkar, 1975; Wicker, 1975; Woodside and Bearden, 1978; Srivastava, 1979; Foxall, 1983).

The effect of situational influences on behavior has been studied extensively. Funder and Ozer (1983) provide an account of the situational influences on attitude change under forced compliance, on bystander intervention and on obedience. They conclude that the effects of situational influence on behavior are important although such effects need not necessarily be large. Other research supports this conclusion. Cote, McCullough and Reilly (1985) studied the effects of unexpected situations on the relationship between behavioral intentions and behavior, in the context of in-home food and beverage consumption. Actual consumption was measured by garbage analysis (see section 6) and self-reports. The effects of a number of unexpected situations that could influence in-home consumption were investigated. Unexpected situations included: time pressure (being very busy), physical surroundings (the weather), social surroundings (shopping for food with family members or others). Their analyses revealed that unexpected situations explained a significant amount of variance in behavior (consumption), in addition to the variance explained by attitudes, behavioral intentions and past behavior, for 13 of the 15 products under study. The largest amount of additional variance explained was about 20 percent.

An in-depth discussion of features of situations and of the size and kinds of effect of situations on behavior is beyond the scope of this chapter. For the present discussion it is important that aspects of the situation can influence behavior directly, independent of their possible effect on attitudes and behavioral intentions. Thus, situational influence can be incorporated explicitly in the Reasoned Action theory as:

$$B = w_1(BI) + w_2(H) + w_3(SI) \tag{7}$$

in which SI refers to situational influence. It should be noted that research is far from conclusive on what exactly constitutes situational influence, and on which aspects of situations under which conditions influence behavior.

Other direct determinants than the ones discussed have been suggested. Wicker (1971) suggested that cognitions have a direct influence on behavior, independent of their indirect impact via attitudes. In Sheth's (1974) model of attitude structure and attitude-behavior relationships beliefs (cognitions) are also assumed to be directly related to behavior. Bentler and Speckart (1979, 1981) found in their studies that beliefs did influence behavior directly. However, as has been noted before, their results should be treated with some caution. Bagozzi (1981a, 1981b, 1982) found that the effect of beliefs was completely mediated by behavioral intention. To date, there is little evidence that, when other determinants of behavior (normative and situational influence, and habit) are taken into account, and when attitudes and behavior correspond in specification elements, cognitions do, in fact, directly determine behavior.

12. CONSISTENCY AND MODERATING VARIABLES

12.1. *Introduction*

Zanna and Fazio (1982) argue that research on attitude-behavior consistency has moved from the "IS" question to the "WHEN" question. One line of research has extensively dealt with the question under which conditions, which attitudes of which people predict behavior. This question refers to the variables moderating attitude-behavior relationships.[7] In this line of research other determinants of behavior independent of attitude are often not explicitly included. Therefore, it is difficult to extend the conclusions of this research to that concerning the other determinants of behavior. For this reason, it is also hard to draw conclusions about the relative utility of this "moderating variable" approach in comparison with the "other determinants" approach. This issue will be returned to in the last section.

Several variables that may moderate the relationship between attitudes and behavior have been suggested, e.g., direct vs. indirect experience (Fazio and Zanna, 1981), the abstractness vs. concreteness of the attitude-object (Breckler, 1984), the amount of information about the attitude-object (Davidson, Yantis, Norwood, and Montano, 1985), the level of involvement with the attitude-object (Petty, Cacioppo, and Schumann, 1983), the interaction between felt norms and the attitude (Warner and DeFleur, 1969), the amount of vested interest (Sivacek and Crano, 1982), the level of self-monitoring of individuals (Snyder and Decker Tanke, 1976), objective self-awareness (Wicklund, 1982). Other moderating variables have been studied as well (see, e.g., Cooper and Croyle, 1984). In this section some of the more established moderating variables will be introduced. Also, some variables, of which research strongly indicates their moderating properties with respect to attitude-behavior consistency, will be discussed.

Variables moderating attitude-behavior consistency can be distinguished on the basis of two criteria. First, a distinction can be made between variables that are specific to certain situations or attitude-objects, and variables that are specific to certain persons – person characteristics. Second, a distinction can be made between variables that are operative during attitude formation, i.e., when the attitude is learned, and variables that are operative during attitude or behavior generation, i.e., at the time the attitude or the behavior is expressed. By definition, person characteristics operate both during attitude formation and during attitude and behavior expression. However, they may have a differential impact on these stages. First, the formation of attitudes will be discussed. Next, the expression of attitudes and behavior will be turned to. Finally, person characteristics that can moderate attitude-behavior relationships will be introduced.

The moderating factors discussed in this section are presented in Table 1.

Table 1. Some factors that may moderate attitude-behavior relationships.

Formation of attitudes :	direct experience, involvement
Expression of attitudes and behavior:	self-awareness, involvement
Person characteristics :	need for cognition, self-monitoring, private self-consciousness, field-dependence/independence.

12.2. *Formation of Attitudes*

As has been noted in the section on definitions of attitude, attitudes are a learned feeling. Different processes can be involved in the learning or formation of attitudes. Attitudes can be learned through operant or classical conditioning or through information processing. Gorn (1982) provides an account of the classical conditioning of positive and negative attitudes towards pens, in which the information about the pens was kept to an absolute minimum. Information processing can be elaborate, or it can be shallow, depending on a number of conditions. The process through which attitude formation takes place has been shown to affect the extent to which attitudes are related to subsequent behavior (Fazio and Zanna, 1981). Consequently, variables affecting the attitude-formation process are likely to affect the extent to which attitudes predict behavior as well.

In a series of studies Fazio and Zanna (1981; see also Zanna and Olson, 1982; Fazio, 1985) found that attitudes based on *direct behavioral experience* with the attitude object are more predictive of subsequent action than attitudes formed via indirect means such as persuasive communication.

Regan and Fazio (1977) studied attitudes and behavior with respect to a set of five types of intellectual puzzles. In their study, the manner of attitude formation was manipulated by varying the way in which subjects learned about the puzzles. Half of the subjects received information about the puzzles, e.g., on how those could be solved, from the experimenter. The other half of the subjects were allowed to work with each of the puzzles for a certain time, without being given information with respect to how the puzzles could be solved. In other words, the former subjects formed their attitudes through indirect means, the latter subjects through direct behavioral experience. After this manipulation, the interest-value, as a measure of attitude, of each of the five puzzles was assessed. After attitude assessment, the subjects were allowed a 15-minute free play with any of the five types of puzzles. The free nature of the play was stressed. Analyses showed that the correlations between interest-value of each puzzle and a) the order in which the puzzles were attempted, and b) the proportion of available problems of each type which were attempted, were higher in the direct experience group than in the indirect experience group. The manipulation had no effect on the absolute amount of interest expressed in any of the puzzles. In other research similar results are reported (see, e.g., Songer-Nocks, 1976).

In a marketing context, Smith and Swinyard (1983) found that attitudes based on product trial predicted attitude-consistent behavior better than attitudes based on advertising. Sherman, Presson, Chassin, Bensenberg, Corty and Olshavsky (1982) found that the correlation of attitudes and behavioral intentions with respect to smoking increased under levels of greater direct experience.

Research on the effects of direct experience has often compared a situation in which subjects have indirect experience with the attitude object, with a situation in which subjects have direct experience with the attitude-object for a relatively short period of time. The effects of prolonged direct experience with the attitude-object on attitude-behavior consistency are less well studied in this tradition. Schlegel and Ditecco (1982) question whether direct experience strengthens attitude-behavior consistency in all instances. They argue that the effect of direct experience on attitude-behavior consistency may be curvilinear in nature. That is, at the initial stages of behavior acquisition (when novel tasks are involved) greater attitude-behavior consistency is obtained with increased experience, whereas at the advanced stages of direct experience, the reverse finding may be obtained. In such later stages, behavior may have habitualized, to the extent that subsequent behavior is determined directly by past behavior, instead of by attitudes. In a study on the factors influencing marijuana smoking, they found indications for such an effect of direct experience (Schlegel and Ditecco, 1982).

Research on the moderating effect of direct experience is strongly related to the effect of habit on behavior, independent of attitude (reported in the previous section). For instance, Bagozzi (1981a, 1981b, 1982) found that the extent of past behavior with respect to the attitude-object tended to reduce the impact of behavioral intentions on behavior. Although in his research intention-behavior consistency, instead of attitude-behavior consistency was studied, the results do seem to support Schlegel and Ditecco's (1982) hypothesis. Thus, direct experience may have two effects on attitude-behavior consistency. First, it may directly influence behavior, even if the impact of attitude on behavior is accounted for. Second, it may influence the extent to which attitude is related to behavior. The conditions under which these two effects of direct experience occur, the exact impact of the effects, and their functional form, have not been studied in depth.

In the research reported, direct experience is compared with indirect experience. In research on the moderating effect of involvement, the effect of differences in indirect experience with the attitude-object are compared.

Involvement is commonly used to refer to the personal relevance of an object, issue or situation (See Mitchell, 1979; Petty and Cacioppo, 1979). Individuals for which a certain object or situation is personally relevant, engage in elaborate information processing with respect to the object or situation. For instance, when confronted with a persuasive message, such individuals thoroughly scrutinize the arguments contained in the message on their merits. The attitudes of such individuals are based on consideration of the issue-relevant arguments. Individuals for which a certain object or situation is not personally relevant, engage in limited information processing. When confronted with a persuasive message, such individuals do not scrutinize the arguments contained in the message. Instead, their attitude with respect to the issue or object is based on one or more of several cues in the message context, e.g., the status of the endorser, or the number of arguments contained in the message (Petty and Cacioppo, 1986).

Most research on involvement has been performed in the context of attitude-change. Only recently, researchers have started to study the effect of involvement on the persistence and resistance of attitudes once they have been changed, and on attitude-behavior consistency.

As has been mentioned, attitudes that have been formed under conditions of high involvement, are better based on issue or object relevant information than attitudes formed under conditions of low involvement. Attitudes based on more issue or object relevant information can be expected to be better predictors of attitude consistent behavior than attitudes based on less issue or object relevant information. Thus, involvement can be expected to moderate the relationship between attitudes and behavior. More specifically, it can be expected that attitudes formed under high involvement predict subsequent behavior better than attitudes formed under low involvement.

In a relevant study on attitudes towards disposable razor blades, Petty, Cacioppo, and Schumann (1983) found that the correlation between attitudes and behavioral intentions was significantly higher under conditions of high involvement, than under conditions of low involvement.

Sivacek and Crano (1982) found that the behavior of students who felt that the imposition of a university-wide senior comprehensive examination was personally relevant[8], was very consistent with their expressed attitudes toward the examination. The behavior of students who felt that the examination would not affect them was not strongly related to their attitude toward it. No differences in attitudes between conditions of either high or low personal relevance were obtained. Snyder and Kendziersky (1982) found similar results in the context of attitude-behavior consistency in courtroom decisions.

Such results indicate that attitudes formed under conditions of high personal relevance, or high involvement, predict subsequent behavior better than attitudes formed under conditions of low personal relevance, or low involvement.

12.3. *Expression of Attitudes and Behavior*

Many behaviors of individuals are automated. Such behaviors are simply triggered in a certain situation, without the individual having to think about their connection with the individual's relevant attitudes (Abelson, 1982; see also section 11 on habit). Not only may overt behaviors be automated, expressing one's attitude may be automated as well.

Wicklund (1975, 1982) argues that the automated verbal responses with respect to a class of stimuli may bear little relation to the automated overt behaviors with respect to the stimuli. Under this condition, attitudes are not consistent with behavior. Automated verbal responses, e.g., filling out an attitude questionnaire, may also (happen to) be consistent with automated overt behaviors. Then, attitude-behavior consistency is obtained. Yet, consistency may not be the result of the individual's conscious effort to act upon attitudes, but instead, only a by-product of both types of automated behavior. In other words, attitudes did not direct behavior, both types of responses happened to coincide. It can be expected that conditions that lead to expressing attitudes and behavior in a less automatic way, in general, lead to increased attitude-behavior consistency, where without such conditions attitude-behavior consistency is expected to be low. Such "individuating" conditions (Abelson, 1982) have been studied.

According to self-awareness theory (Wicklund, 1975, 1982), a certain class of stimuli may bring the individual's attention increasingly onto the self, while another class of stimuli may distract the individual from the self. Both classes can be either object or situation related, or person related. Here, the object or situation related stimuli will be discussed. The person related stimuli will be presented in the next section. A state of attention to the self, *self-awareness*, has certain motivational consequences. According to the theory, it is more difficult for attitudes and attitude-relevant behavior to remain psychologically dissociated when individuals are in a state of self-awareness. As a consequence, attitudes and behavior will be expressed less automatically when being in such a state. Thus, increased attitude-behavior consistency can be expected. Consider an individual who has a negative attitude towards evading taxes. Such an attitude may be expressed frequently in an automatic way. Each year, such an individual may still forget to report on the tax form those extra earnings from giving post doctoral courses, without feeling any guilt, or experiencing any attitude-behavior inconsistency. Both automated responses are "dissociated."

Self-awareness theory predicts that conditions that lead to self-awareness, lead to experiencing (possible) inconsistencies between attitudes and behavior, and thus to increased attitude-behavior consistency, either by attitude or behavior change. In the tax evasion example, the individual may report the extra earning on the tax form, if s/he is aware of his/her attitudes towards tax evasion. Research provides support for the hypotheses derived from self-awareness theory. Pryor, Gibbons, Wicklund, Fazio and Hood (1977) found that the consistency between self-reported sociability and how sociably individuals actually behaved in a dyadic interaction was considerably enhanced when the self-reports were completed while seated in front of a mirror. Sitting in front of a mirror acted as the manipulation to increase self-awareness. Other research, often using the mirror procedure, reports similar results (see, e.g., Carver, 1975; Gibbons, 1978; Snyder and Swann, 1976).

It is not always possible nor practical to place a mirror in front of subjects at the time attitudes or behavior are expressed. Other conditions that lead to increased attention for the self can have similar effects on attitude-behavior consistency, e.g., the presence of an evaluative audience, being observed, and feeling unique (Wicklund, 1982).

Although research is not available, it can be expected that when attitudes and behavior are expressed under conditions of high *involvement*, a strong relationship between attitudes and behavior can be obtained. In this context, involvement can be expected to have similar effects as self-awareness. This issue will be returned to in the section on the availability of attitudes.

12.4. *Moderating Personality Characteristics*

Some individuals seem to follow up more on their attitudes and behavioral intentions than others. While some who have a positive attitude towards buying Government bonds and a negative attitude towards taking care of the garden, actually express the attitude-consistent behaviors, others with the same attitudes don't. Equating personality characteristics directly to overt behavior has a long history in the social sciences, and an almost equally long history of failures to find significant relationships between the two concepts (see, e.g., Mischel and Peake, 1982).

Only fairly recently researchers have started to investigate the moderating effect of personality variables on attitude-behavior consistency. Two personality characteristics will be introduced more in depth. These two personality characteristics, need for cognition and self-monitoring, have been shown to have the moderating qualities mentioned. More importantly, they hold much promise, and seem to be worth the further research that is still needed. Some other personality characteristics that may moderate attitude-behavior relationships will be introduced only briefly.

First, need for cognition will be introduced. Next, self-monitoring will be touched upon. An introduction of the candidate moderators concludes this section.

Cohen, Stotland, and Wolfe (1955) postulated a global personality characteristic referred to as *need for cognition*. Cacioppo and Petty (1982) define need for cognition as "the tendency of individuals to engage in and enjoy cognitive endeavors." Research has shown that need for cognition moderates the relationship between cognitions, attitudes, and behavior (see Petty and Cacioppo, 1986; Pieters, Petty, and Haugtvedt, 1986; Pieters and Verplanken, 1986).

For instance, Cacioppo, Petty, Kao, and Rodriguez (1986) found that individuals who differed in need for cognition also differed in the extent to which their attitudes predicted their voting intentions and subsequent reports of voting behavior. Attitudes toward the Presidential candidates during the 1984 electoral campaign in the U.S. predicted voting intentions and behavior significantly better for individuals who were high than low in need for cognition. Attitudes did not differ in extremity.

This suggests that the extent to which individuals engage in and enjoy cognitive endeavors may moderate the relationship between attitudes, behavioral intentions and behavior. Stated more simply, the attitudes of individuals that think and enjoy to think more, predict subsequent attitude-consistent behavior better than the attitudes of individuals who think and enjoy to think less.

Social observers have proposed that the ability to manage and control expressive behaviors is a prerequisite to effective social and interpersonal functioning (see, e.g., Goffman, 1959). One cannot always express one's inner feelings, and attitudes. In some situations people have to keep a stiff upper lip, laugh with the guys, act cool. Such behaviors are examples of self-presentation. Individuals differ in the extent to which they tend to engage in self-presentation (Snyder, 1974), and research reveals that this personality characteristic moderates attitude-behavior relationships. The tendency to engage more or less in self-presentation behaviors is labelled as *self-monitoring*.

Snyder (1974, 1979) states that individuals high in self-monitoring are particularly sensitive to the expression and self-presentation of others, out of a concern of social appropriateness. Such individuals use these "situational" cues as guidelines for monitoring their own self-presentations. Individuals low in self-monitoring act more on the basis of inner states, personal dispositions and attitudes. Thus, it can be expected that high self-monitoring individuals show minimal attitude-behavior consistency, while low self-monitoring individuals show considerable attitude-behavior consistency. The difference should be particularly large in situations where there is ample room for self-presentation, for instance in social gatherings and parties.

Empirical evidence has provided documentation for these theoretical propositions (see Snyder, 1982; Snyder and Gangestad, 1986). Snyder and Swann (1976) found that the correlation between attitudes toward affirmative action, and verdicts two week later in a mock court case involving sex discrimination was significantly lower for high self-monitoring individuals than for low self-monitoring individuals. Others report similar results (see Zanna, Olson, and Fazio, 1980).

The two personality characteristics described, have not been the only ones suggested. Scheier, Buss and Buss (1978) found that the correlation between scores on a measure of hostility and a behavioral index of aggressiveness, measured on a later point in time, was almost zero (0.09) for individuals low in private self-consciousness, while the correlation was high (0.66) for individuals high in private self-consciousness. Private self-consciousness refers to the tendency of individuals to draw their attention alternately toward or away from the self. Private self-consciousness is the personality equivalent of self-awareness (described in the section on the expression of attitudes and behavior). Unfortunately, research on the moderating effect of private self-consciousness is not abundant. Also, it is not quite clear in which respect private self-consciousness differs from self-monitoring, need for cognition, and other personality characteristics. Other issues with respect to the issue have also been raised (Wicklund, 1982).

Witkin and his associates (Witkin and Goodenough, 1976) have developed the construct of analytical vs. global cognitive style. The construct is labelled field dependence/independence. Field-independent people are active, hypothesis-testing, participant learners, whereas field-dependents are more passive, intuitive, spectator learners. Research suggests that field-dependent persons are more likely than field-independent persons to attend to the social features of a situation. Presently, no research testing the moderating effects of field dependence/independence on attitude-behavior consistency is available. Yet, research in the context of persuasion indicates that field dependence/independence may have similar, though not identical, effects as involvement (Heesacker, Petty, and Cacioppo, 1983). Given the conceptual overlap of field dependence/independence with self-monitoring, it is not unlikely that field dependence/independence moderates the attitude-behavior relationship.[9]

Several factors have been shown to moderate the relationship between attitudes and behavior. Research reporting such factors and their effects is particularly relevant in answering the "when" question of attitude-behavior consistency, i.e., the question under which (theoretical) conditions attitude-behavior consistency can be observed. Some factors that operate during the formation of attitudes, and some that operate during the expression of attitudes and behavior have been introduced. Also, some relevant personality characteristics were described. Briefly, the question as to which processes are responsible for the obtained moderating effects has been touched upon. In the next section the HOW question of attitude-behavior consistency will be addressed.

13. ACCESSIBILITY AND RELEVANCY OF ATTITUDES

13.1. *Introduction*

It has been mentioned that sometimes one may decide to take another way home than the familiar one, and that while driving, one may realize that the same old road home is taken again. Clearly, the positive attitude toward taking the other road was real. Still, the force of habit overruled it. When would the chances of observing attitude-behavior consistency have been higher? Somewhere on the way home, a decision had to be taken to turn left, and take the new way home, instead of driving straight on, and follow the familiar road. Yet, such a decision was never made. At the particular crossroad the attitude did not come into mind, no decision situation arose, and consequently the old road was taken. If, at the crossroad, the attitude had come into mind, the new road home would likely have been chosen. Thus, following this reasoning, an attitude is more likely to direct behavior if it is readily accessible at the time the relevant behavior is to be performed.[10]

13.2. *Moderating Processes*

Fazio and his co-workers (Fazio, Powell, and Herr, 1982, 1983; Zanna and Fazio, 1982; Fazio, 1985) have developed a process model of the attitude-behavior relationship, in which attitude accessibility takes a central position. Their model involves the following sequence:

1. Upon observation of the attitude object, one's attitude must be retrieved from memory.
2. The attitude is apt, through a process of selective perception to "colour" one's perceptions of the object in the situation.
3. These immediate perceptions, filtered through the attitude, influence the individual's behavioral response.

The end result is behavior that is consistent with the attitude that initiated and "guided" the entire process. To date, research has mainly focussed on the first two steps of the suggested process.

The manner of attitude formation has been shown to moderate attitude-behavior relationships. Attitudes formed through direct experience predict behavior better than attitudes formed through indirect experience. Fazio, Powell and Herr (1982) found that attitudes formed through direct experience are usually remembered more quickly than attitudes formed through indirect experience. This finding supports the first step of the proposed process model.

The fact that feelings, such as attitudes, influence the storage and retrieval of information from memory is well established by now (see Bower, 1981; Bower and Cohen, 1982). Fazio, Powell, and Herr (1982) found that attitudes, once they were accessed, colored the perceptions of the individual, even the perception of objects or persons that were irrelevant to the attitude-object. Fazio and Williams (1986) tested the process model of the attitude-behavior relationship in the context of the 1984 Presidential election in the U.S. They found that the individual's (global) attitude towards a candidate colored his/her perception of the candidate's performance during (specific) pre-election debates. They also found that the correlations between attitude measures and actual voting behavior were higher for individuals whose attitudes were highly accessible than for individuals whose attitudes were difficult to access. Thus, attitude accessibility was found to moderate both the attitude-perception and the attitude-behavior relationships (see also Fazio, Sanbomatsu, Powell, and Kardes, 1986). Such findings support the three steps proposed in the process model.

The process model may largely explain why the extent of direct experience, involvement, self-awareness, and need for cognition determines the extent to which attitudes predict behavior. However, it does not explain why self-monitoring is a factor moderating attitude-behavior relationships. Are attitudes less accessible for individuals high on self-monitoring than for individuals low on self-monitoring?

Snyder (1982) explains that "just as it is the case that deficits in the availability of attitudes may contribute to lack of correspondence between attitudes and behavior, so too may deficits in the relevance of attitudes as guides to action create gaps between attitudes and behavior" (p. 113). Individuals can be expected to act upon their attitudes only when it is in their interest to act upon them, i.e., when they feel attitudes are appropriate guidelines for behavior. Yet, for many reasons one may choose to define situational and interpersonal specifications of behavioral appropriateness as the relevant guidelines for behavior. Thus, from the perspective of the relevance of attitudes, low self-monitoring individuals may be more likely than high self-monitoring individuals to act upon their attitudes. For low self-monitoring individuals attitudes are more relevant guides to behavior, than for high-self-monitoring individuals.

Following this reasoning, it can be expected that all conditions stimulating attitudes to become appropriate guidelines to behavior, result in a strong relationship between attitudes and behavior. The results of research (Snyder and Kendziersky, 1982) support this hypothesis. Snyder (1979, 1982) suggests that situations that invoke individuals to ask themselves "What course of action do my attitudes suggest that I pursue in this situation" will lead to behavior that is consistent with prior attitudes. Such a "believing means doing" strategy holds much promise.

13.3. *Summary*

To summarize, in order that attitudes guide behavior, attitudes should be accessible at the time that the behavior is performed, or that the relevant decision is made. Factors that stimulate the accessibility of attitudes, will moderate the relationship between attitudes and behavior. A number of such factors have been introduced in the previous section. Attitude accessibility is not (always) enough. Attitude should also be defined by the individual as the appropriate (relevant) guideline to behavior. Factors stimulating individuals to use their attitudes as the appropriate guidelines to behavior will moderate the relationship between attitudes and behavior.

Finally, it is somewhat unfortunate that many of the studies on moderating variables have not been performed within the framework of the Reasoned Action theory and its extensions. Also, very few studies within the framework of the Reasoned Action theory take account of moderating variables. For this reason, it is difficult to indicate the effect of other factors, besides attitude, on behavior when the effect of moderating factors is accounted for. The opposite is equally true. Studying, in conjunction, the factors moderating the relationship between attitudes, other variables, and behavior is a challenging undertaking. An undertaking that may shed more light on the dynamics of behavior. This issue will be returned to in the next section.

14. DISCUSSION AND CONCLUDING REMARKS

In this chapter, the literature on attitude-behavior relationships was described. Several issues that pertain to the attitude-behavior relationship have not been treated, or have been treated only marginally. The prediction and explanation of behavior from attitudes and other determinants was the main focus. The process by which attitudes are formed, the relationships between attitudes, the relationships between attitudes, values, needs, and other important issues have been given only scant attention. Due to my idiosyncracies and personal hobbies, some issues, e.g., garbology, may have received more attention than others would give them. Hopefully, the present chapter has, despite this, contributed somewhat to a better understanding of the dynamics of attitude-behavior relationships.

In this chapter, a narrow definition of attitude was used. Attitude was defined as an object-related affect (section 3). Although this definition is shared by most attitude theorists, the issue whether attitudes comprise one, two or three components is still not quite settled. Theorists may believe that they have the same notion in mind when they talk about "attitude." However, their conceptions may actually differ in important ways (Berkowitz, 1986: pp. 168-169). Sometimes, an (implicit or explicit) distinction is made between an "affective attitude" and a "cognitive attitude," in which the latter attitude often refers to the beliefs-times-evaluations component of the Reasoned Action theory. The issue whether attitudes comprise one or more components does not seem to be one that can be solved empirically. It is more one of definition. Instead of analyzing whether "attitudes" comprise one or more components, it is more fruitful to analyze the relationships between the affective, cognitive and conative components of human functioning. The latter approach was followed here.

Since the early days of attitude research when LaPiere showed his Chinese guests the American hospitality of the 1930's, our understanding of the dynamics of attitude-behavior relationships has increased considerably. Models in which global attitudes are assumed to direct all kinds of specific behaviors with respect to the attitude object are deemed naive in hindsight. Four general ways to deal with the apparent inconsistency between attitude and behavior, that was found in early studies, were described.

The first way, that of conceiving attitude as a probability rather than a latent process concept, may render the question whether there is a consistent relationship between attitudes and behavior improper (section 9). When adhering to a strict probability conception, the proper question becomes: "which aspects of the situation influence verbal and non-verbal behaviors, and under which conditions can a consistent relationship between verbal behaviors (purportedly measuring attitude) and non-verbal behaviors be expected." Although the probability conceptualization does focus our attention upon the importance of the contextual determinacy of behavior, strict adherence to it sacrifices the attitude-behavior relationship. A mere relationship between situational aspects and classes of (verbal or non-verbal) behavior remains.

The other three ways to deal with the proposition that attitudes do not relate to behavior take a different perspective. Both in a strict methodological and in a strict moderating variables approach, attitude remains the prime determinant of behavior.

Methodological conditions under which attitude-behavior consistency can be obtained, e.g., correspondence in specification elements, have been described in section 10. The methodological approach has its main focus on the prediction of behavior. It has provided valuable insights. However, we agree with Abelson (1982) that a strict methodological approach may lead to a road paved by psychometric considerations, where the intrinsic dynamics of the attitude-behavior relationship may be lost. Adhering to a strict methodological approach may render the attitude-behavior relationship a mere tautology (Verhallen and Pieters, 1984).

Factors moderating attitude-behavior relationships were described in section 12. The moderating variable approach has been very fruitfully followed in the last decade. It has provided insights in the reasons why some attitudes of some individuals in some situations predict some behavior. The primacy of attitudes in the prediction and explanation of behavior is largely saved, although in newer models, such as Fazio's (1985) model, the relationships between attitudes and behavior become quite complex. Adhering strictly to the moderating variables approach may push a fundamental question to the background, i.e., the question whether attitudes are the sole determinants of behavior.

Research concerning possible other determinants of behavior was briefly reviewed in section 11. A purist might remark that a section on other determinants of behavior independent of attitudes, does not belong in a chapter on attitude-behavior relationships. Yet, when, in a broader perspective, the focus is on the prediction and explanation of behavior, other determinants of behavior should be taken into account. Even if methodological conditions are met (section 9), and if moderating factors are taken into account (section 12), complete attitude-behavior consistency cannot be expected in all situations. Research on the Fishbein and Ajzen Reasoned Action theory has clearly dominated the other determinants approach in the last decade. Adhering strictly to the other determinants approach may push an important question to the background, i.e., the question when and why attitudes determine behavior, and when and why other factors determine behavior. Often, attitude and other determinants of behavior are equated with behavior or behavioral intentions, without a priori specification of the weights they are expected to have. Their weights are simply an outcome of the statistical procedure employed (weights are usually empirically derived regression weights). Early attempts to predict the weights of attitude and other determinants in the prediction and explanation of behavior have not been very successful (see, e.g., Glasman and Fitzhenry, 1976). Not taking account of the factors moderating the relationship between attitudes, other determinants, and behavior may, in the extreme, lead to constantly adding new "other" determinants to the list of determinants of behavior.

In view of these considerations, it is not revolutionary to call for a combined approach to the study of attitude-behavior relationships. Insights gained into the factors moderating attitude-behavior consistency can be fruitfully combined with insights into the other determinants of behavior. Which factors determine whether attitudes or normative influence exert the largest influence on behavior? When and why does situational influence come into play? Under which conditions is behavior mainly determined by personal norms? Many other questions can be fruitfully addressed. Such a combined approach does make models on the determinants of behavior more complex than the early "attitude-determines-behavior-when-methodological-conditions-are-met" models. However, such an approach may be the better one when the focus is on the prediction and explanation of behavior, instead of on its mere restricted prediction.

We do not want to imply that the methodological approach is fruitless. In their review study on attitude-behavior relations, Ajzen and Fishbein (1977: p. 913) found that of the seventy one studies in which attitudes and behavior corresponded only partially in specification elements, still four studies reported high attitude-behavior relations. Although there may be statistical reasons for this result (significance level), there may be other reasons as well. Combining the methodological approach with the moderating variable approach may provide answers to the questions why global attitudes sometimes do predict specific behaviors, why specific attitudes sometimes do predict global behaviors, and why some attitudes predict behavior that is assessed well after attitude assessment, while others do not.

In conclusion, it is clear that the study of attitude-behavior relations is very well alive and kicking. Attitude theory is slowly but steadily progressing from the second question, when do attitudes predict behavior, to the third and fourth question, how do attitudes predict behavior, and when and how do other factors determine behavior. The answers to these questions are of central importance when building models that both predict and explain economic behavior.

ACKNOWLEDGEMENTS

I have benefitted much from the help of Fred van Raaij, Erasmus University Rotterdam, and René van der Vlist, State University of Leiden, both in The

Netherlands, who offered detailed and insightful comments on earlier drafts of this chapter.

NOTES

1. Generally, attitudes are assumed to have four functions for the individual holding them (Katz, 1960):
   a. the instrumental or utilitarian function,
   b. the value expressive function,
   c. the ego defensive function, and
   d. the organization of knowledge function.

   ad a. Attitudes guide individuals in fulfilling needs and achieving goals. In general, positive attitudes will be developed toward people and objects that facilitate the achievement of desired end-states, and negative attitudes toward people and objects that frustrate the achievement of desired end-states.

   ad b. Individuals will develop attitudes that are consistent with, and expressive of, their broader value system or self-concept.

   ad c. Individuals may sometimes develop attitudes to shield them from consciously recognizing their own failings and inadequacies. E.g., attitudes of racism can have such qualities.

   ad d. Individuals develop attitudes to structure their world. Attitudes organize the massive information individuals are confronted with daily. They provide ready aids in sizing up the world.

   Equally favorable or unfavorable attitudes toward a certain object may have different functions for the individuals holding them. Lutz (1981) develops a framework for research on advertising themes, based on the functions attitudes might have for individuals.
2. Usually, when using indirect verbal measures of attitude an index over responses to a set of beliefs (cognition) or intention items is computed (Fishbein and Ajzen, 1975: p. 59). The attitude is inferred from the individual score on the index. When measured in such a way, it is assumed that cognitions either follow or precede the attitude, and that intentions follow the attitude. Thus, the individual's position on the evaluative/affective dimension is inferrred from other verbal responses.
3. In fact, as will be discussed in section 12, such a process can be used deliberately to enhance attitude (or intention)-behavior consistency. However, when the process takes place inadvertently, serious problems concerning the assumptions of verbal self-reports arise.
4. The Reasoned Action theory that was formulated by Fishbein and Ajzen in the course of time, will be dealt with in section 11, on attitude-behavior consistency and other determinants of behavior.
5. It has been noted in section 4 that often attitudes are measured indirectly by assessing behavioral intentions. In such measurement practices a strong relationship between attitudes and intentions is assumed. In research within the framework of Sheth's model and the RA theory such relationships are explicitly studied.
6. Mathematical symbols and notations are mainly used here, discursively, i.e., as a convenient replacement for our natural language. They should not be treated as referring to exact mathematical functions.
7. The question does not refer to methodological conditions upon which the attitude-behavior relationship is contingent. Such conditions have been discussed in section 10.

8. Instead of "involvement" or personal relevancy, they used the term vested interest. Vested interest is used to refer to the hedonic relevance of an attitude of the outcome of an attitude-behavior sequence for the individual (Sivaced and Crano, 1982: p. 210). Such a definition almost equals that of involvement.
9. Research on field dependence/independence started in the 1950's. During the construction of the instrument to measure self-monitoring (Snyder, 1974), the instrument was not compared for discriminant validity with measures of field dependence/independence.
10. Memory researchers distinguish between "availability" and "accessibility." In this context, availability refers to the fact that the attitude is stored, while accessibility refers to the fact that it can be retrieved (Lynch and Srull, 1982).

REFERENCES

Abelson, R.P., 1973, "The structure of belief systems," in: R.C. Schank and K.M. Colby (eds.), Computer Models of Thought and Language, San Francisco, CA: W.H. Freeman, pp. 287-339.

Abelson, R.P., 1982, "Three modes of attitude-behavior consistency," in: M.P. Zanna, E.T. Higgins, and C.P. Herman (eds.), Consistency in Social Behavior. The Ontario Symposium, Vol. 2, Hillsdale, NJ: Lawrence Erlbaum, pp. 131-146.

Adelson, S.F., E. Asp, and I. Noble, 1961, Household records of food used and discarded, Journal of the American Dietetic Association, 39, 578-584.

Adelson, S.F., I. Delaney, C. Miller, and I. Noble, 1963, Discard of edible food in households, Journal of Home Economics, 55, 633-638.

Ahtola, O.T., 1976, Contribution of instrumentality and value to attitudinal affect, Advances in Consumer Research, 4, 117-120.

Ajzen, I., 1982, "On behaving in accordance with one's attitude," in: M.P. Zanna, E.T. Higgins, and C.P. Herman (eds.), Consistency in Social Behavior, The Ontario Symposium, Vol. 2, Hillsdale, NJ: Lawrence Erlbaum, pp. 3-15.

Ajzen, I., and M. Fishbein, 1977, Attitude-behavior relations: A theoretical analysis and review of empirical research, Psychological Bulletin, 84, 888-918.

Ajzen, I., and M. Fishbein, 1980, Understanding Attitudes and Predicting Social Behavior, Englewood Cliffs, NJ: Prentice-Hall.

Ajzen, I., C. Timko, and J.B. White, 1982, Self-monitoring and the attitude-behavior relation, Journal of Personality and Social Psychology, 42, 426-435.

Allport, G.W., 1935, "Attitudes," in: C. Murchison (ed.), Handbook of Social Psychology, Worcester, MA: Clark University Press, pp. 798-844.

Anderson, N.H., and J. Shanteau, 1977, Weak inferences with linear models, Psychological Bulletin, 84, 1155-1170.

Atkinson, J.W., 1982, "Old and new conceptions of how expected consequences influence actions," in: N.T. Feather (ed.), Expectations and Actions: Expectancy-value Models in Psychology, Hillsdale, NJ: Lawrence Erlbaum, pp. 17-52.

Bagozzi, R.P., 1981a, Attitudes, intentions and behavior: A test of some key hypotheses, Journal of Personality and Social Psychology, 41, 607-627.

Bagozzi, R.P., 1981b, An examination of the validity of two models of attitude, Multivariate Behavioural Research, 16, 323-359.

Bagozzi, R.P., 1982, A field investigation of causal relations among cognitions, affect, intentions, and behavior, Journal of Marketing Research, 19, 562-584.

Barber, T.X., 1976, Pitfalls in Human Research. Ten Pivotal Points, New York: Pergamon Press.

Beach, B.H., and L.R. Beach, 1982, "Expectancy-based decision schemes: Sidesteps toward applications," in: N.T. Feather (ed.), Expectations and Actions: Expectancy-value Models in Psychology, Hillsdale, NJ: Lawrence Erlbaum, pp. 365-394.

Belk, R.W., 1974, An exploratory assessment of situational effects in buyer behavior, Journal of Marketing Research, 11, 156-163.

Belk, R.W., 1975, Situational variables and consumer behavior, Journal of Consumer Research, 2, 157-164.

Bentler, P.M., and G. Speckart, 1979, Models of attitude-behavior relations, Psychological Review, 86, 452-464.

Bentler, P.M., and G. Speckart, 1981, Attitudes "cause" behaviors: A structural equation analysis, Journal of Personality and Social Psychology, 40, 226-238.

Berkowitz, L., 1986, A Survey of Social Psychology, New York: Holt, Rinehart and Winston (third edition).

Bettman, J.R., N. Capon, and R.J. Lutz, 1975, A multi-method approach to validating multi-attribute attitude models, Advances in Consumer Research, 2, 357-374.

Bower, G.H., 1981, Mood and memory, American Psychologist, 36, 129-148.

Bower, G.H., and P.R. Cohen, 1982, "Emotional influences in memory and thinking: Data and theory,"in: M.S. Clark and S.T. Fiske (eds.), Affect and Cognition, Hillsdale, NJ: Lawrence Erlbaum, pp. 291-331.

Breckler, S.J., 1984, Empirical validation of affect, behavior, and cognition as distinct components of attitude, Journal of Personality and Social Psychology, 47, 1191-1205.

Budd, R.J., and C.P. Spencer, 1985, Exploring the role of personal normative beliefs in the theory of Reasoned Action: The problem of discriminating between alternative path models, European Journal of Social Psychology, 15, 299-313.

Burnkrant, R.E., and T.J. Page, Jr., 1982, An examination of the convergent, discriminant, and predictive validity of Fishbein's Behavioral Intention model, Journal of Marketing Research, 19, 550-561.

Cacioppo, J.T., and R.E. Petty, 1982, The need for cognition, Journal of Personality and Social Psychology, 42, 116-131.

Cacioppo, J.T., and R.E. Petty (eds.), 1983, Social Psychophysiology: A Sourcebook, New York: Guilford Press.

Cacioppo, J.T., M.E. Losch, L.G. Tassinary, and R.E. Petty, 1986, "Properties of affect and affect-laden information processing as viewed through the facial response system," in: R.A. Peterson, W.D. Hoyer, and W.R. Wilson (eds.), The Role of Affect in Consumer Behavior: Emerging Theories and Applications, Lexington, MA: D.C. Heath and Company, pp. 87-118.

Cacioppo, J.T., R.E. Petty, C. Kao, and R. Rodriguez, 1986, Central and Peripheral Routes to Persuasion: An Individual Difference Perspective (working paper).

Campbell, D.T., 1963, "Social attitudes and other acquired behavioral dispositions," in: S. Koch (ed.), Psychology: A Study of Science. Investigations of Man as Socius, Their Place in Psychology and the Social Sciences, Vol. 6, New York: McGraw-Hill, pp. 94-172.

Campbell, D.T., and D.W. Fiske, 1959, Convergent and discriminant validation by the multitrait-multimethod matrix, Psychological Bulletin, 56, 81-105.

Campbell, D.T., and J.C. Stanley, 1966, "Experimental and quasi-experimental design for research," in: N.L. Gage (ed.), Handbook of Research on Teaching, Chicago, IL: Rand McNally College Publishing Company.

Carver, C.S., 1975, The facilitation of aggression as a function of objective self-awareness and attitudes toward punishment, Journal of Experimental Social Psychology, 11, 510-519.

Cialdini, R.B., and D.J. Baumann, 1981, Littering: A new unobtrusive measure of attitude, Social Psychology Quarterly, 44, 254-259.

Cohen, A., E. Stotland, and D. Wolfe, 1955, An experimental investigation of need for cognition, Journal of Abnormal and Social Psychology, 51, 291-294.

Cook, M.P., J.W. Lounsbury, and G.A. Fontenelle, 1980, An application of Fishbein and Ajzen's attitudes-subjective norms model to the study of drug use, Journal of Social Psychology, 110, 193-210.

Cook, T.D., and D.T. Campbell, 1979, Quasi-experimentation: Design and Analysis Issues for Field Settings, Chicago, IL: Rand McNally College Publishing Company.

Cooper, J., and R.T. Croyle, 1984, "Attitudes and attitude change," in: M.R. Rosenzweig and L.W. Porter (eds.), Annual Review of Psychology, Vol. 35, Palo Alto, CA: Annual Reviews, pp. 395-426.

Cote, J.A., 1984, "Use of household refuse analusis to measure usual and period-specific food consumption," in: W.L. Rathje and C.K. Ritenbaugh (eds.), American Behavioral Scientist, Beverly Hills, CA: Sage Publications, pp. 129-138.

Cote, J.A., J. McCullough, and M. Reilly, 1985, Effects of unexpected situations on behavior-intention differences: A garbology analysis, Journal of Consumer Research, 12, 188-194.

Davidson, A.R., and J. Jaccard, 1979, Variables that moderate the attitude-behavior relation: Results of a longitudinal survey, Journal of Personality and Social Psychology, 37, 1364-1376.

Davidson, A.R., S. Yantis, M. Norwood, and D.E. Montano, 1985, Amount of information about the attitude object and attitude-behavior consistency, Journal of Personality and Social Psychology, 49, 1184-1198.

Dawes, R.M., and B. Corrigan, 1974, Linear models in decision making, Psychological Bulletin, 81, 95-106.

DeFleur, M.L., and F.R. Westie, 1963, Attitude as a scientific concept, Social Forces, 42, 17-31.

Deutscher, I., 1966, Words and deeds: Social science and social policy, Social Problems, 13, 235-254.

Dulany, D.E., 1968, "Awareness, rules, and propositional control: A confrontation with S-R behavior theory," in: T.R. Dixon and D.L. Horton (eds.), Verbal Behavior and General Behavior Theory, Englewood Cliffs, NJ: Prentice Hall, pp. 340-387.

Earl, P., 1983, The Economic Imagination: Towards a Behavioral Analysis of Choice, Armonk, NY: M.E. Sharpe.

Ehrenberg, A.S.C., and G.J. Goodhardt, 1980, Models of Change, New York: J. Walter Thompson.

Ehrlich, H.J., 1969, Attitudes, behavior, and the intervening variables, American Sociologist, 4, 35-41.

Falbo, T., and H.A. Becker, 1980, "The Fishbein model: 'Triumphs, problems and prospects'," in: T.K. Burch (ed.), Demographic Behavior: Interdisciplinary Perspectives on Decision-making, Boulder, CO: Westview Press, pp. 125-140.

Fazio, R.H., 1985, "How do attitudes guide behavior?" in: R.M. Sorrentino and E.T. Higgins (eds.), The Handbook of Motivation and Cognition: Foundation of Social Behavior, New York: Guilford Press.

Fazio, R.H., and C.J. Williams, 1986, Attitude-accessibility as a moderator of the attitude-perception and attitude-behavior relations: An investigation of the 1984 Presidential election, Journal of Personality and Social Psychology, 51, 505-514.

Fazio, R.H., and M.P. Zanna, 1981, "Direct experience and attitude-behavior consistency," in: L. Berkowitz (ed.), Advances in Experimental Social Psychology, Vol. 14, New York: Academic Press, pp. 161-202.

Fazio, R.H., M.C. Powell, and P.M. Herr, 1983, Toward a process model of the attitude-behavior relation: Accessing one's attitude upon mere observation of the attitude object, Journal of Personality and Social Psychology, 44, 723-735.

Fazio, R.H., D.M. Sanbomatsu, M.C. Powell, and F.R. Kardes, 1986, On the automatic activation of attitudes, Journal of Personality and Social Psychology, 50, 229-238.

Feather, N.T., 1982, "Human values and the prediction of action: An expectancy-valence analysis," in: N.T. Feather (ed.), Expectations and Actions: Expectancy-value Models in Psychology, Hillsdale, NJ: Lawrence Erlbaum, pp. 263-289.

Fischhoff, B., B. Goitein, and Z. Shapira, 1982, "The experienced utility of the expected utility approaches," in: N.T. Feather (ed.), Expectations and Actions: Expectancy-value Models in Psychology, Hillsdale, NJ: Lawrence Erlbaum, pp. 315-339.

Fishbein, M., 1963, An investigation of the relationships between beliefs about an object and the attitude toward that object, Human Relations, 16, 233-240.

Fishbein, M. (ed.), 1967, Readings in Attitude Theory and Measurement, New York: Wiley.

Fishbein, M., 1980, "A theory of Reasoned Action: Some applications and implications," in: H. Howe and M. Page (eds.), Nebraska Symposium on Motivation, 1979, Vol. 23, Lincoln, NB: University of Nebraska Press.

Fishbein, M., and I. Ajzen, 1972, Attitudes and opinions, Annual Review of Psychology, 23, 487-544.

Fishbein, M., and I. Ajzen, 1975, Belief, Attitude, Intention, and Behavior, Reading, MA: Addison-Wesley.

Fishbein, M., and I. Ajzen, 1976, Misconceptions about the Fishbein model: Reflections on a study by Songer-Nocks, Journal of Experimental Social Psychology, 12, 579-584.

Forbes, G.B., and H.F. Gromoli, 1971, The lost letter technique as a measure of social variables: Some exploratory findings, Social Forces, 50, 113-115.

Foxall, G.R., 1983, Consumer Choice, London, UK: The Macmillan Press.

Foxall, G.R., 1984, Evidence for attitudinal-behavioural consistency: Implications for consumer research paradigms, Journal of Economic Psychology, 5, 71-92.

Funder, D.C., and D.J. Ozer, 1983, Behavior as a function of the situation, Journal of Personality and Social Psychology, 44, 107-112.

Furnham, A., 1983, Inflation and the estimated sizes of notes, Journal of Economic Psychology, 4, 349-352.

Furnham, A., and A. Lewis, 1986, The Economic Mind: The Social Psychology of Economic Behavior, London: Wheatsheaf.

Gibbons, F., 1978, Sexual standards and reactions to pornography: Enhancing behavioral consistency through self-focused attention, Journal of Personality and Social Psychology, 36, 976-987.

Glassman, M., and N. Fitzhenry, 1976, Fishbein's subjective norm: Theoretical considerations and empirical evidence, Advances in Consumer Research, 3, 477-480.

Goffman, E., 1959, The Presentation of Self in Everyday Life, New York: Doubleday.

Gorn, G.J., 1982, The effects of music in advertising on choice behavior: A classical conditioning approach, Journal of Marketing, 46, 94-101.

Gorsuch, R.L., and J. Ortberg, 1983, Moral obligation and attitudes: Their relation to behavioral intentions, Journal of Personality and Social Psychology, 44, 1025-1028.

Greenwald, A., 1965, Effects of prior commitment on behavior change after a persuasive communication, Public Opinion Quarterly, 29, 595-601.

Heesacker, M., R.E. Petty, and J.T. Cacioppo, 1983, Field dependence and attitude change: Source credibility can alter persuasion by affecting message-relevant thinking, Journal of Personality, 51, 653-666.

Hughes, W.W., 1984, "The method to our madness," in: W.L. Rathje and C.K. Ritenbaugh (eds.), American Behavioral Scientist, Beverly Hills, CA: Sage Publications, pp. 41-50.

Jones, E.E., and H. Sigall, 1971, The bogus pipeline: A new paradigm for measuring affect and attitude, Psychological Bulletin, 76, 349-364.

Judd, J.N., and D.A. Kenny, 1981, Estimating the Effects of Social Interventions, Cambridge, UK: Cambridge University Press.

Kassarjian, H.H., and W.M. Kassarjian, 1979, "Attitudes under low commitment conditions,"in: J.C. Maloney and B. Silverman (eds.), Attitude Research Plays for High Stakes, Chicago, IL: American Marketing Association, pp. 3-15.

Katona, G., 1975, Psychological Economics, New York: Elsevier.

Katz, D., 1960, The functional approach to the study of attitudes, Public Opinion Quarterly, 24, 163-204.

Kelman, H.C., 1961, Processes of opinion change, Public Opinion Quarterly, 25, 57-78.

Kidder, L.H., and D.T. Campbell, 1970, "The indirect testing of social attitudes," in: G.F. Summers (ed.), Attitude Measurement, Chicago, IL: Rand McNally, pp. 333-385.

Kok, G., and S. Siero, 1985, Tin recycling: Awareness, comprehension, attitude, intention and behavior, Journal of Economic Psychology, 6, 157-173.

Landis, D., H.C. Triandis, and J. Adamopoulos, 1978, Habit and behavioral intentions as predictors of social behavior, Journal of Social Psychology, 106, 227-237.

LaPiere, R.T., 1934, Attitudes vs. actions, Social Forces, 13, 230-237.

Leibenstein, H., 1976, Beyond Economic Man: A New Foundation for Microeconomics, Cambridge, MA: Harvard University Press.

Lewin, K., 1951, Field Theory in Social Science, New York: McGraw-Hill.

Lutz, R.J., 1981, "A reconceptualization of the functional approach to attitudes," in: J.N. Sheth (ed.), Research in Marketing, Vol. 5, Greenwich, CT: Jai Press, pp. 165-210.

Lutz, R.J., and P. Kakkar, 1975, The psychological situation as a determinant of consumer behavior, Advances in Consumer Research, 2, 439-454.

Lynch, J.G., Jr., and T.K. Srull, 1982, Memory and attentional factors in consumer choice: Concepts and research methods, Journal of Consumer Research, 9, 18-37.

MacFadyen, A.J., and H.W. MacFadyen (eds.), 1986, Economic Psychology: Intersections in Theory and Application, Amsterdam: North-Holland.

Manstead, A.S.R., C. Proffitt, and J.L. Smart, 1983, Predicting and understanding mothers' infant-feeding intentions and behavior: Testing the theory of Reasoned Action, Journal of Personality and Social Psychology, 44, 657-671.

Margolis, H., 1982, Selfishness, Altruism and Rationality: A Theory of Social Choice, Chicago, IL: The University of Chicago Press.

McClelland, D.C., J.W. Atkinson, R.W. Clark, and E.L. Lowell, 1953, The Achievement Motive, New York: Appleton-Century-Crofts.

McGuire, R.H., 1984, "Recycling," in: W.L. Rathje and C.K. Ritenbaugh (eds.), American Behavioral Scientist, Beverly Hills, CA: Sage Publications, pp. 93-114.

McGuire, W.J., 1985, "Attitudes and attitude change," in: G. Lindzey and E. Aronson (eds.), Handbook of Social Psychology, Vol. 2, New York: Random House, pp. 233-346, (third edition).

McGuire, W.J., 1986, The vicissitudes of attitudes and similar representational constructs in twentieth century psychology, European Journal of Social Psychology, 16, 89-130.

Midden, C.J.H., 1986, Individu en grootschalige technologie: Een vergelijkend attitude-onderzoek naar de opwekking van elektriciteit met kolen en uraan, Leiden, The Netherlands: Leiden University (dissertation).

Midden, C.J.H., and B.S.M. Ritsema, 1983, The meaning of normative processes for energy conservation, Journal of Economic Psychology, 4, 37-55.

Milgram, S., 1969, The lost letter technique, Psychology Today, 3, 30-33, 66, 68.

Miniard, P.W., and T.J. Page, Jr., 1984, Causal relationships in the Fishbein Behavioral Intention model, Advances in Consumer Research, 11, 137-142.

Mischel, W., and P. Peake, 1982, "In search of consistency: Measure for measure," in: M.P. Zanna, E.T. Higgins, and C.P. Herman (eds.), Consistency in Social Behavior, The Ontario Symposium, Vol. 2, Hillsdale, NJ: Lawrence Erlbaum, pp. 187-207.

Mitchell, A.A., 1979, Involvement: A potentially important mediator of consumer behavior, Advances in Consumer Research, 6, 191-196.

Mitchell, T.R., 1974, Expectancy models of job satisfaction, occupational preference and effort: A theoretical, methodological, and empirical appraisal, Psychological Bulletin, 81, 1053-1077.

Mitchell, T.R., 1982, "Expectancy-value models in organizational psychology," in: N.T. Feather (ed.), Expectations and Actions: Expectancy-value Models in Psychology, Hillsdale, NJ: Lawrence Erlbaum, pp. 293-312.

Nisbett, R.E., and T.D. Wilson, 1977, Telling more than we can know: Verbal reports on mental processes, Psychological Review, 84, 231-259.

Norman, R., 1975, Affective-cognitive consistency, attitudes, conformity and behavior, Journal of Personality and Social Psychology, 32, 83-91.

Olshavsky, R.W., 1981, Predicting behavior: More theory needed, Advances in Consumer Research, 9, 465-466.

Olshavsky, R.W., 1985, Toward a more comprehensive theory of choice, Advances in Consumer Research, 12, 465-470.

Ostrom, T.M., 1969, The relationship between the affective, behavioral and cognitive components of attitude, Journal of Experimental Social Psychology, 5, 12-30.

Petty, R.E., and J.T. Cacioppo, 1979, Issue-involvement can increase or decrease persuasion by enhancing message-relevant cognitive responses, Journal of Personality and Social Psychology, 37, 1915-1926.

Petty, R.E., and J.T. Cacioppo, 1981, Attitudes and Persuasion: Classic and Contemporary Approaches, Dubuque, IA: Wm. C. Brown.

Petty, R.E., and J.T. Cacioppo, 1986, "The elaboration likelihood model of persuasion," in: L. Berkowitz (ed.), Advances in Experimental Social Psychology, Vol. 19, New York: Academic Press.

Petty, R.E., J.T. Cacioppo, and D. Schumann, 1983, Central and peripheral routes to advertising effectiveness: The moderating role of involvement, Journal of Consumer Research, 10, 134-148.

Pieters, R.G.M., and B. Verplanken, 1986, The Joy of Thinking About Nuclear Energy, paper presented at the 10th Colloquium of the Association for Research in Economic Psychology, Kibbutz Shefayim, Israel.

Pieters, R.G.M., R.E. Petty, and C. Haugtvedt, 1986, The External and Moderating Effect of Need for Cognition on Reasoned Action, Nr. 51, Rotterdam, The Netherlands: Erasmus University (papers on Economic Psychology).

Pryor, J.B., F.X. Gibbons, R.A. Wicklund, R.H. Fazio, and R. Hood, 1977, Self-focussed attention and self-report validity, Journal of Personality, 45, 514-527.

Rathje, W.L., 1984, "Where's the beef?" in: W.L. Rathje and C.K. Ritenbaugh (eds.), American Behavioral Scientist, Beverly Hills, CA: Sage Publications, pp. 71-91.

Rathje, W.L., 1984, "The garbage decade," in: W.L. Rathje and C.K. Ritenbaugh (eds.), American Behavioral Scientist, Beverly Hills, CA: Sage Publications, pp. 9-29.

Regan, D.T., and R. Fazio, 1977, On the consistency between attitudes and behavior: look to the method of attitude formation, Journal of Experimental Social Psychology, 13, 28-45.

Reilly, M.D., 1984, "Household refuse analysis and market research," in: W.L. Rathje and C.K. Ritenbaugh (eds.), American Behavioral Scientist, Beverly Hills, CA: Sage Publications, pp. 115-128.

Rip, P., 1980, The informational basis of self-reports: A preliminary report, Advances in Consumer Research, 7, 140-145.

Ritenbaugh, C.K., and G.G. Harrison, 1984, "Reactivity of garbage analysis," in: W.L. Rathje and C.K. Ritenbaugh (eds.), American Behavioral Scientist, Beverly Hills, CA: Sage Publications, pp. 51-70.

Rosenthal, R., and R.L. Rosnow, 1969, Artifact in Behavioral Research, New York: Academic Press.

Rotter, J.B., 1954, Social Learning and Clinical Psychology, Englewood Cliffs, NJ: Prentice-Hall.

Ryan, M., and E.H. Bonfield, 1975, The Fishbein extended model and consumer behavior, Journal of Consumer Research, 2, 118-136.

Sarver, V.T., Jr., 1983, Ajzen and Fishbein's "Theory of Reasoned Action": A critical assessment, Journal for the Theory of Social Behavior, 13, 155-163.

Scheier, M.F., A.H. Buss, and D.M. Buss, 1978, Self-consciousness, self-report of aggressiveness, and aggression, Journal of Research in Personality, 12, 133-140.

Schlegel, R.P., and D. DiTecco, 1982, "Attitudinal structures and attitude-behavior relation," in: M.P. Zanna, E.T. Higgins, and C.P. Herman (eds.), Consistency in Social Behavior, Vol. 2, Hillsdale, NJ: Lawrence Erlbaum, pp. 17-49.

Schoemaker, P.J.H., 1982, The expected utility model: Its variants, purposes, evidence and limitations, Journal of Economic Literature, 20, 529-563.

Schwartz, R.D., and S. Orleans, 1967, On legal sanctions, University of Chicago law Review, 34, 274-300.

Schwartz, S.H., 1977, "Normative influences on altruism," in: L. Berkowitz (ed.), Advances in Experimental Social Psychology, Vol. 10, New York: Academic Press, pp. 221-279.

Schwartz, S.H., and R. Tessler, 1972, A test of a model for reducing measured behavior-attitude discrepancies, Journal of Personality and Social Psychology, 24, 225-236.

Sechrest, L., and J. Belew, 1983, "Nonreactive measures of social attitudes," in: L. Bickman (ed.), Applied Social Psychology Annual, Vol. 4, Beverly Hills, CA: Sage Publications, pp. 23-63.

Sechrest, L., and M. Phillips, 1979, Unobtrusive measures: An overview, New Directions for Methodology of Behavioral Science, 1, 1-18.

Seibold, D.R., 1980, "Attitude-verbal report-behavior relationships as causal processes: Formalization, test, and communication implications," in: D.P. Cushman and R.D. McPhee (eds.), Message-Attitude-Behavior Relationship: Theory, Methodology, and Application, New York: Academic Press, pp. 195-244.

Selltiz, C., L.S. Wrightsman, and S.W. Cook, 1976, Research Methods in Social Relations, New York: Holt, Rinehart and Winston (third edition).

Sherman, S.J., 1980, On the self-erasing nature of errors of prediction, Journal of Personality and Social Psychology, 39, 211-221.

Sherman, S.J., C.C. Presson, L. Chassin, M. Bensenberg, E. Corty, and R.W. Olshavsky, 1982, Smoking intentions in adoloscents: Direct experience and predictability, Personality and Social Psychology Bulletin, 8, 376-383.

Sheth, J.N., 1974, "A field study of attitude structure and the attitude-behavior relationship," in: J.N. Sheth (ed.), Models of Buyer Behavior, New York: Harper and Row, pp. 242-268.

Shwartz, R.D., and S. Orleans, 1967, On legal sanctions, University of Chicago Law Review, 34, 274-300.

Silverman, I., 1968, The effects of experimenter outcome expectancy on latency of word association, Journal of Clinical Psychology, 24, 60-63.

Sivacek, J., and W.D. Crano, 1982, Vested interest as a moderator of attitude-behavior consistency, Journal of Personality and Social Psychology, 43, 210-221.

Smith, J.L., 1982, A structuralist interpretation of the Fishbeinian model of intention, Journal for the Theory of Social Behavior, 12, 29-45.

Smith, M.B., J.S. Bruner, and R.W. White, 1956, Opinions and Personality, New York: Wiley.

Smith, R.E., and W.R. Swingard, 1983, Attitude-behavior consistency: The impact of product trial versus advertising, Journal of Marketing Research, 20, 257-267.

Snyder, M., 1974, Self-monitoring of expressive behavior, Journal of Personality and Social Psychology, 30, 526-537.

Snyder, M., 1979, "Self-monitoring processes," in: L. Berkowitz (ed.), Advances in Experimental Social Psychology, Vol. 12, New York: Academic Press, pp. 85-128.
Snyder, M., 1982, "When believing means doing," in: M.P. Zanna, E.T. Higgins, and C.P. Herman (eds.), Consistency in Social Behavior, The Ontario Symposium, Vol. 2, Hillsdale, NJ: Lawrence Erlbaum, pp. 105-130.
Snyder, M., and E. Decker Tanke, 1976, Behavior and attitude: Some people are more consistent than others, Journal of Personality, 44, 510-517.
Snyder, M., and S. Gangestad, 1986, On the nature of self-monitoring: Matters of assessment, matters of validity, Journal of Personality and Social Psychology, 51, 125-139.
Snyder, M., and D. Kendziersky, 1982, Acting on one's attitudes: Procedures for linking attitude and behavior, Journal of Experimental Social Psychology, 18, 165-183.
Snyder, M., and W.B. Swann, 1976, When actions reflect attitudes: The politics of impression management, Journal of Personality and Social Psychology, 34, 1034-1042.
Snyder, M., and W.B. Swann, 1978, Hypothesis-testing processes in social interaction, Journal of Personality and Social Psychology, 36, 1202-1212.
Songer-Nocks, E., 1976, Situational factors affecting the weighting of predictor components in the Fishbein model, Journal of Experimental Social Psychology, 12, 56-59.
Srivastava, R.K., 1979, Usage-situational influences on perceptions of product markets: Response homogeneity and its implications for consumer research, Advances in Consumer Research, 7, 644-649.
Stroebe, W., and B.S. Frey, 1982, Self-interest and collective action: The economics and psychology of public goods, British Journal of Social Psychology, 21, 121-137.
Sudman, S., 1983, "Response effects to behavior and attitude questions," in: T. Wright (ed.), Statistical Methods and the Improvement of Data Quality, New York: Academic Press.
Tolman, E.C., 1955, Principles of performance, Psychological Review, 62, 315-326.
Triandis, H.C., 1977, Interpersonal Behavior, Monterey, CA: Books/Cole.
Van Raaij, W.F., 1977, Consumer Choice Behavior: An Information Processing Approach, Tilburg, The Netherlands: Tilburg University (dissertation).
Van Raaij, W.F., 1981, Economic Psychology, Journal of Economic Psychology, 1, 1-24.
Van Raaij, W.F., 1984, Micro and macro economic psychology, Journal of Economic Psychology, 4, 385-401.
Van Raaij, W.F., and T.M.M. Verhallen, 1983, A behavioral model of residential energy use, Journal of Economic Psychology, 3, 39-63.
Verhallen, T.M.M., and R.G.M. Pieters, 1984, Attitude theory and behavioral costs, Journal of Economic Psychology, 5, 223-249.
Verhallen, T.M.M., and W.F. van Raaij, 1981, Household behavior and the use of natural gas for home heating, Journal of Consumer Research, 8, 253-257.
Von Neumann, J., and O. Morgenstern, 1944, Theory of Games and Economic Behavior, Princeton, NJ: Princeton University Press.
Vroom, V.H., 1964, Work and Motivation, New York: Wiley.
Wahlers, R.G., 1982, Number of choice alternatives and number of product characteristics as determinants of the consumers choice of an evaluation process strategy, Advances in Consumer Research, 9, 544-549.
Warner, L.G., and M.L. DeFleur, 1969, Attitude as an interactional concept: Social constraint and social distance as intervening variables between attitude and action, American Sociological Review, 34, 153-169.
Warshaw, P.R., 1980, A new model for predicting behavioral intentions: An alternative to Fishbein, Journal of Marketing Research, 17, 153-172.
Webb, E.J., D.T. Campbell, R.D. Schwartz, and L. Sechrest, 1966, Unobtrusive Measures: Nonreactive Research in the Social Sciences, Chicago, IL: Rand McNally.
Weigel, R.H., and L.S. Newman, 1976, Increasing attitude-behavior correspondence by

broadening the scope of the behavioral measure, Journal of Personality and Social Psychology, 33, 793-802.
Wells, W.D., and L.A. LoSciuto, 1966, Direct observation of purchasing behavior, Journal of Marketing Research, 3, 227-233.
West, S.G., and S.P. Gunn, 1978, Some issues of ethics and social psychology, American Psychologist, 33, 30-38.
Wicker, A.W., 1969, Attitudes versus actions, Journal of Social Issues, 25, 41-78.
Wicker, A.W., 1971, An explanation of the "other variables" explanation of attitude-behavior inconsistency, Journal of Personality and Social Psychology, 19, 18-30.
Wicker, A.W., 1975, Commentaries on Belk's "situational variables and consumer behavior,"Journal of Consumer Research, 2, 165-167.
Wicklund, R.A., 1975, "Objective self-awareness," in: L. Berkowitz (ed.), Advances in Experimental Social Psychology, Vol. 8, New York: Academic Press, pp. 233-275.
Wicklund, R.A., 1982, "Self-focussed attention and the validity of self-reports," in: M.P. Zanna, E.T. Higgins, and C.P. Herman (eds.), Consistency in Social Behavior, The Ontario Symposium, Vol. 2, Hillsdale, NJ: Lawrence Erlbaum, pp. 149-172.
Wilkie, W.L., and A. Pessemier, 1973, Issues in marketing's use of multi-attribute attitude models, Journal of Marketing Research, 10, 428-441.
Witkin, H.A., and D.R. Goodenough, 1976, Field Dependence Revisited, Research Bulletin 76-39, Princeton, NJ: Educational Testing Services.
Woodside, A.G., and W.O. Bearden, 1978, Field theory applied to consumer behavior, Research in Marketing, 1, 303-330.
Wright, P.L., and P. Rip, 1980, Retrospective reports on consumer decision processes: "I can remember if I want to, but why should I bother trying," Advances in Consumer Research, 7, 146-147.
Zajonc, R.B., and H. Markus, 1982, Affective and cognitive factors in preferences, Journal of Consumer Research, 9, 123-131.
Zanna, M.P., and R.H. Fazio, 1982, "The attitude-behavior relation: Moving toward a third generation of research," in: M.P. Zanna, E.T. Higgins, and C.P. Herman (eds.), Consistency in Social Behavior, The Ontario Symposium, Vol. 2, Hillsdale, NJ: Lawrence Erlbaum, pp. 283-301.
Zanna, M.P., and J.M. Olson, 1982, "Individual differences in attitudinal relations," in: M.P. Zanna, E.T. Higgins, and C.P. Herman (eds.), Consistency in Social Behavior, The Ontario Symposium, Vol. 2, Hillsdale, NJ: Lawrence Erlbaum, pp. 75-103.
Zanna, M.P., J.M. Olson, and R.H. Fazio, 1980, Attitude-behavior consistency: An individual difference perspective, Journal of Personality and Social Psychology, 38, 432-440.

Table of Contents

6. Social Influence on Economic Behavior

KARL-ERIK WÄRNERYD
Stockholm School of Economics, Stockholm, Sweden

1. THE NATURE OF SOCIAL INFLUENCE

1.1. *The Importance of Others*

Social psychologists stress the fact that human beings are social beings who are dependent on fellow humans for their survival and comfort. Undoubtedly, many behavioral acts and behavior in general are heavily influenced by other people. Psychology can even be seen as only a subdivision within social psychology and it can be held that psychology takes the individuals out of their natural social habitats and studies them in artifactual isolation. The social psychologist Tarde (1902) complained that economics was not based on social interaction but on the individual pursuit of self-interest, and that it disregarded the importance of the social environment for the individual. It is still true that consumer choices of products and brands as well as saving decisions are treated in economic theory as if a single individual were making the decisions.

In empirical studies of consumer behavior for marketing purposes there is also often a neglect of the fact that choices and decisions both can be joint undertakings of family members and be susceptible to considerable influence from non-family members. In marketing contexts there is high awareness of the significance of social influence on many purchases and through market research attempts are made to study and adapt to such influences. Social interaction within households is, however, not a highly researched area and mostly other types of social influence are studied (Davis, 1976; and Chapter 7 of this Handbook). In economic theory it is generally said that the household, not the individual is the decision unit, but assumptions are made that individuals like "the head of the household" can be taken to represent the whole household (see, e.g., Becker, 1981).

There seems to be consensus that social influence on attitudes and

Van Raaij, W.F., van Veldhoven, G.M. and Wärneryd, K.E. (eds) Handbook of Economic Psychology. ISBN 90-247-3720-6.

behavior is an important area to study. The whole of social psychology concerns, as it were, forms of social influence and their consequences. The methods used in this study tend to be somewhat less neat than those that can be used in individual experimental psychology and the research results appear to be less general and more tentative. The amount of research efforts devoted to different fields of social psychology have varied considerably over time. Many of the methods and results of basic social psychological research have found their way to the study of consumer behavior. Hypotheses have been confirmed in consumer behavior studies, but sometimes research results in a certain area have become facts about economic behavior without further testing. Attitude research provides examples where market research has given rise to reformulation of models from basic research and has thus contributed to theory development. See Chapter 5 of this Handbook.

The first section of this chapter contains a brief review of forms of social influence, a presentation of the concept of social impact and an introduction to attribution theory: people try to understand the social environment and thus attribute causes to the behaviors of others and to the outcomes of their own actions. After that, some collective concepts like social system, group and culture are introduced, followed by a discussion of economic socialization, i.e., how children become consumers and adopt the work roles that are appropriate in their social environments. The next section deals with social comparisons and reference groups, which is followed by a review of the functions and roles of the mass media. The latter can be seen as significant mediators of social influence. Finally, some issues and trends in research on social interaction are treated.

1.2. *Types of Social Influence*

The effects on individual behavior that derive from other people, are commonly referred to as social influence. There are many, highly varying types of social influence encompassing both verbal and non-verbal, often quite subtle influence, which in social interaction is often mutual. While the effects of social influence typically involve increased similarities among the people concerned, enhanced differences are also conceivable effects, for example when youngsters are encouraged to develop their own individuality or when somebody is provoked to become a deviant rather than to conform to group pressures. The latter type of behavior is known as reactance and means acting counter to the gist of the influence received (see, e.g., Verhallen, 1984). Economic behavior involving such activities as consumption and work is exposed to and shaped through social influence even in the very early years of life.

A newborn baby cannot survive without the help of other people. The fact that somebody has to supply the food, drink and care that are necessary for mere survival starts a life-long process of social interaction. This process is at first rather one-sided and little may be seen of social influence effects. According to learning theory, nurturing a child means to administer positive reinforcers that can stamp in certain behaviors and negative reinforcers that can make other behaviors unlikely. Nurturing a baby is normally accompanied by an emotional exchange, e.g., the mother smiles to and hugs the baby and the baby – already a few weeks after birth – smiles back to her. Mead (1934) who was a social philosopher notes:

> The meaning of social acts originates in the ability of children to anticipate the reactions of others to their behavior, an ability that rests in turn on the fact that "vocal gestures" constitute a stimulus for the individual making them as much as they do for those being communicated to (quoted from Pepitone, 1981: p. 975).

Social learning occurs in three ways (Bandura, 1977):

1. *Direct learning.* Economic behavior and other behaviors are learned because other people administer rewards and punishments that are directly related to the individual's actions.
2. *Indirect learning.* This is often called "vicarious learning" since people learn social behavior from watching what other people are rewarded or punished for. Modern mass media seem to provide ample opportunities for such vicarious learning among today's children.
3. *Imitation.* An individual acquires new behavior and performs new acts after observing another individual's behavior.

It should be noted that in psychological laboratory experiments and in simple learning situations in real life the connections between the performance of certain acts and the ensuing consequences may be obvious and easily assessed. Real life, however, offers many situations with complex relations that have to be interpreted. Assessment of causal relations, in social psychology studied under the label of "causal attributions," is a highly important aspect of social learning. Since attribution theory will be dealt with in the next section, suffice it here to say that all three forms of social learning are open to mistakes and without knowing it people may misinterpret the connections between rewards, punishments and behavioral acts.

Imitation, a concept that refers to behavior which apparently can be acquired independently of rewards, can be highly conscious as when a teenager copies some of the behavior of a pop star. It can be barely conscious as when somebody follows a stranger who crosses a street against a red light. Some authors maintain that imitation is the most important form of social learning (Miller and Dollard, 1941). Imitation is thus used to explain how children learn to behave socially and in accordance with social norms. Behaviors that have started as imitation, are in such cases later rewarded by social reinforcers and the tendency to repeat the behavior is further strengthened.

Emulation which involves comparison and imitation in a competitive spirit belonged to the human instincts listed and described by the early social psychologists. This instinct has since time immemorial been encouraged in young people, especially in young men. Humans have a tendency to compare themselves with others to find out whether they are better or at least equally good. Social comparisons have turned out to play an important role in such diverse economic areas as consumption, saving, and work compensation.

There appear to be two components in all kinds of social influence. One component has to do with the knowledge that is somehow imparted. Information about a certain behavior is transferred through direct sense contact or through symbolic means. This component or function should be kept apart from the transfer of values that guide behavior, i.e., the normative component of social influence. People are subtly or frankly told what is expected of them. People acting as individuals or as groups may issue, formally or informally, rules or norms that serve to regulate an individual's behavior. A specific form of social influence may be described in terms of which component or function dominates: the informative or the normative. In practice, it is often difficult to make such distinctions, but the type of effect to be expected as a consequence of certain social influence can vary depending on whether the imparting of knowledge or the instillment of values prevails.

1.3. *Social Impact*

In social psychology many concepts reflect the fact that the existence or presence of others have consequences for human behavior. Social facilitation is an example of such a concept. It means that the presence of others may stimulate and motivate performance. There is little argument about the fact that this effect occurs, but there is a debate over why it occurs. The phenomenon is also known in animal psychology. If a hen is fed grain in sufficient amount, she will start eating, eat for a while and then stop. If another hen is introduced and is similarly fed, the first hen will start eating again, and stop after some time. If a third hen is introduced and fed after the first two hens have both stopped eating, the latter will again start (Katz, 1937). Customer behavior at a popular sale may be an example of social facilitation effects.

A debated question is, whether the social facilitation effect is a "mere presence effect" where the presence of another human in itself increases the drive or arousal level, which Zajonc (1965) maintains. Or do other factors like encouragement or anxiety over evaluation (evaluation apprehension) give a better explanation as Cottrell (1972) asserts? Recent experiments seem to support the hypothesis about the "mere presence effect" (Brody, 1980: p. 148).

Social impact is defined by Latané (1981) in such a way that the concept covers most of the above phenomena: "any of the great variety of changes in physiological states and subjective feelings, motives and emotions, cognitions and beliefs, values and behavior, that occur in an individual, human or animal, as a result of the real, implied or imagined presence or actions of other individuals" (Latané, 1981: p. 343). Latané proposes a theory of social impact based on three principles, one of which is "The Psychosocial Law"

$$I = sN^t; \; t < 1$$

The Law is explained as follows.

> When people are in a multiplicative force field, the amount of social impact, I, they experience, will equal some power, t, of the number of sources, N, times a scaling constant, s. Further, the value of the exponent t should be less than one. Impact will increase in proportion to some root of the number of people present (p. 344).

There is an increase in impact for every person added, only the effect is marginally decreasing.

For inhibiting social impact the Law is in an analogous way:

$$I = sN^{-t}$$

The inhibition or division of social impact occurs when the tendency to do something is inversely proportional to the number of people involved. An example is the disinclination of bystanders to help in an emergency which grows with an increasing number present. Latané (1981) reports on a study in which the amount of tipping per person in a restaurant was investigated and found to be an inverse power function with an exponent of about 2. Individuals dining alone tipped almost 19%, while groups of five to six people tipped less than 13%. Other applications of the social impact theory concern social loafing or free-riding where individuals restrict their inputs to a common task when the number of contributors increases. Free-riding is often seen as a serious problem in welfare states, where people may want to share the social benefits, but try to escape the costs levied through taxes and fees (see Stroebe and Frey (1982) for a review of free-riding studies and a theoretical model).

1.4. *Receiving Social Influence*

Attempts at influencing people are, fortunately, not always successful. Effects as well as failures to achieve effects can be explained through studies of the properties of the social influence, the circumstances characterizing the environment and the situation, and the person him- or herself. The intended receiver of the influence may choose not to heed the attempt at influencing him or her. Even when effects are achieved, there are many differences in the types and degrees of effects. The social influence may affect overt behavior and/or covert behavior, i.e., attitudes. Behavior may change for example through imitation without any change in attitudes or values. The latter may change without any change in pertinent behaviors; people do not always live up to their convictions and they may choose to feign in certain situations.

Kelman (1961) distinguishes among three processes of opinion change as a consequence of social influence. He notes that there can be *compliance*, which encompasses only overt acts and which may not occur when there is no supervision or checking on the part of the influencer. Somebody may perhaps follow the advice of a powerful or respected person to buy a certain make of automobile without being convinced of this make's superiority for his or her own purposes and may even speak deprecatingly about it when the influencer is not around. A second form of yielding to influence is *identification* when people imitate referent individuals whose esteem they want or to whom they want to appear to be related. A typical example is the fan's identification with an idol. The fan wants people to know that s/he feels related to the idol and tries to display characteristics indicating such a relation. This has of course often been exploited in advertising where pop stars and other celebrities of our time help to market a diversity of products. There may, finally, be *internalization* which means that the individual changes both attitudes and behavior in an integrated way. Influencer characteristics are important for the individual's inclination to yield, but once internalization has occurred the relation to the influencer lacks importance. The newly acquired attitudes are part of the individual's own value system.

Intentional similarities in attitudes or behaviors are often referred to as *conformity*. This concept usually involves that a person yields to and is obedient to social norms or other standards of behavior. Yielding to group pressures has been suggested as a general definition of conformity

(Wrightsman, 1977). Sometimes the concept of conformity is used to reflect only correspondence or particular similarity in attitudes or behaviors rather than the yielding to some social pressures. Conformity may be seen as a valuable quality for a member of a group, but it is a fact that group members who completely conform to the norms of the group hardly initiate or support any changes in the behavior of the group and in the norms regulating the behaviors of the individual group members. An agent of change is by necessity at first a deviant. If s/he is not successful in changing the group norms, s/he must in the long run go back to conform to the existing norms or risk sanctions like status loss, rejection or expulsion.

2. CAUSAL ATTRIBUTIONS OF SOCIAL PHENOMENA

2.1. *Attribution Theory*

The behavior of other people is often of great interest to a person, even though s/he may not be directly affected by it. It is natural that people seek explanations for the behavior of others so that they get a feeling of understanding why a certain behavior occurred, of being able to adapt better to the social world and maybe even to attain increased control over some of it. "In common-sense psychology (as in scientific psychology) the result of an action is felt to depend on two sets of conditions, namely factors within the person and factors within the environment" (Heider, 1958: p. 82). When looking for causes that can explain a person's behavior, for example that person A has enjoyed the viewing of a certain movie, another person P may find it useful to know whether the enjoyment was a consequence of factors within the individual (A is perhaps easily pleased) or of factors relating to the quality of the movie. To Heider (1958), the founder of attribution theory, the important question was what made a person attribute effects to objects or events in the environment and what made him or her attribute effects to acts and dispositions of the person involved. Only in the latter case could there be talk about intentional acts and motives. Interpersonal relations depend to a large extent on how each person interprets the other's behavior.

There seem to be characteristic ways of making causal attributions regarding individuals. In some cases, environmental attributions dominate, in other situations, attributions referring to the individual are most frequent. Kelley (1967) has formulated some general criteria for what guides causal attributions. An attribution to an object (an entity) can be explained by the degree of covariation between the effect and the following four criteria:

1. whether there is distinctiveness, i.e., other entities fail to elicit the response, the effect is only there when the object is there,

2. whether there is consistency over time and the entity always elicits the response,
3. whether there is consensus and other people make the same attribution or make the same response to the entity, and
4. whether there is consistency over sense modalities and the entity elicits the same response under varying interactions between the actor and the entity.

In the example given above, the observer P would attribute A's enjoyment of the movie to the properties of the movie if A usually did not like movies (high distinctiveness), A saw the movie more than once (consistency over time), in varying company (consistency over modalities) and critics praised the movie (consensus). A's enjoyment of the movie would be attributed to personal dispositions if there was low distinctiveness, low consensus, and high consistency. In general low consistency seems to favor situational attributions.

Attribution theory also treats how people make causal attributions of effects relating to themselves. They may find reasons for their behavior or outcomes of behavior in their own dispositions or in environmental factors. The theory has inspired a large amount of research (reviews are given by Kelley and Michela, 1980; Crittenden, 1983; Harvey and Weary, 1984; see Van Raaij, 1986, for a review with special attention given to attributions in economic behavior).

2.2. *Attribution of Success and Failure*

The attributors' goal in seeking causality is that they shall become better able to manage themselves and their environment effectively (Kelley, 1973). It can be held that social adaptation is not possible without causal analysis. "The warrior needs to know why he is winning battles so he can survive the next one, just as the union representative needs to explain why the industry is doing poorly in order to urge wiser actions in the future" (Weiner, 1985: p. 549). A lot of recent research interest has been devoted to how causes for success and failure in achievement-oriented situations are attributed. In comparison to the amount of research efforts bestowed on factors influencing attributions, somewhat less empirical study has concerned the question of what people do with their perceptions of causes, i.e., to the adequacy of the causal attributions made and to the behavioral consequences in actual social interactions. The latter type of research is by Kelley and Michela (1980) labeled "attributional theory" rather than attribution theory. Weiner (1985) and his associates have pursued a long series of studies on attributions of success and failure in achievement-oriented situations and the consequences of those in terms of feelings, self-evaluations, and social behavior.

Perceived causes, however wrong, lead to expectancies of future events. If a person analyzes his or her performance and interprets successes and failures as due to external circumstances rather than to personal factors such as competence, the expectations of future performance will be founded on how these circumstances are expected to develop. If, on the other hand, the causes are perceived as pertaining to the individual him- or herself, strategies for the future become quite different and may involve personal development.

Weiner et al. (1972) have systematized the perceived causes reported by subjects into four categories, based on two two-valued dimensions: stability (stable, unstable) and locus of control (internal, external). See Table 1.

Table 1. Attributions of causality.

	Locus of control	
Stability	Internal	External
Stable	ability, skill	task difficulty
Unstable	effort	luck

When a person notices that another person is successful, s/he can attribute this to skill or ability if it is a stable phenomenon and the success is something that differentiates the person from other people. This is an internal attribution. If many people constantly succeed, the task is seen as simple which is an external attribution. If the success occurs once and can be achieved only by a few, it will be attributed to effort on the part of the successful person which is an unstable, internal cause.

In a study of consumer reactions to product failures, it was found that when product failures were attributed to stable factors such as a company with a poor reputation, consumers anticipated similar dissatisfactions in the future and demanded cash refunds. If the product failure was perceived as due to unstable causes such as an occasional bad shipment of goods, the consumers were expecting full product satisfaction in the future and willingly accepted product exchange (Folkes, 1984).

The four categories of perceived causes, based on stability and locus of control, have proved to be useful, but they leave out some significant aspects (Weiner, 1985). Ability can be unstable if there is learning, effort can be seen as a stable characteristic of some people who are considered industrious, and some people are thought of as being lucky (or unlucky) as a stable characteristic. Controllability has thus been added as a third dimension to take care of some of the earlier inadequacies. Some internal causes are perceived to be controllable and the individual can develop strategies to cope with them. In the same way certain external factors may be controllable, while others cannot be influenced.

Typically attributions are subject to four kinds of bias (Kelley, 1967; Crittenden, 1983; Harvey and Weary, 1984).

1. Observers have a tendency to underestimate the influence of situational factors on behavior and overestimate the impact of personal dispositional factors.
2. The observer is prone to see his or her own behavior as normal and appropriate and a different, unexpected response by somebody is thus attributed to the actor's personal dispositions.
3. Affective consequences for the perceiver may bias the attribution; the actor-observer may have an ego-enhancing or ego-protective tendency to take credit for success but to attribute failure to external factors; attributions of causes with respect to one's own behavior tend to be more internal, more variable and more complex than attributions made for causes of other people's behavior.
4. A perceiver may have many illusions about causality, e.g., about freedom of action and possibilities of control.

2.3. *Locus of Control Theory*

Attribution theory focusses on general principles for causal attributions and does not deal with individual differences or the long-term effects of causal perceptions. Locus of control theory had as a starting point the question, what happened to individuals when they were exposed to a skill environment that could be manipulated by the individual, as compared to a chance environment in which personal actions or factors did not affect outcomes. Considerable differences in performance were found when subjects in laboratory experiments thought they were working in skill rather than chance environments. Extinction of learned behavior was much slower in the skill conditions. This led the researchers to investigate, whether there were individual differences in the perception of the reinforcements to be expected from the environment.

> When a reinforcement is perceived by the subject as following some action of his own but not being entirely contingent upon his action, then, in our culture, it is typically perceived as the result of luck, chance, fate, as under the control of powerful other. or as unpredictable because of the great complexity of the forces surrounding him. When the event is inter-

> preted in this way by an individual, we have labeled this a belief in external control. If the person perceives that the event is contingent upon his own behavior or his own relatively permanent characteristics, we have termed this a belief in internal control (Rotter, 1966: p. 1).

Locus of control theory thus classifies people as internally or externally controlled and special personality tests have been developed to make this classification. These tests have been used in a variety of contexts and there is now a rich literature on locus of control theory (Lefcourt, 1984). People who are more internally controlled, tend to be more open to information, take more initiatives, assume more responsibility and be more creative than those who are more externally controlled. It has been shown that business leaders generally have a high degree of internal locus of control. In a Canadian study it was for example found that top executives who were more internal tended to pursue more product-market innovation, undertake greater risks and lead rather than follow competitors (Miller et al., 1982). Entrepreneurs tend to display a high degree of internality (see Chapter 11 of this Handbook).

3. BELONGING TO SOCIAL SYSTEMS

3.1. *The Meaning of Social Systems*

Social systems exist whenever there is an interaction of some duration between people. People belonging to a certain culture form a social system, since they share institutions, customs, etc and interact. The size of a social system can vary considerably from a dyad of two people to the total world population. In connection with economic behavior, groups of rather limited size are usually of most interest in the attempts to explain consumer and household behavior. There are contexts where cultural differences among people play an important role, and a few words will therefore be said about culture.

In social psychology, culture is not equivalent to culture as the concept is used in humanistic contexts, where it conveys a tinge of refinement. According to the anthropologist Herskovits (1948) "Culture is the man-made part of the human environment." Triandis (1980) adds that this includes both physical objects (roads, buildings, and tools) which constitute physical culture, and subjective responses to what is man-made (myths, roles, values, and attitudes) which constitute subjective culture. Another way of defining culture states that a culture means that some kind of "meaning" is shared among the members of a group. This presupposes that there is some commonality in the interpretations of objects and events relating to the man-made environment and that there are generally accepted symbols to express the shared meaning. This way of thinking about culture is characteristic of the study of organizational culture, which has expanded considerably during the last few years. In this type of organizational research special emphasis is laid on the use of symbols (see, e.g., Schein, 1984).

Psychological studies involving cross-cultural comparisons are often made with the purpose of testing general psychological theory (Brislin, 1983). In the consumer behavior area, there are two types of studies of what is often called cultural influence on consumption. One type comprises actual comparisons between nations, rarely more than two in a single study (but see, e.g., Hofstede, 1980; Green et al., 1983). These studies tend to suffer from a lack of defined cultural dimensions that could be used to explain differences. When nations are compared, whole clusters of cultural similarities and differences are actually compared without any means of splitting up the influences of different dimensions. A second type of cultural influence studies relating to consumption is devoted to ethnic minority groups (subcultures). A typical example is the North American research on black consumer groups. It would be to go too far in this context to try to summarize the findings of this research. U.S. textbooks on consumer behavior usually contain summaries of it (see, e.g., Engel, Blackwell, and Miniard, 1986).

3.2. *Small Groups*

The concept of group, often referred to as small group, is fundamental in social psychology. It designates interaction and mutual influence among people. The members of a group accept the influence from the group and from other group members, because the group contributes toward achieving something that the group members value, such as a shared goal involving the satisfaction of some need. It may be a question of collectively carrying out certain tasks which the individual member alone cannot cope with, or of creating need satisfaction through collective pursuits, like games or just fulfilling a need of being accepted and belonging somewhere. All members of the group must adjust their interests and their behavior to that of the other group members for the group to achieve the common goal. They have to sacrifice some of their freedom of action and comply with the norms of the group at least to some minimal extent. In return they get something they value from the group membership. Otherwise they leave the group or behave in such a way that they are rejected by the group members.

There are many types of small groups. They can be highly informal, have rather short duration, and people may not even think of themselves as group members, but just accept the influence from a set of other people. A small number of people who work together daily, can form a small group that exerts a lot of pressure on each individual who feels obliged to heed the other group members' opinions about clothes, choice of automobile make, which sports to pursue, which television programs to watch and many other areas. Some of this group's views may conflict with the opinions, tastes and behaviors favored by the person's family, another small group that has great importance. Consumer behavior research, often carried out for marketing purposes, has devoted a lot of attention to the possible influence of small groups on the consumption of products and brands.

An individual can influence group behavior and promote its best interests through being an exemplary, loyal member and subordinate him- or herself to the group interests. Changes in group opinions and behavior can be brought about by members who have higher status in the group and serve as informal or formal leaders. To continue the example from the work place, somebody in the group may have the greatest influence on what is accepted by the members and be asked about his/her opinion before anything is done. A car is not likely to be bought without at least the tacit approval of the leader who perhaps does not at all act overtly as a leader. Challenging the group norms leads, especially for low-status members, to exposure to ridicule, discontent with the member's behavior and even expulsion from the group. A teenager who buys the wrong type of jeans, may be exposed to rather severe treatment by peers!

Studies of communication in small groups and in organizations have given rise to a number of concepts and hypotheses about the flow of information among group or organization members and the roles played by different members (see, e.g., Rogers and Agarwala-Rogers, 1976). Some people serve as group anchors to whom other people listen and turn for information and advice. An individual can be able to influence the behavior of a group and initiate changes in norms and behavior through the fact of being the best informed member. A certain member of the group may serve as a link to other groups and this way acquire information of value to the former group. According to one set of hypotheses the group members who serve as liaisons to other groups, are typically not well integrated in either group. They still serve an important function as transmitters of information. The hypotheses referred to here have become known under the label "the strength of weak ties" or weak links (Liu and Duff, 1972; Granovetter, 1973).

The idea behind the strength of weak ties which has not been extensively researched, involves that persons with relatively little anchoring in a group account for new information and new impulses coming into the group. Instead of being deeply engaged in the dealings of a single group, these persons maintain more superficial contacts with many groups. They tend to move around. They serve then as bridges (ties) between groups which can be highly different. Studies of information flows and diffusion of innovations in developing countries have indicated that the existence of such liaisons is an important explanatory factor for the success or failure of such programs (Rogers, 1976).

3.3. *Roles and Role Expectations*

In groups that exist for some time, a distribution of roles characteristically develops. Somebody is chosen or emerges as a leader, other members assume or are expected to assume other roles. Roles grow out of all social interaction. Three dimensions of roles are usually distinguished:

1. the actual role behavior,
2. the expectations of relevant others with respect to the role incumbent, and
3. the incumbent's role perception.

A role is seen as an individual's way of living up to the expectations about him regarding a certain set of behaviors. Modern man is exposed to expectations originating from many sources and may easily experience role conflicts when the expectations are at issue with one another. In marketing contexts the role concept is well established. Housewives' perceptions of their roles as a housewife are related to product use. A housewife who perceives her role to be to provide good meals for the family, is not likely to buy ready-prepared food, but may be interested in trying new flavors.

Certain events in a person's life are accompanied by new role expectations. Graduating from school and starting gainful employment, accepting promotion on the job, getting married, having children, and going into retirement are some examples of such important changes in roles with accompanying changes in economic behavior. These changes usually encompass changes in purchase patterns and saving habits, not only on account of changed physical needs such as needs for new lodgings, furniture and clothes, but also because of attempts to live up to new expectations. A promotion of the household head on the job may for example lead the family to look not just for a new residence, but rather for a new residential area, more commensurate with the new role (see Zaltman and Wallendorf, 1983).

Research on roles has often focussed on role conflicts and socalled cross pressures when different expectations are directed toward the person. It has been considered strainful to have several roles. A rather new research orientation instead stresses that it may be agreeable to play many roles (Sieber, 1974). Successful people are assumed to like their tasks and their life in general and they are characterized by the fact that they have accumulated a number of roles. If you are successfully fulfilling the expectations associated with one role, you are likely to be offered positions involving new roles. Failures within one role may be easier to overcome or cover up when the person – the role accumulator – has other roles to fall back on. In Sweden for example, studies show that the chairman of the local section of the Social Democratic party is often also chairman of the local labor union, the consumer cooperative union and maybe other associations like in sports or athletics. Role accumulators probably serve an important function in economic life, because they are effective liaisons between organizations and groups (see Zaltman and Wallendorf (1983) for a discussion).

4. ECONOMIC SOCIALIZATION

4.1. *The Meaning of Socialization*

Socialization is the process of becoming a member of a social system. DiRenzo (1977) who uses "humanization" as a covering concept for four processes that together constitute human development makes the following distinctions between them:

1. *Maturation* is the development of the biological organism and means an innate and relatively automatic process of moving through the life cycle.
2. *Culturation* is a principally anthropological conception of social learning. Its formal object is the content of the learning process or that body of knowledge that is transmitted to the individual. There is enculturation which refers to the culturation of the neonate or culture-free organism, and there is acculturation which is the transmission of a secondary culture.
3. *Socialization* is the purely processual and/or structural dimensions of social learning. In this process uniquely human attributes are developed and/or actualized in the human organism.
4. *Personality* is the internal or psychological development of the organism in terms of its unique or individualizing qualities and/or attributes.

Becoming member of a social system involves learning to interact with other people in the system. The concept of socialization covers the acquisition of the knowledge, skills and values that make it possible for an individual to live and interact with others in a social system. In psychological research socialization is seen either as a social learning process in which the influence of others, so-called socialization agents, is essential, or as a consequence of cognitive development which occurs in stages and which is close to maturation in the sense suggested by DiRenzo (1977). In the former approach the assumption is that children do not learn the abstract, subjective culture through direct experience in the same way as they learn the physical culture. This model stresses the role of the social environment while the latter approach embodies the idea that the individual must have reached a certain stage of maturity before a particular type of social learning can occur. The attainment of a higher stage enables the individual to learn new sets of knowledge, skills and values. Although the models are distinctly different on a theoretical level, in empirical socialization research they are often combined. This is demonstrated by the fact that, e.g., the influence of different socialization agents is studied over age groups of children.

4.2. *Economic Socialization*

Economic socialization is a relatively new concept. It seems to have been first used in neo-Marxist analysis of socialization (Cummings and Taebel, 1978; Stacey, 1982). Independently of this use of the concept, it was employed in a Swedish study to cover three areas of economic behavior: consumption, saving behavior, and gainful employment (Jundin, 1983). The concept was used to indicate that both consumer socialization and work socialization of children were studied. In studies of economic socialization, the interest is focussed on how and when children become involved in the economic realities of the society in which they live. Children's socialization to become consumers in affluent societies has been studied primarily because of an interest in how television advertising affects children. Children's socialization to become productive members of society has received considerably less attention. Berti et al. (1982) and Jundin (1983) find that parents tend to give their children information concerning jobs appropriate to the level of development, at which parents believe their children to be. Furnham and Lewis (1986) who make a thorough review of economic socialization only cite a few studies of work socialization.

4.2.1. *Stages in Economic Socialization*

Stacey (1982) gives a summary of research on economic socialization in the pre-adult years. He deals with economic socialization in four areas:

1. money,
2. possessions,
3. social differentiation and inequality, and
4. socioeconomic understanding.

A common finding is that the first economic socialization that can be traced regards possessing and possessions. "Early in the child's experience with age-mates, possessions and possessive behaviour take on social characteristics involving interpersonal control and power over possessions" (Stacey, 1982: p. 171). Furby (1979) states:

> it is already clear that possessions are related to many areas of psychological development: personal possessions are often an integral part of one's self-concept, possessive behavior has been linked to fundamental motivational constructs such as effectance and competence and possessions are often a focal point in the development of peer relations and social transactions... (p. 181).

The subsequent economic socialization runs through approximately the following stages according to Stacey (1982).

- *4-6 years old*: develop some elementary notions about money and buying; cannot explain any economic phenomena, but realize that money can be used for buying things.
- *6-8 years old*: develop notions about numerical monetary value and they begin to make economic inferences such as seeing work as a source of money.
- *7-9 years old*: grasp the numerical value of money, acquire some personalized understanding of differences between riches and poverty and of socio-economic differences.
- *10-12 years old*: show less personalized, more differentiated economic understanding, ability to construct economic relationships in terms of functional considerations.
- *13-15 years old*: approach adults in knowledge about economic relationships, are aware of socio-economic inequalities and of their own family's position in the social structure.

The research results on which Stacey bases his conclusions all came from cross-sectional studies and not from longitudinal studies as would be appropriate when long-term development is studied. The findings originate from small, purposively selected samples, and are thus not representative in any statistical sense. The fact that the studies have been carried out in widely differing environments, involving both cultural and socio-economic differences, lends some support to the idea that there may be some invariance in the stages of economic socialization in the sense that they follow one another in the same order. The age level at which a certain stage is reached will however vary (see, e.g., Ng, 1985).

An example of cultural differences is given by Ng (1983). Using essentially the same questions as Jahoda (1979, 1981) had earlier posed to Scottish children, Ng interviewed Hong Kong children aged six to twelve. The questions concerned knowledge about banks and about shops. It turned out that the Hong Kong children who came from varying socio-economic backgrounds with some overweight for middle class acquired economic knowledge much earlier than the Scottish children. "A full understanding of the bank emerged at age 10, while that of shop profit emerged at age 6, both showing a precocity over the Scottish sample" (Ng, 1983: p. 209). The author attributes the differences to the socio-economic realities that shape the children's economic understanding. A later study which was conducted in New Zealand confirmed that there was an age-related progression of knowledge and reasoning about banks, but the rate of progression was different with the New Zealand sample lagging behind the Hong Kong children with about two years (Ng, 1985).

Ng (1983, 1985) and also Leiser (1983) who reports on a study of children in Israel, devote their main attention to the cognitive development of the children studied. When children are asked about economic concepts that are related, such as bank profits from differences between interest on deposits and interest on loans on one hand and the salaries paid by the bank on the other, they start to think about the relation at a certain age level. When confronted with conflicting answers they have given earlier, the children between 10 and 13 are increasingly able to identify the contradictions and to overcome them. Leiser similarly finds that about age 11 children become more alert to contradictions in the assumptions they have made and attempt to find solutions. When the cognitive development hypothesis is given priority as in these two studies, the role of socialization agents is made less dramatic than when the social learning hypothesis prevails. The social influence becomes a question of who are around and/or the social environment as a whole when the child reaches the appropriate degree of maturity.

Influences on socialization can be of various types. In economic socialization research the focus is usually on the roles of parents, peers, the mass media and the school (see, e.g., Moschis and Churchill, 1975; Jundin, 1983). These are the socialization agents who mediate the socioeconomic environment. In some studies the emphasis is laid on the economic system as a whole and differences in economic systems are seen as producing major differences among children. This view is represented by Marxist theorists and by some non-Marxist sociologists like Inkeles and his associates who have worked with problems of modernization in ancient cultures (Inkeles and Smith, 1974). In studies of political socialization, events are assumed to have effects on the learning of political attitudes and behavior. It is conceivable that economic events like unemployment in the family or a severe depression may affect the economic socialization of children and leave permanent traces in their economic thinking and behavior as may spells of extreme affluence. Elder (1974) who studied the effects of the Great Depression of the 1930s, found considerable psychosocial effects on the life course of Americans who were born during the early 1920s.

Most studies of economic socialization attempt to assess influences from socialization agents directly through asking children questions and possibly also parents (Jundin, 1983). An example of an indirect approach is shown in studies of the influence of father's occupation on children. It has been found that sons of fathers in entrepreneurial occupations have significantly higher levels of achievement motivation than children whose fathers are in non-entrepreneurial positions (DiRenzo, 1977).

Maital (1982) points out that there is no room in economic theory and little interest among economists in economic socialization. In economic theory the consumer is full-fledged from the beginning. Maital thinks that economic socialization should be a very important area of research for economists since people's economic behavior is guided by the learning in the socialization process. Problems like inflation and tax evasion may according to him have their roots in early childhood socialization when children learn to become competitive.

The acquisition of knowledge, skills and values that are pertinent for living in a social system does not stop with reaching adulthood. Socialization is a process that can be said never to stop. The changes involved may vary considerably between persons and over age brackets. There are probably transitions of special importance like getting the first job and retiring from active work. Very little research attention has been devoted to such transitions from the vantage point of continued socialization.

4.2.2. *Consumer Socialization*

Although studies of consumer socialization indicate that there is little purposive consumer training by parents (Ward and Wackman, 1973; Moschis and Churchill, 1975; Jundin, 1983), they show that parents still have considerable influence on the economic socialization of their children. They make purchases together with their children, they discuss purchases among themselves and with their children, they approve or reject their children's own purchases.

Jundin (1983) presents a study of Swedish school children in third, fifth and seventh grade (9-13 years old). She finds that contacts with parents correlate significantly with knowledge about buying and consumption as measured by a knowledge index. While the influence of parental contacts with children with respect to consumption attitudes vary with age, the peer contacts always show a positive correlation with attitude toward consumption. The more contacts the children have with peers, the more positive is their attitude toward consumption and toward spending money on consumption. As to the mass media, only television watching (which in Sweden is free from advertising) shows significant correlations with both consumption knowledge and consumption attitude. The amount of television watching is not significant, but the motive for watching television is: Children with a stated purpose of getting information from television are significantly better informed on buying and consumption matters and more in favor of such matters.

The U.S. studies on consumer socialization which started with the issue of children's reactions to television advertising have continued over several years and a number of reports are published (see, e.g., Ward and Wackman, 1973; Ward et al., 1975, 1986).

5. THE ROLE OF THE FAMILY

Families are groups, in which most resources are pooled and most consumption of products and services is characteristically a joint preoccupation. The extent of pooling resources can of course vary among families and family members and the joint consumption may nowadays be more a matter of using the same durable goods than of having meals together. While the main breadwinner is expected to and usually does contribute his or her revenues to fulfilling the needs of the family, a teenager who has his or her first gainful employment may only make a minor contribution to joint consumption needs and keep most of the income for his or her own expenditures.

The changing role of the family and the tendency away from small, two-generation families, so-called nuclear families, has given rise to much discussion. Marketing and market researchers have been concerned with the ensuing consequences for the demand for goods, for consumer preferences for different retail outlets, and for the proper format of market communication. Many new tendencies have been discovered and some of these have been intensively studied like the changing gender roles. The fact that more women are gainfully employed seems to affect the division of labor in the household only slowly. The earlier popular "availability theory" which held that the spouse who had most time available would be responsible for more of the household chores, has been repeatedly disconfirmed (Aldous, 1977; Berk and Berk, 1983). The female partner still carries out the main part of such duties in most households. The studies of family interaction patterns which have appeared in increasing numbers over the last decades, focus on the new roles of spouses, the power of children, new divisions of labor, and conflict management as important subjects (Aldous, 1977).

Many purchases are made within the framework of households which are usually equivalent to families. The majority of households comprise more than one member, but in modern welfare societies there are surprisingly many one-person households, because of high divorce rates and because of the fact that young people tend to move away from their parents at an early age. This tendency toward a substantial proportion of one-person households, which still seems to be on the increase, is reflected in the new availability on the market of a steadily growing number of packaged goods for single person consumption. Judging from a multitude of studies in many countries, as far as the frequently bought, so-called convenience goods are concerned, the division of labor in purchasing goods for the household is rather limited. The actual buying is typically, but not exclusively the burden of the housewife. Other family members still seem to have considerable influence on what products and brands are bought. The buying agent of the family does not want to risk negative reactions from family members.

Purchases of durable goods like household equipment and automobiles display more complex influence patterns and joint decision making. Family members may initially have very conflicting opinions and have their own "rules" of conflict management. Davis (1976) suggests that research on household decision making is too much influenced by laboratory research on small groups. The family has since very long been treated as a small group in sociological and social psychological research and the special emotional characteristics of families may have been too much neglected (Aldous, 1977). Basing himself on Weick (1971), Davis (1976) mentions a number of respects in which families are unlike small groups studied in the laboratory:

1. The emotional relationships are vital.
2. Problem solving is a recurring activity over long periods of years.
3. Families are heterogeneous groups.
4. The home environment is not ideal for optimal decision making.

Problem solving that ends with a decision to purchase, say, a new family car, may involve compromises so as not to hurt the feelings of certain family members or it may hurt the feelings of somebody who can then claim or decide to have the next joint problem solved his or her way. Problems arouse emotions which may be threatening to the well-being and survival of the family and thus problem solving processes have to be handled in such ways that tensions, if possible, are reduced (see also Chapter 7 of this Handbook).

It should be mentioned that in family studies Becker (1981) has employed what he calls "the economic approach to human behavior." The theory is applied to such questions as household decisions on the gainful employment of husband and wife, and on having children. A review with some criticism is found in Berk and Berk (1983).

6. SOCIAL COMPARISONS AND REFERENCE GROUPS

6.1. *Economic Effects of Social Comparisons*

Social comparisons and the consequences of these have drawn a lot of attention in research related to consumer behavior. The concept of reference group has often been used to designate all kinds of social comparisons and to explain effects of personal influence on behavior. Economists like Veblen (1899), Duesenberry (1949) and Leibenstein (1950) have directed economists' attention to the roles of others in forming economic behavior. Veblen introduced the concept of "conspicuous consumption" to describe the acquisition and use of objects that could be seen by other people and duly impress those. Leibenstein distinguished between three types of effects on the consumption of goods: the bandwagon effect, the Veblen effect, and the snob effect. The bandwagon effect involves that when more people adopt a product, the more the pressure to adopt increases on the people who have not yet adopted. The Veblen effect refers to the circumstances connected with status motives and conspicuous consumption in that a higher price is assumed to increase the consumption of certain goods, what the economists call a backward-sloping demand curve. The snob effect is opposed to the other two effects in its assumed effect on consumption: A product may become the more attractive, the fewer are the people who possess it. The latter effect can be compared to what has been found in recent studies of the significance of scarcity of products. Certain types of scarcity lead to increased demand whereas other types which have arisen from other causes do not (Verhallen, 1984).

Duesenberry (1949) made an attempt to explain why household savings could be differently affected by income rises. Keynes (1936) had formulated his famous "psychological law" which states that an increase in income leads to increased consumption, but not to the extent that the whole income is consumed. Some of the increase is saved. Keynes discussed why this was so in terms of slow adjusting of the standard of living to the new income standard. Studies of aggregate saving over long time periods have failed to disclose the relation between saving and income that was expected on the basis of the law. Duesenberry suggests that it makes a difference, whether the income increase or, more generally expressed, the income change is general or limited to individual households. The crucial factor is then whether the position of a household in relation to those of other households is changed or not.

Duesenberry's hypothesis which is often referred to as "the demonstration effect" or "relative income hypothesis," gives rise to the question how people actually choose their comparison objects. Reference group theory deals with the effects of social comparisons, but is not explicit about the choice of suitable comparison objects. Festinger (1954) contributes a number of hypotheses about how the individual chooses these comparison objects. The nine hypotheses suggested are to some extent based on earlier research, they have inspired later research and they have been combined with, for example, attribution theory.

The first hypothesis is actually a postulate stating that persons have an innate tendency to evaluate their attitudes and capacity (cf. attribution theory). Another hypothesis states that to the extent that there are no objective, non-social objects of comparison, persons will evaluate their attitudes and capacity through comparison with the attitudes and capacity of other persons. The probability that a person compares himself or herself with another person, decreases with increasing difference between them with respect to the attitudes or qualities which the comparison involves. When a person no longer compares himself or herself with another person or group, devaluation and even hostility arises against the former comparison object. Rijsman (1974) formalizes Festinger's theory of social comparisons to some extent, focussing on the pressures to choose comparison persons in simple and complex situations, and also tests some of the predictions.

Reference group theory systematizes the determinants and consequences of the evaluation processes in which the individual takes over values or standards from other individuals and groups (Merton and Kitt, 1952). In the first uses, reference group was applied to groups of which the individual was not a member, or to other individuals who did not necessarily form a group of any kind. Later the concept has been allowed to include also membership groups on the proviso that the individual compares him- or herself with the group members in some respect. Kelley (1952) makes a distinction between the comparison function, which is primarily informative, and the normative function of a reference group which means that the individual is subject to some kind of power exertion from the group. The person may be rewarded by getting the esteem of the group members, but this is not a necessary condition. The two categories are not mutually exclusive. The reference group may for example give valuable information in matters of taste, i.e., exert expert power.

There are many studies that indicate considerable reference group influence on the buying and consumption of products. They comprise, for example, how neighbors' influence stimulated adoption of such innovations as air-conditioners (Whyte, 1954) and many other diffusion of innovation studies (see Robertson, 1971). The reference group concept at first aroused a lot of interest within consumer behavior research, especially in marketing contexts, but the number of studies now reporting on the influence of reference groups is dwindling (Stafford and Cocanougher, 1981). The reasons are presumably connected with

1. the difficulties of a meaningful operationalization of the concepts,
2. the findings that people tend to have different referents for different behaviors, and
3. the fact that few stable patterns have thus been found.

6.2.1. *Level of Aspiration and Relative Deprivation*

Reference groups influence levels of aspiration, i.e., the goals that people set for themselves with respect to some behavior. A person's own earlier performance seems to be the most important determinant of the level of aspiration, but in particular when the person is lacking in personal experience reference groups appear to be influential. Reference group influence on level of aspiration is similar to the effect that Duesenberry (1949) called "the demonstration effect." Siegel (1957) and Starbuck (1963) have underlined the importance of level of aspiration for the study of decision making. The former author maintains among other things that utility should be seen as a function of the level of aspiration.

The concept of level of aspiration is connected with Simon's (1957) concept of bounded rationality. The latter concept implies that limited information and limited cognitive resources make it impossible for humans to behave rationally in the strict sense of economic theory. Instead of actually maximizing in their choice behavior, people search for alternatives whose qualities are above a boundary line (similar to level of aspiration), which defines what is acceptable or not. As soon as a person finds an alternative that is above the level of aspiration ("satisficing"), the search will stop and this alternative will be chosen.

In prospect theory (Kahneman and Tversky, 1979) the reference point which determines whether something qualifies as a gain or a loss is similar to level of aspiration (see Payne et al., 1980). Katona (1975) uses level of aspiration to explain why a person continues to save money and even may increase saving for old age after becoming member of an old-age pension system. The level of aspiration is often raised after successful performance and the pension system makes the person come close to the previous goal which encourages further efforts.

While there are many discussions about the importance of level of aspiration and its relation to reference group influence, there are very few empirical studies, if any, combining the two concepts. As a matter of fact, there are few attempts actually to measure levels of aspiration in field studies. The interest in a survey is usually rather focussed on satisfaction or dissatisfaction with achievements such as the amount of savings than on goals, probably because the latter are quite difficult to ask meaningful interview questions about.

In the early field studies of level of aspiration it was found that reference groups were significant for a person's assessment of his or her well-being (Merton, 1962). During World War II, American studies showed that black soldiers from the North were more dissatisfied with their lot than their colleagues from the South. It turned out that their reference groups differed. Northern soldiers had their referent persons among rather well-to-do northerners who made money in the armament industries, while southern soldiers had their referent persons among poor people in the South. This led the investigators to create the concept of "relative deprivation." This concept indicates what happens when the level of aspiration which has been set in accordance with what characterizes referent individuals, is not attained. Economists would probably explain the differences in terms of differing opportunity costs.

A person who is well equipped with many things that are assumed to be important in modern life, may still entertain feelings of relative deprivation and feel unjustly treated because his or her standards of comparison are taken from a superior reference group. Persons who lack most of the things considered to be necessary luxuries may feel little deprivation if they compare themselves with people who are even worse off. Reference groups, level of aspiration, and relative deprivation appear to be useful concepts for the study of consumption patterns and subjective well-being, but they seem to be more used in discussions about welfare than in actual empirical studies. In the EC countries data on happiness and satisfaction with life are collected regularly since the early 1970s (Euro-Barometer, 1986). There appears to be some correlation between income per capita in the countries and the stated average degree of happiness and satisfaction with life, but there are clearly deviating countries which are more or less happy than what would be expected on the basis of pure material welfare. A study of levels of aspiration and what influences those would then be of great interest.

6.2.2. *Social Equity*

Relative deprivation can be seen as a special case of the social justice, distributive justice or equity problem (Runciman, 1966). When people perceive that they have got their fair shares of some output, there is equity. Competing principles for dividing some asset are equality in which everybody gets exactly the same, and according to need in which case an assessment of needs must be made (cf. Deutsch, 1975). An essential question concerns what the person's conception of fairness is based on. In psychological theory of social equity, fairness is usually related to the ratio between input and output (Walster and Walster, 1975)

$$\frac{O_A - I_A}{I_A^{K_A}} = \frac{O_B - I_B}{I_B^{K_B}}$$

I is the input of persons A and B.

O is the output A and B receive.

K_A and K_B take on the value + 1 or -1, depending on the sign of A's and B's inputs and the sign of their gains

Walster and Walster (1975) stress that inputs are defined as what persons perceive as their contributions to the exchange. The formula can also be based on objective data and a distinction be made between perceived equity and equity assessed on purely objective grounds. In experiments reported by, e.g., Harris (1979) equity judgments are studied concerning other people, using descriptions of groups in which the subjects are not members. A typical task given to the subjects involves deciding on the split of profits when a group of young people have started a business together. Equity or distributive justice is then what the subjects judge to be a fair distribution of rewards and punishments.

When inputs have varied, an equal split that gives everybody the same amount of reward is simpler than a split proportionate to inputs. Debusschere and Van Avermaet (1984) find that both situational ambiguity and computational complexity lead to decreased quest for equity. There are situations when equality rather than equity can be expected (Walster and Walster, 1975: p. 28):

1. when there are time constraints,
2. when there are substantial costs of communication or negotiation,
3. when there are small potential benefits, given equity (if the sum to be split is small), and
4. when there is little significance for future decisions.

According to the same authors, women tend to be more affiliative in their motivation while men tend to be more assertive and anxious to succeed, especially in challenging tasks. There are some findings indicating that when women do better they favor an equal split and when they do worse an equitable division (see, e.g., Hastie, 1983; Carles and Carver, 1979). Attempts to explain these differences between women and men assume that there may be a difference between two types of relationships, exchange relationships vs. communal relationships: "equity principles may apply in market place or exchange relationships, but not in communal relationships, for example among members of a family" (Hastie, 1983: p. 530).

Some support for the last-mentioned idea is found in Greenberg (1983) who had subjects judge the relationship between two diners who either divided their restaurant checks equally or who paid for exactly what they ordered, i.e., split the check equitably. Those who made equal divisions were perceived as liking each other more, having a closer relationship, being better friends, and being more likely to see each other again than those who divided equitably.

A fundamental question relates to what principle the estimation of inputs is based on (cf. Törnblom, 1977). Many more or less conflicting principles suggest themselves:

1. skill, ability,
2. efforts,
3. investments of assets,
4. productivity, and
5. emotional consequences.

It is obvious that when, for example, equity of pay or income, or profit sharing is under debate, disagreement about what principle to employ for assessing the amount of input will lead to different perceptions of equity. Much of the turmoil and many of the crises in modern welfare states can be seen as instigated by questions of social equity. A pertinent question is what people think of as an equitable distribution of earnings and of taxes. There are some studies of the equity of income distributions (Jasso and Rossi, 1977; Alves and Rossi, 1978; Overlaet and Lagrou, 1981) and some of equity perceptions in tax systems (Lewis, 1982; Furnham and Lewis, 1986).

In two of the above studies, co-authored by Rossi, people were interviewed about their conceptions of fair pay to differently described income earners. Two dimensions were used: *need* which is defined as depending on household size and *merit* which is defined as based on occupation and education. Alves and Rossi (1978) find that both merit and need as defined in the study are important for judgments of equitable pay, but it is not possible to conclude that one is more important than the other. People with higher social status tended to favor merit more than respondents with lower status and the latter tended to favor need more than the former. The authors make rough estimates of what is considered fair pay (in U.S. dollars) for different categories of income earners. In one-person households, the average earner is considered to be fairly paid with an income of $ 19,900, in a husband-wife household a fair pay corresponds to $ 26,122. For a working poor the figures are $ 11,346 and $ 13,655 respectively, for the best merited $ 34,485 and $ 44,466 respectively. Discrepancies are thus accepted by the general public, but the ranges are smaller than in reality. A similar picture was found in the Belgian study by Overlaet and Lagrou (1981) who also conclude that people favor rather large discrepancies according to merit criteria, but on the average prefer more limited ranges than they think now exist.

7. THE MASS MEDIA AS MEDIATORS OF SOCIAL INFLUENCE

7.1. *The Functions of the Mass Media*

In modern societies most citizens spend considerable time every day with the mass media: the daily press, magazines, television, radio, books and movies. Today most of this time is spent with television which is not always actively watched. It is rather a matter of being present in a room where a television set is on most of the time. The average number of hours spent on watching television during one day varies somewhat from country to country. Low figures amount to 1.5-2 hours of daily viewing and high figures to 3-5 hours per day. It is no wonder then that questions are often asked about the effects of mass communication. There is of course no single or simple answer to such a complex question and the debate is often heated. I shall try to delineate some dimensions in this discussion that are of particular consequence for economic psychology. For a fuller treatment of research on mass communication effects, see Roberts and Bachen (1981).

The mass media effects include changes in economic behavior brought about, facilitated, or hampered through mass media influences. Economic information and advertising brought to the receiver/buyer through mass media is not the only way consumer and other economic behavior can be influenced. The mass media carry news about political, social, and cultural events and about people's behavior. Any kind of news may influence economic behavior by affecting expectations, aspirations, and values and under certain circumstances directly inspire actions. The roles of the mass media are often described as a number of functions which the mass media are assumed to serve (Wright, 1959; DeFleur, 1970):

1. surveillance of the environment,
2. interpretations of events and objects,
3. upholding of social norms; education, and
4. entertainment.

The *surveillance function* encompasses that the mass media report news so that people become aware of things and happenings that are of potential importance to them, especially when the news portends some danger. Partaking of news has for most people in modern societies become a well-established habit, almost a ritual. Through the selection of news items, the format of presentation and the editorial comments, the mass media can influence their audiences. While there are many debates over the actual influence on behavior what with the effect of the reported event itself what with the way of reporting it, there is nowadays consensus that the media strongly affect what is in the focus of interest during a given time period. This is referred to as "the agenda setting function" of the mass media. The latter more or less dictate what should be discussed among the audience.

The borderline between news reporting and *interpretations* is not easily drawn and is in practice often disregarded: The mass media mingle evaluations into their news reporting to varying extents. Some predominant theories of the press stress the importance of the distinction between facts and comments and the adherents of this philosophy try to uphold the distinction. Subjective journalism as a philosophy guiding journalistic work seems to have gained increased acceptance among journalists over the last decades or so. Adherents of subjective journalism maintain that since subjective evaluation of news starts already with the selection of news (so-called gate-keeping), no news reporting can be totally objective. Therefore it should be accepted that the message is also subjectively conceived, in particular if the message creator's own evaluations are clearly stated. So-called advocacy journalism is a case in point (Bagdikian, 1974). It is generally agreed that the journalist role has developed in the direction of growing professionalism and awareness of professional responsibilities (cf. Fjaestad and Holmlöv, 1977).

The mass media are assumed to reflect the *prevailing social norms*, tell people about those, and report on punishments for deviations from the norms as well as on rewards for achievements, give the recipients a chance for social learning through vicarious experience. They are important intermediaries of cultural influences and can serve purposes of social and economic development (Davison and Yu, 1974). Education in a somewhat broader sense than just representation of social norms is seen as an essential part of the social responsibility of the mass media.

Entertainment which serves the audience's need for variety, fun and pastimes is a much debated function of the mass media. While all the functions of the mass media can be served well or badly, in the latter case even becoming a dysfunction, the entertainment function has more often been accused of being almost exclusively dysfunctional. The mass media, in later years especially television, and now video cassettes have been the targets of very strong criticisms for providing entertainment (of varying quality) to the detriment of serving the other, more important functions, and for promoting violence through presenting violent contents.

7.2. *Mass Media and Economic Information*

The mass media have been compared to mirrors which reflect society in its multitude of aspects. The mass media would then be less independent instigators of change for good or evil than if they were independent sources of power and causal agents on their own. When such judgments are made, it is of course difficult to distinguish even on a theoretical level between the effects of certain news or certain facts per se and the effects of the circumstance that the report has been given a format and been disseminated to a large number of people through the mass media. It has been remarked that even if the mass media mainly serve as mirrors, they can select, emphasize, distort and dramatize what they mirror and thus manipulate or even delude their audiences. There is plenty of evidence of mass media influences on economic behavior, but the influences only occasionally seem to be dramatic.

Economic behavior is not only affected by economic stimuli, but also by other stimuli such as political and social events. When they are reported by the mass media, such stimuli can in some cases trigger immediate reactions from large groups of people. Economic and other information disseminated by the mass media can according to Katona (1975) give rise to similar expectations and similar actions within large segments of the population. Survey research which investigates how economic and other information is received and used by the general public is necessary for discovering and interpreting such effects. In rational expectations theory, public confidence in government policy makers is a rather crucial explanatory concept. It is likely that the mass media play a major role in increasing or decreasing such confidence (cf. Katona, 1980).

When small group research and mass communication research were brought together, the notion of indirect effects emerged (Katz and Lazarsfeld, 1955). The two-step flow of information hypothesis states that

1. information and opinion formation often flow first to opinion leaders and
2. from opinion leaders to followers who are members of the same primary or secondary small groups.

Based on studies of influences on voting behavior, food buying behavior, magazine reading and a few more, some characteristics of opinion leaders were established (Rogers and Shoemaker, 1971). While opinion leaders are still considered to be important in social influence studies, their role is not as clear as earlier thought. It may more be a matter of exchange of information and opinions among people who are specialized in different areas and who are generally highly active information seekers rather than actual opinion leadership. In the political arena the interest in opinion leaders of various types who relay opinions has decreased with the increased importance of television in political campaigns. Television gives a feeling of personal experience of political candidates which can give direct effects on voting according to many studies. In the consumer area, marketers at first developed a strong interest in finding opinion leaders who could be the first targets of the marketing efforts. While there is still some belief in the importance of getting the right persons to accept a new product first, the role of special influentials has been de-emphasized over the years.

7.3. *Advertising Effects*

As a rule with few exceptions mass media carry advertising. The exceptions are books (for some reason), television and radio in a few countries and some other, minor exceptions. Advertising is debated as a social influence on behavior and there are widely differing views of the economic effects of advertising. Advertising effects have been studied from three major angles:

1. macroeconomic effects,
2. effects on social norms, and
3. effects on individuals and groups.

In macroeconomic thinking advertising is usually judged from the viewpoint of how much information it carries. The judgments of advertising pronounced by economists are as a rule rather based on comparisons between the assumed effects of advertising contents and the effects that would occur if advertising behaved in accordance with an ideal model, derived from theories involving perfect competition. Advertising can contribute to market transparency if it provides the consumers with relevant and adequate information. Or it can increase the opaqueness of the market through fostering monopolistic tendencies. Brand loyalty stimulation means such a monopolistic attempt and is reprehensible especially when based on emotional appeals according to this thinking. The possibilities of actually assessing the effects of advertising at the macroeconomic level are slim. Psychological studies have so far not contributed much to this study, but it is conceivable that in the long run psychological studies of consumer use of advertising can furnish new material of interest (this topic is discussed in Wärneryd, 1986).

Advertising effects on social norms have not been directly studied empirically. There are, however, a few laboratory studies suggesting that children's values can be influenced by advertising (see Roberts and Bachen (1981) for a review). The major type of evidence for advertising effects on social norms is derived from content analyses of advertising. The latter type of study necessitates the assumption that there is a close correspondence between advertising contents and advertising effects. Evidence from psychological research on emotional and non-emotional appeals in communication indicates that this may be a rather tenuous assumption in many cases (see, e.g., Hovland et al., 1953). Content analyses of advertising tend to show that the norms displayed in advertising are the norms prevailing in society (see, e.g., Möller, 1970; Nowak and Andrén, 1982). In general, advertising does not deviate very much from what is commonly accepted in society. There is of course some advertising that is challenging or provocative, but characteristically it either attacks only superficial norms or it is aimed at a specific target group which is judged to be most amenable to that type of approach.

According to one line of reasoning, derived from some new social psychological theory, there is a definite possibility that advertising influences social norms. Branthwaite (1983: p. 33) has formulated the idea in this way:

> that advertising works not by its impact on specific individuals but by influencing the social climate in which action takes place. Advertising affects the shared ideas, common understandings and the social meaning of acts. Advertising does not change individuals as much as the social world in which they operate.

If this idea is applied to tobacco advertising, forbidding tobacco advertising which is an actual fact in many countries since a few years, may serve as stigmatization, suggesting that smoking is not totally socially desirable. Anti-smoking advertising like what was earlier, before the ban of tobacco advertising on U.S. television, mandatory in U.S. television, and cancer warnings on cigarette packages may not convert a single smoker but still be effective through strengthening the position of non-smokers and making them aware of their rights. Incidentally, cigarette smoking increased a little after the ban on tobacco advertising was introduced and anti-smoking television ads also disappeared (Teel et al., 1979). It is possible that, e.g., cigarette advertising or beer advertising can affect the social norms of youngsters so that they accept smoking or drinking without protest although they do not engage themselves in such activities.

Research on advertising effects at the individual level has often been guided by the most recent developments in psychological research. When communication theory, based on learning theory principles, was first developed by the Yale school, headed by Carl Hovland (see, e.g., Hovland et al., 1953), this type of thinking was eagerly adopted by advertising researchers. The latter became involved in the study of the persuasion process and also made contributions to the knowledge in the area of communication effects. After some years, research on the process of persuasion merged more or less with the study of attitude change. The latter is still an object of massive study both in social psychology and in the applied context of advertising (Cialdini et al., 1981; Kassarjian, 1982).

The learning approach to the study of advertising effects which was common in advertising research long before the Yale studies and known as the AIDA formula (Attention → Interest → Desire → Action) has been severely questioned, but still seems to prevail in advertising research for practical purposes. In recent years mass communication research has witnessed an upsurge of interest in the so-called uses-and-gratifications model (Katz et al., 1973; Roberts and Bachen, 1981: pp. 315 ff.). This model focusses on what the individual does with the mass media contents and what needs are gratified rather than on what the media do to the individual. Within advertising research similar ideas are found in discussions of the "hierarchy-of-effects" model which is tantamount to the AIDA formula. There is now some agreement that this model is hardly applicable to advertising for goods bought with low involvement (Ray, 1973; Ehrenberg, 1974).

Judging from the results of many empirical studies, the main effect of advertising is primarily to change market shares for brands while there is practically no evidence that advertising can increase consumption of the product. Econometric studies using advertising as an additional explanatory factor in explaining product consumption have usually not demonstrated any significant contribution to the amount of explained variance (see, e.g., Scitovsky, 1976: pp. 204-205). Advertising may all the same be a very important tool for marketing firms since they are usually interested in promoting their own brands rather than generic products.

8. TRENDS AND ISSUES IN RESEARCH ON SOCIAL INFLUENCE AND ECONOMIC BEHAVIOR

Economic behavior is like all other behavior exposed to social influence. This makes the economist's assumption of independence among household preferences seem problematic at least in some contexts. Social interaction and social influence through the mass media can apparently cause similarities in behavior within small groups as well as in larger social systems with the consequence that economic preferences change and behaviors that were earlier considered unlikely come to prevail in the marketplace. Social psychological research has furnished consumer behavior study with many of the hypotheses and methods that are considered fundamental in this study. Social influence, social interaction, causal attributions, attitude formation, and socialization are well-known and much used concepts in this field. Social psychology has had less influence on economic thinking outside of such aspects of the consumer behavior area that are especially related to marketing of goods and services or public consumer policy. Already Tarde (1902) pointed out that social interaction and social influence should be considered in economic studies.

There are certainly many explanations why economic theory finds little use for social psychology. Part of the explanation can be found in the way economic theory is used to study mainly phenomena at an aggregate level where many distinctions and differences that are important at the individual and small group level cancel out. Part of the explanation can be found in the way social psychology is pursued. The remaining part of this chapter will deal with some ideas relating to the latter issue. One idea pertains to the recent discussion of methods and approaches in social psychology, the other has to do with problem areas which can perhaps develop into something of particular interest for the study of economic behavior.

Social psychology in general and experimental social psychology in particular have been severely attacked by critics for their assumed lack of reality orientation and for not treating subjects/respondents as human beings (see, e.g., Harré and Secord, 1972; Gergen, 1982). Many critics have exhorted researchers to study actual social problems under realistic conditions. Cialdini (1980) made a plea for such studies as part of what he called "full-cycle social psychology." Following his own advice, he spent a long time working as a salesman and in other professional persuader roles while preparing his book on "persuasion" (1985).

Critics emphasize that the variables used in social psychological research must be complex since social reality is complex and tends to become even more complex. It can consequently not be studied experimentally. "The fruits of such experimentation provide only partial knowledge and understanding of social behavior in life situations. Phenomena in open systems require knowledge of additional conditions and contexts, and frequently biographical/historical knowledge as well" (Manicas and Secord, 1983: p. 409). Similar ideas on the proper object of study have been expressed by other authors. Pepitone (1981) concludes his review of the history of social psychology with an emphasis on social psychology as a social science:

> The most important influence on human social behavior is the human social environment. There are two related but conceptually distinct parts: social structures and normative dynamic systems. The former includes group formations and organizations in which individuals exist: family, kinship, roles, hierarchies, communication nets, and so on. Normative systems include all the values and beliefs that groups establish and maintain to affect the behavior of members (p. 983).

Protagonists of social psychology have defended the selection of problems, the theories produced, and the methods employed in social psychological laboratory experiments. They provide arguments for the use of the laboratory experiment involving that laboratory experiments make it feasible to study many problems in simple, flexible and inexpensive ways (Berkowitz and Donnerstein, 1982). It is possible to develop and test theory under conditions which permit a large amount of control and of efficiency. According to this line of reasoning, the intention behind laboratory experiments is not to make immediate generalizations of research results to situations outside the laboratory, but to develop theory which can then be tested on actual social situations (Mook, 1983).

If social psychological research in certain areas is brought closer to social reality, it is conceivable that it can deliver results of more potential interest to economists than at present. This does not imply that laboratory experiments should be given up. On the contrary, theory development of a rather strict kind seems necessary, but subsequent, deliberate testing on social reality through field research is inevitable. The studies must embrace both individual variables and variables relating to the social and economic system. The research results must be put into an economic context and be characterized by methodological rigor. Otherwise they will at best be treated as mere curiosities.

Against the background of criticism hitting social psychology, it is hazardous to select a certain type of primarily laboratory studies and pronounce that it is trendsetting and of particular importance. I would wager to claim that the area which could be called "social dilemmas" (Dawes, 1980) is one of the most interesting areas for economic psychology as far as social psychological contributions to the study of economic behavior is concerned. A rich literature reporting theories and experiments is emerging in this area.

Social dilemmas are characterized by choice situations in which individuals can choose between cooperating socially or pursuing an immediate personal gain. Each individual receives a higher pay off for a socially defecting choice than for a socially cooperative choice, but all individuals will be better off if they cooperate than if all defect. This type of problem which is becoming well-known, for example in environmental economics and analysis of competition within strategic management, is often referred to as the problem of the commons (see, e.g., Edney, 1980). The label comes from a parable proposed by the biologist Hardin (1968). A commons to which all members of a village can take their cattle for grazing can be sufficient and in a state of equilibrium if everybody observes some restraint. If in a state of balanced grazing, somebody increases his/her herd by one cow, s/he can profit while the collective suffers from a decline in total grazing. If another follows the example, the collective effects will become even worse, because the regeneration rate will become even more insufficient. A single individual may win at the expense of others, but if all act in the same uncooperative way they will all lose in the end. Social dilemmas of this kind have definite similarities with the problems that the economist Mancur Olson (1965) brought to public attention in the 1960s: the provision of public goods and free-riding tendencies.

A similar problem concerns the balancing of short-run gains against long-run ill effects which will not appear until after a long delay, sometimes generations later. Platt (1973) calls such phenomena "social traps" and proposes a model based on reinforcement theory for explaining these and possibly remedying them. Edney (1980) reviews some additional theories and discusses suggested solutions to the problems, none of which appear promising for a wide range of situations. Many problems in modern societies are similar to the commons problem: air and water pollution, energy conservation, having additional children in overpopulated countries (Dawes, 1980). Maital (1982) maintains that economic problems like inflation and tax evasion can be explained in terms of the commons problem and he suggests that the solution of this type of problem presupposes a different kind of education and socialization of children, making them more cooperative and less competitive.

A second problem area of great interest to economic psychology concerns social comparisons in economic matters and feelings of social equity. In the modern welfare states, there have been pronounced tendencies towards doing away with discriminations of all kinds and promoting equality. A well-known example is given by the attempts to level the income distribution through progressive taxation. In studies of tax evasion the concept of social equity (or rather social inequity) has turned out to have some explanatory power (Spicer and Becker, 1980; Wärneryd and Walerud, 1982).

There are obviously limits to the degree of equality that can be obtained in a society. Critics of advanced welfare states point to the necessity of providing individual incentives for creative contributions to the welfare of the society. One may think of incentives for saving (which lead to unequal distribution of wealth if everybody does not save the same amount), incentives in terms of high prizes to make people participate in legal, national lotteries and so on. The social psychological study of social comparison processes could be given an important role for elucidating how people compare themselves with others and how equality and equity principles are perceived and valued. This could be of relevance to the construction of taxation systems. Further studies in the area of income evaluation, taking into account also the income distribution and social justice aspects would seem to be highly relevant in this context.

Social influence on economic behavior will no doubt change in the years to come as a consequence of the fact that the potentialities of the presently available communication technology will be more and more utilized. Some channels of social influence, e.g., the mass media in the traditional sense will probably have less significance than now as a consequence of the successively increasing possibilities for the receivers to select and also create their own communication channels. There will be fragmentation of audiences and mass audiences will more rarely be reached with the same messages at the same time. New channels and old channels with added functions such as powerful combinations of microcomputers and telecommunications will enable people to make new social contacts and give new contents to old contacts, but may also serve to impoverish social networks. It will be a challenge for economic psychologists to study the consequences for economic behavior and thus follow up the early work of the British Communications Study Group (see Short et al., 1976).

REFERENCES

Aldous, J., 1977, Family interaction patterns, Annual Review of Sociology, 3, 105-135.

Alves, W., and P. Rossi, 1978, Who should get what? Fairness judgments of the distribution of earnings, American Journal of Sociology, 84, 541-564.

Bagdikian, B.H., 1974, "Professional personnel and organizational structure in the mass media," in: W.P. Davison and F.T.C. Yu (eds.), Mass Communication Research: Major Issues and Future Directions, New York: Praeger, pp. 122-142.

Bandura, A., 1977, Social Learning Theory, Englewood Cliffs, NJ: Prentice-Hall.

Becker, G.S., 1981, A Treatise on the Family, Cambridge, MA: Harvard University Press.

Berk, R.A., and S.F. Berk, 1983, Supply-side sociology of the family: The challenge of the new home economics, Annual Review of Sociology, 9, 375-395.

Berkowitz, L., and E. Donnerstein, 1982, External validity is more than skin deep. Some answers to criticisms of laboratory experiments, American Psychologist, 37, 245-257.

Berti, A., A. Bombi, and A. Lis, 1982, The child's conceptions about means of production and their owners, European Journal of Social Psychology, 12, 221-239.

Branthwaite, A., 1983, Situations and social actions: Applications for marketing of recent theories in social psychology, Journal of the Market Research Society, 25, 19-38.

Brislin, R.W., 1983, Cross-cultural research in psychology, Annual Review of Psychology, 34, 363-400.

Brody, N., 1980, Social motivation, Annual Review of Psychology, 31, 143-168.

Carles, E.M., and C.S. Carver, 1979, Effects of person salience versus role salience on reward allocation in a dyad, Journal of Personality and Social Psychology, 37, 2071-2080.

Cialdini, R.B., 1980, "Full-cycle social psychology," in: L. Bickman (ed.), Applied Social Psychology Annual, Vol. 1, London and Beverly Hills, CA: Sage Publications, pp. 21-47.

Cialdini, R.B., 1985, Influence: Science and Practice, Glenview, IL: Scott and Foresman.

Cialdini, R.B., R.E. Petty, and J.T. Cacioppo, 1981, Attitudes and attitude change, Annual Review of Psychology, 32, 357-404.

Cottrell, N.B., 1972, "Social facilitation," in: G.C. McClintock (ed.), Experimental Social Psychology, New York: Holt, Rinehart and Winston, pp. 185-236.

Crittenden, K.S., 1983, Sociological aspects of attribution, Annual Review of Sociology, 9, 425-446.

Cummings, S., and D. Taebel, 1978, The economic socialization of children: A neo-Marxist analysis, Social Problems, 26, 198-210.

Cyert, R.M., and J.G. March, 1963, A Behavioral Theory of the Firm, Englewood Cliffs, NJ: Prentice-Hall.

Davis, H.L., 1976, Decision making within the household, Journal of Consumer Research, 2, 241-260.

Dawes, R.M., 1980, Social dilemmas, Annual Review of Psychology, 31, 169-193.

Debusschere, M., and E. van Avermaet, 1984, Compromising between equity and equality: The effects of situational ambiguity and computational complexity, European Journal of Social Psychology, 14, 323-333.

DeFleur, M.L., 1970, Theories of Mass Communication, New York: David McKay Company (second edition).
Deutsch, M., 1975, Equity, equality, and need: What determines which value will be used as the basis of distributive justice?, Journal of Social Issues, 31, 137-149.
DiRenzo, G.J., 1977, Socialization, personality, and social systems, Annual Review of Sociology, 3, 261-295.
Duesenberry, J.S., 1949, Income, Saving and Theory of Consumer Behavior, Cambridge, MA: Harvard University Press.
Edney, J.J., 1980, The commons problem. Alternative perspectives, American Psychologist, 35, 131-150.
Ehrenberg, A.S.C., 1974, Repetitive advertising and the consumer, Journal of Advertising Research, 14, 25-34.
Elder, G.H., 1974, Children of the Great Depression, Chicago, IL: University of Chicago Press.
Engel, J.F., R.D. Blackwell, and P.W. Miniard, 1986, Consumer Behavior, Hinsdale, IL: The Dryden Press (fifth edition).
Euro-Barometer, 1986, Brussels: Commission of the European Communities, no. 25, June.
Festinger, L., 1954, A theory of social comparison processes, Human Relations, 7, 117-140.
Fjaestad, B., and P.G. Holmlöv, 1976, The journalists' view, Journal of Communication, 26, 108-114.
Folkes, V.S., 1984, Consumer reactions to product failure: An attributional approach, Journal of Consumer Research, 11, 398-409.
Furby, L., 1979, Inequalities in personal possessions: Explanations for and judgments about unequal distribution, Human Development, 22, 180-202.
Furnham, A., and A. Lewis, 1986, The Economic Mind. The Social Psychology of Economic Behavior, Brighton, Sussex, UK: Wheatsheaf.
Gergen, K., 1982, Toward Transformation in Social Knowledge, New York: Springer Verlag.
Granovetter, M., 1973, The strength of weak ties, American Journal of Sociology, 78, 1360-1380.
Green, R.T., J.-P. Leonardi, J.-L. Chandon, I.C.M. Cunningham, B.J. Verhage, and A. Strazzieri, 1983, Societal development and family purchasing roles: A cross-national study, Journal of Consumer Research, 9, 436-442.
Greenberg, J., 1983, Equity and equality as clues to the relationship between exchange participants, European Journal of Social Psychology, 13, 195-196.
Hardin, G., 1968, The tragedy of the commons, Science, 162, 1243-1248.
Harré, R., and P.F. Secord, 1972, The Explanation of Social Behavior, Oxford, UK: Basil Blackwell.
Harris, R.J., 1979, Equity judgments in hypothetical, four-person partnerships, Journal of Experimental Social Psychology, 16, 96-115.
Harvey, J.H., and G. Weary, 1984, Current issues in attribution theory and research, Annual Review of Psychology, 35, 427-459.
Hastie, R., 1983, Social inference, Annual Review of Psychology, 34, 511-542.
Heider, F., 1958, The Psychology of Interpersonal Relations, New York: Wiley.
Hempel, D.J., 1974, Family buying decisions: A cross-cultural perspective, Journal of Marketing Research, 11, 295-302.
Herskovits, M., 1948, Man and his Works, New York: Knopf.
Hofstede, G., 1980, Culture's Consequences. International Differences in Work-related Values, Beverly Hills, CA: Sage.
Hovland, C.I., I.L. Janis, and H.H. Kelley, 1953, Communication and Persuasion, New Haven, CT: Yale University Press.
Inkeles, A., and D. Smith, 1974, Becoming Modern. Individual Change in Six Developing Countries, Cambridge, MA: Harvard University Press.

Jahoda, G., 1979, The construction of economic reality by some Glaswegian children, European Journal of Social Psychology, 9, 115-127.
Jahoda, G., 1981, The development of thinking about economic institutions: The bank, Cahiers de Psychologie Cognitive, 1, 55-73.
Janis, I.L., 1972, Victims of Groupthink: A Psychological Study of Foreign-policy Decisions and Fiascoes, Boston, MA: Houghton Mifflin.
Jasso, G., and P. Rossi, 1977, Distributive justice and earned income, American Sociological Review, 42, 639-651.
Jundin, S., 1983, Barns uppfattning om konsumtion, sparande och arbete (Children's Conceptions About Consumption, Saving and Work), Stockholm, The Stockholm School of Economics, EFI, (doctoral dissertation, English summary).
Kassarjian, H.H., 1982, Consumer psychology, Annual Review of Psychology, 33, 619-649.
Katona, G., 1975, Psychological Economics, New York: Elsevier.
Katona, G., 1980, Essays on Behavioral Economics, Ann Arbor, MI: Institute for Social Research.
Katz, D., 1937, Animals and Men: Studies in Comparative Psychology, London: Longmans.
Katz, E., M. Gurevitch, and H. Haas, 1973, On the use of the mass media for important things, American Sociological Review, 38, 164-181.
Katz, E., and P.F. Lazarsfeld, 1955, Personal Influence. The Part Played by People in the Flow of Mass Communications, Glencoe, IL: The Free Press.
Kelley, H.H., 1952, "Two functions of reference groups," in: G. Swanson, T.M. Newcomb, and E.L. Hartley (eds.), Readings in Social Psychology, New York: Henry Holt and Company, pp. 410-414.
Kelley, H.H., 1967, "Attribution theory in social psychology," in: D. Levine (ed.), Nebraska Symposium on Motivation, Vol. 15, Lincoln, NB: University of Nebraska Press, pp. 192-238.
Kelley, H.H., 1973, The process of causal attribution, American Psychologist, 28, 107-128.
Kelley, H.H., and J.L. Michela, 1980, Attribution theory and research, Annual Review of Psychology, 31, 457-501.
Kelman, H.C., 1961, Processes of opinion change, Public Opinion Quarterly, 25, 57-78.
Keynes, J.M., 1936, The General Theory of Employment, Interest and Money, London: The MacMillan Press.
Latané, B., 1981, The psychology of social impact, American Psychologist, 36, 343-356.
Lefcourt, H.M. (ed.), 1984, Research with the Locus of Control Construct. Extensions and Limitations, Vol. 3, Orlando, FL: Academic Press.
Leibenstein, H., 1950, Bandwagon, snob, and Veblen effects in the theory of consumer demand, Quarterly Journal of Economics, 64, 183-207.
Leiser, D., 1983, Children's conceptions of economics. The constitution of a cognitive domain, Journal of Economic Psychology, 4, 297-317.
Lewis, A., 1982, The Psychology of Taxation, Oxford: Martin Robertson.
Liu, W.T., and R.W. Duff, 1972, Strength of weak ties, Public Opinion Quarterly, 36, 361-366.
Manicas, P.T., and P.F. Secord, 1983, Implications for psychology of the new philosophy of science, American Psychologist, 38, 399-413.
Mead, G.H., 1934, Mind, Self, and Society, Chicago, IL: Chicago University Press.
Merton, R.K., 1962, Social Theory and Social Structure, Glencoe, IL: The Free Press (revised edition).
Merton, R.K., and A.S. Kitt, 1952, "Contributions to the theory of reference-group behavior," in: G. Swanson, T.M. Newcomb, and E.L. Hartley (eds.), Readings in Social Psychology, New York: Henry Holt, pp. 430-444.
Miller, D., M.F.R. Kets de Vries, and J.-M. Toulouse, 1982, Top-executive locus of control and its relationship to strategy-making, structure, and environment, Academy of Management Journal, 25, 237-253.

Miller, N.E., and J. Dollard, 1941, Social Learning and Imitation, New Haven, CT: Yale University Press.
Möller, C., 1970, Gesellschaftliche Funktionen der Konsumwerbung, Stuttgart, FRG: C.E. Poeschel Verlag.
Mook, D.G., 1983, In defense of external invalidity, American Psychologist, 38, 379-387.
Moschis, G.P., and G.A. Churchill, Jr., 1975, Consumer socialization: A theoretical and empirical analysis, Journal of Marketing Research, 15, 599-609.
Ng, S.H., 1983, Children's ideas about the bank and shop profit: Developmental stages and the influence of cognitive contrasts and conflict, Journal of Economic Psychology, 4, 209-221.
Ng, S.H., 1985, Children's ideas about the bank: A New Zealand replication, European Journal of Social Psychology, 15, 121-123.
Nowak, K., and G. Andrén, 1982, Reklam och samhällsförändring: Variation och konstans i svenska populärpressannonser 1950-1975, (Advertising and Social Change: Variation and Constancy in Swedish Magazine Advertisements 1950-1975), Lund, Sweden: Student-litteratur.
Olson, M., 1965, The Logic of Collective Action. Public Goods and the Theory of Groups, Cambridge, MA: Harvard University Press.
Overlaet, B., and L. Lagrou, 1981, Attitudes towards a redistribution of income, Journal of Economic Psychology, 1, 197-215.
Payne, J.W., D.J. Laughhuhn, and R. Crum, 1980, Translation of gambles and aspiration level effects in risky choice behavior, Management Science, 26, 1039-1060.
Pepitone, A., 1981, Lessons from the history of social psychology, American Psychologist, 36, 972-985.
Platt, J., 1973, Social traps, American Psychologist, 28, 641-651.
Ray, M.L., 1973, Marketing Communication and the Hierarchy-of-effects, Cambridge, MA: Marketing Science Institute (working paper).
Rijsman, J.B., 1974, Factors in social comparison of performance influencing actual performance, European Journal of Social Psychology, 4, 279-311.
Roberts, D.F., and C.M. Bachen, 1981, Mass communication effects, Annual Review of Psychology, 32, 307-356.
Robertson, T.S., 1971, Innovative Behavior and Communication, New York: Holt, Rinehart and Winston.
Rogers, E.M., 1976, New product adoption and diffusion, Journal of Consumer Research, 2, 290-301.
Rogers, E.M., and R. Agarwala-Rogers, 1976, Communication in Organizations, New York: The Free Press.
Rogers, E.M., and F.F. Shoemaker, 1971, Communication of Innovations: A Cross-cultural Approach, New York: The Free Press.
Rotter, J.B., 1966, Generalized expectancies of internal versus external control of reinforcement, Psychological Monographs 80, no. 609.
Runciman, W.G., 1966, Relative Deprivation and Social Justice: A Study of Attitudes to Social Inequality in Twentieth-century England (reprint: 1972, Harmondsworth, Middlesex, UK: Penguin Books).
Schein, E.H., 1984, Coming to a new awareness of organizational culture, Sloan Management Review, 25, 2, 3-16.
Scitovsky, T., 1976, The Joyless Economy, New York: Oxford University Press.
Short, J., E. Williams, and B. Christie, 1976, The Social Psychology of Telecommunications, London: John Wiley.
Sieber, S.D., 1974, Toward a theory of role accumulation, American Sociological Review, 39, 567-578.

Siegel, S., 1957, Level of aspiration and decision making, Psychological Review, 64, 253-262.
Simon, H.A., 1957, Models of Man: Social and Rational, New York: Wiley.
Spicer, M.W., and L.A. Becker, 1980, Fiscal inequity and tax evasion: An experimental approach, National Tax Journal, 33, 171-176.
Stacey, B.G., 1982, Economic socialization in the pre-adult years, British Journal of Social Psychology, 21, 159-173
Stafford, J.E., and A.B. Cocanougher, 1981, "Reference group theory," in: H.H. Kassarjian and T.S. Robertson (eds.), Perspectives in Consumer Behavior, Glenview, IL: Scott Foresman, pp. 329-343 (third edition).
Starbuck, W., 1963, Level of aspiration, Psychological Review, 70, 51-60.
Stroebe, W., and B.S. Frey, 1982, Self-interest and collective action: The economics and psychology of public goods, British Journal of Social Psychology, 21, 121-137.
Tarde, G., 1902, La psychologie économique, Paris: Alcan (2 volumes).
Teel, S.J., J.E. Teel, and W.O. Bearden, 1979, Lessons learned from the broadcast cigarette advertising ban, Journal of Marketing, 43, 45-50.
Törnblom, K.Y., 1977, Distributive justice: Typology and propositions, Human Relations, 30, 1-24.
Triandis, H.C., 1980, "Introduction to Handbook of Cross-cultural Psychology," in: H.C. Triandis and W.W. Lambert (eds.), Handbook of Cross-cultural Psychology. Perspectives, Vol. 1, Boston, MA: Allyn and Bacon, pp. 1-14.
Van Raaij, W.F., 1986, "Causal attributions in economic behavior," in: A.J. MacFadyen and H.W. MacFadyen (eds.), Economic Psychology: Intersections in Theory and Application, Amsterdam, Elsevier, pp. 353-379.
Veblen, T., 1899, The Theory of the Leisure Class, New York: Mentor Books (MD 93).
Verhallen, T.M.M., 1984, Scarcity: Unavailability and Behavioral Costs, Tilburg, The Netherlands: Tilburg University (doctoral dissertation).
Walster, E., and G.W. Walster, 1975, Equity and social justice, Journal of Social Issues, 31, 21-43.
Ward, S., and D.B. Wackman, 1973, Effects of Television Advertising on Consumer Socialization, Cambridge, MA: Marketing Science Institute.
Ward, S., D.B. Wackman, and E. Wartella, 1975, Children Learning to Buy: The Development of Consumer Information Processing Skills, Cambridge, MA: Marketing Science Institute.
Ward, S., T.S. Robertson, and R. Brown, 1986, Commercial Television and European Children – An International Research Digest, Epping, Essex, UK: Gower Publishing Company.
Wärneryd, K.-E., 1986, "Advertising and consumer behavior," in: B. Gilad and S. Kaish (eds.), Handbook of Behavioral Economics, Vol. A, Greenwich, CT: JAI Press, pp. 89-126.
Wärneryd, K.-E., and B. Walerud, 1982, Taxes and economic behavior: Some interview data on tax evasion in Sweden, Journal of Economic Psychology, 2, 187-211.
Weick, K.E., 1971, "Group processes, family processes, and problem solving," in: J. Aldous, T. London, R. Hill, M. Straus, and I. Tallman (eds.), Family Problem Solving: A Symposium on Theoretical, Methodological, and Substantive Concerns, Hinsdale, IL: Dryden Press, pp. 3-32.
Weiner, B., 1985, An attributional theory of achievement motivation and emotion, Psychological Review, 92, 548-573.
Weiner, B., I. Frieze, A. Kukla, L. Reed, S. Rest, and R.M. Rosenbaum, 1972, "Perceiving the causes of success and failure," in: E.E. Jones, D.E. Kanouse, H.H. Kelley, R.E. Nisbett, S. Valins, and B. Weiner (eds.), Attribution: Perceiving the Causes of Behavior, Morristown, NJ: General Learning Press, pp. 95-120.
Whyte, W.H., Jr., 1954, The web of word of mouth, Fortune, 50, no. 5, 140-3, 204,6,8,10,12.

Wright, C., 1959, Mass Communication: A Sociological Perspective, New York: Random House.
Wrightsman, L.S., 1977, Social Psychology, Monterey, CA: Brooks/Cole Publishing Company (second brief edition).
Zajonc, R.B., 1965, Social facilitation, Science, 149, 269-274.
Zaltman, G., and M. Wallendorf, 1983, Consumer Behavior: Basic Findings and Management Implications, New York: John Wiley.

Part II

Household Economic Behaviour

Introduction to Part II: Consumer Behavior

CONSUMER BEHAVIOR

Too Much Consumer Behavior?

Consumer behavior is certainly the most intensively investigated part of economic psychology, due to the interest of marketing scholars, marketing researchers and managers. Many textbooks entitled Consumer or Buyer Behavior exist; these textbooks show a remarkable similarity in their contents and structure. The *Consumer Behavior* textbooks are often modeled after the successful book by Engel, Kollat, and Blackwell, of which the first edition appeared in 1968. The seventeen most familiar textbooks are the ones by Assael (1987), Engel, Blackwell, and Miniard (1985), Hansen (1972), Harrell (1986), Horton (1984), Loudon and Della Bitta (1984), Markin (1974), Mellott (1983), Mowen (1987), Reynolds and Wells (1977), Robertson, Zielinski, and Ward (1984), Runyon and Stewart (1987), Schiffman and Kanuk (1987), Sternthal and Craig (1982), Williams (1982), Wilkie (1986), Zaltman and Wallendorf (1983). Even more textbooks are now being prepared, mainly for the large market of consumer behavior courses at North-American universities.

Next to textbooks, scientific journals populate the bookshelves of consumer behavior researchers and marketing practitioners. We note the *Journal of Consumer Research*, *Psychology and Marketing*, and many marketing journals that publish articles on consumer behavior, e.g. the *Journal of Marketing Research*, *Marketing Science*, the *Journal of Advertising Research*, the *Journal of Advertising*, the *Journal of Marketing*, *Marketing Science*, the *European Journal of Marketing*, the *Journal of the Market Research Society*, the *International Journal for Research in Marketing*, and the *Journal of Retailing*.

The journals mentioned above have a marketing and/or advertising

Van Raaij, W.F., van Veldhoven, G.M. and Wärneryd, K.E. (eds) Handbook of Economic Psychology. ISBN 90-247-3720-6.

perspective in common. The *Journal of Economic Psychology* has a broader perspective on economic behavior, including consumer behavior. Psychological journals occasionally publish consumer studies, e.g. the *Journal of Applied Psychology*, and the *Journal of Personality and Social Psychology*. Economics and business journals publish consumer studies as well, e.g. the *American Economic Review*, and the *Journal of Business*, *Journal of Business Research*, and *Management Science*.

Finally, there are two journals with a consumer protection and policy perspective, the *Journal of Consumer Affairs* in North-America, and the *Journal of Consumer Policy* in Europe.

Too much research has been done in this area, for us to have the illusion that we could completely cover "consumer behavior" in this handbook. With only three chapters we just cover some aspects, although we are confident that these aspects are important ones.

Historical Developments

In the early ages micro-economics was the first systematic approach to the study of consumer behavior. It started from the assumptions of rationality, well-informedness, and utility maximization. Although the economic approach brought us some explanations, e.g. the Engel curves, price and income elasticities, practitioners became dissatisfied with the explanatory power of micro-economic models. Many aspects of consumer behavior, especially the motives and reasons behind this behavior, remained in the dark. Some anomalies, such as price as an indicator of quality, price thresholds, or unstable preferences, puzzled the hard-core micro-economist, but couldn't easily be explained in an economic framework.

In the late 1950s and early 1960s "motivation research" (Dichter, 1964) seemed to fill this knowledge gap. Motivation research had a clinical-psychological background. Consumer behavior was explained by unconscious, often sexual motives, as compensations for sexual deprivations or as sexual symbols.

The 1960s were characterized by partial theories, covering an aspect of consumer behavior, using one or a few concepts, e.g. perceived risk. It was a single-construct approach. Advertising recall was studied, as well as the diffusion of innovations. Personality measurement was also popular, using psychological tests to differentiate between types of consumers and corresponding product purchases.

In the late sixties, we saw the development of "grand theories", covering a variety of determinants and their interrelationships. Friedman discusses these grand theories in Chapter 9. The grand theories mainly had the function of an inventory of what was known about consumer behavior in those years, and provided a state of the art, checklist, and source of creative ideas for the scientist and the practitioner.

The 1970s was the period of the cognitive approach: consumer decision making rules and processes were studied. Herbert Simon's studies on human problem solving were very influential for this development. Concepts such as decision networks, cognitive algebra, information overload, consumer purposeful and incidental learning, and computer simulations were popular. This period was concluded with Bettman's book on consumer information processing (1979). Friedman discusses Bettman's model as well. Parallel to the cognitive approach in consumer behavior, we observed a "cognitivistic" approach to the study of attitudes and attitude-behavior relationships in the Fishbein-Ajzen model of reasoned action.

The 1980s seem to become the period of the study of "emotion": The role of affect (mood, arousal) in consumer behavior. Opportunism is everywhere, but especially in consumer behavior research. Many researchers are now attracted by studies on mood, attitude toward the ad, and affective conditioning. Time will teach us, whether this observation is correct.

New Developments

Consumer behavior research may be criticized in many respects. It is not developed in a balanced way with emphasis on the many aspects. Some aspects are much further developed than others. We will mention eight developments for a healthy developments of consumer behavior, we should welcome in the near future.

Many consumer behavior studies have a narrow focus on purchase processes from a marketing perspective only. A broader focus should include the *complete consumption cycle*: purchase, usage, maintenance, and disposition of the goods. Pinson and Roberto describe in Chapter 8 the consumer behavior research from a marketing perspective, although they include product usage as well. Van Raaij and Verhallen discuss in Chapter 18 product usage, maintenance, and disposition in relation to resource conservation.

Too little is known of the *generic decision-making* of consumers. How do consumers allocate their budget for major categories, such as food, clothing, recreation, transportation, and saving? From a societal perspective it is more interesting to know, how consumer spending and saving patterns develop than which brand of soft drink is most perferred.

Consumer behavior with regard to the *public sector* should be developed, along with the knowledge on consumer behavior in the private sector. In a mixed economy, such as in the European countries, the collective sector provides for many services. How do consumers evaluate these services, if no price or a reduced price is to be paid?

The marketing perspective on consumer behavior should be more often complemented by the *consumer policy perspective*. Consumer organizations and governments, better business bureaus and consumer affairs departments of firms are interested in research on consumer behavior as well. Studies on consumer satisfaction and dissatisfaction and complaining behavior are often initiated from a consumer policy perspective.

The consumer policy perspective should include *"quality of life"*, the environmental and external effects of consumption: The conservation of raw materials and energy, the preservation of nature, and the avoidance of noise pollution.

Cross-cultural and *comparative* studies on consumer behavior should complement the studies done in the Western world. It is unlikely that we could generalize the findings of North-American and Western-European studies to consumer behavior in developing and socialist countries. In these countries scarcity of goods and problems of distribution play a crucial role, rather than, for instance, brand choice in the western supermarket.

Already mentioned is the broadening of the cognitive perspective to include *affective factors*. Chapter 2 by Van Raaij is an example of the cognitive approach, whereas Pieters and Van Raaij discuss in Chapter 6 the role of affect and the cognitive-affective interface. The recognition of the role of affect is a valuable improvement in the understanding and explanation of consumer behavior.

The focus has been too often on the individual consumer, as if consumers are isolated information processors. It is more and more recognized that most consumers live in small groups, called *households* or families, and that the partners decide together about another car or the next summer vacation. Kirchler discusses in Chapter 7 the decision processes in households.

Kirchler concludes in Chapter 7 that the research on household decision making is still in its infancy. Although many studies exist on group decisions, only a few employed the household as a group. The family is a unique group, relatively permanent because of the affective ties between the members. Marital roles in spending pertain to autonomous versus joint decisions, bargaining and conflict management between the partners. Kirchler categorizes the studies on family decision making in three classes: studies on role division, process dynamics, and outcomes. Role division is relatively well studied, whereas process dynamics are underresearched, probably because of the inherent measurement difficulties.

Pinson and Roberto describe the consumer orientation in the marketing of firms: product positioning, market segmentation. They structure Chapter 8 along the marketing mix factors: product, price, promotion (mass communication), and distribution. Consumer perception and evaluation of products, decision rules, and price sensitivity are discussed. The marketing communication process is connected with consumer information processing. Consumer shopping behavior is related to the distribution strategy of firms.

Friedman reviews in Chapter 9 the "grand models" of consumer choice behavior. These models try to be comprehensive by integrating the research findings of explanatory variables that in-fluence consumer choice. Sometimes these models stimulate further research by opening up new research avenues. The grand models were not borrowed from the social sciences, as was done in the years before, but exclusively developed for consumer behavior research. Friedman reviews the models of Andreasen (1965), Nicosia (1966), Howard and Sheth (1969), Engel, Kollat, and Blackwell (1968), later Engel, Blackwell, and Miniard (1985), and the information-processing model by Bettman (1979). He concludes that these models are still very much marketing oriented; and that more work should be done to develop models that include spending and saving, time use, and product usage and satisfaction.

W. Fred van Raaij

REFERENCES

Andreasen, A.R., 1965, "Attitudes and customer behavior", in: L.E. Preston (ed.), New Research in Marketing, CA: Berkeley: University of California, pp. 1-16.

Arndt, J., 1976, Reflections on research in consumer behavior, Advances in Consumer Research, 3, 213-221.

Assael, H., 1987, Consumer Behavior and Marketing Action, Boston, MA: Kent (third edition).

Bettman, J.R., 1979, An Information-Processing Theory of Consumer Choice, Reading, MA: Addison-Wesley.

Dichter, E., 1964, Handbook of Consumer Motivations, New York: McGraw-Hill.

Engel, J.F., R.D. Blackwell, and P.W. Miniard, 1985, Consumer Behavior, Chicago, IL: The Dryden Press (fifth edition).

Hansen, F., 1972, Consumer Choice Behavior. A Cognitive Theory, New York: The Free Press.

Harrell, G.D., 1986, Consumer Behavior, San Diego, CA: Harcourt, Brace, Jovanovich.

Horton, R.L., 1984, Buyer Behavior, Columbus, OH: Charles E. Merrill.

Howard, J.A., and J.N. Sheth, 1969, The Theory of Buyer Behavior, New York: John Wiley.

Loudon, D.L., and A.J. Della Bitta, 1984, Consumer Behavior. Concepts and Applications, New York: McGraw-Hill (second edition).

Markin, R.J., Jr., 1974, Consumer Behavior: A Cognitive Orientation, New York: Macmillan.

Mellott, D.W., 1983, Fundamentals of Consumer Behavior, Tulsa, OK: PennWell Books.

Mowen, J.C., 1987, Consumer Behavior, New York: Macmillan.

Nicosia, F.M., 1966, Consumer Decision Processes: Marketing and Advertising Implications Englewood Cliffs, NJ: Prentice-Hall.

Reynolds, F.D., and W.D. Wells, 1977, Consumer Behavior, New York: McGraw-Hill.

Robertson, T.S., J. Zielinski, and S. Ward, 1984, Consumer Behavior, Glenview, IL: Scott, Foresman and Company.

Runyon, K.E., and D.W. Stewart, 1987, Consumer Behavior, Columbus, OH: Merrill (third edition).

Schiffman, L.G., and L.L. Kanuk, 1987, Consumer Behavior, Englewood Cliffs, NJ: Prentice-Hall (third edition).

Sternthal, B., and C.S. Craig, 1982, Consumer Behavior: An Information Processing Perspective, Englewood Cliffs, NJ: Prentice-Hall.

Williams, T.G., 1982, Consumer Behavior. Fundamentals and Strategies, St. Paul, MI: West Publishing.

Wilkie, W.L., 1986, Consumer Behavior, New York: John Wiley.

Zaltman, G., and M. Wallendorf, 1983, Consumer Behavior, New York: John Wiley.

Table of Contents

7. Household Economic Decision Making

ERICH KIRCHLER
University of Linz, Austria

1. THE UNIT OF ANALYSIS IN HOUSEHOLD DECISION MAKING

1.1. *Definition of the Family Household*

It seems so obvious and commonplace what the concepts "family" and "household" mean that they have frequently been employed loosely without formal definitions. However, the seemingly simple task to define these terms can become a rather complicated matter. The distinctions which seem to be most widely accepted contrast kinship and locality as the crucial characteristics which define membership in the family and household, respectively (Yanagisako, 1979). These features are also the core of the definition offered by the United Census Bureau (Nye and Berardo, 1973), that describes a *family* as "a group of two or more persons, related by blood, marriage, or adoption and residing together"; whereas a *household* consists of "all persons occupying a housing unit" (pp. 31 ff).

The most crucial difference between family and household, relevant to the study of purchasing decisions, concerns the emotional bonds between the members. Whereas the family is characterized by a high degree of intimacy among the members, "strong, frequent, and diverse interdependence that lasts over considerable periods of time" (Kelley et al., 1983: p. 38), individuals in the private household are usually less closely related to each other. Moreover, families generally consist of members differing in sex and age, whereas in a household same-sex and same-age members may co-reside.

Despite these differences, in the following the terms *family, household, and family-household* shall be used interchangeably, referring to a small social group which allies its members through intimate feelings, cooperativeness, mutual assistance, and the need for future cooperation, thus, to parents and children. It should, however, be emphasized here that, although the family usually consists of parents with their children, in research it most frequently is just the husband-wife dyad.

Van Raaij, W.F., van Veldhoven, G.M. and Wärneryd, K.E. (eds) Handbook of Economic Psychology. ISBN 90-247-3720-6.

1.2. *Methodological Problems in Family Decision Making Studies*

This paragraph addresses some questions about the relevant unit to be approached in household decision studies, the subject(s) to be queried, the setting of investigation, and the conceptualization of the phenomenon to be studied.

1.2.1. *Uniqueness of the Family*

In his taxonomy of social groups, Argyle (1969; see also Fraser, 1978) distinguishes between ad-hoc groups, T-groups, committees, work-groups, friends, and families. The family, as the most important group in one's life, is unique, that is, it is crucially different from other groups. Like in no other group, the members interact for long periods of time in a widening array of settings. The mask of impression management which characterizes the everyday world, is counteracted in the family, that is, family members disclose their personal secrets and share physical intimacies. They are less inhibited than members of any other group, more willing to share positive and negative feelings, and to praise and criticize each other. They develop their own communication system, synchronize their goals and behavior, and establish rather stable interaction patterns. The family is a group with a common history, cohesion and solidarity which becomes more and more important and irreplaceable to its members (Huston and Burgess, 1979).

The idiosyncracy of the family has only recently created a surge of interest in its specific dynamics. Most frequently results from ad-hoc groups have been generalized to the family, or "synthetic families," consisting of three unacquainted individuals with family like sex and age composition (Waxler and Mishler, 1970), have been observed in artificial settings with the aim to discover real family functioning. After constantly finding significant discrepancies between family and ad-hoc group dynamics (e.g., status and coalition formation, role differentiation, interaction and communication patterns, problem solving; cf. McGrath, 1984; Sorrels and Myers, 1983; Walters, 1982) it became evident that to understand the family it is necessary to study real families in their natural environment. Moreover, as systems theory emphasizes, the family needs to be studied in full (Kantor and Lehr, 1975), that is, purchase decisions ought to be perceived as transactions between all family members as well as embedded in everyday family life.

1.2.2. *Number of Respondents*

Surveys in which the respondents are asked about their attitudes and behaviors, and observational techniques have been the preferred techniques of collecting information in the family (for a discussion of these methods see Miller, Rollins, and Thomas, 1982; Glick and Gross, 1975). In questionnaire or interview studies researchers often approached only one family member, generally the wife, and relied on her responses. The belief that the wife is the appropriate informant about marital or family purchase decisions, rests on the assumption that she either holds the same attitudes as her husband or perfectly knows his attitudes. Recently, there has been growing concern about this assumption and consequently about the reliability of the reports of a single spouse.

In a study about automobile and furniture purchase decisions Davis (1970) found discouragingly low agreement between the spouses' opinions about their roles. Intrafamily comparisons on the husbands' and wives' responses to the question about one spouse's influence relative to the other for any given subdecision, led to an agreement rate of 62%. In a reanalysis of his study Davis (1971) emphasized that the responses of husbands and wives are very similar when compared on an aggregate level but dissimilar on a within family basis; on the average only 40% of the variance in one spouse's responses to the automobile and furniture decisions was accounted for by the other spouse's responses to the same questions. Similar results have been reported in replications by Shuptrine and Samuelson (1976), Wilkes (1975), and Woodside and Motes (1979). Also Davis and Rigaux (1974) found that the percentage of spouses who agreed about their influence in 25 decisions over three decision stages averages 68%, while 32% of the responses were either modestly biased or the respondents had overestimated their influence (vanity bias).

Moderate agreement between husbands' and wives' responses across specific item categories have also been reported by Granbois and Summers (1975) in a study which compared family purchase plans based on independent responses by husbands, wives, and their joint answers. The correlation between husbands' and wives' responses amounted to r = 0.42 for all items under investigation, whereas the correlations between the single spouses' and the joint plans reached r = 0.71 and 0.76 for wives and husbands, respectively. Interestingly, the husbands' responses correlated higher with the joint responses than the wives' for traditionally typically husband dominated items, automobiles and travel plans (r = 0.85 and 0.76 for husbands and r = 0.54 and 0.67 for wives, respectively), whereas the wives' responses were better predictors of joint responses than the husbands' for appliances (r = 0.88 and 0.68 for wives and husbands, respectively).

Davis and Ragsdale (1983) investigated husbands' and wives' attitude similarity and accurate perception of others for a series of products and services. Also their results clearly show that in marketing situations spouses frequently have different product preferences, are largely unaware of these differences, and perceive the other's preferences inaccurately.

Williams and Thomson (1985) analyzed survey data of husbands' and wives' perceptions of the partner's desire for children and found only moderate correlations between the spouses' desires (r = 0.58) and their perceptions of the other's desires (r = 0.68). The authors, nevertheless, conclude that single spouses can be trusted to some extent; however, having data from both spouses still seems highly desirable. Thus, efforts to enlighten and predict family economic decisions should consider both spouses' perceptions.

1.2.3. *Environment of Investigation*

Direct observation of family interaction usually took place in a rather artificial research setting. Most frequently, husband and wife have been brought to the laboratory, presented a hypothetical gift of money which had to be spent. The decision how to spend the money was assisted by an unfamiliar researcher who recorded the interaction process (e.g., Kenkel, 1957; Arndt and Crane, 1974; Ochsman, 1979). Although simulation of family interaction and the development of behavioral coding systems (e.g., Bales, 1950; Gottman, 1979) are major breakthroughs in the attempt to shift from the "Blood and Wolfe (1960) final-say outcome-focused technique" (Hill and Scanzoni, 1982) to the interaction process, the external validity still needs to be questioned. The possible impact of the setting of research on the respondents' behavior has not attracted much attention, thus, rejection of laboratory research would be premature. However, it could be that in public settings, such as the laboratory, spouses behave differently than at home. Gottman (1979), for instance, found that the interaction of couples at their homes contains much more negative affect and less agreement than the interaction of comparable couples in the laboratory. Also role specialization was found operating differently in artificial and natural settings (cf. Waxler and Mishler, 1970). After considering structuring and interaction in different settings, McGrath (1984) concluded: "The principles identified under artificial conditions are a crucial part of, but not a comprehensive description of, the forces operating in natural conditions" (p. 261).

Another problem inherent to commonly used observation techniques in laboratories is the isolation of the respective decision task from other problems which a couple at home may concurrently face. Almost no empirical studies have controlled the influence of past decision experiences as well as the impact of concurrent transactions between the spouses on decision processes. Although there is no doubt that "the long arm of past events is inevitably felt throughout current events" (Scanzoni and Polonko, 1980: p. 35), in the laboratory, the family generally faces problems in a way like committees that work on a task in isolation of other activities.

Summarizing, there is evidence that progress in research in family purchase decision making depends at least on the right group to be studied, namely the family; the right respondents to be queried, namely both husband and wife (and children); the right environment where to observe ongoing interactions, namely the natural setting. Another basic question is how to conceptualize the phenomenon under investigation.

1.2.4. *Conceptualization of Family Economic Decisions*

Almost all marketing scholars agree that the field of economic decision making can no longer be content with the exclusive focus on the final-say outcome. To ask respondents "Which partner decides what to buy?" in no way taps the complex dynamics of the decision process. However, despite growing urge to shift attention to the process, final-say techniques still predominate. The reason lies probably in the extreme difficulty to conceptualize and to operationalize the process. The following attempt is made to design a frame to study household decision processes. It leans heavily on Scanzoni and Polonko's (1980) "conceptual approach to explicit marital negotiation," which in turn is an expanded version of Strauss' (1978) "general paradigm for negotiation."

The model (Figure 1) suggests to study three interrelated segments, context variables, bargaining processes, and outcomes. It assumes ongoing influence emerging from the variety of context variables and continuing through marital interactions and proceeding to outcomes.

The first set of context variables is called family composition. It includes length of marriage, number and age of children, and social stratification characteristics (Sheth, 1974). A second set is termed task composition and represents characteristics of the task, such as product or service category (Davis and Rigaux, 1974), importance of the issue to the family members (Burns and Granbois, 1977), time pressure to reach a consensus. A third

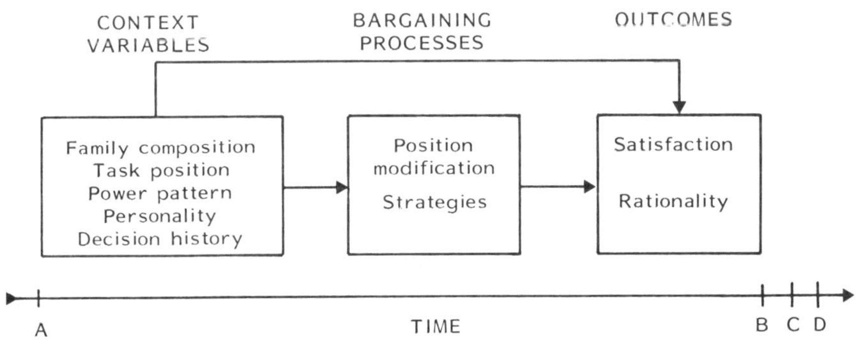

Fig. 1. A model to study household economic decisions (adapted from Scanzoni and Polonko, 1980).

cluster of variables consists of bases of marital power, such as relative contribution of tangible and intangible resources (cf. Blood and Wolfe, 1960; Heer, 1963; Rodman, 1967) and balance of love or involvement within the relationship (Safilios-Rothschild, 1976; for reviews of power see Scanzoni, 1979; Huston, 1983). Next, personality characteristics are considered. As Brandstätter (1985) shows, personality orientations of the interaction partners account substantially for yielding and resistance, respectively, in dyadic discussions. Although his model of reinforcement vs. exchange orientation has been tested only in ad-hoc dyads, it might be useful also in family studies. The fifth cluster of context variables is labeled decision history. It subsumes past experiences which are the "prologue of the present" (Scanzoni and Szinovacz, 1980). Past bargaining experiences which may strongly determine the present transactions are, for instance, trust (Colosi, 1983) and empathy shown by the other party in the past, the other's profit orientation (egoistic vs. joint profit seeking), fairness and utility debts (Pollay, 1968).

The second segment concerns the negotiation process. If family members do not unanimously agree on the utility of a specific commodity or the value of a particular attribute, they need to homogenize their different preferences. In other words, members need to bargain to reach a decision, whether to buy a desired item or to save the money, and/or which alternative to choose. To reach an agreement, at least one of the involved parties must be willing to modify his/her subjective utility function or be able to persuade the other(s) to yield. The rules leading to a mutual gradual adaptation of utility functions are labeled position modification. The attempts to persuade the other to acquiesce are termed bargaining strategies and tactics.

The third segment addresses the results of spousal interaction process in purchasing situations. As Scanzoni and Polonko (1980) repeatedly emphasize, process and outcome are two phenomena which make up an intrinsic whole, separable only theoretically. In the present conceptualization, outcomes refer to those decision patterns which emerge "whenever the mutual give and take "stops" " (Scanzoni and Polonko, 1980: p. 40). Negotiation may either stop, because the spouses have reached a consensus or because they withdraw from the discussion for whatever reason for some time. The most relevant outcome qualities are satisfaction or affective climate and rationality of the decision.

A negotiation outcome A persists indefinitely or at least as long as no party wishes some modifications in it in order to achieve another outcome pattern B. Endeavors to reach outcome B start on the basis of the former process outcomes and are determined by them.

This three-stage model offers a framework to study family economic decision making. In the past, research on family decisions has predominantly focused upon contextual variables in relation to which spouse had the final say. The major concern was who has the power to make decisions, depending on task and family composition. Rather few scholars have addressed the decision process, such as bargaining strategies; and almost no attention has been devoted to emotional and rational outcomes of the family deliberation process. In the following, this chapter collects some results of

1. investigations about marital task and role specialization in purchasing situations,
2. process studies, and
3. research on outcomes.

2. MARITAL ROLES IN ECONOMIC DECISION MAKING

A large body of information has been accumulated about the influence of wives and husbands in economic decisions. It is reasonably certain that spouses' roles differ considerably among decision topics, decision stages, and family composition characteristics.

2.1. *Decision Topics*

Family life consists of a variety of economic decisions. Ferber (1971) distinguishes two types, financial and non-financial economic decisions. Financial decisions encompass money management (e.g., handling of money, payment of bills, budgeting), spending decisions (e.g., purchase of durables, services), saving decisions (e.g., allocation of financial resources for a given period of time), and as a special form of saving behavior, asset management. Non-financial decisions include all other decision topics, e.g., decisions whether to have children, choice of an occupation, choice between work and leisure. Marketing research has mainly focused on spending decisions, whereas saving behavior as well as asset and money management are largely ignored issues.

2.1.1. *Spending Decisions*

Spending behavior has been classified in purchases of durables and non-durables. Other classifications have focused on individual or joint consumption of the commodity, consumption by adults or children, visibility of the brand during the use, etc. Ruhfus (1976) suggested a classification across ten criteria which led to three types of goods: Type A includes convenience goods, such as food, cigarettes, and corresponds to non-dura-

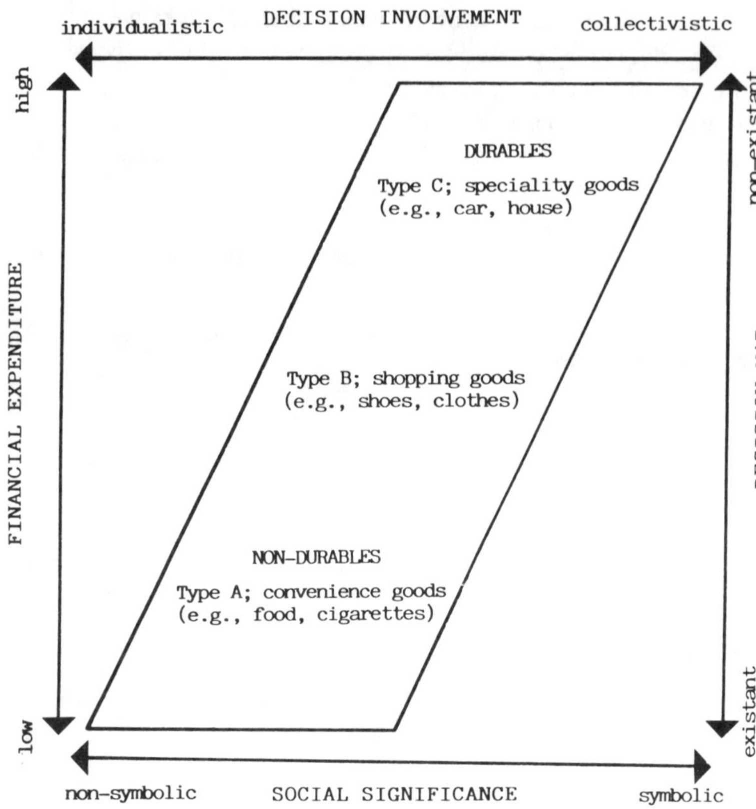

Fig. 2. A typology of spending behavior (adapted from Ruhfus, 1976).

bles. Type C encompasses specialty goods, as for instance, car, housing, thus, durables. Type B is a mixture of types A and C, labeled shopping goods (shoes, clothing, etc.). Figure 2 presents a typology which draws on Ruhfus' (1976) taxonomy. However, the ten criteria have been aggregated to four and the commodity types have been labeled durables and non-durables.

The four classification criteria are

1. *Financial expenditure*, that is the amount of money the item costs,
2. *Decision involvement* accounts for the weight the family members assign to the purchase (the requested commodity can either be useful to only one or more members; the necessary money to buy it could be taken from a single member or from the common budget),
3. *Decision map*: If the family buys the demanded good or service frequently, the decision parties may already possess detailed information about the alternatives and the market conditions, and may have estab-

lished a strategy leading to the optimal or to a satisfying choice. For infrequently demanded durables a decision map usually needs to be developed during the deliberation process, and

4. The *social significance* of the commodity. Durables, such as a car, house or apartment, are highly visible, culturally symbolic items, whereas non-durables usually are less important in terms of social meaning.

Research on frequently purchased goods and services is rather scarce as compared to the interest in durables. As Davis (1976) points out, data on non-durables have almost without exception been collected by the print media. After reviewing nine commercial studies, he concludes that they dispel some of the conventional wisdom that views the world of super-market purchase as women's domain. Although husbands are aware of many brands in many product categories, and are, thus, involved in actual purchasing, wives clearly predominate. This result has been confirmed in other studies which investigated series of products and services. Davis and Rigaux (1974) found, for instance, that purchases of food, cleaning products and kitchen ware are wife-dominated. However, purchases of alcoholic beverages are in some families controlled by the husband (see Figure 3). In a replication also Bonfield (1980) was able to show that in general the family assigns the wife the power to decide about kitchen items, cleaning products, tooth paste, and adhesive bandages. Green et al. (1983) investigated cross-cultural differences in spouses' roles and found in all five European, American, and African countries that groceries are in the wives' domain.

Research identifying spousal roles in buying of durables comes predominantly from marketing and sociological sources. The influence patterns seem to be more complex than those of non-durables and vary across different products considerably. In general, however, the husbands' influence increases with technically complex items (e.g., car), whereas the probability for joint decision making increases with increasing financial cost of the item.

Davis (1970) asked couples about the relative influence of husbands and wives in purchases of a car and furniture for a living room. Generally, he found that the husband has more say in automobile purchases: He decides about when and where to buy the car and how much money to spend. Make, model, and color of the automobile are jointly decided. The wife, on the other hand, has more influence in furniture purchases. She decides color, fabric, and style of the furniture autonomously, and has at least equal say as the husband in deciding what furniture to buy, how much to spend, when and where to buy (Table 1).

Shuptrine and Samuelson (1976) replicated Davis' study some years later and found strikingly similar results. Woodside and Motes (1979), undertaking a similar study as Davis (1970) did, asked husbands and wives about

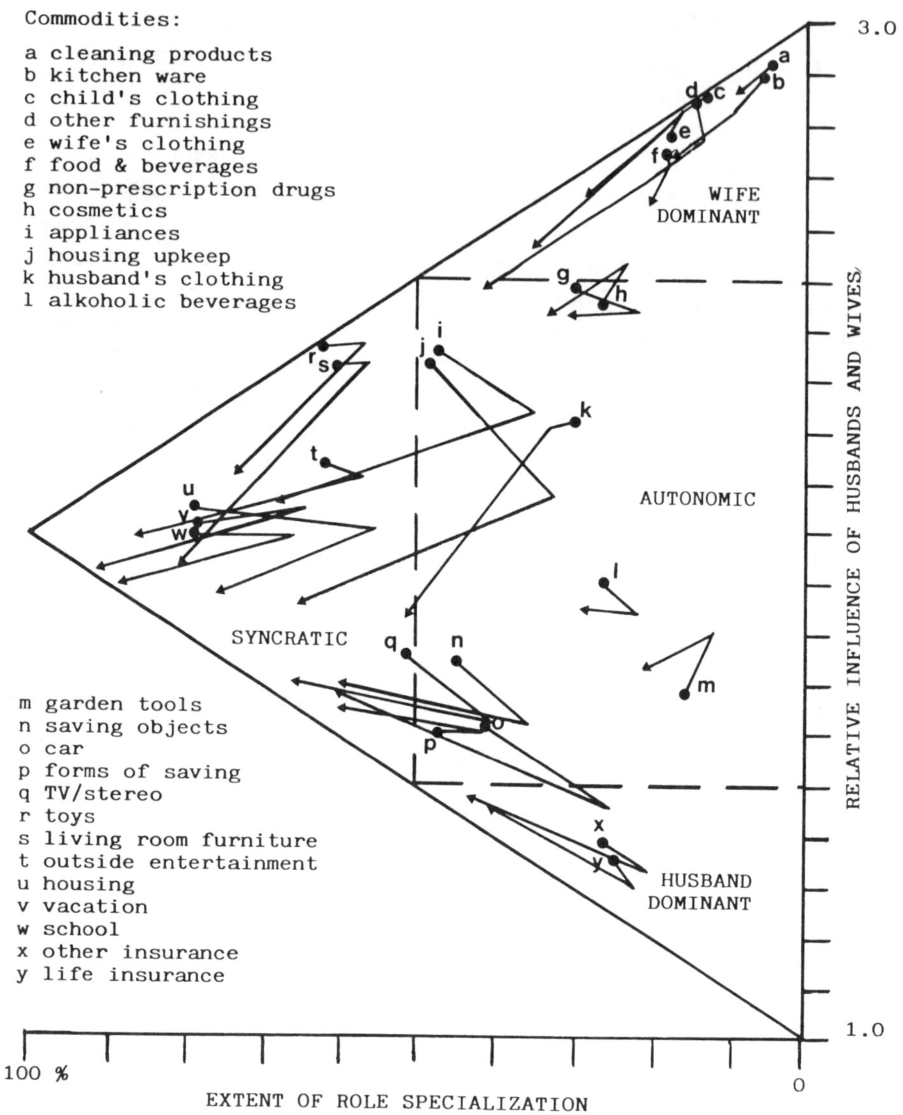

Fig. 3. Changes of marital roles between decision phases 1 (problem recognition), 2 (search for information), and 3 (final decision) (adapted from Davis and Rigaux, 1974).

the relative decision influence each spouse has for several commodities. Also in their study spousal perception about each others' influence varied across subdecisions within each product category. However, it can be summarized that husbands decide most frequently about the car and television set, whereas purchases of a washing machine and rugs are decided jointly or by the wife (cf. Table 2). Similarly, Burns and Ortinau (1979)

Table 1. Marital roles in automobile and furniture purchase decisions as perceived by husbands and wives (adapted from Davis, 1970).

Subdecisions	Patterns of influence (%)		
	Husband has more influence than wife	Both spouses have equal influence	Wife has more influence than husband
Automobile			
When to buy	68/68	29/30	03/02
Where to buy	62/59	35/39	03/02
How much to spend	62/62	37/34	01/04
What make to buy	60/50	32/50	08/00
What model to buy	41/47	50/52	09/01
What color to buy	25/25	50/63	25/12
Furniture			
When to buy	16/18	45/52	39/30
Where to buy	07/06	53/61	40/33
How much to spend	22/17	47/63	31/20
What furniture to buy	03/04	33/52	64/44
What style to buy	02/02	26/45	72/53
What color or fabric to buy	02/02	16/24	82/74

Note: N = 92 couples. Numbers are percentages; the first values are husbands' perceptions of influence, the second values indicate wives' perceptions.

found that the husbands' influence is highest for automobiles, television and stereo sets; the wives exert significant influence if a sofa or dinette is at stake. Moreover, Hendon and Hamilton (1977) found that males are credited with greater power to decide about cars and entertainment, while females show greater influence and independence in the furniture and clothing purchases. These findings are, in general, also consistent with the influence patterns Huszagh and Murphy (1982) found in Mexican households.

Filiatrault and Ritchie (1980) scrutinized vacation decisions and found that husbands' opinions were given the highest weight. In another study, Qualls (1982) observed a slight shift from autonomous to more joint decisions. Husbands and wives decided jointly about vacation, children's education, and housing. Purchases of cars, insurance or saving issues were still dominated by the husband. Male dominance in car and insurance purchases has also been consistently observed by Green et al. (1983) in their cross-cultural study. Moreover, Burns and DeVere (1981) reported husband dominance in life insurance purchases and also in purchases of encyclopedias. The wife decided which pots and pans to buy and had also more say than the husband in purchases of vacuum cleaners. These influence patterns were consistent across various situations, such as in decision settings at home, in the store with a salesman present.

Summarizing, these findings suggest that the wife decides rather autonomously about non-durables. Her influence decreases while the husband's influence increases with augmentation of costs. Moreover, the wife has most say if traditionally female-related commodities are at stake. The husbands' influence is highest for typically masculine items, such as the car, and technical items.

2.1.2. *Other Financial Decisions*

Besides spending behavior, Ferber (1971) enlists money management, saving decisions, and asset management. All three areas have been largely ignored by consumer researchers. As Hempel and Tucker (1980) comment, empirical information about marital task differentiation in these areas is generally derived from a single question about who is responsible to pay the bills or to buy an insurance. We know that family income and wealth are the primary determinants of families' initial decisions to save (Heffran, 1982) but are rather insecure about the roles husbands and wives play in decisions how to save money. According to Ferber (1971) and Ferber and Nicosia (1972), saving decisions are made most frequently on a joint basis. This has been confirmed by a study designed to assess cross-cultural differences in husbands' and wives' involvement in selected household activities (Douglas, 1979). Saving and investment activities are shared between the spouses. Closely related to saving behavior are decisions about assets. Also in this area, scientific information is scarce.

Similarly, disappointingly little attention has been paid to money management. More than a decade ago, Ferber and Lee (1974) investigated the "family financial officer." In their panel study restricted to newly wed couples, both spouses jointly carried the

> main responsibility for the family finances from the point of view of both decision making and execution with reference to (a) looking after the payment of bills, (b) keeping track of expenditures in relation to budgets, (c) use of money left over at the end of a pay period.

After a period of one year, the couples showed a role pattern away from joint performances of these financial tasks to performance by the wife alone. More recently, Rosen and Granbois (1983) investigated financial behavior and included both money management and saving behavior. They found three distinct task types (implementation tasks, long-term, and short-turn adjustments) in financial decisions. The influence structure in these tasks was determined by the spouses' sex role orientations and education (the wife was in charge of implementation tasks in traditional marriages when the educational level was low), by the spouses' locus of control (couples with external locus of control decided separately about long-term adjustments, such as method of saving and financing, handling of residual money, number of ownership of check accounts), and wife's working status (if the wife had a paid job, the spouses decided separately about short-term adjustments, such as the order of bill payment, decisions about payment on credit card accounts; also Hempel and Tucker, 1980, assume that wives committed to a working career have more influence in family saving behavior).

These results do not contribute much to clarify financial decisions; they rather indicate how complex the area is and how urgently systematic theory-led research is needed.

2.2. *Decision Stages*

Purchase decision making is a process which begins with the feelings of uncertainty or discomfort with the present situation and the desire for a commodity. After seeking information about alternative strategies to change the dissatisfying state, evaluation processes and the choice of one alternative follow. Then, the process moves towards the installation of the selected alternative and ends with post-decisional dynamics. Marital role and task division not only varies with the product category but also across the decision process.

Simon (1966) classified decision processes into the following steps: problem recognition, identification of alternatives, evaluation of alternatives, selection of and commitment to an alternative. In the following this sequence has often been applied in consumer research (e.g., Engel, Kollat, and Blackwell, 1968). In their seminal study, Davis and Rigaux (1974) subdivided purchase decisions into three phases, problem recognition, search for information, and final decision. The phases of identification and evaluation have been collapsed because these steps are so closely related to each other that in empirical research it might be difficult for the respondents to distinguish between them.

Davis and Rigaux (1974) presented husbands and wives of a convenience sample of 73 Belgian households separately a questionnaire, in which they had to fill out who had the major influence in 25 purchase decisions. Each respondent gave information about who was the first to recognize the need, who collected the information about possible alternatives, and who made the final decision to buy. The response categories in each of the resulting 75 questions were husband, wife, and joint. The results have been classified in a diagram which, at the vertical axis, represents the scale of relative influence between the spouses and results from the average scores. The horizontal axis, which is not independent from the vertical axis, represents the degree of role specialization. This has been operationalized in terms of the percentage of families reporting that a decision is jointly made. This diagram led to four decision types:

1. typically female dominant,
2. typically male dominant,
3. autonomous decisions dominated either by the husband or wife, and
4. joint or syncratic decisions.

Figure 3 shows the position of the 25 decisions during the three decision phases with reference to the two axes. Task specialization was found to vary throughout the three stages of the decision process. As shown in the diagram, the second phase of information seeking is characterized by more role specialization than phases one and three. The decision to buy was most frequently made jointly. Bonfield (1978) replicated this study for 20 product categories. He found more problem recognition specialization than Davis and Rigaux (1974) did, and consequently less role differentiation during information search phases. Both studies revealed a significant movement to joint decisions in the last phase. Another replication, conducted by Dahlhoff (1980) provided similar results.

Woodside and Motes (1979) analyzed marital influence patterns throughout the decision processes of four products. The authors analyzed who brought up the idea of purchasing (equivalent to phase 1), who decided on style or type, size, price, brand, collected information from stores, visited showrooms, and decided in which store to buy (equivalent to phase 2), and who made the final decision (equivalent to phase 3). The findings were the following (Table 2): Task specialization was high in the first phase and changed toward more joint information collection and joint final choice.

Although the methods used in this study and in Davis and Rigaux' (1974) and Bonfield's (1978) work are not directly comparable, there are some parallels in the results. At the beginning of purchase decisions, families show rather strong role specialization patterns; when the process moves towards information collection and evaluation of alternatives, the initial differentiation changes. The direction of change is, however, not yet predictable due to contradictory findings. When the phase of information accumulation and evaluation ends, usually both spouses jointly decide about the final purchase.

2.3. *Family Composition*

Husbands' and wives' influence on decisions depends also on the family type. Both demographic and sociographic variables of the family account for considerable marital role differentiation.

Some of the most frequently measured demographic characteristics are duration of marriage, number and age of children, income, and spouses' education. Several studies have revealed that joint financial decision mak-

Table 2. Marital roles in purchases of four commodities by decision phase, as perceived by husbands and wives (adapted from Woodside and Motes, 1979).

Influence pattern	Decision phase 1	Decision phase 2	Decision phase 3	Total
	Automobile			
Husband has more influence than wife	71/71	56/56	67/67	58/58
Both spouses have equal influence	18/21	42/42	31/31	39/39
Wife has more influence than husband	11/09	02/02	02/02	03/03
	Washer			
Husband has more influence than wife	12/12	22/20	41/36	23/21
Both spouses have equal influence	20/19	44/45	40/40	41/42
Wife has more influence than husband	68/69	34/34	19/24	36/37
	Rug			
Husband has more influence than wife	09/10	11/13	22/24	12/14
Both spouses have equal influence	31/32	52/51	52/47	50/48
Wife has more influence than husband	60/58	36/36	27/29	38/38
	Television set			
Husband has more influence than wife	53/54	45/42	46/51	46/44
Both spouses have equal influence	33/32	46/48	46/39	44/45
Wife has more influence than husband	14/14	09/10	08/09	09/11

Note: The numbers are percentages of husbands' (first value) and wives' (second value) perceptions of influence.

ing is most probable among newly wed couples. With the duration of marriage, the spouses seem to specialize in their tasks and to divide roles (Ferber and Lee, 1974; Sheth, 1974). A major change of a family occurs with the birth of the first child. In purchasing studies the husband's influence relative to the wife's was found to increase, when the wife became a mother (Filiatrault and Ritchie, 1980).

When the children grow up, they become potential coalition partners of the spouses in conflict and exert some influence in purchase situations. Szybillo and his collaborators (Szybillo, Sosanie, and Tenenbein, 1977; Szybillo and Sosanie, 1977) analyzed children's influence during several stages of decisions for a restaurant and family trip. Children were found to affect decision making, however, their influence is often indirect and varies across products and decision stages. Belch, Belch and Ceresino (1985) asked 260 families with at least one teenager child currently living at home to complete a questionnaire about the relative influence in decisions for different products, across three stages, and for several subdecisions. Also their results indicate that children have some influence. The influence they had was low and varied across products and decision stages. Similar findings have been reported by Ward and Wackman (1973), and Mehrotra and Torges (1977). Another family characteristic associated with role differentiation is income. Joint decision making is typical for young and middle class families. Among the members in both the upper and the lower social classes autonomous buying decisions are more common (cf. Komarovsky, 1961; Sheth, 1974; Kassarjian, 1982; Huszagh and Murphy, 1982).

A summary variable for several demographic indices is the concept of life cycle.

Over time, most families pass through several phases in their career, called the family life cycle. The first phase begins with a newly wed couple without children. Then, the young couple with children under six (full nest 1), the couple with the youngest child over six (full nest 2), and the couple with independent children (full nest 3) follow. The family passes then through the "empty nest-periods": first with the head 45 years of age or older, married, employed, and without dependent children; second, the family with the same constellation except the head being retired. The next stages are with the head widowed and either employed or retired. During these phases marital roles vary from joint to more autonomous decision making. The general flow of variation has been illustrated by Ruhfus (1976; Figure 4).

Social psychological variables of the family have been largely neglected in past consumer research. A taxonomy which deserves consideration is Olson, McCubbin and Associates' (1983) circumplex model, consisting of the dimensions cohesion, adaptability, and communication style. Another powerful tool to control family role structure is Fitzpatrick's (1984)

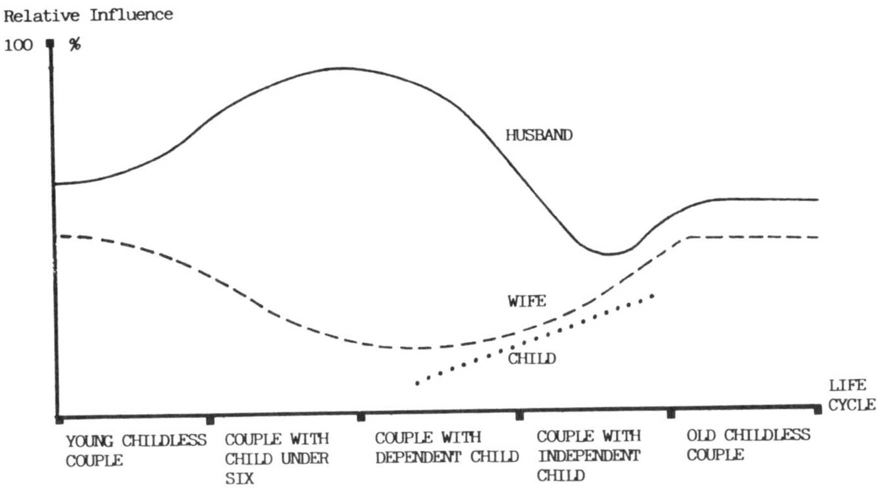

Fig. 4. Relative influence of husband, wife and child over the family life cycle (adapted from Ruhfus, 1976).

taxonomy. She distinguishes between three basic dimensions to describe families:

1. autonomy vs. interdependence,
2. conflict engagement vs. conflict avoidance, and
3. conventional vs. traditional ideology.

The more interdependent the couple, the higher the level of companionship, the more time the spouses spend together, and the more they organize with each other. The second important criterion concerns the way of conflict resolution. In purchasing decisions, couples avoiding conflicts have probably higher role structuration than others. The last dimension relates to the couple's interpretation of masculinity and femininity. Traditional couples hold on norms which associate task completion, problem solving and instrumental behavior to the husband, whereas the wife is seen as socio-emotional-oriented (see Bales, 1950). Traditionals show probably task decision patterns which Kenkel (1957) found in his sample, with the wife being the socio-emotional leader and the husband being the task-oriented leader. Recent studies which investigated Bales' role orientations in purchasing situations, using random or convenience samples, did not find the traditional task division (Arndt and Crane, 1974; Ochsman, 1979), which indicates, that in western societies a distinction needs to be made between traditional and progressive families. In some studies traditionalism has explicitly been investigated. Qualls (1982), for example, found that sex-role modern couples have a more egalitarian distribution of decision influence, and thus, increased interaction between the members as compared to traditional couples.

2.4. *Explanations of Marital Role Differentiation*

Now the question arises why one spouse rather than the other is more influential in family decision making. Among the most frequently mentioned causes, spouses' relative resource contributions, gender norms, and relative involvement deserve special attention.

Blood and Wolfe (1960) rationalized their findings in marital decision research by suggesting that the spouse who contributes the most to the common budget, exercises the most power in purchasing situations. Since in most families the husband contributes most financial resources, and has a higher education than the wife, he is vested with the power to decide about the purchases. Blood and Wolfe's (1960) conceptualization has stimulated extensive research both providing support and contradicting relative resource contribution theory (cf. Berger, 1980; McDonald, 1980). In a recently conducted study on the impact of unemployment on the family, Kirchler (1986) found support for the resource theory. With job loss the breadwinner was found to loose a substantial source to gain financial resources and status for the family. Consequently his power decreased, and dependence on the wife increased in purchase decision situations, whereas the wife became more autonomous. Contradicting results were found in studies investigating the influence of wives' employment on decision making. According to relative resource theory, in dual career families, wives should have more say in purchase decisions as compared to marriages with the husband being employed and the wife being a housewife. In this respect, Blood and Wolfe's theory has not been supported (cf. Arndt and Crane, 1974; Blood and Hamblin, 1958; Draughn and Rutledge, 1982; see, however, Ybarra (1982) who reports a more egalitarian conjugal role structure in Chicano families where the wife was employed). Contradicting results have also been obtained in studies conducted in Greece (Safilios-Rothschild, 1967) and Yugoslavia (Buric and Zecevic, 1967). In both studies an inverse relationship between resource variables and power has been found. However, Rodman (1967) was able to interpret these results by including cultural aspects into the relative resource theory.

Except from economic resources, power may also derive from non-economic contributions. In his least-interested-party theory, Heer (1963) criticized Blood and Wolfe's (1960) theory, arguing that contributions are not only compared between the spouses but also between potential alternative marital partners. Such comparisons may be more important to determine power than relative resource contributions. Safilios-Rothschild (1970) adds that conjugal power is also based on emotional resources. The partner who demonstrates the greater level of emotional involvement in the relationship is more submissive in decisions than the spouse who is least interested in the marriage.

Another source of role differentiation are gender norms. Societal norms prescribe which decision a spouse should make. In the past, the husband was accorded legitimate power to make decisions, independent of his interests and competence. In the recent years, a new perspective has evolved about the division of tasks between the spouses. Young women who in the past planned their adult lifes around marriage and full-time home making, are now engaged in a career themselves and are interested in the conditions of their life and able to control the conditions autonomously. Nowadays social norms change towards a more symmetrical or egalitarian role structure. Formerly institutionalized norms are abandoned and the spouses think of each other more and more in terms of two individuals than of a unit. These ongoing changes in gender norms affect family decisions. Scanzoni and Fox (1980) emphasize three ways of influence: First, spontaneous consensus is increasingly being replaced by negotiation processes. Second, formerly typically male or female preferences shift towards interchangability of roles, and thus, cause conflicts of interest. Third, shifting sex roles influence the style of conflict resolution. These changes of norms lead away from rigid role and task specialization towards a high degree of joint participation in decisions.

A third explanation of the allocation of roles within families views the partner who is most interested in the purchase and the most competent, as the most influential. Burns (1976) and Burns and Granbois (1977) report a study on the influence of spousal involvement and empathy in purchase decisions. The authors investigated the strength of preference for particular features of a product (involvement) and the importance to the respondent of his/her spouse's preference being reflected in the final choice (empathy). The findings were the following: If a spouse was highly involved in a subdecision, the partner's empathy was high. In other words, the higher the interest of one spouse in a subdecision the higher his/her influence. In car purchases, for instance, the husbands were found to be more involved than the wives – it is, thus, not surprising that husbands have more influence in decisions for this particular item. In a review on sex differences and influenceability, Eagly (1978) assumes that higher influence is based on higher interest and expertise, while on the other hand, readiness to yield is based on less interest and less expertise. Further evidence for the importance of motivational factors stems from Corfman and Lehmann (1987).

3. PROCESS OF ECONOMIC DECISION MAKING

An avenue of research was preoccupied with who in the household makes decisions, while little effort has gone into explaining how families decide. Decision making is a process with ongoing movement, directed towards unambivalent group assent and commitment to a course of action or inaction (Turner, 1970). The process may start with a dissension of spouses' aims or positions, and ideally, move through a phase of position modification, driven on by various tactics, towards agreement.

3.1. *Position Modification*

How are spouses' positions defined and which variables need to be changed in order efficiently regulate the distance between the positions to come to a final decision? Pollay (1968) presented an interesting model of the interaction between family members in purchase decisions. In his conceptualization of dyadic interaction he starts with the assumption that a spouse is able to determine both the utility of the product alternatives on the market and which products generate him/her the highest utility. The spouses are assumed to be motivated to maximize their own utility and to maintain distributive justice. Moreover, he defines three basic concepts: First, utility U(sk) to spouse P(s) resulting from product choice P(k) is a function of the need intensity for that spouse N(s), the frequency that spouse uses the respective product F(sk), the satisfaction of needs to the spouse by usage of the product S(sk), and the empathy the spouse feels for the partner E(sp). Empathy may, for instance, result from enjoying that the partner is happy with the respective product and his/her agreement to the purchase. A spouse's position or utility is thus,

$$U(sk) = f(N(s), F(sk), E(sp)).$$

According to Pollay (1968), given a utility each member will derive from a product, a decision is still not described. Since utility functions of the spouses may differ, it is further necessary to add the concept of priorities. In other words, it is necessary to specify the influence power of a spouse relative to the other. At a given point in time, the priority structure for a specific product is dependent on

1. the normal position preference NPP(s), that is for instance, the power assigned to a spouse deriving from his/her relative resource contributions,
2. the relative risk to be assumed by the spouse in the purchase R(sk), that are tangible and intangible costs resulting to a spouse,

3. the utility debt between the spouses D(sp). Utility debts have been neglected in most purchasing studies which conceive of decision processes as isolated events not interrelated to other past, present, and future family decisions. Utility debts are determined by the prior history of a couple. In the past, a spouse may have bought a commodity which was useful only to him/her, by spending money from the common budget.

In an upcoming purchasing decision with the partner having an egoistic desire, s/he might have credit or influence power basing on the net residual of past decisions. Thus, the priority index B(sk) is,

$$B(sk) = f(NPP(s), R(sk), D(sp)).$$

The last concept concerns distributive justice. This principle states that the spouses strive for a proportion distribution of rewards. Adams (1965) has stated that justice is met if the proportions of costs and rewards of each spouse are matched. Mathematically stated, justice is given if

$$U(sk)/B(sk) = U(pk)/B(pk).$$

It should be noted, that in long-term relationships this criterion does not need to be balanced in any single decision. Especially happy couples seem to accept disproportionality for considerable time periods, but strive to reach balance in the long run (Gottman, 1979). If balance is not given on a decision, the privileged partner accumulates utility debts which are included in future decisions. Empirical evidence supporting the assumption of primary importance of the decision history is provided by Corfman and Lehmann (1987) and Kirchler (1987).

Next, the question arises how spouses solve disagreements which result from different utility functions, different opinions about priorities and unjust distributions of rewards. Spouses with different product preferences, seeking to maximize the own utility, will try to convince the other that his/her choice is the most preferable. The spouses will use different strategies to influence the other's utility function. If the spouses fail in their influencing efforts, then the family decision depends on the priority structure, insofar as the more powerful spouse's preference will determine the family choice. The spouses will, thus, focus also on the priority structure and try to negotiate each others' relative power. Bargaining on power role definitions may be intense and a lengthy process since each decision contains implications towards long run priorities. Finally, spouses may negotiate about the net residual from prior decisions, namely the utility debts. They need to come to an agreement about the total amount of debts, and about the time lag they tolerate until the "account" must be balanced out.

Although Pollay (1968) introduced concepts of essential importance in family purchasing interactions, which have unfortunately been ignored in the past, his theory inherits severe shortcomings as well. The critique concentrates on the classical ideals of economic man. Pollay (1968) assumes that spouses are rational, analytical, utility maximizing, they know and assess each others' utility functions and reach an agreement through optimizing strategies. Among others, Braybrooke and Lindblom (1963) criticize the "synoptic type" of decision making and conceptualized decision making as a muddling-through process, called disjoint incrementalism.

In contrast to the synoptic process, Park (1982) has used Braybrooke and Lindblom's (1963) conceptualization to study joint decisions. The "informationally impoverished" decision makers are expected neither to be capable to process the whole information about each others' utility functions nor to identify the other's functions in every detail. Couples are perceived as solving purchasing problems by incremental politics. They solve disagreements by small incremental moves by staving problems off or nibbling at them, often making headway but sometimes retrogressing; often they have plans which are no more than a loosely stated set of goals (Braybrooke and Lindblom, 1963). In his study on joint decisions in home purchasing, Park (1982) characterized decision making by limited knowledge and awareness of each spouse's decision strategies, however, relying on conflict avoiding heuristics. Each spouse is supposed to follow his/her own utility, attempting to avoid marital conflict. Moreover, Park (1982) assumes that "By following conflict-avoiding heuristics, the dyad believes that it 'makes' a decision jointly, when in fact it more or less 'reaches' a decision through a disjoint, unstructured, and incremental strategy" (p. 152). The major heuristics to reach a decision are:

1. "common preference levels on salient objective dimensions,"
2. "task specialization," and
3. "concessions based on preference differences."

First, a spouse is able to identify the partner's preference on a set of salient objective dimensions of a commodity (e.g., number of bedrooms, price) but has difficulties to identify the other's evaluations of subjective dimensions (e.g., interior design of a home, appearance). Since preference differences on objective dimensions can be identified relatively easily, spouses seek to reach agreement on those dimensions at an early stage of decision making. Second, spouses try to avoid conflict by role differentiation. As outlined previously, spouses differentiate purchasing roles according to societal norms, expertise, power bases, etc. The last heuristic subsumes concessions. Differences are sometimes resolved through concessions. For example, if one spouse absolutely wants to go to the theatre while the other accepts both theatre and cinema, the spouses' joint utility enhances if they decide for the theatre (cf. Kelley and Thibaut, 1978). In terms of Pollay (1968), the spouse risking less in the purchase may yield more likely than the other. Park (1982) tested the concept of muddling through by examining husbands' and wives' decision plans in home purchasing. The results showed that spouses are largely unaware of the partner's decision plan net and changes over different decision stages, they are better able to identify salient objective dimensions and reach easier agreement on objective than subjective dimensions. Moreover, the spouses were relatively poor in identifying their mutual influence in the decision process. Park (1982) concludes that in spite of this muddling through, joint decision making effectively leads to a choice by relying on conflict-avoiding heuristics.

Park's (1982) approach bases on more relaxed assumptions about human cognitive capacities than Pollay's (1968) model. However, decisions are still conceived of as processes isolated from family history; also justice as a major value of intimate partners is excluded. It is necessary to start thinking of purchasing decisions as interrelated events. Current decision patterns depend on each other's cooperativeness in the past, trust, fairness, and empathy (Scanzoni and Szinovacz, 1980). In economic terms, marital interaction is an exchange process with the spouses reciprocating rewards. As Gottman (1979), McClintock, Kramer and Keil (1984), Nye (1980), Huesmann and Levinger (1976), Pollay (1968), and others point out, intimate partners with qualities such as trust and commitment may not expect short-term or immediate reciprocation of rewards, but rather are capable of long-term investments, keep book on one another in order to regulate future transactions on the basis of justice. Spouses may seek to maximize joint rather than egoistic utilities (Scanzoni, 1979) and consider the other's costs and rewards in the own utility function. In conclusion, it seems a worthwhile endeavour to include Pollay's (1968) concepts of justice and utility debts into Park's (1982) conceptualizations in future research devoted to develop a language to describe family decision processes.

3.2. *Bargaining Strategies*

Spouses interested in maximizing joint or egoistic utility in purchase decisions may use "appropriate" techniques in order to "move" the other to get the desired outcome. Several studies have addressed the question of what strategies spouses use (Sheth, 1974; Davis, 1976; Scanzoni and Polonko, 1980; Spiro, 1983; Howard, Blumstein and Schwartz, 1986).

In marketing, family purchasing scholars have tempted to categorize strategies and to predict when a particular tactic will be used. Davis (1976; see also Turner, 1970) distinguishes between two basic kinds of decision making: the consensual and accommodative type. Situations where spouses are able to eliminate initial disagreement through discussion and unanimously agree upon the value of outcomes or goals, are consensus decisions. The result of consensus is a decision to which the partners are equally committed without reservation or resentment. On the other hand, if spouses disagree about goals or are not convinced about the decision they finally make, the decision type is accommodative. According to Davis (1976), in the consensus model spouses rely on role structure specialization, pre-agreed budgets, and problem solving strategies to reach a decision. In the accommodative mode spouses use persuasion and bargaining strategies.

Role structure specialization: An approach to manage conflict is to assign to each spouse a role. The family comes to accept the special competence of a member in a particular decision area.

Pre-agreed budgets: Another strategy is to impose an impersonal rule or budget to solve conflicts. Once family members have reached an agreement about the appropriate rules, overt conflict situations can be avoided by applying the "institutionalized" rules.

Problem solving: Role structure and budgets are conflict avoiding strategies. If the family agrees on the goals but does not dispose about an "institutionalized decision map" it may turn to problem solving strategies. The family may consult experts both from within and without the family in order to accumulate relevant information, or repeatedly discuss the purchase to get a better solution.

Persuasion: In situations where family members disagree about goals, strategies of persuasion and bargaining are likely to be implemented. Davis (1976) defines persuasion "as a way of forcing someone to make a decision that they would not otherwise make. Bargaining, on the other hand, leads to willing agreement since by doing so both parties tend to gain" (p. 255). Persuasive strategies are coercion, coalition formation, as well as most of the strategies identified by Scanzoni and Polonko (1980), Spiro (1983), Howard et al. (1986), such as bullying, manipulation, supplication, emotional strategies.

Bargaining: These strategies base on exchange rules. Turner (1970) defines bargaining as "any interaction in which the concessions that one member makes to another are expected to be reciprocated in some manner, so that over the long run the sacrifices of each will balance out" (p. 10). Table 3 enlists the different strategies and ways of implementing them as conceptualized by Davis (1976: p. 255).

To understand how these strategies for conflict management are used, it is necessary to specify the circumstances under which they "operate." Little research has addressed the question on which strategies are applied by

Table 3. Alternative decision making strategies (from Davis, 1976).

Goals	Strategy	Ways of Implementing
"Consensus" (Family members agree about goals)	Role structure Problem solving	"The Specialist" "The Expert" "The Better Solution" "The Multiple Purchase"
"Accommodation" (Family members disagree about goals)	Persuasion	"The Irresponsible Critic" "Feminine Intuition" "Shopping Together" "Coercion" "Coalitions"
	Bargaining	"The Next Purchase" "The Impulse Purchase" "The Procrastinator"

which families, in which decisions and decision stages. Moreover, the few investigations available have usually focused on different strategy taxonomies, which makes it difficult to compare the results.

Madden (1982), for example, conceptualized a model of interspousal conflict in purchasing situations basing on the assumption that in conflict the type of strategy used depends on spouses' awareness of the respective disagreement. If both spouses are unaware of the conflict, they use problem solving strategies. If one spouse is aware of the conflict, whereas the other is not, they use persuasion; and if both spouses are aware of conflict, they use bargaining strategies.

Hill and Scanzoni (1982) distinguished between "verbal persuasion strategies" which range on a continuum from self-interests to collective or family motives, and found that spouses refer to different motives in different decisions. Collective interests have been stressed most frequently in disagreements on child matters, whereas individualistic interests were used in decisions about wife's own activities.

Spiro (1983) conducted a study to isolate influence strategies used by husbands and wives in resolving disagreements in purchasing decisions. She asked 98 couples who had jointly purchased or considered purchasing a major durable in the last three months and said that there had been disagreement, about influence types to resolve those disagreements. The influence types were expert influence (a spouse has more information about an issue than the partner), legitimate (based on role division), bargaining (attempts to turn the joint decision into an autonomous one in return for some rewards to the other spouse), reward/referent (based on a spouse's ability to reward the other or feelings of identification), emotional influence (emotional reactions such as anger, crying), and impression management (premediated persuasive attempts to enhance one's influence). These influence tactics derive from French and Raven's (1960) taxonomy of power bases, and are used by husbands and wives to resolve disagreements. The most frequently used strategy was expert influence. There were, however, differences between the respondents in the frequency and type of used strategies. "Non-influencers" and "light influencers" rarely used influence tactics, and when they attempted to persuade their spouse they used the expert type of influence. "Heavy influencers" used all six types of influence rather frequently, especially reward/referent, emotional, and bargaining tactics. Another group of spouses, "emotional influencers," used especially emotional-laden tactics. These emotional tactics have most frequently been used by spouses with traditional life styles, whereas more modern couples were light or non-influencers. Early in the life cycle spouses were found to use more influence tactics than at later stages, when they have established a role structure and divided tasks.

In a social psychological investigation, Howard et al. (1986) posed to intimate partners the question: "When your partner wants you to do something you do not want to do, how often does s/he do each of the following?" and listed 24 different influence tactics. Also Howard et al. (1986) found six strategy clusters, which were, however, different from those identified by Spiro (1983). They found two weak strategies, manipulation (dropping hints, flattering, reminding past favours) and supplication (crying, acting ill and helpless); two strong strategies, bullying (threats, insulting, ridiculing) and autocracy (claiming greater knowledge, asserting authority); and two moderate tactics, namely disengagement (leaving the scene, making the other feel guilty) and bargaining (trade-offs). Overall, bargaining tactics were used most frequently. Interestingly, strong tactics were used most frequently by those partners who inherited a powerful position in the relationship, whereas weak partners used supplication and manipulation strategies.

These studies show that scientific information about the decision process is poor and by no means apt to clarify and predict ongoing family decision making. Additional research is needed to determine the incidence and nature of purchasing decision processes.

4. OUTCOMES OF ECONOMIC DECISIONS

The family can be defined as a unit with the needs for optimal allocation of its scarce resources and interests in intensifying the emotional bonds between its members. The family will, thus, seek to minimize social and economic costs in decision situations by trying to make an optimal choice after passing through a commonly satisfying interaction process. Reiterating, the outcome of decision processes is twofold: Quality of information processing and choice (rationality) as well as the impact of the deliberation process upon the emotional climate of the family need to be considered.

The optimism that families perform better on purchasing decision tasks than individuals or ad-hoc groups has been sharply disillusioned by Hill (1972). He describes the family system as an inefficient work group due to the age and sex composition. It is "a poor planning committee, an unwieldy play group and a group of uncertain congeniality. Its leadership is shared by two relatively inexperienced amateurs for most of their incumbency, new to the roles of spouse and parent" (p. 14). Due to the impossibility to isolate purchasing decisions from other past and ongoing events in the family, spouses may not only seek to choose the best alternative but to make a choice which satisfies motives which are not "officially" at stake, and are counter-rational. For example, a spouse may be interested to purchase a commodity not only because s/he needs it and it is the best alternative but because it would enhance his/her power in the family, because it is useful to balance out utility debts, etc. Thus, the family is an impoverished decision maker not only because of the incapacity to process the available information accurately but also because "periferal" goals are interwoven in the decision process and detract attention from the central decision problem.

Also according to Weick (1971), families are rather inefficient and ineffective decision makers, especially because of information acquisition depth. Rudd and Kohout (1983) conducted a study to analyze individual and group consumer information acquisition in brand choice situations. They hypothesized that ad-hoc dyads and individuals will acquire more information than spouses. In this study, the subjects were asked to imagine that they were shopping for a particular product and were asked to make a purchase decision from among four alternative brands. They acquired information from an information board and made decisions for four products (toothpaste, television set, vitamins, and hid-a-bed sofa). The dependent variables included depth of information acquisition and decision time. The data showed that spouses were indeed acquiring less information and spending less time than ad-hoc groups. However, spouses accumulated more information and took more time than individuals.

Although the findings of a single study do not justify the conclusion that families are poorer decision makers than other groups, it can be expected that further research will reveal that intimate couples and families frequently fail to process available product information adequately in order to perform purchasing tasks in an optimal way. The particular sources of failure inherent to families and possible strategies to overcome them need to be uncovered in future research.

Another product of marital purchasing decisions is satisfaction. It refers to the spouses' well-being or feelings of resentment and resignation resulting from the purchased or rejected commodity and the interaction process. Dissatisfaction may result not only from unfulfilled expectations about product performance, but also from unexpected stressful confrontation or from the fact that a high-quality decision was purchased at the costs of marital conflict. Satisfaction in purchasing decision situations has rarely been examined. There are, however, a few studies which are concerned with outcome quality, even if merely as a byproduct of decision making.

Kourilsky and Murray (1981) hypothesized that satisfaction with the decision process might be caused by the level of economic reasoning of the involved members, that is, by the use of a common decision process and participation in that process. In their study, 27 parents and 27 children have been taught to apply economic reasoning in budgetary decisions. Pre- and post-training of economic decision making led to a higher level of economic reasoning, which in turn enhanced satisfaction with the decision process. Another determinant of satisfaction is the communication style. Hill and Scanzoni (1982) found that defensiveness causes resignation and resentment. Also if mutuality disparity and disagreement increased, the likelihood of dissatisfaction increased. Similarly, Wagner, Kirchler and Brandstätter (1984) found that both husbands and wives are dissatisfied in disagreement situations. The comparison of well-being in situations where one spouse bought an egoistically desired commodity against the other's will with well-being in situations where the spouse rejected the purchase after disagreement, showed that spouses tended to gain significantly less satisfaction from buying than from not buying when the partner disagreed. Thus, agreement is a major determinant of satisfaction. However, the importance of marital consensus depends largely on dominance patterns and gender: The husbands' well-being was less dependent on the wives' agreement in patriarchal than in egalitarian families. Wives, on the other hand, felt bad in disagreement situations, independent of the power distribution.

While these studies examined satisfaction as outcome variable of a single decision process, Schaninger and Buss (1986) investigated the aggregated impact of processes of consumption and finance handling over considerable periods of time on marital happiness. Their longitudinal comparison of economic decisions between happily married and divorced couples revealed that happy couples practice more role specialization, with greater influence of the wife and less husband dominance in family finance handling, and greater joint and wife influence in decision making. These results are in line with Gray-Little and Burks' (1983) conclusion of a literature review, indicating that highest levels of satisfaction were most often found among egalitarian couples. However, if the wife had more power than the husband, marital quality was lowest.

5. SUMMARY

In the last decade there has been a growing wealth of publications attesting to the importance of the family as a major economic decision making unit. Most attention has still been devoted to marital role and task specialization. There are, however, some studies which tap the process and outcome of family decision making.

The field of family decision making suffers a major shortcoming which results from parsimonious theoretical conceptualizations of most studies. As Burns and Granbois (1980) note, "with notable exceptions, the theoretical underpinnings of the research studies are generated from subjective observations and a considerable amount of intuitive reasoning" (p. 221). Marketers have not constructed theories about family decision making, and as Jenkins (1980) puts it in his review, have also "been lethargic in borrowing from other disciplines pertinent theories to test in their study of family decision-making" (p. 208). The increasing efforts, both from sociologists, social psychologists, economists, communication scientists, and marketers in the past years, promise a rapid change in the next future. Economic family decision making may become a major research topic in "famology," the new science of the family (Burr and Leigh, 1983).

In this review, family decision making studies have been categorized in three classes: studies about role division, process dynamics, and outcomes. Considerable scientific information has been accumulated about role division. We are reasonably certain that roles vary with variation of product classes, decision stages, and the family type. Roles are in a permanent state of flux: Societal changes towards more progressive or conservative role structures affect family role division and decision making.

We do not know much about the ongoing process of decision making and are largely unaware of the outcome of family deliberations and its impact on upcoming decisions. Marketing scholars interested in the process might take profit from collaborations with family clinicians, in trying to capture the process dynamics. In marketing research, most information about the process concerns strategies spouses may use to persuade the other. Other variables, such as the impact of time pressure on the process have been largely ignored in the past.

In conclusion, family decision making has become an attractive field of research. The body of scientific information has grown in the past years but there remain still numerous crucial questions unanswered. A statement of Winston Churchill (quoted in Olson, McCubbin, and Associates, 1980) poignantly describes the current state of research: "This is not the end. It is not even the beginning of the end. Let us hope it is the end of the beginning" (p. 239).

REFERENCES

Adams, J.S., 1965, "Inequity in social exchange," in: L. Berkowitz (ed.), Advances in Experimental Social Psychology, Vol. 2, New York: Academic Press, pp. 267-299.

Argyle, M., 1969, Social Interaction, New York: Methuen.

Arndt, J., and E. Crane, 1974, "Marital roles in intrafamilial decision making on spending matters," in R.C. Curhan (ed.), Combined Proceedings. New Marketing for Social and Economic Progress and Marketing's Contributions to the Firm and to the Society, Series 36, Chicago, IL: American Marketing Association, pp. 63-66.

Bales, R.F., 1950, Interaction Process Analysis. A Method for the Study of Small Groups, Reading, MA: Addison-Wesley.

Belch, G.E., M.A. Belch, and G. Ceresino, 1985, Parental and teenage child influences in family decision making, Journal of Business Research, 13, 163-176.

Berger, C.R., 1980, "Power and the family," in: M.E. Roloff and G.R. Miller (eds.), Persuasion: New Directions in Theory and Research, London: Sage, pp. 197-224.

Bettman, J.R., 1986, Consumer psychology, Annual Review of Psychology, 37, 257-289.

Blood, R.O., and R.L. Hamblin, 1958, The effect of the wife's employment on the family power structure, Social Forces, 36, 347-352.

Blood, R.O., and D.W. Wolfe, 1960, Husbands and Wives. The Dynamics of Married Living, Glencoe, IL: Free Press.

Bonfield, E.H., 1978, Perception of marital roles in decision processes: Replication and extension, Advances in Consumer Research, 5, 300-307.

Bonfield, E.H., 1980, Different influences on consumer decision making, Advances in Consumer Research, 8, 748-749.

Brandstätter, H., 1985, "Social emotions in controversial discussions and in group decision making," in: E.E. Lawler (ed.), Advances in Group Processes: Theory and Research, Vol. 2, Greenwich, CT: JAI Press, pp. 249-281.

Braybrooke, D., and C.E. Lindblom, 1963, A Strategy of Decision, Glencoe, IL: Free Press.

Buric, O., and A. Zecevic, 1967, Family authority, marital satisfaction and the social network in Yugoslavia, Journal of Marriage and the Family, 29, 325-336.

Burns, A.C., 1976, Spousal involvement and empathy in jointly-resolved and authoritatively-resolved purchase subdecisions, Advances in Consumer Research, 3, 199-207.

Burns, A.C., and S.P. DeVere, 1981, Four situations and their perceived effects on husband and wife purchase decision making, Advances in Consumer Research, 8, 736-741.

Burns, A.C., and D.H. Granbois, 1977, Factors moderating the resolution of preference conflict in family automobile purchasing, Journal of Marketing Research, 14, 77-86.

Burns, A.C., and D.H. Granbois, 1980, Advancing the study of family purchase decision making, Advances in Consumer Research, 7, 221-226.

Burns, A.C., and D.J. Ortinau, 1979, Underlying perceptual patterns in husband and wife purchase decision influence assessments, Advances in Consumer Research, 6, 372-376.

Burr, W.R., and G.K. Leigh, 1983, Famology: A new discipline, Journal of Marriage and the Family, 45, 467-480.

Colosi, T., 1983, Negotiation in the public and private sectors, American Behavioral Scientist, 27, 229-253.

Converse, P.D., H.W. Huegy, and R.V. Mitchell, 1958, Elements of Marketing, Englewood Cliffs, NJ: Prentice-Hall.

Corfman, K.P., and D.R. Lehmann, 1987, Models of cooperative group decision-making and relative influence: An experimental investigation of family purchase decisions, Journal of Consumer Research, 14, 1-13.

Dahlhoff, H.D., 1980, Kaufentscheidungsprozesse von Familien, Frankfurt am Main, FRG: Lang.

Davis, H.L., 1970, Dimensions of marital roles in consumer decision-making, Journal of Marketing Research, 7, 168-177.
Davis, H.L., 1971, Measurement of husband-wife influence in consumer purchase decisions, Journal of Marketing Research, 8, 305-312.
Davis, H.L., 1972, Household Decision Making, 72/41, Brussels: European Institute for Advanced Studies in Management (working paper).
Davis, H.L., 1976, Decision making with the household, Journal of Consumer Research, 2, 241-260.
Davis, H.L., and E.K.E. Ragsdale, 1983, Limitations and Biases in Perceiving Others, Chicago, IL: University of Chicago (unpublished manuscript).
Davis, H.L., and B.P. Rigaux, 1974, Perception of marital roles in decision processes, Journal of Consumer Research, 1, 51-62.
Douglas, S.P., 1979, A cross-national exploration of husband-wife involvement in selected household activities, Advances in Consumer Research, 6, 364-371.
Draughn, P.S., and C.M. Rutledge, 1982, Working wives: Their impact on perceptions of role competency of middle-age husbands, Home Economics Research Journal, 4, 391-400.
Eagly, A.H., 1978, Sex differences in influenceability, Psychological Bulletin, 85, 86-116.
Engel, J.F., D.T. Kollat, and R.D. Blackwell, 1968, Consumer Behavior, New York: Holt, Rinehart and Winston.
Ferber, R., 1971, Family Decision-making and Economic Behavior: A Review, Urbana-Champaign, IL: University of Illinois (faculty working paper).
Ferber, R., and L.C. Lee, 1974, Husband-wife influence in family purchasing behavior, Journal of Consumer Research, 1, 43-50.
Ferber, R., and F.M. Nicosia, 1972, "Newly married couples and their asset accumulation decisions," in: B. Strümpel, J.N. Morgan, and E. Zahn (eds.), Human Behavior in Economic Affairs, Amsterdam: Elsevier, pp. 161-187.
Filiatrault, P., and J.R.B. Ritchie, 1980, Joint purchasing decisions: A comparison of influence structure in family and couple decision-making unit, Journal of Consumer Research, 7, 131-140.
Fitzpatrick, M.A., 1984, "A typological approach to marital interaction: Recent theory and research," in: L. Berkowitz (ed.), Advances in Experimental Social Psychology, Vol. 18, New York: Academic Press, pp. 2-47.
Fraser, C., 1978, "Small groups. 1. Structure and leadership," in: H. Tajfel and C. Fraser (eds.), Introducing Social Psychology, Harmondsworth, Middlesex, UK: Penguin, pp. 176-200.
French, J.R.P., and B. Raven, 1960, "The bases of social power," in: D. Cartwright and A. Zander (eds.), Group Dynamics. Research and Theory, London: Tavistock, pp. 607-623 (second edition).
Glick, B.R., and S.J. Gross, 1975, Marital interaction and marital conflict: A critical evaluation of current research strategies, Journal of Marriage and the Family, 37, 505-512.
Gottman, J.M., 1979, Marital Interaction, New York: Academic Press.
Granbois, D.H., and J.O. Summers, 1975, Primary and secondary validity of consumer purchase probabilities, Journal of Consumer Research, 1, 31-38.
Gray-Little, B., and N. Burks, 1983, Power and satisfaction in marriage: A review and critique, Psychological Bulletin, 93, 513-538.
Green, R.T., J.-P. Leonardi, J.-L. Chandon, I.C.M. Cunningham, B.J. Verhage, and A. Strazzieri, 1983, Societal development and purchasing roles: A cross-national study, Journal of Consumer Research, 9, 436-442.
Heer, D.M., 1963, The measurement and bases of family power: An overview, Marriage and Family Living, 25, 133-140.
Hefferan, C., 1982, Determinants and patterns of family saving, Home Economics Research Journal, 11, 46-55.

Hempel, D.J., and L. Tucker, 1980, Issues concerning family decision making and financial services, Advances in Consumer Research, 7.

Hendon, D.W., and W.C. Hamilton, 1977, Partner interaction and influence on purchase decision of married, engaged, and "going steady" couples, Journal of the Academy of Marketing Science, 5, 339-348.

Hill, R., 1972, Modern systems theory and the family: A confrontation, Social Science Information, 10, 7-26.

Hill, W., and J. Scanzoni, 1982, An approach for assessing marital decision-making processes, Journal of Marriage and the Family, 44, 927-941.

Howard, J.A., P. Blumstein, and P. Schwartz, 1986, Sex, power, and influence tactics in intimate relationships, Journal of Personality and Social Psychology, 51, 102-109.

Huesmann, L.R., and G. Levinger, 1976, "Incremental exchange theory: A formal model for progression in dyadic social interaction," in: L. Berkowitz (ed.), Advances in Experimental Social Psychology, Vol. 9, New York: Academic Press, pp. 192-229.

Huston, T.L., 1983, "Power," in: H.H. Kelley, E. Berscheid, A. Christensen, J.H. Harvey, C.T. Huston, G. Levinger, E. McClintock, L.A. Peplau, and D.R. Petersen (eds.), Close Relationships, San Francisco, CA: Freeman, pp. 169-219.

Huston, T.L., and R.L. Burgess, 1979, "Social exchange in developing relationships: An overview," in: R.L. Burgess and T.L. Huston (eds.), Social Exchange in Developing Relationships, New York: Academic Press, pp. 3-28.

Huszagh, S.M., and A.D. Murphy, 1982, Patterns of influence in the purchase of consumer durables by Mexican households, American Marketing Association, Proceedings, Series 48, 1-16.

Jenkins, R.L., 1980, Contributions of theory to the study of family decision-making, Advances in Consumer Research, 7, 207-211.

Kantor, D., and W. Lehr, 1975, Inside the Family, San Francisco, CA: Jossey-Bass.

Kassarjian, H.H., 1982, Consumer psychology, Annual Review of Psychology, 33, 619-649.

Kelley, H.H., and J.W. Thibaut, 1978, Interpersonal Relations, New York: John Wiley.

Kelley, H.H., E. Berscheid, A. Christensen, J.H. Harvey, T.L. Huston, G. Levinger, E. McClintock, L.A. Peplau, and D.R. Peterson (eds.), 1983, Close Relationships, New York: W.H. Freeman.

Kenkel, W.F., 1957, Influence differentiation in family decision making, Sociology and Social Research, 42, 18-27.

Kirchler, E., 1986, The Long Arm of Unemployment. Change of Marital Power After Job Loss, paper presented at the International Conference on Economics and Psychology: Choice and Exchange, Kibbutz Sheffayim, Israel.

Kirchler, E., 1987, Daily Marital Purchase Decisions – a Retrospective Diary Approach, paper presented at the 12th IAREP Annual Colloquium, Aarhus, Denmark.

Komarovsky, M., 1961, Class differences in family decision-making on expenditures, in: N. Foote (ed.), Household Decision Making, New York: New York University Press, pp. 255-265.

Kourilsky, M., and T. Murray, 1981, The use of economic reasoning to increase satisfaction with family decision making, Journal of Consumer Research, 8, 183-188.

Madden, C.S., 1982, The Effect of Conflict Awareness on Interspousal Decision Making in Highly Involving Purchases, Lincoln, NB: University of Nebraska (unpublished dissertation).

McClintock, C.G., R.M. Kramer, and L.J. Keil, 1984, "Equity and social exchange in human relationships," in: L. Berkowitz (ed.), Advances in Experimental Social Psychology, Vol. 17, New York: Academic Press, pp. 183-228.

McDonald, G.W., 1980, Family power: The assessment of a decade of theory and research 1970-1979, Journal of Marriage and the Family, 42, 841-854.

McGrath, J., 1984, Groups. Interaction and Performance, Englewood Cliffs, NJ: Prentice-Hall.
Mehrotra, S., and S. Torges, 1977, Determinants of children's influence on mothers' buying behavior, Advances in Consumer Research, 4, 56-60.
Miller, B.C., B.C. Rollins, and D.L. Thomas, 1982, On methods of studying marriages and families, Journal of Marriage and the Family, 44, 851-873.
Nye, F.I., 1980, Family mini-theories as special instances of choice and exchange theory, Journal of Marriage and the Family, 42, 479-489.
Nye, F.I., and F.M. Berardo, 1973, The Family. Its Structure and Interaction, New York: Macmillan.
Ochsman, R.B., 1979, Husband/wife interaction in making purchase decisions, Journal of Psychology, 103, 145-157.
Olson, D.H., H.I. McCubbin, et al., 1980, Families. What Makes them Work, Beverly Hills, CA: Sage.
Park, W.C., 1982, Joint decisions in home purchasing: A muddling through process, Journal of Consumer Research, 9, 151-162.
Pollay, R.W., 1968, A model of family decision making, British Journal of Marketing, 2, 206-216.
Qualls, W.J., 1982, Changing sex roles: Its impact upon family decision making, Advances in Consumer Research, 9, 267-270.
Rodman, H., 1967, Marital power in France, Greece, Yugoslavia, and the United States: A cross-national discussion, Journal of Marriage and the Family, 29, 320-324.
Rosen, D.L., and D.H. Granbois, 1983, Determinants of role structure in family financial management, Journal of Consumer Research, 10, 253-258.
Rudd, J., and F.M. Kohout, 1983, Individual and group consumer information acquisition in brand choice situations, Journal of Consumer Research, 10, 303-309.
Ruhfus, R.E., 1976, Kaufentscheidungen von Familien, Wiesbaden, FRG: Gabler.
Safilios-Rothschild, C., 1967, A comparison of power structure and marital satisfaction in urban Greek and French families, Journal of Marriage and the Family, 29, 345-352.
Safilios-Rothschild, C., 1970, The study of family power structure: A review 1960-1969, Journal of Marriage and the Family, 32, 539-553.
Safilios-Rothschild, C., 1976, A macro- and micro-examination of family power and love: An exchange model, Journal of Marriage and the Family, 38, 355-362.
Scanzoni, J., 1979, "Social process and power in families," in: W.R. Burr, R. Hill, F.I. Nye, and R.I. Reiss (eds.), Contemporary Theories About the Family. Research Based Theories, Vol. 1, London: Free Press, pp. 295-316.
Scanzoni, J., and G.L. Fox, 1980, Sex roles, family and society: The seventies and beyond, Journal of Marriage and the Family, 42, 743-756.
Scanzoni, J., and K. Polonko, 1980, A conceptual approach to explicit marital negotiation, Journal of Marriage and the Family, 42, 31-44.
Scanzoni, J., and M. Szinovacz, 1980, Family Decision-making, Beverly Hills, CA: Sage.
Schaninger, C.M., and W.C. Buss, 1986, A longitudinal comparison of consumption and finance handling between happily married and divorced couples, Journal of Marriage and the Family, 48, 129-136.
Sheth, J.N., 1974, Models of Buyer Behavior: Conceptual, Quantitative, and Empirical, New York: Harper and Row.
Shuptrine, F.K., and G. Samuelson, 1976, Discussions of marital roles in consumer decision making: Revisited, Journal of Marketing Research, 13, 87-91.
Simon, H.A., 1966, New Science of Management Decision, New York: Harper.
Sorrels, J.P., and B. Myers, 1983, Comparison of group and family dynamics, Human Relations, 36, 411-492.

Spiro, R.L., 1983, Persuasion in family decision-making, Journal of Consumer Research, 9, 393-402.

Strauss, A., 1978, Negotiations. Varieties, Contexts, Processes, and Social Order, San Francisco, CA: Jossey-Bass.

Szybillo, G.J., and A. Sosanie, 1977, Family decision making: Husband, wife and children, Advances in Consumer Research, 4, 46-49.

Szybillo, G.J., A.K. Sosanie, and A. Tenenbein, 1977, Should children be seen but not heard?, Journal of Advertising Research, 17, 7-13.

Turner, R.H., 1970, Family Interaction, New York: John Wiley.

Wagner, W., E. Kirchler, and H. Brandstätter, 1984, Marital relationships and purchase decisions – to buy or not to buy, that is the question, Journal of Economic Psychology, 5, 139-157.

Walters, L.H., 1982, Are families different from other groups?, Journal of Marriage and the Family, 44, 841-850.

Ward, S., and D.B. Wackman, 1973, "Children's purchase influence attempts and parental yielding," in: H.H. Kassarjian and T.S. Robertson (eds.), Perspectives in Consumer Behavior, Glencoe, IL: Scott, Foresman, pp. 368-374.

Waxler, N.E., and E.G. Mishler, 1970, "Experimental studies of families," in: L. Berkowitz (ed.), Advances in Experimental Social Psychology, Vol. 5, New York: Academic Press, pp. 250-304.

Weick, K.E., 1971, "Group processes, family processes, and problem solving," in: J. Aldous, T. London, R. Hill, M. Straus, and I. Tallman (eds.), Family Problem Solving, Hillsdale, IL: Dryden Press, pp. 3-32.

Wilkes, R.E., 1975, Husband-wife influence in purchasing decisions: A confirmation and extension, Journal of Marketing Research, 12, 224-227.

Williams, R., and E. Thomson, 1985, Can spouses be trusted? A look at husband/wife proxy reports, Demography, 22, 115-123.

Woodside, A.G., and W.H. Motes, 1979, "Husband and wife perceptions of marital roles in consumer decision processes for six products," in: N. Beckwith, M. Houston, R. Mittelstaedt, K.B. Monroe, and S. Ward (eds.), Educators' Conference Proceedings, Series 44, Chicago, IL: American Marketing Association, pp. 214-219.

Yanagisako, S.J., 1979, Family and household: The analyses of domestic groups, Annual Review of Anthropology, 8, 161-205.

Ybarra, L., 1982, When wives work: The impact on the Chicano family, Journal of Marriage and the Family, 44, 169-177.

Table of Contents

8. Consumer Behavior and the Marketing Activities of Firms

CHRISTIAN R.A. PINSON
INSEAD, Fontainebleau, France

and

EDUARDO L. ROBERTO
Asian Institute of Management, Manilla, Philippines

1. INTRODUCTION

In his 1982 review of the consumer behavior field published in the *Annual Review of Psychology*, Kassarjian (1982) characterized consumer research as being too fragmented and called for the desperate need for "integration of the various topics in the field" (p. 643). To the marketing firm and its strategist, however, the situation does not look that desperate. As Sternthal and Craig (1982: p. 34) suggest, it is those "fragmented" theories and concepts that marketers seem to find of immediate practical use in developing effective marketing strategies.

This chapter is about those supposedly fragmented consumer behavior theories and concepts and how marketers make or more precisely can make practical immediate use of them. The chapter begins with an overview of the firm's marketing decisions and the role that consumer research plays in enabling the marketer to be more effective in those decisions. Then, the consumer behavior basis and dimensions of the marketer's product, pricing, persuasive communication and distribution decisions are examined. The chapter ends with a note on the need for consumer behavior research as a behavioral science research discipline, and the need for researching into marketers themselves especially with regard to their use and application of consumer research.

2. THE CONSUMER ORIENTATION IN MARKETING DECISIONS OF FIRMS

2.1. *Introduction*

Successful firms consider their marketing function to be that of satisfying

Van Raaij, W.F., van Veldhoven, G.M. and Wärneryd, K.E. (eds) Handbook of Economic Psychology. ISBN 90-247-3720-6.

consumer wants and needs so that they may satisfy their own objectives.[1]

To succeed in marketing, the firm's foremost consideration is the choice of the customer and of the industry in which one elects to compete. Having made the choice, the firm must develop skills and resources around the markets it has elected to serve. To implement this consideration in planning the marketing of a product, firms search, source and use, either formally or informally, data on the consumer. The data are intended to answer their basic questions on marketing planning and execution. These questions are:

1. On the market-product fit:

   1.1. Who is my consumer? What are the segments of the market? What are the characteristics of this market and of each of its segments? Who are catering to the consumers' needs and wants?
   1.2. What is my product? What consumer needs or wants does it meet? How different is it from other products in satisfying those needs and wants of the consumer?

2. On realizing the market-product fit:

   2.1. How do I present my product to my market? What name and packaging do I give it?
   2.2. How do I effectively inform and persuade that market about my product?
   2.3. How do I effectively make my product available to my market and at what price?
   2.4. Having done all the above, how do I effectively engineer movement? How do I get consumers to buy now instead of later?
   2.5. How do I put all these foregoing elements together so that I have a consistent and mutually reinforcing whole?

2.2. *The Marketing Mix Concept and the Marketing Plan*

The marketing mix elements as implied in the foregoing are the product decisions of positioning, branding and packaging, the pricing decision, and promotion decisions of advertising and sales promotion, and the place decision of distribution or product availability.

While each of these decisions is or can be made with the backing of the appropriate consumer behavior data to make for the "best" elements, their combination into the marketing mix does not necessarily make for the best mix. This is because a decision about any one of the elements has an effect on the others. This interaction is based on and follows from the consumer behavior fact that a consumer response to a marketing mix element will affect her/his response to other elements. And so the mix itself must be checked for this interaction.

Making the foregoing decisions for all of the firm's products with a view to seeing how each can contribute best to the firm and to one another is what constitutes the firm's marketing planning. The underlying concept is that of interaction between the offered products. Although it is not necessary that the firm makes money on all and each of its products, it is vital that its product portfolio be well balanced in terms of use and generation of resources (Day, 1977).

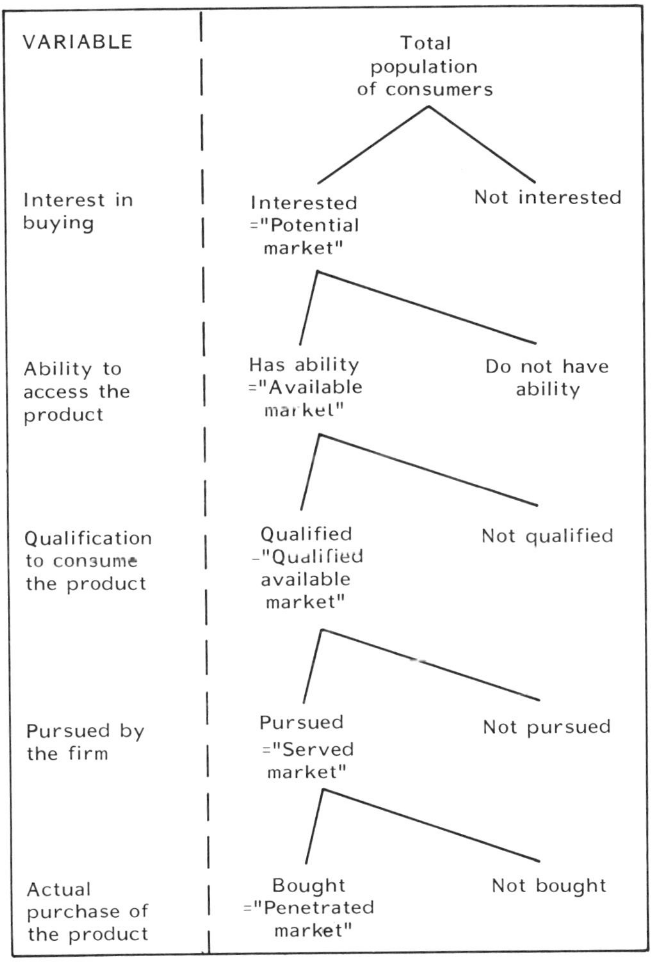

Fig. 1. Kotler's proposed system of defining the market (drawn from the discription of the system in Kotler, 1984).

2.3. *Market Definition and Market Measurement*

In the marketing planning process, the firm's first step is to set the market objectives for the products constituting the objects of the marketing plan. To be able to take this step, the firm must be clear about each product's market and that market's size, growth, potential, and competitive participants. This is the area of market measurement and forecasting.

For an unambiguous market definition, Kotler (1984: pp. 226-227) proposed the use of the variables of consumer interest in buying the product, the consumer ability to access it, the consumer qualification to consume it, the firm's decision to pursue the consumers concerned, and the actual buying of the product. Figure 1 shows how the cumulative consideration of these variables yields different market definitions. Day, Shocker and Srivastava (1979) took this issue one step further by working out a system by which market definition can be "demand or customer-oriented." This system proposed that a market definition should be based on "the set of products judged to be substituted, within those usage situations in which similar patterns of benefits are sought, and the customers for whom such usages are relevant." These authors offer an excellent review of the major methodological approaches available for identifying "products-markets." In a more recent paper, Fraser and Bradford (1983) suggest to use a principal component analysis of revealed product substitutabilities to identify a group of competing brands or products in a market place.

2.4. *Market Segmentation and Consumer Research*

An integral part of the market definition and measurement steps required by the setting of objectives in marketing planning is deciding on a product's target market segment or segments. This means that firms at this stage must engage in market segmentation, a process of dividing the market into segments based on the simple fact that not every consumer will want the same features or services from a product class nor react similarly to marketing stimuli. Therefore the most effective way to meet specific consumer needs is to serve different segments separately. Presumably, consumers have similar needs and response elasticities within the segment they belong to but different from those in other segments. To Lunn (1978), market segmentation provides "the cornerstone for a company's total planning. It helps to set the basic objectives for the whole marketing operation, and to indicate strategies for implementing these objectives" (p. 346).

This high regard for market segmentation comes from the fact that its consumer research base has given firms more than any other market studies, the closest and most intimate knowledge of the consumer. Consumers differ in geographic location, demographics, e.g., age, sex, social class, psychographic characteristics (personality and life style). They may also be segmented on the basis of such behavioral variables as differences in purchase and usage patterns, product benefits sought, and a variety of perceptual and additional variables (Frank, Massy, and Wind, 1972; Young, Ott, and Feigin, 1978).

2.5. *Product Positioning: Concept and Measurement*

Product positioning is the product side of the market-product fit equation referred to and discussed earlier. It is defined as the image consumers have of a given product or brand relative to their perception of competing products or brands (Ries and Trout, 1981). The measurement approaches to product positioning take a direction consistent with its assumed perceptual character. For instance, the most popular of such approaches is the perceptual mapping technique. The output of this technique is a "perceptual map," which "positions" products or brands relative to one another based on how consumers perceive those brands to be similar or dissimilar to one another. The mapping technique processes the similarity and dissimilarity data with the use of multidimensional scaling (MDS) which mathematical psychologists had developed. For a more detailed treatment of MDS and other positioning measurement techniques, the reader is referred to Green and Tull (1978) and Wind (1982).

The resultant plots of the brands on the perceptual map surface for the marketing manager such marketing strategy questions as the following:

1. Is the perception of one's brand as given by the perceptual map compatible with its marketing objectives and with reality?
2. Should repositioning be considered for the brand given the "ideal" brand sought by the chosen market segment?
3. Are there new product opportunities suggested by the perceptual map?

The answers obtained for these questions provide the marketing decision maker a conceptual framework for designing and evaluating marketing strategies. The real value of product positioning however is revealed only where marketers couple it with a thorough analysis of the buying situation.

3. TYPOLOGY OF CONSUMER BUYING SITUATIONS

3.1. *Introduction*

Consumer behavior research started and evolved with a model of the purchase behavior as a decision-making process. Olshavsky and Granbois (1979: p. 98) reviewed the literature and ended up with the conclusion that "a significant proportion of purchases may not be preceded by a decision process" and that in fact "for many purchases a decision process never occurs, not even on the first purchase." This turned the tide of consumer research towards the direction of low-involvement purchasing processes.

Consumer buying situations can be usefully classified by examining:

1. what meanings consumers attach to products,
2. how consumers handle perceived risk, and
3. what impact anticipated product usage and other situational factors have on consumer purchasing behavior.

3.2. *Product Meanings*

Wind (1982) in assessing the use by marketing planners of the Office of Statistical Standards' Standard Industrial Classification (SIC) system of defining and categorizing products concluded that the system was of "little value as a guideline for ... marketing strategy" (p. 68). The useful classification is, it was argued, one that draws upon consumer needs and/or behavior.

It is generally accepted that through their purchase and consumption of products, consumers do not solely try to satisfy physiological or purely functional needs. Rather there is insistent evidence that they frequently see their possessions as social communication tools (Belk et al., 1982; Holman 1981; Hirschman and Holbrook 1981). The intended message is based on the self concept (Sirgy, 1982) and is aimed at projecting an idealized image of the self. Solomon (1983) argues that product symbolism serves an additional function, namely that of helping consumers structure social reality and perform social roles. Products can therefore be looked at as "cultural symbols which may be either referential or expressive" (Robertson et al., 1984: p. 563). Whereas referential symbols represent and indicate tangible objects and their attributes, expressive symbols provide additional information about the consumer's social status, personality and life style.

High involvement products are products that are important to the consumer, because they are closely tied to the consumer's ego and self concept. They also involve financial and/or physical risk. In such cases, consumers are expected to engage in information search and careful consideration of product alternatives. On the other hand, *low involvement* products represent purchases that are much less important to the consumer, in that the financial, physical and psychological risks involved are not nearly so high. Therefore, low involvement products generally entail a habitual or limited process of decision making.

3.3. *Perceived Risk: Definition and Reduction Heuristics*

Since Raymond Bauer (1960) introduced some two and a half decades ago the concept that most of consumer behavior is related to perceived risk, marketing scholars have devoted themselves to studying consumer behavior from that perspective and a considerable volume of research and literature is now available on the subject (Jacoby, 1978; Ross, 1975; Gemünden, 1985).

A product's perceived risk level is defined by what its consumers may see as possible adverse or unpleasant consequences of buying or using it and by the uncertainty that those consumers may feel towards the occurrence of such possible consequences. Any product's risk profile is determined by five types of risk that its consumer may entertain about it. In each of these types, consumers may be thought of as asking themselves:

1. "Will this product do what it is said to do?" (functional risk).
2. "Will this product be worth what I paid for it now?" (financial risk).
3. "Does this product have any side-effects or could it be harmful?" (physical risk).
4. "Will this product deliver its promised psychological reward?" (psychological risk).
5. "Will this product be socially acceptable?" (social risk).

This typology of perceived risk is thought to be of practical significancc to marketing practitioners. It directs them to the specific action they are to take to help consumers reduce their perceived risk about the product. For example:

1. Against perceived functional risk, they could explore ways of providing the consumer with information or with free product trial in small sized packages.
2. Against perceived financial risk, they could work on how to best provide prospective consumers with assurance of the product's warranties and guarantees.
3. Against perceived physical risk, they could try finding ways of providing

certificates of approval for the product, such as the "Good Housekeeping" seal.

4. Against perceived psychological risk, they could try to find ways of providing personal service or extensive usage instructions.
5. Finally, against perceived social risk, they could look for ways of providing endorsements of the product from influential opinion molders.

This of course does not preclude the fact that the consumers themselves take both preventive and corrective or remedial measures to handle and manage situations and products with high perceived risk content. The impressive volume of research that has gone into the study of consumer coping behavior produced some of the more provocative and controversial concepts and theories of consumer behavior.

3.4. *Product Usage and the Situational Variables*

Research into product usage situation (Assael, 1981: pp. 420-443) has led to a broadening of the consumer research paradigm. Following Belk's (1975) seminal article on the importance of situational variables, research has stressed and empirically demonstrated that alternative products/brand are evaluated in terms of their appropriateness for particular, anticipated usage situations (e.g., Bearden and Woodside, 1978; Miller and Ginter, 1979; Sharpe and Granzin, 1974; Sandell, 1968).

Reviewing this literature, Dickson (1982) suggested the practical utility to marketing firms of segmenting markets by usage situations. A beer can be positioned as primarily suitable for informal vs. formal social events, for heavy vs. light use, for indoor vs. outdoor consumption and so forth. Such a usage-based segmentation would improve target market selection and competitive positioning. However,

> in some cases, consumers will buy a certain brand regardless of the situation ... For example, a consumer may be very loyal to Michelob beer. The consumer makes no distinction between drinking Michelob when alone, with guests, while watching television, with meals, in-between meals, or any other time (Assael 1981: p. 424).

To ascertain the importance of the situation, Belk (1979) suggests the development and use of "situational inventories" in which a sample of customers are asked to select those situations that seem to be most closely related to brand choice.

Situational variables are not limited to anticipated usage situations. The purchase situation, i.e., the conditions at the time of the purchase, may have a major impact on consumers' decision making. For example, one can speculate that consumers' time resources and predispositions towards time use will have an influence on their problem solving behavior. Similarly decision making is known to be a function of such situational factors as the physical and social surroundings of the decision maker.

4. CONSUMER PERCEPTION AND EVALUATION OF PRODUCTS

4.1. *Introduction*

To best position their products, firms need to examine

1. how consumers gather information about new and existing products,
2. what are the product evaluation rules most often used,
3. what types of cues consumers resort to, when they have to infer uncertain product attributes, and
4. under which conditions brand loyalty is likely to occur.

4.2. *Information Search Behavior*

When confronted with the stimulus product to be evaluated the consumer is pictured as engaging in both internal and external search for information about the triggering stimulus.

In looking at the issue of internal search, McGuire (1976: p. 310) suggested that instead of directing research at uncovering the different kinds of search strategies consumers pursue or use to retrieve from their memory, what they regard as relevant and useful information, there is much more to be gained from focusing the research on "describing the organization of (that) memory." This is because once that organization is understood, according to McGuire, issues like "whether search strategies go deeply or broadly, ... whether there are parallel searches in different memory systems, and how the person monitors the search to determine whether it is getting close, ..." become more meaningful to talk about. Lynch and Srull (1982) claimed that consumer researchers have given exclusive attention to conscious manipulation of product information by consumers. They advocate studying memory and additional processes that may occur below the level of consciousness.

Robertson et al. (1984: pp. 82-91) review of past research on external search behavior shows that the efforts of the past twenty years can be summarized in a state of knowledge contained by the following four propositions. See also Chapter 2 of this Handbook.

1. In general, the consumer's external information search is quite limited. For example, in one survey study, only 53 percent of sampled buyers of cars and household appliances considered more than one brand, while in an experimental study, out of a total of 560 information pieces available for a brand choice decision, only 11 or less than two percent of those pieces were asked for by the consumer before making a choice (Robertson et al., 1984: p. 84).
2. The more experience the consumer has with a product, the less his/her search tends to be and this is generally true for both width (i.e., purchase experiences across brands) and depth (i.e., purchase experiences within individual brands) of experience. There are two qualifications to this generalization. One says that this is true provided the experience was satisfactory, while is in the proviso that the experience is still relevant or applicable. Search is inversely related to satisfactory experience and to relevance or applicability.
3. The more the brand choice involves a selection from a set of differentiated brands, the more information search will take place. This is because the more the differentiation, the more the perceived benefits from the alternative brands will differ, and the higher the perceived risk will be from loss of potential satisfaction arising from a wrong choice.
4. Consumers perceive personal information sources to be more important to them than non-personal sources such as the mass media. This derives from two inherent advantages of personal sources over non-personal. First, personal sources provide two-way communication, while the non-personal is only one-way. Secondly, personal sources are able to provide at the moment of communication more knowledge, create more interest and secure more attention from the consumer.

These insights are taken to have critical marketing communication strategy as well as public policy (Beales et al., 1981) implications. For example, Proposition 1 is seen to provide guidelines for the marketer's decision about the amount and type of information to make available to consumers. Proposition 2, on the other hand, is used as a framework for thinking about strategies for increasing the probability that the marketer's information will be used. The importance of Proposition 3 is seen to be in directing the marketer's thinking about how to encourage the consumer to do information search. Proposition 4 had led to the marketer's consideration of the relative effectiveness of different information sources. This has triggered further investigations. This time they looked into the influence of the nature of the product itself and the role of the different stages of the consumer's product adoption process on the effectiveness question.

Studies cited by Williams (1982) indicate that in the process of adoption, consumers make use of both personal and non-personal sources of information. However, personal and interpersonal sources tend to become more significant to consumers than non-personal mass media sources, as they move from the awareness stage of the process to the adoption stage.

Because one consumer's adoption of a product is not independent of other consumers' completed or prospective adoptions but interacts with these either by the imitation effect (vis-à-vis others' completed adoption) or by the word-of-mouth influencing effect (vis-à-vis other's possible or prospective adoption), the sum total of these interactions across time and across consumers give rise to the process of diffusion. This aggregate process and that of the individual process of adoption have been the subject of voluminous consumer studies. An excellent summary of this literature can be found in Gatignon and Robertson (1985).

4.3. *Product Evaluation Rules*

There has been much research on the way consumers compare alternative products and brands, making use of various evaluative criteria (Pras, 1977; Wilkie and Pessemier, 1973). The rules used by the consumer are called evaluation or decision rules. Whereas some decision rules (compensatory rules) assume that a perceived weakness on one product attribute may be compensated by a strength on others, the alternative to this procedure is a non-compensatory method of evaluation. See also Chapter 3 of this Handbook.

The best known *compensatory rule* is the one developed by Fishbein (1963). In this rule, the individual's attitude toward an object is predicted from a knowledge of his or her beliefs about what attributes an object possesses and evaluations of those attributes. *Fishbein's attitude model* may be expressed algebraically as follows:

$$A_o = \sum_{i-1}^{n} B_i \, a_i \,,$$

where

A_o = the overall attitude towards an object o;
B_i = the belief whether or not object o has some particular attribute;
a_i = the favorableness attached by the consumer to attribute i;
n = the number of beliefs.

For example, if we are concerned with cars, consumers may specify five major attributes: durability, economy, comfort, safety, and service dependability. B_i refers to a consumer's belief about whether or not a particular brand actually is durable, economical, comfortable, safe and comes with a dependable service. This is typically measured on a scale that ranges from "very likely" to "very unlikely." The a_i component allows for ordering these attributes and corresponding needs by favorableness. Greater weight is given to attributes regarded as more favorable. See for attitude research Chapter 5 of this Handbook.

Non-compensatory decision rules assume that a weakness on one dimension is not compensated for by a strength on another dimension. The major types of non-compensatory rules are the conjunctive, disjunctive, and lexicographic decision rules.

When following the *conjunctive rule*, the consumer establishes a minimum acceptable level for each product attribute. A particular brand will be evaluated as acceptable only if each attribute equals or exceeds that minimum level. If a *disjunctive approach* is used, the consumer specifies one or more attributes to be dominant. A brand will be judged as acceptable, only if it exceeds the minimum specified level on these key attributes. The *lexicographic rule* assumes that consumers rank product attributes from most important to least important. The brand that dominates on the most important criterion receives the highest evaluation. If two or more brands tie, the second attribute is examined and so on until the tie is broken.

Both the compensatory and non-compensatory rules describe a multi-attribute approach to consumer decision making. That is, consumers are assumed to use more than one attribute to determine their preferred brand. Most rules assume that consumers process information by evaluating alternative brands on many attributes at a time (*processing by brand*) rather than examining several alternatives on one attribute (*processing by attribute*). The lexicographic rule, on the other hand, suggests processing by attribute, i.e., the alternatives are first compared on the most important attribute, and only if a tie occurs, on a second attribute.

Empirical research (e.g., Bettman, 1975, 1976b, 1979; Pras and Summers, 1978) suggests that processing by attribute is more likely to occur in routinized buying decisions or when the consumer has some prior understanding of the various alternatives and the evaluative criteria to use. When faced with more uncertainty, consumers are expected to favor processing by brand, probably because this is the way information is usually presented in advertising and other forms of marketing communications. There is also growing consensus (see Lussier and Olshavsky, 1979) that consumers may reduce the complexity of product evaluation tasks by adopting a combination of compensatory and non-compensatory decision rules. A non-compensatory strategy is used to eliminate unacceptable brands, followed by a compensatory assessment of the remaining acceptable alternatives. As task complexity increases, multi-stage sequential information strategies are expected to be followed (Park, 1978; Bettman and Park, 1982; Chapter 3 of this Handbook).

Although the various decision rules just described may appear to be rather esoteric representations of actual consumer information processing behavior, this research track strongly indicates the necessity to discover, under which conditions consumers prefer to process product information by either brand or attribute. If processing by brand is the dominant processing mode, then according to Engel and Blackwell (1982: p. 424) "... information on salient attributes should be given in one package, so to speak, in the context of a given brand .... " If processing by attribute is preferred, "... then the attribute itself should be predominantly featured."

Another implication is that there exist at least two main strategies for changing consumers' brand perceptions. A first approach requires convincing consumers to reassess the value of one or more product attributes. A second strategy is one that attempts to convince consumers that the brand has certain positively valued attributes. Experimental tests (e.g., Lutz, 1975) of these two strategies tend to indicate that it is easier to change consumers' perceptions of brand attribute possession rather than their assessment of the importance of product attributes.

4.4. *Product Cue Utilization Behavior*

Past research on consumer cue utilization (see Cohen, 1972; Cox, 1967; Mitchell and Olson 1981; Olson 1978, 1980) has shown that a variety of product attributes and product related attributes serve as cues when consumers have to make product inferences on the basis of incomplete information. Huber and McCann (1982) have demonstrated that these inferences have considerable impact on consumers' final product evaluations and purchase intentions. Consumers frequently form overall, very subjective impressions of the product extending beyond the product information available to them. When evaluating products they often use such cues as odor, noise, color, package, brand name, price and other physical attributes, which have pre-existing interrelationships in the consumers' minds. Pinson (1986) referred to these anticipated interrelationships as the consumer's "implicit product schemata." The combination of schemata that a consumer maintains about a product makes up that consumer's "implicit product theory" about that product.

In addition, there is empirical evidence showing that consumers are often influenced by certain inferential bias and that they may hold and use inferential beliefs which are not warranted by the information available to them (Deighton, 1983; Henry, 1980; Huber, 1975; Ofir and Lynch, 1984; Park and Lessig, 1981; Shugan, 1980; Scott and Tybout, 1983). Several studies (see Schellinck, 1980) have shown that the confidence value attached to the various cues available to the consumer may explain why consumers often do not hesitate to use cues with low predictive value. Confidence value refers to the individual's confidence in correctly using the cue. When confidence value is reasonable, weak cues, i.e., cues with low predictive value, are often found to be favored over cues with high predictive value but low confidence value. It is also well documented (Dillon et al., 1984; Holbrook, 1983; Hutchinson, 1983) that product judgments can take the form of a global and very subjective impression that seeps into the individual perceptions of the product attributes. These evaluation processes may be so subjective or unconscious that the consumers may be unable or unwilling to report them, at least if one uses traditional research methods (Lynch and Srull, 1982).

The marketing strategy significance of understanding consumer implicit product theories extends to the marketing manager's product concept, product development and promotion decisions. For instance, marketing people can determine their product's "cue mix" which can be used to effectively reinforce the image that their product possesses the characteristics desired by consumers. This mix may encompass the kind of raw materials whose texture, size, color, shape and so on convey the suitable psychological meaning to the consumer, the brand name whose connotation will further support the product's image, the pricing which will be seen by the consumer as indication of the quality (Gabor and Granger, 1966) or newness s/he is looking for, and other product characteristics that the consumer associates with other distinctive features of the product.

4.5. *Product or Brand Loyalty Behavior*

A common consumer coping mechanism against perceived risk that will be looked at is the consumer's brand loyalty, another heavily researched area of consumer behavior (Jacoby and Chestnut, 1978).

One of the first things that the brand literature now makes clear is that brand loyal behavior is not only repeat purchase behavior but is also accompanied by some degree of psychological commitment to the brand. The view most commonly held today stems from the distinction made by Day (1969) between "intentional loyalty" and "spurious loyalty." Day contends that loyalty is more than repeat purchase behavior, in that the spuriously loyal customer lacks real attachment or commitment to the brand.

As a perceived risk reducing mechanism, brand loyalty behavior has been found to be the consumer's most used strategy. Roselius (1971) tested eleven consumer risk reduction strategies (i.e., brand loyalty, major brand usage, store image, shopping, free sample trial, word-of-mouth information, government testing, endorsements, money back guarantee, private test, and expensive model preference) against four types of risk (i.e., loss of time to get a product that failed repaired or replaced, risk to health or safety when the product fails, risk of feeling foolish when the product turns out to be defective, and the loss of money to get a product that failed repaired or replaced) and found brand loyalty rated by consumers as the best and most helpful strategy among the eleven risk reduction strategies and across all four risk types.

The managerial marketing implications of the brand loyalty research are probably more developed than any of the other perceived risk minimizing methods of the consumer. The brand loyalty definition alone had inspired the development of the so-called "vulnerability model." This framework developed by Wind (1977) has been presented as useful to the marketing strategies for assessing the degree and distribution of loyalty in the market.

Brand loyalty behavior research (or more accurately its subset, the repeat purchase and brand switching behavior research) has also been responsible for the development of some of the major computer simulation models that are increasingly replacing expensive and time consuming test marketing procedures for new product introductions or product relaunching projects. An example is the ASSESSOR model (Silk and Urban, 1978).

5. CONSUMER BEHAVIOR AND THE PRICING DECISION

5.1. *Introduction*

There are three aspects of consumer price perception that are of particular interest to the marketer. These are the consumers' price awareness and sensitivity, perceived price/quality relationship and their reactions to psychological pricing.

5.2. *Price Awareness and Sensitivity*

The studies reviewed by Assael (1981) and Williams (1982), revealed the following:

1. Price level awareness is mostly low. For instance, a 1974 Progressive Grocer magazine study showed that of 44 supermarket items, consumers identified the correct price in only a fourth of the cases. In another study, Fady (1976) found that two French shoppers out of three were using supermarkets' price images to compensate for their unfamiliarity with the prices of grocery products.
2. About awareness of price changes. Over time, consumers show increasing price awareness for lower priced products and decreasing price awareness for higher priced ones.

3. The price-aware consumer
   - belongs to the higher income group or the very low income group.
   - is highly educated.
   - is single and/or employed full time.
   - has access to more accurate price information.
   - is exposed to more advertising.
   - shops in more stores.
   - goes around shopping for price.
   - uses a shopping list.

Going beyond the simplistic economic concept and assumption of price elasticity of demand, consumer studies of price elasticity or sensitivity behavior (Zeithaml, 1984) have indicated that:

1. Consumers tend to express greater price elasticity to an impending price increase than what actually takes place when the price increase happens. Claimed price elasticity tends therefore to be greater than realized price elasticity.
2. Consumers are more downside elastic, i.e., sensitive to price decreases, than upside elastic, i.e., sensitive to price increases.
3. The consumer's price elasticity decreases when shopping with a friend or when facing a salesman viewed as an expert. It increases when shopping alone and when feeling self-confident about his/her own product evaluation.

A second important aspect of price sensitivity is the consumer's expectations of a normal price level and price range (Monroe, 1976). The product's standard price or what consumers regard as the product's fair price, serves as an anchor for judging other prices. According to Assael (1981: p. 537), "there is a range around the standard price that is not likely to produce a change in quantity consumed or a switch in brands." There is a lower limit to this price range below which consumers begin to suspect that this is "too good a deal" and therefore something must have been sacrificed in the brand, most probably its quality. The range also has an upper limit about which the brand is seen to be just too expensive to be really worth buying.

The range and its threshold points move over time. When a general price increase takes place such as what happens during inflation, the existing acceptable price range when exceeded prompts consumer to take cost-cutting measures. However, Williams (1982), citing the work of Kamen and Toman (1970), says that an adaptation level effect "takes over as consumers become accustomed to the higher prices, and they then abandon their cost-cutting ways" (p. 367).

5.3. *Perceived Price–Quality Relationship*

The literature on consumer perception of the price-quality relationship is extensive and dates far back in time. While the price-quality relationship studies constituted an impressive huge collection, they have not really made clear the exact form of that relationship. There are studies reporting on a linear form, and others on a non-linear, in fact an inverted U-shaped form.

There are also studies (see Zeithaml, 1984) indicating that the relationship may be true only within certain upper and lower limits, or even quite weak or limited, when other cues, such as brand-related knowledge, product test reports, perceived market share, store image and product composition are available.

The consumer's perception of the relationship has been found by still other studies (e.g., Etgar and Malhotra, 1981) to depend on an individual's perception of the product quality concept and to be a function of those occasions or situations, where quality is difficult to judge on the basis of other quality connoting criteria and those where there are perceived variations of quality among brands.

5.4. *Psychological Pricing*

The consumer behavior and price perceptions underlying psychological pricing are largely assumed rather than directly measured through field or experimental research. The exceptions are in the issues of unit pricing, multiple unit pricing, and odd vs. even price endings. But even here, the supporting research base is restricted to a relatively few studies.

When talking about psychological pricing then, reference is much more to the marketer's pricing strategies than to studies of consumer price-related behavior and perceptions. Williams (1982) describes six major psychological pricing strategies of marketing firms. These are:

1. *customary pricing*, where there is strong market resistance to any price changes because the product has been at a certain price level for so long;
2. *odd pricing*, where price is ended with an odd number or near a round number;
3. *price lining*, where a product is priced at different levels "to take advantage of various levels of purchasing power and desire for quality;"
4. *multiple-unit pricing*, where items are priced in multiples, e.g., two for 45ç;
5. *leader pricing*, where price on a certain product is reduced to build store traffic; and
6. *prestige pricing*, where a high price tag is placed on a product to lend it prestige and to create the perception of its limited ownership (scarcity).

These pricing strategies assume that there are numerous curves associated with different products, purchase situations, and consumers. These consumers are in turn, assumed to be sensitive to certain prices so that deviation above or below the critical price will result in decreased demand. Consumer research has not yet provided firm empirical evidence that those pricing strategies are actually effective and further research is clearly called for. A good step toward this is the pricing framework developed by Simon (1982).

6. CONSUMER BEHAVIOR AND THE COMMUNICATION DECISION

6.1. *Introduction*

To reach and communicate persuasively to their market, marketers must decide on what is called their communication mix, their communication targets and goals in the context of their marketing targets, and their persuasive communication factors of source, message, receiver and media. Consumer research and behavior theories of varying complexity and practical value abound to help them make a data- and research-based decision on each of these elements.

The concept of the communication mix relates to the set of mutually reinforcing activities that the marketer has to undertake to have an impact on the communication target. There are four such sets. They are referred to as advertising, selling, sales promotion and public relations. To attain effective communication with his audience, the marketer has the task of combining these four elements in such a way that the total effect is greater than the sum of these parts. This is of course no simple task to undertake. To do it well, Ray (1982: p. 11) suggests that the marketing strategist's starting point is to first understand communication at the individual level (of the receiver).

6.2. *Communication Goals and the Hierarchy of Effects*

The communication receiver effects that have served as sources for specifying communication goals have had a long history of theory building in consumer research. The communication mix component that has been the major recipient of this theory building is advertising.

The communication effects of advertising on its receiver or audience have been hypothesized to take place in a hierarchical sequence. This framework is usually traced back to the AIDA model of the 1920's. This model very simply stated that "any effective sales presentation should attract attention, gain interest, create a desire, and precipitate action." Two other, well known and influential models of this kind are Colley's (1961) DAGMAR (Defining Advertising Goals for Measured Advertising Results) and a six stage model proposed by Lavidge and Steiner (1961). The six stages are: awareness, knowledge, liking, preference, conviction and purchase. Aaker and Myers (1982), Ray (1973, 1982), Assael (1981), Robertson et al. (1984) have discussed the development and limitations of hierarchy of effects models since that early beginning of AIDA to today's more elaborate, more flexible frameworks able to supposedly accommodate all possible major situations of consumer communication behavior.

There are two versions of the current research paradigm that are interesting to contrast. The first of these is Ray's (1982, Chapter 2) rigorously formulated "three-order hierarchy model." The second is Vaughn's (1980) more practitioner oriented formulation that showed a four-order hierarchy model.

In Ray's conceptualization (see Figure 2), there are two major communication variables that will determine the kind of hierarchy model that will prevail. These are felt involvement that the communication audience have on the communication object (i.e., the product), and the brand differentiation condition of the advertised product that exists at the time of the advertising campaign. Dichotomizing these two variables results in the four-quadrant matrix of Figure 2. One quadrant is presumed under Ray's formulation as almost logically impossible: the case where there is a high

	High brand differentiations	Low brand differentiations
High involvement	The learning hierarchy "Learn-feel-do"	The dissonance-attribution hierarchy "Do-feel-learn"
Low involvement	None: not logically possible	The low-involvement hierarchy "Learn-do-feel"

Fig. 2. Ray's three-order model of hierarchy of effects (constructed from the description of the models in Ray, 1982).

degree of brand differentiation, and yet consumers feel a low or no involvement with the product.

The remaining three hierarchy effects possibilities are well documented in Ray's development of these effects both in supporting theories and research findings. Ray (1982: p. 184) describes these three models very simply as consisting of

> the standard stairstep Learning hierarchy, the Dissonance-Attribution hierarchy, which consists of action occurring first followed by attitude change and learning; and finally, the Low-Involvement hierarchy, which consists of a gross awareness occurring first and then action and attitude development in that order.

Vaughn (1980) formulated a framework, now identified simply as the FCB Grid (Berger 1986), consisting of four hierarchical sub-models (see Figure 3). The four hierarchical models are derived from the dichotomous variables of product involvement and a distinction between "thinking" and "feeling" communication tasks. This conceptual framework can be used to select the types of appeals and media most appropriate for each product category. For example, cell 1 products call for communication containing detailed information about the brand's benefits and require more involving media such as magazines or direct mail. If, on the other hand, the product

		Thinking communication task	Feeling communication task
Product	High involvement	1 The economic model "Learn-feel-do"	2 The psychological model "Feel-learn-do"
Product	Low involvement	3 The responsive model "Do-learn-feel"	4 The social model "Do-feel-learn"

Fig. 3. Vaughn's models of hierarchy of advertising effects, the FCB Grid (adapted from Vaughn, 1980).

falls into cell 2, emotional and ego involving appeals are likely to be more effective, particularly if one uses involving media. Communication about cell 3 products should aim at inducing trial through point of purchase displays poster ads, coupons, sample. Finally, in cell 4, the objective is to arouse emotions and to emphasize social connections through high attention getting media.

Vaughn's model suffers from the absence of the kind of rigor of concepts and scientific basis as found in Ray's more carefully worked-out formulation. For example, the concept in the "think-feel" variable is not clear. As Haley et al. (1984: p. 17) cautioned, "it is virtually impossible to deliver a completely cognitive or a completely emotional message." "Think" messages have emotional overtones and "feel" messages are read with logical lenses. At the same time, the measurement of involvement incorporates the think/feel dimension in it which casts doubt on the validity of the model derived from correlated variables. Recent efforts to better operationalize involvement and the think-feel dimension are reported in Ratchford (1985) and Vaughn (1986).

Smith and Swinyard (1982) presented a so-called "integrated information response model" that was able to explain under what conditions, cases such as the following can take place:

1. Direct experience or product trial, and not advertising is used by the consumer as the major information source.
2. Affect has very low correlation to behavior.
3. Apparently the same behavior of purchase responds differently to the same information stimuli.
4. Promotional effects upon conation are found in supposedly the same cases in varying degrees.

The marketing implications of all these are best illustrated, surprisingly, in the work of a non-marketing researcher, William McGuirc (1976, 1978). Applying the Learning Hierarchy model, McGuirc developed from his analysis of the model what he called the "matrix of persuasion" and offered this as a means of developing and evaluating an effective advertising campaign in terms of "the five-component analysis of communication," he identified together with "the six-step behavioral analysis of persuasion" he presented. A campaign is considered to be effective under this matrix "to the extent that it maximizes the probability of occurrence of each of the behavioral steps" (in the matrix's row headings) given the constraints of "its communication components" (in the matrix's column headings).

In his discussion of this act of predicting the probability of occurrence of a behavioral step as a result of a manipulated communication component, McGuire introduced a complication of reality which he called the "compensation effect." This complication works out this way: "Quite frequently, a variable which affects one of the behavioral steps positively, tends to affect other steps negatively." This, according to McGuire, has a critical practical implication to the advertiser. He argues that because the compensation effect renders "the overall relationship between the independent variable (i.e., a communication component) and the dependent variable (e.g., purchasing behavior) ... non-monotonic," it follows that "intermediate levels of communication variables tend to be most efficacious in producing the target behavior such as purchasing" (McGuire, 1978: p. 171).

6.3. *The Communication Process and Information Processing Research*

After setting his advertising's communication goals based on the selection of the application hierarchy of effects model, the marketer must decide on what to do to attain the specified goals. For this decision, s/he has for his/her guidance the concepts from the various models of the communication process and the accumulated findings from the growing field of consumer information processing research (Bettman, 1979).

Like the hierarchy of effects models, the communication process models also started with a very simple formulation and progressed to today's complex comprehensive integrative version. As Robertson et al. (1984) described it, this development started with a "one-way flow or hypodermic-needle model," went on to a "two-way or transactional model" and rests in today's so-called "information processing model (which) elaborates the two-way model and specifies many of the variables determining consumer responses to advertising" (p. 216).

What is referred to as the consumer information processing model as an approach to developing and evaluating advertising is different from considering it as a model of what is happening to the consumer when exposed to advertising. As an approach, it uniformly views the consumer as proceeding through a chain or stages of responses to the advertising ultimately leading to the final stage of product purchase provided that no intervening stage is aborted. As a model of consumer response to advertising, there is no single consumer information processing model. There are several of them differing from each other by the number and complexity of the stages they define and by the nature and measure of each stage that they adopt.

For example, McGuire (1978) formulated his information processing model as consisting of a set of dependent variables made up of the six behavioral steps "through which the individual must pass if he is effectively to be persuaded" and a set of independent variables made up of the five components of the persuasive communication (i.e., source, message, channel, receiver and destination). Assael's (1981: p. 483) version is a process formulation that starts with multiple sources of both mass media and personal sources who all "encode and transmit" information to the consumer. In turn, the consumer processes this multiple source information by evaluating the source of the message itself choosing to search for more information, "when the level of information is considered inadequate to make a choice." This step is then followed by a "brand evaluation" stage, which if favorable leads to the purchase decision.

In the formulation of Smith and Swinyard (1982), the stages proceed from the starting point of the "information source" progressing to "information acceptance" then to "cognition" and then to "affect" and finally ending in "conation." Each of these five stages are however, dichotomously differentiated into:

1. advertising vs. direct experience for the information source;
2. low vs. high information acceptance;
3. lower order vs. higher order beliefs for cognition;
4. lower order vs. higher order affect; and
5. trial vs. commitment for conation.

The chain defined by the first elements in this series of five dichotomies makes up the "low-involvement" information processing situation, while that defined by the second elements makes up the traditional learning hierarchy of effects situation. Finally, Robertson et al. (1984) present probably the most complex formulation using the concept of mediators consisting of "situation factors" and "consumer information-processing factors" (p. 22[illegible]).

The research base for each of the several components of any of these models is almost overwhelming if account of the work that has been done in the social and behavior sciences aside from consumer research is considered. For a review of recent information processing research in advertising the reader is referred to Harris (1983) and to Percy and Woodside (1983).

The most impressive bases and the most helpful so far to the marketing practitioners are those that have been directed at studying the persuasion factors in the source, message, receiver and media components of the communication process and consumer information processing. The specific ones that have found frequent reference and use from among both marketing researchers and practitioners are the following:

1. *Source factors*:
   1.1. credibility: expertness and unbiasedness, and
   1.2. attractiveness: prestige, similarity and physical attractiveness,

2. *Message factors*:
   2.1. for creating positive attitudes,
      - message focus: ethos, pathos, logos,
      - implicit vs. explicit conclusions,
      - one vs. two sided arguments,
      - positive vs. negative emotions/appeals, and
   2.2. for building resistant attitudes,
      - inoculation/immunization messages,
      - refuting vs. ignoring opposition arguments, and
   2.3. for changing negative attitudes,
      - refutational messages,
      - audio, visual, behavioral distraction, and

3. *Receiver factors*:
   3.1. learning: wearout, memory, recall, recognition,
   3.2. attitude: active vs. passive role, high vs. low commitment/involvement,
   3.3. personality: self-confidence, authoritarianism, aggressiveness, dogmatism, anxiety, and sociability,
   3.4. social class, and
   3.5. culture.

4. *Media factors*:
   4.1. high vs. low involvement media,
   4.2. modality, e.g., eye vs. ear,
   4.3. reach, frequency, and repetition,
   4.4. continuity,
   4.5. dominance: advertising intrusiveness, and
   4.6. mood: emotional and imagination stimulation.

Listing is of course hardly an appropriate way to do justice to the richness of the consumer research literature and finding behind the specific factors included in the above list. But because of the relative abundance of comprehensive reviews of this literature such as those cited earlier, it is inefficient and repetitive to simply repeat a summary here. What is important to note is that many of the studies have really progressed to the point where it is now becoming more and more possible for the marketers to know from their results, specifically under what condition or conditions, for example, source credibility is effective in raising message acceptance, and not simply whether source credibility is important or not.

Some of the research issues which are recently receiving increasing attention include the role of memory stores and cognitive structures (e.g., Olson and Reynolds, 1983; Toy, 1982), levels of processing and consciousness (e.g., Derbaix and Vanden Abeele, 1985; Krugman, 1977; Saegert and Young, 1983), message evoked thoughts (e.g., Wright, 1980), mood effects (e.g., Lutz et al., 1983), the mediating effect of visual, verbal and emotional elements (e.g., Mitchell, 1983; Rossiter and Percy, 1983) and the study of brain waves responses to advertising (Hansen, 1981; Ray and Olson, 1983).

7. CONSUMER BEHAVIOR AND DISTRIBUTION STRATEGY

7.1. *Introduction*

As they are planning their communication program, marketers have to also plan their distribution strategy. But in terms of implementation, the latter will have to precede the former, as a consumer persuaded by a communication, who then goes to a store and does not find the product will not "walk a mile" to other stores or wait patiently for the product to come along. This final portion of the consumer's market-product fit equation needs as much consumer research and theory base as the communication portion (Darden and Lusch, 1983).

The field as currently structured consists of such consumer variables and processes as shopping motivations and shopper typology, planned and unplanned shopping and in-store purchasing behavior, store image and store patronage, and store loyalty behavior.

7.2. *Shopping Motivation and Shopper Typology*

The study that is almost always referred to in order to answer the question of what need or needs the consumer is trying to satisfy by shopping is an old one published in 1972.

The Tauber (1972) study identified six personal motivations for shopping and five social motivations. The six personal motivations are:

1. the need to play the shopper role,
2. the diversion need,
3. the self gratification need,
4. the need to learn about new trends,
5. the physical activity need, and
6. the sensory stimulation need.

The five social motivations are:

1. the need for a social experience outside the home,

2. the need to communicate with others having a similar interest,
3. the peer group attraction need,
4. the status and authority need, and
5. the need for the pleasure of bargaining.

A lot more work has been done on looking at shopping motivation not directly but through the study of shopper "personality" or typology. For example, Darden and Reynolds (1971) report a seven category study which typed shoppers into:

1. the apathetic shopper,
2. the demanding shopper,
3. the quality conscious shopper,
4. the fastidious shopper,
5. the stamp prefer shopper,
6. the convenient location shopper, and
7. the stamp hater shopper.

Having available shopper profiles such as the above should be useful in helping retail managers position their store and appeal to different segments of the market by providing them the most appropriate types of information and products/services.

A recent typology was developed by Verhallen and De Nooij (1982), based on the shoppers' sensitivity for price, quality, assortment, and locational convenience of supermarkets.

7.3. *Planned and Unplanned Shopping and In-store Purchasing Behavior*

While consumers may plan their store shopping, this does not also mean that what they buy in the store is also planned. This suggests that it is useful to distinguish between planned vs. unplanned shopping behavior and planned vs. unplanned in-store purchasing behavior. A planned in-store purchasing behavior is likened to a high involvement consumer decision making while an unplanned purchasing behavior is said to conform to the predictions of the low involvement consumer decision making model. The few consumer studies available have directed their attention to the unplanned purchasing behavior.

The first categorizing of the types of unplanned in-store buying behavior came out in 1962 (Stern 1962) and has not, to the present, been significantly improved upon. There were four types identified, i.e., pure impulse buying, reminder buying, suggestion buying and "planned" impulse buying. A decade later, D'Antoni and Shenson (1979) picked up the subject and proposed a new approach to it. According to D'Antoni and Shenson, the 1962 ideas of Stern and those that came after, were based on a questionable concept of impulsiveness. That concept saw impulse buying to be "unplanned as a result of the buying decision being in-store" (D'Antoni and Shenson, 1973: p. 66). These authors proposed a definition of the impulse buying decision as one in which "the bits of information processed and thus the time taken relative to the normal decisional time lapse are significantly less with respect to the same or quite similar products or services." The emergent impulse buying "theory" remained unfortunately, as an untested theory. To expect it to have been tested was perhaps not that realistic. In the first place, its authors did not try testing it. In the second place, the "theory" and its proposed measures were never operationalized.

Assael (1981: p. 515) has set aside the above issue and instead looked at the question of what are "the most influential factors" in the in-store purchase decision of the consumer. Arguing on the assumption that most in-store purchases are unplanned (in whatever way this is defined), Assael pointed out that those most influential factors are the "in-store stimuli (of) displays, shelf position, shelf space, information on the package, the nature and attractiveness of the package, (and) the in-store pricing promotions." If this is true, Assael concluded that in-store pricing stimuli deserve to be studied as much as advertising is.

Kotler (1974) has attempted to provide a framework for encouraging research to look at what he regarded to be a major influencing in-store stimulus. He called this stimulus the outlet's "atmospherics," and defined this as the outlet's "buying environments (designed) to produce specific emotional effects in the buyer that enhance his purchase probability" (Kotler, 1974: p. 50). Sommer and Aitken (1982) present additional evidence showing that the location of various product categories inside supermarkets influence customers' recall of these products and presumably their subsequent purchasing behavior.

7.4. *Store Image and Patronage*

The preoccupation of store image studies has been on the measurement issue (Lindquist, 1975). This measurement is based on the definition of store image as "the way in which a store is defined in the shopper's mind, partly by its functional qualities and partly by an aura of psychological attributes."

Various measurement studies of store image have looked at varying store attributes along which to measure store image (for a critical review, see Peterson and Kerin, 1983). The research instruments most often used include the semantic differential, Guttman attitude scaling, multidimensional scaling, multi-attribute modeling, free association and psycholinguistic techniques. The studies reviewed in Assael (1981), Williams (1982), and Engel and Blackwell (1982) made use of a high of 35 attributes. Of all these attributes, location has received the highest share of research (for a review, see Hubbard, 1978; MacKay and Olshavsky, 1975).

In conceptualizing the shopper's store patronage behavior of the first time kind (i.e., store choice behavior), marketing authorities have defined the role of store image as a very major one (May, 1974-1975). In the model of store choice processes that Williams (1982: p. 458) discussed, it is in fact the major factor together with the "evaluation criteria" or "important store attributes" that shoppers use in their evaluation of alternative stores. The same is true in the more elaborate model suggested by Monroe and Guiltinan (1975).

This model uses path-analysis to describe the probable direction of influence between sets of variable thought to influence store patronage. The first set includes the consumer's demographic, life style, and personality characteristics. These variables lead to the development of general opinions and activities concerning shopping and search for information (set 2). These variables then influence the importance attached to the various store attributes and the perception of the various store alternatives. If the consumer is satisfied with the store visited, then a positive image of this store is reinforced and may result in store loyalty. Other attempts to use a causal modelling approach to store patronage are described in Darden et al. (1983) and Mason et al. (1983). A more ambitious paper is Sheth's (1983) attempt to develop an integrative theory of patronage behavior. Sheth presents a case for distinguishing between two subtheories of patronage behavior: The first subtheory describes shopping preferences as a function of shopping predispositions motives, choice calculus and shopping options. The second subtheory tries to integrate the market, firm, product and personal determinants of store choice.

7.5. *Store Loyalty Behavior*

Store patronage behavior of the same kind is store loyalty behavior. Different ways of operationalizing store loyalty have been suggested (e.g., Carman, 1970; Charlton, 1973; Lessig, 1973; Enis and Paul, 1970; Samli, 1975). It can be measured by the percentage of customer's budget allocated to a certain store for one or more product classes, by the percentage of purchase of certain products done at a given store, by the number of stores patronized or by the number of trips made to the favorite store during the survey period or by the combination of the above. Alternatively, store loyalty can be measured by using psychographic scales.

Variations in store loyalty have been explained by a variety of factors

(Charlton, 1973). Store loyalty is believed to vary across product classes and customer type. Store loyals tend to engage in less information search, have a low knowledge of existence of other stores, to be older, have a lower educational level and family income. They also tend to be more risk adverse and less confident in their information processing skills. In his review of the literature Goldman (1977-78) concluded that store loyalty behavior appears to be "part of a low search, low knowledge and low utilization level shopping style." This conclusion is supported and extended by a more recent study of the personal characteristics of those customers who tend to be loyal to banks (Jain et al., 1987).

Store and brand loyalty are apparently negatively related to variety-seeking behavior (McAlister and Pessemier, 1982) and new product trial. It is positively related to convenience and tradition-related factors. Store loyals tend to patronize local stores and place greater emphasis on the human, interpersonal aspects of shopping. These findings have obvious implications for retailers in terms of store location strategy and the kind of store image that would best appeal to customers with a high store loyalty propensity.

8. CONCLUSION

All review articles on consumer behavior research invariably start by pointing out how critical and indeed indispensible the understanding of consumer behavior is to an effective marketing strategy. This chapter did not take any exception to this pattern and it looked at consumer behavior under this perspective. In 1976, writing an octennium review of the consumer behavior field for the *Annual Review of Psychology*, Jacoby (1976: pp. 344-345) estimated that about 85% of published work in the area prior to 1968 was probably "rather low and of questionable worth." Between 1968 and 1975, he put the proportion at probably 50%. His anticipation over the years following his review was however optimistic.

To Jacoby, there are at least four major research issues that consumer behavior studies needed to address, if consumer behavior as a discipline were to rise to a respectable behavioral science research area. These issues say that consumer behavior research should or need to:

1. start undertaking "the rudimentary task of ascertaining the validity, reliability, and sensitivity of (its) measures, and their relationship with other indices (measuring) the same phenomenon,"
2. move "from simplistic dependent variables toward employing multiple measures of the same dependent variable and to multiple dependent measures,"

3. work toward "greater conceptual specificity and clarity, especially in regard to definitions of terms and constructs," and
4. have more "programmatic research" (in contrast to the typical "terrain mapping and nose counting"), and "replication and crossvalidation of findings."

If the consumer behavior studies and "theories" discussed in this chapter were subjected to and evaluated by these four criteria, it can be concluded that:

1. they are all still weak on the first criterion;
2. except for the product perception area and some of those in communication behavior area, all others are also weak on the second criterion,
3. price-related consumer behavior and consumer shopping behavior researches have been particularly weak on the third criterion,
4. shopper behavior research work has been conspicuously very weak on the need for more programmatic research.
5. with the exception of product perception studies, all others have been weak on the need for replication and cross-validation of findings.

Insofar as applications and use by the marketing strategies of those consumer behavior concepts and research discussed in this chapter are concerned, at least two things are apparent. The first is that users are not mindful of the violation of the Jacoby criteria and simply just use whatever they seem to find useful. This of course is an unverified impression which leads to the second need.

It seems clear that there is no research looking into the actual incidence and extent of usage by marketers of consumer behavior studies. There have on occasions been articles reporting on surveys of what marketing input variables are held important over other by marketers or what type of marketing research projects they commission. However, there are no existing reports on studies on their consumer research using behavior.

NOTE

1. The formal definiton of marketing offered by the American Marketing Association (AMA) is: "Marketing is the process of planning and executing the conception, pricing, promotion, and distribution of ideas, goods, and services to create exchanges that satisfy individual and organizational objectives" (AMA President S.W. Brown, quoted in Marketing News, March 1, 1985, p. 1).

REFERENCES

Aaker, D.A., and J.G. Myers, 1982, Advertising Management, Englewood Cliffs, NJ: Prentice-Hall.

Assael, H., 1981, Consumer Behavior and Marketing Action, Boston, MA: Kent.

Bauer, R.A., 1960, "Consumer behavior as risk taking," in: R.S. Hancock (ed.), Dynamic Marketing for a Changing World, Proceedings of the 43rd Conference, Chicago, IL: American Marketing Association, pp. 389-400.

Bass, F.M., and W.W. Talarzyk, 1974, An attitude model for the study of brand preferences, Journal of Marketing Research, 9, 93-96.

Beales, H., M.B. Mazis, S.C. Salop, and R. Staelin, 1981, Consumer search and public policy, Journal of Consumer Research, 8, 11-22.

Bearden, W.O., and A.G. Woodside, 1978, Consumption occasion influence on consumer brand choice, Decision Sciences, 9, 237-284.

Belk, R.W., 1975, Situational variables and consumer behavior, Journal of Consumer Research, 2, 157-164.

Belk, R.W., 1979, "A free response approach to developing product-specific consumption situation taxonomies," in: A.D. Shocker (ed.), Analytic Approaches to Product and Market Planning, Cambridge, MA: Marketing Science Institute, pp. 177-196.

Belk, R.W., K.D. Bahn, and R.N. Mayer, 1982, Developmental recognition of consumption symbolism, Journal of Consumer Research, 9, 4-17.

Berger, D., 1986, Theory into practice: The FCB grid, European Research, 14, 35-46.

Bettman, J.R., 1975, Issues in designing consumer information environments, Journal of Consumer Research, 2, 169-177.

Bettman, J.R., 1979a, Memory factors in consumer choice: A review, Journal of Marketing, 43, 37-53.

Bettman, J.R., 1979b, An Information Processing Theory of Consumer Choice, Reading, MA: Addison-Wesley.

Bettman, J.R., and C.W. Park, 1980, Effects of prior knowledge and experience and phase of the choice process on consumer decision processes: A protocol analysis, Journal of Consumer Research, 7, 234-48.

Carman, J.M., 1970, Correlates of brand loyalty: Some positive results, Journal of Marketing Research, 7, 67-76.

Charlton, P., 1973, A review of shop loyalty, Journal of the Market Research Society, 15, 35-51.

Cohen, O., 1972, Surrogate indicators and deception in advertising, Journal of Marketing, 36, 10-15.

Colley, R.D., 1961, Defining Advertising Goals for Measured Advertising Results, New York: Association of National Advertisers.

Cox, D.F., 1967, "The Sorting Rule model of the consumer product evaluation process," in: D.F. Cox (ed.), Risk Taking and Information Handling in Consumer Behavior, Boston, MA: Harvard Graduate School of Business Administration, pp. 324-369.

D'Antoni, J.S., and H.L. Shenson, 1979, Impulse buying revisited: A behavioral typology, Journal of Retailing, 49, 63-76.

Darden, W.R., and R.F. Lusch (eds.), 1983, Patronage Behavior and Retail Management, New York: North Holland.

Darden, W.R., and F.R. Reynolds, 1971, Shopping orientations and product usage rates, Journal of Marketing Research, 8, 505-508.

Darden, W.R., O. Erdem, and D.K. Darden, 1983, "A comparison and test of three causal models of patronage intentions," in: W.R. Darden and R.F. Lusch (eds.), Patronage Behavior and Retail Management, New York: North Holland, pp. 29-43.

Day, G.S., 1969, A two-dimensional concept of brand loyalty, Journal of Advertising Research, 9, 29-35.

Day, G.S., 1977, Diagnosing the product portfolio, Journal of Marketing, 41, 29-38.

Day, G.S., A.D. Shocker, and R.K. Srivastava, 1979, Customer-oriented approaches to identifying product markets, Journal of Marketing, 43, 8-19.

Deighton, J., 1983, How to solve problems that don't matter: Some heuristics for uninvolved thinking, Advances in Consumer Research, 10, 314-319.

Derbaix, C., and P. Vanden Abeele, 1985, Consumer inferences and consumer preferences. The status of cognition and consciousness in consumer behavior theory, International Journal of Research in Marketing, 2, 157-174.

Dickson, P.R., 1982, Person-situation: Segmentation's missing link, Journal of Marketing, 46, 56-64.

Dillon, W.R., N. Mulani, and D.G. Frederick, 1984, Removing perceptual distortions in product space analysis, Journal of Marketing Research, 21, 184-193.

Enis, B.M., and G.W. Paul, 1970, Store loyalty as a basis for market segmentation, Journal of Retailing, 20, 42-56.

Engel, J.F., and R.D. Blackwell, 1982, Consumer Behavior, Hinsdale, IL: The Dryden Press.

Etgar, M., and N.K. Malhotra, 1981, Determinants of price dependency: Personal and perceptual factors, Journal of Consumer Research, 8, 217-222.

Fady, A., 1976, Les clients connaissent-ils les prix des articles courants?, Coopération, Distribution, Consommation, 12, 2-7.

Fishbein, M., 1963, An investigation of the relationships between beliefs about an object and the attitude toward that object, Human Relations, 16, 233-240.

Frank, R.E., W.F. Massy, and Y. Wind, 1972, Market Segmentation, Englewood Cliffs, NJ: Prentice-Hall.

Fraser, C., and J.W. Bradford, 1983, Competitive market structure analysis, Journal of Consumer Research, 10, 15-30.

Gabor, A., and C.W.J. Granger, 1966, Price as an indicator of quality: Report on an inquiry, Economica, 33, 43-70.

Gatignon, H., and T.S. Robertson, 1985, A propositional inventory for new diffusion research, Journal of Consumer Research, 11, 849-867.

Gemünden, H.G., 1985, Perceived risk and information search. A systematic meta-analysis of the empirical evidence, International Journal of Research in Marketing, 2, 79-100.

Goldman, A., 1977-78, The shopping style explanation for store loyalty, Journal of Retailing, 53, 33-46, 94-95.

Green, P.E., and D.S. Tull, 1978, Research for Marketing Decisions, Englewood Cliffs, NJ: Prentice-Hall.

Haley, I.H., J. Richardson, and B.M. Baldwin, 1984, The effects of nonverbal communications in television advertising, Journal of Advertising Research, 24, 11-18.

Hansen, F., 1981, Hemispheral lateralization: Implications for understanding consumer behavior, Journal of Consumer Research, 8, 23-36.

Harris, R.J.(ed.), 1983, Information Processing Research in Advertising, Hillsdale, NJ: Lawrence Erlbaum.

Henry, W.A., 1980, The effect of information processing ability on processing accuracy, Journal of Consumer Research, 7, 42-48.

Hirschman, E.C., and M.B. Holbrook (eds.), 1981, Symbolic Consumer Behavior, Ann Arbor, MI: Association for Consumer Research.

Holbrook, M.B., 1983, Using a structural model of halo effect to assess perceptual distortion due to affective overtones, Journal of Consumer Research, 10, 247-252.

Holman, R.H., 1981, "Product as communication: A fresh appraisal of a venerable topic," in: B.M. Enis and K.J. Roering (eds.), Review of Marketing, Chicago, IL: American Marketing Association, pp. 106-119.

Horton, R.L., 1984, Buyer Behavior, Columbus, OH: Charles E. Merrill.

Hubbard, R., 1978, A review of selected factors conditioning consumer travel behavior, Journal of Consumer Research, 5, 1-21.

Huber, J., 1975, Bootstrapping of data and decisions, Journal of Consumer Research, 2, 229-234.

Huber, J., and J. McCann, 1982, The impact of inferential beliefs on product evaluations, Journal of Marketing Research, 19, 324-333.

Hutchinson, J.W., 1983, On the locus of range effects in judgment and choice, Advances in Consumer Research, 10, 305-308.

Jacoby, J., 1976, Consumer psychology: An octennium, Annual Review of Psychology, 27, 331-358.

Jacoby, J., 1978, Consumer research: A state of the art review, Journal of Marketing, 42, 87-96.

Jacoby, J., and R.W. Chestnut, 1978, Brand Loyalty: Measurement and Management, New York: John Wiley.

Jain, A.K., C. Pinson, and N.K. Malhotra, 1987, Customer loyalty as a construct in the marketing of banking services, International Journal of Bank Marketing, 3, 49-72.

Kamen, J.M., and R.J. Toman, 1970, Psychophysics of prices, Journal of Marketing Research, 7, 27-35.

Kassarjian, H.H., 1982, Consumer psychology, Annual Review of Psychology, 3, 619-649.

Kotler, P., 1973-74, Atmospherics as a marketing tool, Journal of Retailing, 49, 48-64.

Kotler, P., 1984, Marketing Management, Englewood Cliffs, NJ: Prentice-Hall (fifth edition).

Krugman, H.E., 1977, Memory without recall, exposure without perception, Journal of Advertising Research, 17, 7-12.

Lavidge, R.J., and G.A. Steiner, 1961, A model for predictive measurements of advertising effectiveness, Journal of Marketing, 25, 59-62.

Lessig, V.P., 1973, Consumer store images and store loyalties, Journal of Marketing, 37, 72-74.

Lindquist, J.D., 1974-75, The meaning of image, Journal of Retailing, 50, 29-38, 116.

Lunn, T., 1978, "Segmenting and constructing markets," in: R.M. Worcester and J. Downham (eds.), Consumer Market Research Handbook, New York: Van Nostrand Reinhold, pp. 343-376.

Lussier, D.A., and R.W. Olshavsky, 1979, Task complexity and contingent processing in brand choice, Journal of Consumer Research, 6, 154-165.

Lutz, R.J., 1975, Changing brand attitudes through modification of cognitive structure, Journal of Consumer Research, 1, 49-59.

Lutz, R.J., S.B. MacKensie, and G.E. Belch, 1983, Attitude toward the ad as a mediator of advertising effectiveness: Determinants and consequences, Advances in Consumer Research, 10, 532-539.

Lynch, J.G., Jr., and T.K. Srull, 1982, Memory and attentional factors in consumer choice: Concepts and research methods, Journal of Consumer Research, 9, 18-37.

MacKay, D.B., and R.W. Olshavsky, 1975, Cognitive maps of retail locations: An investigation of some basic issues, Journal of Consumer Research, 2, 197-205.

Mason, J.B., R.M. Durand, and J.L. Taylor, 1983, "Retail patronage: A causal analysis of antecedent factors," in: W.R. Darden and R.F. Lusch (eds.), Patronage Behavior and Retail Management, New York: North Holland, pp. 339-351.

May, E.G., 1974-75, Practical applications of recent retail image research, Journal of Retailing, 50, 15-20.

McAlister, L., and E. Pessemier, 1982, Variety seeking behavior: An interdisciplinary review, Journal of Consumer Research, 9, 311-322.

McGuire, W.J., 1976, Some internal psychological factors influencing consumer choice, Journal of Consumer Research, 2, 302-319.

McGuire, W.J., 1978, "An information-processing model of advertising effectiveness," in: H.L. Davis and A.J. Silk (eds.), Behavioral and Management Science in Marketing, New York: John Wiley, pp. 156-182.

Miller, K.E., and J.L. Ginter, 1979, An investigation of situational variation in brand choice behavior and attitude, Journal of Marketing Research, 16, 111-123.

Mitchell, A.A., 1983, "The effect of visual and emotional advertising: An information processing approach,"in: L. Percy and A.G. Woodside (eds.), Advertising and Consumer Psychology, Lexington, MA: Lexington Books, pp. 197-218.

Mitchell, A.A., and J.C. Olson, 1981, Are product attribute beliefs the only mediator of advertising effects on broad attitude?, Journal of Marketing Research, 18, 318-332.

Monroe, K.B., 1976, The influence of price differences and brand familiarity on brand preferences, Journal of Consumer Research, 3, 42-49.

Monroe, K.B., and J.P. Guiltinan, 1975, A path-analytic exploration of retail patronage influences, Journal of Consumer Research, 2, 19-28.

Ofir, C., and J.G. Lynch, Jr., 1984, Context effects on judgment under uncertainty, Journal of Consumer Research, 11, 668-679.

Olson, J.C., 1978, Inferential belief formation in the cue utilization process, Advances in Consumer Research, 5, 706-713.

Olson, J.C., 1980, Encoding processes: Levels of processing and existing knowledge structures, Advances in Consumer Research, 7, 154-160.

Olson, J.C., and T.J. Reynolds, 1983, "Understanding consumers' cognitive structures: Implications for advertising strategy,"in: L. Percy and A.G. Woodside (eds.), Advertising and Consumer Psychology, Lexington, MA: Lexington Books, pp. 77-90.

Olshavsky, R.W., and D.H. Granbois, 1979, Consumer decision making: Fact or fiction?, Journal of Consumer Research, 6, 93-100.

Park, C.W., 1978, A conflict resolution choice model, Journal of Consumer Research, 5, 124-135.

Park, C.W., and V.P. Lessig, 1981, Familiarity and its impact on consumer decision biases and heuristics, Journal of Consumer Research, 8, 223-230.

Percy, L., and A.G. Woodside, 1983, Advertising and Consumer Psychology, Lexington, MA: Heath.

Peterson, R.A., and R.A. Kerin, 1983, "Store image measurement in patronage research: Fact and artifact," in: W.R. Darden and R.F. Lusch (eds.), Patronage Behavior and Retail Management, New York: North Holland, pp. 293-306.

Pinson, C., 1986, An implicit product theory approach to consumers' inferential judgments about products, International Journal of Research in Marketing, 3, 19-38.

Pras, B., 1977, "Comment les consommateurs opèrent-ils leurs choix?" in: C. Pinson (ed.), Encyclopédie du Marketing, Vol. 2, Paris: Editions Techniques, pp. 1-24.

Pras, B., and J.O. Summers, 1978, Perceived risk and composition models for multi-attribute decisions, Journal of Marketing Research, 15, 429-437.

Ratchford, B.S., 1985, Operationalizing Involvement and Thinking/Feeling in the FCB Grid, Buffalo, NY: State University of New York (working paper).

Ray, M.L., 1973, "Marketing communications and the hierarchy of effects," in: P. Clarke (ed.), New Models for Mass Communication Research, Beverly Hills, CA: Sage, pp. 147-176.

Ray, M.L., 1982, Advertising and Communication Management, Englewood Cliffs, NJ: Prentice-Hall.

Ray, W.J., and J.C. Olson, 1983, "Perspectives on psycho-physiological assessment of psychological responses to advertising," in: L. Percy and A.G. Woodside (eds.), Advertising and Consumer Psychology, Lexington, MA: Lexington Books, pp. 253-270.

Reibstein, D.J., 1985, Marketing, Englewood Cliffs, NJ: Prentice-Hall.

Ries, A., and J. Trout, 1982, Positioning: The Battle for your Mind, New York: Warner Books.
Robertson, T.S., J. Zielinski, and S. Ward, 1984, Consumer Behavior, Glenview, IL: Scott, Foresman.
Roselius, T., 1971, Consumer rankings of risk reduction methods, Journal of Marketing, 35, 56-61.
Ross, I., 1975, Perceived risk and consumer behavior: A critical review, Advances in Consumer Research, 2, 1-19.
Rossiter, J.R., and L. Percy, 1983, "Visual communication in advertising," in: R.J. Harris (ed.), Information Processing Research into Advertising, Hillsdale, NJ: Lawrence Erlbaum, pp. 83-126.
Saegert, J.R., and R.K. Young, 1983, "Levels of processing and memory for advertisements," in: L. Percy and A.G. Woodside (eds.), Advertising and Consumer Psychology, Lexington, MA: Lexington Books, pp. 117-132.
Samli, A.C., 1975, Use of segmentation index to measure store loyalty, Journal of Retailing, 51, 51-60, 113.
Schellinck, D.A., 1980, Determinants of cue choice behavior, Urbana-Champaign, IL: University of Illinois (unpublished doctoral dissertation).
Sandell, R.G., 1968, Effects of attitudinal and situational factors on reported choice behavior, Journal of Marketing Research, 5, 405-408.
Scott, C.A., and A.M. Tybout, 1983, Some indirect effects of case vs. base-rate data on information processing strategies, Advances in Consumer Research, 10, 109-111.
Sharpe, L.K., and K.L. Granzin, 1974, Market segmentation by consumer usage context, Journal of Economics and Business, 26, 227-228.
Sheth, J.N., 1983, "An integrative theory of patronage preference and behavior," in: W.R. Darden and R.F. Lusch (eds.), Patronage Behavior and Retail Management, New York: North Holland, pp. 9-28.
Shugan, S.M., 1980, The cost of thinking, Journal of Consumer Research, 7, 99-111.
Silk, A.J., and G.L. Urban, 1978, Pre-test market evaluation of new packaged goods: A model and measurement methodology, Journal of Marketing Research, 15, 171-191.
Simon, H., 1982, Preismanagement, Wiesbaden, FRG: Gabler.
Sirgy, M.J., 1982, Self-concept in consumer behavior: A critical review, Journal of Consumer Research, 9, 287-300.
Smith, R.E., and W.R. Swinyard, 1982, Information response models: An integrated approach, Journal of Marketing, 46, 81-93.
Sommer, R., and S. Aitken, 1982, Mental mapping of two supermarkets, Journal of Consumer Research, 9, 211-215.
Solomon, M.R., 1983, The role of products as social stimuli: A symbolic interactionism perspective, Journal of Consumer Research, 10, 319-329.
Stern, H., 1962, The significance of impulse buying today, Journal of Marketing, 26, 59-62.
Sternthal, B., and C.S. Craig, 1982, Consumer Behavior, Englewood Cliffs, NJ: Prentice-Hall.
Tauber, E.M., 1972, Why do people shop, Journal of Marketing, 36, 46-49.
Toy, D.R., 1982, Monitoring communication effects: A cognitive structure/cognitive response approach, Journal of Consumer Research, 9, 66-76.
Vaughn, R., 1980, How advertising works: A planning model, Journal of Advertising Research, 20, 27-33.
Vaughn, R., 1986, How advertising works: A planning model revisited, Journal of Advertising Research, 26, 57-66.
Verhallen, T.M.M., and G.J. de Nooij, 1982, Retail attribute sensitivity and shopping patronage, Journal of Economic Psychology, 2, 39-55.

Wilkie, W.L., and E.A. Pessemier, 1973, Issues in marketing's use of multi-attribute attitude models, Journal of Marketing Research, 10, 428-441.

Williams, T.G., 1982, Consumer Behavior, St. Paul, MN: West Publishers.

Wind, Y., 1977, "Brand loyalty and vulnerability," in: A.G. Woodside, J.N. Sheth, and P.D. Bennett (eds.), Consumer and Industrial Buying Behavior, New York: Elsevier, pp. 313-319.

Wind, Y., 1982, Product Policy: Concepts, Methods and Strategy, Reading, MA: Addison-Wesley.

Wright, P.L., 1980, Message-evoked thoughts; Persuasion research using thought verbalizations, Journal of Consumer Research, 7, 151-175.

Young, S., L. Ott, and B. Feigin, 1978, Some practical considerations in market segmentation, Journal of Marketing Research, 15, 405-412.

Zajonc, R.B., and H. Markus, 1982, Affective and cognitive factors in preferences, Journal of Consumer Research, 9, 123-131.

Zeithaml, V.A., 1984, Issues in conceptualizing and measuring consumer response to price, Advances in Consumer Research, 11, 612-616.

Table of Contents

9. Models of Consumer Choice Behavior

MONROE FRIEDMAN
Eastern Michigan University, Ypsilanti, U.S.A.

1. INTRODUCTION

No review of the scholarly literature of economic psychology would be complete without some treatment of the process of consumer choice leading to the acquisition of goods and services. The present chapter examines five conceptual models of consumer choice behavior. None of these models can be considered old. Two originated in the mid-1960's while the remaining three were developed (or revised) in the last ten years. Thus the development of this theoretical area has been a relatively recent phenomenon in economic psychology.

The first section of this chapter presents background information relating to models of consumer choice behavior. This section starts with an examination of models in the context of consumer behavior theory. It continues with a look at the functions served by the models in the scholarly community along with the criteria by which they are often evaluated. This background material is followed by sections describing the five models of consumer choice behavior. The chapter ends with a comparative assessment of the models and a discussion of their role in economic psychology.

2. BACKGROUND INFORMATION

2.1. *Models as Theoretical Constructs*

A first question to be asked about models of consumer choice behavior is how they differ from other theoretical constructs. While some authors draw a distinction between models and theories, many others, such as Horton (1984), Lunn (1974) and Simon and Newell (1963), use the two terms interchangeably.[1] As Lawrence (1966) has noted, "model" has a practical connotation to it which has rendered it more acceptable than "theory" to

Van Raaij, W.F., van Veldhoven, G.M. and Wärneryd, K.E. (eds) Handbook of Economic Psychology. ISBN 90-247-3720-6.

the marketing community. And it is this community which has been primarily responsible for the development of models of consumer choice behavior. (As we shall see shortly, all five models examined in this chapter have been developed by marketing professors). Both terms, however, are concerned with providing a conceptual framework for a field of study which will aid in its understanding. Both "theories" and "models" designate sets of key variables and specify causal relationships among them.

2.2. *Model Characteristics in Common*

The models to be examined herein are similar in several important respects:

1. They all focus on the behavior of individual consumers, rather than groups of consumers, such as families or communal organizations.
2. They all focus on consumer choice behavior associated with the acquisition of consumer commodities, rather than the use or disposal of such commodities.
3. They all view consumer choice behavior as a complex process rather than a simple act.
4. They all attempt to be comprehensive in their explanations of this process; to reach this objective the models make use of elaborate flow diagrams to depict various constellations of endogenous and exogenous variables impacting upon consumer behavior.
5. Unlike earlier conceptual efforts, many of which were simply extrapolations of the work of an individual theorist from the social and behavioral sciences (e.g., Freud, Lewin or Maslow), the models of consumer choice behavior are the original formulations of scholars whose primary academic affiliation is with the field of marketing.

That the models of consumer choice behavior should have many of these characteristics in common will come as no surprise to observers of economic developments in Europe and the United States since World War II.[2] As Sternthal and Craig (1982) have noted, interest in the formulation of consumer choice theories was triggered by the dramatic changes to European and American markets which emerged in the postwar era. Substantial increases in available consumer goods and services, coupled with unprecedented demand for such commodities, as millions of military servicemen returned to civilian life with new interests and aspirations, prompted marketers to look for help in understanding how these postwar consumers would make their purchase decisions.

While the early efforts of marketing scholars to understand this phenomenon were crude, consisting largely of whole-cloth applications of theories from other academic disciplines, the situation improved significantly in the mid-1960's. The models which emerged during this later period were more original in conception, more comprehensive in scope, and more sophisticated in their treatment of relevant research findings.

2.3. *Functions Served by the Consumer Choice Models*

Since the models to be examined herein attempt to account for a wide range of variables impinging upon consumer choice behavior, their function within the consumer research fields is of necessity somewhat different from theoretical formulations with more modest objectives.

Engel and Blackwell (1982: pp. 677-678) note four advantages offered to consumer researchers by these comprehensive models of consumer choice behavior:

1. Explanatory variables are specified.
2. Research findings can be integrated into a meaningful whole.
3. Explanations are provided for the performance of the system.
4. Avenues for fruitful research are revealed.

Taken together these statements point to the importance of models in guiding the planning of research studies and the interpretation of their findings.

That there may be disadvantages associated with the use of models of consumer behavior has also been noted (Walters, 1978; Zaltman and Wallendorf, 1983). Walters identifies four potential disadvantages:

1. Models may oversimplify complex relationships.
2. Models may be substituted in peoples' minds for reality.
3. Models, particularly complex mathematical models, may have an intimidating quality about them which reduces or retards discussion.
4. Models may lack flexibility, especially if they are based upon highly restrictive assumptions.

Despite these potential hazards, most scholars view models of consumer choice behavior as functional, rather than dysfunctional, vehicles for advancing knowledge in the field.

Table 1. Sixteen criteria for theory evaluation (Zaltman, Pinson and Angelmar, 1973).

Criterion	Description
Formal Criteria	
1. Well-formedness	The theory obeys the rules of "formation" and "transformation" (elementary logic).
2. Internal consistency	The theory contains no logical contradictions.
3. Independence	The theory has primitive-concepts independence and axioms independence.
4. Strength	The theory entails other theories.
Semantical Criteria	
5. Linguistic exactness	The theory exhibits minimum intensional and extensional vagueness.
6. Conceptual unity	The components of the theory refer to the same set of behavioral phenomena.
7. Empirical interpretability (or testability in principle)	The theory is operationalizable (interpretable in empirical terms).
8. Representativeness	The theory deals with deep mechanisms.
Methodological Criteria	
9. Falsifiability	The theory is falsifiable – that is, confrontable with reality (facts).
10. Methodological simplicity	The theory is easy to build and test.
Epistemological Criteria	
11. Confirmation	The theory coheres with facts.
12. Originality	The theory increases knowledge by deriving new propositions.
13. External consistency	The theory is consistent with existing knowledge.
14. Unifying power	The theory connects previously unconnected items.
15. Heuristic power	The theory suggests new directions for research.
16. Stability	The theory is able to accommodate new evidence.

This table is based largely on Bunge, Scientific Research, Volumes I and II, 1967ab.

2.4. *Criteria for Evaluating the Models*

Although several scholars (e.g., Markin, 1974) have looked at the problem of establishing criteria for evaluating models of consumer behavior, perhaps no one has done it with the thoroughness of Zaltman, Pinson and Angelmar (1973). As indicated in Table 1, these researchers have borrowed heavily from the work of Bunge (1967a, 1967b) to identify sixteen criteria for theory evaluation. The criteria are of four types: formal, semantical, methodological, and epistemological. Later in this chapter the usefulness of the criteria will be seen when they are individually applied to each of three models of consumer choice behavior.

3. EARLY MODELS OF CONSUMER CHOICE BEHAVIOR

3.1. *Introduction*

In the mid-1960s, two models of consumer choice behavior appeared in the literature which had considerable influence on the consumer research community (Andreasen, 1965; Nicosia, 1966). Both models attempted to account for the consumer buying decision for a new product, but the approaches taken by the two theorists were very different. Let us look at these two models in turn.[3]

3.2. *The Andreasen Model*

The Andreasen model (1965) of consumer choice behavior has attitude formation and change as its focus in partnership with the information processing capabilities of the individual consumer. The model addresses the question of how a consumer decides whether or not to purchase a new product. Andreasen believes that consumers form attitudes about products and that these attitudes influence consumer reactions (favorable or unfavorable) toward products in purchase situations. To understand consumer choice behavior, Andreasen contends that one must determine the present disposition of various attitude subsystems.

Andreasen identifies five formative factors which may influence attitudes about consumer products. These are as follows:

1. the personality of the individual consumer,
2. information and feelings resulting from past experiences involving the satisfaction of wants,
3. information yielded from past experiences not involving want-satisfaction,
4. the individual's social perception, i.e., his or her perceptions of the beliefs, norms and values of significant others, and
5. the individual's attitudes toward objects relating to the product of interest, e.g., product substitutes or complements.

Attitude change toward a product may result, according to Andreasen, from changes to one or more of these five formative factors.

Figure 1 presents the structure of the Andreasen model in the form of a

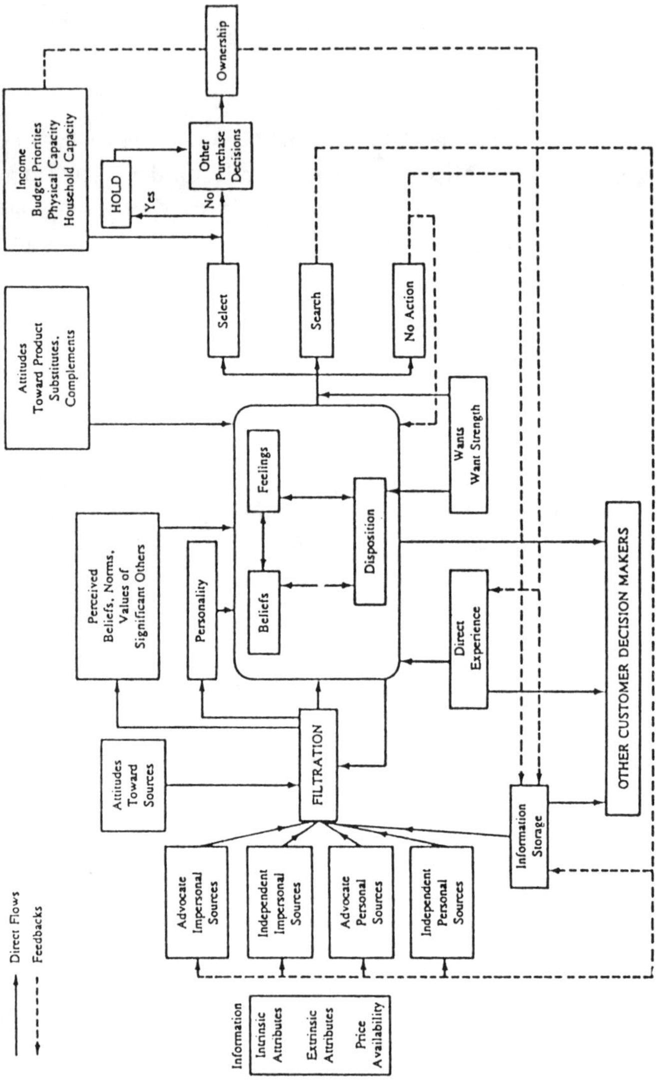

Fig. 1. The Andreasen model (Andreasen, 1965). Reprinted with permission.

flow diagram. The figure depicts various informational and attitudinal "inputs" and behavioral "outputs" (select, search or refrain from action). Information is seen as originating from four sources (advocate impersonal sources, independent impersonal sources, advocate personal sources, and independent personal sources) after which it is acted upon by a "filtration process." This process simply reflects the influence of perceptual mechanisms on stimuli impinging upon the organism.

Once the filtration process is completed, Andreasen contends that information interacts with a variety of entities (e.g., beliefs, feelings and dispositions) yielding a resultant attitude which conditions or affects behavior. As indicated earlier, three consumer choice behaviors are possible. The consumer may select the product, initiate a search process or take no action. The select decision has to take into consideration certain constraints (income, budget priorities, physical capacity, and household capacity) as well as other purchase decisions. The other two decision alternatives (search or no action) contain a feedback mechanism which affects future filtration processes.

Having described the basic components of the Andreasen model and their patterns of interaction, we look next at how the model has been received in the consumer research community. In one word, the reception might be called "mixed." To illustrate, Walters calls the model "a reasonable statement of the major relationships involved in consumer behavior" (1978: p. 58), but is critical of what he sees as its mechanical, stimulus-response character. Walters is also critical of some of the model's variables and the placement of its constraints late in the decision-making process. Moreover, Horton (1984) and Markin (1974) are critical of some of the variables treated by the model and the manner in which their relationships are specified. Horton also notes that the model is limited to explaining new purchase decisions and ignores decisions relating to repeat purchases. Notwithstanding these various criticisms, the Andreasen model should be viewed as a creative contribution to the consumer theory of the mid-1960's. Its emphasis on attitudes and information processes foreshadowed many later theoretical and empirical developments in the field.

3.3. *The Nicosia Model*

A year after the Andreasen model appeared in the consumer behavior literature, Nicosia published *Consumer Decision Processes: Marketing and Advertising Implications* (1966). This book was distinctive in at least two respects. First, it contained a comprehensive review of the consumer behavior literature through the mid-1960's. Second, it presented a highly original model of consumer choice behavior relating to the purchase of new products.

Like Andreasen, Nicosia underscored the importance of the decision processes occurring prior to the act of purchase. Unlike Andreasen, however, Nicosia explicitly recognized the role of the selling firm in his model. The model is cast in a computer simulation framework which stresses the interactive nature of buyer-seller relationships. In particular, sellers communicate with buyers through marketing messages and buyers in turn communicate with sellers through acts of purchase (or non-purchase). Through his use of a computer simulation model of buyer-seller relations, Nicosia demonstrates the circularity of these communication patterns.

To fully understand the intricacies of the Nicosia model it is necessary to examine the detailed computer flow charts contained in his book. For our purposes a summary depiction of the model will suffice and this is presented in Figure 2. As indicated therein the model consists of four basic fields:

1. the chain of events starting with marketing message activation to consumer attitude formation,
2. search and evaluation processes,
3. the purchase act, and
4. the feedback process.

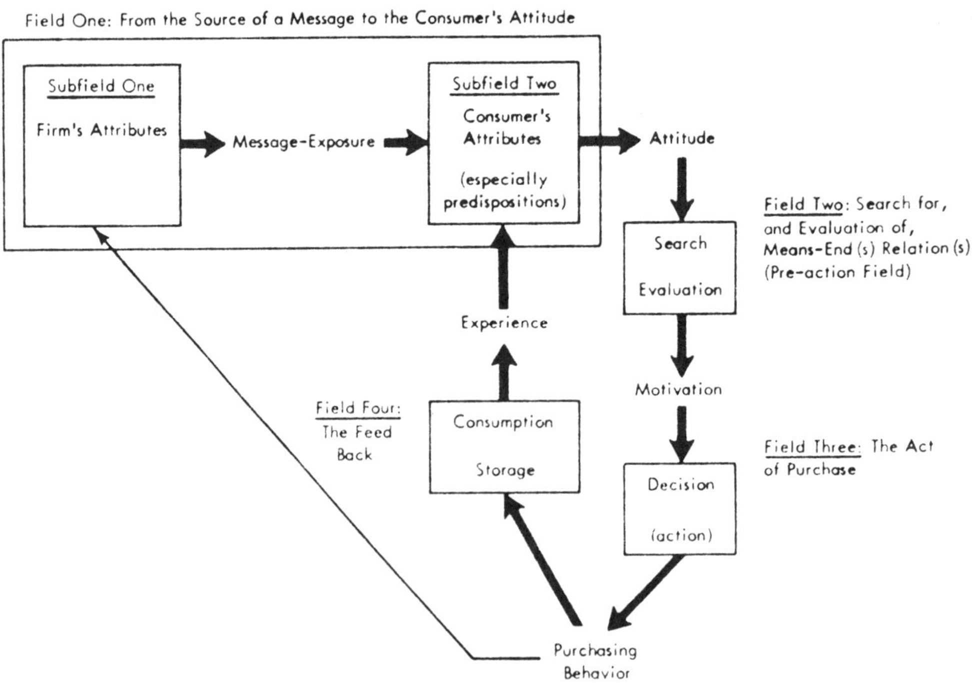

Fig. 2. The Nicosia model (Nicosia, 1966). Reprinted with permission of Prentice-Hall.

The first field of the model is split into two subfields. The first subfield includes those elements of the firm's marketing and communication activities which influence consumer attitudes. The second subfield consists of psychological attributes, particularly consumer predispositions, which affect consumer reception of the firm's marketing messages. The output of the two subfields is a consumer attitude toward the firm's product.

The second subfield of the model consists of search and evaluation processes. In particular, the focus is on searching for relevant purchase information and evaluating the firm's brand relative to other available brands. The output of these processes is motivation to purchase (or not purchase) the firm's brand.

Assuming that the motivation is indeed to purchase, the third field consists of the act of purchase. Following this stage in the Nicosia model is the fourth and final field which provides feedback of two types from the purchase act. The first is feedback to the firm consisting of sales data. The second is feedback to the consumer, consisting of satisfaction or dissatisfaction, resulting from the purchase experience. This second type of feedback affects consumer predispositions relating to future marketing communications from the firm.

What is evident from this description is the adaptive-system nature of the Nicosia formulation, with its emphasis on continuing flows of information through the four components of the model. This feature of the model, as well as several others, such as its explicit recognition of the role of the seller in the buyer-seller relationship, have been commented on favorably by several researchers (Horton, 1984; Markin, 1974; Walters, 1978; Zaltman and Wallendorf, 1983). This is not to say that the model has escaped criticism from consumer researchers. For example, Zaltman, Pinson and Angelmar (1973) contend that many of the model's variables are not satisfactorily specified and Lunn (1974) is critical of Nicosia's definitions of motivation and attitude. Nonetheless, the model is a significant contribution to the consumer behavior literature and it continues to receive the attention of scholars some twenty years after its original formulation.

4. NEWER MODELS OF CONSUMER CHOICE BEHAVIOR

4.1. *Introduction*

As indicated, the Andreasen and Nicosia models of consumer choice behavior were major contributions to the literature of the 1960s. However, their impact beyond this time period was necessarily limited by the absence of revisions of the models incorporating more recent developments in research and practice. Since the mid-1960s, there has been an enormous

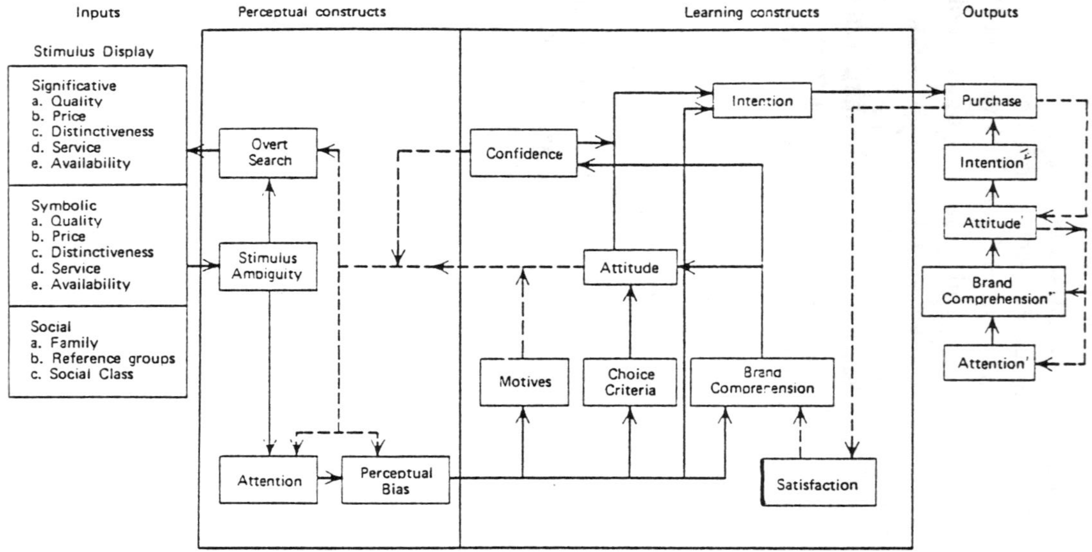

Solid lines indicate flow of information; dashedlines, feedback effects.

Fig. 3. The Howard-Sheth model (Howard and Sheth, 1969). Reprinted by permission of John Wiley & Sons.

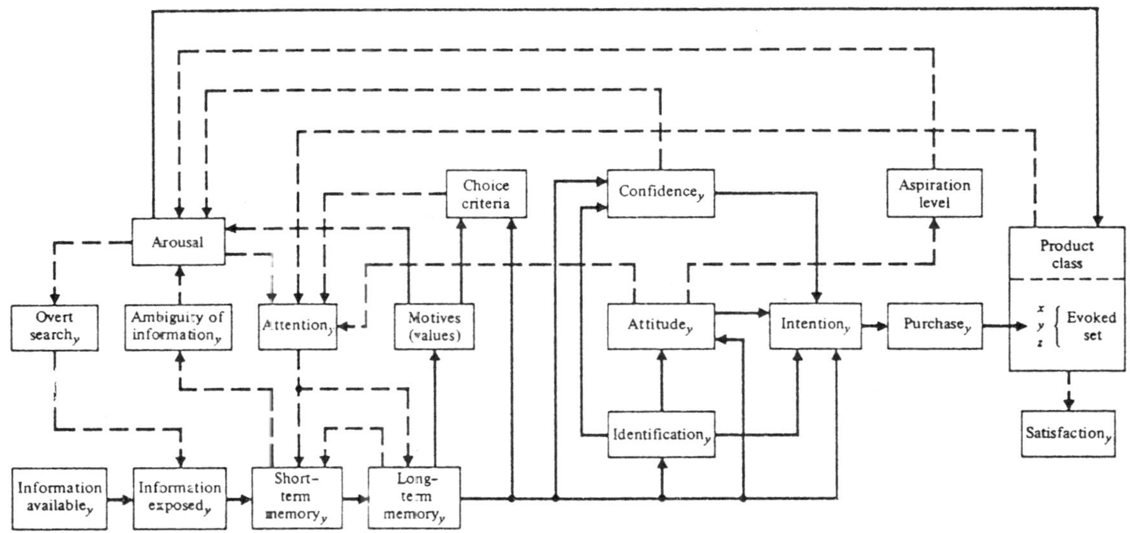

Fig. 4. The Howard model (Howard, 1977). Reprinted with permission of McGraw-Hill.

increase in scholarly research in consumer behavior and much of it has been conducted with a sophistication and rigor which were missing from earlier research in the field. Also occurring since the mid-1960s is a marked increase in consumer movement activities with such consequences as a new emphasis both by government and business on consumer complaint handling – an emphasis with clear implications for the Nicosia model with its focus on feedback to the firm. Thus models which have not undergone further development since the mid-1960s are likely to become increasingly outdated.

The three models explored in this section of the chapter do not suffer from this handicap. The first two to be examined (the Howard-Sheth model and the Engel-Kollat-Blackwell model) have been revised several times since their first versions were published in the 1960s. And the third (the Bettman model) is of such a recent vintage (1979) that "datedness" is not a problem.

4.2. *The Howard-Sheth Model*

This model of consumer choice behavior, first presented in *The Theory of Buyer Behavior* in 1969, is an elaboration of a model first advanced by Howard in 1963. The 1969 version, which is depicted in flow diagram form in Figure 3, conceives of five stages in the consumer decision process: attention, brand comprehension, attitude, intention, and purchase.

In a more recent version of the model (Howard, 1977), which is presented schematically in Figure 4, the model is further developed with the addition of arousal, evoked set, and memory.[4]

Five major types of variables are included in the model: inputs, perceptual constructs, learning constructs, outputs, and exogenous variables. Let us briefly look at each in turn.

Input variables include three types of information in the environment of the consumer. Significative stimuli refer to physical brand characteristics. Symbolic stimuli, as the name suggests, refer to verbal or visual symbolic information which indirectly represent a product. Social stimuli are a special type of symbolic stimuli provided by the consumer's social environment.

Perceptual constructs are used in the model in an effort to explain how consumers select the information which is communicated to the brand choice decision process. The two mechanisms involved in the perceptual process are attention and overt search. Attention is viewed as a passive process while overt search is viewed as an active process. Additional perceptual constructs in the model are stimulus ambiguity and perceptual bias. The first acknowledges that stimuli are frequently not clear and the second that information is sometimes distorted before it is stored in the consumer's memory.

Learning constructs are core constructs in the Howard-Sheth model. They include motives, brand comprehension, choice criteria, attitude, confidence, intention, and satisfaction. The complex interactions among these constructs together with the perceptual constructs are depicted in Figure 3. For example, intention is affected by confidence and attitude (two learning constructs) as well as perceptual bias (a perceptual construct). The learning constructs also interact with purchase variables. To illustrate, intention affects purchase which in turn affects satisfaction. Thus satisfaction is treated as a post-purchase construct.

Unlike the perceptual and learning constructs which are hypothesized as internal, non-observable mechanisms to account for consumer choice behavior, the *output variables* in the model are based directly upon observable data. As indicated earlier, they include, in sequential form, attention, brand comprehension, attitude, intention, and purchase. Except for the last-mentioned (purchase), all the output variables have counterparts among the perceptual and learning constructs. Where the names are the same, a prime superscript is added to the output variable to indicate that it is not a hypothetical construct, but an intervening variable based on observable data.

Exogenous variables. These variables are not part of the decision process and are thus not depicted in Figure 3 or Figure 4. Their inclusion in the model simply reflects the fact that external factors influence the consumer's choice process. Candidates include such diverse entities as time pressure, social class, religion, sex, personality traits, financial status, and organizational setting.

A final noteworthy feature of the model is the useful distinction it draws among three stages of consumer decision making: rationalized response behavior, limited problem solving, and extensive problem solving. The three differ with regard to how completely the consumer has learned the relevant product concepts as well as associated brand concepts. Howard (1977) presents detailed models for each of these stages in a later version of the theory.

Unlike the earlier examined models of consumer choice behavior, the Howard-Sheth model has been extensively tested (e.g., Farley and Ring, 1970). In a review of the empirical tests of the model Holbrook (1974) found that no specific relationship postulated by the model was consistently supported, and that only a small portion of the variance of the empirical data was accounted for by the model. However there are serious methodological problems raised by these empirical tests. As Horton (1984) has suggested, "Perhaps the most important and general methodological limitation is that the sheer complexity of the theory makes a truly comprehensive test at this time virtually impossible" (p. 43). Research by Laroche and Howard (1980) suggests that the introduction of non-linear relationships among variables

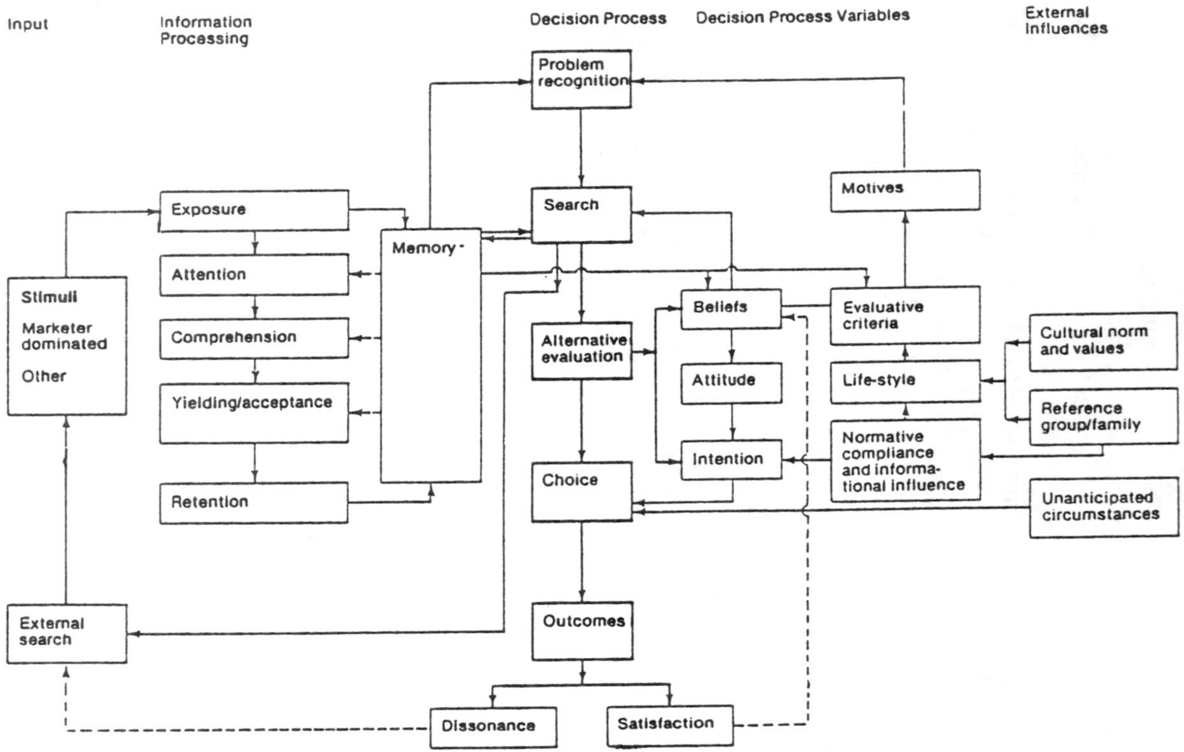

Fig. 5. The Engel-Kollat-Blackwell model (Engel and Blackwell, 1982). Reprinted with permission of the Dryden Press.

may help by making a better fit between the model and behavioral reality.

The Howard-Sheth formulation has been viewed by many consumer researchers as a model for others to emulate with regard to the process of theory development. There are three reasons for this high regard. First, from the outset the model was developed as an integral part of an ongoing program of research which was undertaken to yield a more comprehensive understanding of consumer choice behavior. Second, the model's designers drew upon an unusually rich storehouse of theory from basic academic disciplines, including Hull's learning theory, Osgood's theory of cognition and Berlyne's theory of motivation. And third, the model developers have not strayed from their original course in that the model revisions have incorporated new theoretical and empirical developments (e.g., information processing concepts in Howard's 1977 elaboration of the model) and, equally importantly, the empirical testing of the model has continued.

4.3. *The Engel-Kollat-Blackwell Model*

The three creators of this model were faced in the mid-1960's with the task of writing a comprehensive textbook on consumer behavior. Having found no available model of consumer behavior to use as a guide for this effort Engel, Kollat and Blackwell developed one with the assistance of a former student, M. Lawrence Light. The model first appeared in their 1968 textbook, *Consumer Behavior*. Further elaborations of the model followed in the revisions of the textbook (Engel, Kollat, and Blackwell, 1973, 1978; Engel and Blackwell, 1982; Engel, Blackwell, and Miniard, 1986).

The latest version of the model is depicted in Figure 5. This particular form of the model is for high-involvement purchase decisions; another form has been proposed for low-involvement purchase decisions. As the model developers have noted (Engel, Kollat, and Blackwell, 1978; Engel and Blackwell, 1982), their formulation is similar to the Howard-Sheth model and the Howard model. Engel and his collaborators have made this point by using mathematical symbols to represent the components of these models and then structuring these symbols in general equation form. One similarity among the three models is that "all three hypothesize a hierarchy of effects in which a change in attitude leads to corresponding changes in intention and behavior, all things being equal" (Engel and Blackwell, 1982: p. 689).

With regard to differences, Engel and Blackwell (1982) assert that their "model is unique in highlighting the decision process and explicitly including the proven relationships of the Fishbein behavioral intentions model under alternative evaluation" (p. 688). As Horton (1984) has noted, the claim for uniqueness in highlighting the decision process is questionable, but the use of the Fishbein formulation in the Engel-Kollat-Blackwell model is indeed an original and important contribution.

Before leaving the Engel-Kollat-Blackwell model it should be noted that perhaps its main problem from the perspective of scientific theory is the absence of empirical evidence to support its various propositions. To understand why such evidence is lacking, one must look to the intentions of the authors in creating the model. As indicated, the model was originally seen as a pedagogical device for identifying existing knowledge relating to consumer behavior and organizing this knowledge in a form appropriate for a college-level textbook. With each revision, new scholarly contributions were reviewed and the model changed accordingly. And with each revision the primary function of the model remained pedagogical rather than scientific. As a result, no effort was made over the years to postulate quantifiable functional relationships nor to subject such relationships to empirical test.

4.4. *The Bettman Model*

While the models treated so far in this section are revisions of earlier formulations, Bettman's is new. It first appeared in full form in 1979 in his book, *An Information Processing Theory of Consumer Choice.* As the title suggests, information processing is at the heart of the Bettman model. After reviewing existing models of consumer choice, he saw the need for an integrated framework for studying consumer choice from an information processing perspective and wrote his book to satisfy this need.

The basic structure of the theory is depicted schematically in Figure 6. The key elements presented therein are as follows: processing capacity, motivation, attention and perception, information acquisition and evaluation, use of memory, decision processes, and consumption and learning. The model also included a scanner mechanism for continually monitoring the environment as well as mechanisms for interrupting ongoing behavior (when this proves necessary) and for interpreting and handling conflict situations. Finally, the model incorporates the influences of individual differences, situational influences and different kinds of stimuli. These influences are not shown in Figure 6.

Having provided an overview of the model, we look next at its key elements.

1. *Processing capacity* acknowledges the consumer's limited capacity for processing information. When confronted with "overload" situations consumers are likely to use heuristics, or rules of thumb, as coping mechanisms. As presented in Figure 6, processing capacity is a critical component of the Bettman model with linkages to many other components.
2. Since Bettman views consumer choice as purposeful, *motivation* is a

critical component of his model. Motivation is treated as a set of mechanisms for controlling movement from a consumer's "initial state" to his or her "desired end state." Two basic devices are suggested for performing this function:

a. a hierarchy–of-goals mechanism and
b. a scanning and interrupt mechanism.

The hierarchy-of-goals mechanism is especially important since it guides the consumer choice process. Sometimes this means interrupting the process to cope with unanticipated developments, identified by the scanning mechanism (e.g., conflicting stimuli). Thus we find that the process is goal-directed with active consumer involvement.

3. *Attention and perception* are strongly influenced by the goal hierarchy of the consumer. Following the lead of Kahneman (1973), Bettman makes a distinction between voluntary and involuntary forms of attention. The former is viewed as the conscious allocation of processing capabilities to current goals while the latter is conceived of as the more automatic allocation of processing capabilities to cope with unexpected stimulus events. Bettman also proposes a perceptual coding mechanism which draws upon information stored in memory to interpret stimuli being attended to by the consumer.
4. *Information acquisition and evaluation.* If the information currently available to the consumer in memory is deemed inadequate, information may be sought externally. Although there are exceptions (e.g., low-involvement learning situations), generally the incoming information is actively processed and assessed by the consumer.
5. *Memory*, a key component of the Bettman model, is, of course, the consumer's internal storehouse of information. A distinction is made between short-term and long-term memory. As Bettman notes, memory retrieval is critical in interpreting perceptions and the results of external search activities.
6. *Decision processes.* Bettman views the choice process as a cycling procedure rather than a sequential procedure. At each stage in the cycle choices are made; thus decision processes are critical to the model. As Bettman notes, "decision processes occur throughout the course of choice determining goals, selecting information, comparing purchase alternatives" (1979: p. 35).
7. *Consumption and learning* are concerned with the post-purchase situation. Once a product alternative has been purchased and consumed, feedback from these experiences is made available to the consumer which may affect future choice situations as well as the heuristics used by consumers in such situations.

Having presented an overview of the Bettman model we look next at its contribution to the research literature. Two observations appear appropriate here. First, the Bettman model constitutes a giant step forward for consumer research due to the extent to which it has drawn creatively upon the rapidly growing empirical and theoretical literature in the field of information processing – a literature which draws upon the contributions of the behavior and social sciences as well as the computer sciences. Second, since Bettman deals with highly specific micro-behaviors in the context of a macro-model, his formulation can be expected to provide a highly useful framework for guiding future research on consumer choice processes.

5. OVERALL ASSESSMENT OF THE MODELS

5.1. *Introduction*

This final section of the chapter attempts to provide two overall assessments of the models of consumer choice behavior. The first looks at similarities and differences among the various models. The second examines their collective contribution to the field of economic psychology.

5.2. *Similarities and Differences Among the Models*

Earlier we noted five characteristics common to the models of consumer choice behavior examined in this chapter. To recapitulate, we stated that all of the models

1. focus on individual consumer behavior,
2. attempt to account for consumer choice behavior associated with the acquisition of consumer commodities,
3. view consumer choice behavior as a complex process,
4. attempt to be comprehensive in their explanations of this process, and
5. are the works of marketing scholars.

Differences among consumer choice models have also been noted. Perhaps the most detailed analysis has been conducted by Bettman who compared his model with those of several major theorists. Table 2 presents the results of these comparisons. Inspection of the table reveals considerable overlap among models, and especially among the three models of Nicosia, Engel-Kollat-Blackwell, and Howard-Sheth. Also evident in the table are some of the distinguishing characteristics of individual models. For example, the Bettman model appears to have gone further than all the others in its

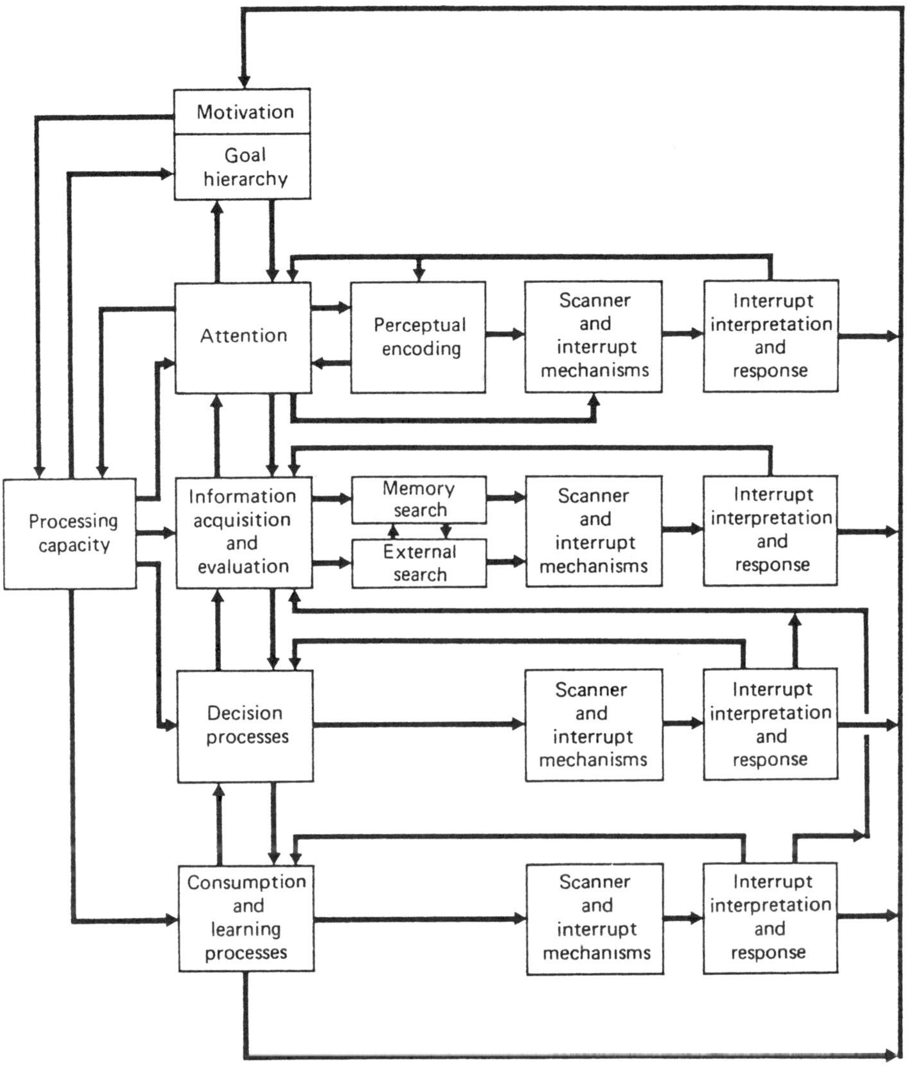

Fig. 6. The Bettman model (Bettman, 1979). Reprinted with permission of Addison-Wesley.

Table 2. A comparison of consumer choice theories (Bettman, 1979).

Aspects compared[a]	Theories				
	Bettman	Nicosia	Engel, Blackwell, and Kollat	Howard and Sheth	Howard
Information processing focus					
Level of detail	Very detailed	Very general	Some detail	Some detail	Moderate detail
Consideration of specific processing notions	Extensive	Very limited	Some detail	Some detail	Some detail
Role of Motivation					
Emphasis in theory	Central	Central	Central	Central	Central
Use of goal hierarchy	Extensive	Not considered[b]	Very limited	Limited	Limited
Nature of consumer	Active	Stimulus-bound	Active	Stimulus-bound	Active
Role of Conflict and Responses to Conflict					
Concept of conflict used	General	Not considered	Not considered	Perceptual and choice distinguished	Perceptual and choice distinguished
Determinant of reactions	Assessment of meaning	Not considered	Not considered	Optimal-level theory	Optimal-level theory and assessment of meaning
Role of Interrupts and Reactions to Interrupts					
Specification of interrupt mechanisms	Extensive	Not considered	Limited	Limited	Extensive

Determinants of reactions	Assessment of meaning	Not considered	Limited	Not considered	Limited
Consideration of specific reactions	Extensive	Not considered	Limited	Not considered	Limited
Role of Memory					
Treatment of memory phenomena	Extensive	Very limited	Some detail	Very limited	Moderate detail
Treatment of semantic structure, language	Not considered	Not considered	Not considered	Limited	Extensive
Treatment of Choice Heuristics and Implementation Methods					
Range of heuristics considered	Very wide	Narrow	Moderate	Narrow	Narrow
Specification of implementation methods	Extensive	Not considered	Not considered	Not considered	Not considered
Specification of form of processing	Extensive	Not considered	Very limited	Not considered	Not considered
Summary of choice research	Extensive	Limited	Limited	Limited	Limited
Is attitude a necessary component of choice?	No	Yes	Yes	Yes	Yes
Analysis of Choice Task Properties					
Treatment of task properties	Extensive	Very limited	Very limited	Limited	Some detail

[a] This comparison focuses on some selected aspects for which the theories appear to differ. Similarities are considered in the text.
[b] "Not considered" means that the phenomenon is either not mentioned at all or is mentioned so briefly that it is not a central part of the theory.

information processing focus, its treatment of memory phenomena, and its extensive analysis of choice heuristics and implementation methods. The Howard model, on the other hand, is the only one to extensively consider the semantic structure of language in memory.

Another attempt to compare models has been undertaken by Zaltman, Pinson and Angelmar (1973) using the criteria listed earlier in Table 1. These criteria were applied to the models of Nicosia, Howard-Sheth, and Engel-Kollat-Blackwell. The results appear in Table 3.

Table 3. An evaluation of three major models of consumer behavior (Zaltman, Pinson and Angelmar, 1973).

Model Criteria	Nicosia	Howard-Sheth	Engel-Kollat Blakcwell
Formal criteria			
1. Well-formedness	very good	very good	good
2. Internal consistency	good – very good	good – very good	good
3. Independence	*	*	*
4. Strength	good	good	good
Semantical criteria			
5. Linguistic exactness	good	fair – good	fair
6. Conceptual unity	good	fair	fair
7. Empirical interpretability	good	good	fair
8. Representativeness	fair – good	good	fair – good
Methodological criteria			
9. Falsifiability	poor – fair	fair	poor
10. Methodological simplicity	poor – fair	poor – fair	poor
Epistemological criteria			
11. Confirmation	(untested)	fair	(untested)
12. Originality	good	good	fair
13. External consistency	fair – good	fair – good	fair – good
14. Unifying power	good – very good	good – very good	good
15. Heuristic power	good	good – very good	fair – good
16. Stability	fair	fair	fair

* The criterion does not apply.

What is evident from perusal of Table 3 is that all three models perform well on formal criteria (well-formedness, internal consistency, independence, and strength); however, on methodological criteria (falsifiability and methodological simplicity), all three perform far less adequately. With regard to each of the remaining two classes of criteria, the verdict is mixed. In particular, with regard to semantical criteria (linguistic exactness, conceptual unity, empirical interpretability, and representativeness), the Nicosia model performs best and the Engel-Kollat-Blackwell model performs worst.

With regard to epistemological criteria (confirmation, originality, external consistency, unifying power, heuristic power and stability), the Nicosia and Howard-Sheth models receive generally "good" ratings while the Engel-Kollat-Blackwell model receives "fair-to-good" ratings.

Perhaps the most disappointing result of the evaluation conducted by Zaltman and his colleagues are the low marks earned by the models on the methodological criteria. Basically these criteria consider the empirical testability of a model and weakness on such a critically important dimension should be a matter of serious concern to the consumer research community. What this result suggests is that the models should perhaps be viewed not as "scientific theories" (in the traditional sense of that term), but rather as conceptual frameworks for organizing the rapidly accumulating research findings on consumer choice behavior.

5.3. *The Contribution of the Models to Economic Psychology*

As indicated, the models of consumer choice behavior offer useful conceptual frameworks for organizing the data of an important area of economic psychology – the study of decisions related to the acquisition of goods and services in the marketplace. The models are major contributions to economic psychology and the appearance of revised and new models in the last decade suggests that the contributions will continue in the years ahead.[5]

While these contributions are welcome by consumer psychologists as well as economic psychologists, it is important to note that the models are extremely limited in their domain of coverage. Although we have referred to them as "comprehensive" in actuality they treat a small subset of consumer behavior and an even smaller subset of economic behavior.

First, with regard to consumer behavior, the models reflect their marketing origins by focusing on acquisition behavior rather than usage or disposal behavior. And further reflecting their marketing origins, the models typically examine one form of acquisition behavior, namely purchase, and one type of commodity, namely mass-produced and mass-marketed new products. Excluded by this focus are other forms of acquisition behavior, such as bartering, borrowing and building; also excluded are various consumer behaviors relating to used goods and hand-crafted items.

With regard to economic psychology, as it has been defined by Van Raaij (1981), the models do not deal with such critical behaviors as the allocation of time and effort as well as economic choices between spending and saving. In addition, decisions relating to investments, taxes and wills are economic in nature but largely untreated by the models.

To conclude, the chapter reveals that much of value has been done to create useful conceptual frameworks for structuring research findings relating to consumer choice behavior. More work is needed on their development and on the development of models to guide research in other less marketing-oriented fields of economic and consumer psychology.

NOTES

1. The semantic problems involved are too complex to consider here. For a philosopher's perspective on these and related theoretical issues see the excellent books by Kaplan (1964) and Nagel (1961). For a likewise excellent treatment of these issues from a marketing theory perspective see Zaltman, Pinson and Angelmar (1973). Other noteworthy contributions of marketing scholars include the works of Lazer (1962) and Mittelstaedt (1971).
2. See Engel, Kollat and Blackwell (1978) for a more detailed treatment of the history of consumer behavior research as it relates to the development of models of consumer choice behavior. These authors distinguish three time periods in this development: pre-1960, 1960-1967, and 1967-1978.
3. Due to space limitations several other early models of consumer choice behavior are not considered in this chapter. They include the models of Britt (1978), Hansen (1972), Kerby (1975), and Markin (1974).
4. Space limitations preclude consideration of the particulars of the Howard model. Interested readers are advised to consult his book (Howard, 1977), especially Chapters 1 through 9. For a brief review of the model see Engel and Blackwell (1972).
5. Affect and emotion are two areas recently noted by Bettman (1986) in which new research findings could be expected to influence models of consumer behavior.

REFERENCES

Andreasen, A.R., 1965, "Attitudes and customer behavior: A decision model," in: L.E. Preston (ed.), New Research in Marketing, Berkeley, CA: University of California, Institute of Business and Economic Research, pp. 1-16.

Bettman, J.R., 1979, An Information Processing Theory of Consumer Choice, Reading, MA: Addison-Wesley.

Bettman, J.R., 1986, "Consumer psychology," in: M.R. Rosenzweig and L.W. Porter (eds.), Annual Review of Psychology, 37, Palo Alto, CA: Annual Reviews Corporation, pp. 257-289.

Britt, S., 1978, Psychological Principles of Marketing and Consumer Behavior, Lexington, MA: Lexington Books.

Bunge, M., 1967a, Scientific Research I: The Search for System, Berlin: Springer.

Bunge, M., 1967b, Scientific Research II: The Search for Truth, Berlin: Springer.

Engel, J.F., and R.D. Blackwell, 1982, Consumer Behavior, Hinsdale, IL: The Dryden Press (fourth edition).

Engel, J.F., R.D. Blackwell, and P.W. Miniard, 1986, Consumer Behavior, Chicago, IL: The Dryden Press (fifth edition).

Engel, J.F., D.T. Kollat, and R.D. Blackwell, 1968, Consumer Behavior, New York: Holt, Rinehart and Winston.

Engel, J.F., D.T. Kollat, and R.D. Blackwell, 1973, Consumer Behavior, New York: Holt, Rinehart and Winston (second edition).

Engel, J.F., D.T. Kollat, and R.D. Blackwell, 1978, Consumer Behavior, New York: Holt, Rinehart and Winston (third edition).

Farley, J.U., and L.W. Ring, 1970, An empirical test of the Howard-Sheth model of buyer behavior, Journal of Marketing Research, 7, 427-438.

Hansen, F., 1972, Consumer Choice Behavior, New York: Free Press.

Holbrook, M.B., 1974, "A synthesis of the empirical studies," in: J.U. Farley, J.A. Howard, and L.W. Ring (eds.), Consumer Behavior. Theory and Application, Boston, MA: Allyn and Bacon, pp. 229-252.

Horton, R.L., 1984, Buyer Behavior: A Decision-making Approach, Columbus, OH: Bell and Howell.

Howard, J.A., 1977, Consumer Behavior: Application of Theory, New York: McGraw-Hill.

Howard, J.A., and J.N. Sheth, 1969, The Theory of Buyer Behavior, New York: John Wiley.

Kahneman, D., 1973, Attention and Effort, Englewood Cliffs, NJ: Prentice-Hall.

Kaplan, A., 1964, The Conduct of Inquiry: Methodology for Behavioral Science, New York: Chandler.

Kerby, J.K., 1975, Consumer Behavior: Conceptual Foundations, New York: Dun-Donnelley.

Laroche, M., and J.A. Howard, 1980, Nonlinear relations in a complex model of buyer behavior, Journal of Consumer Research, 6, 377-388.

Lawrence, R.J., 1966, Models of consumer purchasing behavior, Applied Statistics, 45, 216-233.

Lazer, W., 1962, The role of models in marketing, Journal of Marketing, 26, 9.

Lunn, J.A., 1974, "Consumer decision-process models," in: J.N. Sheth (ed.), Models of Buyer Behavior. Conceptual, Quantitative, and Empirical, New York: Harper and Row, pp. 34-69.

Markin, R.J., Jr., 1974, Consumer Behavior: A Cognitive Orientation, New York: Macmillan.

Mittelstaedt, R.A., 1971, "Criteria for a theory of consumer behavior," in: R.J. Holloway, R.A. Mittelstaedt, and M. Venkatesan (eds.), Consumer Behavior. Contemporary Research in Action, Boston, MA: Houghton Mifflin, pp. 8-13.

Nagel, E., 1961, The Structure of Science, New York: Harcourt.

Nicosia, F.M., 1966, Consumer Decision Processes: Marketing and Advertising Implications, Englewood Cliffs, NJ: Prentice-Hall.

Simon, H.A., and A. Newell, 1963, "The uses and limitations of models," in: M.H. Marx (ed.), Theories in Contemporary Psychology, New York: Macmillan, pp. 89-104.

Sternthal, B., and C.S. Craig, 1982, Consumer Behavior: An Information Processing Perspective, Englewood Cliffs, NJ: Prentice-Hall.

Van Raaij, W.F., 1981, Economic psychology, Journal of Economic Psychology, 1, 1-24.

Walters, C.G., 1978, Consumer Behavior: Theory and Practice, Homewood, IL: Richard D. Irwin (third edition).

Zaltman, G., C.R.A. Pinson, and R. Angelmar, 1973, Metatheory and Consumer Research, New York: Holt, Rinehart and Winston.

Zaltman, G., and M. Wallendorf, 1983, Consumer Behavior: Basic Findings and Management Implications, New York: John Wiley (second edition).

Part III

Business Behavior

Introduction to Part III: Business Behavior

BUSINESS BEHAVIOR AND RATIONALITY

When critics of economic theory cite empirical evidence that businessmen are not rational in their decision making, they hardly get full support from the latter. Being rational has a connotation of being intelligent and capable of planning actions. Such an interpretation is not necessarily warranted by the economists' use of the concept of rationality; in economics the concept merely stands for maximizing behavior which need not always be intelligent.

In marketing and purchasing textbooks industrial buyers are usually described as more rational than ordinary consumers. If ordinary consumers can be assumed to be rational in their economic behavior, there should then be even more reason to make such an assumption about businessmen. Businessmen are assumed to maximize their profits which can be seen as a measure of utility accruing to firms. While the assumptions of maximizing utility or profits have proved to be useful in many contexts in which large enough groups of consumers or business firms are concerned and long-term equilibria are studied, the assumptions do not provide adequate theory for elucidating the processes going on at the individual consumer or firm level. There should be room for supplementing economics with theories and methods from psychology and other behavioral sciences in order to get better descriptions and explanations about what actually happens at the micro level of business firms as well as at the level of households. According to such protagonists of behavioral economics as George Katona and Herbert Simon, this way of constructing theories of economic behavior, i.e. through provision of data on micro level processes is very slow and rather cumbersome in comparison to developing elegant mathematical models.

It is said that Alfred Marshall, who was one of the founders of economics, had some friends who were businessmen and that he sought their advice when he wanted to find out what business behavior was like. An early study

Van Raaij, W.F., van Veldhoven, G.M. and Wärneryd, K.E. (eds) Handbook of Economic Psychology. ISBN 90-247-3720-6.

of business behavior was carried out in the 1930's by two economists, Hall and Hitch, who interviewed business men about how prices were set. The finding that prices were set according to average cost rather than to marginal cost as economic theory would have it, aroused a lot of discussion. Other studies found that business leaders, in economics often called "entrepreneurs", could have personal reasons for not striving to maximize profits. Typical reactions to these studies were that interviews could not be trusted or that short-run deviations from profit maximization would balance out in the long run. Or it is stressed that assumptions are free as long as the predictions made on the basis of the assumptions are good.

Economists generally have a tendency to stick to the profit maximizing assumption despite the fact that empirical evidence from business studies clearly indicate that there are many exceptions. They do not find it reasonable to reject the conclusions derived from profit maximization on the basis of sample surveys in which managers claim that they trade off profit for social good. It is interesting to note here what the psychologist Francis Galton wrote in an appreciative letter to F.Y. Edgeworth in 1881 after having read a review of the latter's *Mathematical Psychics*, published by Jevons in Mind: "As regards a few details: – mixed modes of utilitarianism" – I should have thought your view was the one to be formulated, so as to serve the entire range of cases, the value of a neighbour's happiness as compared to one's own being represented by a variable, =0 in pure economics, =1 in pure altruism."(Quoted from back cover of *The Journal of Political Economy*, 1977, 85, No.1).

The Behavioral Theory of the Firm

An important step in the direction of developing a better descriptive theory of the firm was taken when, in 1963, the economist Richard Cyert and the psychologist James March published their book *Toward a Behavioral Theory of the Firm*. The purpose of the behavioral theory of the firm was to introduce greater process realism into economic theories of the firm. The authors suggest that business firms do not behave as the economic theory of the firm assumes. Firms are organizations with specific characteristics, are capable of learning from experience – so-called organizational learning – and are collections of individuals with often conflicting goals. Firms are in varying degrees capable of handling the problems which are consequences of conflicting goals and of limited cognitive capacity both at the organizational and at the individual level. Simon's concept of bounded rationality is a cornerstone in this treatment.

The concept of bounded rationality is used to signify that lack of information and limited cognitive capabilities make it impossible for humans to be utility maximizing in the strict sense of economics. Instead people accept choice alternatives that are satisficing, i.e. the alternatives chosen coincide with or are above what is the person's level of aspiration. The latter expresses the demands of the person and is the borderline between what is acceptable and what is not. If no satisfactory alternative is immediately available, a search starts and it will continue until a satisfactory choice can be made.

Irrational behavior is often seen as unintelligent behavior. Simon has pointed out that human beings develop decision procedures that are sensible given the constraints they have to face, even though the decision procedures would not be sensible if the constraints were removed.

In their paper, March and Sevón take up the thread from 1963 and give a review of some significant trends in the research relating to the behavioral theory of the firm. As an introduction, they have a look at economic theory's postulate of rationality. They admit the attractiveness of optimal decision making theory, that has made it accepted in other sciences, but they cite evidence against it and emphasize the limitations of human cognitive capacities as well as the limitations of the information environment. Similar to people, firms have no clearcut or stable preferences. They are often ignorant about their preferences, especially what the preferences will be like in the future. For firms there is the additional problem that different people in the firm tend to have conflicting preferences. The authors propose that the theory of attention allocation and search which follows from the theory of bounded rationality catches the most characteristic features of individual and organizational decision making. It is not possible to attend to everything at the same time and neither time nor information are freely available utilities. As a result, much of the theory of the firm must be a theory of attention allocation and search rather than a theory of choice.

March and Sevón's approach to organizational decision making involves that decisions are characterized by uncertainty and ambiguity and by the limited human capabilities of handling these. Behavioral research on decision making and other behavior in firms furnishes economics with empirical data that are replacing and will even more in the future replace economic assumptions. These authors are optimistic about the opportunities for behavioral research to provide theory and data which will be accepted in economics: "Judging from past experience, the behavioral research is likely to continue to lead to adjustments in economic theory, possibly to major ones." It is, however, true that they find economic theory capable of absorbing new findings without changing its basic tenets. "Other observations have become part of the stylized truths with which the theory deals, thus subsumed by some new elaboration of the basic model that retains the axioms of rationality."

In the second paper, Wärneryd introduces psychological contributions to the study of entrepreneurship against a broader background of research on entrepreneurs and entrepreneurship. He notes that there is no complete consensus about what an entrepreneur is like, but that there is a long tradition of including certain characteristics in definitions of entrepreneurship or entrepreneurial acts. An entrepreneur may then be defined as somebody who has displayed entrepreneurship, but such after-the-fact definitions do not lay a foundation for spotting budding entrepreneurs or answering the question whether entrepreneurship can be trained. One of the points of disagreement concerns how much risk taking entrepreneurs have a propensity for. The economist Schumpeter deemphasizes the risk taking component of entrepreneurship, while Knight like most other economists thinks of entrepreneurs as less risk aversive than other people. The psychologist McClelland who devoted many years to the study of achievement motivation in economic life describes entrepreneurs as moderate risk takers, something which is a characteristic trait of people with high need achievement.

While psychological studies of entrepreneurs have mostly concerned their motivation and personality traits, there is now a tendency to look at cognitive aspects as well. Related to studies of achievement motivation are studies of locus-of-control theory, which have shown that entrepreneurs tend to be more internally controlled, i.e. have a feeling that what they do gives them some mastery of the external world. Risk propensity studies fail to show any significant differences between entrepreneurs and others. In the study of entrepreneurs, there are some recent attempts to apply results from cognitive psychological studies of risk perception and decisions under risk.

Small business research has often been equivalent to research on entrepreneurs. There are many studies in many countries, but surprisingly few conclusions that seem to have general acceptance and validity. The use of case studies and informal techniques has not been followed up by more systematic studies to any large extent. There is apparently more than one type of small business owner and entrepreneur. In recent years, the technical entrepreneur who usually has an advanced education has become frequent and attracted researchers' attention.

In the last section, Wärneryd summarizes the state of the art trying to combine and integrate ideas from entrepreneurial research. A psychological model of entrepreneurship should comprise, first, perception of a problematic situation, of personal skills and perhaps of illusion of controlling one's destiny (belief in luck). Secondly, this combination of factors is by the entrepreneur judged as an opportunity and it gives rise to a feeling of excitement as something new and meaningful. Thirdly, an irresistable impulse to proper action is thus born. This psychological model seems to be quite close to McDougall's instinct theories and also to what the economist Kirzner suggests.

Theories of Negotiations and Bargaining

In the third paper, Johnston and Benton review bargaining theories and present an attempt towards an integrated theory. The latter is discussed in connection with a report on a bargaining experiment. The authors note that psychologists have been busy with studying distributive bargaining, in which a party can gain only at the loss of the other, while economists have found integrative bargaining more interesting. In the latter type of bargaining, both parties can make a gain. Consumer bargaining in a retail store is according to the authors an example of distributive bargaining whereas industrial buying often qualifies as integrative bargaining since the outcomes, if negative, can be transferred to the ultimate consumer level. The psychological research on bargaining is described as strictly empirical and fragmented with no attempts at developing a comprehensive theory.

Economists have pursued theoretical work aimed at explaining integrative bargaining. Johnson and Benton start their review of theory with Edgeworth's two-person, two-commodity bargaining situation in which the solutions lie along a curve. There is no way of fixing a point along this curve where the bargain will be settled. Von Neumann and Morgenstern can similarly only explain movement up to the contract curve which shows possible solutions. Movement along the curve is still done by actual bargaining which in the absence of studies of actual processes remains unexplained. The contract curve indicates a range in which the outcome must fall.

Economic theory can according to the authors predict the approximate outcomes of bargaining situations, but psychological conditions will cause the solution actually reached to vary around the predicted outcome point. This is a good illustration of how psychology and economics can work together: economics provides an abstract theory which fixes the theoretical boundaries for the possible solutions; psychology provides empirical data showing how point solutions are achieved in practice.

Johnson and Benton favor a richer description of bargaining situations than either economics or psychology can offer. They provide such a model which is partly based on their own results from experiments on bargaining. One of the related experiments is reported in some detail. The results of the experiment suggest that the way a negotiator is paid will significantly affect the bargaining process and the outcome of the negotiations. The reward practices that exist today in purchasing functions of industrial firms put the buying organization at a distinct disadvantage. Sales organizations have developed reward systems that motivate their personnel through compensation whereas purchasing organizations for the most part have not. The authors suggest that buying organizations should look into the question of rewards contingent upon results.

Conclusion

Compared to consumer behavior, business behavior is still investigated only to a very small extent. In organizational psychology, many studies have undoubtedly been carried out, but they have a rather different slant from economic psychology. The organizational studies do not aim in the first place at explaining variables that can be potentially useful in elucidating or predicting behavior at an aggregated level. In economic psychology, the interest is focussed on explanations at some level of aggregation rather than on the actor's or the firm's own perspectives. Economic psychology tends to take the outsider's vantage point, not that of the insider, in its studies of business behavior. It can all the same produce research results of great interest to business practitioners as well as to policy-makers in government bodies.

Karl-Erik Wärneryd

Table of Contents

10. Behavioral Perspectives on Theories of the Firm[1]

JAMES G. MARCH
Stanford University, California, U.S.A.

and

GUJE SEVÓN
Swedish School of Economics, Helsinki, Finland

1. INTRODUCTION

Economic theories of the firm are theories of rational choice. They use strong assumptions about individual human behavior to derive predictions about aggregate behavior at equilibrium. For the most part, they seek to rationalize observed behavior in markets, to show how it can be imagined to arise from self-interested behavior by individuals and firms. Such theories are somewhat indifferent to two classical distinctions familiar to the behavioral literature. First, they tend to ignore differences between decision making by individuals and decision making by firms, seeing the latter as largely the actions of specific individuals – usually managers but sometimes owners. Second, they move easily from theories of optimal behavior to theories of actual behavior, assuming for the most part that actual human behavior is driven to the optimum by some competitive process.

Since rather little effort has been exerted either to compare economic theories of the firm with plausible alternatives or to examine the behavioral assumptions that are made, the empirical standing of neo-classical theories is not particularly high among behavioral economists (Cyert and Simon, 1983). The skepticism is largely justified from the point of view of conventional behavioral concerns with empirical validation; but it probably misperceives (or rejects) the canonical style of economic reasoning. Modern economic theories of the firm are not empirical in the sense in which that word is normally used among students of behavior. The assumption of rationality is not a hypothesis in economic theory but an axiom, a proposition conceivably subject to doubt but only as a last resort. Although the theories are concerned with real world phenomena, they tend to emphasize the rationalization of stylized facts rather than the empirical exploration of behavior in firms.

The basic intellectual process by which economic theory develops, there-

Van Raaij, W.F., van Veldhoven, G.M. and Wärneryd, K.E. (eds) Handbook of Economic Psychology. ISBN 90-247-3720-6.

fore, is neither through the careful empirical investigation of underlying assumptions, nor through the generation and testing of critical hypotheses, but through the gradual acceptance of behavioral assertions and their incorporation into the theory through an extension of a rational perspective. Behavioral research produces observations that come to be summarized into some broad behavioral generalizations about the firm that, in turn, become stylized facts for economic theorists. From this point of view, organization theory, behavioral decision theory, and the behavioral theory of the firm seek an understanding of actual choice behavior that is intriguing enough to stimulate the rationalizations of economic theory.

In this chapter we try to suggest some of the history and recent work on a behavioral theory of the firm, drawing from research on individual and organizational choice behavior more generally as well as on the economic firm. In section 2, we consider the background for contemporary research, classical theories of choice and the outline of a behavioral theory. Thereafter, we report several different kinds of elaborations of behavioral ideas. In section 3, we examine some contributions of behavioral decision theory. In section 4, we explore ideas of search and attention as factors in organizational choice. In section 5, we look at adaptation in organizations and its implications for theories of the firm.

2. THE BASIC THEORETICAL FRAMEWORK

2.1. *Introduction*

The background for behavioral perspectives on decision making in business firms is the neo-classical theory of the firm and its more modern variants drawing from n-person game theory. Such theories are built on assumptions of action that emphasize the willful, self-interested, anticipatory bases of human choice. Behavioral students of decision making have exposed various ways in which actual behavior in firms differs from the assumptions and apparent expectations of these rational theories of choice. Some of their observations have been ignored by economic theory, treated as inaccurate or uninteresting. Other observations have become part of the stylized truths with which the theory deals, thus subsumed by some new elaboration of the basic model that retains the axioms of rationality. Since any interesting fact can find a rationalization but the converse is not true, the role has an appropriate delicacy and primacy to match its traditional modesty.

2.2. *Economic Theories of Decision Making in Firms*

Neo-classical economic theories of the firm presume that decisions are made intentionally on the basis of expectations about future consequences of current actions. Within such theories a decision depends on four things:

1. A *knowledge of alternatives*. Decision makers are assumed to have a set of alternatives for action. These alternatives are defined by the situation and are known unambiguously.
2. A *knowledge of consequences*. Decision makers are assumed to know the consequences of alternative actions, at least up to a probability distribution.
3. A *consistent preference ordering*. Decision makers are assumed to have objective functions by which alternative consequences of action can be compared in terms of their subjective value.
4. A *decision rule*. Decision makers are assumed to have rules by which to select the best alternative on the basis of its consequences for the preferences.

In the most familiar form of the model, we assume that all alternatives, the probability distribution of consequences conditional on each alternative, and the subjective value of each possible consequence are known; and we assume a choice is made by selecting the alternative with the highest expected value. The details of organizational processes involved in decision making may vary from one firm to another and they may appear to differ substantially from the assumptions specified explicitly in the theory, but decisions are uniquely determined by environmental constraints. Subject only to variations attributable to variations in preferences, therefore, such theories assume that choice is dictated by environmental conditions and is predictable from them. Heterogeneity in preferences tends to be denied, ignored, or assumed away by some kind of natural selection argument with respect to the requirements for survival.

The durability of simple choice models in the economic study of the firm is both impressive and understandable. Choice is a faith as well as a theory; it is linked to ideologies of the Enlightenment; it is associated with definitions of the nature of the species. Rational theories of decision making in firms have somewhat more mundane claims also. The models capture some truth. Demand curves for consumer products generally have negative slopes, and labor unions usually are more resistant to wage cuts than to wage increases. Moreover, the core ideas are flexible. When the model does not seem to fit, it is often possible to reinterpret preferences or knowledge and preserve the axioms. The prevalence of choice models of behavior not only in economics, but also in political science, sociology, psychology, linguistics, and anthropology attests to the attractiveness of choice as a theoretical vision of human behavior.

The same basic structure underlies modern decision engineering. Operations analysis, management science, decision theory, and the various other analytical approaches to improving choices are variations on a theme of rational choice, as are standard ideas for determining the value of information and the design of information systems. The attraction extends to ordinary discourse. Ideas of willful, rational choice are the terms of discourse for answering the generic questions: Why did it happen? Why did you do it? The standard explanation provided for the actions of individuals or institutions involves two assertions: Someone decided to have it happen. The decision was made because it was in the self-interest of the decision maker to make it. In cases involving multiple actors, a third assertion may be added: Different people, in their own self-interests, wanted different things and people got what they wanted in proportion to their relative power, or as a result of a process of bargaining, coalition formation, and exchange.

2.3. *Behavioral Theories of the Firm*

The basic theory of choice sketched above has guided most modern empirical efforts to observe how firms make decisions. Many of the empirical observations, however, have proven to be inconsistent with the relatively pure theory we have outlined (Simon, 1979). Thirty years ago, students of organizations made two major criticisms of the existing theory of organizational decision making. The first criticism was that the theory made extraordinary time and information demands on organizations (Simon, 1955; Miller, 1956; March and Simon, 1958). Information and time were treated as freely available resources. To ask that all consequences of all alternatives be known precisely seemed unreasonable in the face of empirical evidence that organizations considered only a small number of alternatives, examined only a small number of consequences related to only a subset of organizational goals, and made relatively imprecise estimates.

The second criticism was that the theory assumed that the preferences of the firm were not problematic, that decision makers in an organization had identical preference functions, or if they did not, that conflict among them could be readily managed through the terms of some prior agreement (March, 1962; Cyert and March, 1963). In the case of a political organization, the agreement was a coalition contract, or constitution, by which all members of a coalition, or polity, agreed to be bound to the policies specified through bargaining, or legislation. Thus, the familiar distinction between politics and administration. In the case of a firm or other Weberian bureaucracy, the agreement was an employment contract by which employees, in return for the payment of wages, agreed to act as though they had the same goals as the owner, or other legitimate policy maker. Empirical studies, on the other hand, seemed to indicate that conflict was endemic in organizations, that it tended to be interminable rather than settled by prior agreements.

The behavioral theory of the firm developed by Cyert and March (1963) was an effort to attend to such criticisms, to introduce greater process realism into economic theories of business firms. They summarized their basic ideas in terms of four concepts: The first concept is the *quasi-resolution of conflict*. It was argued that organizations make decisions in such a way that conflict is often neither resolved nor confronted. Local rationality shields subunits from each other and the combination of acceptable-level decision rules and sequential attention to goals makes it less likely that conflict will be made relevant to the choices as they are made.

The second concept is *uncertainty avoidance*. It was argued that organizations face uncertainty about future outcomes conditional on present actions, but that the response to such uncertainty is not to try to use probabilistic calculations or decision theory guides but rather to try to reconstruct the environment to avoid uncertainty. There is extensive use of incremental, feedbackreact procedures rather than forecasting, and organizations are inclined to negotiate agreements with other actors that eliminate uncertainty as much as possible.

Third there is *problemistic search*. It was argued that search for new alternatives or new information is motivated by a problem and proceeds in a relatively simple way to consider alternatives in the neighborhood of existing alternatives before going further afield. Search was also seen as biased, as reflecting the private agendas, training, and expectations of subunits and individuals.

The fourth concept is *organizational learning*. It was argued that organizations learn from their experiences. They modify aspiration levels to conform to their own performance and the performances of others to whom they compare themselves. They modify attention rules on the basis of experience in finding different patterns of attention differentially rewarding. They modify search rules on the basis of experience in finding (or failing to find) things through search.

Subsequent to 1963, the general notion that the theory of the firm needed a stronger basis in the behavioral study of decision processes within firms became common, as did specific applications of the behavioral theory of the firm framework. For example, Aharoni (1966) studied foreign investments, and Carter (1971) examined corporate financial management and capital budgeting from that perspective; Swieringa and Waterhouse (1982) looked at transfer pricing; Hopwood (1983) made a more general application to accounting practices; Eliasson (1974) studied planning processes; Joskow (1973) investigated the pricing behavior of regulated firms; and Bazerman and Schoorman (1983) considered interlocking directorates. Kay (1979, 1982, 1984) extended and elaborated the framework to consider many of the conventional concerns of neo-classical theories of the firm, including resource allocation, organizational structure, and economic growth. In addition, a rather large number of studies (e.g., Allison, 1971; Padgett, 1980a, 1981; Olsen, 1983) applied ideas of bounded rationality to behavior in non-economic organizations.

Observations suggesting that behavior within economic firms deviated from the canons of theories of the firm were well-known and widely-accepted for some time before they penetrated formal theories of choice; but ultimately they were translated into doctrinally acceptable form through the development of information economics and theories of agency. Such theories consider information as a scarce resource subject to strategic manipulation by self-interested rational actors. Ideas drawn from organizational studies of bounded rationality and internal conflict permeate modern economic theory in the form of discussions of moral hazard, asymmetric information, agency, signalling, and optimal information strategies (Ross, 1973; Hirschleifer and Riley, 1979; Fama, 1980). Increasingly, this attention has been extended to a concern for the normative rules and institutions within which choice takes place (Kreps and Wilson, 1982; Milgrom and Roberts, 1982; Shepsle, 1983). Although most behavioral students of organizations would argue that these theories are also incomplete and to some degree perversely inattentive to the way organizations operate, the earlier empirical criticisms have reformed theoretical thinking.

3. BEHAVIORAL DECISION THEORY

3.1. *Introduction*

Extensive reviews of behavioral decision theory and related studies of human cognitive processes have appeared elsewhere (Slovic, Fischhoff, and Lichtenstein, 1977; Nisbett and Ross, 1980; Einhorn and Hogarth, 1981; Kahneman, Slovic, and Tversky, 1982; Kiesler and Sproull, 1982; Schoemaker, 1982; Pitz and Sachs, 1984). Those reviews make it unnecessary for us to do more than suggest here some of the key results particularly relevant to a behavioral theory of the firm.

Although primarily concerned with empirical studies of individual decision making, behavioral decision theory has features in common with the theory of economic behavior of firms, particularly its model of rational decision making. As a result, there are complementarities between the development of behavioral decision theory and the development of a behavioral theory of the firm. The details of future links between the two fields are hardly clear (March and Shapira, 1982), but there is no question that ideas flow rather easily from one domain to the other, despite apparent differences in the disciplinary backgrounds of the researchers, the methodologies for doing research, and the orientation to rationality.

Most students of decision behavior have assumed that decision problems are well-defined, and decision makers are rational, although rational only within the boundaries set by human cognitive limitations (Simon, 1955). Given these limitations, behavior can be explained by features of the decision task and its content, by the way problems and information are perceived, coded, and judged, and by the rules of choice that are applied (Ungson, Braunstein, and Hall, 1981). A central presumption of behavioral decision theory is that a decision maker acts within serious cognitive limitations while judging and choosing something that is ambiguously described or partly unknown.

The research has depicted both automatic, perception-like heuristics involved in most judgment and decision making (e.g., Kahneman, Slovic, and Tversky, 1982) and more deliberate information processing strategies (Montgomery and Adelbratt, 1982). It has produced a catalogue of interesting biases in human judgment (Einhorn and Hogarth, 1981; Kiesler and Sproull, 1982; Pitz and Sachs, 1984), and has led to studies of how people notice problems (Kiesler and Sproull, 1982), how they learn from experience (Brehmer, 1980), how a decision problem is framed (Tversky and Kahneman, 1981), how cognitive maps are developed (Sevón, 1984), and how these maps relate to choices (see also Berkeley and Humphreys, 1982). The research also suggests that a decision maker's preferences can be labile, ambiguous, partly, or totally unknown, or, even undeveloped (Fischhoff, Slovic, and Lichtenstein, 1980). These concerns bear some resemblance to those of behavioral theories of the firm described earlier and also to the garbage can perspectives discussed below (March and Olsen, 1976).

Some studies have focussed on problem sensing, the ways in which things are noticed, coded, and interpreted in the environment. Other studies have described inferential behavior, for example, how people judge the probability of the occurrence of events. Other studies have centered on choices, for example, on what rules people use to decide which alternative to choose in different situations of risk and uncertainty, and for different decision problems. Still other studies have been concerned with the development of decision aids, with procedures for helping people and organizations make good decisions. We describe some empirical findings of importance to the theory of the firm, concentrating on empirical findings concerning judgment and choice, and omitting studies of decision aids.

3.2. *Problem Sensing*

Kiesler and Sproull (1982) have summarized studies of social cognition relevant to the ways in which individuals in organizations notice problems and define their causes. They identify five basic concepts from attribution theory and social perception:

1. The *augmentation principle* (Kelley, 1971): Decision makers are likely to exaggerate the importance of a factor that might plausibly be imagined to produce an effect if there is a plausible inhibiting effect present at the same time.
2. The *discounting principle* (Kelley, 1971): Decision makers are likely to overestimate the importance of the more powerful causal agents in a situation, underestimate the importance of lesser agents.
3. *Illusory correlation* (Smedslund, 1963; Hamilton and Gifford, 1976): Decision makers are likely to see two events as correlated when they occur together, appear similar, or were in some other way fortuitously linked.
4. *Illusory causation*: Decision makers are likely to see conspicuous events as causally important (Taylor and Fiske, 1978); they are likely to see others as having greater causal effects than themselves (Jones and Davis, 1965); they are likely to attribute causation to another individual's wishes or attitudes rather than to situational factors (Ross, 1977); they are likely to assign greater significance than warranted to recent events (Wyer, 1980).
5. *Automatic scanning*: Decision makers scan automatically for cues and are likely to exaggerate the importance of cues that are salient and frequent (Hasher and Zacks, 1979).

Problem sensing also depends on motivational factors in the uses of information and on the ways in which information is processed. Kiesler and Sproull (1982) detail some of the factors affecting the ways in which mental representations are developed on the basis of experience. They note that decision makers are most likely to notice and incorporate information that is salient and relevant to an existing schema for organizing the knowledge (Rothbart, Evans, and Fulero, 1979), that they are more likely to accept information that confirms their prior beliefs or their own self-worth (Deutsch and Gerard, 1955; Weary, 1979).

3.3. *Decision Framing and Decision Rules*

People seem to treat decisions in isolation. They do not have the kind of portfolio perspective required by rational choice. Most decisions are made in a decomposed fashion using comparisons, following conjunctive or disjunctive rules. When a conjunctive rule is used, alternatives are compared against a preset standard and eliminated, if they fail to measure up. People use disjunctive rules, if satisfaction of at least one dimensional standard is sufficient. When alternatives and dimensions are numerous, subjects tend to use conjunctive and lexicographic models as initial screening rules (Payne, 1976). With fewer attributes, holistic evaluations are more probable. The uses of these rules in business and other decision making have been shown in a number of studies (e.g., Reder, 1947; Einhorn, 1970; Libby and Fishburn, 1977; Hey, 1982; see also Chapter 3 of this Handbook).

3.4. *Probability Processing*

People seem to disobey many of the classical rules for probabilistic reasoning, when they are asked to judge the likelihood of occurrence of events. For example, they overestimate low probabilities and underestimate high ones (Lee 1971). In addition, Slovic (1966) found that subjective probabilities became higher as outcomes became more desirable (i.e., wishful thinking). Kahneman, Slovic, and Tversky (1982) have examined two judgmental heuristics frequently observed in human actors. The first is an availability heuristic, assessing the frequency or probability of an event by the ease with which instances can be brought to mind. Utilizing an availability heuristic, leads to an overestimation of the likelihood of occurrence of easily retrievable events (e.g., dramatic, highly negative, or positive events). The second is the representativeness heuristic, by which the strength of a link between objects or events is inferred from the extent to which the two objects or events appear similar. The representativeness heuristic is one way in which people ignore base-rate information in judging the frequency of an event. Sevón (1977) has shown that people use different judgment heuristics in situations involving different degrees of subjective uncertainty. She found that if people felt uncertain about their probability judgment, their judgments showed wishful thinking. When they were fairly certain, they followed an availability heuristic.

Some attention has been given to the way individuals relate their experience in the past to their estimates about the future. Fischhoff (1975) found that events that actually happened appeared in retrospect more likely than they did before the outcome was known, and that events that did not happen appeared in retrospect less likely ("hindsight"). The updating of subjective probabilities was more extreme than would be expected from a simple Bayesian perspective. Sevón (1984) has shown that managers conceive past causes for an economic event, such as inflation and unemployment, as less dramatic and more complex than future causes of the same events.

3.5. *Preference Processing*

As long as preferences are considered to be fixed and known, there is no need to study if and how preferences develop or relate them to task characteristics, choice and context. However, a behavioral perspective on decision making raises questions of preference processing. For example, one of the earliest speculations in a behavioral theory of the firm was the idea that alternatives are evaluated in terms of gains and losses relative to some targets, rather than in terms of their effects on final wealth levels (Simon, 1955). This was shown empirically by Ortiz (1980) who collected data on Colombian coffee farmers' expectations. He found that farmers retain:

1. prices, yields and returns in terms of categories;
2. incomes as ranges rather than as sequential numerical lists;
3. prices and yields as judgments integrated into ranges and/or numerical ranges; and
4. actual prices remembered only as an illustration of a judgment category or when the price has significantly affected the return.

Recently, there has been increased theoretical attention to difficulties with conventional assumptions about human goals. Theories of rationality assume that individuals in organizations have preferences and that preferences drive their actions. Moreover, the assumptions about preferences are strong ones. Individual preferences are expected to be stable. Action taken now presumes that current preferences will be unchanged, when the consequences of action are realized. Preferences are expected to be consistent. Any possible inconsistency is removed through the specification of trade-offs. Preferences are expected to be precise. Whether a particular outcome is consistent with a particular taste must be clear. Preferences are expected to be exogenous. In particular, they are presumed to be unaffected by choices made in their name.

All of these features of preferences as they appear in the theory seem incongruent with observations of choice behavior by individuals and organizations. Preferences are expressed but not followed. Preferences change; and they change as a result of choice (March and Olsen, 1976). They may be inconsistent and imprecise (Fischhoff, Slovic, and Lichtenstein, 1980). It seems clear that organizations routinely and habitually make decisions without the kind of preferences that would satisfy the axioms of rational choice.

This behavioral research on the treatment of preferences by human subjects also raises doubt about the normative position of standard models of rational choice. Most discussions of preferences have assumed that normatively appropriate preferences are those close to the consistent preferences found in rational models of choice, although actual preferences may deviate from that ideal. Not everyone agrees on the optimality of consistent, stable preferences, however (Dykman, 1981). March (1978) has argued not only that ordinary human preferences are quite different from the preferences presumed by the theory, being characterized by inconsistency, change, and lack of clarity, but also that such preferences may make normative sense. Cohen and Axelrod (1984) and Cohen (1986) have shown how adaptive, changing preferences can lead to better performance than performance produced by unambiguous, stable preferences, even where the criterion of goodness is defined in terms of a known prior objective function.

3.6. *Attitudes Towards Risk*

Riskiness is a feature of decision problems. A risky decision is one with a relatively large variance over the possible outcomes as seen at the time of the decision. Risk aversion and risk proneness have sometimes been seen in the psychological literature as stable traits, and successful entrepreneurship has sometimes been associated with a willingness to take risks. In most modern economic theories of risk, however, all individual rational actors are assumed to be risk averse. That is, it is assumed that the greater the risk associated with a choice, the greater must be the expected value to warrant its selection.

The empirical research suggests that attitudes toward risk are not stable but shift across decision problems and frames (Wolf and Pohlman, 1983). Specifically, Laughhunn, Payne, and Crum (1981) found executives to be risk-seeking, when presented with gambles having outcomes below break-even returns of investments. However, when the gambles involved ruinous losses, the executives were often risk-averse. Hershey and Shoemaker (1980) similarly have shown that the response to formally equivalent choice situations depends on whether the choices are presented as a gamble or an opportunity to purchase insurance. The "insurance" option is much more likely than the "gamble" option to elicit the risk averse choice even though the choice situation is equivalent in the two contexts. Several studies have indicated that gains are evaluated differently from losses (Fishburn, 1977; Kahneman and Tversky, 1979). People act as though their utility functions are convex for losses and concave for gains, a result consistent with the original search ideas of the behavioral theory of the firm. Interviews with executives similarly suggest that managerial risk taking is responsive to the relation between expected return and both the level of aspiration and the survival level, but that managers distinguish risk taking from gambling through a belief in their ability to beat the odds (MacCrimmon and Wehrung, 1985; March and Shapira, 1987).

4. ATTENTION IN DECISION MAKING

4.1. *Introduction*

The behavioral theory of the firm assumes that human actors have limited cognitive capabilities. In particular, they cannot attend to everything at once. As a result, much of the theory is a theory of attention allocation and search rather than a theory of choice. The focus is on how problems, solutions, and other information come to the attention of decision makers, and on how decision makers ration their scarce attention resources (Radner and Rothschild, 1975; Winter, 1981).

4.2. *Success, Slack, and Search*

The basic structure of the original model is simple. Organizations, or the decision makers within them, are assumed to have performance targets, normally called goals or aspiration levels. When performance exceeds a goal (success), two things happen: The goal is increased and the search for new alternatives is decreased. On the other hand, when a goal exceeds performance (failure), the goal is decreased and search for new alternatives is increased. Thus, the theory pictures an equilibrating organization that tends to keep a firm's performance and goals close to each other, subject to exogenous factors affecting them.

Variations in the search level for new alternatives result in variations in organizational slack (the difference between potential and actual performance). Successful organizations accumulate slack; unsuccessful organizations reduce slack. Slack, therefore, serves to smooth performance, making it less variable than would be expected simply from variations in environmental conditions. During adverse times, the firm discovers opportunities for cost reductions and alternative strategies that were "stored" during better times (Radner, 1975a, 1975b; Winter, 1971). As a result, slack is both a source of inefficiency in a firm and a protection against the dangers of unpredictable shocks. Leibenstein (1966, 1976) uses a somewhat different formulation of the same phenomenon in his analysis of X-inefficiency in firms and provides examples drawn from the utilization of labor, capital, and information within business organizations. This fundamental relation between success and search was elaborated by Cyert and March (1963), and subsequently by others (Knight, 1967; Kay, 1979; Levinthal and March, 1981), to distinguish between search stimulated by failure, which was assumed to be focused and relatively narrow, and search encouraged by slack, which was assumed to be less controlled, broader, and with a wider variance on the outcomes. The elaboration seemed warranted by observations of firms, but it had the consequence of making the net effect of current success on subsequent success equivocal. The basic ideas are summarized in Figure 1.

A number of subsequent studies have explored the relationship between slack and organizational behavior. Both Lane (1954) and Staw and Szwajkowski (1975) found that organizations that were failing were more likely to be found to be engaged in illegal acts. Manns and March (1978) found that curricular innovation at a university was more likely to occur under conditions of relative adversity than during relatively good times, particularly among departments of lesser prestige. Several studies have indicated that reduced performance leads to tightening of controls and a centralization of authority (Burns and Stalker, 1961; Pfeffer and Leblebici, 1973; Smart and Vertinsky, 1977; Staw, Sandelands, and Dutton, 1981; Czarniawska and Hedberg, 1985), a result that Pfeffer (1978) associates with the influence of variations in slack. However, Sevón and Sundin (1985) found an opposite

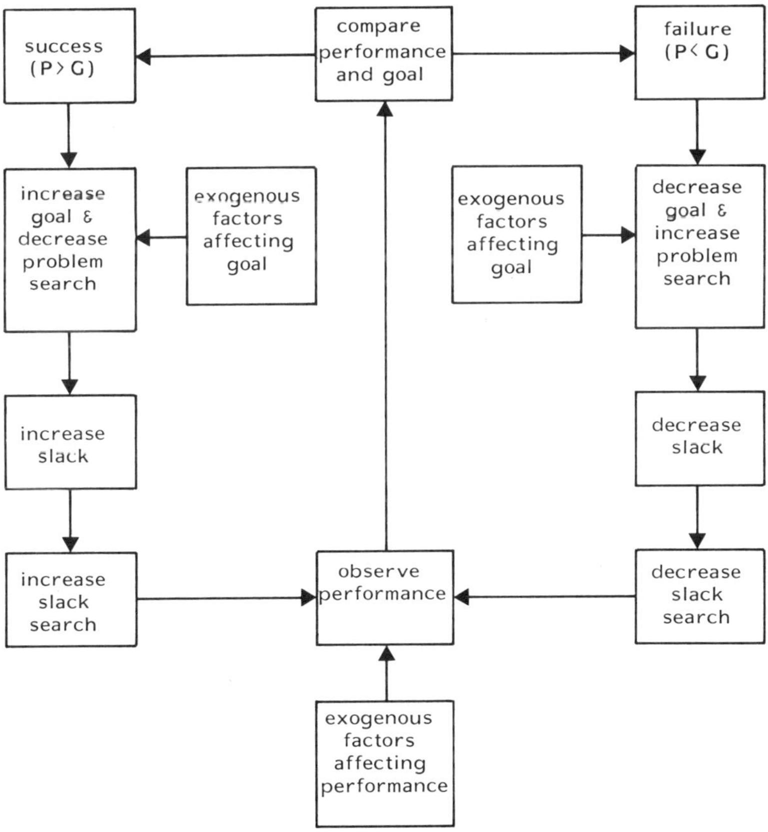

Fig. 1. Goal, performance, slack, and search.

tendency in the public sectors of Finland and Sweden, i.e., decentralization of authority in the face of austerity.

Building on such findings and also on a distinction between absorbed and unabsorbed slack (Bourgeois, 1981; Bourgeois and Singh, 1983), Singh (1986) found that performance and risk taking were negatively related and that the relationship was partly direct and partly indirect, mediated through absorbed slack. The result that performance (or return) and risk taking are negatively related (see also Bowman 1980, 1982; Brenner and Shapira, 1983) is not anticipated by theories that assume general risk aversion. Risk averse decision makers need to be compensated for variability in possible outcomes; thus the greater the risk, the greater should be the return on an investment (Fisher and Hall, 1969).

4.3. *Loose Coupling and Garbage Can Models*[2]

As early as 20 years ago, it was observed that theories of choice underestimate the confusion and complexity surrounding actual decision making. Observations of decision making suggested that the link between problems and solutions was often tenuous, that many decisions were made by default, that decision processes frequently seemed to exercise problems rather than solve them, that the attention of participants was difficult to predict simply from properties of the choices being considered. The instrumental linkages between means and ends, between action today and action tomorrow, between action in one part of the system and action in another, between plans and decisions, between decisions and implementation all tended to be obscure. The generic observation was that organizations could be seen as relatively loosely coupled systems; and although the term was used in many different, and not entirely consistent ways, it seemed to fit (March and Olsen, 1976; Weick, 1976).

Since the original discussions of garbage cans and loose coupling, numerous empirical observations of organizations have confirmed a relatively confusing picture of decision making. Many things seem to be happening at once; technologies are changing and poorly understood; alliances, preferences, and perceptions are changing; solutions, opportunities, ideas, people, and outcomes are mixed together in ways that make their interpretation uncertain and their connections unclear (Kingdon, 1984). It has been observed, for example, that organizations ignore information they have, ask for more information, then ignore the new information when it is available (Feldman and March, 1981; March and Sevón, 1984); and that managers spend substantial amounts of time in activities that appear to have few consequences beyond acknowledging the importance of others, as well as themselves (Cohen and March, 1974). Such observations could be explained in other ways, but they support a perspective that sees decision making as an occasion for exercising problems and solutions more than connecting them, for displaying decision making more than profiting from it, and for exhibiting virtue more than using it.

The apparent disorderliness of many things in decision making has led some people to argue that there is very little order to organizational decision making, that it is best described as bedlam. A more conservative position is to assume that the ways in which organizations bring order to disorder is somewhat different from the ways anticipated by conventional theories. The garbage can model is an effort to define an alternative way for seeing order in decision making processes (March and Olsen, 1984), thus an alternative basis for managing them (Cohen and March, 1974; Padgett, 1980b).

In pure form, the garbage can model assumes that problems, solutions, decision makers, and choice opportunities are independent, exogenous streams flowing through a system (Cohen, March, and Olsen, 1972). They are linked in a manner determined by their arrival and departure times and any structural constraints on the access of problems, solutions, and decision makers to choice opportunities. In the absence of structural constraints within a garbage can process, solutions are linked to problems, and decision makers to choices, primarily by their simultaneity.

Empirical students of decision making in organizations have noted how garbage cans are affected by structural features of organizational life. March and Romelaer (1976) pointed out that the drift of decisions within a garbage can situation is not random but occurs in a context of beliefs, norms, and institutions that produce systematic biases. Powell (1978) found that timing was important to publishing decisions but so was the structure imposed by company traditions, by the academic status of the author, and by whether the initiative was taken by the author or the publisher. Rommetveit (1976) showed that moving a decision from one arena with certain structural features to another with different characteristics apparently changed the decision. Weiner (1976) explored the consequences of having flows of problems and participants interconnected and showed that imposing deadlines on choices makes a difference in a garbage can process. The effect of belief structures and normative duties on the flows of participants was observed by Enderud (1976) and Olsen (1976a). Various studies have examined the structural constraints imposed by demographic orders (Stinchcombe, McDill, and Walker, 1968; March and March, 1977, 1978; Pfeffer, 1981b), symbolic orders (Meyer and Rowan, 1977; Pondy, 1978; March, 1981a; Pfeffer, 1981a; March and Olsen, 1983), historical orders (Etheredge, 1976; Olsen, 1976b, Chapter 15; Levinthal and March, 1981), normative orders (Christensen, 1976; Kreiner, 1976; Olsen, 1976c; Rommetveit, 1976; Stava, 1976), formal organizational charts (Egeberg, 1981;

Olsen, 1983), and accounting systems (Cooper, Hayes, and Wolf, 1981).

Events within a garbage can decision process are understandable and in some ways predictable, but typically neither the processes nor the outcomes appear to have a close relation with the explicit intentions of actors. In situations, in which load is heavy and the structure is relatively unsegmented, intention is lost in context dependent flows of problems, solutions, people, and choice opportunities. Indeed, outcomes are frequently sufficiently dependent on elements of exogenously determined timing as to make the differences between what happens and what does not happen deceptively significant.

4.4. *Generalized Contextual Perspectives*

Observers of decision making in organizations usually assume that the primary results of a decision process are decisions, that decisions can be understood by an analysis of the process, and that the centrality of a particular decision for an observer assures its centrality for participants. Such an exclusive focus on results and the implicit projection of their theoretical importance onto a belief in their subjective centrality and unity can be contrasted with the contextual perspective of temporal orders, such as those found in garbage can models. Without denying that organizations and the individuals in them pursue intentions and that organizational decision making sometimes can be understood in such terms, these alternative orders emphasize rule-bound decision making and the adaptation of rules over time, temporal linkages between problems and solutions, and the symbolic and ritual aspects of choice in organizations.

Two general elaborations of this contextual view have been suggested. The first emphasizes the context of intertwined individual lives. Any specific decision process involves a collection of individuals and groups who are simultaneously involved in other things. It is hard to understand the way decisions are made in one arena without understanding how those decisions fit into the lives of participants. Each participant is involved in a life with a variety of changing demands. The meaning, importance, and accessibility of any decision to any one participant depend on the mosaic of demands on that individual at that time.

Understanding the course of a decision in full cross-sectional detail requires fitting a decision and the process that generates it into the life of each participant (Krieger, 1979, 1983), but a less comprehensive form of the multiple lives perspective focuses on the allocation of attention. The idea is simple. Each potential participant in a decision process is faced with a personal decision problem: how to allocate scarce attention across various demands for attention. The attention given to a particular decision will depend both on attributes of that decision and on alternative claims for the attention of possible decision participants. Since those claims are neither homogeneous across participants nor synchronous, the attention that any particular decision will receive can be both quite unstable and remarkably independent of the properties of the decision (Olsen, 1976c; Weiner, 1976).

The second elaboration of decision contexts emphasizes the symbolic aspects of decision making. Decision processes are sacred rituals, and decision making is linked to important symbolic concerns of organizations and society (Olsen, 1970; Edlefson, 1978; Bartunek and Keys, 1979; Roos and Hall, 1980). As a result, many of the phenomena within a decision process are better understood as part of a symbolic process than as a way to produce substantive decision results. Organizations and the individuals in them need to communicate to their observers that the decisions they make are legitimate (Meyer and Rowan, 1977). Since it is often hard to demonstrate a linkage between decision and outcome, legitimacy often depends on the appropriateness of the process as much as it does on the outcomes. Thus, we would expect a proliferation of plans (Cohen and March, 1974), information gathering (Feldman and March, 1981; March and Sevón, 1984), analysis (Weiss, 1977; Feldman, 1986), consultation, and other observable features of normatively approved managerial decision making (Pfeffer, 1981a).

Ambiguity, conflict, and loose coupling make it difficult to sustain decision commitment in an organization. It has been observed that individuals fight for the right to participate in decision making, then do not exercise that right with any vigor (Olsen, 1976a); that minor issues create a governmental crisis and unexpected patterns of political activation, then drift away again (Olsen, 1983: Chapter 5); that organizational participants contend acrimoniously over adoption of a policy, but once the policy is adopted, the same contenders appear to be largely indifferent to its implementation, or lack of it (Christensen, 1976; Saetren, 1983; Baier, March, and Saetren, 1986). Since it has been shown that, in the absence of behavioral compensation, sensible decision procedures introduce a structural bias toward disappointment (Harrison and March, 1984), it is not surprising that behavioral processes in organizations are marked by mechanisms that facilitate commitment. These include ego-defensiveness and self-justification (Weick, 1964; Staw, 1974, 1981), the framing of decisions (Whyte, 1986), impression management (Schwenk, 1986), and the buffering of organizational processes of thought from processes of action (March, 1984; Brunsson, 1982, 1984).

5. ADAPTATION IN THE FIRM

5.1. *Introduction*

Theories of organizational choice probably exaggerate the importance of systematic decision making in producing action within an organization. Most action results neither from deliberate, willful choice, nor from extraordinary organizational processes or forces, nor from uncommon imagination, persistence or skill, but from relatively stable, routine processes that relate organizations to their environments (March, 1981b). What we commonly call organizational adaptation is the consequence of an ecology of such processes occurring concurrently in various parts of an organization (Day and Groves, 1975). Environmental change produces response (innovation, change, instability) by stable organizations.

5.2. *Comparative Statics of the Structure of Firms*

Attention to adaptation in firms is partly an outgrowth of a traditional emphasis in economic theory on the analysis of equilibria. The conceptual and mathematical attractiveness of the comparative statics of equilibria has led economic theory to a conception of historical processes that emphasizes their efficiency, the ways in which history moves quickly and inexorably to a unique equilibrium, normally in some sense an optimum (March and Olsen, 1984; Simon, 1984). This assumption of historical efficiency makes it possible to be largely indifferent to behavioral description of the micro processes by which equilibria are achieved.

Students of organizational structure typically explore differences in structure associated with differences in technology or other features of the environment within which the organization must function. Although it has been argued that efforts to relate technical and structural measures at the organizational level are extremely hazardous because organizations tend to employ a variety of technologies and to be structurally complex (Scott, 1981), a substantial amount of research effort has been devoted to explore how features of organizational structure are related to features of the environment (Woodward, 1965; Khandwalla, 1974; Yasai-Ardekoni, 1986).

At the most general level, it seems obvious that firms and other organizations exist in different cultural contexts, which in turn may have some effect on how they organize. Researchers have been interested in describing these relations. One problem has been to find general dimensions, on which cultural values and beliefs could be measured and compared. Another problem has been to get meaningful comparative data on organizations in different cultures. Nevertheless, some work has been done. In order to find general value dimensions, Hofstede (1980) conducted a survey study among employees of one large U.S.-based multinational corporation in 40 different countries. He found national differences in beliefs and values on four dimensions: power distance, individualism-collectivism, uncertainty avoidance, and masculinity-femininity.

Lammers and Hickson (1979) summarized several studies aiming at detecting cross-cultural differences. They argued that there are at least three distinctive cultural forms:

1. a Latin type, exemplified by French, Italian, and Spanish organizations, which seem often to have relatively high centralization, rigid stratification and sharp inequalities among levels,
2. an Anglo-Saxon type, represented by firms in the United States, Great Britain, and Scandinavia, which is characterized by more decentralized, less rigid stratification, and more flexible approach to the application of rules, and
3. a third world type, typified by paternalistic leadership, implicit rules, and ill-defined or minimal separation between organizational and non-organizational roles.

Studies of cultural differences have also been part of several historic efforts to borrow organizational solutions across countries. This happened among European researchers looking at American corporations in the 1960's and 1970's. Now, U.S. researchers are doing the same with Japanese firms (see, e.g., Ouchi and Jaeger, 1978; Vogel, 1979). There is, however, some doubt whether an ideal model of a firm in one culture can be successfully transferred to another culture. There is in the particular case of Japanese firms also some doubt, whether what is said to be typical features of Japanese firms, as "lifetime employment" really is related to productivity growth (Nelson, 1981), or even are accurate portrayals of Japanese firms (Sethi, Namiki, and Swanson, 1984).

Much of the recent research in the United States on the structure of firms has been stimulated by the work of Williamson (1975), who uses an efficiency-seeking view of rationality to address the issue of structure and technology. Williamson assumes that transaction costs arise because of the following conditions in exchange relations:

1. small numbers or non-competitive markets,
2. opportunism,
3. uncertain future environment and uncertainty about how to cope with it, and
4. cognitive limits on information-processing.

Williamson asks the following questions:

1. Why are there organizations at all, as contrasted with having transactions, conducted solely through markets. And given that there are organizations, which transactions are more efficiently organized by markets rather than by hierarchies (the efficient boundary question)?
2. Given the fact of organizations, how can such entities be structured to economize on transaction costs within the firm (the "efficient form" question)?
3. What is the most efficient way of organizing and managing human assets in the firm, in the sense of structuring the exchange relations and incentives between the firm and its workers?

The second of these questions has been the starting point for a comparative evaluation of alternative modes of organizing in terms of their transaction costs, particularly an investigation of the conditions for efficiency of the multidivisional structure (M-form). Williamson (1980) compared the M-form with other forms, as did Armour and Teece (1978), who looked at firms in the petroleum industry. When they controlled factors like size, they found the M-form to have a significant impact on performance, but only until the multidivisional structure had been widely adopted within the industry. Teece later (1981) extended the test of the M-form argument to consider a set of matched firms (to control for interindustry differences) in 20 industries. The first firm to adopt ("the lead firm") was matched and compared with another firm similar in terms of product line and size. Teece measured differences in performance within pairs of firms over two periods: a "before period" in which the lead firm had the M-form, and an "after period," when both firms had the M-form structure. The M-form hypothesis was supported by the results.

Teece has also outlined a theory of the multiproduct firm (Teece 1982). Important building blocks of this theory include excess capacity, and its creation, market imperfection, and the peculiarities of organizational knowledge, including its tacit character. Teece adopts a framework in which profit seeking firms are seen to diversify in order to avoid high transaction costs associated with using markets to trade the services to various specialized assets.

5.3. *Epidemiological Theories of Firms*

Students of comparative statics assume some form of relatively efficient process by which organizational structures are matched appropriately to organizational environments. Only recently, however, has much close scholarly attention been directed to the precise mechanisms of these adaptive processes. For example, adaptation can be seen as resulting from conflict and shifts in the mobilization of participants and the resources they control (March, 1962; Gamson, 1968; Pfeffer, 1981c). Adaptation can be seen as resulting from regeneration, from changes in the competencies and intentions of organizational participants as a consequence of turnover in personnel (Stinchcombe, McDill, and Walker, 1968; White, 1970; McNeil and Thompson, 1971; Brittain and Freeman, 1980). Adaptation through conflict and regeneration have had some attention in the literature on the firm, but the major recent focus has been on ways in which organizations adapt either through some form of natural selection, through experiential learning (Day and Groves, 1975), or through contagion and imitation.

As has long been noted, adaptation in a population of firms can be seen as resulting from the spread of action from one organization to another through a contagious process (Rogers, 1962; Mansfield, 1968, 1971; Walker, 1969; Rogers and Shoemaker, 1971; Nelson, 1981). Contagion as a fundamental feature of organizational action has been given a new impetus in recent years by interest, particularly among sociologists, in the ways in which technologies, procedures, rules, and organizational forms spread among organizations as they pursue legitimacy. The central assertion is that organizations do not act on the basis of calculations of the technical contribution to be made by a procedure or form. They are driven by a need to fit into a social order rather than a technical order. This may be because the technical order is obscure (DiMaggio and Powell, 1983; Meyer and Scott, 1983) or that it is subordinated to a normative structure (Zucker, 1977). Empirical studies within this tradition show that early adoptions of organizational innovations tend to be predicted by features of the technical match between the innovation and the organization but that later diffusion is less well predicted by such factors (Tolbert and Zucker, 1979; Fligstein, 1985; Baron, Dobbin, and Jennings, 1987). They also indicate that the spread of procedures or forms is related to classical diffusion variables, such as rate and ease of contact (Knoke, 1982).

5.4. *Evolutionary Theories of Firms*

Some elementary forms of evolutionary theories have, of course, long been maintained as justification for rational models of choice in economics (Alchian, 1950). The core argument is that competitive pressures assure survival of only those organizational procedures and forms that optimize, thus that the actual behavior of firms will be a solution to an appropriate optimization problem even though the individuals in the firm could neither solve nor formulate the problem analytically. For example, we might predict the outcome of a complicated contractual negotiation by assuming that the actors are each acting rationally on the basis of complete information about each other and the world, even though we recognize that such assumptions are quite false as a description of individual behavior. Standard examples include theories of market equilibria, such as those found in recent ideas of efficient capital markets (Sharpe, 1970). Similarly, there has been interest in the conditions under which firms operating under the incomplete rules associated with limited rationality approach the optimality defined by conventional analysis (Day, 1967; Radner, 1975b).

Behavioral theories of the firm are also interested in selection and learning, but they are somewhat more inclined to argue that history cannot be guaranteed to be efficient. An equilibrium may not exist. Even if there is an equilibrium, it may not be unique and the historical processes can easily be slow enough relative to the rate of change in the environment that the equilibrium of the process is unlikely to be achieved before the environment, and thus the equilibrium, changes. As we move from a purely deductive economic theory of selection or learning in firms to a more behavioral one, we devote more theoretical attention to the inefficiencies of history, i.e., historical processes that do not have equilibria, take extended periods of time, lead to non-unique equilibria, or result in unique but suboptimal outcomes (Day, 1984; Iwai, 1984).

Sociologists (see, e.g., Hannan and Freeman, 1977; Carroll and Delacroix, 1982; Delacroix and Carroll, 1983), in particular, have pursued the population biology model by looking particularly at birth and death processes in families of organizations and the ways, in which the population of organizational types adapts to features of the environmental structure. They argue that the structure of an individual organization is hard to change because of prior investments and commitments, limited information, internal political constraints, and historical and legal traditions (Stinchcombe, 1974). Nevertheless, the population of organizational structures changes in response to selection processes. For the most part, students of population ecology have not emphasized uncovering the organizational features associated with adaptation to selective pressure. In that sense, they pursue a strategy similar to that of other students of comparative statics. However, they have illuminated some important features of the adaptation to environments (Wholey and Brittain, 1986). Beginning with Stinchcombe (1965), there are numerous studies that support the proposition that the survival of organizations is positively related both to age and to size (Carroll and Delacroix, 1982; Carroll, 1983; Freeman, Carroll, and Hannan, 1983; Singh, Tucker, and House, 1986). Somewhat more problematic is the research on the relative mortality of specialist and generalist organizational forms, since both the complexity of the theoretical argument and the complications of operationalizing concepts of organizational specialization make the empirical results difficult to assess. Nevertheless, Carroll (1984, 1985,

1986) has been able to identify some aspects of the circumstances, under which an environment dominated by generalists leaves safe niches for specialists.

Nelson and Winter (1973, 1982), Winter (1964, 1971, 1975), and Nelson, Winter, and Schuette (1976) have developed a different form of an evolutionary model that is similar in spirit to that of the population ecologists but is more closely linked to research on internal decision processes within the firm. Within a context of competition and the pursuit of profit, behavior in the firm is assumed to be driven by rules and standard operating procedures. However, these rules can change endogenously as a result of search. Organizational forms are only semi-stable and "mutations" are produced not only by chance but also by deliberate problem-induced search. The distribution of rules changes over time as a result of differential growth and survival of firms using them and imitation. Nelson and Winter use such ideas to develop alternatives to conventional economic models of comparative statics, growth, Schumpeterian competition, and economic policy. In a somewhat similar spirit, Axelrod (1984) has developed some evolutionary understanding of the ways in which reciprocity and cooperation develop within a world of self-interested actors.

5.5. *Experiential Learning Theories of Firms*

Business firms learn from their experience. That is, actions and beliefs in the firm change as a result of monitoring and interpreting the consequences of past actions (Day and Groves, 1975). Learning occurs concurrently along at least three dimensions (Herriott, Levinthal, and March, 1985). First, firms learn what resource *allocations* to make. They adapt to their experiences by coming to allocate more resources to those activities that have, in the past, been associated with success and less resources to those activities that have been associated with failure (Cyert and March, 1963; Levinthal and March, 1981). Second, firms learn (and forget) *competence*. They become more able at those things they do frequently, lose abilities that are not used (Arrow, 1962). There are numerous organizational mechanisms by which an increased potential gained from experience may be captured by individuals or subunits in the form of organizational slack, but we generally expect that organizations will become better at what they do the more they do it, but that experiential competence decays with time. Third, firms change their *aspirations*, or expectations, as a result of their experience. They learn what they can reasonably expect from their environment. They discover what a reasonable profit is, what kind of sales to expect, what kinds of governmental regulations to anticipate (Cyert and March, 1963; March and Olsen, 1976).

For the most part, discussions of learning in business firms and other organizations treat each of these three forms of learning separately and develop the implications of each without attention to parallel implications of the others, or to the ways in which they interact. Yet, it is clear that the three learning dimensions are not independent. The interrelations make it difficult to examine any of the three dimensions without attention to the others. These interactions among the dimensions of learning are further complicated by the fact that a firm is a collection of subunits that are simultaneously changing their own allocations, competencies, and aspirations on the basis of their own experiences. Since the separate decisions made by the several subunits and the firm affect the outcomes for the others, their learning experiences are intertwined (Herriott, Levinthal, and March, 1985; Lounamaa and March, 1987). In addition, firms that are learning allocations, competencies, and aspirations (while adapting to subunits that are simultaneously developing their own allocations, competencies, and aspirations) compete in an environment consisting of other firms that also are learning (and also contain learning subunits). As a result of competition and imitation, the learning of one firm depends on the actions and learning of the others (Cyert and De Groot, 1975; Herriott, Levinthal, and March, 1985).

Recent work on organizational learning and decision making has emphasized the importance of uncertainty and ambiguity to an understanding of modern organizations. It is easy to show that prima facie sensible learning procedures may produce anomalous results under conditions in which learning is affected by various forms of "noise" (Levinthal and March, 1981; March, 1981b). For example, performance may not be precisely determined by actions; environmental constraints may not be precisely specified; goals may be ambiguous, as may be results or their causes (March and Olsen, 1975). Moreover, it can be shown that in many situations experiential learning does better if it is slow rather than fast, imprecise rather than precise, and jerky rather than smooth (Herriott, Levinthal, and March, 1985; Lounamaa and March, 1987).

6. CONCLUDING REMARKS

Work on a behavioral theory of the firm has challenged important assumptions in economics and led to some significant changes in economic theory. At the same time, however, it is clear that there is no single substitute behavioral theory of the firm. Rather, there are a number of ideas suggesting additional empirical research. The inability to specify a comprehensive competing theory has been both criticized (Baumol and Stewart, 1971) and praised (Simon, 1984). Judging by past experience, the behavioral research is likely to continue to lead to adjustments in economic theory, possibly to major ones; but regardless of the impact on the economic theory of the firm, the behavioral theory of the firm provides some serious empirical and theoretical alternatives to a simple model of rational choice and some opportunities for research that will both clarify fundamental issues in understanding human behavior and contribute to an improvement of decision making within modern organizations such as the business firm.

NOTES

1. This research has been supported by grants from the Swedish School of Economics (Helsinki), Societas Scientarium Fennica, the Spencer Foundation, the Mellon Foundation, the Stanford Graduate School of Business, and the Hoover Institution. We are particularly grateful for the collaboration of Johan P. Olsen.
2. This section draws heavily on March and Olsen (1986).

REFERENCES

Aharoni, Y.A., 1966, The Foreign Investment Decision Process, Cambridge, MA: Harvard Graduate School of Business Administration.

Alchian, A.A., 1950, Uncertainty, evolution and economic theory, Journal of Political Economy, 58, 211-222.

Allison, G.T., 1971, Essence of Decision, Boston, MA: Little, Brown.

Armour, H.O., and D.J. Teece, 1978, Organizational structure and economic performance. A test of the multidivisional hypothesis, Bell Journal of Economics, 9, 106-122.

Arrow, K.J., 1962, "Economic welfare and the allocation of resources for invention," in: National Bureau Committee for Economic Research, The Rate and Direction of Inventive Activity: Economic and Social Factors, Princeton, NJ: Princeton University Press, pp. 609-625.

Axelrod, R., 1984, The Evolution of Cooperation, New York: Basic Books.

Baier, V.E., J.G. March, and H. Saetren, 1986, Implementation and ambiguity, Scandinavian Journal of Management Studies, 3, 197-212.

Baron, J., F. Dobbin, and P.D. Jennings, 1987, War and peace: The evolution of personnel administration in American industry, American Journal of Sociology, 92, 350-383.

Bartunek, J.M., and C.B. Keys, 1979, Participation in school decision making, Urban Education, 14, 52-75.

Baumol, W.J., and M. Stewart, 1964, Rules of thumb and optimally imperfect decisions, American Economic Review, 54, 23-46.

Baumol, W.J., and M. Stewart, 1971, "On the behavioral theory of the firm," in: R. Marris and A. Wood (eds.), The Corporate Economy: Growth, Competition and Innovative Potential, London: Macmillan, pp. 118-143.

Bazerman, M.H., and F.D. Schoorman, 1983, A limited rationality model of interlocking directorates, Academy of Management Review, 8, 206-217.

Berkeley, D., and P. Humphreys, 1982, Structuring decision problems and the bias heuristic, Acta Psychologica, 50, 201-252.

Bourgeois, L.J., 1981, On the measurement of organizational slack, Academy of Management Review, 6, 29-39.

Bourgeois, L.J., and J.V. Singh, 1983, "Organizational slack and political behavior among top management teams," in: K.H. Chung (ed.), Academy of Management Proceedings, pp. 43-47.

Bowman, E.H., 1980, A risk-return paradox for strategic management, Sloan Management Review, 21, 17-31.

Bowman, E.H., 1982, Risk seeking by troubled firms, Sloan Management Review, 23, 33-42.

Brehmer, B., 1980, In one word: Not from experience, Acta Psychologica, 45, 223-241.

Brenner, M., and Z. Shapira, 1983, "Environmental uncertainty as determining merger activity," in: W. Goldberg (ed.), Mergers: Motives, Modes, Methods, New York: Nichols, pp. 51-65.

Brittain, J.W., and J.H. Freeman, 1980, "Organizational proliferation and density-dependent selection," in: J. Kimberley and R. Miles (eds.), Organizational Life Cycles, San Francisco, CA: Jossey-Bass, pp. 291-338.

Brunsson, N., 1982, The irrationality of action and action rationality: Decisions, ideologies, and organizational actions, Journal of Management Studies, 19, 29-44.

Brunsson, N., 1984, The Irrational Organization, Chichester, Sussex, UK: John Wiley.

Burns, T., and G.M. Stalker, 1961, The Management of Innovation, London: Tavistock.

Carroll, G.R., 1983, A stochastic model of organizational mortality: Review and reanalysis, Social Science Research, 12, 93-113.

Carroll, G.R., 1984, Organizational ecology, Annual Review of Sociology, 10, 71-93.

Carroll, G.R., 1985, Concentration and specialization: Dynamics of niche width in populations of organizations, American Journal of Sociology, 90, 1262-1283.

Carroll, G.R., 1986, Publish and Perish, Greenwich, CT: JAI Press.

Carroll, G.R., and J. Delacroix, 1982, Organizational mortality in the newspaper industries of Argentina and Ireland: An ecological approach, Administrative Science Quarterly, 27, 169-198.

Carter, E.E., 1971, The behavioral theory of the firm and top level decisions, Administrative Science Quarterly, 16, 413-428.

Christensen, S., 1976, "Decision making and socialization," in: J.G. March and J.P. Olsen (eds.), Ambiguity and Choice in Organizations, Bergen, Norway: Universitetsforlaget, pp. 351-385.

Cohen, M.D., 1986, "Artificial intelligence and the dynamic performance of organizational designs," in: J.G. March and R. Weissinger-Baylon (eds.), Ambiguity and Command: Organizational Perspectives on Military Decision Making, Cambridge, MA: Ballinger, pp. 53-71.

Cohen, M.D., and R. Axelrod, 1984, Coping with complexity: The adaptive value of changing utility, American Economic Review, 74, 30-42.

Cohen, M.D., and J.G. March, 1974, Leadership and Ambiguity: The American College President, New York: McGraw-Hill.

Cohen, M.D., J.G. March, and J.P. Olsen, 1972, A garbage can model of organizational choice, Administrative Science Quarterly, 17, 1-25.

Cooper, D.J., D. Hayes, and F. Wolf, 1981, Accounting in organized anarchies: Understanding and designing accounting systems in ambiguous situations, Accounting, Organizations and Society, 6, 175-191.

Cyert, R.M., and M.H. De Groot, 1975, "Adaptive Utility," in: R.H. Day and T. Groves (eds.), Adaptive Economic Models, New York: Academic Press, pp. 223-246.

Cyert, R.M., and J.G. March, 1963, A Behavioral Theory of the Firm, Englewood Cliffs, NJ: Prentice-Hall.

Cyert, R.M., and H.A. Simon, 1983, The behavioral approach: With emphasis on economics, Behavioral Science, 28, 95-108.

Czarniawska, B., and B. Hedberg, 1985, Control cycle response to decline, Scandinavian Journal of Management Studies, 2, 19-39.

Day, R.H., 1967, Profits, learning and the convergence of satisficing to marginalism, Quarterly Journal of Economics, 81, 302-311.

Day, R.H., 1984, Disequilibrium economic dynamics: A post-Schumpeterian contribution, Journal of Economic Behavior and Organization, 5, 57-76.
Day, R.H., and T. Groves (eds.), 1975, Adaptive Economic Models, New York: Academic Press.
Delacroix, J., and G. Carroll, 1983, Organizational foundings: An ecological study of the newspaper industries of Argentina and Ireland, Administrative Science Quarterly, 28, 274-291.
Deutsch, M., and H. Gerard, 1955, A study of normative and informational social influences upon individual judgment, Journal of Abnormal and Social Psychology, 51, 629-636.
DiMaggio, P., and W.W. Powell, 1983, The iron cage revisited: Institutional isomorphism and collective rationality in organizational fields, American Sociological Review, 48, 147-160.
Dykman, T.R., 1981, The intelligence of ambiguity, Accounting, Organizations and Society, 6, 291-300.
Edlefson, C.J., 1978, Participatory Planning for Organizational Change: The Case of Project Redesign, Stanford, CA: Stanford University, School of Education (doctoral dissertation).
Egeberg, M., 1981, Stat og organisasjoner, Bergen, Norway: Universitetsforlaget.
Einhorn, H.J., 1970, The use of non-linear, non-compensatory models in decision making, Psychological Bulletin, 73, 221-230.
Einhorn, H.J., and R.M. Hogarth, 1981, Behavioral decision theory: Processes of judgment and choice, Annual Review of Psychology, 32, 53-88.
Eliasson, G., 1974, Corporate Planning – Theory, Practice, Comparison, Stockholm: Federation of Swedish Industries.
Enderud, H., 1976, "The perception of power," in: J.G. March and J.P. Olsen (eds.), Ambiguity and Choice in Organizations, Bergen, Norway: Universitetsforlaget, pp. 386-396.
Etheredge, L.S., 1976, The Case of the Unreturned Cafeteria Trays, Washington, DC: American Political Science Association.
Fama, E.F., 1980, Agency problems and the theory of the firm, Journal of Political Economy, 88, 288-307.
Feldman, M.S., 1986, The Invisible Mind: Order Without Design, Ann Arbor: University of Michigan (unpublished manuscript).
Feldman, M.S., and J.G. March, 1981, Information as signal and symbol, Administrative Science Quarterly, 26, 171-186.
Fischhoff, B., 1975, "Hindsight ≠ foresight: The effect of outcome knowledge on judgment under uncertainty," Journal of Experimental Psychology: Human Perception and Performance, 1, 288-299.
Fischhoff, B., P. Slovic, and S. Lichtenstein, 1980, "Knowing what you want: Measuring labile values," in: T.S. Wallsten (ed.), Cognitive Processes in Choice and Decision Behavior, Hillsdale, NJ: Lawrence Erlbaum, pp. 117-141.
Fishburn, P.C., 1977, Mean-risk analysis with risk associated with below-target returns, American Economic Review, 67, 116-126.
Fisher, N., and G.R. Hall, 1969, Risk and corporate rates of return, Quarterly Journal of Economics, 83, 79-92.
Fligstein, N.J., 1985, The spread of the multidivisional form among large firms, 1919-1979, American Sociological Review, 50, 377-391.
Freeman, J.H., G.R. Carroll, and M.T. Hannan, 1983, The liabilities of newness: Age dependence in organizational death rates, American Sociological Review, 48, 692-710.
Gamson, W.A., 1968, Power and Discontent, Homewood, IL: Dorsey Press.
Hamilton, D.L., and R.K. Gifford, 1976, Illusory correlation in interpersonal perception: A cognitive basis of stereotypic judgments, Journal of Experimental Social Psychology, 12, 392-407.

Hannan, M.T., and J.H. Freeman, 1977, The population ecology of organizations, American Journal of Sociology, 82, 929-964.
Harrison, J.R., and J.G. March, 1984, Decision making and postdecision surprises, Administrative Science Quarterly, 29, 26-42.
Hasher, L., and R.T. Zacks, 1979, Automatic and effortful processes in memory, Journal of Experimental Psychology: General, 108, 356-388.
Herriott, S.R., D. Levinthal, and J.G. March, 1985, Learning from experience in organizations, American Economic Review, 75, 298-302.
Hershey, J.C., and P.J.H. Schoemaker, 1980, Risk-taking and problem context in the domain of losses: An expected utility analysis, Journal of Risk and Insurance, 47, 111-132.
Hey, J.D., 1982, Search for rules for search, Journal of Economic Behavior and Organization, 3, 65-82.
Hirschleifer, J., and J.G. Riley, 1979, The analytics of uncertainty and information. An expository survey, Journal of Economic Literature, 17, 1375-1421.
Hofstede, G., 1980, Culture's Consequences: International Differences in Work-related Values, Beverly Hills, CA: Sage.
Hopwood, A.G., 1983, On trying to study accounting in the contexts in which it operates, Accounting, Organizations and Society, 8, 287-305.
Iwai, K., 1984, Schumpeterian dynamics: An evolutionary model of innovation and imitation, Journal of Economic Behavior and Organization, 5, 159-190.
Jones, E.E., and K.E. Davis, 1965, "From acts to dispositions: The attribution process in person perception," in: L. Berkowitz (ed.), Advances in Experimental Social Psychology, Vol. 2, New York: Academic Press, pp. 219-266.
Joskow, P.L., 1973, Pricing decision of regulated firms: A behavioral approach, Bell Journal of Economics, 4, 118-140.
Kahneman, D., and A. Tversky, 1979, Prospect theory: An analysis of decision under risk, Econometrica, 47, 263-291.
Kahneman, D., P. Slovic, and A. Tversky, 1982, Judgment under Uncertainty: Heuristics and Biases, Cambridge, MA: Cambridge University Press.
Kay, N.M., 1979, The Innovating Firm: A Behavioral Theory of Corporate R & D, New York: St. Martin's Press.
Kay, N.M., 1982, The Evolving Firm, London: Macmillan.
Kay, N.M., 1984, The Emergent Firm: Knowledge, Ignorance and Surprise in Economic Organisation, London: Macmillan.
Kelley, H.H., 1971, Attribution in Social Interaction, Morristown, NJ: General Learning Press.
Khandwalla, P.N., 1974, Mass output orientation of operations technology and organizational structure, Administrative Science Quarterly, 19, 74-97.
Kiesler, S., and L.S. Sproull, 1982, Managerial response to changing environments: Perspectives on problem sensing from social cognition, Administrative Science Quarterly, 27, 548-570.
Kingdon, J.W., 1984, Agendas, Alternatives, and Public Policies, Boston, MA: Little, Brown.
Knight, K.E., 1967, A descriptive model of the intra-firm innovation process, Journal of Business, 40, 478-496.
Knoke, D., 1982, The spread of municipal reform: Temporal, spatial, and social dynamics, American Journal of Sociology, 87, 1314-1339.
Kreiner, K., 1976, "Ideology and management in a garbage can situation," in: J.G. March and J.P. Olsen (eds.), Ambiguity and Choice in Organizations, Bergen, Norway: Universitetsforlaget, pp. 156-173.
Krieger, S., 1979, Hip Capitalism, Beverly Hills, CA: Sage.
Krieger, S., 1983, Mirror Dance, Philadelphia, PA: Temple University Press.

Kreps, D., and R. Wilson, 1982, Reputation and imperfect information, Journal of Economic Theory, 27, 253-279.

Lammers, C.J., and D.J. Hickson, 1979, "A cross-national and cross-institutional typology of organizations," in: C.J. Lammers, and D.J. Hickson (eds.), Organizations Alike and Unlike, London: Routledge and Kegan Paul, pp. 420-434.

Lane, R.E., 1954, The Regulation of Businessmen, New Haven, CT: Yale University Press.

Laughhunn, D.J., J.W. Payne, and R. Crum, 1980, Managerial risk preferences for below-target returns, Management Science, 26, 1238-1249.

Lee, W., 1971, Decision Theory and Human Behavior, New York: John Wiley.

Leibenstein, H., 1966, Allocative efficiency vs. X-efficiency, American Economic Review, 56, 392-415.

Leibenstein, H., 1976, Beyond Economic Man: A New Foundation for Microeconomics, Cambridge, MA: Harvard University Press.

Levinthal, D., and J.G. March, 1981, A model of adaptive organizational search, Journal of Economic Behavior and Organization, 2, 307-333.

Libby, R., and P.C. Fishburn, 1977, Behavioral models of risk-taking in business decisions: A survey and evaluation, Journal of Accounting Research, 15, 272-292.

Lounamaa, P., and J.G. March, 1987, Adaptive coordination of a learning team, Management Science, 33, 107-123.

MacCrimmon, K.R., and D.A. Wehrung, 1985, Taking Risks: The Management of Uncertainty, New York: Free Press.

Manns, C.L., and J.G. March, 1978, Financial adversity, internal competition, and curriculum change in a university, Administrative Science Quarterly, 23, 541-552.

Mansfield, E., 1968, Industrial Research and Technological Innovation, New York: Norton.

Mansfield, E., 1971, Research and Innovation in the Modern Corporation, New York: Norton.

March, J.C., and J.G. March, 1977, Almost random careers: The Wisconsin school superintendency, 1940-1972, Administrative Science Quarterly, 22, 377-409.

March, J.C., and J.G. March, 1978, Performance sampling in social matches, Administrative Science Quarterly, 23, 434-453.

March, J.G., 1962, The business firm as a political coalition, Journal of Politics, 24, 662-678.

March, J.G., 1978, Bounded rationality, ambiguity, and the engineering of choice, Bell Journal of Economics, 9, 587-608.

March, J.G., 1981a, "Decisions in organizations and theories of choice," in: A.H. Van de Ven and W.F. Joyce (eds.), Perspectives on Organization Design and Behavior, New York: John Wiley, pp. 205-244.

March, J.G., 1981b, Footnotes to organizational change, Administrative Science Quarterly, 26, 563-577.

March, J.G., 1984, "How we talk and how we act: Administrative theory and administrative action," in: T.J. Sergiovanni and J.E. Corbally (eds.), Leadership and Organizational Culture, Urbana, IL: University of Illinois Press, pp. 18-35.

March, J.G., and J.P. Olsen, 1975, The uncertainty of the past: Organizational learning under ambiguity, European Journal of Political Research, 3, 147-171.

March, J.G., and J.P. Olsen, 1976, Ambiguity and Choice in Organizations, Bergen, Norway: Universitetsforlaget.

March, J.G., and J.P. Olsen, 1983, Organizing political life: What administrative reorganization tells us about government, American Political Science Review, 77, 281-296.

March, J.G., and J.P. Olsen, 1984, The new institutionalism: Organizational factors in political life, American Political Science Review, 78, 734-749.

March, J.G., and J.P. Olsen, 1986, "Garbage can models of decision making in organizations," in: J.G. March and R. Weissinger-Baylon (eds.), Ambiguity and Command:

Organizational Perspectives on Military Decision Making, Cambridge, MA: Ballinger, pp. 11-35.

March, J.G., and P.J. Romelaer, 1976, "Position and presence in the drift of decisions," in: J.G. March and J.P. Olsen (eds.), Ambiguity and Choice in Organizations, Bergen, Norway: Universitetsforlaget, pp. 251-276.

March, J.G., and G. Sevón, 1984, "Gossip, information and decision making," in: L.S. Sproull and P.D. Larkey (eds.), Advances in Information Processing in Organizations, Vol. l, Greenwich, CT: JAI Press, pp. 95-107.

March, J.G., and Z. Shapira, 1982, "Behavioral decision theory and organizational decision theory," in: G.R. Ungson and D.N. Braunstein, (eds.), Decision Making: An Interdisciplinary Inquiry, Boston, MA: Kent Publishing, pp. 92-115.

March, J.G., and Z. Shapira, 1987, Managerial perspectives on risk and risk taking, Management Science, 33, 1404-1418.

March, J.G., and H.A. Simon, 1958, Organizations, New York: John Wiley.

McNeil, K., and J.D. Thompson, 1971, The regeneration of social organizations, American Sociological Review, 36, 624-637.

Meyer, J.W., and B. Rowan, 1977, Institutionalized organizations: Formal structure as myth and ceremony, American Journal of Sociology, 83, 340-363.

Meyer, J.W., and W.R. Scott, 1983, Organizational Environments: Ritual and Rationality, Beverly Hills, CA: Sage.

Milgrom, P., and J. Roberts, 1982, Predation, reputation, and entry deterrence, Journal of Economic Theory, 27, 280-312.

Miller, G.A., 1956, The magic number seven plus or minus two: Some limits on our capacity for processing information, Psychological Review, 63, 61-97.

Montgomery, H., and T. Adelbratt, 1982, Gambling decisions and information about expected value, Organizational Behavior and Human Performance, 29, 39-57.

Nelson, R.R., 1981, Research on productivity growth and productivity differences: Dead ends and new departures, Journal of Economic Literature, 19, 1029-1064.

Nelson, R.R., and S.G. Winter, 1973, Toward an evolutionary theory of economic capabilities, American Economic Review, 63, 440-449.

Nelson, R.R., and S.G. Winter, 1982, An Evolutionary Theory of Economic Change, Cambridge, MA: Harvard University Press.

Nelson, R.R., S.G. Winter, and H.L. Schuette, 1976, Technical change in an evolutionary economy, Quarterly Journal of Economics, 90, 90-118.

Nisbett, R., and L. Ross, 1980, Human Inference: Strategies and Shortcomings of Social Judgment, Englewood Cliffs, NJ: Prentice-Hall.

Olsen, J.P., 1970, Local budgeting: Decision making or a ritual act?, Scandinavian Political Studies, 5, 85-118.

Olsen, J.P., 1976a, "University governance: Non-participation as exclusion or choice," in: J.G. March and J.P. Olsen (eds.), Ambiguity and Choice in Organizations, Bergen, Norway: Universitetsforlaget, pp. 277-313.

Olsen, J.P., 1976b, "The process of interpreting organizational history," in: J.G. March and J.P. Olsen (eds.), Ambiguity and Choice in Organizations, Bergen, Norway: Universitetsforlaget, pp. 338-350.

Olsen, J.P., 1976c, "Choice in an organized anarchy," in: J.G. March and J.P. Olsen (eds.), Ambiguity and Choice in Organizations, Bergen, Norway: Universitetsforlaget, pp. 82-139.

Olsen, J.P., 1983, Organized Democracy, Bergen, Norway: Universitetsforlaget.

Ortiz, S., 1980, "Forecast, decisions and the farmers' response to uncertain environments," in: P.F. Bartlett (ed.), Agricultural Decision Making, New York: Academic Press, pp. 177-200.

Ouchi, W.G., and A.M. Jaeger, 1978, Type Z organization: Stability in the midst of mobility, Academy of Management Review, 3, 305-314.

Padgett, J.F., 1980a, Bounded rationality in budgetary research, American Political Science Review, 74, 354-372.
Padgett, J.F., 1980b, Managing garbage can hierarchies, Administrative Science Quarterly, 25, 583-604.
Padgett, J.F., 1981, Hierarchy and ecological control in Federal budgetary decision making, American Journal of Sociology, 87, 75-129.
Payne, J.W., 1976, Task complexity and contingent processing in decision making: An information search and protocol analysis, Organizational Behavior and Human Performance, 16, 366-387.
Pfeffer, J., 1978, Organizational Design, Arlington Heights, IL: AHM Publishing.
Pfeffer, J., 1981a, "Management as symbolic action: The creation and maintenance of organizational paradigms," in: L. Cummings and B.M. Staw (eds.), Research in Organizational Behavior, Greenwich CT: JAI Press, pp. 1-52.
Pfeffer, J., 1981b, "Some consequences of organizational demogra]phy: Potential impacts of an aging work force on formal organizations," in: S.B. Kiesler, J.N. Morgan, and V.K. Oppenheimer (eds.), Aging: Social Change, New York: Academic Press, pp. 291-329.
Pfeffer, J., 1981c, Power in Organizations, Marchfield, MA: Pitman.
Pfeffer, J., and H. Leblebici, 1973, The effect of competition on some dimensions of organizational structure, Social Forces, 52, 268-279.
Pitz, G.F., and N.J. Sachs, 1984, Judgment and decision: Theory and application, Annual Review of Psychology, 35, 139-163.
Pondy, L.R., 1978, "Leadership as a language game," in: M.W. McCall, Jr., and M.M. Lombardo (eds.), Leadership, Where Else Can We Go?, Durham, NC: Duke University Press, pp. 87-99.
Powell, W.W., 1978, Publishers' decision-making: What criteria do they use in deciding which books to publish?, Social Research, 45, 227-252.
Radner, R., 1975a, A behavioral model of cost reduction, Bell Journal of Economics, 6, 196-215.
Radner, R., 1975b, Satisficing, Journal of Mathematical Economics, 2, 253-262.
Radner, R., and M. Rothschild, 1975, On the allocation of effort, Journal of Economic Theory, 10, 358-376.
Reder, M.W., 1947, A reconsideration of the marginal productivity theory, Journal of Political Economy, 55, 450-458.
Rogers, E.M., 1962, Diffusion of Innovations, New York: Free Press.
Rogers, E.M., and F.F. Shoemaker, 1971, Communication of Innovations, New York: Free Press.
Rommetveit, K., 1976, "Decision making under changing norms," in: J.G. March and J.P. Olsen (eds.), Ambiguity and Choice in Organizations, Bergen, Norway: Universitetsforlaget, pp. 140-155.
Roos, L.L., Jr., and R.I. Hall, 1980, Influence diagrams and organizational power, Administrative Science Quarterly, 25, 57-71.
Ross, L., 1977, "The intuitive psychologist and his shortcomings: Distortion in the attribution process," in: L. Berkowitz (ed.), Advances in Experimental Social Psychology, 10, New York: Academic Press, pp. 174-220.
Ross, S.A., 1973, The economic theory of agency: The principal's problem, American Economic Review, 63, 134-139.
Rothbart, M., M. Evans, and S. Fulero, 1979, Recall for confirming events: Memory processes and the maintenance of social stereotypes, Journal of Experimental Social Psychology, 15, 343-355.
Saetren, H., 1983, Iverksetting av offentlig politikk: Utflytting av statsinstitusjoner fra Oslo, Bergen, Norway: Universitetsforlaget.

Schoemaker, P.J.H., 1982, The expected utility model: Its variants, purposes, evidence and limitations, Journal of Economic Literature, 20, 529-563.
Schwenk, C.R., 1986, Information, cognitive biases, and commitment to a course of action, Academy of Management Review, 11, 298-310.
Scott, W.R., 1981, Organizations: Rational, Natural, and Open Systems, Englewood Cliffs, NJ: Prentice-Hall.
Sethi, S.P., N. Namiki, and C.L. Swanson, 1984, The False Promise of the Japanese Miracle, Marshfield, MA: Pitman.
Sevón, G., 1977, Subjective probabilities and values of socio-economic events at different degrees of uncertainty, Scandinavian Journal of Psychology, 18, 127-129.
Sevón, G., 1984, Cognitive maps of past and future economic events, Acta Psychologica, 56, 71-79.
Sevón, G., and E. Sundin, 1985, The municipality pinch: Slack reducation in state and firms, Scandinavian Journal of Management Studies, 2, 71-75.
Sharpe, W.F., 1970, Portfolio theory and capital markets, New York: McGraw-Hill.
Shepsle, K.A., 1983, Institutional Equilibrium and Equilibrium Institutions, Chicago, IL: American Political Science Association (paper for the section on formal political theory).
Simon, H.A., 1955, A behavioral model of rational choice, Quarterly Journal of Economics, 69, 99-118.
Simon, H.A., 1979, Rational decision making in business organizations, American Economic Review, 69, 493-514.
Simon, H.A., 1984, On the behavioral and rational foundations of economic dynamics, Journal of Economic Behavior and Organization, 5, 35-56.
Singh, J.V., 1986, Performance, slack, and risk taking in organizational decision making, Academy of Management Journal, 29, 562-585.
Singh, J.V., D.J. Tucker, and R.J. House, 1986, Organizational legitimacy and the liability of newness, Administrative Science Quarterly, 29, 171-193.
Slovic, P., 1966, Value as a determiner of subjective probability, IEEE Transactions on Human Factors in Electronics, HFE-7(1), 22-28.
Slovic, P., B. Fischhoff, and S. Lichtenstein, 1977, Behavioral decision theory, Annual Review of Psychology, 28, 1-39.
Smart, C., and I. Vertinsky, 1977, Designs for crisis decision units, Administrative Science Quarterly, 22, 640-657.
Smedslund, J., 1963, The concept of correlation in adults, Scandinavian Journal of Psychology, 4, 165-173.
Stava, P., 1976, "Constraints on politics of public choice," in: J.G. March and J.P. Olsen (eds.), Ambiguity and Choice in Organizations, Bergen, Norway: Universitetsforlaget, pp. 206-224.
Staw, B.M., 1976, Knee-deep in the big muddy: A study of escalating commitment to a chosen course of action, Organizational Behavior and Human Performance, 16, 27-44.
Staw, B.M., 1981, The escalation of commitment to a course of action, Academy of Management Review, 6, 577-587.
Staw, B.M., and E. Szwajkowski, 1975, The scarcity-munificence component of organizational environments and the Commission of Illegal Acts, Administrative Science Quarterly, 20, 345-354.
Staw, B.M., L.E. Sandelands, and J.E. Dutton, 1981, Threat-rigidity effects in organizational behavior: A multilevel analysis, Administrative Science Quarterly, 26, 501-524.
Stinchcombe, A.L., 1965, "Social structure and organizations," in: J.G. March (ed.), Handbook of Organizations, Chicago, IL: Rand McNally, pp. 142-193.
Stinchcombe, A.L., M.S. McDill, and D.R. Walker, 1968, Demography of organizations, American Journal of Sociology, 74, 221-229.

Stinchcombe, A.L., M.S. McDill, and D.R. Walker, 1974, Creating Efficient Industrial Administration, New York: Academic Press.
Swieringa, R.J., and J.H. Waterhouse, 1982, Organizational views of transfer pricing, Accounting, Organizations and Society, 7, 149-155.
Taylor, S.E., and S.T. Fiske, 1978, "Salience, attention, and attribution: Top of the head phenomena," in: L. Berkowitz (ed.), Advances in Experimental Social Psychology, 2, New York: Academic Press, pp. 250-288.
Teece, D.J., 1981, Internal organization and economic performance: An empirical analysis of the profitability of principal firms, Journal of Industrial Economics, 30, 173-199.
Teece, D.J., 1982, Towards an economic theory of the multiproduct firm, Journal of Economic Behavior and Organization, 3, 39-63.
Tolbert, P., and L.G. Zucker, 1979, Institutional sources of change in the formal structure of organizations: The diffusion of Civil Service Reform, 1880-1935, Administrative Science Quarterly, 28, 22-39.
Tversky, A., and D. Kahneman, 1981, The framing of decisions and the psychology of choice, Science, 211, 453-458.
Ungson, G.R., D.N. Braunstein, and P.D. Hall, 1981, Managerial information processing: A research review, Administrative Science Quarterly, 26, 116-134.
Vogel, E.F., 1979, Japan as Number One: Lessons for America, Cambridge, MA: Harvard University Press.
Walker, J.L., 1969, The diffusion of innovations among the American states, American Political Science Review, 63, 880-899.
Weary, G., 1979, Self-serving attributional biases: Perceptional or response distortions, Journal of Personality and Social Psychology, 37, 1418-1420.
Weick, K.E., 1964, Reduction of cognitive dissonance through task enhancement and effort expenditure, Journal of Abnormal and Social Psychology, 56, 152-155.
Weick, K.E., 1976, Educational organizations as loosely coupled systems, Administrative Science Quarterly, 21, 1-19.
Weiner, S.S., 1976, "Participation, deadlines, and choice," in: J.G. March and J.P. Olsen (eds.), Ambiguity and Choice in Organizations, Bergen, Norway: Universitetsforlaget, pp. 225-250.
Weiss, C.H., 1977, Research for policy's sake: The enlightenment function of social science research, Policy Analysis, 3, 531-545.
White, H.C., 1970, Chains of Opportunity: System Models of Mobility in Organizations, Cambridge, MA: Harvard University Press.
Wholey, D.R., and J.W. Brittain, 1986, Organizational ecology: Findings and implications, Academy of Management Review, 11, 513-533.
Whyte, G., 1986, Escalating commitment to a course of action: A reinterpretation, Academy of Management Review, 11, 311-321.
Williamson, O.E., 1975, Markets and Hierarchies: Analysis and Antitrust Implications, New York: Free Press.
Williamson, O.E., 1980, The organization of work. A comparative institutional assessment, Journal of Economic Behavior and Organization, 1, 5-38.
Winter, S.G., 1964, Economic "natural selection" and the theory of the firm, Yale Economic Essays, 4, 225-272.
Winter, S.G., 1971, Satisficing, selection and the innovating remnant, Quarterly Journal of Economics, 85, 237-261.
Winter, S.G., 1975, "Optimization and evolution in the theory of the firm," in: R.H. Day and T. Groves (eds.), Adaptive Economic Models, New York: Academic Press, pp. 73-118.
Winter, S.G., 1981, Attention allocation and input proportions, Journal of Economic Behavior and Organizations, 2, 31-46.

Wolf, C., and L. Pohlman, 1983, The recovery of risk preferences from actual choices, Econometrica, 51, 843-858.

Woodward, J., 1965, Industrial Organization: Behaviour and Control, London: Oxford University Press.

Wyer, R.S., 1980, The acquisition of social knowledge: Basic postulates and representative research, Personality and Social Psychology Bulletin, 6, 558-573.

Yasai-Ardekani, M., 1986, Structural adaptations to environments, Academy of Management Review, 11, 9-21.

Zucker, L.G., 1977, The role of institutionalization in cultural persistence, American Sociological Review, 42, 726-743.

Table of Contents

11. The Psychology of Innovative Entrepreneurship

KARL-ERIK WÄRNERYD
Stockholm School of Economics, Stockholm, Sweden

1. INTRODUCTION

Many industrialized countries are somehow losing momentum in their economic development. This seems to be the case with the West European countries and the U.S.A. Lack of entrepreneurial activities is one of the major factors blamed for the negative development. Politicians and mass media in many countries frequently stress the need for innovative entrepreneurship. It is noted that Japanese entrepreneurship has made Japan prosper in an impressive way since the end of the second world war. Great expectations are founded on the possibilities of using the potentials of high technology. High technology industries provide an interesting story of innovative exploitation of research ideas in enterprises that have started out small, but rapidly grown into large complexes. Rogers and Larsen (1986) who have published a study of the rise and continued fortunes of Silicon Valley firms, talk about a Silicon Valley "fever" spreading to nations all over the world and even including the People's Republic of China.

The quest for entrepreneurship is also notable in the discussions of the future economic development of non-industrialized, mostly underdeveloped countries. In the latter cases, more emphasis is laid on initiative and managerial skills than perhaps on real innovative ideas for new industrial development.

The potentials of high technology are there. It takes entrepreneurship to exploit them and the question arises what entrepreneurship is. Rogers and Larsen comment in their preface to the paperback edition of their book that they "thought that entrepreneurism was as important as the microelectronics technology that it shaped. We are now even more convinced of this point." They add: "The technology is rarely the main cause of corporate failure; it is the human and attitudinal components that are most vulnerable."

The purpose of the chapter is to give an overview of the research on

Van Raaij, W.F., van Veldhoven, G.M. and Wärneryd, K.E. (eds) Handbook of Economic Psychology. ISBN 90-247-3720-6.

entrepreneurs with special emphasis on innovative entrepreneurship and to review in this context some of the major theories in the field that have psychological content. This means that the individual and not the group nor the organization is the primary focus.

This chapter will only deal with certain aspects of entrepreneurship. In the first place it will focus on studies which have used psychological variables to describe and explain these phenomena and only to a lesser extent on other types of explanations such as those exclusively based on social structural factors or economic factors. The relevant research emanates from three approaches:

1. empirical psychological research on motivation, personality, risk perception and judgment that bears any relation to entrepreneurship or to a presumed dimension of entrepreneurship,
2. economic research, mostly involving attempts to create theory of entrepreneurship and innovation, and
3. organizational research on entrepreneurs. This research has been both extensive and intensive, especially in the area of small business and has usually incorporated economic, psychological and social structural variables.

First, some definitions of entrepreneurship will be presented and an attempt will be made to clarify the relations between entrepreneurs and inventors. After that, a review of pertinent psychological theory follows, notably achievement and power motivation, risk taking and, to a more limited extent personality theory. In neo-classical economic theory, there is little room for entrepreneurship studies and this inadequacy has in recent years led to many discussions among economists of the possibilities for new additions to economics to fill this gap. Variables connected with risk bearing are examples of such additions. After a review of some of these ideas, studies of small business will be discussed which usually combine approaches. The question will be touched upon to what extent entrepreneurship is different from management and can be taught and enhanced in an economy. Finally, the state of the art of research on innovative entrepreneurship will be assessed.

2. WHAT IS AN ENTREPRENEUR?

2.1. *Definitions of "Entrepreneur"*

Dictionary definitions of "entrepreneur" vary somewhat over time and between dictionaries (Ronen, 1983: p. 158; Brockhaus, 1980), but it may still be wise to borrow from a dictionary a succinct statement of what characterizes an entrepreneur. Webster's New Collegiate Dictionary (1977) gives the following definition of "entrepreneur": "One who organizes, manages, and assumes the risks of a business or enterprise." The question is whether a failure to fulfil one of the three functions mentioned is enough to disqualify somebody from being called an entrepreneur. There seems to be general agreement that risk bearing is a necessary, but not sufficient prerequisite for being called an entrepreneur and also that just providing capital is not enough and may not even be an indispensable requirement. It seems necessary to include in the risk bearing also psychological and social risks. Organizing and managing functions are by themselves far from enough qualifications for being an entrepreneur.

In economic theory, the concept of entrepreneur is used to designate the owner-manager of a firm (see, e.g., Bannock et al., 1985) and is more or less an abstraction used for convenience while it is generally realized that most entrepreneurs in this sense are bodies of directors who are separate from financiers. The concept in this use has little to do with entrepreneurship of an innovative kind and is on the whole synonymous to management functions.

In the literature, there is considerable agreement around the characteristics of entrepreneurship, more than about those of the entrepreneur. The major characteristics are commonly described in terms that are ascribed to John Stuart Mill (1848) who in his *Principles of Political Economy* discussed four entrepreneurial functions: direction, control, superintendence, and risk bearing. In Mill's view, the risk bearing criterion was what most distinguished the entrepreneur from a manager (Brockhaus, 1980; Kirzner, 1979). While students of entrepreneurship generally accept these functions, they can put more or less emphasis on the risk bearing function. The economist Knight (1921) was for example particularly concerned with the risk taking function and characterized the entrepreneur as a taker of non-quantifiable uncertainties (Kets de Vries, 1977). Knight ascribed two functions to the entrepreneur:

1. exercising responsible control, and
2. securing the owners of productive services against uncertainty and fluctuation in their incomes (Kihlstrom and Laffont, 1980: p. 746).

An individual was assumed to make a choice between becoming a worker or an entrepreneur, based on a calculation of what s/he could get from either occupation and taking risk into account.

The Austrian economist Schumpeter (1934), on the other hand, saw the entrepreneur as an innovator who disrupted the economic equilibrium and thus initiated new development. The entrepreneur is never a risk bearer according to Schumpeter; risks are borne by those who invest capital. The entrepreneur is the "creative destructor" who is necessary for the changes that can make the economy flourish (Kirzner, 1979; Elliott, 1983; Giersch, 1984). The entrepreneur is a deviant, a contrast to economic man,

> ... the entrepreneur must be a man of "vision", of daring, willing to take chances to strike out, largely on the basis of intuition, on courses of action in direct opposition to the established, settled patterns of the circular flow. The entrepreneur is more of a "heroic" than an economic figure; s/he must have the drive and the will to found a private kingdom as a "captain of industry", the will to conquer, to fight for the sake of fighting rather than simply the financial gains of the combat, the desire to create new things – even at the expense of destroying old patterns of thought and action (Elliott, 1983: p. 284).

Kirzner (1979) who up to a point shares the Schumpeterian view sees the entrepreneur "... as the prime agent in the process from disequilibrium to equilibrium" and thus of particular importance in the context of economic development. Kirzner describes the main characteristics of the entrepreneur in the following way which often has been cited by other students of entrepreneurship.

> In addition to the exploitation of perceived opportunities, purposive human action involves a posture of alertness toward the discovery of as yet unperceived opportunities and their exploitation. This element in human action – the alertness toward new valuations with respect to ends, new availability of means – may be called the entrepreneurial element in the individual decision. ( ) Awareness of this element in human action leads to the recognition that knowledge by the outside observer of the data surrounding a decisionmaking situation is not sufficient to yield a prediction of the decision that will be made. The observer's calculation of the optimum choice relevant to the data may be profoundly irrelevant (Kirzner, 1979: p. 109).

Behavioral scientists tend to define the entrepreneur something like this:

> Entrepreneurs are found in all professions – teaching, medicine, research,

> law, architecture, engineering, social work, and distribution. Therefore, to account for any type of entrepreneurial behavior, our definition is: Entrepreneurship is the process of creating something different with value by devoting the necessary time and effort, assuming the accompanying financial, psychic, and social risks, and receiving the resulting rewards of monetary and personal satisfaction (Hisrich and Brush, 1985: p. 15; cited from Bowen and Hisrich, 1986: p. 394).

An entrepreneur is then a person who has displayed entrepreneurship; to what extent s/he must have done this, is open to discussion.

Here is another, more succinct behavioral science definition of entrepreneurship: "[Entrepreneurship] is concerned with the creation of a set of social relations – the firm – where none existed before" (Stanworth and Curran, 1973: p. 15). The same authors find that management, on the other hand, centres on the maintenance and extension of an existing business enterprise.

Since one of the great problems in entrepreneurial research is to get an opportunity to study entrepreneurs with adequate methods, there is a tendency among researchers to adapt the definition to what samples they can get. Operationally, entrepreneur is consequently often defined as owner-manager of a firm or founder of a firm. Some students of entrepreneurship have added the criterion of success (see, e.g., Ronen, 1983; Gilad et al., 1986). In extensive surveys, those who state that they are self-employed are sometimes called entrepreneurs. McClelland (1961; McClelland and Winter, 1969) did not include ownership as a criterion and defined any innovative manager who had decision making responsibility as an entrepreneur. If ownership is abolished as a criterion, it follows that entrepreneurs can be found also in public administration (see, e.g., Ramamurti, 1986) and in socialist economies, however pure (cf. McClelland, 1961).

It seems possible to reach a fair degree of consensus on what characterizes entrepreneurial activities and consequently on what are the important dimensions of entrepreneurship. An entrepreneur can then be classified as somebody who has pursued entrepreneurial activities and demonstrated entrepreneurship. Post-hoc definitions are, however, not very interesting. Rather, there is a demand for a definition in such terms that it has predictive value in the sense that

1. it makes it possible to identify an entrepreneur before the activity,
2. it suggests ways of training persons to become entrepreneurs. This explains the general interest in psychological factors that can conceivably lie behind entrepreneurship.

2.2. *Inventors, Innovations, and Entrepreneurs*

Some authors make a distinction between "routine entrepreneurs" and "innovative entrepreneurs" (Leibenstein, 1968). Commonly, there is a stress on the fact that the entrepreneur accomplishes something new. Peterson (1981: p. 65) aptly draws attention to entrepreneurship as the process of unprogrammed innovative recombinations of preexisting elements of activity. This definition makes entrepreneurs distinctly different from inventors who also come up with something new. The distinction between the two is in principle clear. Inventors create a new product or process that is a new combination of material things, whereas entrepreneurs focus on combinations of activities, seize an opportunity for activity or use a situation to their advantage. They may create new services and can then be very close to inventors or they can find new uses for products which is also similar to what inventors can do. Entrepreneurship is necessary to bring inventions to production and successful marketing.

A special type of entrepreneur is the technical entrepreneur who is of particular importance in connection with the high expectations on the growth potential of technology and who is in many respects quite similar to the inventor. The technical entrepreneurs found science- or technology-based firms, something which usually presupposes an advanced level of technical competence in addition to whatever characterizes entrepreneurial spirit. They come from two major suppliers: academic research and R & D departments in business and industry; these suppliers are referred to as "incubator" organizations. There seems to be consensus about the essential role of such incubators for the place, time and field of application of technology-based industrial firms (Cooper, 1973; Watkins, 1973; Eisenhardt and Forbes, 1985; Rogers and Larsen, 1986). While entrepreneurs are mostly depicted as lonely wolves, technical entrepreneurs characteristically work in teams the members of which complement each other in competence and skills.

Figure 1 describes the steps in the innovation process and shows the overlap between the functions involved in the process over time. An inventor may be an entrepreneur, but s/he usually is not (which some inventors have been too slow to realize). Although there is not too much published research illuminating the relations between inventors and entrepreneurs, there is enough evidence to suggest that inventors have a tendency to be suspicious of entrepreneurs who are willing to exploit their inventions. Case studies in Sweden give such indications (Grönstedt et al., 1981; Broström and Holmlöv, 1984). In a way, the whole problem is pure arithmetic from the point of view of the entrepreneur. The latter usually has to exploit more than one invention to find one that is profitable. This invention will then have to pay for the non-successful attempts, something the successful inventor may not appreciate.

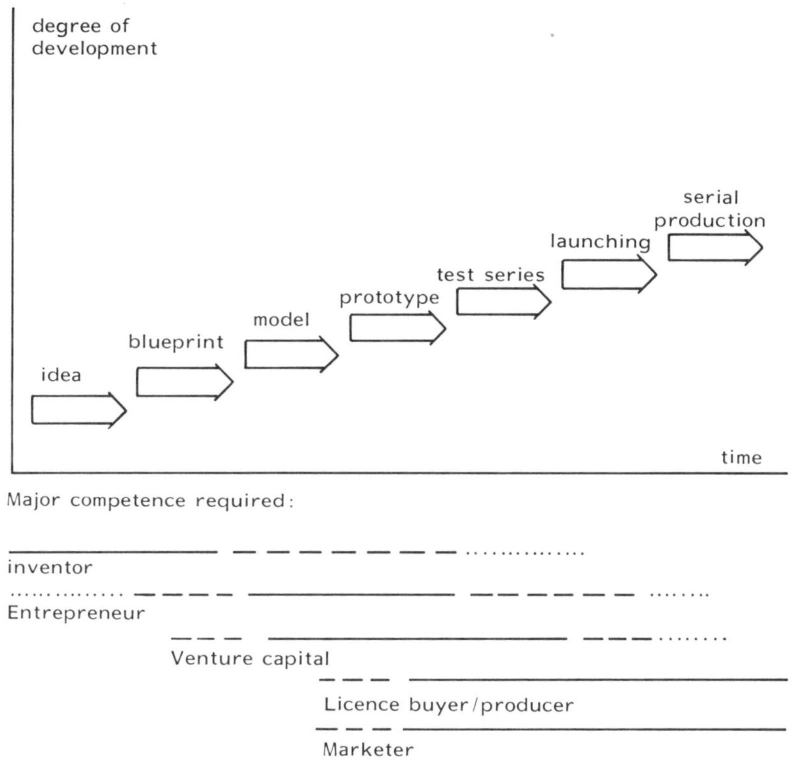

Fig. 1. The innovation transfer process with distribution of roles, from idea to market. *Source*: Grönstedt, Julander and Wärneryd (1981).

Entrepreneurs are people who exploit other people's ideas when they see opportunities in the exploitation. Without the supply of outside entrepreneurship the inventors would often gain little or nothing from their inventions. In rare cases, inventors have founded companies on the basis of their inventions and brought the companies to success. This has been the case in some high technology fields. In the typical development process, the entrepreneur is replaced at a later stage in the firm's life cycle by the manager. The transition of leadership from entrepreneur to manager is often described as a period of internal conflict in the firm after market failures or other difficulties. The need for entrepreneurship and the type of entrepreneurship needed seem to vary considerably over the firm's life cycle (see, e.g., Maidique, 1980; Churchill and Lewis, 1983; Schein, 1983; Kets de Vries, 1985; Rogers and Larsen, 1986).

3. PSYCHOLOGICAL RESEARCH ON ENTREPRENEURSHIP

3.1. *Introduction*

Psychologists interested in studying entrepreneurship have often applied motivational concepts such as need for achievement and risk propensity in their attempts to explain entrepreneurial behavior. Psychologists interested in motivation have wanted to test their ideas on entrepreneurs. Propensity to take risk is not only studied in research on motivation, but also in personality research and has been a major focus of interest in cognitive psychology for the last 15-20 years. The next section presents research in these three areas. Since creativity research mainly deals with generation of ideas (cf. Stein, 1968), while entrepreneurship rather concerns putting ideas into action, it will not be covered here.

3.2. *The Study of Motivation*

3.2.1. *Early Instinct Theories and Dimensions of Entrepreneurship*

Although entrepreneurship is not a very common concept in psychological literature on motivation, concepts with a similar meaning or some presumably integral dimensions of entrepreneurship have had a place especially in the early instinct theories of motivation. William James (1890) defined instinct as "the faculty of acting in such a way as to produce certain ends, without foresight of the ends, and without previous education in the performance" (quoted from Atkinson, 1964: p. 16). Among the instincts were emulation or rivalry, pugnacity (anger and resentment), sympathy, constructiveness, play, curiosity. James says about emulation or rivalry:

> Emulation or rivalry, a very intense instinct, especially rife with young children, or at least especially undisguised. Everyone knows it. Nine-tenths of the work of the world is done by it. We know that if we do not do the task someone else will do it and get the credit. So we do it. It has very little connection with sympathy, but rather more with pugnacity, which we proceed in turn to consider (quoted from Atkinson, 1964: p. 17).

The early social psychologist McDougall (1908, 1923) defined instinct in the following manner the relevance of which we shall see later.

> We may therefore define "an instinct" as an innate disposition which determines the organism to perceive (to pay attention to) any object of

> a certain class, and to experience in its presence a certain emotional excitement and an impulse to action which find expression in a specific mode of behavior in relation to that object (quoted from Atkinson, 1964: p. 122).

One of the instincts cited by McDougall was "constructiveness."

Instinct theories have since long been abandoned. Instincts really only constitute summaries of certain behaviors and can consequently not be used to explain the same behaviors. Instinct theories have left some traces in modern motivation theories and also in studies of entrepreneurship. McDougall defined three steps in instinctive behavior: perception of a phenomenon, emotional excitement, and impulse to proper action. These components appear in one form or another in many discussions of entrepreneurship and the corresponding concepts are used in such a way that theories of instincts which were assumed to be innate, come to mind.

Maslow's (1954) well-known theory of motivation is like instinct theories a listing, although in this case a listing of needs. Maslow conceives of the needs as being hierarchically ordered from the physiological needs which, when not satisfied, to a certain degree dominate behavior to the highest needs, the self-fulfillment needs. Where if at any place would entrepreneurship be placed in this hierarchy? An obvious answer would be and has as a matter of fact often been suggested: in the highest group, namely self-fulfillment. Further reflection leads to the question whether entrepreneurship cannot be evoked in any one of the need groups. Does not hunger at least in some cases lead to entrepreneurship to secure food in the long run?

Even though motivation theories have in general lost some of their earlier importance in psychology and in the study of entrepreneurship, there are still many references made to achievement motivation. Before proceeding to achievement motivation, here is a definition of motivation that also seems appropriate in the context of entrepreneurship. Motivation refers to "How behavior gets started, is energized, is sustained, is directed, is stopped. And what kind of subjective reaction is present in the organism while all this is going on" (Jones, 1955; quoted from Atkinson, 1964: p. 1). Notice that the last part of the definition resembles McDougall's idea of "a certain emotional excitement."

Instinct and need theories only become meaningful if motivation can be measured or assessed independently of the behavior to be explained. It must furthermore be possible to study differences among individuals and over time for one and the same individual. None of the theories mentioned so far fulfill these requirements.

3.2.2. *Achievement Motivation*

Murray's (1938) theory of psychogenic needs corresponds to the two requirements just mentioned: independent measurement and measurement of individual differences. He describes a need as:

> ... a construct (a convenient fiction or hypothetical concept) which stands for a force (the physico-chemical nature of which is unknown) in the brain region, a force which organizes perception, apperception, intellection, conation and action in such a way as to transform in a certain direction an existing, unsatisfying situation (Murray, 1938: pp. 123-124).

Among the needs so defined is the need for achievement, often abbreviated as nAch. The Thematic Apperception Test (TAT) was designed to serve as an instrument for assessment of a person's needs. It consists of a number of pictures that show people in somewhat vaguely indicated situations and the subjects/respondents are asked to tell who the people are, what they are doing and what their history is. The answers are scored according to how much of the need they express which is judged with the help of a manual.

The TAT furnished the researcher with a possibility to assess individual differences in motivation. Some of the pictures elicited more achievement responses than the others. The early experimental studies of the achievement need, using a set of four of the TAT pictures, showed that the test scores were influenced rather heavily by instructions, situational pressures, and a variety of cues in the immediate situation (Atkinson, 1964: p. 230). The achievement score is then a function of the person studied, the stimuli used and the situation, but so is actual performance in a particular situation according to the achievement researchers (Atkinson, 1964).

The studies of achievement motivation were developed into a theory of achievement-oriented performance through the work of McClelland and his coworkers (McClelland, 1961). They define need for achievement as "a competition with some standard of excellence" or some variation on that theme. A long series of laboratory experiments gave a large number of ideas as to how achievement motivation was composed and how it was related to behavior. McClelland and Winter comment:

> Laboratory studies of individuals with high nAch show that in general they behave like successful, rationalizing, business entrepreneurs. That is, they set moderately difficult goals for themselves, neither too easy nor too hard, so as to maximize the likelihood of achievement satisfaction (McClelland and Winter, 1969: p. 11).

McClelland (1961) formulated three conditions for the achievement motive to be aroused in performance of an activity:

1. The individuals must consider themselves as being responsible for the outcome.
2. There must be explicit knowledge about the results so that the individual knows whether s/he has succeeded or failed.
3. The success must not be certain, but connected with risk at a moderate level.

These conditions were found to obtain not only for college students in laboratory experiments, but also for business executives in actual situations. McClelland felt that entrepreneurs were people who took responsibility. On the basis of the earlier mentioned laboratory findings on high need for achievement, McClelland hypothesized that business executives would score higher than professionals on need for achievement and that they would be moderate risk takers. His studies in a number of countries, including socialist Poland, bore out this expectation.

When McClelland's book *The Achieving Society* appeared in 1961, it was something of a sensation since it was a grandiose attempt to use psychological theory and methods to tackle a major economic problem, that of economic growth. In addition to his studies of managers in different countries, McClelland analyzed differences in the achievement need by examining and scoring the need for achievement content of popular literature and children's textbooks. He found for example that those countries that scored high in need for achievement in 1925 and again in 1950 subsequently developed at a faster rate economically than countries that scored lower.

Two features in McClelland's work should be specially noted. In the first place, it is important to be aware of the fact that he favors the TAT as the only direct approach to study individual achievement motivation. He emphasizes that direct questions to the respondents tend to give socially acceptable answers and have a tendency to be wrong also for other reasons. Content analysis of material representing symbolic behavior produced for other purposes may also be used.

Secondly, McClelland prefers to use Alfred Marshall's view on entrepreneurs as expressed in the latter's *Principles of Economics* (1890). This leads to the following description: "... the entrepreneur, through vigorous activity, combines the factors of production – labor and capital – so as to produce an increased output of goods and services, thus increasing the total wealth or material welfare of the society" (McClelland and Winter, 1969: p. 214). In congruence with this view, McClelland and his associates use as criteria for entrepreneurs' performance: changes in entrepreneurial activity such as hours worked, use of labor, capital invested, and output such as gross income.

3.2.3. *Atkinson's Achievement Motivation Theory*

The study of achievement motivation has also developed in another direction than the one represented by McClelland. Since there is an affinity between this development and the locus of control theory which is applied in studies of entrepreneurs as a recent fashion, some space will be devoted to a discussion of Atkinson's theory of success and failure.

Atkinson's theory is a continuation of McClelland's theory and takes its departure in some observations in the experimental situations in class rooms that students reacted differently to success. Some who seemed to be characterized by high need for achievement took a pride in being successful. Others, usually with a low need for achievement, were more concerned about avoiding failure than achieving success. Atkinson (1957, 1964) postulates that the motivation for performing a certain activity is a function of the expectancy of success and the expectancy of failure and suggests the following formulas

$$T_s = M_s \times P_s \times I_s \qquad (1)$$

where

T_s is the tendency to achieve success through an activity;
M_s is the motive to achieve success which is a stable characteristic of the individual;
P_s is the expectancy or probability of success;
I_s is the incentive value of success at a particular activity defined as $I_s = 1 - P_s$.

The lower the probability of success is, the higher is the incentive value. $P_s x I_s$ reaches a maximum, if $p = 0.50$.

The tendency to avoid failure through the performance of an activity is defined in a similar way:

$$T_{AF} = M_{AF} \times P_F \times I_F \qquad (2)$$

where the terms indicate the motive to avoid failure (M_{AF}), the probability of failure (P_F) and the "disincentive" value of failure (I_F). In congruence with I_s, I_F is set to $I_F = -P_s$.

This means that failure at an easy task, i.e., with a high probability of success, is more embarrassing than failing at a difficult task, which certainly agrees with common sense. If $T_s > T_{AF}$, the individual will perform the activity.

These formulas give rise to a number of interesting questions. Entrepreneurs are according to McClelland and others characterized by high need achievement implying that they tend to choose tasks (activities) with moderate probabilities of success, in laboratory studies approximated as $p = 0.50$. They want to succeed and they want to be proud of their achievements which they cannot be if the success is too easily won. If on the other hand, the task is too difficult, they may not be able to succeed without the help of some luck. So far the theory implies that there is a free choice of activities at least to some extent so that the individual can choose among more or less risky alternatives.

An interesting question concerns what happens as a result of experiences with success or failure. Weiner (1972: pp. 229-230) suggests the following generalizations after examining experimental results:

1. Motivation is enhanced following failure among individuals high in resultant achievement motivation.
2. Motivation is inhibited following failure among individuals low in resultant achievement motivation.
3. Motivation is decreased following success among individuals high in resultant achievement motivation.
4. Motivation is enhanced following success among individuals low in resultant achievement motivation.

These generalizations contain implications for learning achievement motivation and for stimulating entrepreneurship.

The Achieving Society and its followers applying achievement motivation theory to economic development were severely criticized and challenged because many factors were left out from consideration. In actual situations there is rarely free choice of activities, rather a limited set of opportunities if any. It was pointed out by several critics that social structural variables were necessary to get a satisfactory explanation of the role of achievement motivation in economic growth. What happens for example to high need achievement motivation if there are no opportunities? McClelland and Winter (1969) deal with this issue. They review some studies in which opportunities have been studied or can be inferred from the general situation and they find that high need for achievement does not help when opportunity is low. It may even have contrary effects on economic development.

The authors adopt Atkinson's theory of success and failure motivation and compare three individuals with different characteristics in the terms of this theory. They consequently assume that, for a person with high need for achievement, there is a curvilinear relation between tendency to choose a task and the probability of success, with a pronounced peak at p = 0.50 and very low tendency at the low and at the high extremes. For a person with a low need for achievement the corresponding curve is almost flat; it makes little difference, whether the probability is moderate or extreme, the tendency is only insignificantly higher when the probability of success, which here is interpreted as opportunity, is moderately high. For a person with high fear of failure the curve is the reverse of the high need for achievement curve. The tendency to avoid the task has a peak at moderately high probability of success and is considerably lower for either extremely low or extremely high probabilities of success.

According to McClelland and Winter (1969), the model implies that if a government can increase the probability of success for business from low to moderate, the high need achievers and low need achievers will be attracted to business. If high fear of failure prevails, however, the effects will rather be for people to leave business, if the probability of success increases from low to moderate. If the probability of success increases from moderate to high, high need achievers will find business uninteresting and seek other challenges with moderate levels of success probabilities. Those with high fear of failure, however, will be attracted. This kind of reasoning leads us to the further development of achievement motivation theory.

3.2.4. *Attribution Theory*

The only cognitive component in Atkinson's theory is the subjective probability of success. Atkinson belongs like McClelland among those who do not want to take the full step to cognitive motivation theory. They tend to see reports on cognitive events as merely unreliable indicators of motivational processes. Weiner (1974) criticizes these aspects of the theory and suggests a somewhat changed theory, which can explain the same research results as achievement motivation theory and make even more predictions. Weiner's expanded or alternative theory incorporates hypotheses about causal attributions, first formulated in Heider's (1958) attribution theory which has given rise to an enormous amount of research in both basic and applied contexts. Successes and failures can be attributed to essentially four factors: ability and effort which are internally controlled factors and luck and task difficulty which are externally controlled factors. While ability and task difficulty are stable factors, effort and luck are unstable. Persons with a stronger hope for success than fear of failure tend to ascribe success to ability and effort (internal factors) and failure to a lack of effort which is an internal, unstable, i.e., changeable factor. Persons who are characterized by a predominantly fear-of-failure orientation ascribe failure to a lack of ability which is an internal, stable factor and seem to have no characteristic way of attributing success. It follows from this that there are affective and expectancy effects. Those who believe that failure at a task was caused by lack of ability will continue to expect failures. Those who attribute failure to lack of effort will, if the goal of success seems worth it, work harder next time.

Weiner's cognitive theory of motivation which he recently has presented in a full, revised version (Weiner, 1985), has been tested in controlled laboratory experiments and in a number of cross-cultural studies (see, e.g., Betancourt and Weiner, 1982), but it has as far as I know not been applied in studies of entrepreneurs. It is an elaborated and extended version of Heider's original theory of interpersonal behavior (Heider, 1958). The original theory and especially Kelley's (1967) interpretation and extension of it has given rise to an enormous amount of research also in organizational contexts. It competes with locus of control theory which seems simpler and which is connected with a simple test procedure that can easily be used. Before the latter theory is treated, a brief assessment of the state of achievement motivation theory should be made.

3.2.5. *The Role of Achievement Motivational Dimensions in Entrepreneurship*

McClelland's imaginative work on the basis of the need for achievement motive inspired a large number of studies, many of them in underdeveloped countries (Jahoda, 1980). The concept of achievement motivation was originally used in much the same way as McClelland did, but it soon lost most of its contact with economic growth and entrepreneurship and much of the interest became focused on cultural differences affecting the achievement scores. While McClelland used Weber's work on the Protestant ethic and capitalism (Weber, 1904) as a starting point and saw achievement as an important mediating factor between religion and economic effort, other researchers have preferred to look into cultural differences and emphasized that the meaning of situational cues varies between cultures. Some cultures like the Japanese culture are collective-oriented rather than individual-oriented. The individual with a high need for achievement is a lone hunter according to McClelland and achievement motivation consequently means something different in Japan than in the United States (see, e.g., Kashima and Triandis, 1986). An increased interest in cognitive processes has promoted research on success and failure and the learning effects of such experiences rather than achievement motivation. Another development is seen in attempts to differentiate between different kinds of achievement motivation. Nicholls (1984) suggests two kinds: task involvement and ego involvement. Kukla and Scher (1986) propound, in their critique of

Nicholls, the idea that there may be at least four kinds of achievement motivation in applied contexts.

Reviewers of achievement motivation theory seem to agree that the theory set off a lot of interesting research, that it proved some influence of the achievement motive on behavior, but that the influence at best was small compared to the influence of other factors such as opportunity structure. Berry (1980), Jahoda (1980), Kornadt et al. (1980), Peterson (1981), Segall (1986) and others all see a vanishing interest in McClelland's idea of achievement motivation, but a growing concern with a more differentiated theory of motivation encompassing causal attributions (for examples of cross-cultural studies, see Chandler et al., 1981; Betancourt and Weiner, 1982; Chandler et al., 1983, who also deal with gender differences; and Kashima and Triandis, 1986).

My own feelings about McClelland's work on achievement motivation is that he should be lauded for his attempt to create a macropsychological theory, something which in my opinion is badly needed. He provided one of the simple relationships that economists want from psychology and ascribed universal validity to the concept of achievement motivation. Through his analyses of symbolic production either from TAT or from existing fictional sources he provided impressive support for his theory. The theory has not failed, but in a (micro)psychological perspective it has a number of weaknesses. Some comments are given below.

1. The achievement motive is not conceptually clear, indicated by the fact that phrases with slightly varying sense are used to describe it. "The wish to do better" or "Comparison with a standard of excellence" can be interpreted in more than one way.
2. There are measurement problems. The direct measurement is based on the use of four TAT pictures; the scoring is sometimes dubious although interrater agreement is quite high (indoctrination?).
3. Group means are used. No individual predictions can be made. The data from the laboratory experiments refer to groups, which are compared in terms of standard scores.
4. Assessment of achievement motivation has thus found little use in organizations (cf. Peterson, 1981).

Convinced that the evaluations made by venture capitalists encompassed achievement motivation and that such judgments were important for the fate of risky undertakings, Khan (1986) carried out a mail survey in which venture capital sources were asked questions. It was hypothesized that, similar to McClelland's theory, these experts would rank the entrepreneurs' achievement motivation very highly in their evaluations of the risk involved in supporting the entrepreneur. This expectation was clearly borne out in the results, only the correlations of the experts' judgments with venture outcome were poor. The creativity and ingenuity of the entrepreneurs as also judged by the venture capitalists were much better predictors of actual outcome.

3.3. *Locus of Control*

Locus-of-control theory was developed by Rotter (1966) in an attempt to explain long-term effects of reinforcement in a person's dealings with his/her environment. Rotter made a distinction between those who were more internally controlled and those who were more externally controlled. In the literature, many authors wrongly use the expressions "internal" and "external," while it rather should be "more internal" and "more external," since there is no clear borderline between internal and external. The former have lower scores on the I-E scale or Rotter scale as it is called. Every externally oriented answer to a scale item is given one point. Thus a high score means a high degree of externality. The I-E scale comprises a number of broad attitude statements indicating different beliefs about how the run of the world and one's own destiny are determined. A more internally controlled person believes in his/her ability to influence and control both the run of the world and private destiny, whereas the more externally controlled person believes in the power of external circumstances which cannot be influenced and is at the extreme end a pure fatalist.

The locus-of-control theory and various forms of the scale have been extensively applied in a large number of contexts. There seems to be good support for the hypothesis that the entrepreneur is more internally controlled and that the more internally controlled manager is more active and more innovative (cf. Dailey and Morgan, 1978; Panday and Tewary, 1979). Kets de Vries (1977) and Brockhaus (1982) mention some studies that support this hypothesis. Miller et al. (1982) also refer to a few earlier studies which they say indicate that internals are more activity oriented and more likely than externals to possess entrepreneurial qualities and they set up some hypotheses to this effect. They find that in their Canadian sample, more internally oriented chief executives tended to demonstrate more innovativeness with respect to products and markets, were more willing to take risks and to lead rather than follow competition. Johannisson (1984) who is a Swedish researcher with an interest in entrepreneurship and small business development, reports on his studies in which locus-of-control, i.e., low, internal scores gave clear indications of more entrepreneurial spirit in some medium-sized U.S. companies.

Serious criticism has been directed against the theory of locus-of-control and against the scale. This has led to some revisions, not by Rotter but by other researchers. The statements used in the original scale have often been found to be a bit vague in some contexts and suggestions have been made that more specific sub-scales, for example concerning economic or social affairs, should be constructed. In some developing countries, factor analyses of the scale have revealed that by the external attributions a distinction is made between "fate" and "the power of others." The latter is an important reason for external attributions in some population groups in some countries (see Niles, 1981).

3.4. *Other Motivation and Personality Characteristics of Entrepreneurs*

3.4.1. *An Adaption-Innovation Scale*

Basing himself on the observation that people seem to be very consistent over time in the way they deal with similar problems, Kirton (1976) developed a bipolar scale of cognitive style, reflecting adaptive or innovative style. The scale, KAI (Kirton Adaption Innovation theory) consists of 32 items which make it possible to locate people on an adaptor-innovator personality continuum. The highly adaptive person, say a manager, produces a sufficiency of ideas within an accepted pattern. Such persons are inclined to deal with details and to change things by doing them better than at present within the established norms of the organization. The highly innovative people, on the other hand, create discontinuities and are more concerned with doing things differently than better (Lowe and Taylor, 1986). The KAI has been used in comparative studies and yielded the result that entrepreneurs scored significantly higher, i.e., they were more on the innovative side, than the comparison group of government officials (Kirton, 1984).

3.4.2. *Need Power and the Differences Between Entrepreneurs and Managers*

When studying achievement motivation which he saw as "the need to do something better than it has been done before," McClelland realized that the entrepreneurs who created the growing business firms, were seldom leaders of men (McClelland, 1975: pp. 252-253). "The reason for this is simple: nAchievement is a one-man game that need never involve other people." When firms grow they must develop an organizational structure which involves relationships among people. Stimulating achievement motivation in others presupposes other motives and an obvious candidate for consideration is the need for power. On the basis of his studies of the relationships between need for power and leadership, McClelland (1975; McClelland and Burnham, 1976) declares that managers as distinct from entrepreneurs have a high need for power and that power is actually their great motivator. In his interpretation, the power need of the good manager does not involve personal aggrandizement, but rather a need to influence others' behavior "for the good of the whole organization." Managers have a low need for affiliation which means that they have little need for association with other people. Power can lead to authoritarianism so it must be tempered by maturity and a high degree of self-control. The strength of the power motive as well as that of the affiliative motive was measured through the use of TAT pictures.

In a study of what McClelland calls the "Leadership Motive Pattern" which involves moderate-to-high nPower, low nAffiliation, and high Activity Inhibition (operationally defined as the number of times the word "not" appears in the respondent's imaginative stories), the hypotheses were essentially confirmed for higher level non-technical managers. At lower levels, success was also associated with nAch which was explained as a consequence of the fact that at lower levels individual contributions are more important than the ability to influence people. The sample consisted of 237 managers who had been tested with TAT when they were recruited many years ago and for whom success data were available (McClelland and Boyatzis, 1982). Other researchers do not seem to have picked up McClelland's ideas on nPower to any large extent. In one recent study, it was found that the hierarchical importance of the manager's position was correlated with the Leadership Motive Pattern, but there was no correlation with administrative job performance or subordinate morale (Cornelius III and Lane, 1984).

McClelland is not the only one to make a distinction between the characteristics of entrepreneurs and managers (cf. 2. What Is an Entrepreneur?). An interesting and pertinent question concerns whether entrepreneurs (when necessary) can develop into good managers and thus become more dominated by power motivation. Rogers and Larsen (1986: p. 270) provide a line of reasoning and some examples of such development from entrepreneur to manager (and then to politician). They conclude that when the entrepreneurs are engineers, those have a feeling that they can apply the scientific method to solving practical problems, rather independently of the type of problem. The engineer entrepreneurs use the "scientific method" to solve also management problems when their firms grow in size.

3.5. *Gender Differences in Motivation for Entrepreneurial Activities*

Psychological research dealing with the question of why there are relatively few female managers and business owners has been preoccupied with motivational questions in the spirit of McClelland and his followers. The findings of Horner (1972) in her dissertation that women students were characterized by what she called "fear of success" aroused a lot of interest and has been a recurrent theme in the debate also outside of research circles ever since. Using achievement oriented success stories relating to academic pursuits, she found that women students tended not only to be afraid of failure as postulated by Atkinson (see above), but also of success in achievement oriented areas. The fear of success is assumed to arise from a conflict between achievement and femininity.

There is no need here to go into the critique that has been raised against the concept of fear of success both on methodological and conceptual grounds. For good reviews, see, e.g., Ward (1978) and Riger and Galligan (1980). The latter stress the well-known fact that a behavioral phenomenon can be a function of two sets of variables, one of which has to do with a person's psychological characteristics, and the other with situational or environmental variables. They put more faith into the second type of variables for explaining the low number of women in management.

In Kirton's comparative studies of entrepreneurship, female entrepreneurial managers in India turned out to score in an even more innovative way than their male counterparts. Kirton comments: "They had to cross two boundaries: they broke with tradition by becoming a manager in the first place, and they had succeeded in becoming a manager in a risky entrepreneurial business" (Kirton, 1984).

Bowen and Hisrich (1986) use a career development perspective in their thorough comparison of male and female entrepreneurs and find some interesting differences. The conclusion that may be drawn is that psychological variables do not appear as yet to have contributed substantially to the explanation of the lower frequency of entrepreneurial activities among women. In the section on small business below, more will be reported about women entrepreneurs.

3.6. *Perception and Judgment of Risk*

3.6.1. *Risk Propensity*

It is commonly assumed in economic discussions of entrepreneurship that entrepreneurs are less risk aversive than other people (Knight, 1921; Kihlstrom and Laffont, 1979). On a common-sense level, it is of course easy to draw the conclusion after somebody has failed with an enterprise that s/he has willingly taken too large a risk, and failures are no rare thing. The failing entrepreneur may think of her/his failure as bad luck which attribution theory suggests. If the enterprise is successful, an outside observer may still think of the enterprise as involving a high risk, but surviving thanks to good luck. The successful entrepreneurs probably do not invoke good luck in the first place to explain their success. McClelland hypothesizes that high need achievers seek moderate risks and he seems to have found a lot of corroboration in his own studies. He has not done any studies aimed at finding out what dimensions are actually involved in entrepreneurial risk taking such as perception of environmental opportunities and of personal ability.

Some of the definitions of entrepreneur cited earlier include several aspects of risk taking such as risking financial well-being, career opportunities, and social relationships. Some authors stress the emotional risks the entrepreneurs take and which hit them if they fail in their endeavors. Despite this discussion there seem to have been precious few attempts to make direct studies of the risk propensity of entrepreneurs. Brockhaus (1982) cites a few, including his own studies. Brockhaus (1980) found in a study which compared managers and entrepreneurs, the latter defined as operators and at the same time owners of firms, that there were no significant differences in risk propensity between the two groups. Moreover, when the distributions of their scores were compared to norms, both groups seemed perfectly normal.

Brockhaus (1980) used the Wallach and Kogan Choice Dilemmas Questionnaire (Kogan and Wallach, 1964). This test presents the subjects/respondents with situations, in which they can choose between a safe alternative and a more risky, but more attractive one. A situation involves for example that somebody is offered a new job and the task may be formulated as follows: "Please check the lowest probability that you would consider acceptable to make it worthwhile for Mr. A to take the new job. The chances are 1 in 10 that the company will prove financially sound." This is then followed by increasingly higher probabilities presented in the same way: 3 in 10, 5 in 10, 7 in 10, 9 in 10, and finally the advice to Mr. A not to take the new job. Risk aversive persons may choose the last alternative or some of the high probabilities and they receive a low score on the test.

Given the nature of the test, it does not seem surprising that there were no differences among Brockhaus' groups. The probabilities stated in the hypothetical situations are objective probabilities or are at least seen as such by the respondents. If the probabilities are the described actor's subjective probabilities, the subject would face the additional task of judging the adequacy of an unknown person's perceptions. The important part to study in entrepreneurial risk taking may be the perception of risk, i.e., how a person arrives at the conclusion that a risk in an uncertain situation is high, low, or moderate. This has been pointed out by many authors, including Brockhaus (1982), but so far nobody seems to have heeded this advice. Note in this context, what Arrow (1974) says:

> It may be argued that the gambler is one who believes the odds are more favorable to him than they really are; according to his subjective probabilities, the bet is favorable to him, but there is, for one reason or another, a divergence between the subjective and objective probabilities (p. 91).

In principle, the scores of entrepreneurs may be spread over the whole length of the scale of risk propensity, if the scale is based on statements of objective risk and still be different from other groups in the way they perceive risk, when no objective references are there. Attribution theory implies that such factors as ability and effort play an important role in causal assessments of success and failure. There is a lot of anecdotal evidence suggesting that entrepreneurs think that what they do may be connected with a much greater risk, if done by other people who do not have their own ability in the field or are not willing to spend the same amount of effort.

3.6.2. *Perception of Risk*

There is as far as I know, no direct study of how entrepreneurs perceive risk. There are reports on risk perception deriving from interviews in case studies, sometimes from so-called depth interviews. The latter are unstructured, informally conducted, lengthy interviews. Risk perception is usually not treated as a major dimension, rather as a small part of a long story.

In cognitive psychology over the last two decades, considerable interest has been devoted to studying decision making in risky situations (for comprehensive reviews, see Libby and Fishburn (1977), and Abelson and Levi, 1985). Although these studies deal with judgments that are presumably of a different type than those in entrepreneurial contexts, they do provide some ideas which have now also entered the discussion of entrepreneurs' characteristics (see Ronen, 1983; Gilad et al., 1986). Some concepts from judgment and decision research will therefore be briefly discussed here, more for their potential contributions than for what they have already contributed to the discussion and the study of entrepreneurs. They can be said to represent an attempt at generative use of theory which involves the wide application of a theory to problems of reality (Gergen, 1982).

A persistent finding in judgment studies is the fact that judgments are affected by serious biases. Tversky and Kahneman (see Kahneman et al., 1982) who have studied how people handle probabilities in uncertain situations, mention and illustrate three such biases or heuristics as they are often referred to: availability, representativeness, and anchoring. Slovic (1972) speaks of a fourth heuristic: concreteness. The assumption is that the use of heuristics makes perception easier and increases our confidence in our judgments.

Availability applies to situations in which people assess the frequency of a class or the probability of an event by the ease with which instances or occurrences can be brought to mind.

The *representativeness* heuristic is connected with situations where the question is for example: What is the probability that object A belongs to class B? If people are asked about the probability that person A belongs to, for example, different vocational groups and A is somebody with traits that are part and parcel of the stereotype of a certain vocational group, they will rather use the degree of similarity than the statistical probability as a basis for their estimates. This is a case of representativeness where similarity prevails over statistical considerations of frequencies.

When people have to make estimates in some situations, they tend to use a starting point, then make adjustments and stay rather close to the starting point. Depending on the starting point the estimates can become very different. This heuristic is called *anchoring*.

Concreteness, finally, points to the fact that people have a tendency to remember information in exactly the same form as it was given to them.

Ronen (1983) suggests that entrepreneurs may function somewhat differently from other people in availing themselves of these heuristics. It is, however, not quite clear how entrepreneurs may differ from other people. One possibility is that they are more resistant, for example in relation to the availability heuristic and instead of immediately accepting something as the truth have an inquisitive inclination. There is in the verbal descriptions of entrepreneurship some support for such an idea and as was shown earlier, Kirzner's notions go in that direction. Another possibility is that entrepreneurs are quicker than others to see similarities between situations and act upon such perceived similarities before anybody else. Such behavior may of course be dangerous and lead to failures, but the availability heuristic has given them the necessary confidence to carry out an idea.

Similar reasoning can be applied to the other heuristics. Entrepreneurs may be expected to resist the temptations of representativeness and secure new niches of their own creation. Or they may get their confidence to act from the fallacy of this heuristic. For lack of empirical studies, there is as yet no way to tell which alternative is more likely, or if both occur under what circumstances one or the other prevails. With respect to concreteness it seems plausible on the basis of some entrepreneurial success stories that entrepreneurs may be able to reformulate a given form of information so that it can be meaningfully interpreted in a new way or in a way consistent with the entrepreneur's earlier conceptions.

Following Kirzner's observation that perception is an important clue to entrepreneurs and that entrepreneurs have a special kind of alertness, and also Leibenstein's notion (1968) that entrepreneurs are "gap-fillers," Gilad et al. (1986) in a new not yet finished study concentrate on the information processing aspects of entrepreneurship. They make informal interviews with a limited number of entrepreneurs and focus their interviews on three areas of interest:

1. the discovery of opportunities (informational aspects of "alertness"),
2. the biases in information processing for decision making,
3. information-processing mechanisms in instances of failure.

With respect to the second area of interest, the research attempts to identify the existence of such biases as Tversky and Kahneman (1982) have described. So far the authors report only preliminary results from their work. It is interesting to note that in their small sample of successful entrepreneurs (drawn from a list of the fastest growing new companies), they find support for their notions about the unique information processing abilities of entrepreneurs. These seem to be on constant look-out for information, which is processed with relative immunity of the biases mentioned. Other findings of interest indicate that the entrepreneurs in the group are not afraid of admitting and talking about failures they have had, in contrast to managers who never want to speak about failures according to the authors. Money as a reward for "excellence" or "veridical perception" is much more important in the early days of the entrepreneur's activities and is later supplanted by "vision" as the main driving force according to these authors.

Prospect theory, also developed by Kahneman and Tversky (1979), makes an important distinction between losses and gains in risk taking behavior. People are according to this theory risk aversive when there is a choice between a sure gain and a gain with an attached probability less than one, even though the expected value is the same or even higher in the latter case. In the choice between a sure loss and a loss with a probability less than one and the same expected value, people in general prefer the risky alternative. The value function looks different for gains and losses. Both gains and losses are defined in relation to a reference point by the individual himself/herself. The gain function is concave while the loss function is convex and steeper implying that a certain amount is worth more on the loss side than on the gain side.

In Ronen's (1983) view, prospect theory can reconcile the entrepreneur's exhibited risk seeking behavior with a marginal utility that increases with wealth. Ronen also notes that Fishburn's (1977) model of target returns and prospect theory give similar predictions as demonstrated in an experiment by Payne et al. (1980). The latter defined both target return and reference point as level of aspiration, i.e., a subjectively fixed zero point deciding whether something is a success or a failure, and found support for the importance of level of aspiration in estimations of gains and losses. One of the groups studied consisted of managers. These authors conclude that there is now a consensus emerging among researchers implying that "risk preference when ruinous loss is not a concern, is a mixture of risk seeking for losses and risk aversion for gains" and that "ruinous loss considerations lead to lexicographic choice behavior that screens alternatives out from further consideration" (Ibid.: p. 1054). In a later publication the same year (Laughhunn et al., 1980), the authors report an experiment using U.S., Canadian, and European managers as subjects and confirming these hypotheses. A good-sized majority was risk seeking for non-ruinous losses below target returns, but switched to risk aversive behavior when ruinous losses were introduced.

Support for prospect theory can also be found in a totally different type of study, also concerning managers and their risk taking behavior, but based on questionnaires sent out to a large number of Canadian and U.S. business executives. Of those, 509 submitted usable answers (MacCrimmon and Wehrung, 1986: p. 99). The study reports that the executives were risk taking for business decisions involving only losses whereas risk aversion was more common when only gains were possible. The authors even suggest an extension of prospect theory (p. 195): "Finding greater risk taking when chances of loss are higher suggests an extension of prospect theory that incorporates probability along with the value dimension." They also found greater risk taking with lower vs. higher stakes which to them "seems contrary to prospect theory." It seems possible to accommodate this finding in the framework of prospect theory, if the possibilities of making manipulations at the editing stage of the risk handling process and of changing reference points (levels of aspiration) are considered.

Despite the fact that the last mentioned study concerned top level executives and consequently is a little off our main interest in this chapter, something more should be said about it. It is based on ideas and guidelines provided from among other fields also cognitive psychology. The authors complain that in the whole process of risk taking the predominant focus has been on the choice among alternatives rather than on other steps. They set up and use in their analysis a model, which they call REACT, and which incorporates the following five steps

Recognition (of risk)
Evaluation
Adjustment (of time, information, and control)
Choice
Tracking the outcome.

This model seems to have something in it also for studies of entrepreneurship and risk taking. The Risk Portfolio presented in the book for the reader to use in testing his/her own willingness to take risks can possibly be used in such studies. The Risk Portfolio consists of a series of questionnaires that were used in the authors' own study. The book itself will probably lead to attempts in many other countries to study risk taking among business executives and entrepreneurs since it is interesting and provocative.

3.6.3. *A Non-Cognitive View of Entrepreneurial Information Handling*

What has just been said, using cognitive psychology as a vantage point, can be contrasted with what Kets de Vries (1977) calls the "Reactive" model of the entrepreneur. It points out the entrepreneur (at least before s/he succeeds) as a deviant with a low tolerance for frustration and tension and a low attention span,

> seemingly in pursuit of immediate gains and satisfactions. For the entrepreneur the initial impression, "the hunch", often becomes the final conclusion without a further serious search and deliberation process. There seems to be an absence of concentration, of logical objectivity, judgment and reflectiveness, as if the process of cognition is impaired and does not fulfil its integrative function. A lack of analytical thinking, an absence of active search procedures and self-critical reflections becomes a predominant mode (Ibid.: p. 49).

This rather negatively formulated view of the entrepreneur – which would hardly be appreciated in workshops held jointly by researchers and entrepreneurs – is made the basis of some speculations about the conflicts between the entrepreneurial role and the subsequent fate of an organization built on entrepreneurship. This line of reasoning reflects the often found distinction between entrepreneur and manager and is further pursued by the same author in a recent article on "the dark side of entrepreneurship" which spells out the conflicts that may arise in an entrepreneurial organization (Kets de Vries, 1985).

4. ECONOMIC THEORY AND THE STUDY OF ENTREPRENEURSHIP

Economic theory has been severely criticized by many economists for not having anything to say about entrepreneurs in the sense of innovators and generators of new business developments. To cite one of the foremost critics who has formulated a theory which is intended to handle entrepreneurship and other micro-microeconomic phenomena, Leibenstein:

> The received theory of competition gives the impression that there is no need for entrepreneurship. If all inputs are marketed and their prices are

known, and if all outputs are marketed and their prices are known, and if there is a definite production function that relates inputs to outputs in a determinate way, then we can always predict the profit for any activity that transforms inputs into outputs. If net profits are positive, then this should serve as a signal for entry into this market. The problem of marshaling resources and turning them into outputs appears to be a trivial activity. From this point of view it is hard to see why there should ever be a deficiency of entrepreneurship. But there is frequently a lack of entrepreneurship. The answer is that the standard competitive model hides the vital function of the entrepreneur (Leibenstein, 1968: p. 72).

Leibenstein continues to give a model for entrepreneurship while blaming the conventional theory of the production function for being the main obstacle to an understanding of the entrepreneurial role. Similar criticisms can be found in Casson (1982: p. 9): "Indeed, almost all the social sciences have a theory of the entrepreneur, except economics." He finds that the villain is the extreme assumption of neo-classical theory of access to information which renders decision making the mechanical application of mathematical rules for optimization.

Baumol (1968) who wrote an article in the same issue of the American Economic Review as Leibenstein, is less critical of economic theory, but admits in an article fifteen years later (1983) that "the subject of entrepreneurship looms as a continuing reproach to the theory of the firm and to the formal analysis of economic growth." He then proceeds to develop models for studying the influences that encourage or discourage entrepreneurship since the latter phenomenon itself is non-standardized and cannot because of its very nature be subjected to systematic analysis.

Kirzner (1979) says that in the eighteenth century world of commerce the figure of the entrepreneur was fairly well recognized and finds it surprising that the English classical economists when constructing their system "so completely submerged the entrepreneurial function, jumbling it so unhelpfully with that of the capitalist" (p. 37). Adam Smith, Kirzner notes, was so preoccupied with the long-run tendencies in production that he could overlook the new adventurous speculator-projector. The same thing happened with post-Walrasian theory which emphasized equilibrium. The exception to this tendency is the Austrian tradition.

It may seem as though economics has little to offer in terms of what is studied in this chapter. This is, however, not the whole truth. Economists have, as said earlier, developed ideas and in some cases models that are imaginative and provocative and thus apt to stimulate new research. The economist Schumpeter who was an offspring of the Austrian school – albeit a somewhat deviant innovator, being the cofounder of the Econometric Society – is still often cited as the leading source of inspiration for studies of entrepreneurs. Non-economists, e.g., Brockhaus (1980), Kets de Vries (1977) and Peterson (1981), all indicate their respect for Schumpeter's ideas and find them useful in their discussions.

It is not possible to give a complete and accurate review of Schumpeter's ideas within the limited space here. Let me therefore rely on a few summarizing statements cited from some authors who have given recent overviews of Schumpeter's work. One of the main characteristics of Schumpeterian thinking, which is also a prominent feature of the present-day Austrian school, is the emphasis on processes rather than equilibria or outcomes. Economic life consists of discontinuities which may be described as cycles: business cycles, product cycles, fashion cycles, seasonal cycles and "technological revolutions and all sorts of lagged adjustments and overreactions to unanticipated events in the markets for factors and products, for assets and monies" (Giersch, 1984: p. 105).

> Emphasis, therefore, is on the growth and dissemination of knowledge, on pathbreaking entrepreneurs who create new markets and successful "intrapreneurs", who rejuvenate old firms, on credit creation for the supply of venture capital, and on Schumpeterian competition (i.e., on innovative monopolistic competition rather than sterile perfect competition, on oligopolistic rivalry rather than collusive equilibria, on aggressive trading rather than mere arbitrage transactions) (Ibid.: p. 105).

For Schumpeter, entrepreneurship was the novel combination of pre-existing factors of production where the outcome of the recombination cannot be well predicted (Peterson, 1981: p. 66). Schumpeter saw the presence of potential entrepreneurs everywhere, but he thought that the ability for those actually to practice entrepreneurship was a function of socioeconomic conditions. He pointed to overregulation as an important factor to keep entrepreneurship at a low level or make entrepreneurs devote their efforts to non-productive undertakings. (Elliott, 1983; Giersch, 1984). In a similar way, Kirzner (1979) emphasizes the importance of markets for productive entrepreneurship to be developed. With Schumpeter's way of thinking entrepreneurship becomes a rather elusive phenomenon and the implication is that, in the same way as Baumol (1983) does, economists should study factors influencing entrepreneurship rather than the phenomenon itself.

Schumpeter (1934) proposed according to Carland et al. (1984) five criteria for classifying somebody as an entrepreneur:

1. introduction of new goods,
2. introduction of new methods of production,
3. opening of new markets,
4. opening of new sources of supply, and

5. industrial reorganization.

Leibenstein (1968, 1976, 1979), whose ideas about entrepreneurs are basically very similar to those of Schumpeter, identifies four functions for innovative entrepreneurs:

1. They connect different markets.
2. They are capable of making up for market deficiencies ("gap-filling").
3. They are "input-completers."
4. They create or expand time-binding, input-transforming entities (i.e., firms).

The basic assumptions in Leibenstein's model follow from his X-efficiency theory which is rather complex, due among other things to the fact that he creates and labels a number of highly abstract concepts. Suffice it then to say that he stresses the importance of both market factors (market imperfections as a positive factor) and factors inside the firm and the individual such as knowledge and motivation.

These criteria for what is entrepreneurial behavior seem generally accepted, but there is still confusion as to what characterizes an entrepreneur. Attempts have been made to distinguish between different types of entrepreneurs, from two categories, like the "routine" entrepreneurs and "new type," innovative entrepreneurs of Leibenstein's (1968) description, to a continuum along which many types of entrepreneurs exist (Ronen, 1983). Kirzner (1983) lists twelve different ways of identifying entrepreneurs in the economic literature.

A dichotomy that is apparently not mentioned by economic theorists involves a distinction between, on one hand, a craftsman-entrepreneur, who is assumed to have low education and training, low social skills, and a narrow time horizon, and on the other hand, the opportunistic entrepreneur, who knows how to seize opportunities (Kets de Vries, 1977). The former now frequently appears to be replaced by the highly educated R & D entrepreneur who works in an organization (Ibid.: p. 42). This is the technical entrepreneur who was mentioned earlier and who is evidently becoming increasingly important for industrial development (Eisenhardt and Forbes, 1985).

In this section some ideas emanating from economists' works have been described for two reasons. In the first place, it is important for psychologists also to observe variables at the system level such as market factors. Economic-psychological research on entrepreneurship should include consideration of such variables. Secondly, although, when treating the topic of entrepreneurs, economists rarely make references to scientific psychology (except maybe for a line or two about McClelland's *The Achieving Society*), they use psychological concepts. Psychologists can give more precise, operational meaning to such concepts and perhaps also get some inspiration for their own work on entrepreneurship encouraging them to become more generative (Gergen, 1982).

5. SMALL BUSINESS RESEARCH AND THE STUDY OF ENTREPRENEURSHIP

5.1. *Some Characteristics of Small Business Research*

Small business research and research on entrepreneurs have since long been intimately connected. One reason for this is probably that there is general acceptance of the notion that real innovation can be pursued only in small firms and that entrepreneurs capable of pushing such endeavors to a successful end can only function in environments which they can dominate and completely control (see, e.g., Arrow, 1983; Ronen, 1983).

Small business research is pursued in many countries and seems to be attracting an increasing number of researchers, but since the reports are mostly not published in English, little is actually known about their findings. Some of the studies may in fact be quite as interesting as the North American studies that now dominate the literature. There appear to be three major reasons why the findings of this research are rarely reported in the international journals:

1. The research often has the normative purpose of stimulating small business, possibly in combination with some sort of help or training given to the entrepreneur.
2. The research is so conceived and planned that close cooperation with one or a few small business firms is necessary, even apart from the normative purposes under 1.
3. The research is aimed at the specific case, not at finding generalities because generalities tend to be abstract and seemingly removed from concrete reality. The researcher may entertain the hope that s/he will be able to do something more generally valid in the long run based on a number of case studies.

The strength of small business research on entrepreneurship is that it has usually not been dogmatic, on the whole very pragmatic and eclectic in its use of assumptions, hypotheses and methods. There has been a predilection for informal approaches, which no doubt give full descriptions and realistic details at a common-sense level, but the impression that every case is more or less unique. This has at the same time been its weakness, since it does not seem possible to make valid generalizations about the factors contributing to shaping entrepreneurial behavior. There are now claims for stricter research methods, more representative and larger samples making regular comparisons employing multivariate statistical methods feasible. Sexton and Smilor (1986) who suggest this, note a clear trend in this direction.

Psychological research on entrepreneurs in small business has dealt with entrepreneurial motivation and attempts to stimulate entrepreneurship. Again, McClelland should be mentioned. He has demonstrated that motivational training can produce effects (McClelland and Winter, 1969; Miron and McClelland, 1979), although there still remains some doubt as to what should be trained: motivation or skills or perhaps both.

Another area in which psychologists have been deeply involved concerns testing instruments where the hope is that it shall become possible to sort out among aspiring entrepreneurs those who will have success. As yet there does not seem to be available any really good instrument for doing this (Sexton and Smilor, 1986).

5.2. *Some Characteristics of Entrepreneurs in Small Business*

There is a debate about whether all small business firms can be seen as entrepreneurs or a distinction should be made, and if so, where the borderline should be drawn (Carland et al., 1984; Sexton and Smilor, 1986). There seems to exist some consensus that only small business firms which are in some defined way innovative should be counted. Carland et al. (1984) go so far as to suggest a distinction between an entrepreneur, who is interested in profit and the growth of his/her firm and on the other hand a small business owner who establishes and manages a business for the principal purpose of furthering personal goals like creating a living for members of the family or having everything under personal control. There is some support for this idea in a Belgian study (Ettinger, 1983). The author of the study distinguishes between independence seeking and power seeking entrepreneurs. The latter want growth whereas the former are careful not to sacrifice their quest for independence, which they would risk with further growth. In the sample, the size and origin of which are not presented in the article, these hypotheses were evidently borne out.

In studies of entrepreneurs, certain variables are with few exceptions examined. Among these are family background, membership in minority groups like immigrants, age, education, and previous work experience. A brief resumé will be given here, followed by some findings on female entrepreneurs.

In comparison with the population in general and managerial groups, entrepreneurs are much more often found to have fathers who are or have been entrepreneurs. They may have inherited a firm, but in the majority of cases they seem to have founded their own firms. Stimulation from other entrepreneurial members of families has also been a characteristic feature.

Membership in minority groups has since long been noted by many authors as a common characteristic of entrepreneurs. Creating new activities appears to minority groups often to be the only or the main way to reach an acceptable standard of living. Being considered to be different can serve as a motivator for some people to create a road of their own. Little is known about how this factor interacts with individual factors.

Younger people are more entrepreneurial than older people. It is often said that the typical age for an entrepreneur is 30-35, i.e., an enterprise is usually founded after a person has had some work experience. A common assumption with respect to work experience is that the entrepreneurs have been rather dissatisfied with their previous occupations. Some of them have jumped from one job to another. There are also findings that entrepreneurs are not very different from other job holders in their attitudes to jobs held (see, e.g., Watkins, 1973).

With respect to educational background, it seems safe to say that there are two different groups of entrepreneurs, one with an education lower than the average in the population and the other with a higher than average education. Entrepreneurial activities in certain industries presuppose high technical competence. An interesting question is whether the room for non-technology based entrepreneurship is shrinking so that future entrepreneurs will primarily be recruited from among university graduates.

Finally, something referred to as "attitudes" is commonly reported in the studies. These include values like the striving for independence and the value attributed to family life in comparison to the interest of the enterprise. The typical entrepreneur puts more value on independence than do employees and tends to treat his/her family as second to the interest of the enterprise (see, e.g., Brockhaus, 1982; Gasse, 1982; Donckels and Degadt, 1986; Holmquist and Sundin, 1986).

Researchers who make surveys of managers and of entrepreneurs tend to complain that they find few if any female respondents in their samples. (see, e.g., MacCrimmon and Wehrung, 1986). Statistics show that there are comparatively few female entrepreneurs, but that their number is increasing (Riger and Galligan, 1980; Bowen and Hisrich, 1986; Donckels and Degadt, 1986). The number of businesses started by and operated by women is in the U.S. estimated to be from 4.6 to 5.7 percent of total business ownership according to different estimates (Bowen and Hisrich, 1986). Many countries seem to show tendencies toward increased entrepreneurial undertakings among women. It is noted that female entrepreneurship defined and assessed in this way has a tendency to be concentrated in certain industries like retailing and personal service (Holmquist and Sundin, 1986). In Belgium, the proportion of female self-employed amounts to 29 percent for all industries, is highest in the sector of services with 47.3

percent and is lowest in the sector of manufacturing with 12.6 percent (Donckels and Degadt, 1986). A recent discovery in the area of female entrepreneurship is the role played by so-called contributing wives, who participate in their husband's enterprise. This has also attracted attention to how entrepreneurial families experience their situation (see, e.g., Rosenblatt et al., 1985; Miettinen, 1986).

Female entrepreneurs show pretty much the same characteristics as male entrepreneurs. They seem to have slightly higher educational level. When personality inventories or scales are used, female entrepreneurs are more internal on the I-E scale, more innovative on KAI than male entrepreneurs and more masculine and achievement oriented than other women according to other personality tests. Like their male counterparts they tend to set their families second to the interest of the firm (see Kirton, 1984; Bowman and Hisrich, 1986; Holmquist and Sundin, 1986; Donckels and Degadt, 1986).

5.3. *Organizational Culture and the Functions of the Entrepreneur*

Every new trend in organizational research adds new features to the picture of the entrepreneur. The recent attention bestowed on organizational culture – a concept which I shall refrain from defining because of its rather complex nature – has also revealed some novel aspects of entrepreneurship. Entrepreneurs when founding enterprises do not only create the more rational and tangible characteristics of firms, but they also create ideologies and means to control symbolic behavior (Pettigrew, 1979). Studies of entrepreneurship will then focus less on the individual and more on the interaction with the social environment.

Schein (1983) who in an article pays special attention to the role of the founder, suggests that there are essential differences between founders/entrepreneurs and professional managers. The founders by virtue of the fact that they are founders/owners are more able to pursue independent objectives in running the enterprise and neglect objectives that may in the long run be more in line with the growth and survival of the firm. The founders/owners tend to fulfill some unique functions which are important in the early history of their enterprises:

1. Containing and absorbing anxiety and risk. The founders have to reassure the organization that it will survive, and to inspire confidence and commitment. This can be compared to McClelland's earlier mentioned notion of the importance for high need achievers to assume responsibility.
2. Embedding non-economic assumptions and values. This includes the identity which founders/owners want to impose on their enterprise and

which is variously labeled image, personality of the firm or style. The encouragement of a certain style and value system may occur at the expense of more profitable business values.
3. Stimulating innovation. Because of their secure position in the organization founders/owners can take larger risks and with their personality orientation they are uniquely willing to try innovations. This can be compared with Kirton's (1984) discussion of innovators vs. adaptors.
4. Originating evolution through hybridization. This essentially involves preparing for transition from an early entrepreneurial stage to a more managerial stage. As noted before, some entrepreneurs seem to be able to make it while others fail with crises and conflicts as a consequence (cf. Churchill and Lewis, 1983).

This is not the place to try to evaluate organizational culture theories, but it may be appropriate to note that the ideas above are still rather new and based on a few case studies. The most interesting hypothesis for further research on entrepreneurs is in my opinion the anxiety-absorbing function of the entrepreneur. It seems hard to reconcile with what has often been said about entrepreneurs: that they are lonely wolves, deviant and dominant persons. An idea for a possible reconciliation implies a leadership of a fatherly type.

6. CONCLUDING ASSESSMENT OF THE STATE OF THE ART

6.1. *Summing up the Research*

It seems clear that research on the psychology of innovative entrepreneurship has not reached a point where any single or simple explanation can be generally accepted. It is hardly likely that any such point will ever be reached for good reasons that have been convincingly demonstrated by research. Let me summarize these in three categories:

1. Entrepreneurial activities are a function of environmental/structural factors, situational events and certainly individual variables.
2. In so-called entrepreneurial activities, the amount of entrepreneurship displayed or required varies from a very small amount to something really innovative, never before thought-of.
3. Entrepreneurship is multidimensional, based on patterns of variables rather than on outstanding values on a single variable.

The hypothesis that entrepreneurship is motivated by high need achievement has had some success, but it is obvious that this way of thinking at best gives only a very partial explanation. The hypothesis can, however, play a part in developing training programs in certain managerial areas, particularly if coupled with other insights.

Personality theories of many kinds have been employed to characterize entrepreneurs, but none are totally convincing. The description of the entrepreneur as a deviant, who cares little about social skills and who is preoccupied with an idea does not seem wholly adequate and can hardly serve as a complete explanation of entrepreneurship. Locus-of-control theory has shown some promise in studies of entrepreneurs, but is obviously insufficient, when standing alone, since there are many people who are highly internal without being entrepreneurs. The successful explanations using locus-of-control theory are of the type that in a given context people who are more internal are more entrepreneurial. Further development along this line of thought would probably best be based on Weiner's (1985) recently published, revised attribution theory of achievement motivation.

With respect to risk taking behavior, the early assumption, still apparently held by many economists who are nonSchumpeterians, that entrepreneurs are low in risk aversion, i.e., are conscious takers of great risks has yielded to some confusion. Obviously, many entrepreneurs may be only moderate, and some of them even low risk takers, at least in their own view. The latter point may be a very essential one. Some people, like myself may avoid to climb steep mountain sides, not because we are highly risk-averse, but because our climbing ability would make the climbing extremely risky. Other people who are actually more risk-averse may do the climbing – to get to an attractive panorama or for the joy of climbing – since they believe in their own ability, a well-founded belief or not. The self-confidence of entrepreneurs and their perceptions of their risk taking with respect to the particular enterprise they are involved in deserve no doubt to be looked into, but the first consideration should be the attractiveness of the enterprise, and risk perception, which may be an illusion of control of chance (cf. Langer, 1975), should be second.

The research based on modern cognitive psychology is as yet new and although promising has still to prove that it can explain any significant amount of entrepreneurship. Prospect theory and the judgmental heuristics that Kahneman and Tversky (1982) have brought forward, provide interesting ideas. This theory comes close to being a general theory of decision behavior which should make it appealing also to economists, but the use by Gilad et al. (1986) and MacCrimmon and Wehrung (1986) presupposes that attention is paid to individual differences. If so, this theory can perhaps be coupled with motivational theory such as attribution theory in its recent shape and give a new perspective to the question of entrepreneurs and risk taking. So far these two theories do not seem to have mixed very well (see, e.g., Kahneman et al., 1982).

6.2. *A Two-dimensional Model of Entrepreneurship*

From the discussion above it appears to be clear that there are not two distinctly different groups of humans: a small group consisting of entrepreneurs and a huge one consisting of nonentrepreneurs. There are differences among people in how many entrepreneurial activities they initiate and in the degree of entrepreneurship embedded in the activities. Several authors have suggested that entrepreneurship varies along a continuum. Ronen (1983) says:

> To summarize: there is a continuum of decision making under uncertainty. At its lowest extreme is the laborer, his/her routine tasks characterized by minimal uncertainty. At the other extreme stands the most innovative entrepreneur. Along the continuum, the most discriminative characteristic is the quest for novelty (p. 149).

In another context, Ronen stresses "the purposefulness of action of entrepreneurs," which can be seen as another important dimension with the

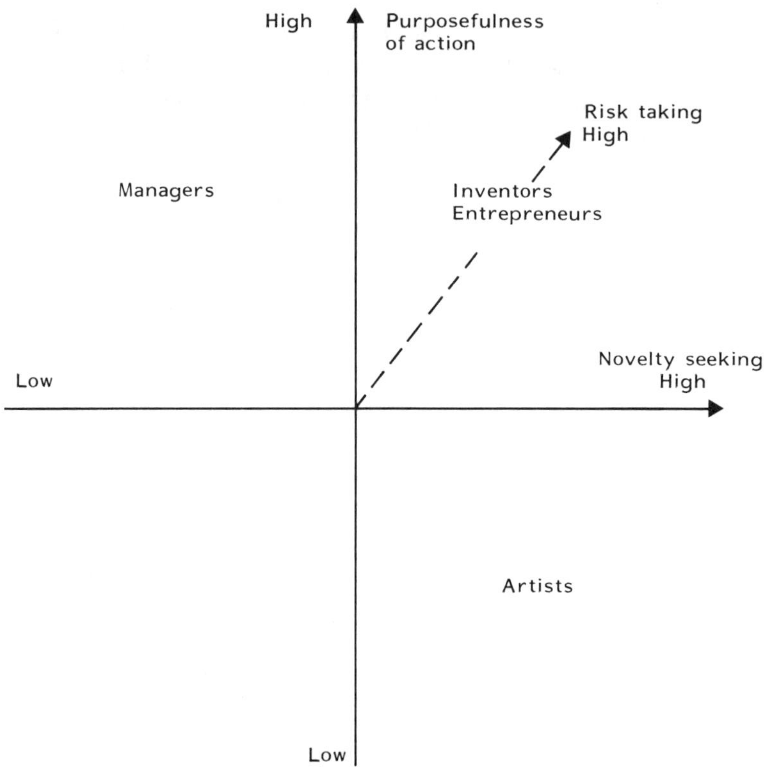

Fig. 2. Dimensions of entrepreneurship.

possibility of varying values for different activities. Both of these dimensions are clearly psychological and can furthermore be assessed or even measured using psychological scales. If these two dimensions are crossed, an interesting pattern emerges as can be seen in Figure 2.

This crossing of the two dimensions seems to bring forward some of the generally known characteristics of entrepreneurs and illuminates the presumed and sometimes found differences between managers and entrepreneurs. It does not clarify the distinction between creative people like inventors and entrepreneurs unless it is assumed that inventors are low on purposefulness of behavior. If persistence is an indication of high purposefulness of action, then inventors must be said to be high on this dimension. They are even higher than entrepreneurs since they often set out to solve a specific problem that troubles them.

The distinctions made between entrepreneurs and managers could be interpreted as though managers were always shy of novelty. This is of course not true. Being a manager in the sense of being a leader of a company without owning it, no doubt requires (access to) entrepreneurship in many situations for the mere survival of the company. Again it seems necessary to start with the entrepreneurial acts and look at how much novelty they involve and how much purposefulness of action is required. Business firms are assumed to have varying needs for entrepreneurial activities over their life cycle and could be (and certainly are) analyzed from that point of view. The strategic management literature contains many such discussions (see, e.g., Drucker, 1985). There is an ever increasing, already large literature covering entrepreneurship in organizations. Most of it is not research oriented or research based, but it affords plenty of cocksure advice to unwary managers. The reader who has a research interest in entrepreneurship in organizations may find Peterson (1981), Miller and Friesen (1982), and Tushman and Moore (1982) useful for reviews and references.

The two dimensions just discussed and shown in Figure 2 are not sufficient to explain entrepreneurial behavior. Judging from the discussion of risk taking, it is desirable to add a risk taking dimension. This has been done in the figure. Risk increases with increased novelty seeking and with increased purposefulness of action. How, then, do entrepreneurs perceive risks when investing their (perceived) skills and other resources in risky enterprises? Do they see risk mainly as a constraint and do they tend to set a definite cut-off point for action where the risk could involve ruinous losses? Do they or some of them feel exhilarated when taking what they think are tractable risks? There are indications that entrepreneurs indeed perceive risks as tractable in their own areas of competence or skill even where other people may fear to tread. They seem willing to take risks if necessary, but only up to a point, and they do not think of themselves as high risk takers. To what extent is this an illusion of control, i.e., a feeling of being able to influence one's luck (Langer, 1975)?

The question to what extent there are people who are consistently more entrepreneurial than others, over many or in specific areas, and whether they can be identified early as promising entrepreneurs, can perhaps be answered through the use of these dimensions in the study of entrepreneurship: the motivating effect of novelty seeking and of purposefulness of action and the supporting effect of risk-reducing perception, based on self confidence. It should be possible to develop tests, questionnaires, interview and observational methods to study these dimensions.

On the whole, the phenomena to be studied are surprisingly similar to McDougall's earlier mentioned components of instinctual behavior. Phrased in accordance with McDougall's instinct theory, the dimensions involve studies to determine:

1. whether people perceive certain problematic situations as opportunities,
2. whether they get a feeling of positive excitement facing such situations,
3. whether this tends to result in irresistible impulses to proper action.

These ideas are illustrated in an integrated way in Figure 3 which can be said to show a psychological model of entrepreneurship. It is an attempt to bring some order among a number of variables introduced in the earlier discussion.

There is no reason to assume that these are innate behaviors. The question is rather: How do budding entrepreneurs learn from their attempts

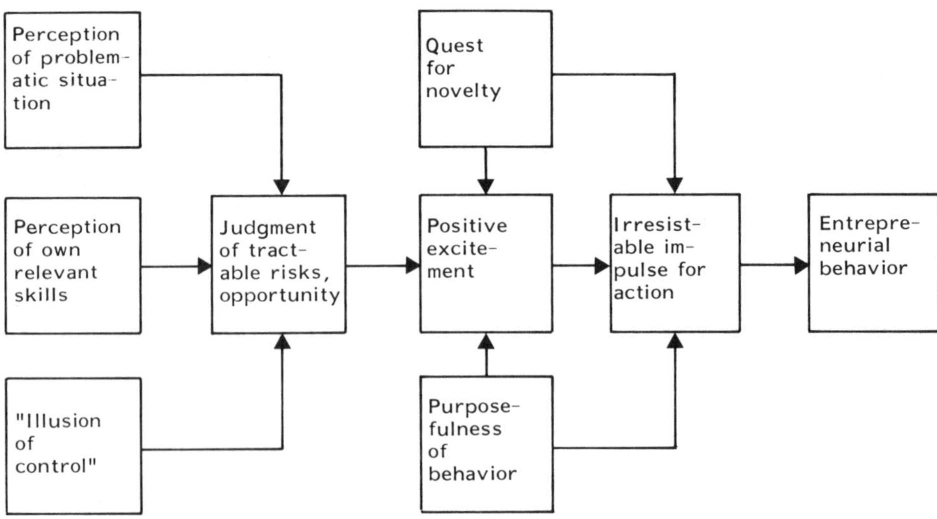

Fig. 3. A psychological model of entrepreneurship.

at entrepreneurship? The last question again draws attention to the possibilities of combining risk perception theory and attribution theory in the study of entrepreneurship. These questions should be challenging to researchers.

REFERENCES

Abelson, R.P., and A. Levi, 1985, "Decision making and decision theory," in: G. Lindzey and E. Aronson (eds.), Handbook of Social Psychology, Vol. 1, New York: Random House, pp. 231-309 (third edition).

Arrow, K.J., 1974, Essays in the Theory of Risk Bearing, New York: North-Holland.

Arrow, K.J., 1983, "Innovation in large and small firms," in: J. Ronen (ed.), Entrepreneurship, Lexington, MA: Lexington Books, D.C. Heath, pp. 15-28.

Atkinson, J.W., 1957, Motivational determinants of risk taking behavior, Psychological Review, 64, 359-372.

Atkinson, J.W., 1964, An Introduction to Motivation, New York: American Book/Van Nostrand/Reinhold.

Bannock, G., R.E. Baxter, and R. Rees, 1985, Dictionary of Economics, Harmondsworth, Middlesex: Penguin Books (third edition).

Baumol, W.J., 1968, The entrepreneurship in economic theory, American Economic Review, 63, 64-71.

Baumol, W.J., 1983, "Toward operational models of entrepreneurship," in: J. Ronen (ed.), Entrepreneurship, Lexington, MA: Lexington Books, D.C. Heath, pp. 29-47.

Berry, J.W., 1980, "Social and cultural change," in: H.C. Triandis and W.L. Lonner (eds.), Handbook of Cross-cultural Psychology, Vol. 5, Boston, MA: Allyn and Bacon, pp. 211-279.

Betancourt, H., and B. Weiner, 1982, Attributions for achievement-related events, expectancy, and sentiments: A study of success and failure in Chile and the United States, Journal of Cross-Cultural Psychology, 12, 362-374.

Bowen, D.D., and R.D. Hisrich, 1986, The female entrepreneur: A career development perspective, Academy of Management Review, 11, 393-407.

Brockhaus, R.H., Sr., 1980, Risk taking propensity of entrepreneurs, Academy of Management Journal, 23, 509-520.

Brockhaus, R.H., Sr., 1982, "The psychology of the entrepreneur," in: C.A. Kent, D.L. Sexton, and K.H. Vesper (eds.), Encyclopedia of Entrepreneurship, Englewood Cliffs, NJ: Prentice-Hall, pp. 39-57.

Broström, K., and P.G. Holmlöv, 1984, Innovationstransfer. Två praktikfall om uppfinningar. Förstudie 2 (Innovation Transfer. Two Case Studies of Inventions. Pilot Study 2), Stockholm: Stockholm School of Economics, Economic Research Institute.

Carland, J.W., F. Hoy, W. Boyton, and J. Carland, 1984, Differentiating entrepreneurs from small business owners: A conceptualization, Academy of Management Review, 9, 354-359.

Casson, M., 1982, The Entrepreneur: An Economic Theory, Oxford, UK: Martin Robertson.

Chandler, T.A., D.D. Shama, and F.M. Wolf, 1983, Gender differences in achievement and affiliation attributions, Journal of Cross-Cultural Psychology, 14, 241-256.

Chandler, T.A., D.D. Shama, F.M. Wolf, and S.K. Blanchard, 1981, Multi-attributional causality for achievement across five cross-national samples, Journal of Cross-Cultural Psychology, 12, 207-221.

Churchill, N.C., and V.L. Lewis, 1983, The five stages of small business growth, Harvard Business Review, 61, 30-51.

Cooper, A.C., 1973, Technical entrepreneurship: What do we know?, R & D Management, 3, 59-64.

Cornelius, E.T. III, and F.B. Lane, 1984, The power motive and managerial success in a professionally oriented service industry organization, Journal of Applied Psychology, 69, 32-39.

Dailey, R.C., and C.P. Morgan, 1978, Personal characteristics and job involvement as antecedents of boundary spanning behavior. A path analysis, Journal of Management Studies, 15, 330-339.

Donckels, R., and J. Degadt, 1986, "Women in small business. The Belgian experience," in: R. Donckels and J.N. Meijer (eds.), Women in Small Business. Focus on Europe, Assen/Maastricht, The Netherlands: Van Gorcum, pp. 45-64.

Donckels, R., and J.N. Meijer (eds.), 1986, Women in Small Business. Focus on Europe, Assen/Maastricht, The Netherlands: Van Gorcum.

Drucker, P., 1985, Innovation and Entrepreneurship, New York: Harper and Row.

Eisenhardt, K.M., and N. Forbes, 1985, Technical entrepreneurship: A global perspective, Economic Impact, 4, 56-62.

Elliott, J.E., 1983, Schumpeter and the theory of capitalist economic development, Journal of Economic Behavior and Organization, 4, 277-308.

Ettinger, J.C., 1983, Le profil psychologique du créateur d'entreprise, Revue Française de Gestion, Juin-Juillet- Août, 24-29.

Fishburn, P.C., 1977, Mean-risk analysis with risk associated with below-target returns, American Economic Review, 67, 116-126.

Gasse, Y., 1982, "Elaborations on the psychology of the entrepreneur," in: C.A. Kent, D.L. Sexton, and K.H. Vesper (eds.), Encyclopedia of Entrepreneurship, Englewood Cliffs, NJ: Prentice-Hall, pp. 57-71.

Gergen, K., 1982, Toward Transformation in Social Knowledge, New York: Springer-Verlag.

Giersch, H., 1984, The age of Schumpeter, American Economic Review, 74, 103-109.

Gilad, B., S. Kaish, and J. Ronen, 1986, The Entrepreneurial Way with Information, paper presented at SABE/IAREP International Conference on "Economics and Psychology," Kibbutz Shefayim, Israel.

Goffee, R., and R. Scase, 1983, Business ownership and women's subordination: A preliminary study of female proprietors, Sociological Review, 31, 625-648.

Grönstedt, L.O., C.-R. Julander, and K.-E. Wärneryd, 1981, Skatter och innovationer – en pilotstudie om uppfinnares problem vid utveckling av innovationer (Taxes and Innovations – a Pilot Study of Inventors' Problems Developing Innovations), Stockholm: Stockholm School of Economics, Economic Research Institute.

Heider, F., 1958, The Psychology of Interpersonal Relations, New York: John Wiley.

Hisrich, R.D., and C.G. Brush, 1985, The Woman Entrepreneur: Characteristics and Prescriptions for Success, Lexington, MA: Lexington Books.

Holmquist, C., and E. Sundin, 1986, "Female entrepreneurs: A newly discovered group," in: R. Donckels and J.N. Meijer (eds.), Women in Small Business. Focus on Europe, Assen/Maastricht, The Netherlands: Van Gorcum, pp. 33-44.

Horner, M., 1972, Toward an understanding of achievement-related conflicts in women, Journal of Social Issues, 28, 157-176.

Jahoda, G., 1980, "Theoretical and systematic approaches in cross-cultural psychology," in: H.C. Triandis and W.W. Lambert (eds.), Handbook of Cross-cultural Psychology, Vol. 1, Boston, MA: Allyn and Bacon, pp. 69-141.

James, W., 1890, The Principles of Psychology, Vols. I and II, New York: Henry Holt.

Johannisson, B., 1984, Entreprenören – både meningsbyggare och företagsbyggare (The Entrepreneur – Creator of Meaning and Enterprise), paper presented at workshop "Ekonomi och psykologi," Gothenburg, Sweden: University of Gothenburg, Department of Psychology.

Jones, M.R., (ed), 1955, Nebraska Symposium on Motivation, Lincoln, NB: University of Nebraska Press.

Kahneman, D., and A. Tversky, 1979, Prospect theory: An analysis of decisions under risk, Econometrica, 47, 263-291.

Kahneman, D., P. Slovic, and A. Tversky (eds.), 1982, Judgment under Uncertainty: Heuristics and Biases, Cambridge, MA: Cambridge University Press.

Kashima, Y., and H.C. Triandis, 1986, The self-serving bias in attributions as a coping strategy. A cross-cultural study, Journal of Cross-Cultural Psychology, 17, 83-97.

Kelley, H.H., 1967, "Attribution theory in social psychology," in: D. Levine (ed.), Nebraska Symposium on Motivation, Lincoln, NB: University of Nebraska Press, pp. 192-238.

Kent, C., D.L. Sexton, and K.H. Vesper (eds.), 1982, Encyclopedia of Entrepreneurship, Englewood Cliffs, NJ: Prentice-Hall.

Kets de Vries, M.F.R., 1977, The entrepreneurial personality: A person at the crossroads, Journal of Management Studies, 14, 34-57.

Kets de Vries, M.F.R., 1985, The dark side of entrepreneurship, Harvard Business Review, 63, 160-167.

Khan, A.M., 1986, Entrepreneur characteristics and the prediction of new venture success, Omega, 14, 365-372.

Kihlstrom, R.E., and J.J. Laffont, 1979, A general equilibrium entrepreneurial theory of firm formation based on risk aversion, Journal of Political Economy, 87, 719-748.

Kirton, M.J., 1976, Adaptors and innovators: A description and measure, Journal of Applied Psychology, 61, 622-629.

Kirton, M.J., 1984, Adaptors and innovators: Why new initiatives get blocked, Long Range Planning, 17, 137-143.

Kirzner, I.M., 1973, Competition and Entrepreneurship, Chicago, IL: University of Chicago Press.

Kirzner, I.M., 1979, Perception, Opportunity, and Profit, Chicago, IL: University of Chicago Press.

Kirzner, I.M., 1983, "The entrepreneurial function," in: J. Ronen (ed.), Entrepreneurship, Lexington, MA: Lexington Books, D.C. Heath, pp. 281-290.

Knight, F.H., 1921, Risk, Uncertainty, and Profit, New York: Houghton Mifflin.

Kogan, N., and M.A. Wallach, 1964, Risk Taking, New York: Holt, Rinehart, and Winston.

Kornadt, H.J., L.H. Eckensberger, and W.B. Emminghaus, 1980, "Cross-Cultural research on motivation," in: H.C. Triandis and W.W. Lambert (eds.), Handbook of Cross-Cultural Psychology, Vol. 3, Boston, MA: Allyn and Bacon, pp. 223-321.

Kukla, A., and H. Scher, 1986, Varieties of achievement motivation, Psychological Review, 93, 378-380.

Langer, E.J., 1975, The illusion of control, Journal of Personality and Social Psychology, 32, 311-328.

Laughhunn, D.J., J.W. Payne, and R. Crum, 1980, Managerial risk preferences for below target returns, Management Science, 26, 1238-1249.

Leibenstein, H., 1968, Entrepreneurship and development, American Economic Review, 63, 72-83.

Leibenstein, H., 1976, Beyond Economic Man, Cambridge, MA: Harvard University Press.

Leibenstein, H., 1979, A branch of economics is missing: Micro-micro theory, Journal of Economic Literature, 17, 477-502.

Libby, R., and P.C. Fishburn, 1977, Behavioral models of risk taking in business decisions: A survey and evaluation, Journal of Accounting Research, 15, 272-292.

Lowe, E.A., and W.G.K. Taylor, 1986, Creativity in life sciences research, R & D Management, 16, no. 1, 45-61.

MacCrimmon, K.R., and D.A. Wehrung, 1986, Taking Risks: The Management of Uncertainty, New York: The Free Press.

Maidique, M.A., 1980, Entrepreneurs, champions and technological innovation, Sloan Management Review, 21, no. 2, 59-76.
Marshall, A., 1890, Principles of Economics (reprint: 1961, London: MacMillan, ninth edition).
Maslow, A.H., 1954, Motivation and Personality, New York: Harper and Row.
McClelland, D.C., 1961, The Achieving Society, Princeton, NJ: D. Van Nostrand.
McClelland, D.C., 1975, Power: The Inner Experience, New York: Irvington.
McClelland, D.C., and R.E. Boyatzis, 1982, Leadership motive pattern and long-term success in management, Journal of Applied Psychology, 67, 737-743.
McClelland, D.C., and D.H. Burnham, 1976, Power is the great motivator, Harvard Business Review, 54, 100-111.
McClelland, D.C., and D.G. Winter, 1969, Motivating Economic Achievement, New York: The Free Press.
McDougall, W., 1923, Outline of Psychology, New York: Scribner.
McDougall, W., 1908, An Introduction to Social Psychology, London: Methuen.
Miettinen, A., 1986, "Contributing spouses and the dynamics of entrepreneurial families," in: R. Donckels and J.N. Meijer (eds.), Women in Small Business. Focus on Europe, Assen/Maastricht, The Netherlands: Van Gorcum, pp. 78-86.
Mill, J.S., 1848, Principles of Political Economy with Some of Their Applications to Social Philosophy, London: John W. Parker.
Miller, D., and H. Friesen, 1982, Innovation in conservative and entrepreneurial firms: Two models of strategic momentum, Strategic Management Journal, 3, 1-25.
Miller, D., M.F.R. Kets de Vries, and J.-M. Toulouse, 1982, Top executive locus of control and its relationship to strategy-making structure, and environment, Academy of Management Journal, 25, 237-253.
Miron, D., and D.C. McClelland, 1979, The impact of achievement motivation training on small businesses, California Management Review, 21, 13-28.
Munro, D., 1979, Locus-of-control attribution factors among blacks and whites in Africa, Journal of Cross-Cultural Psychology, 10, 157-172.
Murray, H.A., 1938, Explorations in Personality, New York: Oxford University Press.
Nicholls, J.G., 1984, Achievement motivation: Conceptions of ability, subjective experience, task choice, and performance, Psychological Review, 91, 328-346.
Niles, F.S., 1981, Dimensionality of Rotter's I-E scale in Sri Lanka, Journal of Cross-Cultural Psychology, 12, 473-479.
Panday, J., and N.B. Tewary, 1979, Locus of control and achievement values of entrepreneurs, Journal of Occupational Psychology, 52, 107-111.
Payne, J.W., D.J. Laughhuhn, and R. Crum, 1980, Translation of gambles and aspiration level effects in risky choice behavior, Management Science, 26, 1039-1060.
Peterson, R.A., 1981, "Entrepreneurship and organization," in: P.C. Nystrom and W.H. Starbuck (eds.), Handbook of Organizational Design, Vol. 1, Oxford, UK: Oxford University Press, pp. 65-83.
Pettigrew, A.M., 1979, On studying organizational cultures, Administrative Science Quarterly, 24, 570-581.
Ramamurti, R., 1986, Public entrepreneurs: Who they are and how they operate, California Management Review, 28, 142-158.
Riger, S., and P. Galligan, 1980, Women in management: An exploration of competing paradigms, American Psychologist, 35, 902-910.
Roberts, G.B. (ed.), 1986, Proceedings: Venturing into Entrepreneurship and Small Business. 31st Annual World Conference International Council for Small Business, Marietta, GA: Kennesaw College.
Rogers, E.M., and J.K. Larsen, 1984, Silicon Valley Fever. Growth of High Technology Culture (reprint: 1986, New York: Basic Books).

Ronen, J., 1983, "Some insights into the entrepreneurial process," in: J. Ronen (ed.), Entrepreneurship, Lexington, MA: Lexington Books, D.C. Heath, pp. 137-173.

Rosenblatt, P.C., L. de Mik, R.M. Anderson, and P.A. Johnson, 1985, The Family in Business: Understanding and Dealing with the Challenges Entrepreneurial Families Face, San Francisco, CA: Jossey-Bass.

Rotter, J.B., 1966, Generalized expectancies for internal versus external control of reinforcement, Psychological Monographs: General and Applied, 80, no. 609.

Schein, E.H., 1983, The role of the founder in creating organizational culture, Organizational Dynamics, 12, 13-28.

Schumpeter, J.A., 1934, The Theory of Economic Development. An Inquiry into Profits, Capital, Credit, Interest, and the Business Cycle, Cambridge, MA: Harvard University Press.

Segall, M.H., 1986, Culture and behavior: Psychology in a global perspective, Annual Review of Psychology, 37, 523-564.

Sexton, D.L., and R.W. Smilor, 1986, "Research needs and issues in entrepreneurship," in: G.B. Roberts (ed.), Proceedings: Venturing into Entrepreneurship and Small Business. 31st Annual World Conference International Council for Small Business, Marietta, GA: Kennesaw College, pp. 135-141.

Slovic, P., 1972, From Shakespeare to Simon: Speculations – and some evidence – about Man's ability to process information, Eugene, OR: Oregon Research Institute.

Stanworth, M.J., and J. Curran, 1973, Management Motivation in the Smaller Business, Epping, Essex: Gower.

Stein, M.I., 1968, "Creativity," in: E.F. Borgatta and W.W. Lambert (eds.), Handbook of Personality Theory and Research, Chicago, IL: Rand McNally, pp. 900-942.

Tushman, M.L., and W.L. Moore (eds.), 1982, Readings in the Management of Innovation, Boston, MA: Pitman.

Tushman, M.L., and D. Nadler, 1986, Organizing for innovation, California Management Review, 28, 74-92.

Tversky, A., and D. Kahneman, 1982, "Judgment under uncertainty: Heuristics and biases," in: D. Kahneman, P. Slovic, and A. Tversky (eds.), Judgment under Uncertainty: Heuristics and Biases, Cambridge, MA: Cambridge University Press, pp. 3-20.

Vesper, K.H. (ed.), 1981, Frontiers of Entrepreneurship Research, Wellesley, MA: Babson College.

Ward, C., 1978, Is there a motive to avoid success in women?, Human Relations, 31, 1055-1067.

Watkins, D.S., 1973, Technical entrepreneurship: A cis-Atlantic view, R & D Management, 3, 65-70.

Weber, M., 1904, The Protestant Ethic and the Spirit of Capitalism (reprint: 1958, New York: Scribner).

Weiner, B., 1972, Theories of Motivation – from Mechanism to Cognition, Chicago, IL: Rand McNally.

Weiner, B, 1974, Achievement Motivation and Attribution Theory, Morristown, NJ: General Learning Press.

Weiner, B., 1985, An attributional theory of achievement motivation and emotion, Psychological Review, 92, 548-573.

Table of Contents

12. Bargaining, Negotiations, and Personal Selling

WESLEY J. JOHNSTON

University of Southern California, Los Angeles, CA, U.S.A.

and

W.C. BENTON

Ohio State University, Columbus, OH, U.S.A.

1. INTRODUCTION

This chapter examines the important human interactions called bargaining and negotiation in the setting of personal selling. Economics and psychology provide important concepts and variables which, when combined, produce favorable insights to bargaining, negotiations, and personal selling. Whenever the terms of a sales transaction are determined, or a business deal is settled, bargaining is likely. In a sense, everyone becomes a bargainer at one time or another. Bargaining occurs between all forms of human groupings: individuals, groups, organizations, and countries. The conditions under which "*bargaining*" takes place are when two or more parties have divergent interests or goals and communication between the parties is possible. Three additional conditions must also exist in order for bargaining to occur (Chertkoff and Esser, 1976):

1. Mutual compromise must be possible. If one of the parties must choose between total victory or complete loss, no bargaining occurs. Bargaining situations require intermediate solutions for the parties involved.
2. The possibility must exist for provisional offers to be made by those involved in the situation.
3. The provisional offers must not determine the outcome of the situation, until the terms are accepted by all parties.

A bargaining situation can then be defined as an interaction where parties with certain disagreements confer and exchange ideas about a possible solution until a compromise is reached or the bargaining is terminated. This definition of bargaining is what Schelling (1963) referred to as explicit bargaining.

In this chapter, we will only consider the kind of bargaining that occurs

Van Raaij, W.F., van Veldhoven, G.M. and Wärneryd, K.E. (eds) Handbook of Economic Psychology. ISBN 90-247-3720-6.

between two parties who possess resources the other desires. Bargaining often occurs in what has been referred to as multiple-opponent bargaining situations, where a consumer visits several dealerships when shopping for a new automobile or where an industrial buyer negotiates a new purchase with several alternative suppliers. This will not be the main focus of this chapter. Instead, the emphasis will be on bargaining in a "bilateral monopoly" system. This does not rule out the influence of others on the two bargainers such as their constituencies, but it does limit the bargaining to only two parties.

Two-party bargaining can be divided into two types: distributive and integrative. The parties in *distributive bargaining* are in basic conflict and competition because of a clash of goals: The more one party gets, the less the other gets. That is, the total gains from the situation must be "distributed" between the two parties involved and each party usually wants as much as they can get. However, if either party is too greedy, an agreement will not be reached. In dealing with distributive bargaining, the influence of both parties must be considered. Discussion, understanding and agreements are vital to distributive bargaining. By the very nature of the situation, cooperation is important. Without some degree of cooperation, either party can block trading and reduce individual gain to zero.

Distributive bargaining can, therefore, be modeled and examined by using "game theory." Either two-party, varying-sum or zero-sum are suitable depending upon the payoff schedule involved. In a varying-sum schedule bargaining situation, the profits (and/or losses) of the respective bargainers, when added together, need not equal the same fixed amount, thus, the term "varying sum." While the payoff schedules are usually inversely related – if one gains the other must lose – there can be some situations where both parties realize a gain (or loss) not in direct proportion to what happens to the other bargainers. In the zero-sum bargaining situation, the profits (and/or losses) of the respective bargainers always sum to the same fixed amount. The term zero-sum stands for the fact that what one bargainer gains the other loses and the net gains (and/or losses) are zero. Both of these situations readily exist in the business environment. The varying-sum schedule is often found in customer service situations, where the supplier is at or above the 90% service level. To go from the 90% level to the 95% level, a gain of only 5% improvement for the customer can often mean a doubling of the costs to the supplier to attain that increased level. The zero-sum schedule is usually found in retail situations where the merchant's costs are relatively fixed. The less the consumer pays for a product, the less profit there is for the retailer almost on a dollar-for-dollar basis.

Integrative bargaining exists, where there are areas of mutual concern and complementary interests. The situation is a varying-sum schedule such that by working together both parties can increase the total profits available to be divided between them. This is often the case between manufacturers and distributors because of the existence of an ultimate consumer. If the ultimate consumer can be persuaded to pay more for a product, there is more to be divided between the manufacturer and the distributor. At this point we are tempted to generalize that integrative bargaining is more common to industrial markets and interactions while distributive bargaining is more common to consumer markets and interactions.

In most bargaining situations there is usually a preliminary discussion, called negotiation. The word "negotiation" is derived from Latin and in civil law means "trading on deliberations leading to an agreement." The modeling approach to bargaining is to determine what contract, i.e., agreed joint strategy, might or should be reached. The bargaining model offers an agreement (solution). Other researchers (Rubin and Brown, 1975), however, have felt the similarities of definition are so strong that the terms "bargaining" and "negotiation" can be used interchangeably even though occasional distinction is made between the terms.

A model of a bargaining problem calls for an asymmetric form of analysis and both a normative focus on one's own behavior and a predictive view of one's opponent. The bargainer needs to determine how s/he, as a decision maker, *ought* to behave in light of his/her analysis of how his/her opponent *might* behave. And, of course, as the decision maker analyzes the problem, s/he should bear in mind that the opponent is also thinking how the decision maker is thinking, and so on. The minimum necessary variables for a model of the overall bargaining process include both the decision maker's and his/her opponent's initial offers, desired outcomes, maximum level of concession (zero profit level) and rate of concession.

Two parties can bargain over price; the seller usually wants the price to be high, the buyer wants the price to be low. The seller is often working under a profit maximization strategy and the buyer is more interested in minimizing cost. Sometimes the resource in contention may be time. The building contractor wants more time; the future owner wants the building completed in less time.

The distributive bargaining situation has been most fully explored by psychologists. The results of this research are a myriad of small laboratory studies which have not generated a general theory of bargaining or a comprehensive model to incorporate the many isolated findings. Economists, on the other hand, have seen distributive bargaining as a problem that only involves two parties dividing fixed resources with no opportunity for any outside influence of third parties. Economists, therefore, have seen the solution to distributive bargaining as indeterminable and left its exploration to others. Economists have spent most of their effort in examining bargaining in integrative bargaining situations.

2. PSYCHOLOGICAL BARGAINING LITERATURE[1]

2.1. *Introduction*

The findings from empirical research by psychologists can be categorized under six areas, each representing a major factor assumed to affect bargaining. These six factors are explained below and examples of each are provided (Chertkoff and Esser, 1976):

1. *General bargaining predispositions.* Individual differences in bargaining predispositions may affect bargaining behavior. For example, bargainers may have a cooperative or competitive general orientation.
2. *Pay-off system.* Payoffs result from various aspects of the negotiated agreement. For example, certain terms may yield a specific amount of profit, or there may be a bonus for attaining a specified agreement, or the time spent in bargaining may involve certain costs.
3. *Social relationship with the opponent.* This factor refers to the social relationship existing between the bargainers. Examples are degree of friendship or differences in status or power.
4. *Social relationship with significant others.* This factor refers to the relationships of the bargainers to significant others not participating directly in the bargaining. Examples of significant others are the bargaining constituents or a mediator.
5. *Situational factors.* The physical and social setting of the bargaining may have an effect. Is the bargaining being conducted in the home territory of one of the bargainers or on neutral ground? What, if any, is the seating arrangement?
6. *Bargaining strategy.* This factor includes the specific actions of the bargainer during bargaining. How extreme is his opening? Does he concede frequently or infrequently?

Payoff system and bargaining strategy are highly relevant at this point in the chapter and worth exploring further at this time. Later, using a conceptual model developed in Bonoma and Johnston (1978), the other four areas will be brought together and applied to buyer-seller negotiations and bargaining.

2.2. *Payoff System*

The actual payoff system that bargainers face in an interaction must certainly be a major determinant of bargaining behavior. Several different factors related to the payoff system have been studied. They include (Chertkoff and Esser, 1976):

1. the amount that has to be exceeded if the bargainer is to realize a profit,
2. the cost of time spent in bargaining,
3. the cost of failure to reach agreement,
4. added benefits achieved by obtaining a specific threshold value,
5. qualitative or quantitative variations in the general level of payoff values,
6. whether payoffs are based solely on one's own profit schedule or are based, in whole or in part, on the degree to which one's profits exceed those of others,
7. whether conflict is constant-sum or varying-sum, and
8. penalties the bargaining opponent (or perhaps a third party) is likely to impose for failure to yield.

A discussion of these factors and the research findings follow. Only directly pertinent findings will be presented. There is a voluminous amount of research on bargaining, a great deal of which is only tangential to this discussion.

2.3. *Breakeven Point*

Various names have been used to describe the amount that must be exceeded in the bargaining interaction in order to obtain a profit: maximum concession point, *breakeven point*, zero profit point, minimum necessary share, resistance point, or minimum disposition (Chertkoff and Esser, 1976). Most experimental research has treated this point as being fixed. However, it has been argued (Ikle and Leites, 1962) that the value in natural settings, including business, is frequently uncertain. The bargaining that takes place is often an attempt to convince the other person that s/he can profitably accept a lower value than the one s/he maintains is necessary. This is true in most business situations where future profits are being negotiated. Without a knowledge of future costs and revenues, the breakeven point would remain uncertain.

Kelley, Beckman and Fischer (1967) assume that a bargainers' resistance to making concessions is positively correlated to both the time required to make a further concession and the probability of withdrawing from the negotiations. The level of resistance is also assumed to be related to the minimum necessary share. As bargainers concede toward their minimum necessary share, their resistance should increase. The Kelley et al. model also predicts that for a given offer, the higher the minimum necessary share, the greater the resistance, and for a given level of profit, the lower the minimum necessary share, the greater the resistance. A good deal of subsequent research supports the model but a number of questions remain unanswered as to why bargainers should behave in the manner predicted by the Kelley et al. model.

For instance, why should resistance mount as the minimum necessary share is approached? Chertkoff and Esser (1976) feel a number of theoretical interpretations are possible. The interpretations they see as possible include behavior in terms of a utility model and a face-saving model.

> A utility model might contain the assumption that the utility of profit is a negatively accelerated function of the amount of profit, so that a reduction in profit by X amount leads to a greater loss in utility the closer that reduction is to the minimum necessary share. A face-saving model might contain a similar assumption, that the loss in face produced by a concession of X amount increases as the minimum necessary share is approached. So far, no research has been directed toward determining what psychological factors underlie the assumptions of the model (Chertkoff and Esser, 1976: p. 471).

2.4. *Time Pressure*

The time remaining before bargaining must be concluded is also believed to have a significant impact on bargaining behavior. Consider the situation in many labor-management negotiations. If the contract is not successfully renegotiated prior to the expiration of the existing contract, a labor walkout may occur. In cases of buyer-seller negotiating time, pressure may be created by the buyer's imminent need for the product or service, the length of delivery time possible being extended by long negotiations. Sellers may realize time pressure by quotas for sales that must be accomplished in set time periods. The greater the time pressure, the faster the concession making. Time pressure in psychological experiments has been exerted in various ways:

1. high or low probability that the present round of offers would be the last;
2. warning that time was almost up;
3. number of offers remaining before penalties for additional offers; and
4. cost of each of the trial offers.

More rapid yielding under greater time pressure may reflect the desire of bargainers to avoid either the undesirable costs associated with making offers or zero profit (which results from no agreement).

2.5. *Cost of No Agreement*

In most of the psychological research, the majority of experiments have been structured so that the alternatives of reaching an agreement and its possible terms are usually preferable to no agreement. Warning the subjects that the end of negotiations is imminent often produces extremely rapid concession making, so uniformly rapid, in fact, that any differences in levels of toughness prior to the warning may be obliterated (Benton, Kelley, and Liebling, 1972; Esser and Komorita, 1975). This is not necessarily true in buyer-seller negotiations because negotiations can usually be resumed in some future time period and other buyers or sellers exist for future interactions.

2.6. *Multiple Bargaining Interactions*

In most psychological research, participants are given the goal of maximizing their own gain; however, they may also be interested in outperforming the other bargainers. In personal selling situations where the same salesperson often negotiates with the same buyer, this may be an important issue. The question is, "What is the effect of being bested on a previous bargaining encounter?" How will this translate into bargaining strategy on subsequent interactions with the same opponent? It appears that in the second encounter, those who had failed on the first encounter bargain in a tougher manner than those who had succeeded (Esser, 1975).

In conclusion, any theoretical model of bargaining must include assumptions about the payoff system under which the bargainers are operating. The breakeven point, the cost of time spent in bargaining, the cost of failure to reach an agreement, time pressure, the effect of previous bargaining outcomes, and other factors all have an effect on bargaining behavior and need to be incorporated into the bargaining process. A great amount of psychological research has examined the effect of the payoff system on bargaining. Some of this research has direct implications for buyer-seller interactions. When buyers and sellers are negotiating over future profits, outcomes may have a wider variance than when the payoff is known with certainty. Resistance to making concessions is related to time pressure, breakeven point, the cost of no agreement, and perhaps previous bargaining outcomes.

2.7. *Bargaining Strategy*

Usually a tougher bargaining strategy – one using a more extreme opening position, fewer concessions, and/or smaller concessions – can obtain a more favorable final agreement (Bartos, 1966, 1970). There appear to be exceptions to such a conclusion, however. Never making a concession may be responded to by the other side in a similar fashion, leading to little or no convergence in the bargaining interaction (Komorita and Brenner, 1968). When time allotted to bargaining (or that which is left) is very short and when not reaching an agreement is clearly disadvantageous, toughness may be a poor strategy because it could result in no agreement (Benton et al., 1972). Also, when bargaining is deadlocked, toughness is counterproductive (Hamner, 1974). Excessive toughness in bargaining could be a particularly bad strategy in buyer-seller interactions where future interactions were expected. If one party always chose a very tough stance the other party will develop a similar approach to the bargaining interaction. This could result in high transaction costs, lack of future agreements, and where possible, replacement of the bargaining opponent.

Esser and Komorita (1975) (also Komorita and Esser, 1975) concluded that the best strategy is to give the other side the impression that one is tough, but fair. A strategy of always reciprocating both the frequency and magnitude of the other bargainer's concessions was found to be more effective in obtaining concessions from the other bargainer than strategies involving less reciprocation. Conceding only in response to a concession by the other side gives the impression that one is strong, while always reciprocating a concession gives the impression that one is fair. Dispositions attributed to the other party in a bargaining situation are crucial in mediating yielding. If you give a little, I will give a little, and vice versa. Concession begets concession and reciprocal concessions can lead to reaching agreement. This leads to the general conclusion that every agreement ought to lie somewhere between the two starting points of the bargainers. Obviously, some agreements are closer to one bargainer's starting position than others because of tough or skillful bargaining tactics. A problem, however, is what the other party thinks of his opponent's reasons for tough negotiation, particularly if there are to be other instances of bargaining between the two parties.

> An attributional analysis suggests that for tough bargaining to be successful, a bargainer must become convinced that the toughness being exhibited by the opponent is not due to excessive greed. As long as an opponent shows some willingness to compromise, his protracted toughness may convince a bargainer that he is not trying to win an overwhelming victory, but rather is merely responding to his profit schedule. Hence, yielding finally occurs (Chertkoff and Esser, 1976).

In support of this, Chertkoff and Baird (1971) found that when a high demand was supported by the assertion that one's breakeven point was high, the other side rapidly made substantial concessions. In conclusion, giving a bargaining opponent the impression that tough bargaining is because of one's payoff system and that one is firm but fair is the best strategy. This will lead to greater yielding on the part of the other party in the bargaining interaction. Another important aspect of the perceived bargaining strategy deals with whether the opponent attributes the need for the level of toughness in bargaining to the opponent or to the opponent's constituency. If the level of toughness is because of the opponent's constituency, it may be beneficial for the bargainer to directly contact the constituency and deal with their expectations before returning to the negotiations. An example of this in an industrial setting is when a salesperson must contact other members of the "buying center" before continuing negotiations with a purchasing manager who is under pressure to obtain a "very low price" from his/her constituency.

3. ECONOMIC BARGAINING LITERATURE

3.1. *Introduction*

While most of the empirical research to date has been in distributive bargaining and done by psychologists, most of the work done on integrative bargaining has been of the theoretical nature and accomplished by economists. At this point, it is appropriate to review the economic theories concerning bilateral bargaining of an integrative nature and then examine a sample problem.

3.2. *Edgeworth*

Edgeworth's (1881) solution for a two-person, two-commodity bargain has been demonstrated for many years by the use of the simple box diagram (see Figure 1).

In Edgeworth's paradigm, Firms 1 and 2 start with a given quantity of A and B (say money and raw materials). Indifference curves for each firm can be drawn where a certain amount of one quantity is willingly exchanged (interchangeable) to obtain an amount of the other quantity. Along any one indifference curve the utility to that firm remains the same.

Edgeworth noted that trading will be carried on until a point on the contract curve CC′ is reached. The contract curve is a solution to the bargaining problem in the game theory sense. It consists of a set of imputations which do not dominate each other. Any point lying off the contract curve is not jointly optional. This means that for any distribution off the contract curve there exists at least one imputation on the curve that will be preferable to both bargainers. Under the Edgeworth assumptions, a multi-imputation solution is obtained (any point along the contract curve

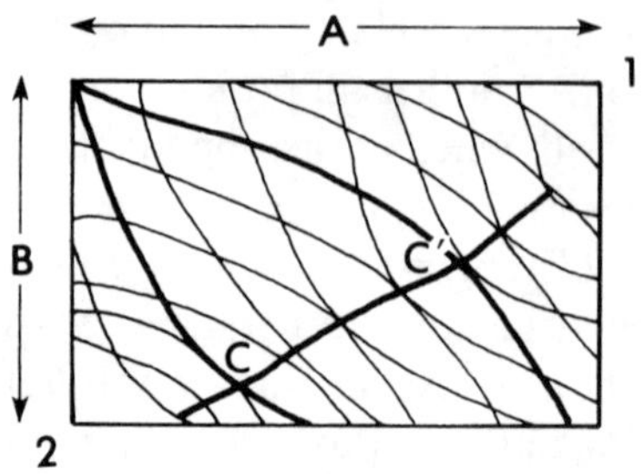

Fig. 1. Edgeworth's box.

CC′ is a solution). This solution to the bargaining problem has been called "indeterminate."

Edgeworth believed in the measurability of utility and in the possibility of making interpersonal comparisons. Consistent with this, then, there is one imputation on the contract curve that jointly maximizes the utility of both players called the "utilitarian point." If $U_1(x,y)$ and $U_2(x,y)$ are the bargainer utilities for the amounts X of the first good and Y of the second good, the maximum of $U_1(x,y) + U_2(x,y)$ is the utilitarian point. Edgeworth did not advocate this as the actual solution to a bargain because such a solution might be too disadvantageous to one side. Nor did he consider the possibility of side payments.

3.3. *Von Neumann and Morgenstern*

In another classical economic approach, Von Neumann and Morgenstern (1944) assume that *individual utilities are comparable*. Under this assumption there is only one point on the contract curve of bargains which is jointly maximal (point corresponds to Edgeworth's utilitarian point). This bargain would be selected and a possible side payment of money or "utility" made.

This bargaining model requires us to treat the money payment made by the buyer as though it were a transfer of a number of units of a measure of utility. To do so appears reasonable, however, in the special case of bilateral monopoly it makes more sense to treat the money payment in terms of utility. Consider two firms, where one firm is a primary producer to the second who, in turn, sells his product to the market. The second firm, or middleman, determines the best pricing and production policies for his final product on the assumption that he can buy from the first firm or manufacturer at marginal cost. The two firms then set their outputs to maximize the revenue of the middleman from the final market. A side payment may settle any differences in utilities. The outputs of both goods and the market price of the consumer good sold by the second firm are all determinant, but the actual price paid for a monopolist's good must be bargained for in this model of bargaining.

The Von Neumann and Morgenstern (1944) solution is equivalent to "Pareto optimality." The players jointly maximize and split the profits in such a manner that each gets at least as much as he could have obtained by himself. Pareto's criterion, upon which the Von Neumann and Morgenstern model relies, states: "Any change which harms no one and which makes some people better off (in their own subjective utility estimation), must be considered to be an improvement." Pareto optimality, then, occurs when no one can be made better off without someone being made worse off. Unfortunately, there are many bargaining situations which cannot be modeled with the aid of this criterion. The Pareto criterion does not apply to any zero-sum or inversely related varying-sum, two party bargaining situations. Movement to the contract curve can be explained by the Pareto criterion, but movement along the curve is still done by "bargaining," which remains unexplained.

3.4. *Nash*

In the Nash (1950) solution, which developed out of the work of Von Neumann and Morgenstern, the bargaining problem is conceived in the usual game theoretic terms. He considers as relevant data only the utilities which each alternative point of agreement provide to the players.

Nash suggests that it is reasonable to expect the outcome of a bargaining process to satisfy the following three conditions:

1. *Pareto optimality*: The outcome will lie on the northeast boundary of the outcome set. The solution to the situation should be such that no other settlement exists which is preferred by both bargainers.
2. *Independence of irrelevant alternatives*: Consider two different bargaining situations with the same mathematical origin, and in which all the possible outcomes of one are included in the other; then, if the actual outcome of the larger bargaining situation is also a possible outcome in the smaller, it will be the final outcome for the smaller bargaining situation as well. If X is the solution to a situation consisting of a given set of alternative settlements, X should also be the solution to any situation consisting of some subset of these settlements, provided that X is present in the subset.
3. *Symmetry*: If the set of possible utility outcomes happens to be symmetric (that is, if for every point $U_1 = a$, $U_2 = b$ in the outcome set, the point $U_1 = b$, $U_2 = a$ is also in the set), the outcome of the bargaining will give $U_1 = U_2$ or equal utility to both partners.

Three other properties of Nash's solution have also been identified:

1. *Individual rationality*: The solution to the bargaining situation should leave both bargainers better off than they would be, if they did not achieve a settlement.
2. *Feasibility*: The solution to the bargaining situation will be a feasible outcome chosen from the set of all possible outcomes to the negotiation.
3. *Independence of utility function scale*: The solution to the bargaining situation will not depend on the scale used to measure the utility function of the participants.

Nash originally took the position that his model constituted a positive theory and that it would describe actual bargaining outcomes, but it is now much more common to give a normative interpretation to the analysis and to treat the Nash solution as a "desirable" outcome of the bargaining process.

The actual result of any bilateral bargain will only be a single imputation, but the economic assumptions made are usually not strong enough to enable the economist to forecast the specific imputation that will be chosen. Often all that s/he can do is to indicate a range in which the outcome must fall (the contract curve). In that case, the specification of this range constitutes the solution in the sense that it fully utilizes the available economic information. In order to single out an imputation within this range, dynamic sociological and psychological information may be needed.

The Nash solution assumes individual utilities are not comparable. The Nash solutions are of a normative nature and assume away such features as bargaining ability. In the Von Neumann and Morgenstern solution, the quantity to be traded is determined, but no price within a range could be determined (side payments place the price anywhere). The Nash solution to the bargaining problem suggests a method of *fair division*. It suggests a way of dividing joint profits that is "fair" in the sense that a referee or judge "should" follow, if called upon to settle a division between two corporations.

The contract should be Pareto optimal (see Figure 2). However, some points on the Pareto optimal joint strategy curve leave a player worse off than if he had not made an agreement. The subset of Pareto optimal joint strategies offering each player at least his security level is called the negotiation set (contract curve).

Siegel and Fouraker (1960) conducted simulated bilateral monopoly bargaining experiments. One subject played the part of the sole manufacturer of a product, and the other subject played the part of the sole distributor. To do business and make money, both players have to deal with each other. Bargaining concerned the quantity of goods the distributor would take and the price he would pay per unit.

A Pareto optimal solution requires a contract with a specific quantity of goods, calculable from the economic model. This quantity maximizes joint profit. Assuming both players agree on the Pareto optimal quantity of goods, there remains the division of the joint profit between the players. This is determined by the price the distributor agrees to pay the manufacturer and the manufacturer accepts. The unit price in a Pareto optimal contract can vary anywhere between the two limiting prices, the higher of which would give all the joint profit to the manufacturer while the lower would give all the joint profit to the distributor.

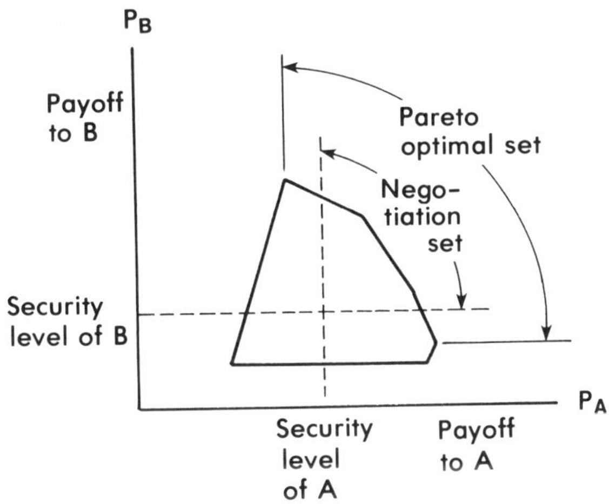

Fig. 2. Nash model.

The actual subset of contract quantities varies around the Pareto optimum; the more complete the information each had about the other, the less the variability of different pairs of bargainers around the Pareto optimum.

The tendency in this situation is to split the joint profit evenly between the buyer and the seller. This seems to agree with all proposed theories yielding a specific Pareto optimal strategy (when utility is linear with money). For example, the only reasonable status quo point seems to be no-deal, in which case the Nash solution requires a 50-50 split of the profits. Neither player can enforce a relative advantage over the other, this also leads to an even split.

Neslin and Greenhalgh (1983) also conducted empirical research within a Nash model. Their research supports the usefulness of the Nash model in predicting the outcomes of buyer-seller negotiations. The results suggest that an understanding of any conflict prior to the actual bargaining is key to predicting the actual outcome. They also found it is important for management to accurately communicate its preferences to the negotiators, because the negotiator preferences strongly affect the outcome. Weakness in bargaining skills also has an effect on the outcome of bargaining situations according to their findings. While the outcomes of the bargaining situations were distributed around the Nash solution, other psychological variables or individual differences affected the actual outcome.

Given the results of the Siegel and Fouraker (1960) study, and the Neslin and Greenhalgh (1983) research, it appears that the following generalization can be made:

Economic theory can help predict the approximate outcome of bargaining situations, but psychological conditions will cause the true solution to vary around the predicted outcome point. An economic-psychological approach will help provide the truest solution and best approach to understanding bargaining and negotiation situations and their outcomes.

Or as Wroe Alderson (1957) stated it:

> Transactions between two operating systems always involve the two factors of economic values and the balance of power. The ideal of a system in which market values alone control, is impossible of realization because goods always move through a power structure and not through the neutral type of facility which may be suggested by the term "marketing channel" (p. 130).

4. AN EXPERIMENT IN DISTRIBUTIVE BARGAINING

To better illustrate both the effects of economic and psychological aspects on the outcome of bargaining situations, it is necessary to turn to an experiment in distributive bargaining. The experiment examines the effect of contingency compensation on both buyers and sellers. It also allows speculation about the differences in the power systems of buyers and sellers, and how they affect the outcome of bargaining situations.

Consider the typical sales situation, where an agreement has to be reached on the specifications of the product to be bought and the money to be paid. Both the seller and buyer can make concessions. To simplify matters, also assume the following bargaining conditions:

1. Only one deal is being negotiated.
2. The bargainers are honorable people.
3. The decisions made are binding.
4. No arbitration or third party is available to assist bargainers.

5. Any party can break off the negotiation and continue as before.
6. The setting and language are not important.

Sellers and buyers tend to have conflicting bargaining goals. The aim of a selling organization is to instill in its salespeople the objective of influencing buyers' actions to the advantage of the seller. This goal is effectively communicated and reinforced by the seller's compensation system. Salespeople are often compensated on the basis of salary plus commission, making their earnings directly contingent upon some measure of sales effectiveness. Logic dictates a similar objective for the buying organization. Since purchases represent costs to the buyers, professional buyers are encouraged to reduce costs. The seller's reservation price (R_s) is usually his or her minimum selling price for any final deal, δ^*. This price includes the total costs plus an expected profit margin. The buyer's reservation price (R_b) represents the maximum amount that s/he is willing to pay for any final deal, δ^*. To pay more than the reservation price, R_b, the buyer would be better off with no agreement (see Figure 3).

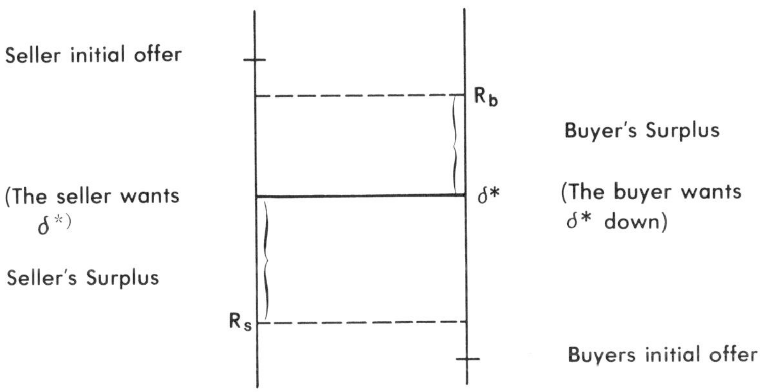

Fig. 3. Distributive bargaining model (note: If $R_b < R_s$, there is no bargaining zone).

If $R_s < R_b$, the bargaining zone is the interval from R_s to R_b. Suppose that the final deal is some value of δ^*, where δ^* is between R_s and R_b, the buyer's marginal gain in value is: $R_b - \delta^*$, and the seller's marginal dollar gain is: $\delta^* - R_s$. At first glance, it appears that a final deal is easily obtained if a bargaining zone exists. This is not really the case simply because the buyer and seller might not agree to settle for an even division of the bargaining zone value. The bargainers generally do not know the exact size of the bargaining zone, $R_b - R_s$. Each party usually knows his or her reservation price. Each party must assess the other party's reservation price. The negotiation process is used to uncover the other party's (buyer's) reservation price. At the same time, the seller may often lead the buyer to think that his reservation price is higher than it really is.

A simple bargaining example will be presented to illustrate concession behavior for distributive bargaining. The instructions for the example are: A bargaining experiment run at the Ohio State University (Columbus, OH, U.S.A.) informed the sellers that they had been hired to represent an individual, who wished to sell an office building (McFillen, Reck, and Benton, 1983). Because of the owner's financial situation, the building could be sold for no less than $ 100,000, R_s. The buyers were told that they had been hired to represent a person, who wished to purchase an office building, but that the potential buyer could afford to pay no more than $ 150,000, R_b. A bargaining zone exists, because $R_s < R_b$. The bargaining game was designed such that no party had a relative advantage over the other due to either the urgency of settlement or to the possession of more complete information. The time limit for the game was 25 minutes. Half of the sellers were told that they would be contingently compensated and they would be rewarded in cash in proportion to the final negotiated price of the building. In their instructions, they were told that they would receive one dollar for each $ 5,000, by which the final price exceeded the $ 100,000 minimum required by the owner, up to a maximum of ten dollars. The participants in this research would actually be allowed to keep this money as an incentive to make the bargaining more extrinsically involving. If no agreement was reached, the contingently compensated sellers would receive no commission. The remaining half of the sellers were told that they would be paid ten dollars for having represented the owner during the negotiations, regardless of whether or not a sale was negotiated. Similarly, half of the buyers were told that they actually would be compensated according to the final agreed price. They were informed that they would receive one dollar in cash for each $ 5,000, by which the final price was lower than the $ 150,000 maximum that the potential purchasers could pay, up to a maximum of ten dollars. No agreement, therefore, meant no money for the contingently compensated buyer. The remaining half of the buyers were told that they would receive ten dollars for having represented the potential purchase in the negotiations, regardless of the outcome of the negotiations. These instructions constituted the contingent and noncontingent reward conditions. No buyer or seller knew whether the opposing negotiator was being contingently or noncontingently rewarded.

The results yielded a number of interesting findings. First, the initial offer from the Buyer was always consistently above the Seller's reservation price. This case will result in an agreement favorable to the seller in each situation.

Second, the results suggest that the way a negotiator is paid will significantly affect the process and outcome of the negotiations. As shown in Figures 4a through 4d, the effects of contingent rewards are to shift the seller's marginal surplus upward and the buyer's marginal value downward. When only one party is contingently rewarded, the effect is to shift the

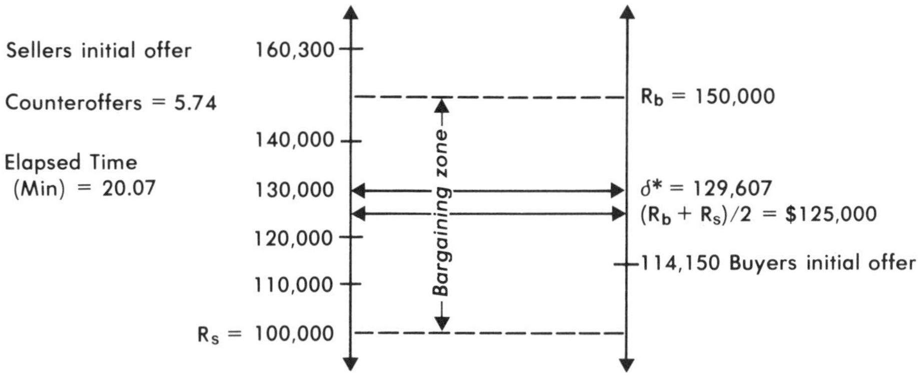

Fig. 4a. Seller contingent/buyer contingent.

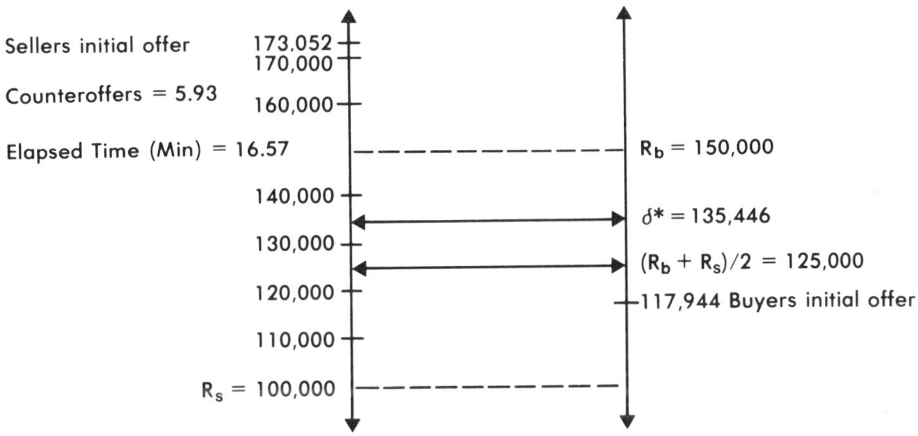

Fig. 4b. Seller contingent/buyer noncontingent.

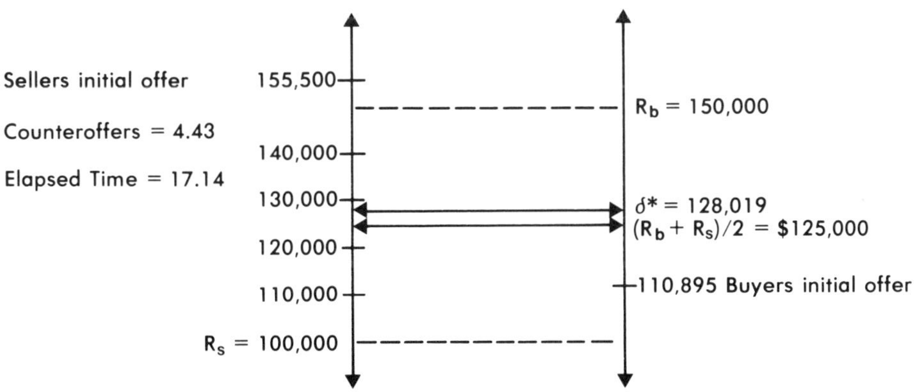

Fig. 4c. Seller noncontingent/buyer contingent.

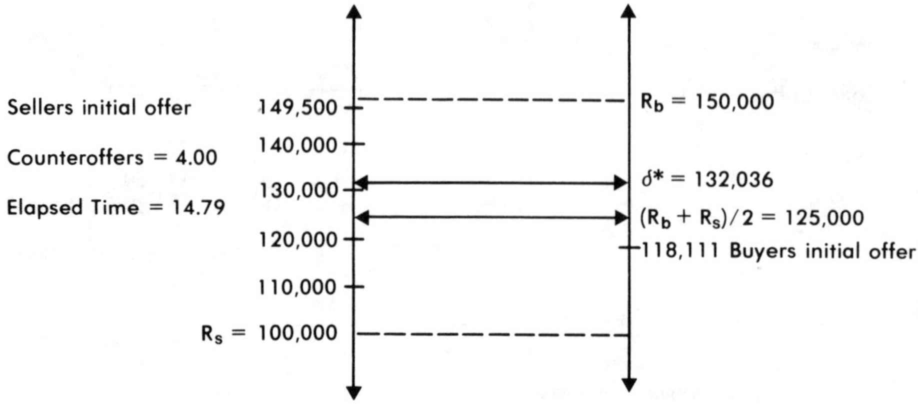

Fig. 4d. Seller noncontingent/buyer noncontingent.

settlement in that party's favor. When both parties are contingently rewarded, the result is a much longer and more difficult negotiation process.

This study, like much of the bargaining research, focused exclusively on price as the relevant criterion. While this is not always true of bargaining situations, the results of this study have three specific implications for understanding bargaining and negotiations, and helps to merge economic considerations with psychological variables. First, contingent rewards make a difference in negotiation outcomes. The reward practices that exist today in purchasing put the buying organization at a distinct disadvantage. Although the sales activity is essentially a mirror image of the buying activity, sales organizations have developed reward systems that motivate their personnel through compensation; purchasing organizations, for the most part, have not.

Second, purchasing organizations need to be aware of the salesperson's reward system. By knowing about the contingencies created for sellers, the buying organization can develop competing contingencies for its personnel where the efforts would have the greatest benefit. A purchasing representative also can take advantage of the seller's own motivation to maximize some element of the negotiation by seeking important concessions on other elements of the negotiation.

The third implication is that management must develop stronger contingencies to encourage purchasing effectiveness. This can be done by concentrating on the most critical areas of purchasing, recognizing the most important variables involved in the negotiations for any given purchase, and improving performance appraisal processes to reflect purchasing effectiveness in relation to the reward system.

5. A RICHER MODEL OF THE BUYER-SELLER INTERACTION

What should be clear by now is that, while both economics and psychology offer useful insight into bargaining and negotiation, a richer conceptual model of the buyer-seller interaction process is necessary. This model needs to capture both the economic and psychological aspects of the bargaining situation. To this end, we propose the adoption of the exchange model of industrial marketing developed by Bonoma and Johnston (1978).

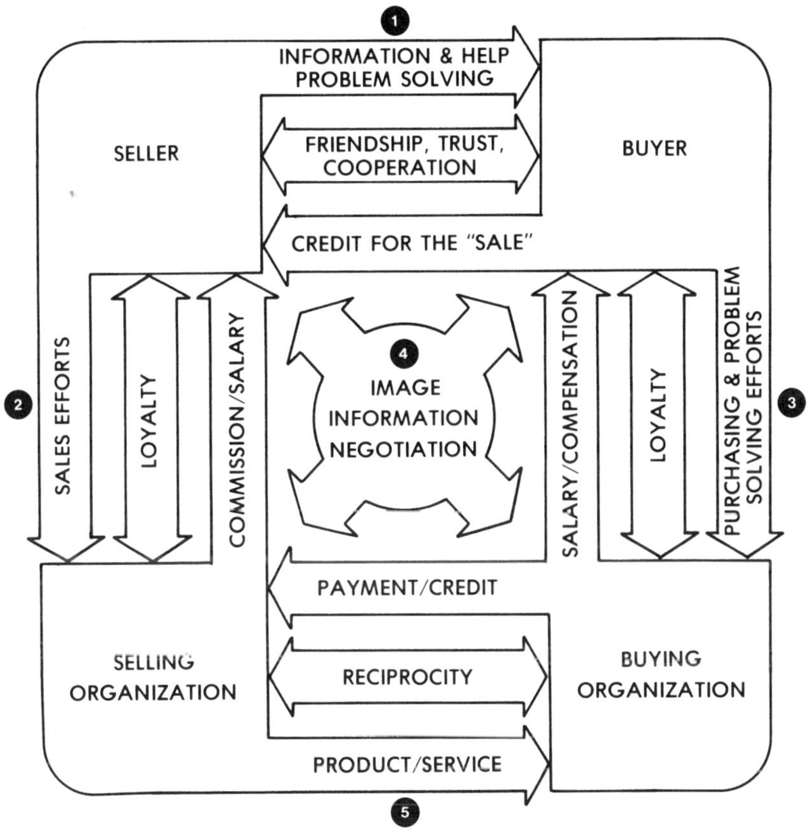

Fig. 5. Exchanges in buyer-seller interactions.
Adapted from Bonoma and Johnston (1978).

The exchange model of industrial marketing captures both the economic aspects and the surrounding psychological variables of the bargaining situation. It allows for the effects of constituents for both the buyer and seller, and permits contingency compensation for either side of the bargaining dyad. The model is built upon the relationships inherent in a bargaining situation and illustrates at least five major types of relations that can be affected by any bargaining interaction:

1. The *buyer-seller relationship* might be an exchange of information and help in problem solving on the part of the seller for credit for the specific "sale" given by the buyer. Cooperation, trust, and mutual liking are variables that can develop in a positive interaction between buyer and seller. The parties in the salespurchasing relationship usually share some values and have mutual interests. Each may want something the other has and can give or in some way be dependent. This mutuality of interests can take the form of alliances, coalitions, contract purchasing agreements, or other relationships.

   Conflict between the buyer and seller may also be a common variable. Just how conflict or disagreement over issues is resolved is a key subject for continued investigation. In situations, where a long-term relationship between parties is desired, mutual problem solving may be the appropriate conflict resolution mode. In other situations of a deteriorated nature, or where a "one time only" sale is sought, fraud and pressure to buy may be exchanged for future distrust.

   The dyadic relationship will invariably exhibit social influence attempts by the seller and the buyer. These social influences attempts can involve a number of strategies including the use of promises, threats, warnings, recommendations, and/or the control of information or other cues.
2. The *seller exchanges sales efforts with the selling organization* for money in the form of a commission or salary. Often there are side payments, such as a trip to the Bahamas, for meeting a special sales quota. Recognition and praise are also often exchanged for loyalty. This dyadic relationship has received considerable research effort. Sales territory allocation, compensation systems, sales force motivation, and sales force selection and management are all aspects of this particular dyad in the model.
3. The *buyer exchanges his/her talents and abilities of buying* and problem solving efforts with his/her organization for money, usually a salary. However, buyers are sometimes rewarded in the form of a percentage of the volume of purchases, or from a cost-savings perspective. The status that an organization awards the buyer, and that buyer's efforts and loyalty toward the organization, are further examples of exchanges that take place between the buyer and the buying organization. If the rewards that the buying organization is willing to exchange with the buyer seem insufficient to the buyer, s/he may look elsewhere for more rewarding exchanges, by moving to another organization or seeking to increase the rewards that accrue by accepting benefits from interested sellers.
4. *Images of the buying organization are held by the seller while the buyer harbors feelings and images about the selling organization.* The images held

by the buyer and other members of the buying organization have been examined frequently in the literature. However, the images held by the seller have received little attention. It would make sense to examine these perceptions because they determine what type of marketing approach or product characteristics the seller will emphasize to the buyer. Dyadic relations depend upon the individual actions and purposive behavior of the parties involved. The seller and the buyer have plans, goals, set ways of behaving, and intentions they hope to satisfy. Sometimes, these are the subject of negotiation. Invariably, they set restrictions on what is acceptable or not in an exchange and serve as the starting point for the interaction process. Clearly, each one's image of the other helps to establish the boundaries of the purchasing interaction.

5. The *primary economic exchange occurs between the buying and selling organizations,* where the product/service is exchanged for money or credit. Reciprocal trade relations or some form of appendix may develop between the two organizations. The supply and demand parameters of each individual bargaining situation dictate what type of interaction develops between buying and selling organizations.

Under this conceptual approach most purchases are better viewed as negotiated settlements between all individuals involved internally in the buying organization and those external to it (i.e., intermediate marketers, competing sellers, the government and the general public). These interactions lead to a purchase decision that is truly some social resultant of those interactive forces rather than any individual response. The outcome of these interactions also has economic and psychological consequences.

6. CONCLUSION

This chapter examines the important human interactions called bargaining and negotiation in a setting of personal selling. Bargaining occurs between individuals, groups, organizations, and countries. In this chapter we considered bargaining between two parties, each possessing resources the other side desires. Two party bargaining can be divided into two types: distributive and integrative. Distributive bargaining is a situation where the parties are in basic conflict and competition because of a clash of goals: The more one party gets, the less the other gets. Integrative bargaining is a situation where some areas of mutual concern and complementary interest exist. The situation is a varying-sum schedule such that by working together, both parties can increase the total profits available to be divided between them.

The distributive bargaining situation has been fully explored by psychologists. Economists, on the other hand, have spent most of their efforts in examining bargaining on integrative bargaining situations. A brief literature review was provided on distributive and integrative bargaining situations.

Next, an experiment in distributive bargaining was presented to better illustrate both effects of economic and psychological aspects on the outcome of bargaining situations. The experiment examines the effect of contingency compensation on both buyers and sellers. It also allows speculation about the differences in the power system of buyers and sellers and how they affect the outcome of bargaining situations.

The chapter ended with the introduction of an exchange model of industrial marketing, which captured both the economic aspects and the surrounding psychological variables of the bargaining situation.

NOTE

1. For more thorough reviews than space permits here, see either Chertkoff and Esser (1976) or Rubin and Brown (1975). This chapter relies, in part, upon the review by Chertkoff and Esser.

REFERENCES

Alderson, W., 1957, Marketing Behavior and Executive Action, Homewood, IL: Richard D. Irwin.

Bartos, O.J., 1966, "Concession making in experimental negotiations," in: J. Berger, M. Zelditch, and B. Anderson (eds.), Sociological Theories in Progress, Vol. 1, Boston, MA: Houghton Mifflin, pp. 3-28.

Bartos, O.J., 1970, "Determinants and consequences of toughness," in: P. Swingle (ed.), The Structure of Conflict, New York: Academic Press, pp. 45-68.

Benton, A.A., 1972, "Accountability and negotiations between group representatives," in: E. Mallinoff (ed.), Proceedings of the 80th Annual Convention of the American Psychological Association, Washington, DC: American Psychological Association, pp. 227-228.

Benton, A.A., H.H. Kelley, and B. Liebling, 1972, Effects of extremity of offers and concession rate on the outcomes of bargaining, Journal of Personality and Social Psychology, 24, 73-83.

Bonoma, T.V., and W.J. Johnston, 1978, The social psychology of industrial buying, Industrial Marketing Management, 17, 213-224.

Chertkoff, J.M., and S.L. Baird, 1971, Applicability of the big lie technique and the last clear chance doctrine to bargaining, Journal of Personality and Social Psychology, 20, 298-303.

Chertkoff, J.M., and J.K. Esser, 1976, A review of experiments in explicit bargaining, Journal of Experimental Social Psychology, 12, 464-486.

Edgeworth, F.Y., 1881, Mathematical Psychics: An Essay on the Application of Mathematics to the Moral Sciences, London: C. Kegan Paul.

Esser, J.K., 1975, Effects of Prior Success or Failure on Subsequent Bargaining, Bloomington, IN: Indiana University (unpublished doctoral dissertation).

Esser, J.K., and S.S. Komorita, 1975, Reciprocity and concession making in bargaining, Journal of Personality and Social Psychology, 31, 864-872.
Hamner, W.C., 1974, Effects of bargaining strategy and pressure to reach agreement in a stalemated negotiation, Journal of Personality and Social Psychology, 30, 458-467.
Ikle, F.C., and N. Leites, 1962, Political negotiation as a process of modifying utilities, Journal of Conflict Resolution, 6, 19-28.
Kelley, H.H., L.L. Beckman, and C.S. Fischer, 1967, Negotiating the division of a reward under incomplete information, Journal of Experimental Social Psychology, 3, 361-398.
Komorita, S.S., and A.R. Brenner, 1968, Bargaining and concession making under bilateral monopoly, Journal of Personality and Social Psychology, 9, 15-20.
Komorita, S.S., and J.K. Esser, 1975, Frequency of reciprocated concessions in bargaining, Journal of Personality and Social Psychology, 32, 699-705.
McFillen, J., R. Reck, and W.C. Benton, 1983, An experiment in purchasing negotiations, Journal of Purchasing and Materials Management, 19, 2-9.
Nash, J.F., 1950, The bargaining problem, Econometrica, 18, 155-162.
Neslin, S.A., and L. Greenhalgh, 1983, Nash's theory of co-operative games as a predictor of the outcomes of buyer-seller negotiations: An experiment in media purchasing, Journal of Marketing Research, 20, 368-379.
Rubin, J.Z., and B.R. Brown, 1975, The Social Psychology of Bargaining and Negotiation, New York: Academic Press.
Schelling, T.C., 1963, The Strategy of Conflict, New York: Oxford University Press.
Siegel, S., and L.E. Fouraker, 1960, Bargaining and Group Decision Making, New York: McGraw-Hill.
Von Neumann, J., and O. Morgenstern, 1944, Theory of Games and Economic Behavior, New York: John Wiley.

Part IV

The Societal Perspective

Introduction to Part IV: The Societal Perspective

In part IV of the Handbook, we turn to the societal perspective of economic psychology. The theoretical approaches were discussed in part I. Consumer and entrepreneur behavior have been dealt with in parts II and III, respectively. These topics were largely of an individual (micro) level. The topics of part IV, however, are micro and macro. How do consumer and business expectations affect spending, saving, and investment? Which persons evade taxation, and which measurement methods are used in tax research? Are work experiences and leisure patterns related? Could we integrate consumer, income and job satisfaction in a concept such as economic well-being? What are the social and psychological consequences of unemployment? And, how could we change consumer behavior in order to conserve natural resources?

Other societal issues could be mentioned than just these, for instance poverty in the western and in the third world, consumer problems, consumer policy, saving and credit, economic development, and investment behavior. This shows that a selection had been made among the possible issues and among prospective authors who could write a review chapter about the research on one of these issues. Although we, as editors, are satisfied with the chapters selected for this part, other chapters could have as good as or even better than the chosen ones.

Five aspects should be discussed in this introduction. First, research may contribute to a *better understanding of the societal* issues involved. One step further, research may help to find solutions to the issues, or, more modestly, may guide the policy of the government and business in these matters. The contribution from psychology pertains to the antecedent factors determining the societal issues, and the consequences for the individuals involved and society at large. For instance, which factors determine tax evasion, and what are the consequences, both for the tax evaders and for others? How do people experience unemployment, and how does this experience affect

Van Raaij, W.F., van Veldhoven, G.M. and Wärneryd, K.E. (eds) Handbook of Economic Psychology. ISBN 90-247-3720-6.

the search for work? Evaluation studies also belong to this aspect. How do people react to policy measures, and what are the intended and real effects of these measures?

A better understanding of the societal problems can be obtained *taking economic, psychological, and sociological variables into account.* Economic models often consider only the "rational" behaviors, i.e., the "best" one can do, ignoring that people have incomplete knowledge and ability, and insufficient willingness to behave in a rational manner. The "rational expectations hypothesis" is an extreme example of this approach (see Chapter 13). One may even argue that people are only rational under exceptional circumstances (extensive problem solving; see Chapter 2). Etzioni (1988) states that in most cases normative-affective approaches overrule rational-cognitive ones. Normative-affective approaches are not necessarily inferior to rational-cognitive ones. A psychological approach contributes to a better understanding, how people really behave.

A third aspect is the *micro-macro dimension.* Psychological research typically starts from the micro, individual-level approach, and often stays there (e.g., psychotherapy). Economic psychologists try to bridge the gap between the micro and the macro (societal) level (Van Raaij, 1984). From the measurement of individual behavior conclusions are drawn for the meso (groups and segments in society) and the macro level. The Index of Consumer Sentiment (Chapter 13) is a typical macro indicator measured at the micro level of the individual consumer or business person.

A fourth aspect is the mundane *reality of the economic world.* All, or at least most, people have income, consume, spend and save money and time, chose among alternatives, and try to make the best of it in this materialistic world of goods. The omnipresence and the high level of reality make economic behavior an attractive behavior for developing and testing hypotheses. The real world is the testing ground for economic psychologists, although they don't eschew the laboratory (see, e.g., Chapter 12). Respondents may sometimes hesitate to report their income, savings, and their tax payments, in most cases they are willing to inform us about their purchases, worries, and economic outlook.

Economic-psychological theories are up to now often borrowed from social and cognitive psychology. There is less development of *purely economic-psychological theories.* The combination of economic and psychological factors is, however, a promising area. It is likely that we will see theories develeoped in economic psychology, e.g., the macro-psychology of expectations and economic behavior, the perception of scarcity, and the cost concepts (out-of-pocket and oportunity costs) in economics and pychology.

Let us introduce the chapters that follow. In Chapter 13, Piet Vanden Abeele discusses consumer and business expectations. The concept of expectation is central in cognitive approaches in psychology and very relevant for economic behavior. He summarizes the research on the measurement of consumer and business expectations as sentiment indexes. These indexes partly explain and predict, in conjunction with economic variables, the spending, saving and borrowing of consumers, and the investments of business people.

Dick Hessing, Henk Elffers, Karyl Kinsey, and Russell Weigel (Chapter 14) review the societal problem of tax evasion, and describe several theoretical models of tax evasion behavior. They focus on the measurement strategies for tax evasion behavior, and recommend to collect unobtrusive (tax files) as well as self-report measures.

Gordon O'Brien describes in Chapter 15 the relationships between work experiences and leisure patterns. Three main hypothesis are identified: generalization, compensation, and segmentation. Work activities affect leisure, and this has implications for ecconomic theories of time allocation.

Theo Poiesz and Jasper von Grumbkov, in Chapter 16, relate consumer and worker satisfaction under the heading of economic well-being. They try to converge to a synthesis of the studies in the various fields of economic well-being, and relate this synthesis to practical considerations and recommendations.

Adrian Furnham reviews in Chapter 17 the psychological literature on unemployment. He emphasizes the attributions people make about the causes of unemployment, both of their own unemployment and that of others. The type of attribution may influence the consequent behavior, such as labor market activities. The deterioration of mental and physical health is a frequent consequence of unemployment.

In the last chapter (18), Fred van Raaij describes the consumer use of natural resources, i.e., goods, materials and energy. A behavioral model is proposed to encompass all relevant factors, and to point to policy measures to promote ecologically conscious consumption behavior and energy conservation.

W. Fred van Raaij

REFERENCES

Etzioni, A., 1988, Normative-affective factors: Toward a new decision-making model, Journal of Economic Psychology, 9, in press.

Van Raaij, W.F., 1984, Micro and macro economic psychology, Journal of Economic Psychology, 5, 385-401.

Table of Contents

13. Economic Agents' Expectations in a Psychological Perspective

PIET VANDEN ABEELE
Catholic University of Leuven, Leuven, Belgium

1. INTRODUCTION

A quick overview of the literature on the psychology of human behavior will reveal that the concept of expectation is a very central one for the explanation of real-life behavioral phenomena. This is true especially for cognitively oriented approaches, but also for behavioristic or learning approaches (e.g., Tolman's concept of expectation in learning theory). Since economic psychology, as an applied discipline, has real-life behavior as its concern, it is to be "expected" that the expectations concept plays a major role in this field. This chapter, which is devoted to the concept of expectations in economic psychology, will first explore the theoretical standing of the expectations concept in psychology, in economics and in economic psychology. Next, the operational aspects of measuring expectations and of using them in behavioral forecasts and control will be the concern.

2. EXPECTATIONS IN A PSYCHOLOGICAL PERSPECTIVE

Psychology is a discipline devoted to the scientific, objective registration of behavior in order to detect its empirical regularities. Next, models for these regularities are proposed and tested; if they prove acceptable, these models are used for the prediction and control of behavior. While psychology focuses on behavior it can, like other disciplines, apprehend its object with varying levels of detail. Human behavior can rather easily be isolated and studied as a separate category of observable phenomena, even though we know that it cannot occur independently of underlying biophysical or biochemical processes. Neither can disciplines such as economics or sociology proceed without acknowledging that the phenomena they study depend on the human behavior that underlies them.

Van Raaij, W.F., van Veldhoven, G.M. and Wärneryd, K.E. (eds) Handbook of Economic Psychology. ISBN 90-247-3720-6.

Micro- or molecular psychology studies the, often non-psychological (e.g., physiological), underpinnings of behavior by isolating component elements or processes; it often achieves high precision at the expense of mundane realism.

Macropsychology studies broader phenomena (e.g., social, societal, environmental) as they result, at least in part, from human behavior.

Molar psychology or "meso-psychology" studies complete behavioral phenomena as objects, which exist in their own right and therefore warrant abstraction or isolation from the wider context in which they occur or to which they give rise. In the sense of this distinction, economic psychology belongs, in many respects, to the category of macropsychology and feeds on molar psychology for its models and explanations.

Two features of molar behavior stand out: its temporal nature and its integration. The temporal nature of behavior is given relatively little emphasis in psychology. Yet, behavior appears as a sequence of acts, often displaying an orderly nature. Behavior occurs in time; it requires time. Since only a finite amount of time is available to every person, time may appear as the one inexorably binding constraint. Since behavior occurs in time, it has a past, a present and a future. Expectations occur in the present, point to the future and are shaped by the past. As a theoretical concept, they are invoked to account for the temporal integration of behavior.

The second feature of behavior is its integration, its coherence. Multiple concepts are used to account for behavior: motivation, perception, learning, etc. Yet, all these concepts are abstracted from the same behavioral data (Derbaix and Vanden Abeele, 1985). In observable behavior, these various aspects are naturally integrated. Our theoretical models for behavior reflect this by showing these diverse facets as mutually interacting and, even more, as feeding on the same latent or intervening variables or processes. The concept of an intervening variable such as an expectation is popular in psychology and, indeed, in economic psychology. An observed empirical regularity, consistency or coherence in varied behaviors is apprehended and abstracted by positing a hypothetical underlying variable or process. While such an intervening variable is only an abstraction, i.e., only exists by grace of the observables from which it is inferred, it helps scientific inquiry by making our models parsimonious and by guiding our attempts at operationalization.

Expectations, then, are only an abstraction, a hypothetical concept to account for the temporal integration observed in behavior. As they are only an abstraction, it matters to give a definition or to explore various definitions proposed for the term. Newcomb (1972) studies the definition of expectations and of related concepts (mainly in the domain of social psychology) and notes the following descriptions and comments in psychological dictionaries.

Expectancy: an intervening process variable, e.g., attitude or set, attributed to animals or men as parallel to what is subjectively experienced as an expectation; an acquired disposition whereby a response to a certain sign or object or cue stimulus is expected to bring about a certain other situation; it is not to be read subjectively; it is inferred from an animal's behavior. Expectancy theory holds that what is acquired in learning is a disposition to react to certain objects as signs for certain further objects.

Expectation: a tense and somewhat emotional attitude toward the prospect of a certain event. In the social psychological literature, Newcomb notes, the term expectancy emphasizes psychological states of set, involving some sort of preparatory adjustment to anticipated events or situations. There is some motivational or affective aspect in these, as the effects of disconfirmed expectations tend to show. The term expectation commonly refers to the content of what is expected. Expectation, however, is also commonly used in the literature on social interaction, where social norms and role refer to the expectations or assumed expectations of others regarding one's behavior.

These definitions are instructive in what they do and do not delineate. Any attempt to define a psychological concept exhaustively is beset by problems resulting from the avoidance of "type I" and "type II" errors. A definition which avoids the undue exclusion of some behavioral aspects will soon include all behavior; the property of behavior, as we noted indeed, is its integration and coherence. Definitions which are restrictive will be less satisfactory because they will soon be shown to exclude some aspects which could also be typical of many expectational phenomena. In our discussion below, we opt for definitions which are exclusive rather than all-embracing. Our definition will be built from the following considerations:

1. Expectations are acquired rather than innate. Since they are learned, they can be unlearned or changed. As a result, expectations have some variability (over time, objects, subjects, etc.).
2. Expectations belong to the category of intervening variables or attitudes. Attitudes are hypothetical constructs developed in order to account for the organization of inferent (perceptual, information acquiring) and efferent (action producing) behavior with regard to a particular class of objects. Expectations are therefore held with regard to particular objects ("object," here is to be understood in a broad sense and includes things, people, acts, states, etc). One may hold many expectations, corresponding to many objects. The object of expectations is located in the future and is therefore restricted to events or situations (one cannot "expect John," but one can expect John to come, John to be there, etc).
3. As expectations are held toward future events or objects and since our control of the environment is not perfect, expectations are inherently

characterized by uncertainty. Whether an expectation holds true appears only after the facts.

4. Expectations, like attitudes, may cover various behavioral aspects. In the traditional trimodal conception (Day, 1973) attitudes are assumed to cover cognitive aspects of behavior as well as emotional and conative (behavioral) aspects. An attitude is revealed by people knowing certain things about the object, by having certain feelings and by acting out certain behaviors toward it. Likewise, expectations are characterized by knowledge, evaluation and action. Although these components cannot be dissociated in real life, it helps to distinguish them for conceptual purposes, if we do not forget to put the puzzle back together at the time of application.

   The *knowledge* component of expectations consists of opinions as to what is to be expected. These opinions can be considered as associations between temporal or causal ("psycho"-logical) antecedents and consequences (if X happens, then Y will happen in the future; X today causes Y tomorrow). As we note below, one should not, as a rule, expect these associative linkages to be elaborate or sophisticated. Yet, since expectations refer to things still to occur, they may require recourse to an individual's representational and reasoning functions and therefore have a rather marked cognitive component. It matters, then, to investigate what people expect and why they expect it.

   The *feeling* component involves the evaluation of the expected event. While expectations are generally thought of as rather more cognitive and less affective, there is reason not to leave out affect altogether. Firstly, sufficient proof exists to support the concept of attitude as a tricomponent variable, which always involves knowledge, feeling and action when activated. Second, the cognitive component of attitudes, on closer inspection, is often very limited, leaving as it where "much room" for affective contents. Third, the expected events are not, as a rule, experienced as neutral. These events often carry with them strong positive or negative evaluations or will lead to expectation formation only if the related affect is sufficiently strong. Lastly, the expected events are often partially under the control of the person holding the expectation and may involve an active attempt to further or to ward off the oncoming of the event; this, again, implies an affective component for the expectation.

   The behavioral or *action* component refers to a tendency to prepare for or to control the event. Expectations can be held about events which have no obvious behavioral implication, but one may doubt that many such "gratuitous" expectations will be held in the normal walk of life.

5. As with attitudes, the definition does not imply that expectations should necessarily be experienced consciously. One can demonstrate that the human organism is capable of knowing about future events, to react

affectively to them and to exercise covert anticipatory action, outside of conscious awareness (Derbaix and Vanden Abeele, 1985). Broadening the definition of expectation to these phenomena, however, would lead us into such a broad area of study as to imperil our effort in the context of economic psychology. Rather than making the distinction between conscious and unconscious processes, we will adhere to the more novel differentiation between controlled and automatic processes. Controlled processes are those of which we are aware and which require the conscious mobilization and concentration of mental capacity in order to reason, judge and act. Controlled processes consume mental energy, have severely limited capacity and cannot occur in parallel (simultaneously). They are activated to cope with important and novel situations. But the reality with which we usually have to cope is that of constant, multiple, repetitive and less important demands upon our cognitive, affective and conative functions. Automatic processes, some innate, but many the result of overlearning, allow us to categorize and judge incoming stimuli upon only superficial analysis and to expedite behavior as a matter of routine. While these processes often operate unconsciously, they are by no means subconscious: They can be brought into conscious awareness (sometimes only by appropriate methods to make them conscious and fit for expression).

In accordance with Katona (1975), therefore, we allow for expectations activated under controlled processing ("original problem solving behavior") and under automatic processing ("habitual" or routine behavior). These "habits," however, are not merely habitual acts or action tendencies, but contain cognitive as well as affective elements. Cognitive habits, some more and others less conscious, have been discussed in psychology under such names as scripts, schemata, personae. These cognitive structures assist us in perceiving, organizing and interpreting our environment. Nisbett and Ross (1980) have shown that these cognitive habits usually serve us well in order to expedite our behavioral affairs efficiently; yet, they are far remote from scientific knowledge and may sometimes lead us astray. Further, individuals are often not aware of the knowledge structures they develop and of how these affect their thinking, feelings and action. One must conclude that particular care will be needed in order to "unearth" expectations belonging to this kind of cognitive structures. Cognitive structures of the "automatic" variety need not necessarily result from overlearning. Langer et al. (1978) has shown that new knowledge, acquired unintentionally or under low involvement (latent learning), may result in structures which will later be activated when they become relevant and which will organize knowledge, affect and action without deliberate attempts to consciously apprehend the novel situation.

> The reliance upon automatic affective processes is documented, e.g., in the consumer behavior literature, where feelings may have become functionally rather autonomous and where choices proceed on the basis of affect referral (Bettman, 1979).

Our previous comments allow us to venture the following definition of *expectations*:

> An expectation is an attitude with regard to a specific future event, which may or may not be under partial control of the person holding the expectation. The expectation organizes the individual's knowledge, evaluation and behavior, towards the future event in a consistent way. While initially often formed by means of conscious reasoning, the expectation many times functions as an automatic cognitive, affective and conative process.

The definition allows for some differentiation between types of expectations. A *contingent expectation* refers to future contingencies, i.e., events or situations over which the individual has no control. My expectation that there will be substantial solar flare activity next year, or that unemployment will increase, is a contingent expectation. Contingent expectations may differ from each other by the extent to which they are the result of reasoning or of overlearned habits, by the extent to which they are based on elaborate knowledge, etc. That expectations are contingent, i.e., deal with events beyond my control, does not confine them to the status of a pure opinion. Future contingencies may be threatening or desirable; they may have implications for the actions I should undertake. Some contingent expectations, of course, are fairly devoid of emotional or conative implications.

The extent to which events are under one's control is not only a matter of objective facts, but also of one's perception. The literature on the *locus of control* highlights the fact that the feeling of being in control of one's fate differs between people. Some expectations are held with respect to future events that one feels are, at least partially, under his control. If the personal control over the outcome is perceived as being significant, the expectation becomes an intention or *intentional expectation*. Related to the concept of intentional expectation are those of aspiration, goal and plan. We take a goal to refer to the nature or content of the intended outcome, whereas aspiration (level of aspiration) specifies more precisely the extent to which the goal-event is pursued. Plans are more specific than goals or aspirations; they refer to the actions to be undertaken in order to reach the target outcomes; they tend to specify target objects, moments, etc. Since intentional expectations relate to one's goal-directed behavior, we expect them to be relatively more affective and conative than contingent expectations.

Plans and goals commonly imply a controlled processing framework in which the individual takes conscious stock of his motives and constructs behavioral sequences which are expected to lead to the attainment of the desired outcome.

Normative expectations also refer to outcomes dependent on one's own behavior, namely the behavior one presumes (specific or generalized) others expect one to enact in a social context. The Theory of Reasoned Action (Ajzen and Fishbein, 1980) proposes normative expectations as one of the determinants of behavioral intention, i.e., of intentional expectation; the extent of determination depends on the motivation to comply.

Various concepts having been defined, it is only fair to warn the reader that these concepts or constructs have to be further developed. It is not because one defines goals and plans as different constructs that this distinction will also be validated by the facts. One central debate in economic psychology, for example, deals with the desirability of distinguishing between contingent and intentional expectations.

Having defined, or attempted to define, the notion of expectation, we should next consider

1. how expectations are formed, and
2. how they influence behavior.

These questions are best dealt with in the context of economics and of economic psychology.

3. EXPECTATIONS IN AN ECONOMIC PERSPECTIVE

3.1. *Introduction*

A quick inspection of the subject index of most economics textbooks will show that the concept of expectations is an integral part of economic theory. Economic behavior is decision behavior between alternative allocations of means in the face of scarcity. The allocation is influenced by the nature of the scarcity, e.g., income and prices in the case of consumption decisions. The decision problem of economic agents, i.e., producers or consumers, is resolved by assuming that they optimize some criterion. In the case of producer behavior the criterion is the maximization of profit; in the case of the consumer it is utility maximization. In his static analysis the economist assumes that the decisions, their outcomes and antecedents occur simultaneously. While static analysis suffices to derive some major economic insights, its framework is too restrictive to have mundane realism. In economic behavior, decisions often have to be made at one moment, while the outcomes or their determinants will only be known at some future time. The decisions are therefore characterized by a time perspective and by uncertainty. The dynamic aspect of economic behavior has been acknowledged in theoretical thinking about the consumer, but especially about the producer.

3.2 *Expectations and Producer Behavior*

Expectations play a role in theoretical models of multiple aspects of producer behavior. The most common reference probably is to the investment decisions of the firm. Investment, by definition, is an outlay whose returns will be spread over a number of future time periods. The profit-maximizing entrepreneur is assumed to invest only if the marginal return of the investment at least equates its marginal cost. The cost may be known today, but the future returns are uncertain. The entrepreneur, then, is assumed to form an expectation of future returns and to invest only if the expected marginal return exceeds the marginal cost. Many influences make for the uncertainty of the returns: the technological evolution, the general economic conditions, competitive actions, etc. For many investment projects, where the outlays are themselves spread in time, the investment costs are also uncertain and the subject of expectations. Investment spending has generally been considered an autonomous factor, in economics; this component of spending is also seen as a potent, but volatile determinant of macroeconomic equilibrium. Hence the interest which always existed for the assessment of investment-related expectations and for the study of their formation.

There are, in fact, two facets to investment-related expectations. First, there are the contingent expectations about the future returns of investment outlays. Second, there are intentional investment expectations. Investment decisions are usually major decisions which are carefully deliberated and require advance planning. Investment decisions can thus be observed in their "formative" stage as plans or intentions. Information concerning the latter can be of much use for producers of investment goods and for macroeconomic policy makers.

The temporal separation of outlay and return which holds in the case of investment decisions can also be observed for production decisions. The production and the sale of output very often do not occur simultaneously, so as to allow immediate adjustment of production to demand; in other cases, while production and sales may be concurrent, prior decisions will have to be made concerning the volume of output, so that discrepancies between production and demand are met by inventory changes, if at all. This shows that production decisions are often based on expectations concerning demand.

Profit is the difference between income and cost. If producer decisions are made on the basis of expected returns, they depend not only on future-income expectations but also on future-cost expectations. Expected cost decreases in the future, e.g., may lead to a delay in the making or implementation of decisions and vice versa.

Producer expectations are the clearest case of the intrusion of psychological concepts into economic reasoning. Economists have long considered these expectations as an exogenous factor, as a foreign body not amenable to economic analysis. As will be discussed below (cf. rational expectations), economics has since taken on the study of the formation of expectations.

3.3. *Expectations and Consumer Behavior*

The economic theory of consumer behavior has little use for an expectations concept. This is largely the result of an approach to consumption as passive and static. It is seen as passive, to the extent that consumption is seen as determined mainly by income which is assumed to be exogenous to the consumer's decisions. It is seen as static, since the consumer's decision span is confined to the ongoing period.

In the conception of a passive and static consumer decision making process, expectations are relevant only in the case of very short and acute episodes. The concept of inflationary expectations, coupled with inflation hysteria and hoarding, for example has always been popular. Such bouts of inflation were seen as short-lived, since inflation hysteria is a self-fulfilling and self-liquidating prophecy.

Gradually, however, as consumer well-being increased, a dynamic, multiperiod view of consumption behavior emerged. The consumer increases the time-span of his decisions by being able to accumulate future wealth. The dynamic consumer is viewed as planning his life-time consumption and as balancing his needs and means over his lifetime. Expectations are very central to the multiperiod consumption decision. The maximization of an intertemporal utility function assumes a consumer able to gauge the satisfaction derived from future consumption. Since present consumption decisions may not always provide a clue as to the utility of future consumption, a new field opens up in which the formation of future utilities, of aspirations, is to be investigated. The more recent attention for economic well-being and for *quality of life* research exemplifies the quest for such knowledge (Strümpel, 1976).

The dynamic consumer is assumed to form expectations not only on future utilities, but also on future means and on future scarcity. His consumption during a period is constrained by his wealth, not by his income in the period, and ex ante lifetime wealth is a psychological concept akin to an expectation (e.g., the concept of "permanent income"). Future scarcity translates into price expectations, price level expectations, inflation expectations, interest rate expectations, etc.

The multiperiod consumer who plans his lifetime consumption can further be seen as formulating intentional expectations. While there appears to be much opportunity for introducing expectations-based concepts in consumption analysis, relatively little formal work has been done in this area. A possible reason lies in the idea that consumer expectations, unlike entrepreneurial expectations, are to be considered as idiosyncratic variables, exerting only a random effect on behavior and cancelling out in the aggregate. Barring contrary evidence, consumer expectations can then be dismissed as irrelevant to economic analysis. As one knows, economic psychology brings much evidence to bear on this point.

3.4. *The Formation of Expectations*

Economic theory has gradually striven to slim down its models by relaxing the most restrictive assumptions and by appealing as little as possible to unobservable variables. It proceeds in a hypothetical-deductive way.

Expectations concepts in economics go counter to this tendency towards parsimony, by requiring the addition of new variables (expectations) which do not belong to the category of readily observable and objectively measurable constructs. It is not surprising then, that economic theory attempts to deal with the expectations phenomenon in a hypothetical-deductive rather than in an empirical inductive way. Economic psychology proceeds by asking the question of what expectations are and how they influence behavior. Economists are rather inclined to ask what expectations should optimally be and how they should optimally affect behavior. Their next effort is to study empirically whether registered expectations and expectation-induced behaviors sustain the hypotheses.

The *Theory of Rational Expectations* covers a diverse body of research approaches embodying the latter approach. It is at times very complex and mathematically involved and it lies outside the scope of this contribution to review or to criticize this subfield of economics. Stated succinctly, the Theory of Rational Expectations formulates the following hypotheses (Muth, 1961):

1. Rational (i.e., good) expectations should be such that they allow a perfect or at least a good forecast of future events. If they are not, in fact, functional in making good forecasts, there is no reason, in an evolutionary sense, to rely on such expectations and thus to form them.
2. Rational expectations will be based on all available knowledge concern-

ing the future event. If some important information were available at the moment of formulating expectations and if that information were not incorporated into them, then a better, more rational expectation could be formed. As a result of the attempt to optimize, of learning from one's own successes and mistakes in the past, the economic agent's expectations will become rational.

3. If rational expectations contain all the information that is predictive of the future event (i.e., the predictors and the predictive relationship), both future events and the expectations should bear identical functional relationships to the predictors. If the relationship between predictors and future events can be described and shown to be the same as that between predictors and expectations, there is no reason to measure expectations directly any more. Expectations can then be replaced by some fixed function of past and contemporaneous "observable" or "objective" variables.

The Theory of Rational Expectations is an excellent demonstration of the scientific method of economic research. Many a behavioral scientist gets upset by what is perceived as a blatant attempt to negate subjective elements and the possibility of not strictly rational behavior.

It should be pointed out that the Rational Expectations Theory is just a theory, i.e., a set of hypotheses awaiting falsification. Very few, if any, alternative theories are available concerning the formation and properties of expectations. In addition, the theory is a very elegant, parsimonious one and its rejection, as well as its non-rejection have clear and important implications. The Theory of Rational Expectations should be rejected on the basis of objective, empirical testing rather than on the basis of subjective prejudice.

This theory is one of the few, if not the only one, to grapple with the question of how expectations are formed and how this formation relates to past and present information. The student of expectations may have the secret hope that s/he will discover expectations components that are highly predictive of the future, yet unrelated to the past. Expectations surveys would then become "crystal balls." We trust that few would rely on this crystal ball component, until they understood why it predicts and how it is formed.

4. EXPECTATIONS IN PSYCHOLOGICAL ECONOMICS

4.1. *Introduction*

If social psychology has at times been defined as the study of attitudes, then economic psychology could, at a certain time, have been defined as the study of consumer expectations. George Katona can safely be credited as the scientist, who brought the study of expectations to fruition in the context of consumption economics by reflecting on the impact and formation of such expectations.

4.2. *The Impact of Consumer Expectations*

As we noted above, expectations have a long history in economic thinking, but were mostly reserved to the business sector of the economy. In contrast, the consumption sector was viewed as relatively limited in its decision autonomy. The consumer's spending decision was viewed as a periodic decision derived automatically from the period income. The composition of the periodic consumption package, likewise, derived mainly from income through the operation of Engel's law. Katona rightfully points to the substantial degree of consumption autonomy in the affluent society of the 20th Century West. The consumption autonomy is related mainly to the following observations:

1. *Discretionary income*: A substantial number of spending units have periodic income in excess of vital consumption and saving requirements. The margin of disposable over vital income is called "discretionary" because of the wide decision latitude it allows. Discretionary income can be freely spent or saved. If it is to be spent, the time of spending and the object on which one will spend are becoming gradually less dependent on income. At least from the perspective of the spending unit, the periodic income is not entirely given. The amount of income disposable for the period can be influenced by the spending unit. More (or less) income can be earned by working more, or differently. The income can be supplemented by borrowing from past or future savings
2. *Time perspective in consumption*: The decision autonomy expands into future periods. This is due on the one hand to the possibility of saving and dissaving. On the other hand, there are consumption projects which span the boundaries of several consumption periods. This becomes especially clear in consumption projects involving consumer investment in durable goods. Durable goods, by their very nature, involve multi-period consumption and outlays.

   Since consumer investments are lumpy and represent major non-repetitive outlays, they tend to occur as the result of careful deliberation and planning. Major consumer expenditures can therefore be observed ex ante from many preparatory activities. The elements discussed above make that a number of consumer decisions, the so-called discretionary decisions (spending or saving), are autonomous rather than lawfully dictated by contextual conditions. Even if this autonomy does not hold over the life-span, where consumer spending and saving will necessarily bear some relationship to lifetime wealth, it will at least hold for shorter time spans. Discretionary consumer decisions, both individually and in the aggregate, can therefore display some volatility. Inspection of economic series shows that aggregate discretionary spending and saving series do indeed display substantial fluctuations. Katona (1975) concludes that such discretionary behavior is determined not only by enabling factors, by the ability to engage in discretionary behavior, but also by the willingness to engage in it. The latter willingness is seen as an underlying variable, as an attitude. An attitude, we have seen, is an intervening variable organizing knowledge, affect and action with regard to a category of objects. If it is to be useful as an hypothetical construct, it requires that one specify its domain. In Katonian thinking, the purpose is not to predict individual discretionary consumer decisions of a very specific nature, e.g., whether family X will purchase a dishwasher. Rather, Katona is interested in forecasting the evolution of the aggregate in broad categories of spending or saving over the typical span of the business cycle. His attitude concept should therefore allow generalization across households, across specific saving or spending instances and have a variability commensurate with that of the business cycle.

Survey research shows that consumers hold such attitudes. These are not very elaborated cognitively but center on a rather unifactorial optimism/pessimism dimension with affective overtones. They have the property of energizing or of inhibiting discretionary behavior.

Since much discretionary behavior has a future-time perspective to it, the optimism/pessimism dimension also has an expectational characteristic. In the Katonian theory, therefore, expectations have a very straightforward impact on behavior: The attitude of optimism/pessimism has the effect of eliciting or of inhibiting the discretionary behavior which is made possible by the enabling conditions. It should be stressed that relatively little emphasis was put, in economic psychology, on the exact nature of the processes by which expectations actually influence behavior.

Our discussion stresses mainly the role of attitudinal variables in the determination of cyclical spending/saving variations. A part of Katonian economic psychology is devoted to the more structural impact of attitudes, expectations and aspirations. This aspect falls outside the scope of this contribution.

4.3. *The Formation of Expectations in Economic Psychology*

Katona's distinction between habitual behavior and original problem solving behavior is applicable to the formation and working of expectations. These, like behavior, have a tendency to persist and to become routine. They provide stable structures for organizing incoming information and for expediting behavior efficiently. Only when it dawns upon the individual that the attitudes and expectations he holds are at odds with the new circumstances and that the routinely applied behavior is inappropriate, does he proceed to the task of formulating new attitudes and expectations. The individual is then out to find information and an organization for that information which allow him to make sense out of the new situation and to produce new and more appropriate behaviors.

Katona describes this process as one which occurs very much in *social interaction*: The relevant pieces of information and the appropriate organization are handed by the social environment, filtered and amplified by it. The result of this process is not only cognition which is socially determined, but an attitude which is socially homogeneous. Not only are new attitudes and expectations formed by households, but the same attitudes and expectations are acquired. These underlying variables can then no longer be dealt with as idiosyncratic information which becomes irrelevant when considered in the aggregate. Rather, homogeneous attitudes and expectations make for societal waves of optimism and pessimism with a noticeable impact on aggregate behavioral phenomena (spending, saving).

As above, we do not discuss the formation of longer-term and structurally more relevant attitudes and expectations, but rather limit ourselves to the components of cyclical relevance.

Katonian economic psychology provides us with an impressive contribution on the processes that rule over the acquisition of attitudes and expectations. Yet, the focus is more on how they are acquired than on what is acquired. As a result, very precise and testable hypotheses, such as offered by the Rational Expectations Theory are missing.

5. THE MEASUREMENT OF ATTITUDES, EXPECTATIONS AND INTENTIONS

5.1. *Introduction*

There is an abundant literature on the measurement of attitudes, and a lot of it certainly is relevant to the topic of measuring consumer or producer attitudes in studies with an emphasis on cyclical economic variations. Some specific properties of economic-psychological studies have to be taken into account, however

1. Economic psychology is applied psychology with a concern for the collection of information that is relevant for macroeconomic policy-making. This leads to an overriding concern for the representativeness of the results.
2. Economic attitudes and expectations are generally rather less involving topics for the modal citizen. It is not so likely that an individual will attempt to conceal or to distort his opinions and feelings when interrogated about his expectations concerning the future course of the economy. Rather, the problem may be that his opinions, feelings and plans are inarticulate and that he will need some assistance to express them.
3. Attitudes and expectations can be measured in a number of ways, ranging from structured through unstructured and from obtrusive to unobtrusive. The nature of economic attitudes/expectations and the need to collect the observations quickly on an extensive sample makes the unstructured or unobtrusive methods less viable and compels one to use structured, undisguised and very expedient observation methods.

The measurement methodology will therefore usually have the following characteristics:

1. The observations are made with rather large respondent samples. Large samples have the advantage of leading to reliable aggregate results and to allow studies in subsamples of comfortable size. The sample should be representative of its universe. Representativeness is achieved by size on the one hand and by randomness on the other. Representativeness is further enhanced by specific provisions for the replacement of refusals, not-at-homes, etc. Unfortunately, large representative samples are costly. Various sampling schemes have been developed to guarantee unbiased results, while allowing the researcher to trade off cost and reliability of results.
2. The observation of attitudes is normally based on verbal self-reports elicited by means of scales in structured questionnaires. Verbal self-reports assume that the respondent is willing to report his attitudes and able to do so verbally. As stated, we think that the willingness may be less of a problem than the ability. Suitable psychometric methods, however, exist to assist in the elicitation of attitudes in a reliable and valid way. The scales typically used in economic-psychological research have only a low level of psychometric sophistication. They are often rather crude, based on single or few items and have not been developed in the typical psychometric tradition. On the other hand, crude scales are easy to administer. Modifying them could also jeopardize the continuity of the research, the value of which depends much on the availability of sufficiently homogeneous long time series.

3. Economic attitudes and expectations are measured by means of interviews. Personal interviews are conducted at the home of the respondent or by means of telephone surveys. Nonpersonal interviewing is carried out by mail. The advantages, disadvantages and intricacies of each type of interview is well documented in most research handbooks. Suffice to say that several studies have revealed a significant method component in survey results, so that it pays to consider the potential biases of the method a priori. Further, questionnaire studies give rise to numerous error sources, starting with erroneous answers by the respondent up to errors in the transformation of responses into machine-readable codes. Any serious survey operation will therefore soon experience the necessity to install a quality control procedure on the data at the various stages of its manipulation.

5.2. *The Measurement of Consumer Attitudes, Expectations and Intentions*

Having considered the general research design for the gathering of consumer or producer attitudes, expectations and intentions, our attention now shifts to specific operationalizations. Since various existing operationalizations are rather similar, we will use concrete examples when useful and avoid the straight enumeration and comparison of alternative operationalizations.

Consumer attitudes and expectations are measured by means of responses to such items as:

> "What do you think the general economic situation of the country is going to be 12 months from now as compared to today?"
> (A lot better, a little better, the same, a little worse, a lot worse, don't know).
> "Why do you think so?"

Table 1 contains the content of the questions, the response scales (and the weights applied to the percentage response in each category in order to obtain an average score), for the EC Survey of Consumer Attitudes.

Several comments on these items are in order:

1. There is no compelling reason why precisely these items and only these appear in the survey. As we have stated, the survey of economic attitudes and expectations is not the result of a typical psychometric program to develop constructs, validate scales, etc. The items appearing in Table 1

Table 1. European Community Consumer Survey.

The questions asked in the EC Consumer Survey and the Consumer Confidence Index are listed below.

The numbers in parentheses are the weights given to each percentage response to obtain the average answer to each question.

- Financial situation of your household now compared to 12 months ago?
- Financial situation of your household, prospects over the next 12 months?
- General economic situation in the country now compared to 12 months ago?
- General economic situation in the country, prospects over the next 12 months?

For the above four questions the possible responses are: a lot better (+ 1), a little better (+ 1/2), the same (0), a little worse (– 1/2), a lot worse (– 1), don't know.

- Price levels now compared to 12 months ago? Much higher (+ 1), moderately higher (+ 1/2), a little higher (0), about the same (– 1/2), lower (– 1), don't know.
- Price trends over the next 12 months? More rapid increase (+ 1), same increase (+ 1/2), slower increase (0), stability (– 1/2), fall slightly (– 1), don't know.
- Unemployment level in the country over the next 12 months? Increase sharply (+ 1), increase slightly (+ 1/2), remain the same (0), fall slightly (– 1/2), fall sharply (– 1), don't know.
- Major purchases (furniture, washing machine, TV, etc.) at present? Yes, right time (+ 1), neither right nor wrong time (0), wrong time, should postpone (– 1), don't know.
- Major purchases next 12 months compared to last 12 months? Much more (+ 1), a little more (+ 1/2), the same (0), a little less (– 1/2), much less (– 1), don't know.

- Savings at present, a reasonable time to save?
- Savings by you or your household over the next 12 months?

For the above two questions the possible answers are: yes, certainly (+ 1), yes, perhaps (+ 1/2), probably not (– 1/2), certainly not (– 1), don't know.

- Financial situation of households at present-financial asset accumulation? Borrowing (– 1), drawing on savings (– 1/2), just making ends meet (0), saving a little (+ 1/2), saving a substantial amount (+ 1), don't know.

The *Index of Consumer Sentiment (ICS)* is an arithmetic average of the answers to the four questions on the financial situation of households and general economic situation (past and future) together with that on the advisability of making major purchases.

are included mainly on the basis of their face validity. The same holds with respect to the response categories and their weights.

2. The items tap a fair number of different aspects in consumer attitudes and expectations. The questionnaire can be said to "sample" from the domain of interest. In particular, some items involve an assessment of the present situation (commonly referred to as "evaluation") and some an assessment of the future situation ("expectation").

3. Several items require a comparison, e.g., of the present and the past or of the future and the present. The responses to these items are therefore detrended or without level: When consumers report that they expect a sharp improvement in economic conditions, the expected level of economic activity could still be very unsatisfactory to them. It is important to keep this property in mind when attempting to relate consumer attitudes to economic variables: Detrended consumer responses should be used to predict differences between observed economic magnitudes rather than to predict their level.
4. Each response scale allows for a "don't know" category. The EC results are reported after having redistributed these responses over the other categories in proportion to their relative frequency. As usually in scaling studies, one can only guess the real meaning of a "don't know." It has been suggested that a high percentage of such answers is indicative of high uncertainty among the respondents and that this uncertainty (more than or in addition to the extent of pessimism) is an indicator of certain behaviors. The issue is unresolved as yet and remains one for empirical verification.
5. The structured questions can be complemented by a further probe as to the reason for one's answer, for the reasoning behind one's response. This further information is collected in a semi-structured or unstructured way. It is said to add much diagnostic, insight-stimulating data to the structured response. The reason given for one's answer, its quality and depth, could add a lot to the researcher's understanding, interpretation and predictive use of the more quantifiable information.

Item batteries such as those in Table 1 naturally lead to the question of the interrelationship between these items, e.g., of the factorial structure underlying their correlation matrix. A repeated multinational survey such as the EC consumer survey allows the computation of a multiplicity of correlation matrices between the items. The basic data matrix consists of the individual responses to the items given by the respondents in a given country at a particular time (with N countries and T time periods, there are NT such data matrices). Starting from these basic data matrices, several new matrices can be derived by pooling them or by computing averages, giving rise to new correlation matrices.

Factor analyses of correlation matrices computed from aggregate time series data have been performed by various researchers. These correlation matrices contain a substantial number of very pronounced correlations and only a very small proportion of insignificant ones. As a result, the first two principal components in the analysis (and often, but not systematically for each country participating to the EC survey, the first component) account for a very high percentage of total variance (depending on the country, from about 65% to about 85%). It is an important finding that five items usually load highly on the first factor or component, namely those relating to the general economic and personal financial situation and the item concerning the evaluation of the present situation for major purchases. These items, indeed, are often selected for the construction of a synthetic index (see below).

Factor analyses of cross-sectional data, as expected, show a less pronounced factorial structure as a result of the relatively low reliability of the individual responses. Still, there is a predominance of one factor which accounts for some 20% of total variance and which tends to regroup the items concerning the general economic and personal financial situation. Other factors typically regroup items according to their key topics: saving, prices, purchasing, etc. While further tests are required, the latter factors could be the result of semantic rather than of substantial causes. The first factor obtained from cross-sectional results is rather congruous with that obtained in longitudinal studies.

The factor analyses discussed above bear a relationship to both theoretical and pragmatic issues.

- On the pragmatic side, high correlations between aggregate time series of the items make for collinearity problems when dependent variables are regressed on attitudinal and expectational variables. A common fixture to resolve this problem is to regress the dependent variable on the principal components of the original regressors. Alternatively (and more meaningful intuitively) there is the practice of using as regressors one or the sum of several items most strongly associated with the principal components.
- On the theoretical side, the items in the consumer survey constitute a "test battery" which can be investigated for its underlying structure. In the analysis of psychological test batteries an important question is the unidimensionality of the items or at least the predominance of one factor. Although the conclusions differ according to the set of items analyzed, the country and the time period, there is a fair degree of evidence in support of such a unifactorial interpretation, certainly in longitudinal data. We believe this to be a confirmation of the original thought in economic psychology, namely that consumer attitudes/expectations are a rather less elaborate or differentiated domain, so that separate items are just samples from the domain of interest, each one tapping the same underlying disposition. While each item is representative of the underlying construct, it is possible that separate items load on it to a different extent, or even that these loadings are time-varying. The underlying optimism/pessimism construct could therefore best be operationalized as a weighted sum of the most representative items, eventually with time-varying weights.

It is common for consumer attitude surveys to provide one synthetic index, the "*Index of Consumer Sentiment*" as a combination of the responses to various items. This practice is parallel to that of using summated scales in testing, since such summated scales are presumably more reliable and more valid. In the EC consumer surveys, an index of consumer sentiment is computed as the unweighted arithmetic average of the answers to the items concerning the general economic situation, the personal financial situation and concerning the appropriateness of the situation for major purchases ("market conditions"). The Index of Consumer Sentiment (ICS), in fact, is the single most used and most referred to piece of information. The ICS weighs its component items equally and constantly over time. While one could regret the latter, it is also true that the correlation between equally weighted and differentially weighted-time variant averages is close to 1.O under normal conditions. Besides, the problem of assigning differential (especially time-varying) weights is not trivial. If the weights are actually time-variant, but hard to obtain, the unweighted average solution provided by ICS-type statistics may be the most expedient and satisfactory approach.

The scaling of the responses to individual items is usually resolved arbitrarily, e.g., according to the EC coding scheme in Table 1. The aggregate response to the item is then obtained as the weighted average response, the weights being the proportions in each response category. This aggregate has the advantage of summarizing the data but does, of course lead to the loss of the original information. The following two distributions of responses, for instance, lead to the same aggregate figure.

15%	0%	70%	0%	15%
a lot better	a little better	the same	a little worse	a lot worse
(+2)	(+1)	(0)	(−1)	(−2)
50%	0%	0%	0%	50%

This leads to the question of which summary statistic is to be used and which additional statistics are required in order to reflect the remaining information. When there are n response categories (e.g., 5 in the example above), constrained by their relative frequencies having to sum to 100%, at least (n − 1) independent pieces of information can be used.

Several statistics can be suggested instead or in addition to the weighted average:

1. Use n − 1 independent response categories. This has the advantage of preserving all information. The disadvantage is that many variables have to be dealt with and that these will tend to be collinear because of the sum constraint on the n categories.

2. Use the modal answer category. The mode disregards the distribution of answers, while it expresses the majority opinion. The modal opinion may be only slightly dominant, however. Additionally, it is not unusual in survey research, to always find the mode on the uncommitted category, thus eliminating any useful variance in the series.
3. Use the percentage of "uncertain" or "no change" answers. The relative frequency of such answers may be indicative of impending shifts in the direction (positive or negative) of opinions. It may be used to accentuate or to attenuate the direction expressed in the other answer categories. On the other hand, this percentage does not in itself give an indication of the direction of opinions.

Our general position is that the results are best expressed by an index which summarizes most of the available information, while giving an indication of direction. In this respect, the overall weighted average or a (weighted) balance of positive and negative opinions are favored. In addition, two further statistics may be useful, one to indicate the concentration or dispersion of opinions (e.g., the standard deviation or some measure for departure from a uniform distribution), another to indicate the relative frequency of uncommitted answers.

These additional statistics can be used in two ways at the analysis stage, i.e., when expectations attitudes are used to explain or predict some other variable: They can be entered as additional explanatory variables in their own right or they can be used to moderate the impact of the major statistic on the dependent variable (e.g., as components of a variable regression coefficient or as a variable weight on the major index).

The scaling itself of the response categories of an item, as we noted, is arbitrary. The numbers which have been assigned, e.g., "a lot better = + 2," or the intervals between those numbers do not necessarily correspond to the underlying psychological intensities. More appropriate values could be derived by using appropriate scaling methodologies (e.g., Thurstone equal-appearing interval scaling) or by resorting to logit or probit type models (Hanssens and Vanden Abeele, 1986).

The measurement of *consumer buying intentions* involves the registration of an intentional expectation. This requires that the attitudinal object be explicitly described. In the case of consumer purchases, it will be necessary to specify the object and the time span of the purchase very clearly. This specificity may mislead one to think that the measurement will be easier for intentions than for attitudes, since intentions are presumed to be more conscious and tangible.

Measuring whether someone is planning the purchase of a major item looks simple, since he will either entertain such plans or not. The planning variable could therefore presumably be measured by means of a dichotomous “yes I do,” “no I do not.” Problems arise when doing so, however, because respondents do not always experience the extent of planning as a dichotomy, but rather as an ordinal multichotomy (“yes certainly,” “yes most likely,” “yes perhaps,” etc.); further, it appears that many respondents categorizing themselves as not planning, do nevertheless purchase the item considered. Indeed, the majority of purchases in a market may be due to non-planning respondents. If one is not measuring the occurrence of plans, strictly spoken, what then is one measuring? Someone who is not explicitly planning a purchase, may still entertain a vague intention to purchase. There may be an aspiration rather than a plan. Another suggestion is that, irrespective of whether one is planning or not, s/he may still have a feeling for the (subjective) probability of making a given purchase within a given time period.

The *U.S. Survey of Consumer Buying Expectations* measures (or rather measured, since the survey has been discontinued; see McNeil, 1974) the subjective probability of buying using the scale shown in Table 2.

Table 2. Scaling of intentional expectations in the U.S. Survey of Consumer Buying Expectations and in the EC Consumer Survey.

U.S. Survey	(scale value)	EC Survey	(scale value)
Absolutely certain to buy	10	Yes, certainly	1,0
Almost certain to buy	9	Yes, perhaps	0,5
Much better than even chance	8	Probably not	0,3
Somewhat better than even chance	7	Certainly not	0
Slightly better than even chance	6	Don’t know	0,3
About even chances (50-50)	5		
Slightly less than even chance	4		
Somewhat less than even chance	3		
Much less than even chance	2		
Almost no chance	1		
Absolutely no chance	0		

The same table also shows the scale for the questions in the *EC survey.* The latter asks for respondent intentions to buy selected items within the next 2 years.

Since the respondents can be assumed to report a psychological intensity similar to a subjective probability, and since probabilities are measured on better than an interval scale, one presumes that the scores or scale values could be important in making a forecast of the sales volume to be expected. The possibility exists for checking the actual percentage of purchasers among the respondents giving each answer in order to assign to that answer a value which is as close as possible to the "objective" probability of the realization of intentions.

As a final note concerning the measurement of intentions, one should note that there has been a rather intense debate between the proponents of contingent expectations measures and the proponents of intentions measures. The latter based their preference for intentions variables on the more tangible and hence more face-valid nature of plans as indicators for future purchasing and on the more detailed, i.e., more object-specific nature of the information thus obtained. In the view of the former, planning variables are usually not what they indicate at their face value. Explicit plans appear only late in the decision process and do not occur with high frequency. Their precise elicitation misleadingly suggests that they are a hard forecast of a specific purchase in the future. Consumer plans, unlike entrepreneurial investment plans, are vague and provisional. They are at most an indicator of optimism, of willingness to buy and should certainly not be interpreted as point forecasts. The experience with intentions surveys seems to have been in favor of the latter view.

5.3. *The Measurement of Business Attitudes, Expectations and Intentions*

Business people are presumably more rational, or at least more conscious decision makers, pondering over the future and taking appropriate actions in order to prepare for it. One should therefore expect business attitudes, expectations and intentions to be more explicit, aware and the subject of explicit or even quantified planning.

In view of the importance given to the business sector, both in theory and in practice, business surveys have since long been conducted in many countries with often high periodicity. Moreover, the results are made available in much detail (e.g., by industrial sector), not only to report future trends but also to obtain a timely and detailed appraisal of the recent evolution.

Table 3 shows the content of the *EC Business Survey*, which is compiled on the basis of mail interviews with some 20,000 business firms every month. The survey comprises both evaluation questions (assessment of the present situation) and expectation questions. The information is mostly collected in a qualitative way, i.e., by means of multiple choice responses over ordered categories; some other questions require a quantified assessment. Several evaluation questions imply a report of facts rather than of evaluative judgments. It should also be noted that the expectations refer to a rather short term future and have a strong intentional, rather than contingent nature. Still it is an empirical question whether the expectations (and even the evaluations) are a report of forecasted or present facts rather than mere indicators of a general attitude or mood of optimism/pessimism.

The EC survey of business attitudes, expectations and intentions is only

Table 3. European Community Business Survey.

The questions asked in the EC Business Survey are listed below.

Industry survey

Monthly questions:

1. Production trend in recent months: up, unchanged, down?
2. Order-books: above normal, normal, below normal?
3. Export order-books: above normal, normal, below normal?
4. Stocks of finished products: above normal, normal, below normal?
5. Production expectations for the months ahead: up, unchanged, down?
6. Selling price expectations for the months ahead: up, unchanged, down?

Bi-annual questions (carried out in June/July and October/November):

7. Employment expectations for the months ahead: up, unchanged, down?

Questions asked three times a year (carried out in January/February, June/July and October/November):

8. Limits to production: none, insufficient demand, shortage of labour, lack of equipment?

Quarterly questions (carried out in January, April, July and October):

9. Production capacity: more than sufficient, sufficient, not sufficient?
10. Duration of assured production (in months)?
11. New orders in recent months: up, unchanged, down?
12. Export expectations for the months ahead: up, unchanged, down?
13. Capacity utilization (in percentage)?
14. Stocks of raw materials: high, normal, low?

Investment Survey

Bi-annual questions (carried out in March/April and October/November):

- Investment trends and prospects: annual percentage change of investment expenditure at current prices.

Building Survey

Monthly questions (except for France and the United Kingdom, where the survey is carried out quarterly):

1. Trend of activity compared with preceding months: up, unchanged, down?
2. Limits to production: bad weather, shortage of manpower, lack of equipment, none?
3. Order-books or production schedules: above normal, normal, below normal?
4. Employment expectations for the months ahead: up, unchanged, down?
5. Price expectations for the months ahead: up, unchanged, down?

Quarterly questions (carried out in January, April, July and October):

6. Months of assured production?

one example of an impressive list of such endeavors conducted in many countries of the world. Rather than providing a list, we mention the major ways in which these surveys differ:

1. *Measured variables*: Surveys attempt to measure one or several of the following variables: evaluations or reports of the present activity of the firm (mainly production level, order situation, stock situation, employment level), contingent expectations about the market situation of the firm (sales, expectations, price expectations), contingent expectations about the general economic environment of the firm (GNP, inflation, unemployment, interest rates), intentional expectations for the medium term (one-, two- or four-year investment plans).
2. *Sample base*: Some surveys are based on extensive samples of business people, others on rather limited samples of them; alternatively, surveys may be conducted with experts, who are not themselves directly involved as business people (e.g., inflation expectations obtained from expert economists)
3. Some surveys attempt to obtain a *point estimate of the level of the variable concerned* (e.g., the 3-month lending rate of interest for commercial banks next month). Other surveys collect only qualitative information, usually referring to evolution rather than level (e.g., inflation rate compared to last quarter: up, unchanged or down?).

6. EVALUATION OF ECONOMIC ATTITUDE AND ANTICIPATIONS DATA

6.1. *Introduction*

The usefulness of economic attitudes and anticipations should be a matter for empirical investigation. It is to an eclectic overview of the rather extensive literature on this topic that we now turn.

The literature deals mainly with two questions:

1. Are economic attitudes and anticipations useful for explaining or, better, forecasting economic outcomes, and
2. How are economic attitudes and anticipations formed?

6.2. *Evaluation: The Formation of Expectations*

Expectation theorists in economic psychology are caught somewhat in a dilemma when it comes to the evaluation of the forecasting power of anticipations variables. If expectations reflected only publicly available information, there would be little reason for direct survey measurement of anticipations. Rather, one could then substitute a function of the public information for the expectations. Measuring expectations directly would serve little purpose if these did not contain some "crystal ball" component which behaves independently of the publicly available knowledge and which has forecasting power.

On the other hand, expectations which are formed and behave independently of contextually available information would make many a scientist skeptical. The formation of such expectations would require invoking a gift of God or some sixth sense.

The formation of expectations is a topic of theoretical and of pragmatic importance. The pragmatic importance lies in the eventual possibility of replacing expectations by some function of already available economic information ("hard" or "objective" data). This would allow one to do without the survey measurement of expectations altogether or to forecast future economic outcomes dependent on future but yet unknown expectations. The theoretical interest for psychology lies in the opportunity for learning more about the formation or change of attitudes.

The theoretical importance for economics lies in the relationship with the assumed rationality of behavior as expressed in the Theory of Rational Expectations explained above.

Rational expectations are only a hypothesis. Yet, they provide a useful theoretical framework for studying the formation of expectations. In comparison with the tests carried out under this hypothesis, most other studies of the relationship between anticipations and available public knowledge are only ad hoc empirical investigations, subject to the vagaries of empirical curve fitting.

The *rational expectations hypothesis* looks at the informational basis of expectations in a normative way. In general terms, it states that economic agents form their expectations on the basis of all information available and that they combine this information optimally. Various stringent tests of the rationality of expectations can be performed. From the literature (see, Ahlers and Lakonishok, 1983; Friedman, 1980) it appears that anticipations will generally fail to pass one or several of the tests of unbiasedness, efficiency, consistency, orthogonality of forecast errors, etc. Especially concerning the latter, anticipations data seem to fail to incorporate all relevant information available. That survey based expectations fail the rationality test does not of course imply that they are irrational. Expectations will be shown below to often allow remarkably good forecasts, so that the rationality must be violated only mildly. Rational expectations is a hypothetical concept; "the" rational expectations formation mechanism will never be found. It can only be approximated, and survey anticipations seem to provide a fair approximation. Finally, all intricacies of testing for rationality seem to be far from resolved at this point (Brown and Maital, 1981).

Nerlove (1983) states that the stringent rationality tests may be unreasonable and proposes the weaker criterion that expectations be shown to present no pattern of systematic error. He adds that when economic outcomes are not undergoing structural change, one will generally find a univariate time series relationship between a variable and its own past; then quasi-rational expectations (i.e., containing no pattern of systematic error) can generally also be generated as a time series forecast from the past realizations of the outcome concerned.

It is fair to assume that attitudes with respect to objects which change over time (e.g., attitudes related to the business cycle) are based on experience and insight and evolve rather smoothly. This intuitively acceptable point of view leads economists to model expectations as extrapolative, based on the past accounts of the series itself, on the past of the attitudes and eventually on the past accounts of other relevant series. The Error Learning Model a special and popular case of extrapolative expectations. It is found to give a good and parsimonious explanation of expectations by several authors, e.g., Nerlove (1983) for demand, price and production expectations and Carlson and Parkins (1975) for inflation expectations.

Some extrapolative expectations studies have used univariate or multivariate time-series techniques. Joyeux (1980) regresses business investment anticipations on their own past, but does not study their formation deeper. Dramais and Waelbroeck (1986) apply an ARMA (autoregressive moving average) model to an evaluation series and find its forecasting RMSE (root mean square error) generally larger than for econometric forecasts on the basis of past expectations. Praet (1985) regresses consumer sentiment indicators on their prior one- or two-lagged values and finds R^2 values in the order of 0.90; objective economic indicators can improve the fit only marginally in view of the already excellent fit. In a time series perspective, his results show that the consumer sentiment series can be explained by simple ARMA models. Hanssens and Vanden Abeele (1986) find several cases of bias and suboptimal use of information in the EC Survey production expectations by business people. All of these results confirm that anticipations evolve rather smoothly and can be well fitted from their own immediate past.

Survey based expectations seem to conflict with the rationality requirements on one or more scores. This appears particularly damaging for the forecasting performance if they fail to incorporate some available predictive information. Yet, this is not a compelling reason to discard survey-based expectations.

Firstly, rationality tests are normally carried out by retrospective fitting of regression relationships; it is well known that the forecasting performance and fitting performance of relationships do not always run in parallel. Second, rationality tests are quite rigorous; anticipations that fail on the rationality requirements may still prove to be relatively good forecasts and their "rationality" drawbacks may trade off favorably with more pragmatic advantages of survey based expectations. Among the latter advantages one counts the earlier availability of survey based expectations compared to that of the formal economic accounts of variables which could substitute for expectations in forecasts.

Several examples are available of studies relating anticipations to their possible antecedents outside of the rational expectations framework. The purpose of such efforts is either to test the hypothesis that anticipations can be accounted for by publicly available antecedent knowledge or to develop equations for expectations formation in econometric models which use expectations in forecasting equations. As mentioned above, these equations are usually of a rather ad hoc nature, barring a priori hypotheses concerning the mechanisms guiding the formation of expectations. When reviewing the evidence, one must conclude that both consumer attitudes/expectations and business expectations (concerning investment) are usually fitted well by means of rather simple functions of "objective" economic data. Moreover, there is evidence to show that the unexplained variance of anticipations data in such relationships has little or no further forecasting virtues (Shapiro, 1972). These results, which are rather against the idea that economic sentiment data have an independent predictive component, should be mitigated as above: Most studies rely on retrospective fitting rather than on pure forecasting testing and the results do not impair potential pragmatic advantages of survey-based expectations.

The result that survey based expectations can be well approximated by functions of select economic indicators led to a counterargument by economic psychologists. Global sentiment indicators, as for example the Index of Consumer Sentiment, are indeed based on an appraisal of the available economic information. The function according to which economic agents integrate such information into a global appraisal would be time-varying and hard to specify a priori. The particular virtue of survey based sentiment measures would therefore lie in the implicit integration rule applied by economic agents. The single test of this issue of which we are aware fails to reject the hypothesis that the Index of Consumer Sentiment is a time-invariant function of economic indicators (Shapiro, 1972).

6.3. *Evaluation: The Forecasting Performance of Economic Attitudes, Expectations and Intentions*

In contrast with the studies on the formation of anticipations, investigations of the forecasting performance of intentions, expectations and attitude data are abundant. An exhaustive report of the results of these studies appears less useful than an attempt to categorize the approaches and to summarize the results which find confirmation across a number of investigations.

The studies can be grouped according to several criteria:

1. *Cross-section* vs. *time series*. Since the survey based anticipations are psychological variables, the basic unit for investigations is the individual. Cross-section studies attempt to show that attitudes and anticipations of individuals are related to (correlated with) their present or future behavior. Such studies may involve repeated interviews, so as to measure anticipations at one time and to measure the realizations or behavior of the same individual at another time. Time series designs are normally carried out using aggregate or average sentiment series and by correlating these over time with aggregate economic series.
2. *Fitting* vs. *forecasting*. Relationships between sentiment variables and realizations are based on retrospective fitting, e.g., by computing the multiple regression of the economic realizations on likely explanatory and forecasting variables. The forecasting performance can be assessed by means of the fit (usually adjusted for the number of available degrees of freedom) on the retrospective data. The actual performance in forecasting can ultimately only be assessed by examining the correspondence between predictions and realizations outside of the data sample used for fitting. Whereas earlier studies assessed the predictive accuracy merely by the degree of retrospective fit, more recent studies often also verify the true predictive accuracy on a holdout sample.
3. *Anticipations* vs. *sentiment* measures. Anticipations are quantitative forecasts of the level of an economic variable; they provide a direct forecast of the concerned variable. Sentiment measures operationalize some hypothetical causative variable. Sentiment measures will therefore appear as explanatory variables in a forecasting model. Pure sentiment models attempt a forecast only on the basis of sentiment variables. Mixed models will include both economic variables and sentiment measures as explanatory factors.

Predictive models are not developed with a mere forecasting purpose. The nature of the forecasting model itself may be of interest. The models to be discussed are usually linear regression models. In these models the size, sign and significance of the regression coefficients and the overall degree of fit, i.e., the degree of explained variance, are of interest.

Some warning should be given concerning such analyses, especially on aggregate time series data. Aggregate time series data have the property of being strongly autocorrelated. Mere autoregressive relationships will often provide an excellent degree of fit for the same series, whereas different series will easily present spurious correlation. Even when there is no true underlying relationship, multivariate autoregressive models can result in mistakingly high degrees of fit (Granger and Newbold, 1974). When this situation is coupled with a "random" search among potential explanatory variables as, e.g., in stepwise regression, one is easily misled to attribute causation where there may be none. For this reason, it is recommended to build aggregate time series models on detrended data, e.g., by differencing the dependent variable. Even more stringent is the concept of Granger causation: Causation between two series should only be concluded to if the residuals from autoregressive models on both variables separately display correlations which remain significant. The forecasting performance of a model can be assessed on the fitting sample, but even better on a holdout or prediction sample. In the former case the forecasting performance is best assessed by the squared multiple correlation adjusted for degrees of freedom (adjusted R^2) or by the standard error of the regression. The forecasting performance on the prediction sample can likewise be assessed by means of the correlation between prediction and realization. This correlation, however, conceals possible biases of level and of regression. Alternative assessments of the forecast are provided by:

1. the average forecast error,
2. the average absolute forecast error, and
3. the mean squared forecast (percentage) error.

The most complete forecast evaluation statistic is Theil's inequality coefficient, which provides an over-all quantitative statistic that can be decomposed into the error components due to level, regression and random error (Naert and Leeflang, 1978).

6.3.1. *Forecasting Performance of Quantitative Anticipations*

Direct quantitative anticipations are mainly found in the business sector, where survey based anticipations are collected concerning such magnitudes as sales, production level, investment spending, rate of interest, etc. These survey measures are direct forecasts of specific variables, usually with a clearly specified time lag (e.g., one month, one-quarter or one-year anticipation). The latter precludes difficulties with the implied forecasting lag of the anticipations data, at least in principle. The possibility still remains that these anticipations measure something else than a specific forecast or that the prediction lag is different from what is implied by the survey question. Several studies have shown that such anticipations allow reasonably good forecasts. In particular, it appears that these anticipations measure up to or are better than alternative forecasting models.

Direct anticipations have been demonstrated to forecast better than naïve models, i.e., time-series models predicting the future of an economic variable from its own past, or than complex econometric models. The latter appear particularly weak when it comes to forecasting turning points in the variable of interest, i.e., decreases following increases or vice versa. The reasons for this finding still beg a satisfactory explanation; it shows that the human integration complexity outdistances that of even complex econometric models by far. Notwithstanding this good performance of direct anticipations, one observes that they tend to underestimate the magnitude of changes, even where they succeed in detecting its direction.

The Livingston data (Ahlers and Lakonishok, 1983) have been a favorite testing ground for economic anticipations. They provide a consensus point-forecast among a panel of economic experts of the changes in a number of economic series. Ahlers and Lakonishok find that the forecasts are biased over the 1947-1978 period. The bias amounts to an understatement of the trend component and an overstatement of deviations from the trend. The forecasts are not consistently able to outperform naive extrapolation models. The predictive performance of the direct forecasts is known to improve markedly over time, so that the survey forecasts generally outperform naive models in the 1970-1978 period, which can be characterized as rather volatile. The unbiasedness of the Livingston series has been tested in other papers. Brown and Maital (1981) point to weaknesses in Ordinary Least Squares-estimation methods and, after a more appropriate estimation, find many of the series unbiased, thus confirming conclusions of others cited by these authors. Zarnowitz (1979) reports similar findings concerning forecasts of GNP change. Forecasts, whether survey- or model-based tend to beat naive and more complex time-series forecasts, and direct survey forecasts perform about equally well as econometric model forecasts. At least for GNP-change forecasts, survey anticipations perform well, absolutely and comparatively. Zarnowitz subscribes the often heard conclusion that no single forecasting method can be shown consistently and generally superior to others.

Next to the direct forecasts of future contingencies, expectations surveys of a more intentional kind are conducted with business people concerning investment spending, sales, production, etc. Rippe and Wilkinson (1974) investigate 1- to 4-year anticipations of investment, sales and capacity and show their predictive performance to be better than for naive extrapolation models or econometric functions. Similar findings were reported by Jorgensen, Hunter and Nadiri (1970) and by Liebling and Russell (1969) for the 1950's and 1960's. Liebling, Bidwell and Hall (1975) confirm the conclusion for the 1973-75 period in a test of direct vs. model (Chase, DRI, Wharton) forecasts. A number of other positive references are cited by Rippe, Wilkinson and Morrison (1976). All these results are fairly encouraging and in line with the early findings by Modigliani and Weingartner (1958):

Business survey anticipations (eventually after some bias correction) allow for a rather good performance in forecasting.

6.3.2. *Forecasting Performance of Sentiment Data*

The largest number of studies consist of econometric model building in which economic variables are regressed on sentiment data as well as on other economic series. Consumer sentiment data have provided the opportunity for cross-section work on the basis of re-interview samples. The initial finding of a weak or nonexistent relationship between individual economic realizations and individual measures of consumer sentiment, combined with the observation of strong correlations between aggregate time series on the same data was labeled the "cross section time series paradox." This outcome is to be expected, however, if one considers that both the economic realizations and the economic sentiment measures at the individual level should have a low cross-sectional reliability and validity. Later research has shown that significant, though modest cross-sectional correlations can be found providing sufficient attention for reliability and validity issues. One should, for example, eliminate from the cross-sectional variation in the economic realizations that part which is little influenced by economic sentiment, such as non-discretionary expenditures.

Economic attitude surveys do not necessarily yield quantitative forecasts in the guise of an anticipation for a well-defined economic outcome. In many cases the survey data are categorical (e.g., production is expected to decrease, remain unchanged or increase) or are not direct indicators of specific categories of economic behavior (e.g., consumer sentiment data). Such data, eventually after rescaling, can be entered as regressors in econometric equations in order to explain economic phenomena; the fitted equations then also become available for forecasting purposes.

Pure survey equations forecast economic outcomes only on the basis of survey data, and mixed equations contain both standard economic regressors and survey data.

Adams and Duggal (1974) study the forecasting performance of three versions of the *Wharton model*, namely the version without, with endogenized and with exogenous (survey based) anticipations. They find that the forecasting performance improves in that order, with the strongest gain for the "hard" anticipations (business investment, housing starts) and with modest gains for "soft" consumer sentiment data. These conclusions were already arrived at earlier by Adams and Klein (1972). Juster and Wachtel (1972), focusing on consumer spending and saving, conclude that consumer intention and sentiment data do come in as significant regressors next to standard economic variables. The marginal increase in the fit is however rather small in most cases, while the "non-survey" part of the equations is fairly simple and the equations show substantially autocorrelated errors. The forecasting performance of consumer sentiment data is a much debated issue between proponents and opponents of "soft" (survey) measures. Rather negative evidence is obtained by Shapiro (1972), who demonstrates that consumer sentiment data fail to improve forecasts provided by econometric models of reasonable complexity.

Hanssens and Vanden Abeele (1986), applying the time series methodology in the framework of the Granger Causality framework, show that business sentiment data "cause" production expectations but, strangely enough, not the corresponding (objective) realizations.

The experience with consumer intentions data in the U.S.A. was largely negative and led to the termination of related survey efforts (McNeil, 1974). On the other hand, an optimistic report is given by Praet and Vuchelen (1984) on EC consumer survey data.

Cross-sectional studies of the relations between anticipations, judgments and accounts do not abound. Dunkelberg (1972) finds a significant although modest explanatory power of consumer sentiment data for subsequent durable goods spending. In the business sector, Nerlove (1983) studies the relationship between short term anticipations (production, demand, prices, etc.) and the subsequent judgments for a German and a French sample of firms. The marginal distribution of anticipations and of evaluations, given expectations, is temporally stable for one sample, but not for the other. These results indicate that in evaluating forecasts from anticipations, a correction for bias is needed and this correction may have to be temporally variable. The bulk of the relevant studies for this section are based on aggregate time series and are, again, too numerous to report individually. The findings are both positive and negative and should be qualified on many points:

1. For business anticipations data and for rather "hard" consumer anticipations such as housing starts, the contribution to the forecasting power of models is substantial. In these instances the anticipatory information is more "firm."
2. For consumer sentiment data in pure sentiment models, a good forecasting performance can generally be obtained. The net contribution of sentiment data in mixed models of reasonable complexity is relatively modest. Consumer sentiment data, in such models, will regularly turn out to be significant regressors, but their net contribution to the explanation of the variance in the dependent variable is often modest. These results should be qualified both in a positive and in a negative way.

On the negative side, the following remarks should be made. There is no strict theoretical framework dictating which sentiment figures should be brought into the equations nor how they should be brought in (e.g., with what time lag). The same is not so often true for other regressors of an economic nature. As a result, the regression equations reported are usually the result of a fitting exercise subject to the danger of a biased search for what may be spurious correlation. The latter holds especially for those regressions that explain the level rather than the departures from the level in economic time series. The collection of regression equations reported presents so much diversity as to confound any effort at generalization. The forecasting tests reported are not always pure forecast assessments but rather evaluations of fit. This optimum lag in forecasting often differs strongly from one study to the next; in addition, the optimum lag is regularly found to be very small or even zero.

On the positive side, sentiment variables do regularly turn up significant in regression relationships. Some studies which investigate the forecasting power on a holdout sample have been able to demonstrate the superiority of sentiment-based models or of mixed models.

Even though the evidence is not overwhelming, it is certainly not negative, both for business and for consumer data. Further efforts at refining the models, e.g., by better scaling of the sentiment data or by building variable regression coefficients can result in fine tuning the contribution of such sentiment data. Still, no major net contribution to the explanation of economic variables should be expected in general.

6.3.3. *Consumer Intentions Data*

Consumer purchase intentions with regard to specific categories of goods appear to be relatively firm data and could therefore be expected to yield good forecasts. The explanatory power of consumer intentions shows clearly in cross-section tests, where planners have a significantly higher purchase probability than non-planners. At the same time, it is somewhat bothersome that the majority of recorded purchases is due to non-planning individuals. As mentioned above, this latter finding leads researchers to operationalize intentions as subjective probabilities rather than as plans.

Unfortunately, the clear predictive superiority of consumer intentions over consumer sentiment data in the cross section was not translated into a similar performance in aggregate time series tests, resulting in another "cross-section vs. time series paradox," at least for the U.S.A. (McNeil, 1974). In time series, aggregate consumer intentions data either fail to come up significant or, if significant, have rather unstable regression coefficients, depending on what other variables are entered into the models. Consumer intentions data loose their net explanatory power when entered in models next to consumer sentiment data.

CONCLUSION

Expectations variables play an important role in (models of) economic decision making. The increasing autonomy of economic actors should increase the prominent role of such sentiment variables. The empirical evidence on expectations variables shows a confused picture of positive, negative and mixed results. It seems that progress in our insight now hinges most of all on the availability of theories that predict

1. when expectations matter, and
2. how these impact on economic decision making.

Both economics and psychology have embryonic concepts to offer concerning this problem. A fusion of both theoretical contributions is needed in order to make progress possible.

REFERENCES

Adams, F.G, 1964, Consumer attitudes, buying plans and purchases of durable goods: A principal components – time series approach, Review of Economics and Statistics, 46, 347-335.

Adams, F.G., 1965, Prediction with consumer attitudes: The time series–cross section paradox, Review of Economics and Statistics, 47, 367-378.

Adams, F.G., and V.O. Duggal, 1974, Anticipation variables in an econometric model: Performance of the anticipation version of Wharton Mark III, International Economic Review, 15, 267-284.

Adams, F.G., and L.R. Klein, 1972, "Anticipations variables in macro-econometric models," in: B. Strümpel, J.N. Morgan, and E. Zahn (eds.), Human Behavior in Economic Affairs, Amsterdam: Elsevier, pp. 289-319.

Ajzen, I., and M. Fishbein, 1980, Understanding Attitudes and Predicting Social Behavior, Englewood Cliffs, NJ: Prentice-Hall.

Ahlers, D., and J. Lakonishok, 1983, Economists' consensus forecasts, Management Science, 25, 1113-1125.

Bechtel, G.G., 1981, Measuring subjective social indicators, Journal of Economic Psychology, 1, 165-181.

Bettman, J.R., 1979, An Information Processing Theory of Consumer Choice, Reading, MA: Addison-Wesley.

Brown, B.W., and S. Maital, 1981, What do economists know? An empirical study of experts' expectations, Econometrica, 49, 491-504.

Carlson, J.A., and M. Parkins, 1975, Inflation expectation, Economica, 42, 123-38.

Commission of the European Communities, Results of the Business Survey Carried out Among Managements in the Community, Brussels: Various issues.

Day, G.S., 1973, "Theories of attitude structure and change," in: S. Ward and T.S. Robertson (eds.), Consumer Behavior: Theoretical Sources, Englewood Cliffs, NJ: Prentice-Hall, pp. 303-353.

Derbaix, C., and P. Vanden Abeele, 1985, Consumer inferences and consumer preferences. The status of cognition and consciousness in consumer behavior theory, International Journal of Research in Marketing, 2, 157-174.

Doornbos, G.J., and W.F. van Raaij, 1983, The Impact of Economic Conditions and Expectations on Household Saving, 28, Rotterdam, The Netherlands: Erasmus University (Papers on Economic Psychology).

Dramais, A., and E. Waelbroeck-Rocha, 1987, A probabilistic approach to the quantification of business survey data, Journal of the American Statistical Association, 82, 335-379.

Dunkelberg, W.C., 1972, "The impact of consumer attitudes on behavior: A cross-section study," in B. Strümpel, J.N. Morgan, and E. Zahn (eds.), Human Behavior in Economic Affairs, Amsterdam: Elsevier, pp. 347-371.

Feige, E.L., and D.K. Pearce, 1979, The causal relationship between money and income: Some caveats for time series analysis, Review of Economics and Statistics, 61, 521-533.

Friedman, B.M., 1980, Survey evidence on the "rationality" of interest rate expectations, Journal of Monetary Economics, 6, 453-465.

Friend, I., and W. Thomas, 1970, A reevaluation of the predictive ability of plant and equipment anticipations, Journal of the American Statistical Association, 65, 510-519.

Furnham, A., and A. Lewis, 1986, The Economic Mind, The Social Psychology of Economic Behaviour, Brighton, Sussex, UK: Wheatsheaf Books.

Granger, C.W.J., and P. Newbold, 1974, Spurious regressions in econometrics, Journal of Econometrics, 2, 111-120.

Hanssens, D., and P. Vanden Abeele, 1986, A Time-series Study of the Formation and Predictive Performance of EEC Production Survey Expectations, Los Angeles, CA: University of California, Graduate School of Management (working paper).

Hymans, S.H., 1970, Consumer durable spending: Expectation and prediction, Brookings Papers on Economic Activity, 1, 173-206.

Jorgensen, S.W., T. Hunter, and M. Nadiri, 1970, The predictive performance of econometric models of quarterly investment behavior, Econometrica, 38, 213-224.

Joyeux, R., 1980, Relationships between economic time-series and their anticipations, Quarterly Review of Economics and Business, 20, 7-15.

Juster, F.T., and P. Wachtel, 1972, Inflation and the consumer, Brookings Papers on Economic Activity, 3, 71-114.

Katona, G., 1957, Federal Reserve Board Committee report on consumer expectations and saving statistics, Review of Economics and Statistics, 39, 40-45.

Katona, G., 1975, Psychological Economics, New York: American Elsevier.

Langer, E., A. Blank, and B. Chanowitz, 1978, The mindlessness of ostensibly thoughtful action, Journal of Personality and Social Psychology, 36, 635-642.

Liebling, H.I., and T.M. Russell, 1969, Forecasting business investment by anticipation surveys and econometric models in 1962-1968, Proceedings of the Business and Economic Statistics Section, American Statistical Association, pp. 250-255.

Liebling, H.I., P.T. Bidwell, and K.E. Hall, 1975, The recent performance of anticipation surveys and econometric model projections of investment spending in the United States, Journal of Business, 49, 451-477.

McNeil, T., 1974, Federal programs to measure consumer purchase expectations, 1946-1973: A post-mortem, Journal of Consumer Research, 1, 7-10.

Mishkin, F.S., 1981, Are market forecasts rational?, American Economic Review, 71, 195-236.

Modigliani, F., and H.M. Weingartner, 1958, Forecasting uses of anticipatory data on investment and sales, Quarterly Journal of Economics, 72, 23-54.

Mullineaux, D.J., 1978, On testing for rationality: Another look at the Livingston price expectations data, Jounal of Political Economy, 86, 329-336.

Muth, J.F., 1961, Rational expectations and the theory of price movements, Econometrica, 29, 315-335.

Naert, P., and P.S.H. Leeflang, 1978, Building Implementable Marketing Models, Leiden, The Netherlands: Martinus Nijhoff.

Nerlove, M., 1983, Expectations, plans and realizations in theory and practice, Econometrica, 51, 1251-1279.

Newcomb, T.M., 1972, "Expectations as a social psychological concept," in: B. Strümpel, J.N. Morgan, and E. Zahn (eds.), Human Behavior in Economic Affairs, Amsterdam, Elsevier, pp. 109-118.

Nisbett, R.E., and L. Ross, 1980, Human Inference Strategies and Shortcomings of Social Judgment, Englewood Cliffs, NJ: Prentice-Hall.

Papadia, F., and V. Basano, 1981, EEC-DG II Inflationary Expectations: Survey Based Inflationary Expectations for the EEC Countries, 1, Brussels: Commission of the European Communities (economic papers).

Praet, P., 1984, The Integration of EEC Qualitative Consumer Survey Results in Econometric Modelling: An Application to the Consumption Function, 30, Brussels: Commission of the European Communities (economic papers).

Praet, P., 1985, Endogenizing consumers' expectations in four major EC countries, Journal of Economic Psychology, 6, 255-269.

Praet, P., and J. Vuchelen, 1984, The contribution of E.C. consumer surveys in forecasting consumer expenditures: An econometric analysis for four major countries, Journal of Economic Psychology, 5, 101-124.

Rippe, R., M. Wilkinson, and D. Morrison, 1976, Industrial market forecasting with anticipations data, Management Science, 22, 639-50.

Shapiro, H.T., 1972, "The Index of Consumer Sentiment and economic forecasting: A reappraisal," in: B. Strümpel, J.N. Morgan, and E. Zahn (eds.), Human Behavior in Economic Affairs, Amsterdam, Elsevier, pp. 373-396.

Strümpel, B. (ed.), 1976, Economic Means for Human Needs, Ann Arbor, MI: University of Michigan, Institute for Social Research.

Vanden Abeele, P., 1983, The Index of Consumer Sentiment: Predictability and predictive power in the EEC, Journal of Economic Psychology, 3, 1-17.

Zarnowitz, V., 1979, An analysis of annual and multiperiod quarterly forecasts of aggregate income, output and price level, Journal of Business, 52, 1-33.

Zimmermann, K.F., 1984, On rationality of business expectations: A micro analysis of qualitative responses, 270-84, Mannheim, FRG: Universität Mannheim, Institut für Volkswirtschaftslehre und Statistik.

Table of Contents

14. Tax Evasion Research: Measurement Strategies and Theoretical Models

DICK J. HESSING
Erasmus University, Rotterdam, The Netherlands,

KARYL A. KINSEY
American Bar Foundation, Chicago, IL, U.S.A.,

HENK ELFFERS
Erasmus University, Rotterdam, The Netherlands,

and

RUSSELL H. WEIGEL
Amherst College, Amherst, MA, U.S.A.

1. INTRODUCTION

In recent years, policy makers as well as social scientists have begun to recognize that income tax evasion is a behavioral problem that seriously threatens the capacity of government to raise public revenue. It is a problem that transcends cultural and political boundaries. For example, estimates have indicated that the equivalent of 7,5% of Britain's gross national product escapes legitimate taxation, while 17% of the taxable income in Belgium remains undeclared (Lewis, 1982). In the United States, the Internal Revenue Service (IRS, 1983) has estimated that the tax gap (the difference between taxes owed and taxes filed) was $ 81,5 billion for 1981; an amount that exceeded the federal deficit for that year. Beyond the prospect of substantial deficit reductions without spending cuts or tax increases, other benefits would be derived from minimizing tax evasion. As Spicer (1975) has noted, tax evasion tends both to undermine the resolve of honest taxpayers and, insofar as it occurs more frequently in some segments of the population than in others, to hinder realization of the distributional and equity goals of taxation.

If social science is to contribute to an understanding of tax evasion behavior, the ideas and data generated to this point merit re-examination with respect to two issues:

1. the measurement strategies employed to assess tax evasion (Elffers et al., 1987) and
2. the theoretical models for tax evasion behavior (Kinsey, 1986).

Van Raaij, W.F., van Veldhoven, G.M. and Wärneryd, K.E. (eds) Handbook of Economic Psychology. ISBN 90-247-3720-6.

2. MEASUREMENT STRATEGIES FOR TAX EVASION BEHAVIOR

2.1. *Introduction*

Previous studies have typically defined taxpayer behavior in one of two ways. "*Noncompliance*" represents the most inclusive conceptualization referring to the failure to meet tax obligations whether or not that failure is intentional. "*Tax evasion*" refers to a deliberate act of noncompliance that results in the payment of less taxes than actually owed. Tax evasion, then, is a more restrictive term which excludes inadvertent noncompliance resulting from memory lapses, calculation errors, inadequate knowledge of tax laws and the like. The distinction merits note because the variables that mediate intentional evasion behavior may be quite irrelevant for mediating inadvertent noncompliance.

With respect to income taxes, evasion behavior usually takes the form of deliberately underreporting income or claiming unwarranted deductions (e.g., Loftus, 1985; Wallschutzky, 1984). Since the specific behaviors comprising income tax evasion cannot be directly observed in natural settings, researchers have tended to use one of three types of measurement strategies to detect its occurrence.

2.2. *Behavioral Simulation Measures*

A number of laboratory experiments have attempted to approximate direct observation by having subjects complete simulated tax returns (Friedland, 1982; Friedland et al., 1978; Spicer and Becker, 1980; Spicer and Thomas, 1982; Spicer and Hero, 1985; Webley and Halstead, 1985; Webley et al., 1985, 1988). Typically, subjects are given tax forms and receive a salary for each of several pay periods. For each pay period, the subjects decide how much of their salary they wish to declare as income and compute the taxes due on that amount. Within the experiments, the effects of the independent variables manipulated (e.g., audit probabilities, severity of fines, tax rates) are assessed in terms of the frequency of underreporting income and the amount of income undeclared. Following the example of the pioneering study by Friedland et al. (1978), subjects tend to be explicitly instructed to maximize their net income (total income across all pay periods less taxes and fines) and are awarded cash prizes based on their performance.

Presumably, by randomly assigning subjects to experimental treatments, properly designed laboratory simulations would permit convincing tests of causal hypotheses. Three general problems, however, tend to compromise the persuasiveness of the experimental work published to date. First, the small sample sizes and almost uniform reliance on college students as subjects seriously limits the generalizability of the results obtained. Only Webley et al. (1985) used members of the general public, but their sample sizes remain small. Second, questions have been raised (Webley and Halstead, 1985) regarding the degree to which the experimental situation parallels taxpayers' decisions in natural settings. In particular, concerns have been expressed with respect to both the transparency of purpose and instructions that literally demand evasion behavior. Underreporting income is the subject's only means of maximizing net income; an option that does not invoke any of the moral constraints that might inhibit such behavior in non-laboratory settings. One consequence is that laboratory experiments have typically reported much higher rates of evasion behavior than are plausible given the estimates of the actual frequency of such behavior. Friedland (1982), for example, found that his subjects underreported their income on 93% of the opportunities available. Preliminary data from postexperimental interviews conducted by Webley and Halstead (1985) suggested that these extraordinary rates of evasion behavior can be attributed to subjects' perceptions of the simulation as a profit maximizing "game." In this investigation, evasion behavior was much less prevalent among the few subjects who described their experience as similar to a tax declaring situation. Two recently published studies (Webley et al., 1985, 1988) have begun to confront this problem by embedding the tax declarations within a variety of decisions comprising a business management task. The frequency of evasion behavior among their subjects was still high (56% and 40%), but more realistic than that observed in previous experiments. A third problem involves the quality of the dependent variable. All of the published experimental simulations have operationalized tax evasion as the frequency or amount of undeclared income across a series of pay periods. Experimental subjects have only had to specify how much of their taxable income they wish to declare; never has a subject calculated a deduction or even had to consider that some fraction of his income may have limited vulnerability to third party documentation.

In short, despite their potential advantages, it is questionable whether experimental simulations up to the present have provoked valid approximations of taxpayers' behavior. It remains to be determined, whether future simulation studies can overcome the artificialities of past experiments and that measures of evasion behavior can be developed that go beyond repetitious confrontations with simplistic tax decisions.

2.3. *Self-report Measures*

Given the difficulty of field observation and the confidentiality requirements surrounding individual tax returns, it is hardly surprising that most empirical investigations have relied on survey methodologies and respondents' verbal descriptions of their past behavior to assess the occurrence and extent of tax evasion. As Lewis (1982: p. 140) suggested, "why not just ask respondents whether they evade tax or not? If they admit it, ask them how much this amounts to and perhaps even why they do it? What could be simpler?" Nevertheless, Lewis (1982) also noted that there were reasons to temper this enthusiastic appraisal.

Although the results of some comparisons between self-reports and measures of overtly documented behavior have been impressive (e.g., Stacey et al., 1985; Warrinier et al., 1984) other results have been more problematic especially when the information sought involved deviant behavior (e.g., Hauser, 1969; Sudman and Bradburn, 1974). Two types of distortion have been implicated in the context. In some instances bragging has produced reports that have exaggerated the range and frequency of deviance (e.g., Bell and Buchanan, 1968; Cahalan, 1968). The most persistent concerns, however, have focused on respondents' tendencies to underreport their involvement in socially proscribed activities (e.g., Clark and Tifft, 1966; Phillips 1971, 1973). For example, Robins (1966) compared interview data with data obtained from various official records as part of a longitudinal investigation of deviance. Of 164 persons who had been arrested at least once, 30% gave accurate information, 29% reported fewer arrests than records indicated, and 41% denied any arrest history. In a different investigation, Farrington (1973) found a significant correlation between self-reports and official records of delinquency for 405 teenagers. However, when 397 of these boys were interviewed again two years later, nearly half of all the seriously delinquent acts (those involving theft and physical aggression) which had been acknowledged on the previous interview, were denied.

The difficulties of evaluating the usefulness of self-report data for tax behavior are compounded by the added element of intentionality in defining tax evasion. Tax authorities can document noncompliant behaviors, and may make judgments, veridical or not, of their intentionality. Survey respondents cannot by definition reveal unintentional noncompliance; they cannot reveal what they do not know. They can, however, reveal deliberate tax evasion if they so choose, and one might speculate that the most accurate reports would come from those who feel immune to official detection and for whom evasion does not threaten the self concept.

An inevitable result of the different capabilities of methods is that official records of noncompliance will differ from self-reports. Discrepancies will reflect the effects of unintentional mistakes, denials by tax evaders that they had evaded, and, in the other direction, failures by authorities to detect evasion that respondents are willing to admit. Empirical evidence indicates that the net effect of these discrepancies is for survey reports to yield lower estimates of noncompliance than official estimates. For example, intensive research audits of a sample of 1979 U.S. tax returns produced estimates that 43% of returns contained errors resulting in tax underpayment (Kinsey, 1986). In comparison, a national survey conducted that same year found that 27-32% (depending on survey method) of respondents admitted being less than absolutely honest on their previous year's return (Aitken and Bonneville, 1980).

The same survey found that admissions of tax evasion were highly sensitive to question wording and methods. Admitted tax evasion was greater with randomized response methods than with locked box methods. The framing of questions also appears to be important: Only 9-18% admitted "stretching the truth," compared to the 27-32% saying they had been less than absolutely honest. A 1986 survey of Oregon adults found similar framing effects: In a design counterbalancing question order, 55% stated they definitely had not left income off their tax returns, while 68% said they had definitely reported all of their income (American Bar Foundation (ABF), 1986). Further, in-person interviews tend to yield higher levels of admitted tax evasion than those conducted by telephone (Westat, 1980a) and there is some evidence to suggest that admitted tax evasion is greater among household members who take primary responsibility for family tax matters, perhaps because they are in a better position to know (Kinsey, 1986; ABF, 1986).

Clearly, much work is needed in refining survey sampling, interview, and question wording procedures to encourage admissions of tax evasion. In addition, the introduction of questions measuring the perceived threat of items measuring tax evasion may be useful in segmenting those with many incentives to lie from those with few incentives. Self-report data will probably never be useful for generating estimates of the incidence and dollar amount of deliberate tax evasion, but then, neither is any other method used to date. The key issue in evaluating the scientific usefulness of self-reports is whether the denials of tax evasion are randomly distributed across taxpayer types, and if non-randomly distributed, the type of bias they introduce in statistical models. If denials are randomly distributed, then the results would be conservative but unbiased estimates of effects. If non-randomly distributed, the effect could be either underestimates or overestimates of the strength of effects, depending on the direction of the bias. Systematic investigation of this issue has yet to be undertaken, but it is worth noting that there are some convergences between the findings of survey and official data. Both sources consistently find greater noncompliance among the self-employed, those in complex financial situations, and those with income not subject to withholding or third-party reports, variables which reflect the situational opportunities of taxpayers which serve to reduce their likelihood of detection during routine enforcement actions.

Research to be described in the next section, though, suggests that different social psychological models are obtained from self-report of tax evasion and tax agency attributions of tax evasion.

Aside from admitted tax evasion, an unexplored area of survey methods is the use of unobtrusive measures in which the economic situations of taxpayers are matched with their reported filing behavior. Kinsey (1987) for example, found that 12% of self-employed taxpayers in a U.S. survey reported filing simple tax forms, although legal requirements are such that most self-employed persons should be filing complex forms. The discrepancies between the person's work situation and filing status may reflect ignorance of filing requirements, but in many cases would also result in underpayment of self-employment taxes, which in the U.S. are self-assessed and paid while filing income taxes. Key advantage of unobtrusive measures is that they minimize the sensitivity of questions and can capture both intentional and unintentional noncompliance.

2.4. *Behavioral Outcome Measures*

A limited number of studies have attempted to measure individual tax evasion behavior by assessing the occurrence of some outcome that is contingent on that behavior. For example, Wallschutzky (1984) capitalized on the Australian policy of publishing the names of convicted income tax evaders. In his study, Wallschutzky compared survey responses of a sample of these convicted evaders to those of a "non-evader" group drawn at random from voting registration lists. Actual conviction, then, was the outcome taken to indicate that evasion behavior had occurred. As Wallschutzky (1984) noted, however, it was quite likely that his sample of registered voters was contaminated by substantial numbers of unconvicted but culpable tax evaders; a problem that could account for the non-significant differences that typically emerged on the attitude measures used to compare the two groups.

Two studies (Clotfelter, 1983; Witte and Woodbury, 1983) analyzed data from sample audits conducted by the Internal Revenue Service (IRS) in the United States to identify individual cases of noncompliance with income tax laws. For both studies the outcome variable was operationalized in terms of the difference between the taxable income reported by the individual and that calculated by the auditors. As such, these measures of noncompliance have three major limitations:

1. They could assess only those instances of tax evasion that are detected in the normal course of an audit.

2. They could not distinguish between unintended errors and deliberate deception.
3. Since the anonymity of the individuals comprising the sample precluded subsequent contact, the measures did not permit investigation of the social or psychological conditions associated with noncompliance.

Elffers et al. (1987) tried to overcome these limitations. Using a contrast-group design the researchers developed a rather elaborate procedure for identifying individuals who tax authorities had labeled as tax evaders and non-evaders, using official records, while simultaneously preserving the confidentiality of that information. In consultation with the Dutch Ministry of Finance and the Tax Inspectorate of Rotterdam two groups of taxpayers were selected:

1. tax evaders, whose tax forms were evaluated by the tax agency as requiring corrections on clearly reproachable grounds for two years in a row, and
2. non-evaders, whose returns were judged to require no corrections whatsoever for two consecutive years.

A number of steps were taken to assure that the anonymity of the respondents was protected. Once the two groups of respondents were identified, the chief of the Office of the Tax Inspectorate sent the individuals' names, addresses, telephone numbers, and coded information regarding the evaluation of their tax returns to a bonded third party (in this case, a notary, which in the Netherlands is a specialized lawyer). He then sent each of the potential respondents a letter asking for their cooperation in a scientific study of citizens' attitudes toward the Dutch tax system and assuring them that the anonymity of their responses would be guaranteed. Persons who were willing to participate returned a card to the notary and a convenient interview date was established. At the outset of the interview, the data collection procedure was explained more fully with emphasis on the safeguards that protect respondents' anonymity. The interviewer also explained that the notary would supply the research team with coded information regarding any tax violations by the respondent. The respondents were then asked to sign a consent from permitting the notary to release the coded information on the past tax corrections to the research team. If consent was given, the respondent was administered the research questionnaire. Each of the questionnaire items was read aloud to the respondent who was seated behind a portable screen that shielded the answer sheet from the interviewer's view. When the interview was completed, the consent form and answer sheet were sealed in an envelope and mailed to the notary. The notary checked the consent form, attached the coded tax information to the respondents answer sheet, removed the respondent's name from both of the latter two documents and mailed them to the researchers. When all of the interviews were completed, the Tax Inspectorate mailed the decoding key for the tax information directly to the researchers.

Despite this elaborate research design to safeguard the respondents' anonymity, the correlations obtained between self-report scores and scores on the various behavioral outcome measures were uniformly negligible. When self-reports were combined into a 2-year index, scores on this index did not correlate either with respondent's actual status as evaders or non-evaders during that period ($r = .06$) or the magnitude of the average post-audit correction levied against them for those years ($r = -.03$). Quite simply, no evidence of correspondence between self-reports and the behavioral outcome measures emerged from these data. Inspection of these data revealed that inconsistencies between the self-report and behavioral outcome measures obtained for 45% of the respondents. Examination of the frequencies of over- and underreporting of tax evasion behavior indicated that while both types of discrepancies occurred, underreporting was much more prevalent. Twenty-five percent of the non-evaders reported some misrepresentation of income or deductions during the years under consideration, whereas 69% of the evaders denied evading taxes in either year. The extent of the denial of past tax evasion behavior was highlighted when the self-reports of the most flagrant evaders were examined. Among the 57 individuals whose audits resulted in corrections of more than ƒ 1000 (approximately $ 600 in terms of purchasing parity estimates) in both 1981 and 1982, more than 70% denied any misrepresentation of income or deductions in their returns for either year.

The circumstances surrounding acquisition of the self-reported data were compatible with obtaining accurate descriptions of past behavior: The behavior in question was likely salient for the respondents, elaborate safeguards protected respondents' anonymity, the respondents' actual tax liabilities had already been exposed and resolved without protest, and respondents exhibited nearly uniform willingness to participate in the research once the purposes and safeguards were explained. Two cautions must be noted though. Intentionality is a key determining factor in criminal prosecutions of tax evasion, and the circumstances of the official evader group – repeated official detection of substantial noncompliance which the tax authorities consider reproachable – may predispose them to be concerned about potential criminal prosecutions. Such respondents may be not only wary about admitting evading under any circumstances, but even may view denial as a defensive tactic to head off prosecution. Second, contesting deficiencies assessed by a tax agency can be expensive, time consuming, stressful, and uncertain as to outcome. Some taxpayers may prefer to concede and pay the assessed deficiency, even though they disagree with it, rather than undertake these uncertain costs.

3. THEORETICAL MODELS OF TAX EVASION

3.1. *Introduction*

The following ten models, some previously summarized by Kinsey (1986), were developed by researchers and tax officials specifically interested in tax evasion as a social problem. These models can be grouped into two broad categories: those incorporating aspects of tax policy and administration, and those focusing primarily on individual perceptions, attitudes, and beliefs. Lewis (1982) and Weigel et al. (1987) bridge these two categories with one model.

Some of these models are essentially compilations of the results from a particular research project (Strümpel, 1969; Ekstrand, 1980), and others have been proposed, but only partially tested by their authors (e.g., Spicer, 1974; Spicer and Lundstedt, 1976; Weigel et al., 1987; Elffers et al., 1987). This discussion will describe the general frameworks and major variables in each model, and highlight some of the empirical findings.

3.2. *Strümpel's Model*

During the 1960s, a multinational study of factors affecting taxpayer compliance was conducted by researchers from the University of Cologne. The study focused on the British, French, Italian, Spanish, and German tax systems, and the "*tax mentality*" – norms and attitudes shared by tax enforcers and taxpayers – in each nation. In each country, the characteristics of tax policies and tax enforcement were delineated, and self-employed taxpayers were surveyed. The Cologne researchers found that in France, Spain, and Italy the tax systems were both inefficient and expensive, with large gaps between tax laws and tax enforcement. The problems of tax collection arose primarily from the country's tax mentality. When norms, attitudes, and beliefs are fundamentally hostile to taxes, attempts at rigid enforcement will be counterproductive because they create even more of the resistance they are designed to overcome. As a result, neither the revenue nor the distributional goals of the tax laws are met.

In Germany, the tax system is efficient, but also expensive. The goals of taxation, for both revenue and income distribution, are realized. However, they are achieved primarily through strict and relatively coercive tax enforcement. The intensive confrontation of taxpayers with tax enforcement agencies leads to alienation, which then decreases taxpayers' willingness to cooperate with tax requirements. In contrast, tax administration in England is generally cautious and somewhat lenient. Audit levels are lower, fewer accounting procedures are imposed by authorities, and the law contains more opportunities for legal tax avoidance. This strategy may avoid friction and resentment on the part of taxpayers, but also allows easy opportunities for evasion and avoidance. The result is a system that is inexpensive, in that little tax resistance occurs, but which is also inefficient, in that the allocative and distributional goals of the tax laws are not met.

The results were formalized in a model of taxpayer compliance using two general categories of independent variables:

1. "Rigidity of assessment" describes the extent of confrontation between the tax administration and taxpayers, including the amount of tax, the level of fines, the inquisitiveness of tax assessment, and the level of red tape.
2. "Willingness to cooperate" represents individual attitudes toward and perception of the tax system (see Figure 1).

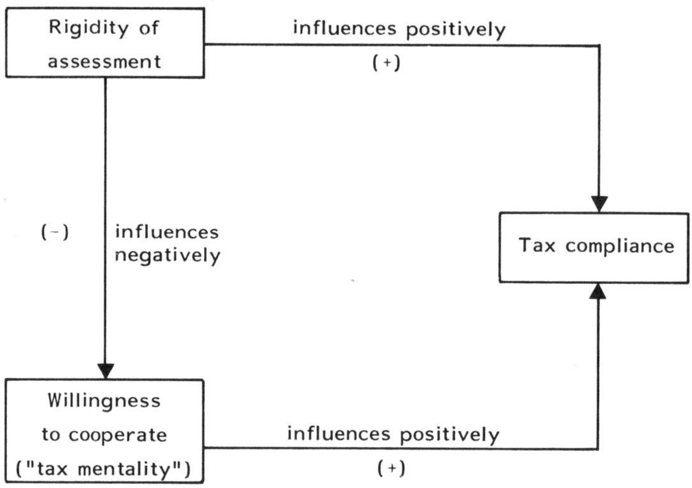

Fig. 1. Strümpel's model of tax compliance (1969).

While willingness to cooperate is positively related to compliance, rigidity of assessment has two opposing effects, a deterrent effect as well as a negative effect through the intervening variable of willingness to cooperate. This model provides an interesting counterweight to traditional deterrence models. It suggests that in the absence of supporting norms, strict law enforcement can create negative reactions in taxpayers that may eventually undermine taxpayer compliance.

3.3. *The U.S. IRS' Model of Taxpayer Compliance*

During the early 1970s, the Internal Revenue Service (IRS) constructed an analytic model of factors affecting three aspects of taxpayer compliance: voluntary filing, accurate assessment of taxes owed, and full payment of the tax liability (IRS, 1970). These aspects of compliance are determined by taxpayers' willingness and technical ability to comply, and the IRS's administrative capability of ensuring compliance. Administrative capability is viewed as having indirect effects on compliance through the agency's influence on taxpayers' ability and willingness to comply. In this view, the tax agency is not solely a law enforcement body, but also a service agency seeking to prevent noncompliance (Smith and Kinsey, 1985).

The previous two models focused primarily upon motivation as the primary individual-level factors affecting taxpayer compliance. The IRS model incorporates motivation, but also specifically includes the taxpayers' knowledge and the complexity of tax situations as important factors. Some of the variables affecting technical ability to comply may also affect taxpayers' technical ability not to comply. For example, taxpayers with more experience with the tax system may have learned more about how to avoid being caught when they evade taxes. This is analogous to the "experiential effect" described in the deterrence literature, and suggests an interaction between willingness and technical ability to comply.

3.4. *Vogel's Model of Taxpayer Compliance*

Vogel (1974) reported on a comprehensive survey of Swedish taxpayers conducted in 1968. In his theoretical framework, three objective factors – exchange relationships with the government, general social orientations, and objective opportunities for tax evasion – have both direct and indirect effects upon tax attitudes and behavior. The indirect effects of these objective variables are mediated through attitudes toward taxes, the tax system, and government spending, as well as perceptions of illegal opportunities. Contact with tax evaders is also found to be a strong factor affecting tax evasion attitudes and behavior.

The empirical analysis was primarily bivariate, but a factor analysis suggested two dimensions of tax fraud, a "learning factor," which was strongly related to contact with delinquent taxpayers, and a "control system factor," which involved opportunity factors like self-employment and the receipt of income subject to withholding.

Vogel constructed a typology of taxpayers based on Kelman's (1965) description of three *processes of attitude change*: compliance, identification, and internalization. *Compliance* occurs when people accept influence solely to gain rewards and avoid punishments, and thus exemplifies classic deterrence. *Identification* occurs when people accept influence because the induced behavior is associated with a satisfying, self-defining relationship with those exerting influence. In this case, the norms of specific valued reference groups will be paramount, even in the absence of informal sanctions. *Internalization* occurs when people accept influence because the induced behavior is already congruent with their own value systems. In such cases, the only sanction feared is guilt.

In Vogel's typology, individual adaptations to the tax system involve not only these processes, but also the specific character of ideological and social referents. Conformist internalizers will pay fully despite opportunities to evade while deviant internalizers will break the law and accept punishment to express their beliefs. Conformist identifiers will pay taxes because they value their identity as citizens, but deviant identifiers will value noncompliant reference groups more highly. Conformist compliers will focus primarily upon legal sanctions. Deviant compliers may believe legal sanctions are weak or may operate in arenas (e.g., organized crime) where extrajudicial sanctioning agents explicitly discourage obedience to tax laws.

3.5. *Spicer's Model of Tax Evasion*

Spicer (1974; Spicer and Lundstedt, 1976) developed a model focused primarily on the internal system of the actor. Concepts from deterrence, equity and reference group theories are used to delineate patterns of interaction between the social system and the individual. These interactions shape generalized beliefs and values concerning the tax system, the importance of money, the likelihood and severity of sanctions, and the tax behaviors of other citizens. In turn, these beliefs and values play a major role in developing the preferences (affective orientations about outcomes), instrumentalities (beliefs about instrumental links among outcomes), and expectancies (subjective probabilities associating specific acts with specific outcomes) associated with particular outcomes. Expectancies, preferences and instrumentalities combine to produce a performance vector, a summary variable representing all the behavioral forces motivating particular acts of compliance and evasion (Lewin, 1935). This model is complex, and the empirical work could provide only a partial test due to data restrictions. A scale of tax resistance, used to measure the performance vector, was developed and pre-tested, and applied to a survey of residents in two middle-class suburbs in Ohio. Predictions derived from reference group theory and equity theory were confirmed for both the tax resistance scale and index of admitted tax evasion. Deterrence predictions were generally not confirmed. The perceived probability of detection was related to tax resistance, but not to tax evasion and perceived severity was unrelated to both.

3.6. *Song and Yarbrough's Model*

Song and Yarbrough (1978) published a study of tax ethics among residents of a North Carolina city. Their model views compliance as a function of the environment, the tax ethics of individuals, and opportunity and other situational factors. The legal environment in the model is structured by

1. the legitimacy of the laws of the state,
2. the effectiveness of the law enforcement process, and
3. citizens' understanding and acceptance of legal obligations.

Situational factors include income level, the unemployment rate, tax rates, and the effectiveness of tax administration agencies. Tax ethics are defined as the norms of behavior governing citizens as taxpayers in their relationship with the government. Both the legal environment and situational factors interact with tax ethics to affect citizens' self-assessment of tax obligations, which is then directly related to tax payment.

The empirical research focuses on developing and analyzing a measure of tax ethics. Tax ethics are defined in an absolute sense; the scale is used as if it were an absolute measure, without consideration of competing ethical stances. When converted to a 100 point scale, the mean was 60.3, which the authors considered "barely passing" (p. 451). This judgment has been widely quoted as an indication that tax ethics are low.

However, in conceptualizing and measuring such a variable, it is important to recognize that there may be a multiplicity of possible – and defensible – ethical stances. A better understanding of how moral commitments to obeying tax laws are developed and sustained will provide greater insight into problems of tax compliance and will point more easily to potential solutions.

3.7. *Westat's Model of Taxpayer Compliance*

In the late 1970s, Westat, Inc., conducted several studies of taxpayer compliance under contract to the IRS, including development of an econometric model of optimal audit coverage (Westat, 1980b), qualitative research using focus groups (Westat, 1980c), and a pilot survey of self-reports of income tax noncompliance in South Bend, Indiana and San Jose, California (Westat, 1980a).

Focus group discussion led to the identification of six basic motives for tax cheating: economic utility, fear of the IRS, moral latitude toward tax evasion, political attitudes, social comparison, and personal control over taxes (Ekstrand, 1980). Tax dollars appear to have differential utility; taxes paid out-of-pocket and on income from second jobs were begrudged more. Contrary to deterrence theory, the IRS was feared more for bureaucratic entanglement than for its sanctions. Political attitudes were germane primarily through perceptions of government waste. Non-itemizers subject to full withholding expressed the greatest frustration with the tax system, but were among the most compliant. This points to the need to control for opportunity to evade when investigating the relationship between tax attitudes and tax behavior.

Key variable groups from the pilot survey (see Ekstrand, 1980) included opportunity to comply, past enforcement contact with the IRS, tax attitudes and differential association with noncompliers. Not surprisingly, self-admitted evaders had more opportunities for noncompliance, had previous enforcement contact with the IRS, condoned tax evasion and had friends who had been contacted by the IRS for enforcement purposes. Unlike focus group results, perceptions of government waste and fear of bureaucratic hassles were not related to tax evasion. As predicted by deterrence theory, perceived certainty of detection was related to tax evasion, but perceived severity of punishment was not.

3.8. *Lewis' Models of Income Tax Compliance*

Lewis (1982) developed a model of taxpayer compliance in which policy concerns of economic research are modeled in parallel with psychological and sociological perspectives (see Figure 2). Beginning with the policy level, the nature of government fiscal policy and policy makers' assumptions about taxpayers affect the structure and policies of tax enforcement agencies, which in turn affect the level of tax compliance and tax evasion. In turn, their level of tax cheating and the successes and failures of tax enforcement affect government policies and policy makers' assumptions about taxpayers. However, policy makers' assumptions about taxpayers are relatively resistant to change.

At the individual level, attitudes and perceptions about the tax system affect taxpayer compliance and tax evasion. These attitudes and perceptions about government policies are, at least in part, the result of actual as well as perceived fiscal policies and structure. Similarly, objective and

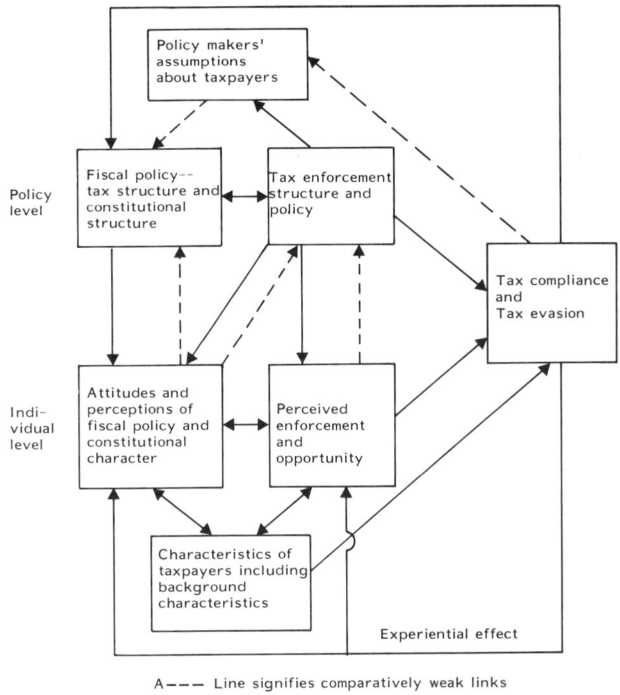

Fig. 2. Modified version of Lewis' parallel model of income tax evasion (1982).

perceived tax enforcement activities affect attitudes toward fiscal policies and perceptions of opportunities for evasion. Lewis' parallel model is complex, with many simultaneous effects and feedback loops, as well as bridges between aggregate and individual levels of analysis that remain unspecified. As such, it is not easily amenable to empirical investigation. A particularly problematic area in this and other models concerns the link between attitudes and behavior, which Lewis addresses in the context of Ajzen and Fishbein's (1980) theory of reasoned action. This theory specifies mathematically the relationship among beliefs, attitudes and behaviors, and assumes that most human behaviors can be predicted and explained almost exclusively in terms of individual beliefs and attitudes. In the model, the best predictor of actual tax evasion is the intention to evade. However, intentions are themselves determined by personal attitudes toward tax evasion and subjective norms about it, weighted by their relative importance to the individual.

Ajzen and Fishbein's (1980) model has been successfully applied to such areas as family planning behavior, adult and adolescent alcohol use, and cheating on college exams. However, Lewis doubts that the model can be adequately tested because of questions about the validity of self-reported intentions and behavior.

3.9. *Groenland and Van Veldhoven's Model of Tax Evasion*

Groenland and Van Veldhoven (1983) proposed a model of tax evasion in which personality and situational characteristics interact to affect knowledge of and attitudes toward the tax system, which then affect personal dispositions to evade taxes. Both situational characteristics and personal dispositions have direct effects on tax behavior. Groenland and Van Veldhoven suggest "locus of control" as a promising personality construct to examine (Rotter, 1966). This model was tested using a small-scale study of two groups of workers in the Tilburg region of the Netherlands and a similar study conducted in Sweden (Wärneryd, 1980). Neither study could examine variations in tax system characteristics, but for other variables the results were similar for both studies, and provided tentative support for aspects of the model. In particular, those with an internal locus of control were more likely to have favorable attitudes toward the tax system. In the Dutch sample, locus of control interacted strongly with education: Better educated internals were more likely, and internals with lower education were less likely, to evade taxes.

3.10. *Weigel, Hessing and Elffers' Social Psychological Model of Tax Evasion Behavior*

The central notion of this model (Weigel et al., 1987) is that evading taxes as a deviant act can be defined as defective behavior within the context of a social dilemma (see Figure 3).

Their theoretical framework specifies two sets of variables in the social environment – situational instigations and situational constraints – which are conducive to tax evasion and their analogous counterparts within the individual – personal instigations and personal constraints. By describing situationally defined instigations such as financial strain and social norms, and constraints like opportunity and legal and social controls, the framework accounts for the concentration of evasion behavior among certain social groups. Location of an individual's position in terms of exposure to these conditions yields an estimate of the probability that s/he will engage in acts of tax evasion. According to the model this probability is increased when it can be shown that the hypothesized effects of such exposure have occurred; the individual actually possesses the psychological characteristics which are expected to flow from exposure to the conditions specified. These

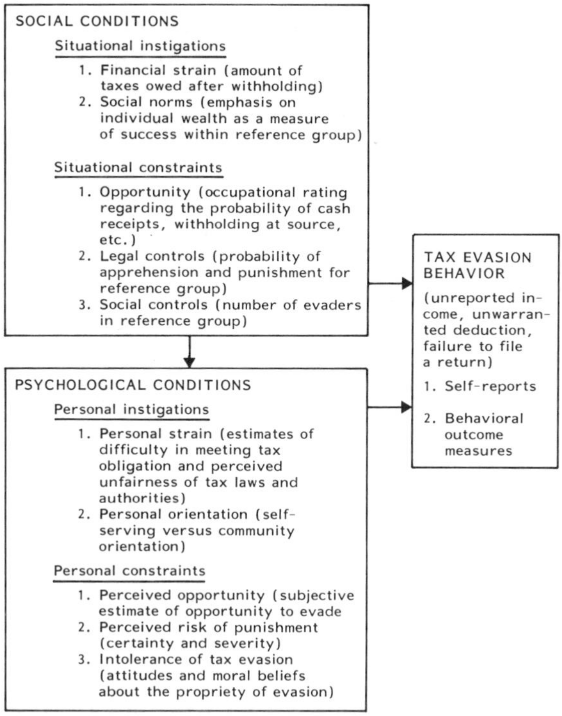

Fig. 3. Weigel, Hessing and Elffers's social psychological model of tax evasion behavior (1987).

psychological characteristics are personal strain and self-serving orientation as personal instigations, and perceived opportunity, perceived risk of punishment, and intolerance of tax evasion as personal constraints.

In general, then, the theoretical scheme conceptualizes tax evasion as the outcome of interacting instigations and constraints operating both within the individual and within the confronting situation. Two aspects of the relationships between the social and psychological elements of the framework deserve emphasis. First, the structure of the social and psychological domains described is formally parallel. Each proposes two major sources of instigation to engage in tax evasion and three major constraints against the occurrence of such behavior. Second, since the variables comprising the psychological domain are the individual analogues of the variables comprising the social domain, the framework permits a systematic basis for examining the role of individual attributes in mediating the impact of social conditions on behavior.

This framework also underscores the need to attend more carefully to the measurement of the dependent behavioral variable. The authors propose that both self-reports and officially documented behavioral measures will be part of future tax evasion studies.

In a first empirical study the authors tested part of their model: the influence of personal instigations and constraints on tax evasion. In cooperation with the Dutch Ministry of Finance they were able to measure both self-reported behavior and officially documented behavior on an individual level (see section 2.4 of this chapter). The unexpected results showed a negligible correlation between the two behavioral dependent variables. Furthermore, the personal constraint variables (fear of punishment, social controls and attitudes toward underreporting income and claiming false deductions) were reasonably strongly correlated with self-reported behavior, but unrelated with the behavioral outcome measures. With regard to the personal instigation variables (dissatisfactions with tax authorities and tax rules, and self-serving orientation variables such as competitiveness, alienation and tolerance of deviance) the results were in the opposite direction: no correlations with self-reported tax evasion and significant correlations with officially documented behavior. This remarkable pattern was replicated in a behavioral simulation study by Webley et al. (1986): The personal constraints were unrelated to tax evasion behavior, while the personal instigation variables were significantly related to the evasion behavior in this simulation study.

Although the first results of Elffers et al. (1987), together with the replication by Webley et al. (1986), support their hypothesis that the system is perceived by the taxpayer as a social dilemma, further research is needed to validate the usefulness of their complete theoretical framework.

4. TAX EVASION RESEARCH: THE FUTURE

With the introduction of taxes society was immediately confronted with tax evasion. This serious societal problem has received considerable attention in recent decades from both tax officials and researchers. Tax evasion studies have been characterized by more theoretical attention than empirical research. Only a few of the theoretical models that were discussed in this chapter were (partially) tested. The different measurement strategies that have been used so far have shown that these different strategies resulted in different empirical results.

All social science methodologies have their weaknesses and strengths, and it is important that researchers be sensitive to limitations and select the methodology that is most appropriate for their research goals. The most convincing evidence that a variable plays a key role in affecting taxpayer decisions to evade taxes is replication of findings across methodologies. Otherwise, we cannot be sure if the finding reflects a true state of nature, or is simply an artifact of the research method used.

When findings diverge across methodologies, the really intriguing question becomes why they do diverge. The final answer may be that one method is superior to another, but it also may reflect interactions of the knowledge and motives of research subjects with the particular measurement situations presented to them by researchers.

REFERENCES

Aitken, S.S., and L. Bonneville, 1980, A General Taxpayer Opinion Survey, IRS, Office of Planning and Research.

Ajzen, I., and M. Fishbein, 1980, Understanding Attitudes and Predicting Behavior, Englewood Cliffs, NJ: Prentice-Hall.

American Bar Foundation, 1986, Frequency Code Book and Selected Cross-tabulations of Survey of Oregon Adults.

Bell, C.G., and W. Buchanan, 1966, Reliable and unreliable respondents: Party registration and prestige pressure, Western Political Quarterly, 19, 37-43.

Cahalan, D., 1968, Correlates of respondent accuracy in the Denver reliability survey, Public Opinion Quarterly, 32, 608-621.

Clark, J.P., and L.L. Tifft, 1966, Polygraph and interview validation of self-reported deviant behavior, American Sociological Review, 31, 516-523.

Clotfelter, C.T., 1983, Tax evasion and tax rates: An analysis of individual returns, Review of Economics and Statistics, 65, 363-373.

Ekstrand, L., 1980, "Factors affecting compliance: Focus group and survey results," Proceedings of the 73rd Annual Conference on Taxation, National Tax Association, "Tax Institute of America", pp. 253-263.

Elffers, H., R.H. Weigel, and D.J. Hessing, 1987, The consequences of different strategies for measuring tax evasion behavior, Journal of Economic Psychology, 8, 311-337.

Farrington, D.P., 1973, Self-reports of deviant behavior: Predictive and stable?, Journal of Criminal Law and Criminology, 64, 99-110.

Friedland, N., 1982, A note on tax evasion as a function of the quality of information about the magnitude and credibility of threatened fines: Some preliminary research, Journal of Applied Social Psychology, 12, 54-59.

Friedland, N., S. Maital, and A. Rutenberg, 1978, A simulation study of income tax evasion, Journal of Public Economics, 10, 107-116.

Groenland, E.A.G., and G.M. van Veldhoven, 1983, Tax evasion behavior: A psychological framework, Journal of Economic Psychology, 3, 129-144.

Hauser, P., 1969, "Comments on Coleman's paper," in: R. Bierstedt (ed.), A Design for Sociology: Scope, Objective, Methods, Philadelphia, PA: American Academy of Political and Social Science, pp. 122-136.

Internal Revenue Service, 1970, Factors Affecting Taxpayer Compliance with Federal Tax Laws, Planning and Analysis Division, Washington DC: U.S. Government Printing Office (staff paper).

Internal Revenue Service, 1983, Income Tax Compliance Research: Estimates for 1973-1981, Research Division, Washington DC: U.S. Government Printing Office.

Kelman, H.C., 1965, "Compliance, identification and internalization: Three processes of attitude change," in: H. Proshansky and B. Seidenberg (eds.), Basic Studies in Social Psychology, New York: Holt, Rinehart and Winston, pp. 140-156.

Kinsey, K.A., 1986, Theories and models of tax cheating, Criminal Justice Abstracts, 18, 403-425.

Kinsey, K.A., 1987, Advocacy and Perceptions: The Structure of Tax Practice, revision of paper presented at the 1986 Law and Society Meetings.

Lewin, K., 1935, A Dynamic Theory of Personality, New York: McGraw-Hill.
Lewis, A., 1982, The Psychology of Taxation, Oxford: Martin Robertson.
Loftus, E.F., 1985, To file, perchance to cheat, Psychology Today, 19, 35-39.
Phillips, D.L., 1971, Knowledge from What? Theories and Methods in Social Research, Chicago, IL: Rand McNally.
Phillips, D.L., 1973, Abandoning Method, San Francisco, CA: Jossey-Bass.
Robins, L.N., 1966, The reluctant respondent, Public Opinion Quarterly, 27, 276-286.
Rotter, J.B., 1966, Generalized expectancies for internal versus external control of reinforcement, Psychological Monographs, 80, no. 609.
Smith, K.W., and K.A. Kinsey, 1985, Cooperation and control: Strategies and tactics for tax examination, Tax Administration Review, 1, 13-29.
Song, Y., and T.E. Yarbrough, 1978, Tax ethics and taxpayers attitudes: A survey, Public Administration Review, 38, 442-452.
Spicer, M.N., 1974, A Behavioral Model of Income Tax Evasion, Columbus, OH: Ohio State University (unpublished dissertation).
Spicer, M.N., 1975, New approaches to the problem of tax evasion, British Tax Review, 152-154.
Spicer, M.N., and L.A. Becker, 1980, Fiscal inequity and tax evasion: An experimental approach, National Tax Journal, 33, 172-175.
Spicer, M.N., and R.E. Hero, 1985, Tax evasion and heuristics: A research note, Journal of Public Economics, 26, 263-267.
Spicer, M.N., and S.B. Lundstedt, 1976, Understanding tax evasion, Public Finance, 31, 295-305.
Spicer, M.N., and J.E. Thomas, 1982, Audit probabilities and the tax evasion decision: An experimental approach, Journal of Economic Psychology, 2, 241-245.
Stacey, A.W., R.H. Widaman, R. Hays, and M.R. DiMatteo, 1985, Validity of self-reports of alcohol and other drug use: A multitrait-multimethod assessment, Journal of Personality and Social Psychology, 49, 219-232.
Strümpel, B., 1969, "The contribution of survey research to public finance," in: A.T. Peacock (ed.), Quantitative Analysis in Public Finance, New York: Praeger, pp. 13-22.
Sudman, S., and N.M. Bradburn, 1974, Response Effects in Surveys: A Review and Synthesis, Chicago, IL: Aldine.
Vogel, J., 1974, Taxation and public opinion in Sweden: An interpretation of recent survey data, National Tax Journal, 27, 499-513.
Wallschutzky, I.G., 1984, Possible causes for tax evasion, Journal of Economic Psychology, 5, 371-384.
Wärneryd, K.-E., 1980, Psychological reactions to the tax system, Skandinaviska Enskilda Banken Quarterly Review, 3-4, 75-84.
Warrinier, G.K., G.H.G. McDougall, and J.D. Claxton, 1984, Any data or none at all? Living with inaccuracies in self-reports of residential energy consumption, Environment and Behavior, 16, 503-526.
Webley, P., and S. Halstead, 1985, Tax evasion on the micro: Significant simulations or expedient experiments? Journal of Interdisciplinary Economics, 1, 87-100.
Webley, P., I. Morris, and F. Amstutz, 1985, "Tax evasion during a small business simulation," in: H. Brandstätter and E. Kirchler (eds.), Economic Psychology. Proceedings of the 10th IAREP Annual Colloquium, Linz, Austria: Rudolf Trauner Verlag, pp. 233-242.
Webley, P., H. Robben, and I. Morris, 1988, "Social comparison and tax evasion in a shop situation," in: S. Maital (ed.), Applied Behavioural Economics, Vol. 2, Brighton, Sussex: Wheatsheaf, pp. 553-561.
Weigel, R.H., D.J. Hessing, and H. Elffers, 1987, Tax evasion research: A critical appraisal and theoretical model, Journal of Economic Psychology, 8, 215-235.

Westat, 1980a, Self-reported Tax Compliance: A Pilot Survey Report, Rockville, MD: Westat.

Westat, 1980b, A Procedure for Estimating Taxpayer Response for Changes in IRS Coverage, Rockville, MD: Westat.

Westat, 1980c, Individual Income Tax Compliance Factors Study: Qualitative Research Results, Rockville, MD: Westat.

Witte, A.D., and D.F. Woodbury, 1983, The Effect of Tax and Tax Administration on Tax Compliance, 83-1, Chapel Hill, NC: University of North Carolina, Department of Economics (working paper).

Table of Contents

15. Work and Leisure

GORDON E. O'BRIEN
The Flinders University of South Australia, Bedford Park, Australia

1. INTRODUCTION

The study of the relationship between work and leisure has been largely influenced by economic, historical and technological factors. Although some writers (e.g., Wilensky, 1960) have maintained that a sharp distinction between work and leisure only appeared with the advent of the industrial revolution, it is possible to trace the distinction between the two concepts to much earlier periods. Earlier Greek writers, for example, often made it clear that manual work was an unfortunate necessity, while leisure provided opportunities for the pursuit of truth and personal fulfillment. Work was an activity of sorrow, "ponos," that prevented the contemplation of truth and beauty (Tilgher, 1930). This elevated view of leisure declined in value after classical Greece. With the development of the modern industrialism, leisure even became an activity that was considered relatively unimportant or even inimical to personal development. In modern times, the creative function of leisure has again become a subject for debate. This has been large due to a recognition that many jobs in industrialized societies do not provide much opportunity for personal fulfillment. They do not provide many employees with tasks that fully use valued skills nor do they often provide a means of allowing employees to exert a moderate degree of personal control over their work activities.

The potential for leisure as a means of compensating for dissatisfying work was stressed by some writers in the nineteenth and twentieth century but the exact meaning of the term "leisure" depended on particular economic and historical circumstances (Hunnicutt, 1980). In England during the nineteenth century it appears that many factory employees did use their free time as a means of personal development as well as a means of shaping a working class culture (Cunningham, 1980; Thompson, 1968). However, this did not develop into a popular movement due to both political control of leisure and free-time activities as well as the debilitating effect of factory work on the health and energy of the employed. It was difficult

Van Raaij, W.F., van Veldhoven, G.M. and Wärneryd, K.E. (eds) Handbook of Economic Psychology. ISBN 90-247-3720-6.

for exhausted workers to be self-directed and persistent in the pursuit of leisure.

The public debate about the function of free time only emerged after a sharp decrease in working hours. The largest decline took place in the first 20 years of the twentieth century. In the United States, for example, the average work week dropped from 58 to 48 hours a week and the decline since then has been slower and has levelled out at about 40 hours. The increased abundance of free time in the present century initially generated a debate about the functions of free time for the working population. A common view was that free time was important for work efficiency and the maintenance of physical health. Politicians and reformers frequently saw free time as an opportunity for employees to improve their health and strengthen family bonds. Businessmen gradually accept shorter working hours on grounds of efficiency rather than the positive virtues of free time. They were influenced by industrial consultants like Frederic Taylor who believed that employee efficiency declined after about eight hours work. In the early part of the century the creative personal function of leisure was not a public issue. Some, such as Veblen (1899), actually counselled against increases in leisure for it could lead to employees mimicking the self-indulgent life of "conspicuous consumption" adopted by capitalist owners.

The positive virtues of leisure were raised by unionists who, after World War I, campaigned for reduction in hours. Not only would shorter hours, for them, decrease unemployment and raise the value of labour, shorter hours would also compensate men for poor jobs. In the United States, unionists believed that machines and management techniques had reduced the capacity of work to provide psychological growth. Their reaction to these changes in work did not lead to large-scale protests about the negative effects of work, but to a demand that leisure be seen as a way of compensating for work that was destroying craftsmanship, personal control and creativity.

The arguments lost their impetus after the Great Depression of the thirties. This occurred for a number of reasons. One reason was that leisure came to be associated with the misery of unemployment. "The shorter hour movement and the share-the-work movement were both branded as regressive and cosmetic devices to disguise the tragedy of unemployment by distributing its misery" (Hunnicutt, 1980: p. 207). Furthermore, economic growth was seen by economists and businessmen as dependent on increased consumer demand that could only be generated by increased work and wages. According to this view, increases in leisure would militate against economic growth.

This view has tended to prevail in the decades of social reconstruction after World War II. Leisure time for most employees has not increased and furthermore little public debate focused on the creative potential of leisure activities. Although many claim that this is the beginning of the age of leisure, there has been little change within industrialized countries in the amount of time spent on work and leisure in the last thirty years (Evans, 1975). Leisure time might have increased, if nonwork time devoted to household maintenance activities (e.g., cooking, cleaning) had declined. However, this does not seem to have happened as household maintenance has not declined much despite the availability of time-saving devices and take-away food outlets (Lindner, 1970; Vanek, 1974). Increased income over this period has, it appears, been used to buy increasing quantities of household goods that require time to purchase and time to install and maintain. Also, the time available for leisure has been restricted within households due to the increased number of married women who have entered the workforce.

Leisure as a social issue has begun to emerge again with the onset of increasing unemployment. Jenkins and Sherman in a book titled *The Collapse of Work* (1979) argued that the modern situation requires us to rethink the nature of work and leisure. Recession, technological change, and the decline of the manufacturing industries have led to unemployment rates which doom millions of workers to a life where paid employment will not be a possibility. Their adjustment to unemployment is poor because, they argue, their belief in the importance of work prevents them from seeing their increased free time as an opportunity for creative leisure. Their work orientation is not innate but a conditioned response that has been reinforced by education, social pressures and the trade unions. Leisure has not been emphasized as a source of life satisfaction or as an activity that can be constructive for society as well as the person. Jenkins and Sherman do not provide evidence for their propositions about the meaning of work and leisure but they do raise one of the main problems amenable to research.

Prior to *The Collapse of Work*, many social scientists had also argued that leisure studies were necessary in order to establish its potential for personal development as, and if, working time decreased. For them it was necessary to identify the kind of leisure that could compensate individuals who may, in the future, have little work to do and work that may be of poor quality (e.g., Dumazedier, 1967; Fourastié, 1965; Emery, 1977).

Others have argued that it is necessary to study leisure in order to understand work. Social scientists have tried to identify the general nature of jobs that could improve the quality of working life. As leisure activities are typically chosen to allow autonomy and personal fulfillment, then the study of leisure activities could help identify the dimension of jobs that, in a sense, could turn work into play or leisure (Csikszentimihalyi, 1975; Dunnette, 1973; Porter, Lawler, and Hackman, 1975).

The call for a re-direction of orientations towards leisure assumes that re-conditioning might be a fairly simple matter of changing self-awareness through public education. However, existing work structures may have left enduring effects on values personality that will prevent individuals from having the capacity to change their leisure behaviour. Hence another reason for examining leisure is to establish the manner in which work experiences have shaped leisure needs and behaviours (Kohn and Schooler, 1983). Has work a dominant influence on nonwork activities or is there independence between the two sets of activities? Or is it possible that leisure is indeed an unrecognized source of compensation for deprivations at work? Before it is possible to address these questions it is necessary to have some way of measuring and comparing work and leisure activities.

2. WORK, EMPLOYMENT AND LEISURE

At a general level, work is the exertion of effort in the performance of a task. Hence work can occur either in paid employment, in household maintenance activities, or in the pursuit of hobby or leisure pastimes. Although this distinction between work and employment is frequently made, the common usage of the term "work" refers to paid employment. People "go to work" and relax in their free time after work. Common usage will be adopted here in the discussion of work-leisure relationships but it is acknowledged that work, in a general sense, is expended during the performance of task.

The problem of distinguishing work activities in employment from activities outside of employment has been examined in a variety of ways. The simplest approach has been to define them in terms of the social setting and the meaning ascribed to the activities. Work, in employment involves the performance of prescribed tasks associated with a position in a work organization. The organization is usually considered to be a work organization if there is a contract specifying that wages are to be paid for a specified amount of work. Whereas activities in work organization are largely imposed and evaluated by agents external to the individual, activities in free time are selected by the individual to satisfy personal goals and needs. The main problem with the separation of activities into those associated with work and free time is that free time activities include activities not usually associated with leisure. Outside of work organizations, people sleep, wash, eat and maintain household property. These tasks have the quality of necessity and it is necessary to distinguish them from leisure tasks which are freely chosen. Thus it seems possible to describe leisure activities as a set of freely chosen tasks performed outside of employment and not done for the purpose of essential personal and household maintenance.

A contrary view is that leisure cannot be defined by activities and tasks because leisure is a state of mind (De Grazia, 1964; Neulinger, 1974). We are at leisure, according to such views, when we choose activities that result in a state of enjoyment. Thus, it is possible for people to be at leisure when they are working for others. Conversely, non-work activities may not be leisure ones, even if they are freely chosen. If they become tedious or too stressful, they cease to be leisure activities.

This subjective approach has the advantage of looking at work and leisure in a way that could eliminate the value overtones of the distinction between work and leisure. Work activities are not necessarily unpleasant but can become pleasurable, if they are experienced as freely chosen, enjoyable and use one's talents. However, the main disadvantage of this framework is that it makes the study of the relationship between work and leisure extremely difficult. Any given activity may be classified as a leisure activity, provided that the mental state of the actor is one of enjoyment in the expression of valued capacities. In order to study leisure it would be necessary to have continuous access to the mental state of the actor and this would be very difficult. Furthermore, it is doubtful that such peak mental experiences are a stable and continuous product of activities that are freely chosen and challenging. Even our most enjoyable activities often require periods of neutral emotion and even some unpleasantness. A keen gardener maybe delighted in monitoring healthy growth in his plants but is unlikely to be in a state of ecstasy when digging, fertilizing and weeding.

A preferable way of studying the relationship between work and leisure is to define them as tasks performed in different social settings (Kabanoff and O'Brien, 1980; O'Brien, Dowling, and Kabanoff, 1978). This does not preclude the possibility of investigating the mental states associated with these tasks. But the main advantage of this task attributes approach is that it allows comparisons to be made between work and leisure tasks – provided some common task attributes have been defined which allow inferences to be made about their similarities and differences. This is an important advance because much of the work and leisure literature assume that people either generalize from or compensate for work activities. But what do they generalize from? And what do they compensate for? Generalization implies similarity in work and leisure activities while compensation implies some form of difference. It is probable that difficulties in integration of the literature in this area are due to the failure of most writers to specify the dimensions on which work and leisure activities can be compared.

Tasks can be described on many dimensions (Table 1), but it was assumed that there were five main dimensions which determined an actor's evaluation of task activities. These were defined as follows:

1. *Skill utilization* is the degree to which a task uses a person's skills and personal capacities.

Table 1. Mean dimensions for leisure activities (from Kabanoff and O'Brien, 1982). (Maximum = 5, Minimum = 1, Range 1-5)

	Influence	Variety	Pressure	Skill utilization	Inter-action
Home gardening	3.78	3.33	2.78	3.11	1.83
Home improvements	3.56	3.78	3.33	3.77	2.11
Sewing	2.94	3.61	2.78	3.44	1.56
Handicrafts	2.77	3.69	2.46	4.00	2.00
Photography	3.07	3.46	2.31	4.08	2.46
Cooking	3.28	4.44	3.17	3.44	2.06
Reading	2.56	3.94	2.00	2.67	1.28
Debating	3.92	3.38	3.92	3.77	4.00
Model building	2.67	3.67	2.72	3.28	1.56
Playing musical instrument	3.06	3.44	3.72	4.28	1.94
Stamps (collecting)	2.11	2.33	1.61	2.17	1.22
Cards alone	2.06	1.77	1.61	1.72	1.00
Cards with others	2.28	2.67	2.78	2.78	3.11
Chess	2.83	2.67	3.72	3.94	2.89
Draughts	2.61	2.11	2.50	2.83	2.78
Dice games	1.67	1.72	2.06	1.94	2.33
Billiards/pool/8-ball	2.78	2.22	3.11	3.22	2.72
Darts	2.56	1.89	2.56	2.89	2.39
Monopoly	2.50	2.33	2.67	2.50	3.00
Scrabble	2.78	2.61	3.11	3.33	2.94
Records	2.50	3.33	1.50	1.78	1.61
Playing football	3.22	2.72	4.00	3.50	3.83
Playing soccer	3.31	3.23	3.92	3.77	3.85
Football (spectator)	1.72	1.94	2.06	1.28	2.33
Hockey	2.04	2.44	3.67	3.33	3.50
Squash	2.78	2.44	4.33	3.78	3.28
Running	2.56	2.27	3.94	2.94	1.89
Tennis	2.62	2.92	3.62	3.77	2.92
Swimming	1.77	2.23	3.54	3.38	2.08
Surfing	2.08	2.76	3.46	3.69	2.08
Fishing	1.85	2.46	1.92	3.00	1.85
Exercise	2.28	2.00	4.06	3.22	1.61
Cricket	2.83	2.50	3.72	3.72	3.44
Croquet	2.56	1.89	2.94	3.06	2.83
Bowls	2.61	2.11	2.94	3.17	3.06
Basketball	2.94	2.61	3.89	3.61	3.56
Lacrosse	2.78	2.39	3.78	3.50	3.44
Golf	2.15	3.00	3.23	3.92	3.00
Judo, Yoga	3.28	2.56	3.78	3.94	2.89
Horse riding	2.38	3.15	3.15	3.46	2.31
Bush walking	2.83	3.44	2.72	2.78	2.33
Camping	3.11	3.61	2.78	2.94	3.00
Sailing	2.83	3.00	3.67	3.94	3.27
Parachuting	2.83	2.78	4.17	3.78	2.22

Table 1. *(continued)*

Gliding	3.15	2.85	4.00	4.15	2.77
Trail bike riding	2.83	3.00	3.11	3.17	1.89
Motor bike riding	2.85	3.15	3.46	3.46	2.77
Watching television	1.89	1.94	1.44	1.00	1.28
Listening to radio	1.08	3.23	1.62	1.53	1.54
Going to the pictures	1.83	2.28	1.44	1.22	1.50
Sleeping	2.17	1.06	1.00	1.00	1.00
Drinking by yourself, away from home	1.89	1.61	1.44	1.00	1.11
Drinking with friends, away from home	2.44	2.61	1.72	1.44	3.28
Drinking alone at home	2.11	1.56	1.39	1.00	1.06
Drinking with friends at home	2.72	2.56	1.56	1.39	3.22
Dances, cabarets, etc.	2.61	3.00	2.22	1.89	3.11
Meet friends at milk bars, etc.	2.39	2.78	1.78	1.56	3.11
Local outings alone	2.72	3.00	1.83	1.44	1.50
Outings with friends	2.78	3.33	2.17	1.67	3.28
Horse racing	1.78	2.17	2.06	1.83	1.94
Dog racing	1.72	1.94	2.00	1.78	1.94
Scouts or Girl Guides	2.46	3.84	2.62	2.69	4.08
Youth clubs	3.00	2.78	2.28	2.11	2.94
Lifesaving	3.46	3.30	3.77	3.62	3.54
Attended lectures	2.39	2.94	2.44	2.22	2.36
Emergency fire fighting	3.15	3.00	4.31	3.69	3.85
Visited museum	2.33	2.94	1.72	2.11	1.67
Visited zoo	2.44	2.94	1.56	1.72	1.72
Visited relative	2.78	3.05	2.11	1.67	3.39
Entertained friends	3.17	3.50	2.50	2.28	3.61
Attended local council meeting	2.11	2.00	2.00	1.83	2.72
Attended school committee	2.78	1.94	2.11	1.72	2.67
St. John's Ambulance	3.23	3.62	4.23	3.92	4.08
Rotary, Lions, Apex, etc.	2.67	2.11	2.11	1.83	2.78
Attended religious meeting	2.22	2.27	2.17	1.83	2.83
Attended sporting organization meeting	2.28	2.39	2.50	2.06	2.89
Attended charitable organization	2.37	2.17	2.11	1.83	2.94
Attended trade union meeting	2.44	2.28	2.11	1.78	2.88
Attended political meeting	2.22	2.22	2.56	1.94	2.88
Letter writing	2.83	2.50	2.39	2.61	1.78
Sitting and thinking	2.83	3.28	1.67	2.39	1.05
Writing	3.00	2.94	2.83	3.39	1.33
Sculpture	3.39	3.72	3.50	4.39	1.44
Attended live plays	3.72	3.78	3.28	4.44	1.72
Attended ballet	3.61	3.72	3.39	4.39	1.61
Attended musicals	1.94	3.44	2.28	2.11	2.28
Attended strip shows	1.94	3.22	2.06	2.06	2.17
Attended opera	1.89	3.06	1.89	1.56	2.22
Attended pop concerts	1.78	2.17	1.83	1.33	2.33
Attended orchestral concerts	1.78	2.17	1.83	1.33	2.33
Attended jazz concerts	2.22	3.11	2.28	1.50	2.50
Composing music	2.00	3.28	2.17	1.94	2.22
Painting	2.22	3.28	2.22	1.83	2.44

2. *Influence* is the amount of control that a person has over task procedures. It refers to the extent to which a person can set goals, decide how best to meet these goals, influence the actions of other people and generally determine the cause of events.
3. *Variety* is the amount of change or mixture of activities, behaviours and interests involved in task performance.
4. *Pressure* is the degree to which a task puts stress or strain, mental or physical, upon a person's capacities.
5. *Interaction* is the degree to which the task involves competing or cooperating with other people.

The extent to which work tasks involve these attributes were measured by self-report scales developed in earlier studies (O'Brien, 1980, 1982). In order to minimize the possibility that obtained correlations between work and leisure attributes were due to method similarity, leisure attributes were determined by using independent ratings of leisure activities. Individuals first identified their main leisure activities from a checklist of 93 activities. All of these 93 activities were classified by independent raters using the same task attributes as were used by respondents to describe their jobs. In order to allow for differential rates of responding, each respondent's score on the five leisure attributes is calculated as the average score over all the activities chosen. For example, if the respondent chosen of the 93 activities then leisure influence is estimated by the following formula.

$$\text{Leisure influence} = \frac{\begin{array}{c}\text{Influence}\\ \text{activity 1}\end{array} + \begin{array}{c}\text{Influence}\\ \text{activity 2}\end{array} + \cdots + \begin{array}{c}\text{Influence}\\ \text{activity n}\end{array}}{n}$$

The leisure attributes measures for each of the 93 activities is shown in Table 1. These are mean ratings obtained from 18 raters and the intraclass correlations for each attribute all exceeded 90. The validity of these attributes were established by Kabanoff (1981).

Respondents' leisure attributes were significantly correlated with personality measures of extraversion, affiliation, dominance, need for control, achievement, endurance, and locus of control. Weighing leisure attributes by frequency of activity, or perceived importance of the activity, did not significantly increase the correlations between personality measures and leisure attributes. Consequently it was concluded that this method of measuring leisure attributes was a reliable and valid method of describing leisure activities. It also allowed one to compare profiles of leisure and work activities across similar dimensions.

3. THE RELATIONSHIP BETWEEN WORK AND LEISURE ACTIVITIES

The two main hypotheses about the effect of work on leisure attributes are derived from the writings of Engels (1892) and Marx (1844): the compensation and the generalization hypotheses. Engels saw some of the excesses of the nineteenth century English working man as providing release or *compensation* for work activities that provided little opportunity for autonomy and self-expression. Drinking and sexual promiscuity were, for Engels, leisure activities that provided some degree of self-expression that compensated for the monotony of simplified and externally controlled work tasks. Engels clearly saw the compensations of the English working class as being self-destructive but later writers have defined compensation as a more positive process whereby employees choose, in leisure, activities which provide creative self-expression that is denied them at work (Kando and Summers, 1971; Parker, 1976).

A contrasting hypothesis is that employees choose leisure activities that are similar to those performed at work: the *generalization hypothesis*. This hypothesis was not stated formally by Marx but it is implicit in some of this writings on alienation from work. For him, the working man had the opportunity to be himself only in leisure but the effects of working separated him from this tasks, his co-workers and knowledge of his inner needs. Powerless to fulfil his needs at work and physically exhausted by his job the tended to choose activities that were consistent with his sense of powerlessness. He did not pursue knowledge or engage in creative political, social, or artistic activities. Like his work, his leisure was marked by routine, involved little skill, and was shaped by external influences.

There has been some support for both compensation and generalization hypotheses but no studies have been able to identify clearly the conditions under which one or the other hypothesis applies. Mansfield and Evans (1975) found some support for compensation, while other studies have found that generalization from work to leisure is the dominant pattern (e.g., Kohn and Schooler, 1973; Kornhauser, 1965; Meissner, 1971; Rousseau, 1978). The relationships between work and leisure appear to be fairly weak and this has led some writers to advocate a third interpretation: the *segmentation hypothesis*. This hypothesis states that work and leisure form fairly distinct and independent role systems (Bacon, 1975; Dubin, 1956, 1958, 1973; London, Crandall, and Seals, 1977).

The relevance of most of these studies to an understanding of work-leisure relationships can be questioned. Except for the study by Rousseau (1978), no attempt was made to compare work and leisure activities on the same dimensions. Objective comparison of the quality of work and leisure was not possible. The Rousseau study did support the generalization hypothesis but the results could have been due to correlated response errors as respondents described their work and leisure on very similar scales (Kabanoff, 1980).

In order to overcome some of these difficulties, a recent study used different methods to measure the attributes of work and leisure activities (Kabanoff and O'Brien, 1980). Work attributes were measured on skill utilization, influence, variety, interaction and pressure using self-report ratings developed in earlier studies (O'Brien, 1980, 1982). Leisure activities were identified by employees from a checklist of 93 different activities. All of these activities were classified by independent raters using the same task attributes as were used by respondents to describe their jobs. Thus it was possible to compare work and leisure attributes on the same dimensions.

The study was not only designed to examine the correlation between work and leisure attributes. It was designed to explore the evidence for one process, whereby work could affect leisure. Marx's (1844) theory of work alienation suggests that work providing little opportunities for skill utilization and influence produces a stable belief, in the employee, of external control. Employees with a work-induced belief that their major life satisfactions were largely determined by other people, fate, or luck, would be less likely to seek leisure activities that required self-direction and internal control. The predicted process is as follows.

Low skill-utilization and influence in work activities	→	External control beliefs	→	Low skill-utilization and influence in leisure activities
High skill-utilization and influence in work activities	→	Internal control beliefs	→	High skill-utilization and influence in leisure activities

If this is the process whereby work activities determine leisure activities, a generalization rather than a compensation hypothesis should be supported by research findings. With a representative sample of 1,700 employees in a medium-sized Australian city it was found that the correlations between work and leisure attributes were very small. Thus, it seems there was more support for the segmentation than for the generalization hypothesis. However, belief in internal or external control, as measured by Rotter scale (1966), was a significant predictor of leisure attributes. Internals were more likely to choose activities requiring greater skill utilization, influence, variety, and pressure. In order to see whether control beliefs distinguished between people who adopted different work/leisure patterns, some further analyses

Table 2. Verbal description of work/leisure groups based on discriminant analysis (adapted from Kabanoff and O'Brien, 1980: p. 604).

Group	Influence	Variety	Attribute Pressure	Skill utilization	Interaction
Low work/low leisure (generalization)	Low income, low intrinsic work orientation, high extrinsic work orientation, low education, male single.	Low extrinsic work orientation, high extrinsic work orientation, male, low income, work shorter hours, younger.	Low income, low intrinsic work orientation, older, high extrinsic work orientation, children <15, external.	Low income, low intrinsic work orientation, male, external, low educatrion.	Male younger, internal, high income.
Low work/high leisure (supplemental compensation)	Female, older internal, low income, low extrinsic work orientation, children <15 years.	Female, older, internal.	Work shorter hours, low extrinsic work orientation, internal, younger, no children <15 years.	Low extrinsic work orientation, work shorter hours, high intrinsic work orientation, younger, low income.	Low income, male, children <15 years.
High work/low leisure (reactive compensation)	Male, younger, external, high income, high extrinsic work orientation, no children <15 years.	Male, younger, external.	Work longer hours, single, high extrinsic work orientation, external, older, children <15 years.	High extrinsic work orientation, work longer hours, low intrinsic work orientation, older, high income.	Female, older, external, lower income.
High work/high leisure (generalization)	High income, high intrinsic work orientation, low extrinsic work orientation, high education, female, married.	High intrinsic work orientation, low extrinsic work orientation, female, high income, work longer hours, older.	High income, high intrinsic work orientation, younger, low extrinsic work orientation, no children <15, internal.	High income, high intrinsic work orientation, female, internal, high education.	Male, younger, internal, high income.

were conducted. Table 2 shows the variables that discriminated between the different forms of generalization and compensation.

These results show that the adoption of a given work-leisure pattern is determined by many variables including income, gender, education, marital status, locus of control beliefs and work orientation. In this study, work orientation was measured by the relative importance to the employee of intrinsic rewards (e.g., job satisfaction, challenge) compared to extrinsic rewards (e.g., pay, security). However there is some support for the effect of personal control beliefs on the relationship between work and leisure activities. This is strongest for the attribute of skill utilization. Employees in low skill-use jobs tend to be externally controlled and tend to have a low skill use in their leisure. Those in high skill utilization jobs tend to be internally controlled and have a high skill use in their leisure. The results are only suggestive of the manner in which work/leisure relationships are formed by control beliefs. The study is a cross-sectional one and cannot provide strong evidence to demonstrate that work determines control beliefs which, in turn, determines choice of leisure activities.

Certainly the results cannot be used to support theories that predict a general negative effect of poor quality jobs on leisure (e.g., Emery, 1977; Gardell, 1976; Meissner, 1971). Many people with poor quality jobs had high quality leisure. Whether or not people are generalizers or compensators depends on their personal characteristics. Some of these characteristics, such as control beliefs and work orientation, might depend on the degree to which they have experienced certain types of jobs, but longitudinal research is required to demonstrate that work attributes actually determine leisure attributes through a process of personality shaping. It may be argued that it is necessary to establish the function of leisure for different individuals. The task attribute approach to leisure may omit the attributes that individuals, themselves see as important. Some research on this problem has been conducted and it shows that, while there are considerable individual differences in leisure needs, there is also general similarity in the extent to which leisure satisfaction is determined by task attributes.

4. LEISURE NEEDS AND LEISURE SATISFACTION

Leisure needs are partly shaped by work experiences and partly by other factors such as personality (Crandall, 1980; Kabanoff, 1982; Tinsley, Barrett, and Kass, 1977), the social environment (Cheek and Burch, 1976; Kelley, 1978), and demographic variables such as age, sex, marital status and socio-economic standing (e.g., Gentry and Doering, 1979; Kabanoff and O'Brien, 1982; Rapaport and Rapaport, 1975).

The general implication of these results is that an individual's leisure needs may vary considerably. Although this is true it does not necessarily imply that there are no general attributes of leisure activities that are important for all people. The content of the activity may vary but the type of activity may be constant. For example, relaxation may be important for most people but the form of the activity may vary. Some people might relax via reading, others by jogging, and others by playing chess. Individual differences in personality, socialization and occupation might determine the form of the activity but the function of the activity might be similar.

A contrary view is that the leisure needs and functions depend on a person's occupation. The generalization or spillover hypothesis would predict, for example, that occupations where people experience low autonomy, skill utilization and variety, would choose leisure activities that do not require high levels of autonomy, skill utilization and variety. Compensation, if of the supplemental kind, would mean that people in lower quality jobs would seek out activities high in autonomy, skill use and variety. If either the generalization or the compensation hypothesis is confirmed, it means that there should be considerable differences in leisure needs and leisure satisfaction across various occupations that vary in job quality.

A recent study provided evidence that bears on this problem (Kabanoff, 1982). Using a cluster sample of employed people who were chosen to vary in socio-economic status and occupation, Kabanoff measured the extent to which employees used their leisure to satisfy various needs. The eleven needs are shown in Table 3 and were partly derived from Crandall's analysis (1980) and partly from an analysis of work needs and satisfactions.

People were asked to rate the extent to which they used their leisure time to meet each need. Leisure satisfaction was used using items from Beard and Ragheb's (1980) leisure satisfaction scale. The scale measures satisfaction with six different aspects of leisure (psychological, educational, social, relaxation, physiological, and aesthetic).

Table 3 shows the leisure needs ranked from most to least frequent. Autonomy, relaxation and family activity are the most important leisure needs as rated by respondents, while esteem, competition and social power are the least important needs. There were only a few occupational differences in leisure needs. Professional employees had higher needs on skill utilization and autonomy than clerical or blue-collar employees.

Kabanoff recognized that what employees say is important in their leisure, does not necessarily predict their satisfaction with leisure. Just as people do not always have insight into what really determines their work satisfaction, so they may not also understand what attributes of their leisure activities predicts their leisure satisfaction.

Table 3. Leisure needs and items used to measure them (adapted from Kabanoff, 1982).

Leisure needs	Items comprising need scale	Mean	Standard deviation
1. Autonomy	Organize own projects and activities. Do things you find personally meaningful.	6.17	1.66
2. Relaxation	Relax and take it easy. Give mind and body a rest.	6.15	1.71
3. Family activity	Bring family closer together. Enjoy family life.	6.11	2.17
4. Escape from routine	Get away from responsibilities of everyday life. Have a change from daily routine.	5.97	1.14
5. Interaction	Make new friends. Enjoy people's company.	5.90	1.78
6. Stimulation	To have new and different experiences. For excitement and stimulation.	5.54	1.97
7. Skill utilization	Use skills and abilities. Develop new skills and abilities.	5.51	1.85
8. Health	Keep physically fit for health reasons.	4.93	1.92
9. Esteem	Gain respect or admiration of others. Show others what you are capable of.	4.26	2.06
10. Challenge/ competition	Be involved in competition. Test yourself in difficult or demanding situations.	4.18	1.93
11. Leadership/ Social power	Organize activities of teams, groups or organizations. To gain positions of leadership.	3.28	1.68

Note: (i) Means based on sample of 210.
(ii) All scales have range 2-10.
(iii) Median reliability of scales = .65 (alpha).

> Four leisure needs contributed significantly and positively to leisure satisfaction – skill utilization, health, interaction, and autonomy, while one is negatively related -esteem. Skill utilization clearly has the strongest relation to leisure satisfaction accounting for 26% of the total variance (Kabanoff, 1982: p. 239).

The dominance of skill utilization occurred across all occupational groups. There where no significant differences in overall leisure satisfaction between occupations and it is therefore clear that a substantial amount of the variance in leisure satisfaction within occupations was attributable to variations in the capacity of the employee to use leisure to exercise abilities or learn new ones. There were a few interesting sex differences. Females rated interaction needs higher, while males tended to rate competition needs higher. However, for both males and females skill utilization was a relatively strong predictor of leisure satisfaction.

The major conclusions of this study were:

1. Individuals tend to rate autonomy, relaxation and family activities as the most important functions of their leisure.
2. The rated importance of leisure needs do not predict leisure satisfaction. Rather leisure satisfaction is high to the extent that leisure activities involve skill utilization, promote health, and allow reasonably high levels of interpersonal contact and autonomy.
3. Occupational differences in leisure needs, leisure satisfaction, and sources of leisure satisfaction are not large.

This is contrary to the expectations of those who would promote a generalization or compensation view of leisure. This does not necessarily mean that leisure activities are unrelated to work activities. Although work activities may have a small direct effect on leisure needs, the attributes of work that determine satisfaction are similar to the attributes of leisure that determine leisure satisfaction. It seems that most people are satisfied with activities, either at work or play, that allow them to use their abilities and provide a reasonable amount of personal control or autonomy. Although skill utilization and autonomy are important for all occupational groups, there seem to be some characteristics of jobs, or the people who hold them, that makes these factors more important. Professional people experience skill use as a very strong predictor of their leisure satisfaction. As professional occupations have the highest level of job skill utilization (Kabanoff and O'Brien, 1982) it is suggests that the regular experience of skill utilization at work engenders a greater desire for, and appreciation of, skill utilization outside of work.

One way of assessing the potentiality of leisure to fulfill the psychological needs which are normally considered to be satisfied by work is to examine the leisure behaviour of those who are unemployed. There are two kinds of unemployment. One is involuntary due to job loss. The other is voluntary (at least for many employees) when employment ceases due to retirement. If leisure activities are capable of promoting psychological functions such as identity based on high skill utilization, time structure, and life purpose then studies of the unemployed should show that a considerable number of people develop leisure interests which promote psychological development. A different hypothesis, which follows from the generalization theory, is that the quality of leisure activities is dependent on past employment experiences. If employees had jobs which provided little opportunity for identity formation through skill use, and little opportunity for autonomy and goal setting, then they will tend to choose leisure activities with similar attributes. Conversely the leisure quality of the employed should be high, i.e., high influence, skill use and interaction, if they had previously experienced jobs which were of high quality.

5. ACTIVITIES AND LEISURE OF THE UNEMPLOYED

Broadly there are two views about the activities of the unemployed. One view is that the unemployed become idle and make little use of their time to improve themselves through educational, political, religious or creative leisure activities (Jahoda, 1979, 1981, 1982). A contrasting view is that the majority of the unemployed are not idle (Bakke, 1933, 1940a, 1940b). They do have initial difficulties in structuring their time but they expend considerable energy in job seeking, managing a limited income, child caring, maintaining social relationships that do not require much money, and expanding past leisure activities provided that these activities do not require large expenditure.

Both views originated from studies undertaken during the Great Depression. Jahoda and her associates reported the enforced idleness and uncreative leisure activities of former employees in a small Austrian town – Marienthal. Significantly this was a one-factory town and thus when the factory closed there was no point in looking for jobs. Examination of the data furthermore reveals that the unemployed were not idle. Idleness was a term used to explain diverse activities such as walking, talking, in the streets and reading at home. Also minor household work was described as inactivity (e.g., fetching water, shopping). It is probable that the kind of activities indulged in were quite similar to the unemployed activities when employed. No data on employed activities were reported. But most men who were unemployed were unskilled and semi-skilled and thus it would be expected that they would not have high educational levels. Their main nonwork pursuits, apart from family activities, were probably those they did when unemployed. They socialized, played cards and chess at the workmen's club. They rarely used the library or engaged in educational or creative handicraft activities.

Jahoda's later writings are devoted to developing a theory of the function of work and leisure which is based on the Marienthal and later unemployment studies (Jahoda, 1979, 1981, 1982). This theory maintains that work has psychological functions that cannot be served by leisure. The manifest function is income while the latent functions are time structure, identity, collective purposes, rational social relationships and activity. Although work in employment may, depending on the content of work, exercise these functions, it is not possible to conclude from a study of unemployment activities that absence of work necessarily deprives the person of means of exercising Jahoda's latent functions.

Firstly, many studies of the unemployed during the depression showed that the unemployed developed time structures, a sense of identity, social purposes and non-family social relationships. The extensive studies of Bakke (1933, 1940a, 1940b) in England and North America showed that the unemployed were, as a group, active and self-reliant in those activities where they still had some freedom of movement. However, there was, for his samples, little use of time for self-development and cultural activities. This was due, according to Bakke, not to loss of employment activities but rather to economic deprivation and past work experience.

Activities requiring money (movies, excursions, social visits) were curtailed, whereas activities involving little expenditure (walking, radio listening, chatting, gardening) increased. Cultural and educational activities did not increase in frequency during employment. Bakke argued that this was due to past work experiences which had severely limited the ability of employees to engage in self-directed learning or actively participate in any group that required member initiative and participation in decision making. This view was also supported by findings reported by the Pilgrim Trust (1938) and the Carnegie Trust (1943).

Thus, the majority of the Depression studies do not support Jahoda's view that employment activities were essential to maintain time structure, social purpose and activity. At the same time, these studies do not show that the unemployed were inclined to increase leisure activities, so that they provided the involvement, challenge and autonomy once provided by work. This appears to be due to lack of money and the shaping effects of past work experiences and not to the inherent deficiency of leisure activities to provide enriched experiences. Hence the studies tend to provide evidence for a generalization position. Workers who experienced jobs that provided little opportunity for developing self-worth based on skill use and autonomy, develop a low level of personal control or self-direction. When they became unemployed, these external control beliefs predisposed them to engage in activities which had attributes similar to the ones possessed by their previous jobs. However, a major problem with this interpretation is that it neglects the importance of income as a determinant of leisure quality. The early studies were unable to disentangle the effects of income and past work content upon unemployment activities.

Unfortunately, recent studies, although more sophisticated in their methods, are unable to address this problem adequately because income levels are rarely considered as determinants of leisure quality. Cross-sectional or correlational studies show that unemployed persons report difficulty in organizing their time but they do learn to structure their time by engaging in domestic and leisure activities (Feather and Bond, 1983;

O'Brien and Kabanoff, 1979; Swinburne, 1981; Trew and Kilpatrick, 1983). The only study that compared the quality of leisure activities of the employed and unemployed reported no significant difference in skill utilization, influence and interaction (O'Brien and Kabanoff, 1979). Hardly any studies were designed to examine the effect of past work experiences on the leisure of the unemployed. Most have concentrated on showing that unemployment generally leads to poor psychological well-being as measured by life satisfaction, depressive affect and vulnerability to psychiatric disorder (O'Brien, 1986; Warr, 1983). However, one study reported that previous job dissatisfaction could lead to more creative leisure activities after job loss. Little (1976) found that 48% of this sample of technical and professional workers were not greatly upset by job loss, but expressed positive satisfaction. Those who felt relatively positive about job loss, had previously been dissatisfied with their jobs and saw unemployment as an opportunity to engage in self-development activities. This reaction seemed to be confined to those with financial resources, high education and a belief that they would soon find better jobs. These people were also likely, due to their income and education, to possess beliefs in the possibility of internal control. Thus, in an unstructured life situation, they were more likely than externals to be self-directed in their choice of leisure activities. So far, no longitudinal research has been conducted to show that past job experiences affect the leisure activities of the unemployed. Hence detailed conclusions about the relationship between past work activities and unemployment activities are not possible. Current studies show that unemployment induces initial stress which could be due to either income loss or loss of job activities. The "free-time" activities of the unemployed generally do not show that unemployment is associated with the adoption of high quality leisure activities. Nor does it show that the quality of leisure activities decreases although the nature of these activities may, for some, be affected by reduced income. See also Chapter 17 of this Handbook.

6. LEISURE AND RETIREMENT

The previous section on work and leisure in the employed showed that the characteristics of job activities that determined job satisfaction were also the characteristics of leisure that determine the leisure satisfaction of employed men and women. It also showed that people were more likely to enjoy leisure to the extent that their jobs provided them with opportunities for skill utilization and autonomy. These findings on the effect of work activities on non-leisure attributes and leisure enjoyment can be used to understand retirement, which is commonly seen as either voluntary or socially enforced unemployment.

There is a large amount of research on the life satisfaction of retired people (Adams, 1971; Chatfield, 1977; Fine, 1975; Larson, 1978; Lemon, Bengston, and Peterson, 1972; Maddox and Eisdorfer, 1962; Markides and Martin, 1979; Medley, 1976; Spreitzer and Snyder, 1973), but few studies have investigated the relationship between the quality of retirement activities and retirement satisfaction. Some authors claim that retirees give the same meaning to leisure as they once gave to work (Havighurst, 1977; Kleemeier, 1961). This could mean that the dimensions of work that gave them satisfaction, could also be the dimensions of leisure that predict satisfaction in retirement.

Few studies have directly examined this although a number of factors have been shown to affect satisfaction and adjustment to retirement. These include health, finances, personality, and amount of interaction and activity (Lemon et al., 1972; Markides and Martin, 1979). In order to investigate the relationship between leisure quality and satisfaction in retirement it is necessary to have a set of dimensions that define leisure quality as well as a measure of satisfaction that clearly distinguishes satisfaction with activities from satisfaction with health and finances. One study that did attempt this, used the dimensions of skill utilization, influence, variety, pressure and interaction to define leisure quality and separate measures of satisfaction for activities, health and finances (O'Brien, 1981a). The main aim was to test the hypothesis that satisfaction with retirement activities was determined by leisure quality. Another aim was to examine the extent to which previous occupation determined overall adjustment to retirement.

Contrary to expectations, it was found that participation in activities requiring skill utilization and autonomy did not predict satisfaction with activities or life satisfaction. The main predictors of satisfaction for both men and women was the amount of interpersonal interaction experienced and the total number of different activities engaged in. One possible explanation is that retirement, at least in Australian culture, is experienced as a state of social isolation and people are happy to the extent that they have a lot of contact and social activities. Also it could be a period where personal identity has been largely formed. The identity of retirees may be largely shaped by previous work and non-work experiences where the exercise of autonomy and valued skills did contribute to identity and personal adjustment. However, identity based on personal control and skill use is not salient for those who are no longer employed as society does not judge retirees on their contribution to and involvement in tasks requiring self-direction and personal control. Lacking any strong linkage to social goals and work organizational, life meaning is imparted rather by the extent and quality of social interaction. Hence interaction and activity level determined satisfaction with activities. If the number of leisure activities is an index of activity or arousal then the results support those of Markides and Martin

(1979). They also showed that retirees then are satisfied to the extent that they have a high activity level and meaningful social interactions.

The only significant differences in leisure attributes were on skill utilization and the number of leisure activities. Retirees from white-collar occupations had higher skill utilization and a greater number of activities than those from blue-collar occupations. These differences in leisure attributes may partly explain the difference in retirement satisfaction. However, it does seem that previous occupation also determines satisfaction with retirement because occupation determines income, health and the ability to enjoy retirement. White-collar occupations do have higher income levels than blue-collar occupations and this should explain why there are variations in financial security. However, work experience could also have shaped personality to some extent. Kohn and Schooler (1973, 1978, 1981) have shown that people from occupations with jobs that are intellectually complex and varied, are more self-directed and flexible than those from jobs that are relatively low in complexity and variability. To some extent this is due to the effect of personality on job choice. However, even after they controlled for selection effects they found that prolonged job experiences involving self-direction induced stable increases in self-direction and flexibility. The suggests that retirees from white-collar jobs, which involve more complexity and self-direction than blue-collar jobs, would produce retirees with the ability to cope more adequately with the stresses associated with retirement. Kohn and Schooler did not investigate this possibility but some evidence to support this interpretation comes from other studies.

A number of studies have found that adjustment to retirement is partly determined by an individual's locus of control (Kuypers, 1971; Palmore and Luikart, 1972; Reid, Haas, and Hawkings, 1977; Reid and Zeigler, 1981). Internally controlled retirees, who believed that their desired goals were largely determined by their own effort, skill and motivation, reported higher levels of contentment and happiness than externally controlled individuals who placed greater emphasis on chance and environmental factors as explanations for their own achievement. The relationship between locus of control and life satisfaction was generally stronger for males than for females. One problem with these studies is that they did not control for health. Poor health, either physical or mental, could strongly determine an individual's perception of personal control and the reported association between locus of control and satisfaction could disappear when health is partialled out. Furthermore, the studies did not examine retirees' previous occupation as a determinant of locus of control. If work determines personality, and locus of control is a personality variable, then it is reasonable to expect that work experiences could affect retirement adjustment via personality.

One study examined this possibility (O'Brien, 1981b). A large sample of

Australian retirees were interviewed and information obtained about their physical health, life stress, locus of control and satisfaction with life in retirement. Those who had been regularly employed prior to their retirement, provided information about their occupation. From previous studies with employed samples it was possible to assign to each occupation a score on skill utilization. These scores had been obtained by estimating the mean amount of skill utilization reported by employees from a wide range of jobs.

Results showed that, for both males and females, that previous occupation determined the degree to which retirees experienced personal control over their lives. If they had held a job which enabled them to use their skills, they tended to feel internally controlled and able to use their own initiative in obtaining personally rewarding experiences. However, if they came from occupations which prevented a reasonable amount of skill utilization, they tended to believe they were externally controlled. They saw that their lives were largely determined by fate or social forces like government and authority figures. These results held even when reported physical health and stress (mental strain) were controlled.

The relation between locus of control and satisfaction in retirement can be interpreted in terms of what is known about the behavioral correlates of locus of control. Externals, compared to internals, are less efficient users of environmental resources and have greater difficulty in maintaining self-directed activity (Lefcourt, 1976; Phares, 1976). Those in retirement have a considerable amount of free time and thus the success of their activities in achieving personal satisfaction depends, to a large extent, on personal initiative. Hence internals are more likely to seek out congenial activities while externals tend to be locked in, accept unwanted and personal associations, and believe that there is a little they can do to make the environment more satisfactory.

However, while this explanation may be true for males, it does not explain why there is a relatively weak relationship between locus of control and life satisfaction for females. Perhaps males experience more free time than females. The majority of females in the Australian study were married and it is likely that they performed a substantial number of domestic tasks before and after retirement. If these tasks were experienced as unfulfilling and boring, it could have led to stress or mental strain. If so, this might explain why the main determinant of female dissatisfaction in retirement was mental strain. Sex differences in the relationship between locus of control, skill utilization and life satisfaction could also be due to a failure to consider domestic activities as work occupations. Greater similarity between men and women might have been found if the occupational skill utilization measure was based in activities in both home maintenance and paid employment.

The relationships between locus of control and retirement satisfaction suggests a number of ways of improving the experience of retirement. If jobs were designed to give people a reasonable amount of skill utilization then they would develop a sense of personal control. With moderate levels of personal control, they would have the personal competence necessary to shape their environment by choosing tasks that suited their interests and capacities. An internal locus of control could also facilitate adjustment by allowing people to seek out and develop alternative methods of coping with the stresses caused by financial worries, isolation and failing health. There is, however, a major problem in understanding the adjustment of retirees. The attributes of their activities such as skill utilization and autonomy, do not predict adjustment. This is a surprising result. One possible explanation is that there is little variation in retiree activities and so it is statistically difficult to find an association between leisure attributes and adjustment. Another interpretation is that satisfactory retirement activities should not only use valued skills but be socially useful. Many writers have pointed out that western societies fail to provide retirees with activities that use their skills and are socially useful (e.g., Parker, 1982). Many retirement activities may use considerable skill such as chess, golf or gardening. Yet these may be unsatisfactory as occupations because the elderly do not feel they are socially useful. Some cultures, such as Australian aboriginal culture, integrate the elderly into the social fabric by giving them senior administrative positions and making them the guardians and teachers of social history and religion. The main implication of this is that future research on leisure in retirement should examine the social role that they are required to fill and the extent to which their adjustment, or lack of it, is due to tasks which lack social significance.

Generally, the studies on unemployment and retirement provide little encouragement for writers who believe that leisure has the potentiality for promoting the psychological well-being of those who have been deprived of employment. Certainly, there are some people who are able to engage in high quality leisure when deprived of work but they may be those with relatively high income and high quality work experiences which have engendered strong beliefs in personal control. The results suggest more support for a generalization type of process whereby past work experiences determine personal control and income which, in turn, limits the quality of leisure activities chosen by the unemployed and retired.

7. WORK ATTRIBUTES, HOURS AND INCOME AS DETERMINANTS OF LEISURE ATTRIBUTES

7.1 *Introduction*

The preceding sections have shown that the relationship between work and leisure is complex. Most of the research has concentrated on the effects of work upon leisure and has sought to confirm the rather simplistic hypotheses termed compensation, generalization and segmentation. No studies have been identified which investigated the effect of leisure upon work activities. Hence it is not surprising that there are no theories about the reciprocal interaction between work and leisure. Research in the future should utilize longitudinal rather than correlational studies in order to test more complex hypotheses. Furthermore, they should use activity measures that enable work and leisure to be compared. This chapter advocated a task attribute approach which assumed that skill utilization, influence, variety, pressure and interaction were common and relevant dimensions of work and leisure. However, other dimensions, such as Holland's occupational categories, may also be useful (Taylor et al., 1979).

This review cited studies which, overall, show very limited support for the three traditional work/leisure hypotheses. Certainly there are studies which can be used to support either one of the hypotheses of compensation, generalization or segmentation but, taken as a whole set, it must be concluded that the results are inconsistent. Progress is likely to be dependent on the development of more complex hypotheses about the processes whereby work and leisure interact. One such model was discussed which describes leisure activities as being determined by personal control beliefs which, in turn, had been determined by previous work experiences. Although there is some evidence to support this model, particularly with respect to skill utilization and influence, the model omits many variables which are known to predict leisure quality. Two additional variables which are likely to be important are working hours and income.

7.2 *Working Hours*

Leisure time and leisure quality may be determined as much by working hours as work content. There has been some experimentation with changing work schedules, but the effects on leisure, productivity and social adjustment have not often been systematically evaluated. The two main innovations have been flexible working hours and compression of the five-day working week into four days. The results on flexitime are difficult to interpret, as conclusions are often based on observation of changes within a particular group of employees without comparison to comparable control groups. The few studies with control designs suggest that flexitime has no adverse effects on productivity and can improve the satisfaction of employees whose work schedules conflict with home duties and shopping opportunities. As a general solution for improvement in leisure and productivity it is clearly inadequate.

The four-day week has been investigated experimentally by a number of psychologists in the United States and Canada (Goodale and Aagaard, 1975; Ivanavich, 1974; Ivanavich and Lyon, 1977; Nord and Costigan, 1973; Steward and Larsen, 1971). The effects of a compressed working week are complicated but some broad generalizations can be tentatively made. In the short term, employees respond favourably to the four-day week and there are no adverse effects on productivity. Occasionally improvement in productivity is reported. The quality of leisure activities is most likely to be improved if the four working days are continuous thus providing a three day period of free time. However, it appears that this results in employees spending more money on consumer and leisure goods.

In the long term, productivity is unaffected but a significant minority of employees report negative effects on sleep, home life and fatigue. Older workers are most affected by fatigue, while workers find that they have little home involvement or contact on working days. The results so far suggest that not all workers experience favourable effects of a compressed work week. There is a general increase in leisure quality but certain classes of employees also experience extra fatigue and poor family contact.

The main implication for leisure is that a small reduction in hours per day is unlikely to affect leisure patterns as most of the extra time is likely to be spent on household maintenance and passive leisure activities like watching television. This suggests that the leisure benefits of a 35 or 30 hour week may only be realized if it is associated with the introduction of a three- or four-day working week.

The only models of work and leisure which take account of working hours and income have been developed by economists.

7.3 *Work, Leisure and the Allocation of Time*

They have tried to account for the relative stability of working hours and associated leisure time in terms of the choice behaviour of employees. Although it is doubtful that employees have much choice in the decisions about basic working hours, they have some degree of choice in decisions about overtime and the way they spend their free time. Hence the economic models may be useful to psychologists who wish to understand why individuals might choose more work rather than more leisure. The initial difficulty with these models is that they are based on simple models that view the employee as a decision maker who makes decisions about the allocation of time and effort on the basis of his preferences for either income or "leisure consumption." The possibility that judgments about work and leisure may depend on the nature and quality of the work activities does not enter their equations. The most recent theory is that of Owen (1979) which is more complex than the early ones of Becker (1965) and Gronau (1977).

Owen divides non-working time up into household production time and consumption time (leisure). After allowing for variable preferences between income and household time, plus variable preferences between leisure time and household production, he developed a mathematical equation connecting the rate of change in leisure time to the rate of change in working hours. After allowing for a range of preferences he infers that, in most cases, reduction in working hours will increase leisure time provided that there is no reduction in income. The model assumes that an individual allocates time so as to maximize the amount of satisfaction he obtains from consumption activities. Time required for consumption activities is equated with time for leisure. The two main problems with this model are:

1. No information is available to allow a realistic estimate of employee preferences for various life spheres.
2. It seems dubious to assume that leisure can be equated with consumption. Perhaps it could be argued that consumption could include the "taking in" of sights, sounds, information and food as well as economic purchases. However, this still tends to assume that leisure is a passive activity. It may be for some, but a considerable number of studies show that it has an active, self-directing quality for many.

To the extent that an individual has a choice between time for work, leisure and household maintenance, it is likely to depend on income and the quality

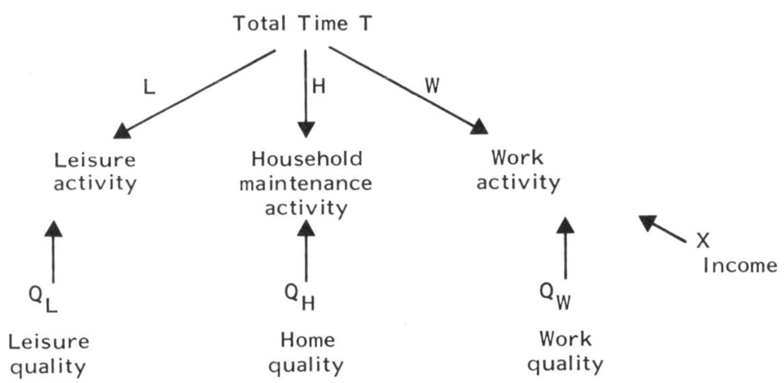

Fig. 1. Determinants of the allocation of time.

of the activities. The quality of leisure (Q_L), home activities (Q_H) may be presumes to depend on the degree to which employees perceive that they have skill utilization, influence, interaction, variety and pressure.

A general model of allocation of time is necessary. A basic structural model is outlined in Figure 1.

Some basic equations would be:

Total time available = T = L + H + W.	L,H,W = time devoted to leisure, home maintenance and work, respectively.
and X = r.W.	r = hourly pay rate
	X = income

The individual can be assumed to maximize life satisfaction, L_S.

Then $L_S = L_S$ (a S_W, b S_H, c S_L)
where S_W, S_H and S_C represent satisfaction with work, home and leisure activities, respectively,

and a, b, c are the weights given by individuals to the personal importance of work, home, and leisure activities, respectively.

and $S_W = S_W$ (Q_W, X)
$S_H = S_H$ (Q_H, X, H)
$S_L = S_L$ (Q_L, L)

then change in leisure time (L) with respect to work time (W) can be predicted. The model predicts that increases in leisure time due to reduction in working time will depend on work quality, income and the weights (a,b,c,) given by the individual of the extent to which work, home and leisure are important determinants of life satisfaction.

Provided that reliable and valid measures of the main concepts are used, this model could be used to guide research on the inter-relationship between work and leisure hours. It could also be useful to identify the relationships between work and leisure quality, when quality is measured on common task attributes such as skill utilization, influence and interaction. Using calculus it would be possible to identify theoretically the conditions of work and leisure that maximize life satisfaction and then compare predictions with observations. The model, as stated, omits personality variable such as personal control, but those could be included in more complex versions. For some, such an approach may introduce unwarranted complexity into a field at an early stage of development. However, complex models are needed to explain observed complexities in work/leisure relationships – complexities that cannot be explained by simple hypotheses of compensation, generalization and segmentation.

REFERENCES

Adams, D., 1971, Correlates of satisfaction among the elderly, Gerontologist, 11, 64-48.

Bacon, A.W., 1975, Leisure and the alienated worker: A critical assessment of three radical theories of work and leisure, Journal of Leisure Research, 7, 179-190.

Bakke, E.W., 1933, The Unemployed Man: A Social Study, London: Nisbet.

Bakke, E.W., 1940a, Citizens Without Work, New Haven, CT: Yale University Press.

Bakke, E.W., 1940b, The Unemployed Worker, New Haven, CT: Yale University Press.

Beard, J.G., and M.G. Ragheb, 1980, Measuring leisure satisfaction, Journal of Leisure Research, 12, 20-33.

Becker, G.S., 1965, A theory of the allocation of time, Economic Journal, 75, 493-517.

Carnegie Trust, 1943, Disinherited Youth, Edinburgh, UK: T and A Constable.

Chatfield, W., 1977, Economic and sociological factors influencing life satisfaction of the aged, Journal of Gerontology, 32, 593-599.

Cheek, N.H., and W.R. Burch, 1976, Social Organization of Leisure in Human Society, New York: Harper and Row.

Crandall, R., 1980, Motivations for leisure, Journal of Leisure Research, 12, 45-54.

Csikszentimihalyi, M., 1975, Beyond Boredom and Anxiety, San Francisco, CA: Jossey-Bass.

Cunningham, H., 1980, Leisure in the Industrial Revolution, London: Croom Helm.

De Grazia, S., 1964, Of Time, Work, and Leisure, New York: Doubleday.

Dubin, R., 1956, Industrial workers' worlds: A study in the central life interests of industrial workers, Social Problems, 4, 131-142.

Dubin, R., 1958, The World of Work: Industrial Society and Human Relations, Englewood Cliffs, NJ: Prentice-Hall.

Dubin, R., 1973, "Work and non-work: Institutional perspectives," in: M.D. Dunnette (ed.), Work and Non-work in the Year 2001, Monterey, CA: Brooks/Cole, pp. 53-68.

Dumazedier, J., 1967, Toward a Society of Leisure, New York: Free Press.

Dunnette, M.D. (ed.), 1973, Work and Non-work in the Year 2001, Monterey, CA: Brooks/Cole.

Emery, F.E., 1977, Futures We Are in, The Hague, The Netherlands: Martinus Nijhof.

Engels, F., 1892, The Condition of the Working Class in England in 1844, London: Allen and Unwin.

Evans, A., 1975, Hours of Work in Industrialised Countries, Geneva, Switzerland: International Labour Organization.

Feather, N.T., and P.R. Bond, 1983, Time structure and purposeful activity among employed and unemployed university graduates, Journal of Occupational Psychology, 56, 241-254.

Fine, M., 1975, Interrelationships among mobility, health, and attitudinal variables in an urban elderly population, Human Relations, 28, 451-474.

Fourastié, J., 1965, Les 40,000 Heures, Paris: Gonthier.

Gardell, B., 1976, Relations at work and their influence on non-work activities: An analysis of a socio-political problem in affluent societies, Human Relations, 29, 885-904.

Gentry, J.W., and M. Doering, 1979, Sex role orientation and leisure, Journal of Leisure Research, 11, 102-111.

Goodale, J.G, and A.K. Aagaard, 1975, Factors relating to varying reactions to the 4-day work week, Journal of Applied Psychology, 60, 33-88.

Gronau, R., 1977, Leisure, home production, and work – theory of the allocation of time revisited, Journal of Political Economy, 85, 1099-1123.
Havighurst, R.J., 1977, "Life-style and leisure patterns in later years," in: R.A. Kalish (ed.), The Later Years: Social Applications of Gerontology, Monterey, CA: Brooks/Cole.
Hunnicutt, B., 1980, Historical attitudes toward the increase of free time in the twentieth century: Time for work, for leisure, or as unemployment, Society and Leisure, 3, 195-215.
Ivanavich, J.M., 1974, Effect of the shorter work-week on selected satisfaction and performance measures, Journal of Applied Psychology, 59, 717-721.
Ivanavich, J.M., and H.C. Lyon, 1977, The shortened work-week: A field experiment, Journal of Applied Psychology, 62, 34-37.
Jahoda, M., 1979, The impact of unemployment in the 1930s and 1970s, Bulletin of the British Psychological Society, 32, 309-314.
Jahoda, M., 1981, Work, employment, and unemployment: Values, theories and approaches in social research, American Psychologist, 36, 184-191.
Jahoda, M., 1982, Employment and Unemployment: A Social-psychological Analysis, Cambridge, UK: Cambridge University Press.
Jenkins, C., and B. Sherman, 1979, The Collapse of Work, London: Eyre Mathuen.
Kabanoff, B., 1980, Work and nonwork: A review of models, methods, and findings, Psychological Bulletin, 88, 60-77.
Kabanoff, B., 1981, Validation of a task attributes description of leisure, Australian Journal of Psychology, 33, 383-391.
Kabanoff, B., 1982, Occupational and sex differences in leisure needs and leisure satisfaction, Journal of Occupational Behaviour, 3, 233-245.
Kabanoff, B., and G.E. O'Brien, 1980, Work and leisure: A task attributes analysis, Journal of Applied Psychology, 65, 596-609.
Kabanoff, B., and G.E. O'Brien, 1982, Relationships between work and leisure attributes of occupational and sex groups in Australia, Australian Journal of Psychology, 34, 165-182.
Kando, T., and W. Summers, 1971, The impact of work on leisure, Pacific Sociological Review, 14, 310-327.
Kelley, J.R., 1978, Situational and social factors in leisure decisions, Pacific Sociological Review, 21, 313-330.
Kleemeier, R.W., (ed.), 1961, Aging and Leisure, New York: Oxford University Press.
Kohn, M.L., and C. Schooler, 1973, Occupational experience and psychological functioning: An assessment of reciprocal effects, American Sociological Review, 28, 97-118.
Kohn, M.L., and C. Schooler, 1981, "Job conditions and intellectual flexibility: A longitudinal assessment of their reciprocal effects," in: D.J. Jackson and E.F. Borgatta (eds.), Factor Analysis and Measurement in Sociological Research, Beverly Hills, CA: Sage, pp. 281-313.
Kohn, M.L., and C. Schooler, 1983, Work and Personality, Norwood, NJ: Ablex.
Kornhauser, A.W., 1965, Mental Health of the Industrial Worker, New York: John Wiley.
Kuypers, J.A., 1971, Internal-external locus of control and ego functioning correlates in the elderly, Gerontologist, 12, 168-173.
Larson, R., 1978, Thirty years of research on subjective well-being of older Americans, Journal of Gerontology, 33, 109-125.
Lefcourt, H.M., 1976, Locus of Control: Current Trends in Theory and Research, New York: John Wiley.
Lemon, B., V. Bengston, and J. Peterson, 1972, An exploration of the activity theory of aging: Activity types and life satisfaction among inmovers to a retirement community, Journal of Gerontology, 27, 511-523.
Lindner, S.B., 1970, The Harried Leisure Class, New York: Columbia University.
Little, C.B., 1976, Technical-professional unemployment: Middle-class adaptability to personal crisis, Sociological Quarterly, 17, 262-274.

London, M., R. Crandall, and G.W. Seals, 1977, The contribution of job and leisure satisfaction to the quality of life, Journal of Applied Psychology, 62, 328-334.

Maddox, G., and C. Eisdorfer, 1962, Some correlates of activity and morale among the elderly, Social Forces, 41, 254-260.

Mansfield, R., and M.G. Evans, 1975, Work and non-work in two occupational groups, Industrial Relations, 6, 48-54.

Markides, K., and H. Martin, 1979, A causal model of life satisfaction among the elderly, Journal of Gerontology, 34, 86-93.

Marx, K., 1844, Economic and Philosophic Manuscripts of 1844, Moscow: Progress Publishers (reprint: 1977).

Medley, M.L., 1976, Satisfaction with life among persons 65 years and older, Journal of Gerontology, 31, 448-455.

Meissner, M., 1971, The long arm of the job: A study of work and leisure, Industrial Relations, 10, 239-260.

Neulinger, J., 1974, The Psychology of Leisure, Springfield, IL: Charles C. Thomas.

Nord, W.R., and R. Costigan, 1973, Worker adjustment to the 4-day week: A longitudinal study, Journal of Applied Psychology, 53, 60-66.

O'Brien, G.E., 1980, "The centrality of skill-utilization for job design," in: K.D. Duncan, M.M. Gruneberg, and D. Wallis (eds.), Changes in Working Life, Chichester, Sussex, UK: John Wiley, pp. 167-187.

O'Brien, G.E., 1981a, Leisure attributes and retirement satisfaction, Journal of Applied Psychology, 66, 371-384.

O'Brien, G.E., 1981b, Locus of control, previous occupation and satisfaction with retirement, Australian Journal of Psychology, 33, 305-318.

O'Brien, G.E., 1982, The relative contribution of perceived skill-utilization and other perceived job attributes to the prediction of job satisfaction: A cross-validation study, Human Relations, 35, 219-237.

O'Brien, G.E., 1984, "Locus of control, work, and retirement," in: H.M. Lefcourt (ed.), Research with the Locus of Control Construct, Vol. 3, New York: Academic Press, pp.

O'Brien, G.E., 1986, The Psychology of Work and Unemployment, Chichester, Sussex, UK: John Wiley.

O'Brien, G.E., and B. Kabanoff, 1979, Comparison of unemployed and employed workers on work values, locus of control and health variables, Australian Psychologist, 16, 184-202.

O'Brien, G.E., P. Dowling, and B. Kabanoff, 1978, Work, Health and Leisure, 28, Bedford Park, Australia: Flinders University of South Australia, National Institute of Labour Studies (technical report).

Owen, J.D., 1979, Working Hours: An Economic Analysis, Lexington, MA: Lexington Books.

Palmore, E., and C. Luikart, 1972, Health and social factors]related to life satisfaction, Journal of Health and Social Behavior, 13, 68-80.

Parker, S., 1976, The Sociology of Leisure, London: George Allen]and Unwin.

Parker, S., 1982, Work and Retirement, London: George Allen and Unwin.

Parker, S., 1983, Leisure and Work, London: George Allen and Unwin.

Phares, E.J., 1976, Locus of Control in Personality, Englewood Cliffs, NJ: General Learning Press.

Pilgrim Trust, 1938, Men Without Work, Cambridge, UK: Cambridge University Press.

Porter, L.W., E.E. Lawler, and J.R. Hackman, 1975, Behaviour in Organizations, New York: McGraw-Hill.

Rapaport, R., and R.N. Rapaport, 1975, Leisure and the Family Life Cycle, London: Routledge.

Reid, D.W., and M. Zeigler, 1981, "The desired control measure and adjustment among the elderly," in: H.M. Lefcourt (ed.), Research with the Locus of Control Construct, Vol. 1, New York: Academic Press, pp. 127-159.

Reid, D.W., G. Haas, and D. Hawkings, 1977, Locus of desired control and positive self-concepts of the elderly, Journal of Gerontology, 32, 441-450.

Rotter, J.B., 1966, Generalized expectancies for internal versus external control of reinforcement, Psychological Monographs, 80, no. 609.

Rousseau, D.M., 1978, Relationship of work to nonwork, Journal of Applied Psychology, 63, 513-517.

Spreitzer, E., and E. Snyder, 1973, Correlates of life satisfaction among the aged, Journal of Gerontology, 29, 454-458.

Steward, G.V., and J.M. Larsen, 1971, A 4-day – 3-day per week application to a continuous production operation, Management of Personnel Quarterly, 10, 13-20.

Swinburne, P., 1981, The psychological impact of unemployment on managers and professional staff, Journal of Occupational Psychology, 54, 47-64.

Taylor, K.F., G.I. Kelso, G.N. Cox, W.J. Alloway, and J.P. Matthews, 1979, Applying Holland's vocational activities to leisure activities, Journal of Occupational Psychology, 52, 199-207.

Thompson, E.P., 1968, The Making of the English Working Class, Harmondsworth, Middlesex, UK: Penguin Books.

Tilgher, A., 1930, Work: What it Means to Men Through the Ages, New York: Harcourt Brace.

Tinsley, H.E.A., T.C. Barrett, and R.A. Kass, 1977, Leisure activities and need satisfaction, Journal of Leisure Research, 9, 111-120.

Trew, K., and R. Kilpatrick, 1983, The Daily Life of the Unemployed, Belfast, UK: Queen's University of Belfast, Department of Psychology.

Vanek, J., 1974, Time spent on housework, Scientific American, 231, 116-120.

Veblen, T., 1899, The Theory of the Leisure Class, New York: MacMillan.

Warr, P., 1983, Work, jobs, and unemployment, Bulletin of the British Psychological Society, 35, 305-311.

Wilensky, H.L., 1960, Work, careers, and social integration, International Social Science Journal, 12, 543-560.

Table of Contents

16. Economic Well-being, Job Satisfaction, Income Evaluation and Consumer Satisfaction: An Integrative Attempt

THEO B.C. POIESZ
Tilburg University, Tilburg, The Netherlands

and

JASPER VON GRUMBKOW
Open University, Heerlen, The Netherlands

1. INTRODUCTION

Economic situations or developments, be it on the aggregate, market, or individual level, can be assessed both objectively and subjectively. In an *objective approach*, economic conditions are described with the help of known parameters that allow objective assessments and comparisons across time periods and across population segments. A *subjective approach* addresses the question whether and how economic conditions in an objective sense correspond with the subjective perceptions and evaluations of these conditions.

The two approaches are complementary in that the subjective approach acts as a validity check on the objective approach. Often, however, the validity check is deemed unnecessary under the implicit assumption that a quantitative analysis provides an accurate description of the subjective aspect as well. "The richer, the happier" would be an example of such an assumption. Economic and financial affairs form an important aspect of human life. Political, collective, and individual decision making often involves trade-offs regarding economic effects. However, assumptions underlying economic decisions are seldom made explicit, so that a mere objective approach is sometimes used when a combination of objective and subjective approaches would be more appropriate.

Corresponding to the two approaches are, in principle, two types of measures. We may identify objective and subjective indicators, corresponding to the objective and the subjective approach, respectively. Both objective and subjective indicators may refer either to the macroeconomic level or to the microeconomic level (Van Raaij, 1984):

Van Raaij, W.F., van Veldhoven, G.M. and Wärneryd, K.E. (eds) Handbook of Economic Psychology. ISBN 90-247-3720-6.

1. *Objective macro indicators* are, for example, a nation's economic growth and unemployment figures.
2. *Subjective macro indicators* provide evaluations of macroeconomic conditions such as experienced by individual persons. Economic pessimism or optimism may be regarded as a subjective macroeconomic indicator.
3. An *objective micro indicator* refers to measures of an individual product's or brand's market performance as expressed, for example, in sales figures or in market share.
4. *Subjective micro indicators* are individual consumer measures of satisfaction with or preference for a particular product or brand.

The advantage of objective indicators is their reliability, ease of interpretation, and cost. However, objective indicators are problematic in the sense that, if they are taken as proxy measures for the more qualitative aspects, their external validity is doubtful. For example, the gross national product of a country does display a nation's general productivity level, but this may not have a simple relation to individual well-being. First, productivity and the associated income effects may be distributed unequally over segments of the population. Second, individuals differ in the extent to which they relate personal productivity and wealth to well-being.

Subjective indicators, on the other hand, attempt to tap well-being at the level where it actually counts: the individual level. This may solve the validity problem of the objective indicators. Moreover, the subjective measures allow for greater sensitivity.

However, subjective measures are associated with a number of problems. These are the reverse of the advantages of the objective indicators: there may be reliability and possible operationalization and interpretation problems, and the cost of data collection is relatively high. A general problem is, for example, the problem of dimensionality. What particular aspects of an issue have to be dealt with and in what detail?

Sometimes a third type of indicator is distinguished: the *social indicator.* This indicator combines, in fact, a number of the advantages – but also disadvantages – of the objective and subjective indicators. As such, it is a third, but not necessarily a better alternative. A social indicator may be described as an objective macro indicator from which subjective associations may be inferred more easily than from pure objective indicators. For example, an indicator such as the number of suicides has the advantage of relating directly to well-being. On the other hand, this measure does not consider explicitly and directly the amount of well-being in the population and does not allow for individual differences.

Where appropriate, the objective, social, and subjective indicators will be distinguished in the sections to follow. In the remainder of this chapter, we will emphasize the potential functions of subjective indicators. In an economic psychological analysis these measures may be taken as dependent variables or as mediating variables between economic conditions and economic decisions. As such, they are important for theoretical and practical reasons.

The subjective approach employs a number of concepts, each associated with a particulate domain in the economic area. The most general concept is that of *happiness*. This concept comprises the subjective perceptions and evaluations of noneconomic life domains. The same is true for the "*quality of life*" concept. "*Economic well-being*" is the term used in connection with societal, market, and individual conditions of an economic nature. A term reserved for the financial aspect of economic well-being is "*income evaluation*." At the market level, we may distinguish the job market and the consumer market.

Subjective approaches have been employed in both, focusing on, respectively, "job satisfaction" and "consumer satisfaction."

The set of the various concepts can be divided both chronologically and hierarchically. Chronologically, income acquisition precedes income spending. Similarly, job satisfaction, income evaluation and consumer satisfaction each cover a part of the qualitative income-related dimension. Hierarchically, economic well-being may be seen as a more general concept comprising the combination of job satisfaction, income evaluation and consumer satisfaction. Economic well-being is to be viewed as hierarchically lower than happiness or quality of life. In Figure 1 the structure of interrelationships among the various concepts is shown. In the remainder of this chapter the emphasis will be on the economic domain of quality of life/happiness.

Our objectives in this chapter are:

1. to identify the common and unique theoretical and methodological aspects in the various fields of economic well-being;
2. to provide a synthesis of the various approaches; and
3. to relate this synthesis to practical considerations.

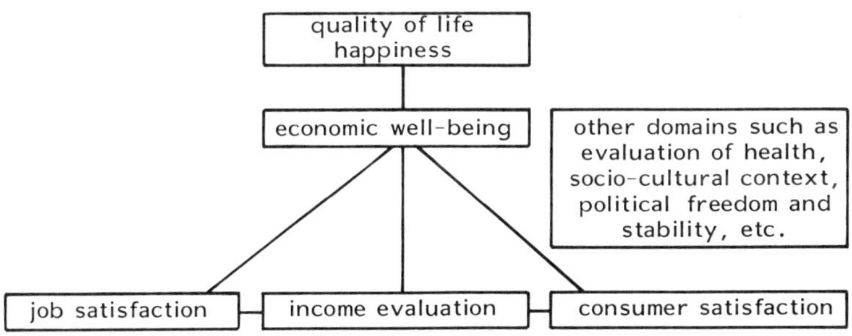

Fig. 1. The relationships among well-being related concepts.

In the following, we will first review the literature on job satisfaction, income evaluation, and consumer satisfaction.

2. JOB SATISFACTION

Job satisfaction, the affective state experienced as a consequence of some job related characteristics or events, is a central issue from the viewpoint of society, economists, organizations and the individual him/herself. Job satisfaction as a social indicator may provide a monitoring and diagnostic aid for early warning of societal dislocations, policy and program failures (Seashore and Taber, 1975). Dissatisfaction is a source of concern for economists, who relate it to labor costs and production level. At the organizational level, it codetermines the psychological bond between the individual and the organization/employer s/he works for.

The emphasis here is on the individual and psychological explanation of (dis)satisfaction differences not accounted for by objective work characteristics. In the following we will discuss several subject aspects and will relate these to the corresponding psychological theories.

A general observation is that work is subjectively important and serves many functions. *Work* is a "central life interest" (Dubin, 1956). First, work has a regulatory, controlling, and financial meaning and significance. Work structures time and provides money, security, and stability. Money, in turn, determines personal life style and consumption level. Second, social contacts are regulated by work, and the social aspect of work is expressed in the social identity, in status and prestige. Personal growth is the third function of work. Experience, skill, autonomy and responsibility are the job elements that contribute to personal development and intrinsic satisfaction.

The importance of work is also mirrored by the psychological effects observed the (forced) transition from work to non-work: the dramatic case of unemployment. Generally, unemployment produces physical and psychological problems, such as depression and a subjective sense of powerlessness (Warr, 1983; Schoormans and Von Grumbkow, 1985).

In the literature, each of these different functions of work has been considered exclusively by different "schools." The Scientific Management school sees job satisfaction as primarily determined by physical working conditions and financial reward. The Human Relations school (Mayo, 1949) focuses upon the relationships between the individual and the group, the supervisor and the management. The social context is the critical factor. Finally, challenges, skills, advancement, and responsibility are primarily considered by the Individual Growth school (Maslow, 1970). The various schools have produced a variety of theories. The most important can be summarized in two broad classes: *content or need theories*, and *process theories*. The first class focuses upon the specific needs or objects that ultimately cause the behavior of an individual and affect his/her well-being. The second class stresses the process by which objects or needs influence what an individual does and how this relates to feelings and emotions. Below, we will briefly elaborate upon each of these classes.

3. NEED THEORIES

Dissatisfaction, according to the need theories, is equated with a psychologically uncomfortable tension caused by deprivation. Satisfaction occurs when this tension is absent. According to Maslow (1970) a *hierarchy of needs* exists so that lower level needs must be satisfied before a higher level need is satisfied. Maslow identified five levels of needs: physiological, safety, social, ego and self-actualization. This model of *self-actualization* is based on the idea that every individual has an innate need to grow. A satisfied need will activate a new, yet unsatisfied need at a higher level in the need hierarchy. A state of satisfaction acts as a releaser for the next need level.

Alderfer (1969) combined these levels to three core needs: maintenance of material existence (*existence needs*), maintenance of interpersonal relationships with significant people (*relatedness needs*), and the need to find opportunities for personal development (*growth needs*). Alderfer does not assume that lower-level needs must be satisfied before higher-order needs can emerge.

For the Human Relations school, social needs are the most important job related needs. Practical suggestions based on this theoretical approach stress direct face-to-face contacts and group cohesiveness. Job characteristics themselves receive only marginal attention.

Herzberg's two-factor theory (Herzberg, Mausner, and Snyderman, 1959), one of the most influential theories, attempts to combine work and social aspects. According to Herzberg, there are two subsets of factors related to job evaluation: satisfiers and dissatisfiers or hygiene factors. These factors cannot be placed on the same continuum. *Satisfiers*, if present, produce satisfaction. If absent, they do not result in dissatisfaction, however. Satisfiers activate the so-called *motivator needs*, needs related to personal growth: responsibility, advancement, autonomy, and recognition. Job satisfaction is precluded by the presence of dissatisfiers. *Dissatisfiers or hygiene factors* can only produce job dissatisfaction. Their prevention or diminution cannot result in satisfaction. They pertain to job context: material labor conditions, interpersonal relations within the group and with the supervisor, and the organization's policy and stability.

4. PROCESS THEORIES

In contrast with the need theories, process theories are not concerned with motivators or satisfying factors. They only describe the interrelationships between factors and disregard the specific nature of these factors. Several theories may be distinguished: the discrepancy theory, the reference group theory, the balance theory, the inequity theory, and the social comparison/social competition theory.

1. *Discrepancy theory* regards satisfaction as a cognitive experience. The individual compares his perception of the present situation with his perception of the desired situation (Cantril, 1965; Locke, 1976; Porter, 1961; Tannenbaum and Kuleck, 1978). Satisfaction depends on the discrepancy between the observed and the desired. The discrepancy theory describes intra-personal comparisons. In this respect, it may be distinguished from the reference group theory.
2. *Reference group theory* (Merton and Lazarsfeld, 1950) produced the concept of *relative deprivation.* Satisfaction is dependent upon the outcome of the comparison between the personal situation and the situation of relevant others (e.g., Hulin, 1966). A related theory is the *Social Influence theory* (Salancik and Pfeffer, 1978): An individual's satisfaction is determined by informational cues provided by others as to their satisfaction. Research has shown that informational cues have a greater impact on satisfaction than the objective characteristics of the work.
3. In the *balance theory* the individual cognitively compares expected and actual outcomes. The evaluation of the comparison produces satisfaction or dissatisfaction. Note the similarity with the discrepancy theory. The balance theory describes the consequences of imbalance. The uncomfortable tension associated with imbalanced functions acts as a need and the individual will attempt to reduce the tension. A dissonant set of cognitions constitutes a negative motivational state, which an individual is motivated to reduce. Reduction mechanisms are described by Adams' (1965) Inequity theory.
4. *Inequity theory* (Adams, 1965) is a special case of the balance theory. (Dis)satisfaction is the result of three comparisons. An individual compares his/her inputs with his/her outputs, the inputs with the outputs of (an)other person(s), and s/he compares the results of the two comparisons. In other words, s/he compares his/her job input/output ratio with the corresponding ratios of relevant others. Inputs are, for example, the amount of time and effort spent; salary, security, and status are examples of output. If the two ratios are the same, the individual is satisfied. A relatively high input compared to the input of the other (with outputs

constant) leads to dissatisfaction, possibly in the form of guilt feelings. This is not unequivocally supported by empirical evidence (see Syroit, 1984).

The variety of ways in which dissatisfaction may occur indicates a similar variety of possible corrective/adaptive activities. The inequity theory presumes a consensus on what are to be considered inputs and outputs. However, individual differences may be considerable.

5. According to the *social comparison/social competition theory* (Rijsman, 1983) people strive for a small difference with others on a positively evaluated dimension. A slightly superior position, for example in the case of work, generates a positive personal identity. This position can be attained either by achievement or by a bias in the interpretation of achievements. The positive personal identity can also be secured by taking another person as the comparison-other, in order to (relatively) improve one's personal position. The theory has much in common with the self-competence theory. Individuals will be motivated to perform a job in a manner consistent with the self-image with which they approach the job situation. They will be motivated to effective performance to the extent that their self-concept requires effective performance in order to result in consistent cognitions.

5. JOB SATISFACTION: THEORETICAL DISCUSSION

Job satisfaction represents a generalized affective orientation to all aspects of the job. But it can also be seen as a job-facet satisfaction referring to the various aspects of the job. A job taken as a whole seldom serves as an unitary attitude object; the attitude is rather the degree of satisfaction with a number of different facets of the job. An important question is, which set of facets are common to most jobs.

There are different operational deficiencies and these are probably related to the complex nature of job satisfaction as a theoretical construct. With respect to job satisfaction, there is no comprehensive theoretical model. There are, however, some integrative models and one of the promising ones is *Lawler's facet model.*

Lawler's model (Lawler, 1973) may be viewed as a hybrid theory in that it attempts to integrate many of the elements discussed above. It is a pragmatic model referring to the discrepancy between "the perceived amount of rewards that should be received" and "the perceived amount received." These perceptions are determined by comparisons with others on input and output (facet) dimensions. If the positions on the dimensions are equal, satisfaction will result. Outcomes are broadly defined in this model so as to include social outcomes (Human Relations) and task intrinsic outcomes (Herzberg).

The overall satisfaction can be a complex function of satisfaction with specific job facets. The nature of this function is unknown. It can be compensatory linear, in which a high score on one facet compensates for a low score on another facet, it can be disjunctive, in which the scores do not compensate, or conjunctive, i.e., a non-linear model in which high satisfaction on one facet is enough to outweigh low satisfaction on all other facets.

6. INCOME EVALUATION

6.1. *Introduction*

Although income evaluation will be treated as a separate aspect of economic well-being, it is hard to separate from the other two aspects, job satisfaction and consumer satisfaction. First, there is an overlap between job satisfaction and income evaluation to the extent that job satisfaction may be taken as the outcome of either the sum or the ratio of personal investment in the job and the financial income received in return. On the other hand, in the case of income evaluation the income of partner or other household members may have an effect. This aspect is not included in job satisfaction. Second, income evaluation is not independent from consumer satisfaction. The expenditure level is determined by the income level. It is positively related to purchase quality and negatively related to consumer vulnerability to bad buys.

On the other hand, some differences between the concepts warrant a separate consideration of income evaluation. One of the differences is that there are more psychological aspects to income than just the job compensatory aspect. Income is also the expression of social status and recognition beyond the working place and as such it is an element in general interpersonal comparisons. Also, income may be subjectively perceived as a source of present and future security. For both reasons, it would be correct to distinguish salary satisfaction and income satisfaction.

The difference between income evaluation and consumer satisfaction is even more clear. Even though we may assume a relationship between income evaluation and consumer consumption quality aggregated over all services and products bought, the concept of consumer satisfaction is more specifically tied to individual goods and services. Consumer satisfaction does not apply to the consumer's general marketplace well-being, it applies to the experience with particular items bought. Just as salary satisfaction and income satisfaction are conceptually separable, we may distinguish general expenditure level satisfaction and specific product and attribute satisfaction as different aspects of consumer satisfaction.

Now that income evaluation has been distinguished from job, salary, and consumer satisfaction, let us briefly consider the way it has been treated in the literature. First, we must note that of the three aspects of economic well-being, income evaluation has received less attention. A possible reason is that income is viewed as a one-dimensional concept synonymous with amount of money. From an economic point of view this would be correct – the economic literature often treats income, income evaluation and economic well-being as identical or at least positively and linearly related. As we briefly suggested above, such an approach would be too limited, if the actual subjective meaning of income is the focus of interest.

The second observation to be made is that when research respondents are requested to evaluate their income, they tend to view income as outcome, that is, as salary obtained through labor. Thus, the research that in the past focused on income evaluation may have been biased by stressing income as salary. An alternative approach might be one in which the financial flows (both in and out) of an individual or an individual household are considered separately.

Here, we want to mention two lines of research. The first line (e.g., Van Praag, 1971) offers an alternative to the strictly economic approach. Van Praag's Welfare Function of Income (WFI) allows for nonlinear (logarithmic) relationships between income and income evaluation. The WFI is assessed individually. Each respondent provides an income amount for each of the following income evaluations: very good, good, sufficient, almost sufficient, bad, and very bad. The result, either individual or aggregated over individuals, is an S-shaped curve with the parameters μ and σ indicating the location of the curve midpoint and the steepness of the curve, respectively; σ is an indication of the sensitivity for income changes as it is expressed in income evaluation changes.

The other line of research was undertaken by Poiesz and Von Grumbkow (1982, 1983). They presented empirical evidence with regard to the psychological basis of income evaluation. Their results indicated that psychological variables such as perceived equity, social comparison, short-term income expectations, motivation, and locus of control have a significant (albeit not always very strong) relationship with income evaluation. One of the most powerful predictors, equity, accounted for as much variance in the evaluation measure as the amount of income. The results of the research reported by Poiesz and Von Grumbkow also suggested that the Welfare Function of Income (Van Praag, 1971) has some validity limitations if considered from a psychological point of view. For example, the relationship between the income evaluation based on the WFI and the equity variable was lower than the relationship between a Likert-type income evaluation and equity. In the Likert-type evaluation question ("how do you evaluate your income"), people simply report their judgment; in the WFI, respondents have to "turn around" the evaluation question and cognitively and affectively construct various income levels. A possible critique of this type of operationalization is that a person might find it cognitively both very hard and unusual to construct income levels that have a considerably different evaluation from his/her present income evaluation. Empirical support for this critique has been provided by Poiesz and Von Grumbkow (1982, 1983).

6.2. *Income Evaluation: Theoretical Discussion*

Few studies are explicitly devoted to the psychological basis of income evaluation, although psychological variables have a considerable influence on income evaluation. Of these psychological variables, perceived equity of income is as much an explanation for variance of income evaluation as the level of income in money terms.

There are several possible operationalizations of income evaluation. These operationalizations are subject to the influence of psychological variables.

Income is spent on consumption and saving. If we may view saving as delayed consumption, income and consumption are financial synonyms. There are reasons to believe that they are not synonymous in a psychological sense. In the following section we will discuss satisfaction or dissatisfaction as it is produced by consumption.

7. CONSUMER SATISFACTION

7.1. *Introduction*

The concept of consumer satisfaction is relevant for a variety of reasons. First, consumer satisfaction is the ultimate goal of aggregate marketing activities. A satisfied consumer is likely to repeat-purchase the particular good or service that produced satisfaction. Also, a satisfied consumer is a non-complaining consumer – no time and money have to be spent on corrective actions by the firm, and no adverse communication among consumers will take place. Similarly, a high level of consumer satisfaction/a low level of dissatisfaction will prevent government intervention so that independence may be maintained. On the other hand, questions regarding long term consumer satisfaction form the raison d'être of institutions for consumer information and protection. Finally, as consumption forms a continuous and important part of everyday life, satisfaction with consumption is a crucial aspect of general well-being and an object of political interest and decision making.

The scientific attention to consumer satisfaction has reflected each of these reasons. After a high level of political interest in consumer affairs in the seventies, the importance of the consumer satisfaction issue declined somewhat in the past few years. This is paralleled by a diminishing number of publications on satisfaction and complaint behavior in the consumer behavior literature. However, the concept remains important as a feedback element for marketing activities and as an aspect of general well-being.

Basically, consumer satisfaction can be approached at the aggregate and at the individual level. For the first level "*consumer welfare*" is the appropriate term. It refers to the efficient allocation of resources in an economy. Here we will disregard the aggregate level, considering that genuine insight into the dynamics of consumer satisfaction may only be obtained if we allow for the maximum variation in the object of study, which is at the individual level. Satisfaction is a behavioural phenomenon and should be examined as such (Vinson, 1977). Additionally, a non-psychological approach to satisfaction constitutes essentially a normative and not a descriptive or explanatory approach (Day, 1980).

In the consumer behaviour literature, satisfaction is generally conceptualized in terms of the confirmation or disconfirmation of expectations regarding product attribute levels. Satisfaction is the affective state associated with the outcome of a comparison between the expected and the experienced product performance. The paradigm that relates initial expectations and perceived performance lends itself most readily to approaches departing from psychological theories. Theories that are frequently referred to are the comparison level theory (LaTour and Peat, 1979; Swan and Martin, 1981), the assimilation-contrast theory (Anderson, 1973; Olson and Dover, 1979), and the adaptation level theory (Oliver, 1980a, 1980b; Oliver and Linda, 1981). Guzzo (1980) has called this group of theories the "*discrepancy theory*".

As comparisons require cognitive processes, the various "discrepancy theories" have an important cognitive component in common. Generally, this component is dealt with more explicitly than the affect component which is often implicitly regarded as directly related to disconfirmation (Swan, 1977; Oliver, 1979; Swan and Combs, 1976; Hunt, 1977). It is not always made clear whether (dis)satisfaction should be interpreted as the label for (dis)confirmation or as the result of (dis)confirmation. In the former case (dis)confirmation is the single and only determinant, while in the latter case (dis)confirmation may be one of the determinants of the affective state called (dis)satisfaction. It is clear that the two alternative conceptualizations would require different theoretical approaches.

A comparable point is raised by Hunt (1977). Is (positive) affect associated with the (positive) experience or the (positive) evaluation of that experience? Does affect precede, or is it concurrent with, judgments of satisfaction and dissatisfaction (Westbrook, 1980)?

In the following we will briefly elaborate on the theories receiving the most attention. Next, an overview will be given of the major points of discussion in the literature. Finally, we will conclude with some general observations with regard to the types of studies and operationalizations of consumer satisfaction.

1. The *comparison level theory* (Thibaut and Kelley, 1959) has been applied to consumer satisfaction by LaTour and Peat (1979). Per product attribute the consumer compares performance to a particular comparison level. This level is dependent upon three possible determinants: past experience, other consumers' experiences, and commercial and noncommercial product information. A relatively favourable product performance leads to satisfaction; a relatively unfavourable performance contributes to dissatisfaction.
2. The *assimilation-contrast theory* (Anderson, 1973; Olson and Dover, 1979) predicts a nonlinear effect of the disconfirmation of expectations on (dis)satisfaction. If the perceived performance differs slightly from the expected performance, the difference is ignored and the expected and the perceived performance are psychologically assimilated, so that no effect will be observed on feelings of (dis)satisfaction. Alternatively, if the difference between performance and expectation exceeds a particular critical threshold, the difference is psychologically "blown up" and a relatively strong effect on (dis)satisfaction results.

   The assimilation-contrast theory may be conceived of as integrating two seemingly contradictory explanations: the *contrast theory* and the *cognitive dissonance theory*. The former theory suggests a magnification of the discrepancy between expectation and performance; the latter theory predicts a diminution – resulting from an adaptation of the evaluation of the performance in the direction of the initial expectations in order to avoid psychological tension.

   Even though the assimilation-contrast theory may be an acceptable compromise, we suggest that the concept of attribution may help explain under what circumstances either a contrast or a dissonance reduction effect will be obtained. It can be hypothesized that if the consumer attributes a discrepancy between expectation and performance to him/herself (e.g., uncareful buying behaviour), a dissonance reduction effect will be observed; conversely, if the discrepancy is attributed to an external source (e.g., uncareful packaging or shipment by the manufacturer), we may hypothesize a contrast effect reflected in relatively high dissatisfaction. Yet, research evidence suggests that consumers are more likely to attribute their product dissatisfaction to the product and/or seller than to themselves (Landon and Emery, 1974; Valle and Wallendorf, 1977). In addition, LaTour and Peat (1979) indicate that only if perceived performance is highly subjective, will assimilation occur.

3. The *adaptation-level theory* (Helson, 1964), as applied to consumer satisfaction (Oliver, 1977; Oliver and Linda, 1980), suggests that the (dis)-satisfaction with a product is affected by the prior experience with similar products. These products combined form the adaptation level. The difference between this theory and the other comparison theories is that the adaptation-level theory departs from satisfaction as an additive function of both expectation and disconfirmation. Empirical evidence (Oliver and Linda, 1981) has shown that of the two determinants of satisfaction, disconfirmation is the more potent one.

7.2. *Consumer Satisfaction: Theoretical Discussion*

The state of the art may be summarized in the following points:

1. The concept of satisfaction is defined in a variety of ways (Day, 1980).
2. Swan and Martin (1980) present as a major conclusion that models of consumer satisfaction need to incorporate the disconfirmation of past performance expectations.
3. According to Guzzo (1980): "Each variation of the general paradigm relating expectation to perceived performance has received empirical support. However, no one variation stands out as an overall explanation of consumer satisfaction." Day (1980): There is a lack of a well-developed and widely accepted theoretical framework.
4. The various components or determinants of satisfaction are not completely clear themselves. It is not well understood how expectations influence the evaluative process (Day, 1980). Although satisfaction has been shown to be directly related to disconfirmation (Swan, 1977; Oliver, 1977, 1979; Swan and Combs, 1976), it was suggested by Swan and Trawick (1980) that satisfaction is related to "desired" expectations but not to "predictive" expectations.
5. It is not clear whether satisfaction is a continuous variable or whether satisfaction and dissatisfaction are different states (Leavitt, 1977, referred to by Swan and Martin, 1980).
6. Finally, Jacoby (1976) suggests a parallel between the two-factor content approach presented in the context of job satisfaction (Herzberg, Mausner, and Snyderman, 1959) and the effects that may be observed in the context of consumer satisfaction. According to Jacoby: "(...) it appears that many factors in buying a product will, by their presence or absence, either positively or negatively affect behavior and/or subsequent behavior, but not both." For example, a product warranty may not increase purchase likelihood or product satisfaction. However, the

absence of a warranty may definitely decrease purchase likelihood or product satisfaction. A dual system is suggested including facilitators and inhibitors. In the consumer behavior literature this distinction has not been elaborated upon.

8. ECONOMIC WELL-BEING: AN INTEGRATIVE CONCEPT?

Now that we have discussed the three aspects of economic well-being as presented in the introduction, what can we say about the various interrelationships? Here we will limit ourselves to conceptual suggestions and save the theoretical discussion for later. In the introduction economic well-being was viewed as a weighted mean of job satisfaction, income evaluation, and consumer satisfaction. A dissection of the general concept of economic well-being might prove helpful. Therefore, we propose the following scheme (Table 1).

In Table 1 a distinction is made between satisfaction with general economic contexts and satisfaction with individual effects of economic or financial events or regulations on either the labor market, the consumer market, or in the relationship between government and citizens. The individual effects are of two types: inputs and outcomes. Satisfaction may relate to either one or to their combination.

Obviously, the overview is not complete. For example, it allows only for one type of comparison: that between individual inputs and outcomes. Another type of comparison is the social comparison. How do my present inputs and/or outcomes compare with those of relevant other persons? A third type of comparison relates to the time dimension: what are the present inputs and/or outcomes relative to those experienced in the past or expected in the future? Both additional types of comparisons will be reflected in individual differences with regard to well-being, the objective situation quality held constant. The overview in Table 1, even if incomplete, means to show that economic well-being can hardly be taken as a unitary concept. If it is to be conceptualized at all, it can only be in very broad terms. However, there is clearly an inverse relationship between breadth of conceptualization and psychological meaningfulness.

What we may suggest, then, is to drop the term "economic well-being" as a psychological variable, and instead limit our attention to either of the domains identified as one of its aspects. We realize that this reduces the term to an umbrella label that identifies general categories for research activities. Psychologically, we can do without it, since individuals are not likely to "add up" their evaluations of the general and specific aspects of economic life. For this they lack the cognitive capability and insight into the interdependencies between these aspects.

Table 1. Possible bases of economic well-being.

Satisfaction with		worker	consumer	citizen
general structure		*labor market*	*product market*	
economic political				
system and		– opportunities	– consumer information	– economic
organization				
order		– central negotiations	– consumer protection	
		– quality control	– labor unions	
	I	– mental effort	– mental effort	– taxes
	N	– physical effort	– physical effort	– premiums
	P	– time	– time	
	U	– psychological	– money	
	T	costs		
	S	– financial investments		
Individual	O	– salary	– product	– economic provisions
effects	U			
general	T			
	C	– fringe	– (status,	
	O	benefits	prestige)	
	M	– social	– consumption	
	E	contacts		
	S	– intrinsic		– economic
progress		motivators		stability
		– status, prestige		
		– equity		
	S			
	U	Perceived economic financial freedom of choice		
	M			

9. INTEGRATION AND DISCUSSION

9.1. *Introduction*

This section will be divided in four parts. In the first part, some general observations are made as an introduction to the discussion. In part two we will consider the similarities and differences between the theoretical approaches to job satisfaction, income evaluation and consumer satisfaction. Third, the various operationalizations will be critically discussed. In the fourth and last part, we will make some suggestions as to the theoretical and operational approach to satisfaction-variables.

9.2. *Some General Points*

For a correct interpretation of the similarities and differences among the various fields of interest it is necessary to briefly review the common and distinctive objects of each of these fields.

Job, income and consumer satisfaction have one important object in common: they are all closely related to money. However, this economic relationship occurs at an abstract level which may not have the same psychological meaning and significance for each of the fields under consideration. In considering differences we may note, first, that the freedom to select from among different jobs and income levels is generally limited compared to the freedom of choice actually experienced by the consumer.

A consumer may even have the opportunity to experiment until she finds a satisfactory alternative. In the process, she may have expectations with regard to product performance formed, disconfirmed, adapted or confirmed. The role of expectations is much less clear in the case of job and income satisfaction. Usually, a person holds a steady job or earns a fixed income. The impact of initial expectations may be assumed to be smaller with the number of years in an unchanged situation. Another difference between the three fields is that a satisfying or dissatisfying experience for the consumer is often less important than his/her job and income experiences. The job and the income have a more profound and a longer lasting impact upon general satisfaction than most consumer experiences. A final difference that must be stressed is that the consumer will likely experience an independent relationship with his supplier whereas the worker may not find it possible or wise to express dissatisfaction to his employer. The various material differences are likely to be reflected in theoretical differences.

9.3. *Theory*

The difference in material object and the different type of context in which they have been considered have developed job satisfaction, income evaluation, and consumer satisfaction along different routes. The three fields do not seem to have been systematically cross-fertilized. The three lines of investigation have, to a large extent, really been three separate lines of investigation.

Yet, looking at the various theoretical views presented in the three domains, we note some overlap. Of course, the nomenclature differs, but the underlying reasoning seems basically similar.

The one single notion that stands out in each domain is the notion of comparison. This means, at the very least, that satisfaction is taken as a concept expressing some degree of relativity. Satisfaction is not an absolute thing, it varies with the circumstances even when the object of satisfaction does not. This observation, while not very dramatic, has both theoretical and operational implications. The theoretical implications are covered by the question "relative to what?" Here we can point out some parallels between the three fields. *Satisfaction* can be seen as the affective outcome associated with a cognitive comparison of the present situation relative to any one or a combination of several reference points:

1. the present and the past situation,
2. the present situation and the situation that was expected in the past,
3. the present situation and the desired situation,
4. the present situation and the situation expected in the future,
5. the situation of others and the personal situation,
6. the outcomes of others and the personal outcomes,
7. the inputs of others and the personal inputs,
8. the personal inputs and the personal outcomes,
9. the sum or ratio of inputs and outcomes of others and the sum or ratio of personal inputs and outcomes, and
10. the present situation and some external norm.

These (and possibly other) types of comparisons have been and/or could be identified in the three areas at issue in this chapter.

We may suggest, then, that theoretical satisfaction research should be directed at the nature of comparisons, at the conditions under which the various types of comparisons tend to occur, and at the dynamics of comparisons. Considering the content of the research that has been conducted so far it seems neither necessary nor efficient to limit research to one particular area of satisfaction. A more worthwhile approach to combine research efforts to assess the underlying general psychological factors influencing comparative judgment and satisfaction. Only in cases of application these factors would have to be translated into domain-specific determinants.

In the consumer satisfaction area, comparisons other than that between expected and actual product performance may become relevant. Maybe it is not the difference itself that produces dissatisfaction, but rather the notion that this difference is greater than that observed in other consumers.

Consumer satisfaction research is characterized by the lack of a well developed and widely accepted theoretical framework (Day, 1980). We can justifiably assert the same for the two other lines of inquiry. A lack of theoretical consensus tends to be accompanied by a lack of agreement on the operationalizations to be used.

9.4. *Operationalization*

The field of well-being and satisfaction is covered by an overwhelming amount of different types of measures. The most important types are the economic, social, life style, and psychological measures. We will discuss each of these types very briefly and then elaborate on specific problems associated with psychological measurement.

Economic measures as indicators of well-being are relatively inexpensive, easy to interpret, easy to compare over time, reliable, and have some self-evident basis to them making then acceptable as valid indicators. However, they do not consider individual differences and they ignore the subjective meaning of what has been expressed in the measure. For example, the percentage of unemployment may be a good indicator of a nation's economic activity level. However, it does not show how employment is distributed nor how the nation's inhabitants experience the threat of unemployment or unemployment itself.

Social indicators, e.g. the number of hospital beds, social security provisions, or the number of suicides, may not have some of the interpretation problems of the economic indicators, but their problem is basically the same. These measures may mean something else at the aggregate level than at the individual level – and it is at the individual level that they are supposed to count.

Life style measures provide an insight into people's activities, interests, and opinions. It is very hard to derive satisfaction from these measures without the application of some external/outside norms (whose norms?).

In this chapter we have focused on the psychological aspect of satisfaction. The advantage is that it directly concentrates on the essential point/crucial issue: the circumstances as they are experienced by the individual. However, psychological measurement is associated with a number of problems as well, some of which may be hard to surmount. Here we will briefly outline some examples of these problems.

First, we have the well-known problems of type of scaling, response tendencies, reliability and dimensionality (number and type). More typical for the issue of satisfaction are the following potential problems:

1. Is satisfaction one single continuous dimension ranging from satisfaction to dissatisfaction, or are there in fact two independent psychological dimensions, the positive dimension and the hygiene (potentially dissatisfying) dimension? A related question is that of intensity – satisfaction as indicated on a particular evaluation scale may actually mean anything from a very positive affect to indifference or dissatisfaction.
2. If comparisons have to be assessed by measuring both the actual and

the reference situation, there could be carry-over effects in either direction. For example, if expectations are measured first, the evaluation of future experiences may be influenced by them; if the evaluation of the present situation is measured first, respondents may rationalize their initial expectations or may have forgotten the exact nature of those expectations.

3. Dissonance reduction effects, habituation effects, and effects of knowledge may all influence satisfaction judgment to the extent that we may question their relevance as a feedback to policy decisions, if not their internal validity.
4. Respondents are known to have a limited time and geographical scope causing them to overstate short-term and small-range effects. For example, respondents are unlikely to incorporate possible detrimental long-term effects of cigarette smoking when stating their satisfaction with a particular brand of cigarettes. As another example, people are likely to be less dissatisfied with the installation of nuclear power plants if this is planned at a greater distance from their own back yard.
5. The *Polyanna hypothesis* (Boucher and Osgood, 1969) predicts that people show a tendency toward the positive. It has been suggested that continued questioning after the initial satisfaction question may reveal dissatisfactory aspects.
6. Is the actual experience of (dis)satisfaction tapped by satisfaction questions or is (dis)satisfaction prompted by the questions themselves?
7. The possibility of bias, a positive self-evaluation, is likely to show up in satisfaction scores (positive bias).

10. RECOMMENDATIONS

Taking these points as a whole, we face a crucial operational question: should we measure subjective satisfaction "as it comes" or should we try to eliminate possible biases in order to obtain "corrected" satisfaction scores?

In discussing the theoretical and operational questions and problems concerning well-being and satisfaction, we did not treat in detail the actual application of their measures as a feedback instrument for policy decisions. In an attempt to more explicitly consider what these measures can mean in actual application, we may point at two distinct ways in which the theoretical and operational problems may be handled.

First, one might recommend the exclusive usage of the more macro-type economic and social indicators and discard the individually based psychological measures. As this option would eliminate not only the problems but also the benefits of these latter measures, we might suggest a second alternative to use the micro measures as an essential addendum to the macro measures, taking the various problems into account so that they may be collected for. (The example is given for product satisfaction. Of course, by changing the object of judgment, the steps would equally apply to job satisfaction and income evaluation). Individual measures have the potential to contribute considerably to the explanation of the subjective meaning of and the variance around macro measures.

How to deal with the theoretical and operational issues? Here, we will propose an approach to well-being and satisfaction that may be helpful in either solving or circumventing them. The general idea is that one may conceive of well-being and satisfaction as syndromes of psychological effects based upon some hierarchy of effects in which the following steps may be hypothesized.

1. A negative evaluative effect, resulting from the comparison(s) referred to earlier, must exceed a particular level or threshold in order to be psychologically significant. A moderate deviation from the expected product performance, for example, will be assimilated into the expected range of product performances (dissonance reduction; assimilation).
2. An extension of step 1 is that the person, if s/he does not assimilate the present experience into the expected range, will judge as to whether the deviation lies in the range of perceived acceptable product performances. This is the range of the perceived experiences that all other consumers would judge to be acceptable. One would not anticipate an unexpected negative experience to lead to dissatisfaction if it falls within the range of perceived acceptability.
3. Should a negative evaluation develop, a person will try to avoid this negative psychological effect, even if there are actually disappointing product characteristics. Consequently, a person will attempt to attenuate the experience by generating compensatory thoughts, balancing positive and negative more evenly. Consider, for example, an unexpectedly inferior product characteristic that is perceived to fall outside of the acceptable range. Compensatory thoughts may be those that stress the positive product characteristics, that involve some future retaliation against the producer or seller (e.g., not to buy products of the same brand again; not to return to the same seller; to counteradvertise among friends), or that deal with some meta-reflection (e.g., "this bad buy was a good lesson for me").
4. If a dissatisfying experience occurs beyond steps 1 and 2 and no compensatory thoughts are available, then, to the extent that the cause of the experience is attributed externally, a trade-off will take place involving the perceived actual and psychological costs (see Verhallen and Pieters, 1984) of complaining and the perceived chance of success.

Of course, individuals are not conceived of here as rational decision makers progressing through the various successive phases by making careful and elaborate comparisons and trade-offs. Rather, we want to introduce this approach as one which allows potentially dissatisfying experiences to be handled psychologically before they eventually do or do not surface. Handling refers to the selective perception, distortion, or ignorance of elements that may enter trade-offs based on limited knowledge and psychological defense mechanisms.

In conclusion, some meta observations and questions on the use of well-being and satisfaction data in policy decisions are in order. First, what is the ultimate goal of these decisions? Are they aimed at the increase of satisfaction or at the reduction of dissatisfaction, and, within these extremes/two options, what is the reference point: the extreme, mode, median or mean? Second, apart from cost-considerations evidently involved in policy trade-offs, what is the psychological effect of the chosen approach? The adaptive nature of human aspirations implies that the attempt to increase satisfaction may be self-defeating: after a short while, the increased satisfaction level is likely to regress towards the initial level as a result of habituation effects and rising aspirations (see Homans, 1961).

REFERENCES

Adams, J.S., 1965, "Inequity in social exchange," in: L. Berkowitz (ed.), Advances in Experimental Social Psychology, Vol. 2, New York: Academic Press, pp. 267-299.

Alderfer, C.P., 1969, An empirical test of a new theory of human needs, Organizational Behavior and Human Performance, 4, 142-175.

Anderson, R.E., 1973, Consumer dissatisfaction: The effect of disconfirmed expectancy on perceived product performance, Journal of Marketing Research, 10, 38-44.

Boucher, J., and C.E. Osgood, 1969, The Polyanna hypothesis, Journal of Verbal Learning and Verbal Behavior, 8, 1-8.

Cantril, H., 1965, Pattern of Human Concerns, New York: Rutgers University Press.

Day, R.L., 1980, How satisfactory is research on consumer satisfaction?, Advances in Consumer Research, 7, 593-597.

Dubin, R., 1956, Industrial workers world: A study of the central life interest of industrial workers, Social Problems, 3, 131-142.

Fornell, C., and W.T. Robinson, 1983, Industrial organization and consumer satisfaction/dissatisfaction, Journal of Consumer Research, 9, 403-412.

Guzzo, R.A., 1980, Paradigms Compared: Consumer Satisfaction and Worker Satisfaction, paper presented to the American Psychological Association, Montreal, Québec, Canada.

Helson, H., 1964, Adaptation-level Theory, New York: Harper and Row.

Herzberg, F., B. Mausner, and B. Snyderman, 1959, The Motivation to Work, New York: John Wiley (second edition).

Homans, G.C., 1961, Social Behavior, New York: Harcourt, Brace and World.

Hulin, L.L., 1966, Effects of community characteristics on measures of job-satisfaction, Journal of Applied Psychology, 50, 185-192.

Hunt, H.K., 1977, "CS/D – Overview and future research directions," in: H.K. Hunt (ed.),

Conceptualization and Measurement of Consumer Satisfaction and Dissatisfaction. Proceedings of Conference Conducted by Marketing Science Institute with Support of National Science Foundation, Cambridge, MA: Marketing Science Institute, pp. 455-488.

Jacoby, J., 1976, "Consumer and industrial psychology: Prospects for theory corroboration and mutual contribution," in: M.D. Dunnette (ed.), Handbook of Industrial and Organizational Psychology, Chicago, IL: Rand McNally, pp. 1031-1061.

Landon, L.E., and D.R. Emery, 1974, Causal Attribution of Consumer Dissatisfaction as a Predictor of Complaint Action: A Preliminary Report, paper presented at the Conference of the Association for Consumer Research, Chicago, IL.

LaTour, S.A., and N.C. Peat, 1979, Conceptual and methodological in consumer satisfaction research, Advances in Consumer Research, 6, 431-437.

Lawler, E.E., 1973, Motivation in Work Organizations, Monterey, CA: Brooks and Cole.

Locke, E.A., 1976, "The nature and causes of job satisfaction," in: M. Dunnette (ed.), Handbook of Industrial and Organizational Psychology, Chicago, IL: Rand McNally, pp. 1297-1349.

Maslow, A.H., 1970, Motivation and Personality, New York: Harper and Row.

Mayo, E., 1949, Human Problems of an Industrial Civilization, New York: Harvard University, Graduate School of Business Administration, Division of Research.

Merton, R.K., and P.F. Lazarsfeld, 1950, Continuities in Social Research, Glencoe, IL: The Free Press.

Oliver, R.L., 1977, Effect of expectation and disconfirmation on postexposure product evaluations: An alternative approach, Journal of Applied Psychology, 62, 480-486.

Oliver, R.L., 1979, "Product satisfaction as a function of prior expectation and subsequent disconfirmation: New evidence," in: R.L. Day and H.K. Hunt (eds.), New Dimensions of Consumer Satisfaction and Complaining Behavior, Bloomington, IN: Indiana University, School of Business, pp. 66-71.

Oliver, R.L., 1980a, A cognitive model of the antecedents and consequences of satisfaction decisions, Journal of Marketing Research, 17, 460-469.

Oliver, R.L., 1980b, "Conceptualizing and measurement of disconfirmation perceptions in the prediction of consumer satisfaction," in: H.K. Hunt and R.L. Day (eds.), Refining Concepts and Measures of Consumer Satisfaction and Complaining Behavior, Bloomington, IN: Indiana University, pp. 2-6.

Oliver, R.L., and G. Linda, 1981, Effect of satisfaction and its antecedents on consumer preference and intention, Advances in Consumer Research, 8, 88-93.

Olson, J.C., and P. Dover, 1979, Disconfirmation of consumer expectations through product trial, Journal of Applied Psychology, 64, 179-189.

Poiesz, T.B.C., and J. von Grumbkow, 1982, On the Reliability and Validity of the Individual Welfare Function of Income (WFI), paper presented at the 7th Annual Colloquium of the International Association for Research in Economic Psychology, Edinburgh, UK.

Poiesz, T.B.C., and J. von Grumbkow, 1983, Psychological Correlates of the Evaluation of Income Levels and Changes, paper presented at the 8th Annual Colloquium of the International Association for Research in Economic Psychology, Bologna, Italy.

Porter, L.W., 1961, A study of perceived need satisfaction in bottom and middle management jobs, Journal of Applied Psychology, 45, 1-10.

Rijsman, J.B., 1983, "The dynamics of social competition in personal and categorial comparison situations," in: W. Doise and S. Moscovici (eds.), Current Issues in European Social Psychology, Vol. 1, Cambridge, UK: Cambridge University Press, pp. 279-312.

Salancik, G., and J. Pfeffer, 1978, A social information processing approach to job attitudes and task design, Administrative Science Quarterly, 23, 224-253.

Schoormans, J., and J. von Grumbkow, 1985, "The perception of employed and unemployed of their economic position: Some empirical results," in: H. Brandstätter and E. Kirchler (eds.), Economic Psychology, Linz, Austria: Trauner, pp. 459-466.

Seashore, S.E., and T.D. Taber, 1975, Job satisfaction indicators and their correlates, American Behavioral Scientist, 37, 352-355.

Swan, J.E., 1977, "Consumer satisfaction with a retail store related to the fulfillment of expectations on an initial shopping trip," in: R.L. Day (ed.), Consumer Satisfaction, Dissatisfaction, and Complaining Behavior, Bloomington, IN: Indiana University, pp. 10-17.

Swan, J.E., and L.J. Combs, 1976, Product performance and consumer satisfaction: A new concept, Journal of Marketing, 40, 25-33.

Swan, J.E., and W.S. Martin, 1981, Testing comparison level and predictive expectations models of satisfaction, Advances in Consumer Research, 8, 77-82.

Swan, J.E., and I.F. Trawick, 1980, Satisfaction related to predictive vs. desired expectations, in: H.K. Hunt and R.L. Day (eds.), Proceedings of the 4th Annual Conference on Consumer Satisfaction, Dissatisfaction, and Complaining Behavior, Bloomington, IN: Indiana University, pp. 7-12.

Syroit, J., 1984, Interpersonal Injustice, Tilburg, The Netherlands: Tilburg University (doctoral dissertatation).

Tannenbaum, A.S., and W.J. Kuleck, 1978, The effect on organization members of discrepancy between perceived and preferred rewards implicit in work, Human Relations, 31, 809-822.

Thibaut, J.W., and H.H. Kelley, 1959, The Social Psychology of Groups, New York: John Wiley.

Valle, V., and M. Wallendorf, 1977, "Consumer attributions of the cause of their product satisfaction and dissatisfaction," in: R.L. Day (ed.), Consumer Satisfaction, Dissatisfaction, and Complaining Behavior, Bloomington, IN: University, pp. 26-30.

Van Praag, B.M.S., 1971, The welfare function of income in Belgium: An empirical investigation, European Economic Review, 2, 337-369.

Van Raaij, W.F., 1984, Micro and macro economic psychology, Journal of Economic Psychology, 5, 385-401.

Verhallen, T.M.M., and R.G.M. Pieters, 1984, Attitude theory and behavioral costs, Journal of Economic Psychology, 5, 223-249.

Vinson, D.E., 1977, "Personal values as a dimension of consumer discontent," in: B.A. Greenberg and D.N. Bellenger (eds.), Contemporary Marketing Thought. Educators' Proceedings, Series 41, Chicago, IL: American Marketing Association, p. 105.

Warr, P., 1983, Economic recession and mental health: A review of research. Proceedings of the ICOMII-conference, Amsterdam: Free University.

Westbrook, R.A., 1980, Intrapersonal affective influences on consumer satisfaction with products, Journal of Consumer Research, 7, 49-54.

Table of Contents

17. Unemployment

ADRIAN F. FURNHAM
University College London, London, U.K.

"If any would not work, neither should he eat"
(2 Thessalonians, 3:10)

1. INTRODUCTION

Research into the social and psychological consequences of unemployment, like unemployment in the Western World itself, tends to be cyclical. Two major periods of research activity coincided with periods where unemployment increased dramatically in the western industrialized world – namely the 1930's and the 1970's and the 1980's. Most of this research has been done in Europe and America but there are exceptions (Feather, 1982). The fact that research has been done in two periods nearly 40 years apart means that interesting and important comparisons can be made. Jahoda (1982) has argued that the literature has revealed a substantial amount of similarity whether focused on physical, social or mental consequences of unemployment; irrespective of where (which country) it was conducted, at what period of time (1930's, 1970's) or with what specific population (males, females; middle class, working class).

This chapter will attempt to describe the diffuse conceptual and empirical psychological literature on unemployment, while also paying attention to the salient literature in allied fields (medicine, psychiatry, economics and sociology).

2. RESEARCH IN THE 1930S

Although there has been sporadic research into unemployment for a very long time (Rowntree and Lasker, 1911) the psychological literature appears to date back to the 1930's which saw the highest levels of unemployment in most European countries this century. (Jahoda et al., 1933; Bakke, 1933; Beales and Lambert, 1934). In a review of the literature Eisenberg and Lazarsfeld (1938) listed over one hundred references from Europe and

Van Raaij, W.F., van Veldhoven, G.M. and Wärneryd, K.E. (eds) Handbook of Economic Psychology. ISBN 90-247-3720-6.

America which has investigated aspects of unemployment. Most of the early literature constituted in-depth case studies of individuals or communities which has suffered unemployment. Hence this work was primarily descriptive "sociography" and made little attempt to use representative samples, test theories empirically. etc. Two of the most important psychological effects of unemployment that were identified by nearly all the researchers were the sense of social stigma attached to being unemployed, and the suffering resulting from the lack of structure that people experience (Kelvin and Jarrett, 1985).

The most celebrated research in 1930's is probably the study of Jahoda et al. (1933) on a small Austrian village, Marienthal. Although an unrepresentative town, a one-factory village in rural Austria, the study is worth considering in some detail for three reasons. Firstly, it is a surprisingly detailed sociography of an unemployed community which has never been repeated since. Secondly, the basic findings from this study were found in other studies in the 1930's (Komarovsky, 1940) and the 1970's and 80's (Marsden and Duff, 1975). Thirdly, it demonstrated quite clearly a perhaps counter intuitive finding that has emerged from studies ever since – namely that unemployment leads more to personal apathy and disintegration than political insurrection or organized revolution.

Fraser (1980) has summarized the findings of Jahoda et al. (1933) part of which are noted here:

1. *Finances*: Despite the fact that wages in the area had already been low, unemployment brought consistent reductions in income. Unemployment relief was payable for a period of about six months, then discretionary emergency assistance could be provided for a further period of up to a year. The maximum relief permissible was 80% of wages in the last week of work; in turn, the maximum emergency assistance possible was 80% of the relief. There were numerous ways in which families failed to be eligible for maximum benefits, but even if they were, within six or seven months of unemployment, the most they could receive was slightly less than two-thirds of their previous, generally low, wages. Many families were even worse off.
2. *Material aspects of life-style*: Obviously drastic economies of all sorts were absolutely essential. Standard items of food, such as coffee and butter were replaced by cheaper alternatives. Carbohydrates dominated at meal-times. Only 30% of families had meat on at least two days per week, and over 90% of that meat was either horse-meat or rabbit. On the day before the fortnightly payments of unemployment benefits, approximately half of the schoolchildren took either dry bread or nothing at all for their lunch at school. Even so, so much of a family's budget had to go on food – perhaps up to 90% – that any other substantial item of expenditure, such as shoe repairs, became a major problem.

3. *Physical well-being*: There was evidence of an overall decline in health standards, despite the equally horrifying fact that there was actually improvement, at least in the short-run, in the health of some adults, namely those who had been prone to tuberculosis as a result of their working conditions in the mill. Even the children suffered, despite the willingness of the unemployed families to spend a disproportionate amount of their income on milk for their children. One-third of the children under 14 were rated, during the study, as being in poor general health. Only 8% of the children had teeth unaffected by caries. There were signs of an inverse correlation between ill-health and family income.
4. *Emotional state*: There were many specific reports of emotionality, upsets, fearfulness and the like. Many of the men, in particular, manifested a blunted sense of time relations. "Apathy," "despair," "depression" were terms frequently used to describe the unemployed. Over one-third of the families were regarded as psychologically "broken." The emotional well-being of the families showed a positive correlation with the amount of weekly income.
5. *Personal relationships*: In some cases, the crisis appears to have actually improved marital relations, by, for example, leaving husbands free to help around the house or forcing them, through financial pressures, to give up drinking. But those were exceptions. The more general picture was one of an increase in minor quarrels and of reports of withdrawal from social relations and friendships. So there was some, although by no means dramatic, evidence of increased interpersonal strains and difficulties. In fact, close personal relationships appear to have held up more effectively than many other facets of individual and family life.
6. *Social interests and activities*: In general, these decreased markedly. Clearly, some of the decrease, such as visits to Vienna or to the theatre, reflected financial pressures. But almost all formal social organizations experienced a decline in membership and participation, even when financial outlay was not involved. Inexpensive or free informal activities, such as visiting friends or going for walks, also declined in popularity. The fate of the village library is instructive. Just before the factory closure, the library, fortuitously, had expanded considerably. Its small borrowing charges were abolished. Yet borrowing dropped markedly, mainly in terms of the number of borrowers, but even in terms of the number of books per remaining borrower.
7. *Political activities*: The unemployment, poverty and shattered lives led to no increase in political action. Quite the reverse. There had been a history of political involvement in Marienthal, but all three of the major political organizations suffered marked losses in membership. Since membership fees for the unemployed were nominal, it is unlikely that the primary reason for such loss was financial, a point supported by the fact

> that the cheaper but more political newspaper lost more readers in the village than the dearer but entertainment oriented one. A striking demonstration of the fact that those who remained politically active tended to be from the minority of people still in work was provided by the Young Socialist Workers, who retained 37 members, of whom only 7 were unemployed. "When one of their officers lost his job he resigned from his position and decided to give up politics entirely" (Jahoda et al., 1933: p. 41).

Researchers and reviewers (Fraser, 1980; Furnham, 1982b; Kelvin and Jarrett, 1985) including Jahoda herself (Jahoda, 1979, 1981, 1982) have been impressed more by the similarities than the differences in research findings in the reactions to and of the unemployed. This is not to say that research is no different now; for instance very little of the early work was concerned with how people explain the causes of unemployment, unemployment among women, and youth unemployment. Furthermore, the early research was more concerned with physical deprivation and hardship consequent upon unemployment, whereas current research has focused more upon psychological – clinical and social – aspects of unemployment. People's expectations are now quite different, and the extent to which they are prepared to discuss personal, social and economic problems may have changed. Social security (welfare) is altogether more substantial, compassionate and comprehensive than it was in the 1930's. Despite this, the same themes and patterns in the results appear to arise in present (altogether more empirically sophisticated studies) than in the earlier descriptive work of researchers in the 1930's.

3. THE FUNCTIONS OF WORK

One way to attempt to understand why the experience of unemployment is so psychologically detrimental is to attempt to understand the beneficial functions of work. What are the beneficial aspects of work, the absence of which leads the unemployed to experience so much difficulty? Jahoda (1979, 1981) following Merton (1957) distinguished between manifest and latent consequences of employment. The *manifest aspects of work* are simply earning a living while the *latent consequences* are unintended by-products of the purposeful action that is necessary to achieve the manifest consequences. While the unemployed quite demonstrably miss the manifest consequences of work such as a (possibly) high standard of income, what is most distressing to them is the latent functions.

The *latent functions of work* include:

1. *Work structures time.* Work structures the day, the week and even longer periods. The loss of a time structure can be very disorienting. Feather and Bond (1983) compared the structure and purposeful activity among employed and unemployed university graduates. They found as predicted, that the unemployed were less organized and less purposeful in their use of time and reported more depressive symptoms when compared to the employed.
2. *Work provides regularly shared experiences.* Regular contact with non-nuclear family members provides an important source of social contact. There is a vast literature on social skills deficits which suggests that social isolation is related to disturbed mental states (Trower et al., 1978) There is now a growing interest in the social support hypothesis which suggests that social support from family and friends buffer the major causes of stress and increase coping ability, so reducing illness (Gore, 1978). If ones primary source of friends and contacts is work colleagues then the benefits of social support are denied, precisely when they are most needed. There are also a wealth of studies in organizational psychology which suggests that one of the most frequently cited sources of job satisfaction is contact with other people (Argyle, 1983).
3. *Work provides experience of creativity, mastery and sense of purpose.* "Both, the organization and the product of work imply the interdependence of human beings. Take away this daily experience that efforts must be combined, and the unemployed are left with a sense of uselessness, of being on the scrap heap" (Jahoda, 1979). Work, even not particularly satisfying work, gives some sense of mastery or achievement. Creative activities stimulate people and provide a sense of satisfaction. A person's contribution to producing goods or providing services forges a link between the individual and the society of which s/he is a part. Work roles are not the only roles which offer the individual the opportunity of being useful and contributing to the community but, without doubt, for the majority they are the most central roles and consequently people deprived of the opportunity to work often feel useless and report that they lack a sense of purpose.
4. *Work is a source of personal status and identity.* A person's job is an important indicator of his/her personal status in society; hence the often amusing debates over job titles such as sanitary engineer for street cleaner! Furthermore it is not only to the employed person that the job gives certain status but also to his or her family. The employed person therefore is a link between two important social systems, family and home. An unemployed person has lost their employment status and hence identity. Not unnaturally there is a marked drop in self-esteem following unemployment.

5. *Work is a source of activity.* All work involves some expenditure of physical or mental effort. Whereas too much activity may induce fatigue and stress, too little results in boredom and restlessness, particularly among extraverts. People seek to maximize the amount of activity that suits them by choosing particular jobs or tasks that fulfill their needs. The unemployed however are not provided with this possibility and have to consistently provide stimulation to keep them active.

A number of points should be made about this list of the functions of work. Firstly it is not exhaustive and the functions are not mutually exclusive. Secondly it is possible that other, even more obvious functions could be mentioned such as providing an income. Thirdly these latent or manifest functions of work can be provided by other social institutions, such as societies and clubs, which provide a source of unpaid work. Finally nothing actually prevents the unemployed from seeking out some of the benefits of work such as creating a stable time structure to their day, though this may

Table 1. Factors that influence job satisfaction.

Challenging work	Work should be interesting, but not fatiguing.
Rewards for good performance	Clear contingencies between performance and rewards are very desirable.
Verbal recognition	Most persons enjoy praise and positive feedback.
Good working conditions	Physical working conditions should be comfortable and facilitate attainment of work goals.
Concerned supervision	Supervisors should demonstrate their concern with helping employees to attain important goals.
Positive interpersonal relations	Satisfaction is strongly enhanced by friendly relations with co-workers and supervisors.
Effective company policies	These should be designed to aid employees in attaining important work goals.
Job security	Employees should feel that if they perform adequately, their jobs are secure.
Pay	Absolute level is important, but the belief that such benefits are fairly distributed may be even more crucial.
Participation in decision-making	Employees generally feel that they know much about their jobs and should be consulted about them.
Degree of autonomy and responsibility	The greater these are, the higher satisfaction tends to be.
Role ambiguity	Individuals wish to know just what is expected of them; ambiguity should be avoided.

(From Baron, 1983: p. 214)

be difficult particularly for those most likely to be unemployed (school leavers, unskilled labourers).

Another way of understanding the benefits of employment and by implication the frustrations of unemployment is to look at the extensive and exhaustive literature on job satisfaction. There are, of course, a number of theories of *job satisfaction* (Maslow, 1970; Herzberg et al., 1959; Vroom, 1964), but all have focused on certain specific factors. The list in Table 1 is not exhaustive neither are the factors in rank order as these differ from one job to another.

Argyle (1983) has divided the causes of job satisfaction into a number of categories:

1. intrinsic variables (variety, autonomy, use of skills and abilities);
2. hours of work;
3. incentive conditions (pay, occupational status, promotion prospects, security);
4. work group (cohesiveness, popularity, size, opportunities for interaction);
5. supervision (consideration, participation in decision making);
6. company (size and shape, participation in management); and
7. individual differences (age, intelligence, personality, belief in the Protestant work ethic).

Some of these sources of satisfaction apply only to the employed but others equally to the unemployed to the extent that they do not have them.

Although it has been challenged (Hulin and Blood, 1968; Guion and Landy, 1972) *Herzberg's two-factor theory* perhaps gives the best insight into the sources of job satisfaction (as opposed to dissatisfaction) which are denied to the unemployed. These look very much like the list of the functions of work given above but include others as well: opportunity for achievement, opportunity for recognition, the work itself, responsibility, advancement and personal growth. It is the consistent emphasis on intrinsic factors associated with job-satisfaction, rather than extrinsic factors, that suggests the unemployed are likely to suffer most from not being in work.

However, the work on job satisfaction has one more important feature of relevance to unemployment. Jobs that lead to a high degree of dissatisfaction may be more unpleasant or unhealthy for the individual than unemployment under good conditions. Warr (1983) has differentiated between *"good" and "bad" jobs* and *"good" and "bad" unemployment* in terms of nine variables that have proved discriminating in previous research (see Table 2). Thus it may be that if a person leaves a bad job, s/he may adapt well to good unemployment and there are many examples of this. The point being made here is that just as not all jobs are satisfying, so not all unemployment is

Table 2. Characteristics of "good" and "bad" jobs, and "good" and "bad" unemployment (from Warr, 1983: pp. 309-310).

	"Good" jobs have	"Bad" jobs have	"Good" unemployment has	"Bad" unemployment has
1. Money	more	less	more	less
2. Variety	more	less	more	less
3. Goals, traction	more	less	more	less
4. Decision latitude	more	less	more	less
5. Skill use/development	more	less	more	less
6. Psychological threat	less	more	less	more
7. Security	more	less	more	less
8. Interpersonal contact	more	less	more	less
9. Valued social position	more	less	more	less

unsatisfying. Depending on the job, the person and the society's reaction to unemployment it may be possible to experience beneficial aspects of unemployment.

Indeed some have argued that the central ethic must move away form work to post-industrial self-fulfillment through the growth of the informal or free economy (Pym, 1980).

The importance of the nature of the job, or organizational climate, was demonstrated in a study by Friedlander and Greenberg (1971) of the *hard-core unemployed* in a period of low unemployment. They investigated 478 hard-core unemployed people, i.e., people who find it difficult to hold down a job for any reasonable length of time. They examined unemployed people's biographic and demographic background, their attitudes to work, the organizational climate in which they were placed, and the effect of a two-week intervention programme. The only correlate of the person's work effectiveness and behaviour was the degree of supportiveness of the organizational climate in which they were placed. Hence the authors concluded that the social structure or climate in most organizations may be more a cause than a cure for the hard-core unemployed's work behaviour.

Most of the work on people's actual reactions to unemployment is speculative. However Warr and colleagues have looked at actual changes in behaviour following job loss. Warr and Payne (1983) looked at social class differences in specific behaviours after job loss which were grouped as: domestic work (household chores, shopping, cooking), domestic pastimes (radio, television), other pastimes (smoking, window shopping), book reading (library visits, extra-mural classes), recreations (sports, hobbies), entertainment through money (drinking, cinema), and social contacts (church, political meetings). Apart from entertainment through money (a set of behaviours which declined) many forms of behaviours appeared, not unnaturally, to increase after job loss. The middle-class group tended to report a significantly greater increase in book reading, and the working-class a greater increase in other pastimes but a greater reduction in entertainment through money. See Chapter 15 of this Handbook for more information on the relationship between work, unemployment and leisure. Furthermore several significant associations between change in behaviour and general health were noted, for instance a reduction of entertainment through money was moderately associated with lower well-being for the middle-class, but not the lower-class respondents. Many of these results are in accordance with other studies such as a reduction of drinking (Smart, 1979) but contrary to older studies which found that apathy associated with unemployment led to a reduction in church and political party attendance (Bakke, 1940) there was no reduction (or increase) in this study.

In another study with a larger population Warr (1984) focused on age and length of unemployment as mediating variables in self reported behaviour after job loss. The same 38 item scale subdivided into seven categories was used. Just over a third of the activities changed with length of unemployment; all forms of domestic work increased as did other pastimes and social contacts. Entertainment through money however declined. Nearly half of the behavioural changes were age related, particularly domestic work, other pastimes and recreations many of which were curvilinear. Predictably sitting around at home and watching television (not for study) were highly correlated with mental mal-adjustment. Warr does point out that the results probably illustrate that there is no overall difference in the *amount* of a person's social contact between periods of employment and unemployment, but that the *content* and *location* of encounters and the *range* of people met are reduced after becoming unemployed.

Warr and Jackson (1984) examined the age and length correlates of unemployment among nearly 1000 men. Psychological distress, financial strain and labour market committment were greatest amongst the middle aged men. There was a positive relationship between length of unemployment and mental and physical illness and the probability of having an unemployed wife was found to be negatively associated with the length of unemployment. They conclude: "Age and duration are themselves not causal variables; they stand as proxies for processes and states which require elucidation" (p. 84).

4. STAGE-WISE THEORIES IN REACTIONS TO UNEMPLOYMENT

A number of attempts have been made to understand the way in which the unemployed adjust, over time to their new circumstances. Nearly all research in this area is cross-sectional rather than longitudinal. Therefor there is more speculation than research with regard to transitional stages or phases for the unemployed. The longitudinal studies which do exist (Warr et al., 1982) are usually less than one year, and have not investigated the reactions of the unemployed over a very long period. Hence the long-term effects of unemployment are not clear.

There is, however, no shortage of theories concerning how the unemployed may react to unemployment (Hopson and Adams, 1976; Harrison, 1976). Because unemployment involves the reactions to *loss*, the extensive literature on grieving and bereavement (Parles, 1975), divorce (Levinger and Moles, 1979), and migration (Furnham and Bochner, 1986) has been seen to be relevant. Researchers in all these areas have relied on early neo-psychoanalytic researchers (Bowlby, 1969) for their ideas.

All stage-wise descriptions have their problems: Stage-wise models are descriptive rather than explanatory; simply describe the typical pattern of response over time. Secondly they rarely specify what factors determine that a person moves on from one stage to another or remains fixated in one stage. All stage-wise models are linear but it is quite possible that patterns of reactions are cyclical: that is there are erratic progressions and regressions. Further crucial individual differences and moderating variables are ignored in these descriptions which are by definition general. Finally, the more stages a theory has the more vulnerable it is to disproof.

Hayes and Nutman (1981) have reviewed a number of stage-wise approaches. They include Hopson and Adams' (1976) seven-stage approach, the four stages of Harrison (1970), three of Hill (1978) and five of Briar (1977). They are listed in Table 3.

Although there are certain similarities between these theories there are clear differences. They are based on qualitatively and quantitatively different research and are often post-hoc categorizations of observed differences. To what extent they predict or explain human behaviour in the area of unemployment must remain questionable.

Table 3. Stage-wise theories of reactions to unemployment.

Hopson and Adams (1976)	Harrison (1976)	Hill (1978)	Briar (1977)
1. Immobilization	1. Shock	1. Trauma/denial	1. Shock
2. Minimization	2. Optimism	2. Depression	2. Optimism
3. Depression	3. Pessimism	3. Adaptation	3. Self blame
4. Acceptance of reality	4. Fatalism		4. Depression
5. Testing			5. Inertia
6. Search for meaning			
7. Internalization			

For over a decade a considerable amount of research has been done on life change and discontinuities in experience and its effects on mental and physical health. A vast literature surrounds the relationship between life events and illness which has shown that a range of physical illnesses are related to social stress. Many scales have been developed to measure these life events which include the Social Readjustment Rating Scale (Holmes and Rahe, 1967), which ranks both being fired at work and retirement highly, and the Cochrane and Robertson (1973) Life Events Inventory, which ranks unemployment and retirement amongst the most stressful of items.

The work on life stresses is extensive yet equivocal. The exact nature of the causal link between personal distress and psychological disturbance is however unclear and many intervening variables have been hypothesized. There are also widely different models or explanations for the relationship including Rahe's Optical Analogy (Rahe et al., 1974) which posits a series of filters and lenses which are between exposure to stress and the reporting of symptoms, and Robertson and Cochrane's (1976) value change model which suggests that people with the new (self-fulfillment, growth, hedonism) as opposed to the traditional value system (stoicism, fulfillment through suffering) will be more aware of and sensitive to social stresses and pressures and less able to cope with them.

Problems in this area are most clearly discussed by Platt (1984) who did a comprehensive and critical review of the literature on unemployment and suicidal behaviour. The author distinguished between fatal and non fatal suicides and four types of study: individual cross-sectional; aggregate cross-sectional: individual longitudinal and aggregate longitudinal. He found that:

> Cross-sectional individual studies reveal that significantly more parasuicides and suicides are unemployed than would be expected among general population samples. Likewise, parasuicide and suicide rates among the unemployed are always considerably higher than among the employed. Aggregate-cross-sectional studies provide no evidence of a consistent relationship between unemployment and completed suicide, but a significant geographical association between unemployment and parasuicide was found. Results from all but one of the individual longitudinal studies point to significantly more unemployment, job instability and occupational problems among suicides compared to non-suicides. The aggregate longitudinal analyses reveal a significant positive association between unemployment and suicide in the United States of America and some European countries. However, despite the firm evidence of an association between unemployment and suicidal behaviour, the nature of this association remains highly problematic (p. 93).

Yet researchers have noted as unemployment is a major life event it may explain the fact that unemployed people are by and large less healthy, well-adjusted and happy than their employed peers. There are three sorts of data which show this relationship.

Firstly there are a number of archival studies which have looked at such things as the relationship between unemployment and social problems over a specific period. For instance Boor (1980) examined the relationship between unemployment rates and suicide rates in eight countries between 1962 and 1976. The question addressed was, whether social and psychological conditions associated with suicide rates were also associated with relatively high suicide rates in these countries during these years (not whether unemployed persons were more likely to commit suicide than employed people). There were significant positive (between 0.53 and 0.79) correlations between annual variations in suicide and unemployment rates for the USA, Canada, Japan and France but no significant relationship for Germany, Sweden and Italy. Great Britain however showed the opposite pattern (– 0.59). Annual variations in the suicide rates of females and males were highly intercorrelated but not associated differentially with unemployment rates, and showed similar patterns within the various age subgroups, thus indicating that cultural factors associated with levels of unemployment had similar effects on the suicidal behaviour of male and females. Boor rather cynically explained the unpredicted British findings thus: The rate of unsuccessful suicides did actually increase during this period primarily due to the reduction of carbon monoxide in the domestic gas supply. Similarly, Schapiro and Ahlberg (1983) found a significant positive relationship between unemployment and suicides for males in America over the period 1946-1976. That is, a one percent point increase in the unemployment rate precipitates over 300 additional suicides per annum. In Britain, Krafchik (1983) found a strong positive correlation between unemployment and vagrancy (measured by admissions to the poor law casual wards) in the 1930's. This is also dealt with in some detail in Orwell's classic *Down and Out in London and Paris* (1933).

A second research area is the extensive research on macroeconomic factors and mental health at the University of California (Catalano and Dooley, 1977, 1979; Dooley and Catalano, 1979, 1980). Catalano and Dooley (1979) argued that recent analyses of annual archival data suggest that admission to mental hospitals is significantly associated with previous macroeconomic changes, but that this relationship is modified by two important intervening variables: stress in day-to-day life and mental depression, both of which vary with economic change. However as they point out it is not clear whether economic changes serve to uncover existing untreated cases or to provoke symptoms in persons previously normal. Their results however indicate that the relationship between economic change and recourse to inpatient mental health facilities was due more to the uncovering, than to the provocation, of behavioural disorders. Their other research in metropolitan communities has found significant time-series associations of monthly unemployment rate with depression (Catalano and Dooley, 1977) of absolute change in employment in the basic economic sector with stressful life events (Catalano and Dooley, 1979) and various psycho-physiological symptoms associated with low income respondents (Dooley and Catalano, 1979).

Dooley and Catalano (1980) propose a model (Figure 1) that attempts to explain economic change as a cause of behavioural disorder.

They believe that this model may help mental health planners to anticipate increases in economically caused symptoms. However these results have not been replicated in Great Britain. Stokes and Cochrane (1984) found the introduction of a time lag between changes in unemployment and changes in hospital admissions did not produce a stronger relationship and that in Britain females were more sensitive to economic fluctuations than were males. However they did find a positive relationship between mental hospital admissions and national unemployment, although this relationship was statistically significant only for males aged 25 to 44, and females between 20 and 54.

The life event hypothesis has also been supported by work on low-income families. Thoits and Hannan (1979) compared the psychological distress of an income maintenance and a control group. Their results were consistent with the life event hypothesis namely that any change (positive or negative) in life circumstances is distressing. Thus promotion as much as unemployment may be seen as leading to psychological problems.

The third more common type of psychological study has concentrated exclusively on the mental/physical health and psychological well-being of unemployed people. This usually involves the administration of a self-report or interview style questionnaire on minor psychiatric morbidity. These tests have been found to be valid, reliable, predictive and discriminatory measures of mental health. Banks et al. (1982) compared the mental health (as measured by the General Health Questionnaire, GHQ) of employees in an engineering firm, recent school leavers and a group of unemployed men. They found, as predicted, that the unemployed group, and women more than men, had scores indicating lower mental health but that these scores were unrelated to age, job level or marital status. Similarly, Warr (1981) has suggested that the unemployed's mental health deteriorates because they are denied many of the positive features of work (money, activity, variety, temporal structure, social, contacts, status and identity within society). Warr notes that a variety of studies looking at such things as depression, anxiety, life satisfaction, minor psychiatric morbidity, self-esteem, and positive and negative affect, consistently show the unemployed to be less well

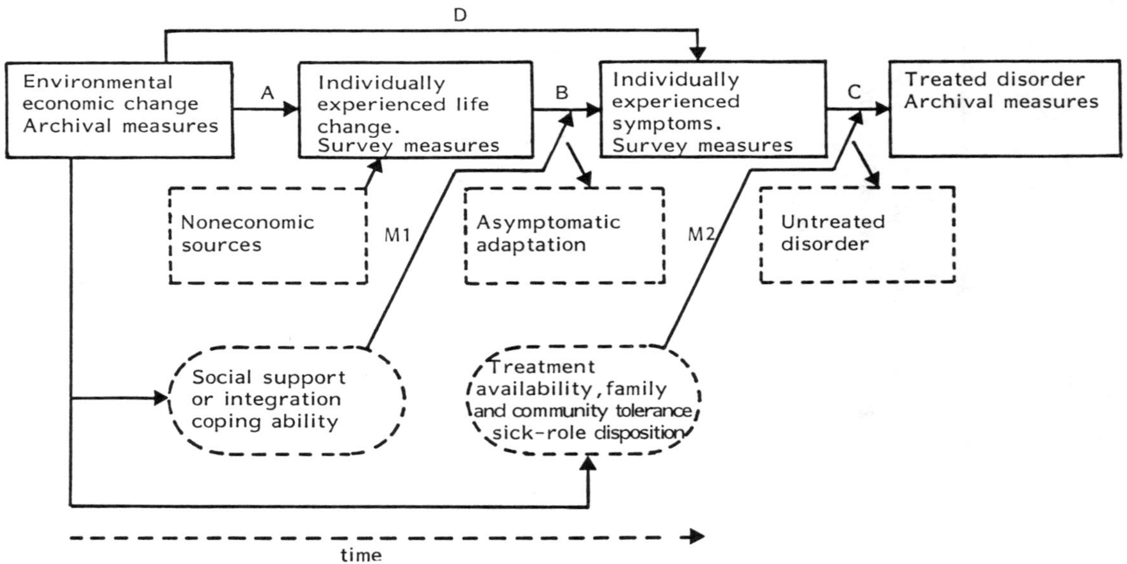

Fig. 1. Hypothetical intervening variables between environmental economic change and treated disorder (source: Dooley and Catalano: p. 461, copywright (1980) by the American Psychological Association, reprinted by permission of the authors).

Relationship

A = cause of life events by economic change.
B = cause of symptoms by stressful life events.
C = translation of experienced symptoms into demand for service.
D = possibility that economic change might affect individual symptoms without mediating life change.

adjusted. However this research has, so far, not answered the following important problems: What other features influence the strength of the association between employment status and psychological health; what is the sequential or longitudinal pattern of reaction to unemployment over time; what sort of people thrive in unemployment? Others (Liem and Rayman, 1982) have suggested that researchers need to concentrate more on mediating processes than on the outcome of unemployment. "We need to know how the costs of unemployment are incurred, what material and social factors moderate their effects, and what conditions exacerbate them" (p. 1122). One area of research that they note is the effects of unemployment of parents on children, the effects of a family history of job loss on the child's adjustment, view of the world of work, and so on.

Furnham (1983a) looked at the mental health (as measured on the Langner index) of five groups depending on their employment status: full-time employed; part-time employed; unemployed; retired; and students. Although there was no age or sex differences in the total mental-health score, there was a significant difference between the five employment groups total score with the full-time employed having the lowest (best adjusted) score, the retired and students having moderately high scores, and the unemployed and the part-time the highest scores.

On the basis of previous findings, one might have expected the part-time employed's adjustment score to be higher than that of students, which in turn would possibly be higher than that of retired people. Yet the part-time employed people's score was almost as high, and not significantly different from that of the unemployed. There could be many reasons for this: Firstly, people seeking full-time work may take a part-time job which they do not like and which is not well paid, simply as an interim measure. Secondly, people with other commitments, such as a family and handicapped relatives, may only be able to take a part-time job which, because of travelling and other stress, is too much for them and leads to mental distress. Thirdly, some part-time work is very casual in that it is for very short periods only: Thus instead of giving the benefits of work, it does the precise opposite. Certainly future studies on the part-time employed would do well to tease apart these various hypotheses by getting subjects to stipulate clearly why they have chosen part-time employment, how long they intend to be in the job, and what the hours are. With the prospect of increased job sharing, the importance of part-time employment is likely to rise.

Warr et al. (1982) have attempted a longitudinal study looking at the duration of unemployment and psychological well-being in young men and women. The importance of longitudinal studies cannot be ignored. To establish a relationship between unemployment and psychological distress tells one nothing of causation, merely correlation. It is possible that the less psychologically adjusted are prone to unemployment or are indeed unemployable! In all two cohorts of recent school-leavers were interviewed over a two-year period but measures of psychological stress and self-esteem were found to be uncorrelated with the duration of unemployment for young men. In fact, in one cohort the women appeared to be better adjusted the longer they were unemployed, apparently because of their reduced commitment to the labour market along with a stronger personal involvement in family matters. The authors offer two (compatible) explanations for their puzzling findings. The association between well-being and length of unemployment may differ between age groups (older people with more commitments may experience greater distress). Also it may only be that longer periods of unemployment than those studied here do lead to distress.

The social and private costs of unemployment naturally lead to various social policy considerations. The financial, psychological and medical costs of unemployment are borne not only by individual workers but also by their families and communities. Liem and Rayman (1982) have suggested a statutory minimum period of notification before workers can be laid off and the creation of a system of medical insurance which is not tied solely to current employment

> nevertheless the primary assumption informing overall policy on unemployment should be that job loss brings costs to personal health and the quality of family and community life. This premise, together with the social ethic of "the right to work" should figure centrally in the formulation of unemployment policy"(Liem and Rayman, 1982: p. 1121).

They also note that one of the most important policy recommendations arising from their own work is to create a medical insurance scheme not tied solely to current employment. Liem and Atkinson (1982) have noted that joblessness should be thought of not only as happening to individuals, but also to families. In their research they found that two or three months after their husbands became unemployed, wives in families with continuing unemployment were significantly more depressed, anxious, phobic and sensitive about their interpersonal relationships than their counterparts in employed (control) families. They conclude:

> Consequently, to the familiar criticisms of official Bureau of Labor Statistics procedures for estimating the nation's unemployment rate we would have to add the shortsightedness of assuming that joblessness only happens to individuals. In terms of serious consequences of being without work the impact of unemployment probably exceeds by a factor of two or three that group of Americans who are counted as unemployed (Liem and Atkinson, 1982: p. 19).

Other social policy implications may be found in studies concerning unemployment and the handicapped which shows firstly that unemployed handicapped people suffer more problems than employed handicapped people (Markova et al., 1980), and that in times of high unemployment the handicapped are more likely to be unemployed, that is, employers discriminate against them.

Another important source of data on the relationship between unemployment and health concerns studying the characteristics of unemployed people admitted to mental hospitals, because this helps to unravel the direction of causality. Fruensgaard et al. (1983a) investigated the psychosocial characteristics of a group of unemployed patients consecutively admitted to a psychiatric emergency clinic in Denmark. They found that alcohol abuse was registered in two-thirds of their sample of 70, and about half were found to be habitual neurotics with a tendency to anti-social behaviour while intoxicated. However only 4% had never suffered from a mental disorder requiring treatment prior to their unemployment – indeed 41% had previously been admitted to a mental hospital and 60% were on sick leave prior to dismissal from unemployment. Despite the fact that this sample was hardly average and that there were other potential causal factors giving rise to mental disease as well as unemployment it was noted that anxiety, depression, neurasthenic and psychotic illness were accentuated by, or commenced with unemployment. In a follow-up study Fruensgaard et al. (1983b) found that in most of the sample there had been a drop in alcohol and drug abuse and an improvement in mental health. Most importantly they found that those who succeeded in getting work and/or those who had favourable employment experiences were "stronger" than those who did not get employment and had a significantly lower frequency of previous admission to the psychiatric department and of sick leave prior to unemployment.

> In addition, the duration of their actual unemployment was shorter and therefore probably less of a strain... Furthermore there was an extremely significant correlation between a favourable course with regard to employment and both improvement of the general mental condition and improvement of the interpersonal relations (p. 135).

Thus it seems that the relationship between mental health and unemployment is bi-directional. The mentally unstable are less likely to find employment than the mentally stable, but lack of employment accentuates the problem, whereas employment does the opposite.

Other attempts to understand the relationship between unemployment and health have been phenomenological. Fineman (1979) has looked specifically at psychosocial stress induced by managerial unemployment. He interviewed 25 unemployed managers and also gave them a battery of tests. Predictably they had high GHQ scores, indicating psychological disturbance almost twice the national average, yet their 16PF (a measure of personality with sixteen dimensions) scores fell within the normal range. Whereas some managers seemed highly stressed by unemployment others seemed to enjoy it. What appeared to characterize the high stress group was prior high personal involvement in the job, belief in personal competence, domestic problems, symbiotic failure in job applications and learned helplessness. Low-stress cases on the other hand perceived their problem in low-threat terms, had previous low job involvement, strong belief in personal worth and a direct, confronting (as opposed to avoidance, passive) approach to problems. From his rich but unquantifiable data Fineman draws a number of conclusions: Stress in unemployment arises from the interaction of four factors: an individual's perception of the environment, personality, experienced threat and behaviour in response to threat. Direct confrontation is the only form of behaviour which can involve mastering the problem of stress; a stressed person needs to be encouraged to examine his perception of environmental demands.

Swinburne (1981) also attempted to look at the psychological impact of unemployment on managers and professional staff. In the interview study she questioned subjects on their feelings about being unemployed, the problems of structuring time, and their job search process. She found that although the experience of unemployment varied according to individual circumstances, certain trends were apparent. Many (50%) reported initial shock and fear/uncertainly about the future, but as few as 10% reported shame, loss of status and self-respect. Although the negativity of their initial reactions appeared less than reported elsewhere, they appeared to pass through the various hypothetical stages much more slowly.

In a study of the effect of social support in moderating the health consequences of unemployment, Gore (1978) interviewed 100 married men who previously had been stably employed but had suddenly been made redundant. The men were interviewed 5 times over a two-year period. She was particularly interested in the effect of supportive and affiliative relations with wife, friends and relatives on the unemployed man's illness symptoms. She found that the rural unemployed, because of the ethnic ties and concern in a small community, had a higher level of support than the urban unemployed. In addition the unsupported unemployed had significantly greater levels of cholesterol illness symptoms and emotional response than did the supported. The author argued that these results demonstrate not so much that support buffers the effects of life stress, but rather a low sense/level of social support exacerbates life stress. Unemployment, in large part, means the inability to make instrumental accomplishments. Thus it might be interpreted that this loss in the absence of a continuing sense of self-worth maintained through supportive relationships contributes to negative health responses. In this research, it is impossible to point to specific behaviors of others which ameliorated life stress, i.e., the buffering effect. It thus makes more sense to explain the more negative responses of some terminees as the exacerbation of the unemployment experience by a low sense of social support.

Finally it should be pointed out that not all studies on unemployment and health are retrospective. Jenkins et al. (1982) carried out a prospective study to examine the effects of the threat of journalists promised redundancy on minor psychiatric morbidity. Each subject was tested three times: two months prior to closure (one month after receiving notice of redundancy), immediately after redundancy notices were revoked and work continued under a new proprietor, and then three months after the threat of redundancy has been removed. Despite various methodological problems it was unambiguously demonstrated that subsequent to the withdrawal of redundancy notices, there was a considerable reduction in minor symptomatology.

Hepworth (1980) looked at moderating factors in the relationship between unemployment and mental health. She found that length of unemployment was inversely correlated with mental health and well-being; semi- and unskilled men were less well adjusted than those of higher occupational status and that the best predictor of the unemployed's mental health was whether or not they felt their time was occupied. In a re-analysis of this data Brenner and Bartell (1983) found that with the passage of time a reciprocal process takes place in which mental health affects subjective well-being and the proportion of time occupied. The authors suggest that there may well be a "critical period" immediately following job loss in which time adaptation may or may not occur. Poor adaptation leads to a vicious circle which results in increased negative effects with time. More recently time-budgeting studies have attempted to investigate this relationship between time-structuring and adaptation. Warr (1984) looked at 38 specific behaviours and asked 954 unemployed British working-class men how being unemployed changed the way in which they spent their time. Home based recreations (gardening, hobbies, etc.) increased, while drinking and smoking decreased. Although the men reported increases in time spent with neighbours and family it seemed that there was no difference in the amount of a persons's social contact between periods of employment and unemployment, but that the content and location of the encounters and the range of people met are reduced after becoming unemployed. There were also numerous age and duration of unemployment effects particularly the latter which indicated that entertainment through money, trips and shopping all exhibited significantly greater decrements with increasing time out-of-work.

In a more detailed study of the leisure behaviour of the unemployed,

Kelvin et al. (1984) did a time budget study in which they found an increase in the unemployed's TV watching, housework, reading and hobbies, a decrease in their social life and no change in their games playing or religious, creative or community activities. The results indicated that the more a given activity was rated in-home rather than out, solitary rather than social, cheap rather than expensive, passive rather than active, the greater the index of change for the activity. Their work seems to suggest that leisure activities are often no more than palliatives, rather than satisfying alternatives to work.

Many writers have noted a change in the self-concept and identity in the unemployed. In their review of the psychological effects of unemployment in the 1930's Eisenberg and Lazarsfeld (1938) note the development of apathy, depression, fatalistic beliefs, lowered self-esteem, resignation, and self-doubt among the unemployed.

As Kelvin and Jarrett (1984) have noted, in a society whose socio-economic structure is defined in terms of its divisions of labour, the unemployed are defined by what they are not – not integrated within that structure. This means that the unemployed person's position is highly ambiguous as saying what a person is not, does not tell us much of what s/he is. It is only the explicit and often unjustifiable assumption that once they find work, that they will once again have an identifiable place in society.

It has been argued that the self-concept is a schema which locates the individual within the social environment and shapes his/her interaction with it. Hence becoming unemployed causes psychological dislocation and disorientation which induces a modification of the self concept. Tiffany et al. (1970) administered the Tennessee Self-Concept Scale to two comparable groups, one in work and one not, and found that the profile of the unemployed group reflected a lower level of self esteem. The unemployed had significantly less faith of confidence in themselves, and saw themselves as less desirable, doubted their worth more, felt more anxious, depressed and unhappy than the unemployed group. This pattern has been studied by Allerhand et al. (1969), Hodgson and Brenner (1968), and Teahan (1969); all of them found lower self-esteem in the previously unemployed compared to the previously employed. Briar (1977) has also noted a desire for secrecy and a distancing in the unemployed which appears to be a means of protecting themselves against being labelled failures and "welfare dependent."

More recently Stokes and Cochrane (1984) completed a longitudinal investigation of the psychological consequences of redundancy and unemployment looking at general symptomatology, hostility, social attitudes, and life satisfaction. The results showed that the redundant workers who remained without work for at least six months had significantly more psychological symptoms; total hostility (including criticism of others, paranoid hostility and guilt); reduced self satisfaction and acceptance by others. They failed to confirm previous stage models of unemployment but felt that that may have been due to the exceptionally good redundancy arrangements for this group which facilitated a lengthy period of constructive adjustment and optimism.

In Canada, Burke (1984) was concerned with the correlates of well-being 16 months after a workforce of 177 were made redundant. He found individuals who found less favourable, less well-paid, or temporary jobs reported less life satisfaction as did those who were currently unemployed. Also individuals earning lower hourly pay rates reported more psychosomatic symptoms and individuals unemployed for more weeks in the intervening 16-month period reported less general satisfaction and greater alcohol consumption. Although the results were consistent with previous studies, the psychological effect of job loss was modest.

Of course one problem plagues the self esteem and unemployment literature and that is correlation and cause. It is possible that those with low self esteem and poor self concept are more susceptible to unemployment rather than unemployment reducing self-esteem. Of course, what is more probable is that both occur together only exacerbating each other. Only longitudinal work can actually determine the direction of causality. This is a central point in this research and will be discussed in the conclusion.

6. UNEMPLOYMENT AMONG ADOLESCENTS, SCHOOL-LEAVERS AND YOUNG PEOPLE

Since the early 70's when the problem became most acute there have been several important studies of youth unemployment (Baxter, 1975; Clark and Clissold, 1982; Fowler et al., 1977; Mair and Raffe, 1983; Roberts et al., 1982). Many of these have looked at the same factors (health, self-esteem, causal explanations) that have been investigated in the adult population, but some have been quite specific to young people.

The underlying causes of increased youth unemployment are of course manifold. They include demographic factors (change in the birth rate and an extension of the school career), micro- and macroeconomic changes (change in technology, different productivity agreements) educational and training factors (the relevance and appropriateness of education). Changes in youth unemployment are naturally associated with changes in adult employment but move with a greater amplitude. It has been calculated that if the unemployment rate for males rises by 1%, the unemployment rate for young males under 20 (excluding school leavers) rises by 1.7% (Makeham, 1980). Compared with other groups, young people change jobs more often or start without jobs hence as the recessions deepens and recruitment is cut, young people are among the most vulnerable. Perhaps the kind of study which is most needed but fairly rare is the path analytic study of Lynn et al. (1984) who tried to determine which variables predicted unemployment in young people. It was found that home background, intelligence, personality, school type and educational attainments all had significant effects on unemployment. For instance home background exerts a direct influence on unemployment but it is also indirect through its effects on intelligence, school-type, educational attainment, psychoticism, and status aspiration. Their model is presented in Figure 2.

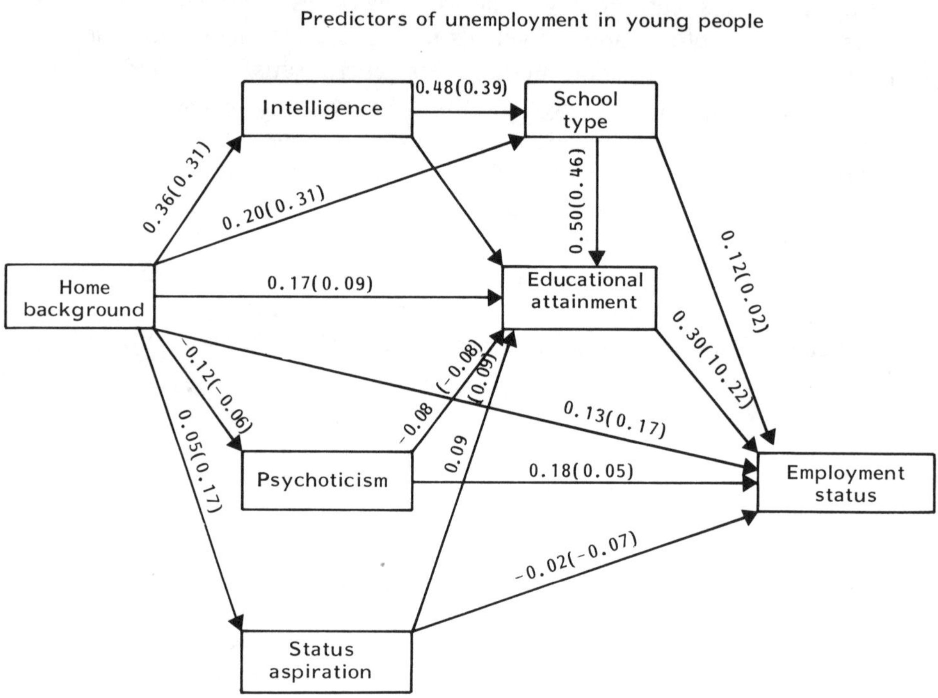

Fig. 2. Path model for employment status for males (followed by females in parentheses).

Some studies have looked at the emotional, social and psychological adjustment of unemployed school leavers. Using a questionnaire developed from the ideas of the neo-psychoanalytic thinker Erikson, Gurney (1980b) looked at over 400 unemployed Australian school-leavers. It was hypothesized that having a job helps school-leavers to clarify their perception of their identity; not being able to get work leads to a confused perception of self or no change due to a moratorium. The hypothesis was confirmed for females but not males. Furthermore the unemployed males showed a significant shift towards the mistrust pole of the first dimension of trust-mistrust and the employed of both sexes shifted significantly on the industry-inferiority subscale. He concludes "it seems reasonable to conclude that unemployment has the effect of inhibiting development in school-leavers, rather than inflicting trauma as is sometimes popularly supposed" (p. 212). Gurney (1980a) also found that over a four-month period after leaving school, self-esteem increased only for those young people who obtained work.

More recently, Donovan and Oddy (1982) investigated the social and emotional development of a small, but carefully matched group of employed and unemployed school-leavers. They found that school-leavers who were unemployed were more depressed and anxious, had lower self-esteem and poorer subjective well-being, were less well socially adjusted and showed a higher incidence of minor psychiatric morbidity than school-leavers who had acquired jobs. They also found a significant interaction between employment status and gender on the locus of control scale: Unemployed males tend to be more external than employed males, whereas these differences were minimal for females. They write: "Certainly the apathy and hopelessness frequently associated with unemployment could be linked to an increased tendency to attribute events to uncontrollable forces" (p. 24).

Similarly, Feather (1982) found both male and female, young unemployed people had higher depression scores, lower self-esteem and Protestant work ethic scores (the belief that personal worth results from self-sacrificing work or occupational achievement) and reported that good and bad outcomes to everyday events were less important to them compared with employed male subjects. He notes:

> These results therefore indicate that both lower self-esteem and less effort to find a job were associated with increasing time out of work. They also show that the active pursuit of employment tended to be more frequent among those with higher self-esteem, stronger Protestant ethic values and higher levels of concern about positive and negative events (lower apathy). But frequency of job search was lower among those unemployed who report more depressive symptoms. These findings may imply a sort of reciprocal determinism in which the state of continued unemployment has effects on the person, so modified by his or her experience, behinds to behave in ways that alter the probability of finding a job (p. 320).

In England, Jackson et al. (1983) found the association between unemployment and reduced psychological well-being to be moderated by a number of factors, particularly employment commitment. In a well designed, two-cohort study using both cross-sectional and longitudinal analyses, they demonstrated that the effects of movement between work and unemployment is greatest for those whose employment commitment is high.

Stafford (1982) examined the impact of the Youth Opportunities Programme (designed to offer 16-18 year olds opportunities for training and work experience to increase employment prospects) on young people's employment prospects and psychological well-being. She found a significant improvement in employment prospects after participation in the scheme which also acts as a buffer against any detrimental effects of unemployment. However the beneficial effects of the programme do not last and the detrimental effects of unemployment return for those ex-trainees who remain unemployed.

Other studies have noted the medical and psychological health costs of being unemployed. In Britain, Banks et al. (1982) gave 647 recent school leavers the GHQ. There was a large significant difference between those unemployed (3.78) and those employed (1.27) but no significant sex differences. Further analysis showed that, although the unemployed scored higher on the GHQ, this relationship was moderated by their motivation to work, such that unemployed with a high motivation to work scored higher than those with lower motivation.

Similarly in an American study, Greenberger et al. (1981) compared the health and behavioural consequences of 16-18 year old school children who had part-time jobs compared to those who had never worked. Although they recognised the potentially positive influence on adolescents their work focused on the costs of job stress. Their study focussed on self-reported frequency of psychological and physical health symptoms, school absence, and the use of cigarettes, alcohol and marijuana. The results indicated that the working youths (especially boys) reported fewer somatic symptoms than the non-working youths, and that even boys who worked under stressful job conditions, report fewer somatic and psychological symptoms than boys who hold less stressful jobs. However the results did show that exposure to job stress is related to alcohol and marijuana use for both boys and girls. The authors proposed four explanations for their finding that work is associated with fewer symptoms in boys but more symptoms in girls:

1. differential selection (hardier boys are likely to take more stressful jobs);
2. differential attrition (hardier boys are likely to remain at stressful jobs, while those less sturdy are likely to leave);
3. differential reporting about health (boys who work under stress are less likely to report problems than are girls); and
4. sex differences in socialization (boys are led to expect more stress than girls).

Other studies have been concerned with the effect of youth unemployment as rapid labour turnover and delinquency. For instance Baxter (1975) studied chronic job changes in the early 1970's. Job changers tended to be less intelligent, more neurotic, from poorer homes and less socially and occupationally skilled than their counterparts who did not change jobs so rapidly. However Raffe (1983) in a study of employment instability in young people found that although instability was generated more by occupational than personal factors (unstable jobs not unstable workers), their changes of finding new employment depended on personal factors more than on their earlier occupational experiences. Similarly, Raelin (1981) found that early career unemployment is not a critical factor in retarding personal economic growth (relative to educational background and first job experience) but does have negative job attitudinal consequences. Young males who are early entrants in the labour force and who spend the bulk of their work in part-time employment, do as well economically and better occupationally in their later work experience than full-time youth.

Milham et al. (1978) in a study of over a thousand boys in approved schools found that employment experiences were a crucial factor in promoting economic and social well-being. Although the authors were careful not to draw causal links between unemployment and delinquency they did find that regular work did build up offending boys' confidence, changed their job aspirations, enhanced their self-perceptions and remotivated their interest in numeracy and literacy.

Banks, Clegg, and Jackson (1982) interviewed two age cohorts of young people up to 2½ years after leaving school to investigate the association between unemployment and risk of minor psychiatric morbidity. They found a positive relationship between unemployment and morbidity after controlling for sex, ethnic group and educational qualifications. Further longitudinal analyses showed that the experience of unemployment was more likely to create increased psychological symptoms, rather than the reverse. More recently Jackson et al. (1983) studied longitudinally two cohorts of young people in the first three years of their working lives. They found, as predicted, that psychological distress is higher for the unemployed than for the employed and that changes in employment status lead to changes in distress score. Virey (1983) attempted to determine which of a number of variables, including age, sex, migrant status and length of unemployment, best predicted the psychological reactions of young people to unemployment. Age was a strong influence on the pattern of psychological adjustment, although depression was found to be better predicted by other factors such as sex and length of unemployment.

Although there have been some studies of adult explanations of unemployment (Furnham, 1982a, 1983b) considerably less work has gone into establishing young people's beliefs about, and actual attempts at getting a job. Feather and Davenport (1981) tested their *expectancy-value theory* on young people: A person's actions are seen to be related to the expectations that a person holds and to the subjective values of the outcomes that might occur following the action. They found, as predicted, that higher motivated, more depressed unemployed youths blamed stable external factors for unemployment and rated the attractiveness of work more highly than less depressed youths. Although incompatible with learned helplessness theory, the results supported their theory which assumes that positive motivation to seek employment is identical to the multiplicative combination of expectancy of success in getting a job and the perceived net attractiveness of unemployment. They note

> One might assume that work will have stronger positive value for individuals with strong Protestant ethic values than for those people for whom these values are weaker. If this assumption is valid, then it follows that people with a strong Protestant ethic value will be more persistent in their efforts to get a job and that they will suffer more negative effects if they fail to obtain employment (p. 337).

Gurney (1981) in fact examined the attributions for the causes of unemployment in both employed and unemployed groups of school-leavers. In a first study he attempted to discover, among a population of Australian school-leavers, whether the unemployed differed in their attributions of employment from those who succeeded in getting work, and secondly, whether any differences were antecedent to or consequent upon unemployment. Subjects were asked to ascribe the ability to get work either to internal or external factors to the job seekers, and to fill out a simple eight-item scale devised by the author. He found that unemployed males attributed both getting and not getting work significantly more to external factors, as has been found previously, but there were no differences in the female groups. Gurney suggested that the lack of differences among the female groups may be due to their lesser defensiveness and need to blame external factors for being unemployed. In a second longitudinal study students were given a twelve-item attribution-for-getting-jobs questionnaire prior to leaving school and then approximately four months later. He suggested that:

> The unemployed may believe themselves powerless to change the circumstances of their lives (external locus) but the fact that they are without work whereas others are not and that they remain so, may lead them eventually to see themselves as responsible for their condition (internal attribution) with consequent self-blame and self-derogation (Gurney, 1981: p. 89).

The results showed that prior to leaving school the groups did not differ, yet later it was not the unemployed who changed their attributions, but the employed who shifted significantly toward a more internal set of causal ascriptions. Overall Gurney (1981) seemed unable to account for his "counter-intuitive and unexpected" findings suggesting perhaps that subjects of this age have their self-esteem based on numerous other things such as parental evaluation and peer groups approval, rather than exclusively on work which is more often the case with adults.

In a rather different study, Dayton (1981) looked at the way in which young people looked for a job. He set out to determine what job-seeking approaches were being used by young people and what factors they found positive and useful (aids) and what negative and worthless (barriers) in a job search. Using a population of 250 young Americans, Dayton found they regarded their own positive personal attributes (personality, flexibility, academic ability) as the most important aids in their job, and external factors (labour unions, welfare and unemployment insurance, government training programmes) as least important. Employment success and satisfaction was correlated with careful analysis of which job suited them best, the assemblance of a placement file, letters of recommendation, and a CV (vita), combined with persistence in the job search.

Research, within the framework of attribution theory, would however lead one to make a number of predictions about school children's expectations and beliefs about getting a job (Furnham, 1982a, 1982b, 1984a). For instance people more prone to unemployment, and the unemployed themselves, tend to make more external attributions for the causes of unemployment in contrast to those in jobs and unlikely to become unemployed. Furthermore, studies have shown external attributions are to some extent protective of self-esteem in the context of achievement (Harvey et al., 1976).

Hence Furnham (1984a) predicted that females more than males and working-class subjects more than middle-class subjects – for whom unemployment is statistically more probable – will be prone to make more external attributions about getting a job. Further it was suggested that these attributions will also be reflected in the number and type of job-search strategies adopted by young people and the barriers and aids that they consider operate in job-hunting success. In this study Furnham set out to examine sex and social-class differences in 240 British school-leavers attributions about unemployment, the most and least useful job-search strategies, and which school course they believed most and least useful in getting a job. The results of the four different parts of this study suggest that, overall, attributions about getting a job are frequently internal (that is to personal attributes or abilities) rather than environmental or societal forces. Confidence, perseverance and qualifications were all considered to be primary factors responsible for success in finding employment, yet this is moderated by the belief that jobs are not currently available (a fact which is attributed to the government). Yet failure to get a job was rarely attributed to the personal short-comings of the job-seeker himself. Thus these results tend to support the well established, attributional finding that success is attributed to internal factors to external factors.

Where there were significant sex differences, it was found that females were more external in their attributions than males. This conflicts with Gurney (1981) who found that unemployed males were more external in their attributions about employment than employed males, but that there were no differences between employed and unemployed females. However, the extensive locus-of-control literature has shown that were sex differences exist in generalized locus of control beliefs, females are more external than males. Similarly, class differences tended to show that working class subjects tend to place more emphasis on structural or external factors (Furnham, 1982a). Again this is to be expected and in accordance with previous literature on the topic (Furnham and Gunter, 1984).

More recently, Feather (1983a, 1983b) examined causal attributions and beliefs about work and unemployment among Australian adolescents in state and independent schools. The results were analyzed for school and sex differences. State-school children tended to blame economic factors, physical appearance and interview inadequacy more than independent-school children, endorsing societal or external explanations. As predicted children from the independent schools (of higher socio-economic status), as opposed to those from state schools, had higher expectations of obtaining employment, higher internal attributions of controllability over their own lives and were more likely to see work as attractive. Also female students tended to have lower expectations about finding employment, compared to their male peers. These results were explained in terms of the current economic situation in Australia, socialization forces in the family, the schools and in peer groups (middle-class children have experience of reward for effort and individual competition; working-class children have lower expectations).

In a more detailed study Feather and Barber (1983) investigated correlates of depressive reactions associated with unemployment in a sample of young unemployed male and female Australians. From studies on depression and attributions three hypotheses were tested and some support was found for each. They were:

1. *Depressive affect* about unemployment is associated with high job expectations, with the rated importance of having a job and with external attributions for the causes of unemployment;
2. *General depressive symptomatology* is associated with low expectation of getting a job, low self esteem, internal attributions abut the causes of unemployment and perceived uncontrollability or helplessness about changing things;
3. *Depressive symptoms* are associated with an unsuccessful employment history.

Overall the findings indicated that attributional variables accounted for only a relatively small proportion of the variance in depression.

> In future investigations of the psychological damage that unemployment may cause, it is important to assess a range of other variables as well, especially those that relate to the personal and social costs of not having a job and the different ways in which people learn to cope with negative outcomes (Feather and Barber, 1983: p. 193).

Doring (1984) investigated the beliefs about the employed and the unemployed in Australian school "leavers" and "stayers." Two hypotheses were stated:

1. School leavers will tend to use more external/socio-environmental beliefs than internal/dispositional beliefs when explaining unemployment status than will those continuing at school.
2. School leavers will use internal/dispositional beliefs rather than external/socio-environmental beliefs to account for employment status.

Both hypotheses received only limited support. For instance, while school leavers indicated less external beliefs than school stayers, they were more inclined to attribute employment to "qualification," "experience," and "luck." Doring argues that by explaining others' success in terms of luck and knowing the right people school stayers can both reconcile their belief in the benefits of the work ethic and believe in the prospect of future employment.

Because it has become so widespread various researchers have argued for some sort of education about the problems and prospects of unemployment (Dancy, 1978; Fleming and Lavercombe, 1982; Lavercombe and Fleming, 1981; Coffield, 1984). Some (Stirling, 1982) have gone so far as to suggest that we need to prepare school leavers for unemployment arguing that because as many as a third of school-leavers in Britain (in 1982/83) may experience unemployment, they need to know what to anticipate and how to cope. Furthermore high levels of youth unemployment have produced a questioning of and disenchantment with the whole education system (Hargreaves, 1981).

Watts (1978) also considered the implications of school-leaver unemployment for Careers Education in Schools. He argues that careers educators have not seriously dealt with the problem of unemployment because they do not feel competent to tackle it effectively. They are aware of its highly political and emotional overtones. It might affect deleteriously the work ethic within and outside the school.

Finally, teachers feel instinctively hostile to the concept of preparation for unemployment. A number of possible curricular objectives are listed including equipping children with employability, survival and leisure skills. Four alternative aims are described depending whether one if focussing on change in society (to help students see unemployment as a phenomenon resolved by social and political measures); change in the individual (to maximize students' chances of finding meaningful employment); status quo in the society (to reinforce students' motivation to seek work) and status in the individual (to make students aware of the possibility of unemployment and how to best cope with it). Much of the educational responses and strategies are dependent on whether one believes unemployment to be voluntary (aversion of the will to work), cyclical (cycles of recession and expansion), or structural (a major change in the relationship between capital and labour). These solutions may include a deeper inculcation of the work ethic, job creation schemes, etc. Careers education is seen as the education of central life interests and personal growth and development, rather than the matching of people to (non-existent) jobs.

7. EXPLAINING THE CAUSES OF UNEMPLOYMENT

A number of writers have suggested that people out of work for long periods of time tend to offer *fatalistic explanations* for the causes of their own and others' unemployment (Hayes and Nutman, 1981; Jahoda, 1979; O'Brien and Kabanoff, 1979). A certain amount of research has gone into lay beliefs about unemployment, including causal attributions may seen as a special case of lay epistemology (Kruglanski, 1980).

Furnham (1982a) set out to examine differences in the explanations for unemployment in Britain as a function of whether people were employed or unemployed as well as their age, sex, education and voting pattern. It was hypothesized that more unemployed people would find *societal* (external) social, economic and political factors and fatalistic (luck, chance, fate) explanations important for unemployment than employed people who would find *individualistic explanations* (internal dispositional and personality factors) more important. It was also hypothesized that Conservative voters would find individualistic explanations for unemployment more important than employed Labour voters who would find societal factors more important. The results showed a predictable pattern of differences between the employed and unemployed, the former believing more individualistic explanations and less in societal explanations than the latter. See Table 4.

However, whereas there were few sex and age differences, education and vote revealed numerous differences in explanations for unemployment. As is the case with explanations for poverty, Conservatives found individualistic explanations for unemployment more important than Labour voters who in

Table 4. Means and F levels for the explanations for unemployment offered by employed and unemployed subjects (these numbers represent the mean on the following scale: Important 1 2 3 4 5 Unimportant).

Explanations	Employed	Unemployed	F level
A. Individualistic			
Unemployed people can earn more money on social security	5.21	5.31	0.17
Lack of effort and laziness among unemployed people	5.13	4.81	1.72
Unemployed people don't try hard enough to get jobs	3.15	4.21	13.22*
Unemployed people are too fussy and proud to accept some jobs	4.89	4.57	1.67
Poor education and qualifications among unemployed people	4.40	3.55	12.94*
Unwillingness of unemployed to move to places of work	4.32	5.51	10.60*
Inability of unemployed people to adapt to new conditions	4.77	4.38	3.44+
Lack of intelligence or ability among the unemployed	5.46	4.76	9.70#
B. Societal			
The policies and strategies of the present government	2.05	2.33	1.48
The policies and strategies of previous British governments	2.82	2.85	0.06
Inefficient and less competitive industries that go bankrupt	3.38	3.45	0.10
An influx of immigrants have taken up all available jobs	5.32	3.92	29.09*
Trade unions have priced their members out of a job	4.37	3.85	4.83+
Overmanning in industry which has occurred for too long	3.53	3.93	2.93
Incompetent industrial management with poor planning	2.94	3.46	5.98#
Weak trade unions that do not fight to keep jobs	4.80	3.58	26.05*
C. Fatalistic			
Sickness and physical handicap among unemployed people	5.14	3.74	29.32*
Just bad luck	5.73	5.27	4.63+
World-wide recession and inflation	2.19	2.57	3.69+
The introduction of widespread automation	3.70	3.09	6.14#

* $p < 0.001$
\# $p < 0.01$
\+ $p < 0.05$

turn found societal explanations more important than Conservative voters. It was suggested that the results confirm the theses of a number of writers in the field (Tiffany et al., 1970) that unemployed people will be more external in their attributions for the causes of unemployment than employed people, although this is only a matter of degree. Furthermore, according to Hayes and Nutman (1981) and others, this pattern should increase the longer a person remains out of work. Yet the overall national unemployment figures would probably affect this relationship. As unemployment grows, even employed people tend to offer societal and fatalistic (external) explanations for unemployment partly as a defense about becoming unemployed themselves.

Furnham (1982b) looked specifically at the relationship between the Protestant work ethic beliefs and attitudes towards and explanations for unemployment. Most of previous research concerned the relationship between work ethic beliefs and paid work, however Furnham's (1983) looked at the relationship between work ethic beliefs and unemployment. As predicted, subjects who strongly endorsed the work ethic endorsed negative individualistic explanations for unemployment and were by-and-large more against welfare payments than subjects who did not strongly endorse these beliefs. This confirms MacDonald's (1971) finding that Protestant work ethic believers were proponents of the ethics of social responsibility which tend to blame people rather than "the system" for the source of their difficulty. It also confirms other findings which suggest that these beliefs, as measured by any of the Protestant work ethic scales, is part of a general conservative attitude pattern. These results are also in accordance with studies of lay-beliefs about economics -poverty, wealth, unemployment, taxation, social security – which suggest that there are coherent lay "theories" about such matters. Thus a high Protestant work ethic scorer is likely to explain poverty in terms of idleness and poor money management; wealth in terms of hard work, honesty, and saving; unemployment in terms of laziness and lack of effort; and s/he is likely to be against both taxation and social security (Furnham, 1982b: p. 283).

Although most of the research on explanations for unemployment has been stimulated by other work within an attribution theory context, other conceptual frameworks have been put forward. Moscovici (1981) has argued that *social representation* (set of concepts, statements and explanations originating in daily life in the course of interindividual communication) in fact determine people's attribution about such things as unemployment benefits. Whereas attribution theory is concerned with the way individuals attribute causes to events that belong to their experience, the theory of social representations concerns how groups or individuals create a stable world in which diverse, unfamiliar or unpredictable behaviours are given meaning familiar and predictable. He maintains that people gather information, classify it into certain categories and then attempt to explain it. He believes that attributions follow from social representation and not the reverse.

> I am convinced that the theory of attribution will become more fruitful and less mechanical as soon as it recognizes the importance of the content of representation and its social character. Any reduction to cognitive patterns and constructs, by eliminating the extraordinary richness of collective thought, its rootedness in a well defined setting, and by flattening all social relation into interaction between two individuals, converts an important problem into a more academic exercise (p. 208).

He in fact illustrates his point by reference to unemployment:

> Some think of the unemployed person as lazy, unlucky or as incompetent in looking for work; others consider him to be the victim of economic downturn, of social injustice and the contradictions of the capitalist regime. The former attribute the cause of unemployment to the individual, to his way of facing the world, and the latter to the general situation, to the individual's class affiliation and to the way in which the world treats him. Obviously this divergence is due altogether to their respective social representations. One representation gives precedence, under all circumstances, to personal responsibility, individual effort, and individual solutions to the problems of society; the other leads to a sharp awareness of social injustice and social responsibility, contemplating collective solutions to individual problems (pp. 107-108).

La France and Cicchetti (1979) were concerned with social class and employment status determinants of the *perceived responsibility* and blame for economic success and failure. Four groups of subjects (middle class employed; middle class unemployed; working class employed; working class unemployed) were asked a series of questions about a stimulus figure that they had read about. They found that subjects were more concerned with praising the successful job seeker than with blaming the unsuccessful. The middle class subjects distinguished significantly more between success and failure than working class subjects, assigning more responsibility to the former and less to the latter. The middle class subjects more than the working class subjects believed personality to be influential. Overall, employed subjects assigned more responsibility to the stimulus person and saw luck as being less influential in the successful outcome than did the unemployed.

Nearly all of the studies in this section on explanations for unemployment used a limited and unrepresentative sample and a structured questionnaire. However, more recent studies have considered a free-response interview format with large, representative samples. In a free-response study Lewis and Furnham (1986) asked 450 people how they believed unemployment could be reduced. Many different answers were given, such as lowering the retirement age, increasing job creation schemes, or increase public spending. Most people gave answers which implied a stimulation of the economy, a number for the redistribution of jobs yet about 15% could provide no answer at all. When given six closed questions is was found that over 90% of the sample believed that the level of unemployment in Britain was unacceptably high, while 66% argued that the government should spend more money in order to reduce unemployment. There were some interesting and predictable sex, age and employment history differences: Women were against sacrificing their jobs if their husbands were unemployed but did favour job sharing and reducing working hours; similarly younger people seemed more liberal than older people in that they did not believe in curbing immigration or women giving up their jobs.

Using a large and representative sample, Lewis, Snell, and Furnham (1987) asked 900 British people to explain the causes of unemployment. Content analysis using 13 economic codes revealed that 28% of the explanations concerned falling demand for goods; 23% the rate of inflation; 18% government policy; 17% high wage demands. Curiously there were very few demographic differences, although many were investigated (sex, social class, age, housing, trade union membership). These explanations (many of which defied coding) were reclassified into the three categories used by Furnham (1982a) – 78% of the explanations were societal, 24% fatalistic, and only 7% societal. What was particularly striking about the explanations offered for unemployment was the fact that so few were purely economic – that is lay explanations for economic phenomena are often normative, moralistic, socio-political as well as economic.

Furnham (1984b) has argued that a potentially important factor in helping to explain an unemployed person's response to unemployment may be how that person or a significant other views the causes of not working. Although causal attributions have in general been studied in relation to psychological well-being, their relevance to the impact of unemployment specifically has received less attention.

Two competing, but related theoretical models have been proposed to explain relationships between causal attributions and reactions to stressful events. The theory of "*learned helplessness*" has shown how attributional/explanational patterns affect levels of depression and other responses to uncontrollable negative events. For instance, internal (self-blame) attributions tend to lower self-esteem whereas external (societal) attributions do not. Furthermore, stable (unchanging) attributions lower expectations of future success and increase the chronicity of helplessness in relation to a particular situation, whereas unstable (changing) attributions do not. Considerable clinical evidence attests to the fact that there is a strong relationship between internal, stable, and global attributions and negative outcomes and depression – that is, people are likely to become particularly depressed if they believe themselves to be the cause of their plight.

The most severe, enduring, and generalized forms of depression and concomitant mental illnesses develop when aversive stimuli (in this case, unemployment) persist despite the person's best efforts to avert them (constantly seeks appropriate employment) and when the person feels hopeless and helpless to change the situation. Thus, one would predict a positive relationship between depressive affect and internal attributions (i.e., a person's holding him/herself responsible) concerning the causes of unemployment. External attributions may also lead to depression and/or anger, but not to the same extent.

A second, related model is based on *expectancy-value theory*, which relates an action (behaviour of cognition) to the perceived attractiveness or aversiveness of expected outcomes. The theory predicts that frustration in the desire to find work is associated with negative affects such as depression and sadness, but that these affects will be most intense among people who perceive work as attractive, have high expectations of getting a job, and are very strongly motivated to find work.

Both models predict a relationship between depressive and other symptoms of mental illness (e.g., anxiety states) and causal attributions, but the direction of the causality is not clear. Hence, it may be that particular attributions follow or co-occur with depression rather than cause it. Moreover, expectancy-value theory suggests that this relationship is mediated by other factors such as the person's desire for work. Finally, whereas learned-helplessness theory would suggest that internal attributions are associated with depression (low self-esteem), expectancy-value theory does the opposite, associating external attributions depression (nothing can be done).

8. UNEMPLOYMENT AMONG WOMEN

Even less research has been devoted to unemployment among women than to the effects of employment on well-being or self-esteem (Spitze and Waite, 1981; Faver, 1982).

In a review of work and well-being in women, Warr and Parry (1982) found that the association between employment status and psychological well-being is mediated by a woman's occupational status, the quality of her non-occupational environment, and the quality of her employment relationship. In certain circumstances psychological well-being is significantly associated with having paid employment – in single rather than married, and working-class rather than middle class women. Although there appears to be paucity of good research in this area, the results seem to indicate that work outside of the home is not generally as important to the well-being of women as it is to the well-being of men.

Indeed various studies have shown deleterious effects of work on physical and psychological health (Zimmerman and Hartley, 1982). In a study of the lives of women managers, Cooper and Davidson (1982) found that compared to men, women have major additional stresses to cope with, and that often their home life obstructs rather than supports their careers. Similarly, Faver (1982) found that a women's labour force participation is partially a function of the interaction between career and family task demands and values.

Almost no work has been done on unemployed women. An exception is Warr and Parry (1982) who looked at depressed mood in working-class mothers with and without paid employment. They compared the depressed mood scores for matched full-time employed, part-time employed and non-employed mothers and they found a large significant difference indicating that the former were least depressed and the latter most depressed. They also looked at various other variables, such as their attitude to employment, strain in coping with domestic and paid work duties, the amount of social support they received and their child care demands. Overall the strain in coping variable was the most predictive of depressed mood in that employed mothers with high interaction strain have mood scores similar to those without paid employment, and part-time employees with high strain have particularly high depressed mood scores. The smallest associations with depressed mood were child-care demands. The authors are conscious of the experimental shortcomings of their and others' work especially in the need to control for various important demographic variables.

Clearly, the fact that there are more women entering the labour market and more being made redundant suggests there is a necessity for studies to be done on the particular problems and processes of being an unemployed woman.

9. CONCLUSIONS

This chapter has attempted to review the now voluminous literature on unemployment under selected headings. Many topics have been neglected, i.e., value changes as a consequence of unemployment.

Penner and Rokeach (1969) hypothesized that there would be certain changes in salient variables as a result of changes in employment conditions. They contacted four groups: temporarily unemployed / subsequently employed; actually unemployed / subsequently employed; temporarily unemployed / still unemployed; and actually unemployed / still unemployed. For the first group the value "broadminded" became significantly more important and "polite" less important, which was also true of the second group. For the unemployed groups the terminal value "equality" became less important especially the third group possibly because they were more concerned with their own well-being. The fourth hard-core group rated "salvation," "tender" and "polite" as more important and patient as less important over time. In Australia, O'Brien and Kabanoff (1979) found that compared to employed workers the unemployed had poorer physical health, lower work values and higher external control orientation and made more use of community helping agencies. The work value differences showed that the unemployed tended to desire less influence, interaction and pressure in their work compared to the employed.

Research on unemployment is scattered across a wide number of disciplines: economics, education, psychiatry, psychology (clinical, educational, occupational and social) and sociology. Although some results are equivocal and others contradictory various themes and established findings emerge. For instance, studies on the psychological consequences of unemployment tend to point in the same direction: namely that unemployment causes stress, a lowering of self-esteem and a change in expectations. Similarly, the work on attributions and explanations has revealed consistent findings. Taken together they show a vicious circle for those who are unemployed. Loss of work leads to lowered self-esteem, and possibly mental and physical illness and low expectations for getting work. These in turn lead to poor or maladaptive job search strategies, so confirming beliefs. Hence we find self-fulfilling prophesies or reciprocal determinism (Feather, 1982). Thus instead of there being a simple unitary direction of causality more and more studies are pointing to the idea of bidirectional causality.

Although research in this area is comparatively recent, difficult and expensive, there is no excuse for poor research which only leads to unreliable, unconfirmed and ambiguous findings. Researchers need to be more specific in the individual difference, organizational and macroeconomic factors which together influence unemployment. For instance three categories of individual difference factors need to be considered: *psychological differences* in personality, self-concept, beliefs, skills prior and subsequent to unemployment. Secondly, there are *demographic differences* in age, sex, religious and ethnic group, schooling, social class which condition expectations and coping strategies. Thirdly, there are *work experience differences* in that some people have had some or all or none of the work experiences possible: full time, part-time, voluntary, none.

Similarly, there are a number of organizational differences which have to be considered such as its size, structure, social support, and manning levels. Finally, gross macroeconomic factors such as the inflation and unemployment rate, levels of social security and employment benefit, must be taken into consideration.

The problem with a lot of research is that, in that it has concentrated on a few specific variables others have been ignored or at worst confounded. The reactions and hardships of people who are jobless seem sufficiently severe and important to merit good research for only sensible policy decisions can be made on the basis of good research findings.

There are, of course, a host of topics like time-budgets of the unemployed, changes in the pattern of spending and saving, intra-family problems, etc. which have only been mentioned peripherally, partly because of the limited research in the area. Perhaps the most important work to emerge from this area are the studies that demonstrate the vicious circle caused by the bi-directional causality between unemployment and deteriorating mental and physical health.

REFERENCES

Allerhand, M., F. Friedlander, J. Marlone, H. Meadow, and M. Rosenberg, 1969, A study of the Impact and Effectiveness of the Comprehensive Manpower Project of Cleveland, Washington, DC: Department of Labour.

Argyle, M., 1983, The Social Psychology of Work, Harmondsworth, Middlesex: Penguin Books.

Bakke, E.W., 1933, The Unemployed Man: A Social Study, London: Nisbett.

Bakke, E.W., 1940, Citizens Without Work, New Haven, CT: Yale University Press.

Banks, M., C. Clegg, and P. Jackson, 1982, Unemployment and risk of minor psychiatric disorder in young people: Cross sectional and longitudinal evidence, Psychological Medicine, 12, 789-798.

Baron, R.A., 1983, Behaviour in Organizations. Understanding and Managing the Human Side of Work, Newton, MA: Allyn and Bacon.

Baxter, J., 1975, The chronic job changer: A study of youth unemployment, Social and Economic Administration, 9, 184-206.

Beales, H., and R. Lambert (eds.), 1934, Memoirs of the Unemployed, London: Gollance.

Boor, M., 1980, Relationships between unemployment rates and suicide rates in eight countries, 1962-1976, Psychological Reports, 47, 1095-1101.

Bowlby, J., 1969, Attachment and Loss, London: Hogarth.

Brenner, S., and R. Bartell, 1983, The psychological impact of unemployment: A structural analysis of cross-sectional data, Journal of Occupational Psychology, 56, 129-136.

Briar, R., 1977, The effect of long-term unemployment on workers and their families, Dissertation Abstracts International, 37, 6062.

Burke, R., 1984, The closing at Canadian Admiral: Correlates of individual well-being sixteen months after shutdown, Psychological Reports, 55, 91-98.

Catalano, R., and C. Dooley, 1977, Economic predictors of depressed mood and stressful life events, Journal of Health and Social Behaviour, 18, 292-307.

Catalano, R., and C. Dooley, 1979, The economy as stressor: A sectoral analysis, Review of Social Economy, 37, 175-188.

Clark, A., and M. Clissold, 1982, Correlates of adaption among unemployed and employed young men, Psychological Reports, 50, 887-893.

Cochrane, R., and A. Robertson, 1973, The life events inventory. A measure of the relative severity of psychological stressors, Journal of Psychosomatic Research, 17, 215-218.

Coffield, F., 1984, Learning to Live with Unemployment: What Future for Education in a World Without Jobs, Durham, UK: University of Durham (unpublished paper).
Cooper, C., and M. Davidson, 1982, High Pressure: Working Lives of Women Managers, London: Fontana.
Dancy, J., 1978, Education about unemployment: A reflective element, Oxford Review of Education, 4, 289-294.
Dayton, C., 1981, The young person's job search: Insights from a study, Journal of Counseling Psychology, 28, 321-333.
Donovan, A., and M. Oddy, 1982, Psychosocial aspects of unemployment: An investigation into the emotional and social adjustment of school leavers, Journal of Adolescence, 5, 15-30.
Dooley, C., and R. Catalano, 1979, Economic, life, and disorder changes: Time-series analyses, American Journal of Community Psychology, 7, 381-396.
Dooley, C., and R. Catalano, 1980, Economic change as a cause of behavioural disorder, Psychological Bulletin, 87, 450-468.
Doring, A., 1984, Beliefs about the employed and the unemployed held by senior high school students in North Queensland, Australian Journal of Psychology, 28, 78-88.
Eisenberg, P., and P.F. Lazarsfeld, 1938, The psychological effects of unemployment, Psychological Bulletin, 35, 79-96.
Faver, C., 1982, Achievement orientation, attainment values, and women's employment, Journal of Vocational Behaviour, 20, 67-80.
Feather, N.T., 1982, Unemployment and its psychological correlates: A study of depressive symptoms of self-esteem, Protestant ethic values, attributional style and apathy, Australian Journal of Psychology, 34, 309-323.
Feather, N.T., 1983a, Some correlates of attributional style: Depressive symptoms of self-esteem, and Protestant ethic values, Personality and Social Psychology Bulletin, 9, 125-135.
Feather, N.T., 1983b, Causal attributions and beliefs about work and unemployment among adolescents in state and independent secondary schools, Australian Journal of Psychology, 35, 211-232.
Feather, N.T., and J. Barber, 1983, Depressive reactions and unemployment, Journal of Abnormal Psychology, 92, 185-195.
Feather, N.T., and M. Bond, 1983, Time structure and purposeful activity among employed and unemployed university graduates, Journal of Occupational Psychology, 56, 241-254.
Feather, N.T., and P. Davenport, 1981, Unemployment and depressive effect: A motivational and attributional analysis, Journal of Personality and Social Psychology, 41, 422-436.
Fineman, S., 1979, A psychological model of stress and its application to managerial unemployment, Human Relations, 32, 323-345.
Fleming, D., and S. Lavercombe, 1982, Talking about unemployment with schoolleavers, British Journal of Guidance and Counselling, 10, 22-23.
Fowler, B., B. Littlewood, and R. Madigan, 1977, Immigrant school-leavers and the search for work, Sociology, 11, 65-85.
Fraser, C., 1980, "The social psychology of unemployment," in: M. Jeeves (ed.), Psychology Survey, No. 3, London: George Allen and Unwin, pp. 172-186.
Friedlander, F., and S. Greenberg, 1971, Effect of job attitudes training and organization climate on performance of the hard-core unemployed, Journal of Applied Psychology, 55, 287-295.
Fruensgaard, K., S. Benjaminsen, S. Joensen, and K. Helstrup, 1983a, Psychosocial characteristics of a group of unemployment patients consecutively admitted to a psychiatric emergency department, Social Psychiatry, 18, 137-144.
Fruensgaard, K., S. Benjaminsen, S. Joensen, and K. Helstrup, 1983b, Follow up of a group

of unemployed patients consecutively admitted to an psychiatric emergency department, Social Psychiatry, 18, 129-135.
Furnham, A., 1982a, Why are the poor always with us? Explanations for poverty in Britain, British Journal of Social Psychology, 21, 311-322.
Furnham, A., 1982b, The Protestant work ethic and attitudes towards employment, Journal of Occupational Psychology, 55, 277-286.
Furnham, A., 1983a, Mental health and employment status: A preliminary study, British Journal of Counselling and Guidance, 11, 199-210.
Furnham, A., 1983b, Attributions for affluence, Personality and Individual Differences, 4, 31-40.
Furnham, A., 1983c, Attitudes to the unemployed receiving social security, Human Relations, 36, 135-150.
Furnham, A., 1984a, Getting a job: School-leavers perceptions of employment prospects, British Journal of Educational Psychology, 54, 293-305.
Furnham, A., 1984b, Unemployment, attributions theory and mental health: A review of the British literature, International Journal of Mental Health, 13, 51-67.
Furnham, A., and S. Bochner, 1986, Culture Shock: Psychological Reactions to Unfamiliar Environments, London: Methuen.
Furnham, A., and B. Gunter, 1984, Just world beliefs and attitudes towards the poor, British Journal of Social Psychology, 23, 265-269.
Furnham, A., and A. Lewis, 1986, The Economic Mind: The Social Psychology of Economic Behaviour, Brighton, Sussex, UK: Wheatsheaf.
Gore, S., 1978, The effect of social support in moderating the health consequences of unemployment, Journal of Health and Social Behaviour, 19, 157-165.
Greenberger, E., L. Stenberg, and A. Vaux, 1981, Adolescents who work: Health and behavioural consequences of job stress, Developmental Psychology, 17, 691-703.
Guion, R., and F. Landy, 1972, The meaning of work and the motivation to work, Organizational Behaviour and Human Performance, 7, 308-339.
Gurney, R., 1980a, The effects of unemployment on the psychological development of school-leavers, Journal of Occupational Psychology, 53, 205-213.
Gurney, R., 1980b, Does unemployment affect the self-esteem of school-leavers, Australian Journal of Psychology, 32, 175-182.
Gurney, R., 1981, Leaving school, facing unemployment and making attributions about the causes of unemployment, Journal of Vocational Behaviour, 18, 79-91.
Hargreaves, D., 1981, Unemployment, leisure and education, Oxford Review of Education, 7, 197-210.
Harrison, R., 1976, The demoralizing experience of prolonged unemployment, Department of Employment Gazette, 4, 339-348.
Hartley, J., 1980, The personality of unemployed managers: Myths and measurement, Personal Review, 9, 12-18.
Harvey, J.H., W.J. Ickes, and R.F. Kidd (eds.), 1976, New Directions in Attribution Research, Vol. 1, Hillsdale, NJ: Lawrence Erlbaum.
Hayes, J., and P. Nutman, 1981, Understanding the Unemployed, London: Tavistock.
Hepworth, S., 1980, Moderating factors of the psychological impact of unemployment, Journal of Occupational Psychology, 53, 139-145.
Herzberg, F., 1966, Work and the Nature of Man, Cleveland, OH: World Publishing Company.
Herzberg, F., B. Mausner, and B. Snyderman, 1959, The Motivation to Work, New York: John Wiley.
Hill, J., 1978, The psychological impact of unemployment, New Society, 43, 118-120.
Hodgson, J., and M. Brenner, 1968, Successful experience: Training hard-core unemployed, Harvard Business Review, 46, 148-156.

Holmes, T., and R. Rahe, 1967, The social readjustment rating scale, Journal of Psychosomatic Research, 11, 213-218.
Hopson, B., and J. Adams, 1976, "Towards an understanding of transition," in: J. Adams, J. Hayes, and B. Hopson (eds.), Transition, London: Martin Robertson.
Hulin, C., and M. Blood, 1968, Job enlargement, individual differences and worker responses, Psychological Bulletin, 69, 41-55.
Jackson, P., E. Stafford, M. Banks, and P. Warr, 1983, Unemployment and psychological distress in young people; The moderating role of employment counsellors, Journal of Applied Psychology, 68, 525-535.
Jahoda, M., 1979, The impact of unemployment in Psychological Society, 32, 309-314.
Jahoda, M., 1981, Work, employment and unemployment: Values, theories and approaches in social research, American Psychologist, 36, 184-191.
Jahoda, M., 1982, Employment and Unemployment: A Social-psychological Analysis, Cambridge, MA: Cambridge University Press.
Jahoda, M., P. Lazarsfeld, and H. Zeisel, 1933, Marienthal: The Sociography of an Unemployed Community, London: Tavistock.
Jenkins, R., A. MacDonald, J. Murray, and G. Strathdee, 1982, Minor psychiatric morbidity and the threat of redundancy in a professional group, Psychological Medicine, 12, 799-807.
Kasl, S.V., and S. Cobb, 1970, Blood pressure changes in men undergoing job loss, Psychosomatic Medicine, 32, 19-38.
Kelvin, P., and J. Jarrett, 1985, Social Psychological Consequences of Unemployment, Cambridge, MA: Cambridge University Press.
Kelvin, P., C. Dewberry, and N. Morley-Bunker, 1984, Unemployment and Leisure, ESRC (report).
Komarovsky, M., 1940, The Unemployed Man and His Family, New York: Dryden.
Krafchik, M., 1983, Unemployment and vagrancy in the 1930's: Deterrence, rehabilitation and the depression, Journal of Social Policy, 12, 195-214.
Kruglanski, A., 1980, Lay epistemologic process and contents: Another look at attribution theory, Psychological Review, 87, 70-87.
La France, M., and C. Cicchetti, 1979, Perceived responsibility and blame for economic success and failure: Social class and employment status comparisons, Journal of Applied Social Psychology, 9, 466-475.
Lavercombe, S., and D. Fleming, 1981, Attitudes and duration of unemployment among sixteen year old school-leavers, British Journal of Guidance and Counselling, 9, 36-45.
Levinger, G., and O. Moles, 1979, Divorce and Separation: Context, Causes and Consequences, New York: Basic Books.
Lewis, A., and A. Furnham, 1986, Reducing unemployment: Lay beliefs about how to reduce current unemployment, Journal of Economic Psychology, 7, 75-85.
Lewis, A., M. Snell, and A. Furnham, 1987, Lay explanations for the causes of unemployment in Britain: Individualistic, societal or fatalistic?, Political Psychology, 8, 427-434.
Liem, R., and T. Atkinson, 1982, The work and unemployment project: Personal and family effects of job loss (unpublished paper).
Liem, R., and P. Rayman, 1982, Health and social costs of unemployment, American Psychologist, 37, 1116-1123.
Lynn, R., S. Hampson, and M. Magee, 1984, Home background, intelligence, personality and education as predictors of unemployment in young people, Personality and Individual Differences, 5, 549-557.
MacDonald, A., 1971, Correlates of the ethics of personal conscience and the ethics of social responsibility, Journal of Consulting and Clinical Psychology, 37, 443.
Mair, B., and D. Raffe, 1983, The transition from school to work in 1980/81: A dynamic account, British Educational Research Journal, 9, 57-70.

Makeham, P., 1980, Youth Unemployment: An Examination of Evidence on Youth Unemployment Using National Statistics, Department of Employment, UK.

Markova, I., R. Lockyer, and C. Forbes, 1980, Self-perception of employed and unemployed haemophiliacs, Psychological Medicine, 10, 559-565.

Marsden, D., and E. Duff, 1975, Workless, Harmondsworth, Middlesex, UK: Penguin Books.

Maslow, A.H., 1970, Motivation and Personality, New York: Harper and Row.

Merton, R.K., 1957, The role-set: Problems in sociological theory, British Journal of Sociology, 8, 106-120.

Milham, S., R. Bullock, and K. Hosie, 1978, Juvenile unemployment: A concept due for re-cycling, Journal of Adolescence, 1, 11-24.

Moscovici, C., 1981, "On social representation," in: J.P. Forgas (ed.), Social Cognition, London: Academic Press, pp. 181-209.

O'Brien, G.E., and B. Kabanoff, 1979, Comparison of unemployed and employed workers on values, locus of control and health variables, Australian Psychologist, 14, 143-154.

Orwell, G., 1933, Down and Out in London and Paris, London: Gollancz.

Parles, C., 1975, Bereavement: Studies of Grief in Adult Life, Harmondsworth, Middlesex, UK: Penguin Books.

Penner, L., and M. Rokeach, 1969, The effects of employment condition on value systems, Papers in Psychology, 3, 47-51.

Platt, S., 1984, Unemployment and suicidal behaviour: A review of the literature, Social Science and Medicine, 19, 93-115.

Pym, D., 1980, Towards a dual economy and emancipation from employment, Futures, 6, 223-237.

Raelin, J., 1981, A comparitive study of later work experience among full-time, part-time, and unemployment male youth, Journal of Vocational Behaviour, 19, 315-327.

Raffe, D., 1983, Employment instability among less-qualified young workers, British Journal of Guidance and Counselling, 11, 21-34.

Rahe, R., I. Floistad, T. Bergan, R. Ringdal, R. Gerhardt, R. Gunderson, and R. Arthur, 1974, A model of life changes and illness research, Archives of General Psychiatry, 31, 172-177.

Roberts, K., J. Duggan, and M. Noble, 1982, Out-of-school youth in high unemployment areas, British Journal of Guidance and Counselling, 10, 1-11.

Robertson, A., and R. Cochrane, 1976, Attempted suicide and cultural change: An empirical investigation, Human Relations, 9, 863-883.

Rowntree, B., and B. Lasker, 1911, Unemployment: A Social Study, Toronto, O.: Macmillan.

Schapiro, M., and D. Ahlberg, 1983, Aspirations, Unemployment and Suicide: An Analysis and Forecast of U.S. Postwar Suicides by Age and Sex, University of Minnesota, Industrial Relations Center.

Smart, R., 1979, Drinking problems among employed, unemployed and shift workers, Journal of Occupational Medicine, 11, 731-736.

Spitze, G., and L. Waite, 1981, Wives' employment: The role of husbands' perceived attitudes, Journal of Marriage and the Family, 12, 117-124.

Stafford, E., 1982, The impact of the Youth Opportunities Programme on young people's employment prospects and psychological well-being, British Journal of Guidance and Counselling, 10, 12-21.

Stirling, A., 1982, Preparing school-leavers for unemployment, Bulletin of the British Psychological Society, 35, 421-422.

Stokes, G., and R. Cochrane, 1984, A study of the psychological effects of redundancy and unemployment, Journal of Occupational Psychology, 57, 309-322.

Stokes G., and R. Cochrane, 1984, The relationship between national levels of unemployment and the rate of admission to mental hospitals in England and Wales, 1950-1976, Social Psychiatry, 19, 117-125.

Swineburne, P., 1981, The psychological impact of unemployment on managers and professional staff, Journal of Occupational Psychology, 54, 47-64.

Teahan, J., 1969, Future Time Perspective and Job Success. A Group Oriented Approach for Facilitating the Work Adjustment of the Hard Core Unemployed, Washington, DC: Department of Labour.

Thoits, P., and M. Hannan, 1979, Income and psychological distress: The impact of an income-maintenance experiment, Journal of Health and Social Behaviour, 20, 120-138.

Tiffany, D., J. Cowan, and P. Tiffany, 1970, The Unemployed: A Social-psychological Portrait, Englewood Cliffs, NJ: Prentice-Hall.

Trower, P., B. Bryant, and M. Argyle, 1978, Social Skills and Mental Health, London: Methuen.

Virey, L., 1983, Psychological reactions of young people to unemployment, Youth and Society, 14, 457-474.

Vroom, V.H., 1964, Work and Motivation, New York: John Wiley.

Warr, P., 1981, Psychological aspects of employment and unemployment, Psychological Medicine, 11, 125-136.

Warr, P., 1982, A national study of non-financial employment commitment, Journal of Occupational Psychology, 55, 297-312.

Warr, P., 1983, Work, jobs and unemployment, Bulletin of the British Psychological Society, 36, 305-311.

Warr, P., 1984, Reported behaviour changes after job loss, British Journal of Social Psychology, 23, 271-275.

Warr, P., and P. Jackson, 1984, Men without jobs: Some correlates of age and length of unemployment, Journal of Occupational Psychology, 57, 77-85.

Warr, P., and G. Parry, 1982, Paid employment and women's psychological well-being, Psychological Bulletin, 91, 498-516.

Warr, P., and R. Payne, 1983, Social class and reported changes in behaviour after job loss, Journal of Applied Social Psychology, 13, 206-222.

Warr, P., P. Jackson, and M. Banks, 1982, Duration of unemployment and psychological well-being in young men and women, Current Psychological Research, 2, 207-214.

Watts, A., 1978, The implications of school-leavers: Unemployment for careers education in schools, Journal of Curriculum Studies, 3, 233-250.

Zimmerman, M., and W. Hartley, 1982, High blood pressure among employed women: A multi factor discriminant analysis, Journal of Health and Social Behaviour, 23, 205-220.

Table of Contents

18. The Use of Natural Resources

W. FRED VAN RAAIJ
Erasmus University, Rotterdam, The Netherlands

1. INTRODUCTION

1.1. *Natural Resources*

Households constitute an important sector in the economy with regard to their use of natural resources (*raw material and energy*) and the disposition of household waste. In The Netherlands, households produce about 20% of the total of solid waste and use about 30% of the total energy, mostly for home heating. The figures for other developed countries do not differ very much from these figures. Household and other waste is used as landfill (40%), is incinerated (40%), or composted (20%).

From different perspectives it is important to reduce the total amount of waste: From an ecological perspective, waste used as landfill and incineration may decrease the ecological value of the countryside. Waste degrades the natural environment, as with "acid rain" and other forms of air pollution. Waste materials are often damaging the health (diseases, stress) conditions of people living in an area. Energy use and its consequences, both for home heating and for transportation, may have the same negative effects on health. Thirdly, there are economic and political consequences. Raw materials and energy supply may make a nation dependent on other nations, e.g., the OPEC cartel. A reduction of the use of resources contributes to the economic independence of a nation.

The use of natural resources is a relevant area of economic psychology. Energy and materials constitute a large part of the consumption budget. Resource conservation is thus relevant from a consumer policy perspective as well. Resource conservation can only partly be reached through technical and economic policy measures, such as improvements of product design or tax measures. It is needed to change the behavior of consumers to reach the full potential of resource conservation.

Van Raaij, W.F., van Veldhoven, G.M. and Wärneryd, K.E. (eds) Handbook of Economic Psychology. ISBN 90-247-3720-6.

1.2. *Raw Materials*

Two main strategies exist for reducing the total amount of household waste (Pieters and Verhallen, 1986). First, less waste may be produced by using less primary materials in the production and packaging process of consumer goods or by designing and manufacturing products that result in less waste in the disposal stage. Second, resources may be recovered by re-using products or by recycling waste as secondary materials.

The re-usage of products or components can be done in at least six ways.

1. Products may be re-used in its original function by other households. Second-hand markets exist for automobiles and clothing. In garage sales, households sell no longer needed pro-ducts, e.g., children's toys and clothing, to other users. The re-use of bottles in their original form is promoted by deposits.
2. Products may be re-used in another function. One may use glass jars and shoe boxes to keep nails and papers.
3. Parts of products may be re-used, as in the case of second-hand car parts.
4. One may re-use the raw material (glass, paper, tin, plastic) to produce new products. The re-usage of glass as a primary material is promoted by containers placed at shopping centers to collect waste glass. Waste separation by households is an almost necessary prerequisite for the re-use of raw material.
5. One may re-use household waste to produce energy, or one may use the energy of household waste to produce heat. And finally,
6. one may re-use the volume of waste as landfill. The latter is a really low-value type of recycling, although there are examples that parks were created on landfill.

Consumer research with regard to raw materials is related to the consumption cycle of purchase → usage → disposition. First it pertains to the study of the importance of ecological product attributes in consumer decision making, choice and purchase. Secondly, the environmental consequences of the usage of products is studied. Does the product, e.g., the washing machine or automobile, need much repair and does it use much energy? Thirdly, what do consumers do with the product after usage? Do they discard the product, do they trade it in, or do they use it for other purposes?

The recycling of solid household waste could be seen as a marketing problem. Household waste becomes a source of raw materials to be distributed to industries for the production of new products. In such a "reversed channels" situation it might be even possible to pay consumers for waste separation in components of paper, glass, tin, plastic, and organic waste. Zikmund and Stanton (1971) discuss the distribution systems for recycling and the feasibility of a commercial operation of the reverse marketing channel.

1.3. *Energy*

Energy conservation creates direct financial benefits for the household itself in the form of lower energy bills for oil, gas and other energy sources. For the country it creates benefits in the form of lower imports of oil. But why do not all consumers behave in a energy-conscious way? Van Raaij and Verhallen (1983a) give seven reasons why consumers do not save as much energy as they can.

1. Energy conservation may not be seen as a problem that concerns them. They consider it to be a problem of industry or the government.
2. They do not behave in a energy-conscious way due to their social environment of energy-wasting relatives, friends and neighbors.
3. They do not always know the energy costs of household and car driving behaviors. They do not consider a behavioral change to be effective in reducing energy use.
4. The feedback information of the energy bills comes too late and is often too general to make them aware of energy wasting types of behavior. The payment at the gas station, however, has a shorter time interval and is thus better feedback information.
5. Some homes and heating systems and automobiles are energy wasting and cannot be managed in an energy-conscious way by the household members.
6. Many consumers are unwilling to give up the comfort of high home temperatures, of a large, but fuel-guzzling car. And finally,
7. energy-conscious behavior asks for some involvement with thermostat settings, heater and stove maintenance, and turning off radiators and engines while idling. Not all consumers are highly involved in energy conservation.

Wilk and Wilhite (1985) add an eighth reason: Strict economic rationality is inadequate in explaining energy conservation behavior; noneconomic goals must be considered as well. Wall cavity insulation of homes, for instance, is not as attractive as it should be from a strict economic savings viewpoint. It may save a lot of money in a heating season, but wall insulation has a low visibility and demonstration value, whereas solar heating and double glazing are better demonstrations of the residents' energy concern and investment.

2. A BEHAVIORAL MODEL

In this chapter we propose a model of consumer behavior with regard to the natural resources (Figure 1). This model is an elaboration of the model of Van Raaij and Verhallen (1983a). Several groups of variables are included that influence the consumers' use of natural resources. First, these groups of variables are discussed:

1. behavior;
2. environmental concern;
3. attitude-behavior relationships;

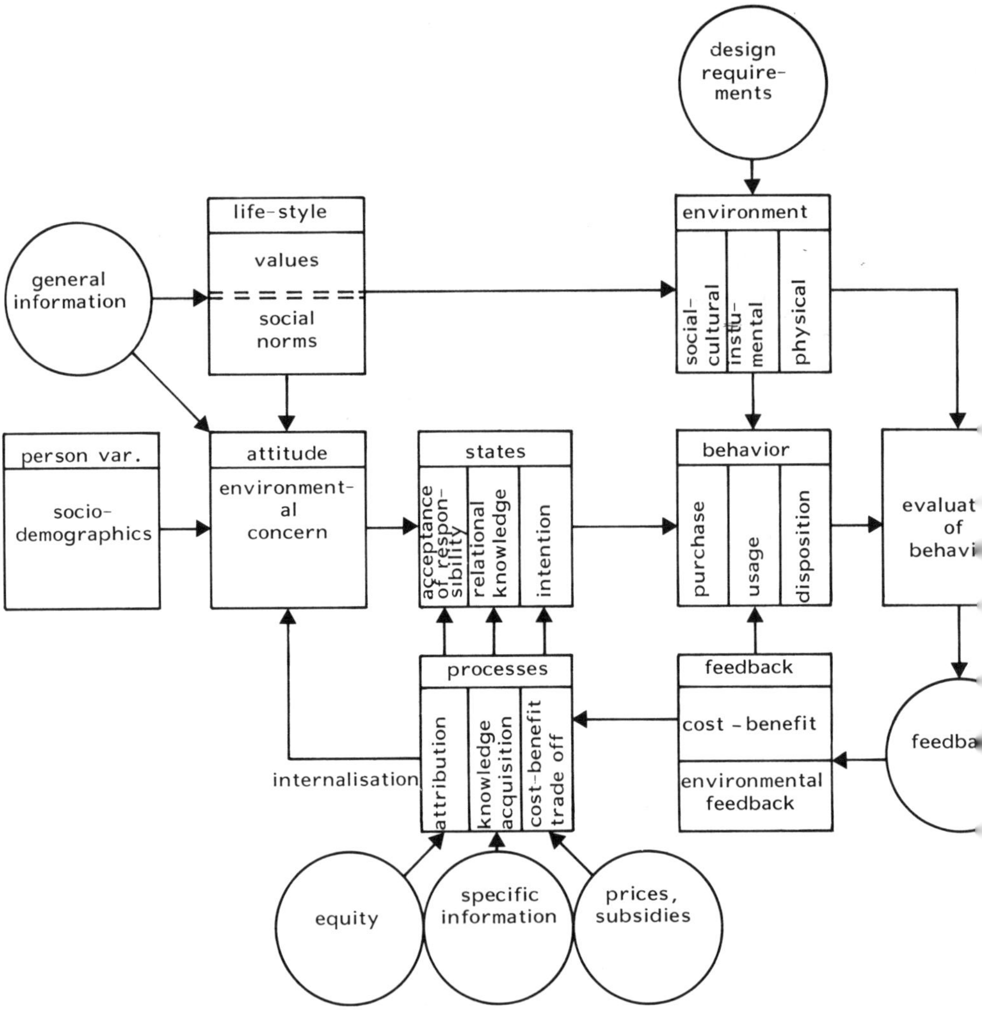

Fig. 1. Model of consumer behavior with regard to the natural resources.

4. evaluation of behavior and feedback from the results of behavior to attitudes and new behavior;
5. contingencies and design of products; and
6. the socio-demographic determinants.

Then the total model is given, with policy implications for the reduction of the use of natural resources.

3. BEHAVIOR

We distinguish three types of behaviors: purchase-related behavior, usage-related behavior, including maintenance, and disposition-related behavior.

With regard to *purchase-related behavior* we are interested, whether consumers consider environmental attributes in their decision process with regard to the purchasing of goods and services. And if they consider any environmental attribute, how important are these attributes compared with other attributes? How are environmental attributes traded off against other attributes? Energy-efficient equipment might, for instance, be more expensive at the point of purchase, but less expensive in use. Environmental attributes are for instance: energy costs, degree of pollution, noise level, repairability, and biodegradability. The feasibility and ease of repair might be an environmental attribute as well.

Anderson and Claxton (1982) and Redinger and Staelin (1981) study the effect of energy labels on the purchase of major household appliances. The labels proved to have a low impact on the choice process, unless salespersons emphasize and explain the energy label to their customers. Hutton and McNeill (1980) provide an overview of current energy labeling research.

Hanna (1978) compared a number of information disclosure methods for energy-saving investments. These methods could be used on energy labels. He recommends the rate of return method (initial investment and annual benefits), because this method is both easy to understand and valid, and corrects for the expected future energy prices.

While purchase-related behavior pertains to a one-time investment in energy-saving, *usage-related behavior* involves the day-to-day handling of the product, e.g., driving the car, setting thermostats, doing the laundry, and using the lawn mower. Usage-related behaviors are very much integrated with behavioral patterns and habits, and are generally hard to change.

Usage of products often interacts with the type of product. Residents of well-insulated homes have lower thermostat settings, but air out their dwellings more often. Van Raaij and Verhallen (1983b) conclude that home characteristics have both positive and negative effects on energy conservation. There are positive effects, in the sense that home insulation may lead to subsequent actions to save energy, possibly due to the self-perception (Bem, 1967) of being energy-conscious. But negative effects are also possible, if the owner of well-insulated home thinks, s/he has contributed enough with home insulation to save energy. Edelson and Olson (1980) found that after a better home insulation had been installed, some residents increase their use of energy by 40 to 50 percent, presumably on the assumption that now their home is well-insulated, they can keep it as warm as they want.

Hamrin (1979) compared the energy use of the residents of homes in two Californian suburbs "Blue Skies Radiant Homes" and "Village Homes." The first type of homes had active solar energy systems and conservation facilities. The second type of homes had passive solar energy and conservation systems, requiring the residents' active involvement by closing shutters and setting thermostats. Contrary to expectations, in the Village Homes less energy was used than in the Blue Skies Radiant Homes. The Blue Skies Radiant Homes residents perceived their homes as a way to conserve energy without changing their life-style and are thus less involved in energy saving. The Village Home people were much more active day-to-day energy conservers and actually used less energy. This means that an active involvement in energy saving leads to a lower energy use, and also that the type of home interacts with the type of behavior of the resident.

Maintenance and operating behavior is also part of the usage-related behaviors. It pertains to the optimal adjustment or tuning of the used equipment in order to reach an acceptable energy use and to prevent unnecessary damage and repair. Regular servicing and correct repairs contribute to an acceptable energy use and diminish wear and tear of parts. Stern and Gardner (1981) conclude that more energy can be saved with increased efficiency of equipment (purchase- and maintenance-related behavior) than with curtailment (usage-related behavior). However, research on how consumers adjust, upkeep, care and maintain their durable goods is almost non-existent, although it is relevant for resource conservation.

Disposition-related behavior is the last stage of the consumption cycle. As stated above, consumers may re-use products with their original or with other functions, may re-use parts of it, or may re-use raw materials. Jacoby, Berning, and Dietvorst (1977) give an overview of consumer disposition behavior.

4. ENVIRONMENTAL CONCERN

Environmental concern can be defined as a general attitude with regard to one's own involvement in maintaining and protecting the natural environment. It is a general attitude that does not refer to specific acts. It includes the beliefs (knowledge), and the evaluations of these beliefs about ideas, objects and behaviors related to the environment and energy. An expectancy-value approach to the formulation of this concern or attitude is very common (Fishbein and Ajzen, 1975). A person has a number of salient beliefs about an idea, object, or act. These beliefs are evaluated on a favorableness dimension. The summation of beliefs * evaluations constitutes the personal attitude toward the idea, object or act. Similarly, social norms multiplied by the motivation to comply with the norms constitute a second component (subjective norms) influencing behavioral intention (subjective probability of performing an act). Behavioral intention determines behavior, along with anticipated and unanticipated situational constraints and possibilities. For instance, a person may have a favorable attitude toward resource conservation (the attitude object); subjective norms also support resource conservation. Both components may create a strong behavioral intention to conserve resources, and, if no situational constraints occur, may also create resource conservation behavior.

Pieters (1987) studied the differences between citizens who had bought a container to compost their vegetable, fruit, and garden waste, and citizens who had not bought such a container. He found that the single most important variable that differentiated between the two groups was environmental concern. The former group had a higher level of environmental concern than the latter group.

Consumers are influenced by the opinions and behaviors of others (see Chapter 6 of this Handbook). If referent persons, such as neighbors, relatives and friends, are environmentally concerned, one is likely to be concerned as well. If the reference group blames others for environmental pollution and resource scarcity, one may accept less responsibility as well.

In the Fishbein and Ajzen model, personal attitudes and subjective norms determine behavior. However, behavioral changes may create attitude changes as well. This possibility is represented in the model by Bentler and Speckart (1979), in which prior behaviors also directly determine present behavior. People do not think about each act they perform; habits and routines partly replace decision processes, especially for daily decisions as to use the car or not, or to purchase certain products.

Environmental concern is a general attitude, often part of a wider attitude. Verhallen en Van Raaij (1981) found that the attitude toward home heating consists of three major factors: energy concern, home comfort, and price concern. Only energy concern could be called an environmental attitude, to be traded off against home comfort. In this example, energy saving and financial saving point in the same direction. Environmental concern may lead to higher costs in other cases: Phosphate-free detergents may be more expensive than "standard" washing powder.

Environmental concern is a general attitude, often composed of a number of more specific attitudes. Leonard-Barton and Rogers (1979) find that specific attitudes about the consequences of energy-conservation actions have more influence on conservation behavior than general attitudes with regard to the energy crisis. General attitudes are not enough; they shape a climate of opinion and facilitate specific behaviors. Environmental concern may lead to a greater sensitivity for specific behavioral recommendations. Specific knowledge and cost-benefit tradeoffs are needed to shape specific behaviors.

5. ATTITUDE-BEHAVIOR RELATIONSHIP

5.1. *Introduction*

Attitudes and behavior are seldom perfectly related. Maloney and Ward (1973) found that Los Angeles residents were very concerned and emotional about the environment, but knew little and did even less to abate the problem. The attitude is general, in this case, whereas the required behaviors may be specific.

In this model (Figure 1) we distinguish three mediating factors between environmental attitude and behavior: acceptance of responsibility, relational knowledge, and behavioral intention. These mediating states are influenced by processes, such as causal attribution, knowledge acquisition, and cost-benefit tradeoffs.

5.2. *Acceptance of Responsibility*

Schwartz's (1977) theory of norm activation predicts performance of pro-ecological behavior, if people accept their own responsibility for the fact that the problem exists and are convinced of their contribution to solve the problem. Acceptance of responsibility, in this case, is the attribution of responsibility for resource conservation to oneself as a consumer or citizen, and not to the government, to agriculture, or to industry. Denying one's own responsibility means that there is no need to change one's behavior or life-style. Hummel, Levitt, and Loomis (1978) studied the "perceived blame" of the energy crisis. They find that self-blame of consumers correlates with a higher willingness to conserve energy. Blaming the environmentalists for the energy crisis concurs with less willingness to conserve energy. This is an interesting example that the environmental concern of some groups, in this case the environmentalists, might have a negative effect on the resource conservation of other groups.

The acceptance of responsibility is the result of a causal attribution process. We may distinguish between the origin and the solution of an environmental problem, such as air or water pollution. Consumers may attribute the cause of the origin of pollution to themselves or to others. They may also attribute the solution to themselves or others. If consumers attribute both the origin and the solution to themselves, they are more willing to contribute to the abatement of environmental pollution. If they attribute the origin, the solution or both to other parties, they are less likely to contribute to the abatement.

Kok and Siero (1985), in an investigation of tin recycling by Dutch consumers, studied the acceptance of responsibility as a variable mediating between attitude and intention. They found no support for the mediating role of this variable. However, according to Fishbein and Ajzen's (1975) theory of reasoned action, persons with a high acceptance of responsibility believe that their ecological behavior has ecological consequences. This was confirmed in their study. High acceptance meant more belief strength with regard to ecological consequences. Respondents with a high acceptance of responsibility had higher scores for pro-ecological consequences of ecological behavior.

5.3. *Relational Knowledge*

Relational knowledge is the knowledge about the specific behavioral acts that have resource conserving consequences, i.e., more that are more conserving than other similar acts. Sometimes consumers really don't know, which behaviors help to save energy, and which behaviors diminish pollution. Relational knowledge may also be called "task knowledge." Consumers may have a positive attitude towards buying in an ecologically conscious way, but may not know which products are better (or less worse) for the environment than other products. In these cases, a lack of relational or task knowledge makes the ecologically conscious consumer behavior similar to the ecologically unconscious consumer behavior.

Part of the relational knowledge are the costs and benefits of environmental behavior. Not only financial costs and benefits are involved in resource conservation, but also behavioral costs and benefits. The behavioral costs are the potential decrease in personal comfort, the low status of traveling with public transit, and the unattractiveness of giving up one's habits and changing one's lifestyle. The behavioral benefits are often minor in comparison with the costs. We mention the pride of the owner of a compost container or heat-pump, and the feeling of being a good citizen. In the financial and behavioral cost-benefit tradeoff, the behavioral costs may be too high for many consumers.

Relational knowledge will help to assess the perceived effectiveness of one's behavior. Relational knowledge mediates the attitude-behavior relationship. Favorable general attitudes is not enough for environmentally conscious behavior. Economic agents need more specific information (relational knowledge) to guide their behavior.

5.4. *Intention*

Intention is related to the cost-benefit tradeoff. For purchase-related behavior the financial cost-benefit tradeoff, e.g., the rate of return on a certain investment, may be most relevant. Prices and subsidies are external factors that influence the cost-benefit tradeoffs, e.g., extra taxation of demerit goods and subsidy to merit goods. For usage-related and maintenance-related behavior the behavioral costs may dominate the cost-benefit tradeoff.

6. EVALUATION OF BEHAVIOR AND FEEDBACK

Feedback is the information that persons obtain about the consequences of their behavior. Feedback about energy-related behavior involves financial information about the energy costs of the expired period (energy bill), numerical information about kWh's electricity or cubic meters natural gas, and social information from referent persons about one's behavior. In general, the shorter the feedback period the more effective the feedback will be in changing behavior. In that case one can easily relate the costs to a certain behavior of wasting or saving energy. Energy bills have long feedback periods. In The Netherlands, consumers pay a fixed monthly amount and a final settlement once a year. The feedback information value of this yearly settlement is very low, because of the long time interval between the usage and the payment. The situation with automobile gas use is somewhat better. Car drivers pay regularly at the gas station and thus may learn about the fuel performance of their cars.

Feedback about garbage-related (disposition) behavior is often general and diffuse, or absent. In The Netherlands, consumers pay a fixed amount a year for garbage pickup and disposal. This amount is only grossly related to the amount of waste.

Feedback information with regard to the environmental effects of the use of resources and energy is generally slow or absent. At the same time it is difficult or impossible to relate the effects to certain behaviors. Acid rain may be a visible environmental effect, and may be attributed to a number of causes or a cumulation of causes, and not to one specific cause. For environmental effects there are several causes, and we have to regulate or change the behaviors of several agents. Positive feedback information, such as the return of salmon in the Thames, may motivate people to continue their efforts.

Feedback information on energy use and costs is more effective to reduce energy consumption than general information on energy conservation, and information prompts. Additional financial rewards increase the effectiveness (Winett and Neale, 1979; Battalio, Kagel, Winkler, and Winett, 1979). Seaver and Patterson (1976) recommend to add social commendation to the feedback information to increase effectiveness. Van Houwelingen and Van Raaij (1988) used an energy display monitor in the home to make the residents aware of their energy use and to help them with energy conservation. The feedback information may be given in quantity of energy used (in cubic meters (m^3) of natural gas or in kWh's) or in monetary terms (of money spent). The feedback period may be one day, one week, or one month.

The content of the feedback information consists of costs and benefits of specific behaviors, and of environmental information about pollution of land, water and air. Feedback information may have three different functions (Van Raaij and Verhallen, 1983a):

1. Acceptable or attractive behaviors are repeated over time, and thus habits and routines are formed.
2. Information about costs and benefits is learned and strengthens relational knowledge, and intentions.
3. Information may be internalized to environmental concern, i.e., repeated environmentally conscious behavior creates or strengthens environmental concern.

Habit formation is a relatively autonomous and unconscious process with a low effort, in which not necessarily much learning will take place. Learning about the costs and benefits may change the utility of the different behaviors and thus lead to a more or less permanent behavioral change. Internalization pertains to an attitude change as a consequence of learning. Internalization is a conscious process and may lead to other environmental behavior as well, because the internalized environmental concern is more general than the specific behavior involved.

7. CONTINGENCIES AND DESIGN OF PRODUCTS

Durable goods as such have an effect on environmental behavior. The design of products determines their environmental effects. Verhallen and Van Raaij (1981) found that home characteristics explain 26% of the residential energy use. Wall-cavity insulation, double glazing, energy-efficient heating, air conditioning and ventilation systems may be important contributions to energy conservation. Rosson and Sweitzer (1981) emphasize the following physical house characteristics determining energy consumption in the home:

1. temperature difference between inside and outside of the house,
2. heat losses through wall, glass, ceiling, floor, and roof transmission,
3. air infiltration and leakage, and
4. efficiency of the furnace, depending on its age and maintenance level.

Van Raaij en Verhallen (1983b) find as important technical home characteristics: home insulation, home attachment (apartment vs. bungalow), energy use of neighbors in attached homes, wind orientation, and temperature difference within the home, e.g., between living room and bedrooms.

Durable goods, such as homes, automobiles, and freezers, may be designed to use less energy. Governments may require minimum performances of these products. In purchase situations the energy and environmental attributes may be stressed (Redinger and Staelin, 1981). This may have a favorable environmental effect, apart from the usage behavior.

Jorden (1986) discusses some rules and regulations to support the recycling of domestic waste. He argues that every product, all other things being equal, should be designed in such a way that it is prepared for the recycling of its parts or components. Durable products, for instance, can be designed in such a way that parts can be taken out easily after the product is disposed of.

8. SOCIODEMOGRAPHIC FACTORS

A number of sociodemographic factors influence environmental behavior, especially energy use. *Household income* is an important factor. Newman and Day (1975) already concluded that the poor use less energy, and that their energy use is largely non-discretionary, i.e., for essentials only. The better-off spend more on natural gas for home heating, because their dwellings are larger and the energy price constitutes less of a cost to them. The poor in the U.S.A. are generally older, have a lower educational level, are more often black, and their families are often incomplete (husband absent) and they do not own the home they live in. Their homes are often of a lower quality, with poor insulation, and a less efficient heating system. Low-income earners cannot easily reduce their energy use any further.

Cunningham and Joseph (1978) concluded that while low-income consumers cannot reduce their energy use, high-income consumers are unwilling to reduce their energy use. Middle-income consumers are the most likely conservers. Low-income consumers accept only short payback periods of energy-saving investments, such as home insulation, while high-income consumers are willing and able to accept longer payback periods. Low-income consumers are more often renters than owners of their home. For renters the home-owner has a crucial role, whether the home will be insulated or not (Van Raaij and Verhallen, 1986).

Other sociodemographic factors have some effect on energy use and conservation, although research is not very conclusive here. Verhage (1980) concluded that early adopters of energy conservation are not significantly different from other respondents with respect to age and educational level. Fritzsche (1981) and Verhallen and Van Raaij (1981) found that household composition (number of persons in the household) and their presence at home are significant determinants of energy use. Pieters (1987) found that consumers that bought and used a compost container possessed a larger garden and had larger household sizes than consumers that did not compost their kitchen and garden waste.

The construct *family life cycle* combines age and household composition. Energy use tends to fluctuate over the family life cycle. Young households without children and both partners working outside the home tend to have a low level of energy use. Households with children at home have a higher energy use. After the children have left home, the energy use decreases, but than gradually increases with age, because in general older persons need a higher room temperature.

Regional differences are another determinant of energy use. Northern countries and northern parts of a country (on the northern hemisphere) have a higher energy use per household, although these regions often have a longer tradition of home insulation. In hot areas, energy is used for air conditioning. This energy use in summer is sometimes higher than the energy use for heating in winter. Rural areas have a higher energy use than urban areas, because of more free standing homes and more wind exposure.

Regional differences may also be related to environmental concern. People that live in areas with visible and smellable pollution may become more concerned and anxious about the environment than people in less polluted areas.

9. POLICY IMPLICATIONS

The policy implications pertain to the ways the behavior of consumers can be influenced. In Figure 1, six ways are indicated (the circles in the figure).

General information may influence the values and attitudes of consumers. Stating environmental problems in mass media may trigger the thinking and environmental concern of consumers. They may become aware of the seriousness of the problem. Messages that certain species of animals may become extinct, will trouble many people, although they do not yet know, what they can do about it, except for giving a donation to Greenpeace or the World Wildlife Fund. General information may be regarded as necessary but insufficient to change consumer behavior in a environmentally beneficial direction, but it might set the agenda for conversations among people (the "agenda setting" function of the mass media, McCombs, 1981; McCombs and Shaw, 1972). Mass media information about the nuclear disasters at Three Miles Island and Chernobyl had a strong effect on the thinking and opinion about nuclear energy. In general, there are however many steps between general information and environmentally conscious behavior.

Design requirements pertain to minimum or maximum standards for products, e.g., the maximum tolerable exhaust pollution of cars or the minimum degree of repairability of durable goods. Strict design requirements may place a country in a disadvantaged position compared to countries with less strict requirements. It is a relatively direct way to abate environmental problems, either through government regulation or through self-regulation by the industry. Design requirements pertain not only to products, but also to the distribution of products. Making environmentally harmful products less easily available, may restrict their use. The permission to use certain products may also be restricted: One may, for instance, restrict the use of motor boats in nature parks.

Feedback information on the effects of behavior is an effective means of changing behavior in a desired direction, or of reinforcing existing desired behavior. Feedback belongs to the consequence strategies, because the information comes after the behavior and is input for subsequent behavior. Positive knowledge of results stimulates to persist in one's endeavors. Goal setting in conjunction with feedback information, whether one comes closer to the goal, is very effective to stimulate energy conservation in the home (Van Houwelingen and Van Raaij, 1988). However, persistent negative results may have a discouraging effect, as if the behavior is not sufficiently under one's volitional control. Feedback information may be about the costs and benefits of certain behaviors, e.g., in energy conservation, or about the condition of the environment as a consequence of one's behavior, or of the behavior of others.

Prices and subsidies change the costs of choice alternatives. If environmentally unfavorable products (demerit goods) will cost more, their demand is likely to decrease with their price elasticity. If favorable goods (merit goods) cost less, their demand is likely to increase. If phosphate-free detergents are more expensive than other detergents, only some very concerned consumers want to pay the extra cost for a better environment. But if phosphate-free detergents cost less than other detergents, more consumers will buy them. Through a system of taxation and subsidies one could reach this favorable price difference. In a similar manner, automobile traffic is taxed, whereas public transport is subsidized.

Specific information on behaviors may help consumers to know, which consequences of behaviors are positive and which are negative for the environment. In this way they can better discriminate between "good" and "bad" behaviors. Specific information and prompts belong to the antecedent strategies, i.e., information before the behavior. Prompts are reminders of the required behavior at the place and time these behaviors should occur, i.e., a reminder placed on the door to shut the door to save energy. Specific information is often a necessary addition to general information. The knowledge acquisition process may also pertain to the costs and benefits of the behaviors.

Equity in this model is the ratio of inputs and outputs for different groups in society, such as industry, agriculture, government. What is the contribution of each of these groups to the origin and the solution of environmental problems? How well-off or worse-off are consumers compared with these groups? What can consumers do to industrial water or air pollution? How effective are consumer efforts in relation to the efforts of the other groups? Consumers tend to attribute the responsibility of pollution to these groups or to themselves. If consumers blame themselves, they may be more willing to contribute to a solution of the environmental problems. Thus, government, industry, and agriculture have an "exemplification" function and should do their part in order not to discourage consumers in their contribution.

ACKNOWLEDGEMENTS

I thank Rik G.M. Pieters, Erasmus University Rotterdam, and Theo M.M. Verhallen, Research International Rotterdam, for their valuable contributions to this chapter.

REFERENCES

Anderson, C.D., and J.D. Claxton, 1982, Barriers to consumer choice of energy-efficient products, Journal of Consumer Research, 9, 163-170.

Battalio, C., J.H. Kagel, C. Winkler, and R.A. Winett, 1979, Residential electricity demand: An experimental study, Review of Economics and Statistics, 61, 180-189.

Bem, D.J., 1967, Self-perception: An alternative interpretation of cognitive dissonance phenomena, Psychological Review, 74, 183-200.

Bentler, P.M., and G. Speckart, 1979, Models of attitude-behavior relations, Psychological Review, 86, 452-464.

Cunningham, W.H., and B. Joseph, 1978, Energy conservation, price increases, and payback periods, Advances in Consumer Research, 5, 201-205.

Edelson, E., and M.E. Olson, 1980, Potential Social Institutional and Environmental Impacts of Selected Energy Conservation Measures in Two Washington Communities, Richland, WA: Battelle (report RAP 39).

Fishbein, M., and I. Ajzen, 1975, Belief, Attitude, Intention, and Behavior. An Introduction to Theory and Research, Reading, MA: Addison-Wesley.

Fritzsche, D.J., 1981, An analysis of energy consumption patterns by stage of family life cycle, Journal of Marketing Research, 18, 227-232.

Hamrin, J., 1979, Energy-saving homes: Don't bet on technology alone, Psychology Today, 12, 18.

Hanna, S., 1978, Evaluation of energy saving investments, Journal of Consumer Affairs, 12, 63-75.

Hummel, C.F., L. Levitt, and R.J. Loomis, 1978, Perceptions of the energy crisis, Environment and Behavior, 10, 37-88.

Hutton, R.B., and D.L. McNeill, 1980, Research issues, empirical findings, and public policy implications for energy labeling, Advances in Consumer Research, 7, 283-289.

Jacoby, J., C.K. Berning, and T.F. Dietvorst, 1977, What about disposition?, Journal of Marketing, 41, April, 22-28.

Jorden, W., 1986, "Recyclingsgerechte Produktgestaltung als Grundlage für ein optimales Stoffrecycling," in: A. Buekens and M. Tels (eds.), Materials and Energy from Refuse. Proceedings of the third International Symposium, Antwerp, Belgium.

Kok, G., and S. Siero, 1985, Tin recycling: Awareness, comprehension, attitude, intention, and behavior, Journal of Economic Psychology, 6, 157-173.

Leonard-Barton, D., and E.M. Rogers, 1979, Adoption of Energy-conservation Among California Home-owners, paper presented at the International Communication Association, Philadelphia, PA.

McCombs, M.E., 1981, "The agenda-setting approach," in: D.D. Nimmo and K.R. Sanders (eds.), Handbook of Political Communication, Beverly Hills, CA: Sage, pp. 121-140.

McCombs, M.E., en D.L. Shaw, 1972, The agenda-setting function of mass media, Public Opinion Quarterly, 36, 176-187.

Maloney, M.P., and M.P. Ward, 1973, Ecology, let's hear from the people, American Psychologist, 28, 583-586.

Newman, D.K., and D. Day, 1975, The American Energy Consumer, Cambridge, MA: Ballinger.

Pieters, R.G.M., 1987, Perceived costs and benefits of buying and using a subsidized compost container, Resources and Conservation, 14, 139-154.

Pieters, R.G.M., and T.M.M. Verhallen, 1986, Participation in source separation projects: Design characteristics and perceived costs and benefits, Resources and Conservation, 12, 95-111.

Redinger, R., and R. Staelin, 1981, "Refrigerator energy labels," in: J.D. Claxton, C.D. Anderson, J.R.B. Ritchie, and G.H.G. McDougall (eds.), Consumers and Energy Conservation, New York: Praeger, pp. 286-292.

Rosson, P.J., and R.W. Sweitzer, 1981, Home heating oil consumption. Profiling "efficient" and "inefficient" households, Energy Policy, 9, 216-225.

Schwartz, S.H., 1977, "Normative influences on altruism," in: L. Berkowitz (ed.), Advances in Experimental Social Psychology, Vol. 10, New York: Academic Press, pp. 221-279.

Seaver, W.B., and A.H. Patterson, 1976, Decreasing fuel-oil consumption through feedback and social commendations, Journal of Applied Behavior Analysis, 9, 147-152.

Stern, P.C., and G.T. Gardner, 1981, Psychological research and energy policy, American Psychologist, 36, 329-342.

Van Houwelingen, J.H., and W.F. van Raaij, 1988, The Effect of Electronic Daily Feedback on Home Energy Conservation, 49, Rotterdam, The Netherlands: Erasmus University (Papers on Economic Psychology).

Van Raaij, W.F., and T.M.M. Verhallen, 1983a, A behavioral model of residential energy use, Journal of Economic Psychology, 3, 39-63.
Van Raaij, W.F., and T.M.M. Verhallen, 1983b, Patterns of residential energy behavior, Journal of Economic Psychology, 4, 85-106.
Van Raaij, W.F., and T.M.M. Verhallen, 1986, Determinants of home insulation intention, Advances in Consumer Research, 13, 476-480.
Verhage, B.J., 1980, Stimulating energy conservation: Applying the business heritage of marketing, European Journal of Marketing, 14, 167-179.
Verhallen, T.M.M., and W.F. van Raaij, 1981, Household behavior and the use of natural gas for home heating, Journal of Consumer Research, 8, 253-257.
Wilk, R.R., and H.L. Wilhite, 1985, Why don't people weatherize their homes? An ethnographic solution, Energy, 10, 621-629.
Winett, R.A., and M.S. Neale, 1979, Psychological framework for energy conservation in buildings: Strategies, outcomes, directions, Energy and Buildings, 2, 101-116.
Zikmund, W.G., and W.J. Stanton, 1971, Recycling of solid wastes: A channels-of-distribution problem, Journal of Marketing, 35, 34-39.

Subject Index

Author Index